Tahiti

& French Polynesia Guide

Jan Prince

Le Meridien Bora Bora

Fakarava

Cruising Around French Polynesia!

Moorea

Kia Ora, Rangiroa

Bora Bora

InterContinental,
Tahiti

Lotus

Traditional Dancers

Outrigger Canoe race,
Bora Bora

Taha'a

Tikehau

Waterfall on Tahiti

Lunch in the
Water, Bora Bora

Paradise in
Moorea

Cruising with
Haumana

Snorkeling with a
great backdrop!

Hotel Bora Bora

Papenoo Valley, Tahiti

Rangiroa

Dive
Tahiti!

Relais Mahana,
Huahine

Tahiti
& French Polynesia Guide

Jan Prince

OPEN ROAD PUBLISHING

We offer travel guides to American and foreign locales. Our books tell it like it is, often with an opinionated edge, and our experienced authors always give you all the information you need to have the trip of a lifetime. Check out our website to see all our titles.

Open Road Publishing
P.O. Box 284, Cold Spring Harbor, NY 11724
www.openroadguides.com

5th Edition

Front cover photo courtesy of Manihi Pearl Beach Resort. Back cover photo copyright©InterContinental Beachcomber Resort Tahiti. Photo insert credits: p. 1, p. 4 middle, p. 7 top, p. 8 middle: Le Meriden; p. 2 top: Frederic Jacquot (wikimedia.com); p. 2 middle: A.www.viajar24h.com (flickr.com); p. 2 bottom, p. 3 bottom: InterContinental Beachcomber Resorts; p. 3 top: Kia Ora; p. 3 middle: tiarescott (flickr.com); p. 4 top, p. 5 top: kckellner (flickr.com); p. 4 bottom, p. 6 top: thelastminute (flickr.com); p. 5 middle: lander2006 (flickr.com); p. 5 bottom, p. 7 bottom: Jean-Sebastien Roy (flickr.com); p. 6 middle: Mr. Dotcom; p. 6 bottom: Haunama; p. 7 middle: veroyama; p. 8 top: Fouka Riddim (flickr.com); p. 8 bottom: Relais Mahana.

Maps by DesignMaps.

All information, including prices, is subject to change. The author has made every effort to be as accurate as possible, but neither she nor the publisher assumes responsibility for the services provided by any business listed in this guide; for any errors or omissions; or any loss, damage, or disruptions in your travel for any reason.

TABLE OF CONTENTS

Sidebars

Maps

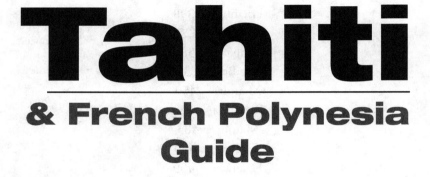

Tahiti
& French Polynesia Guide

1. Introduction

Unlike many armchair travelers and other romantics I harbored no childhood dreams to escape to Tahiti—the Isle of Illusion and Love under the swaying palms. Surely I had heard the magical name "Tahiti" when I saw the old movies about the South Seas, but they made no lasting impression on me.

But when I saw a picture of Bora Bora in a *Sports Illustrated* magazine in January 1968, I was swept away by the beauty of the island. For the next six months I read every book on Tahiti and the South Pacific that I could find in the Public Library in Houston, where I was living at the time.

When I arrived in Tahiti later that year I was prepared to accept Tahiti as she is, not as a starry-eyed tourist. I could even appreciate the wonder and beauty of a volcanic black sand beach. I knew that I would like the smell of a coconut fire and the musty odor of copra. I longed to hear the rumble of the surf crashing on the coral reef and the squawking cries of the sea birds as they fished in the lagoon. I also knew that I would enjoy the fun loving Tahitian people, their dignity, humor and sensuous dances. I understood that it was more important to absorb the colorful sights, sounds and fragrant smells of the people and scenery around me than to see Tahiti through the lens of a camera.

My husband and I spent three weeks on Tahiti, Moorea and Bora Bora, and returned again in 1970 to do it all again. When we moved to Tahiti in 1971, I chose to discover my own Tahiti. That's what I've been doing ever since. I've experienced Tahiti as an American tourist and as an expatriate full-time resident, as a journalist, travel writer and tour guide. I've explored most of the inhabited islands in five archipelagoes, traveling by airplanes, luxury liners, inter-island cargo ships, small fishing boats and by private sail boats. I've stayed in all the best hotels, at several of the pensions and hostels, and I've lived for weeks at a time with Polynesian families in the outer islands. I learned to speak French with an American accent and enough of the Tahitian language to be understood. However, you can get by with English, gestures and smiles almost everywhere you go in these islands.

French Polynesia is not just another destination for vacations. It is a completely different world; a different lifestyle made up of the special light in the sky, the special color of the water, the special smile of the people.

Along with the travel information you'll find in this book are tidbits of my own experiences in Tahiti and Her Islands, which are officially known as French Polynesia. I'm confident that the travel advice in this book will help you discover your own Tahiti!

NEW TO THIS EDITION!
We've added **color photos** and **new maps**, and a new list of *Bests* (see Chapter 3), such as Best Atolls, Best Resort Beaches, Best Luxury Accommodations, Best Seafood Buffet, Best Sunrise, Best Surfing – and much more!

2. Overview

Visitors to **Tahiti** often ask me which is my favorite island in French Polynesia, which island I think is the prettiest and which island I think they would most enjoy visiting.

Although I do have my favorites, each island has its own beauty, charm and specific personality. Almost everywhere you go in French Polynesia you will meet hospitable, friendly people, which helps to give meaning to the natural assets of the island. The latter question is dependent on the amount of time and interest you have to explore the islands, the people and the culture.

From the first moment I laid eyes on the lagoon of **Bora Bora** I was entranced. Each time I have returned to Bora Bora over the years I still gasp in awe at the beautiful colors of the lagoon. I find myself gazing at Otemanu and Pahia mountains from all angles around the island, and especially when I'm taking a boat trip around the lagoon.

The mountains and bays of **Moorea** are simply breathtaking, and this is the cleanest island of the Society group, with neatly trimmed lawns and flower gardens. Here you will find the flavor of the islands by sitting beside the lagoon at a resort hotel and listening to Tahitian musicians playing their guitars and ukuleles and singing their favorite Polynesian songs at sunset time.

Tetiaroa is a sanctuary for thousands of sea birds that lay their eggs on the white powdery sands of the beaches. Here you can easily observe crested terns, brown noddy birds, red- and blue-footed booby birds, white-bellied gannets, petrels, the beautiful white fairy terns with black eyes, and the occasional red-breasted frigate birds, whose fledglings of fluffy white feathers are larger than their mothers are. The Hotel Tetiaroa Village and the airstrip were closed several years ago, prior to the death of owner Marlon Brando on July 1, 2004. You can still visit one part of this lovely atoll by boat. At 42 km. (26 mi.) from Tahiti, it is just the right distance for a day-tour that will take you over in the morning and bring you back at night. You can walk to Bird Island, have a picnic on the beach and swim in the enclosed lagoon. Tahiti Beachcomber SA, which owns the Intercontinental hotels in Tahiti, Moorea and Bora Bora, plans to have Tetiaroa atoll classified as a protected marine sanctuary. The airstrip will be rebuilt and the 40 villa Hotel Brando will be constructed on part of the airport motu. This eco-friendly deluxe resort and spa is planned to open in 2010, and will not include any overwater bungalows.

The island of **Huahine** is very special to me because of the Polynesian people who live in the quiet little villages, fishing and planting vegetables and fruit in their little *fa'apu* farms in the valley. As you drive around the island you can still feel the history of Huahine when you visit the stone *marae* temples in Maeva Village.

Raiatea and **Taha'a** are ideal for sailboat chartering, and there are 4 yacht charter companies based in Raiatea. There are numerous *motu* islets inside the protected lagoon where you can drop anchor, watch a magnificent sunset behind Bora Bora, and listen to the roar of the surf on the reef as you fire up the barbecue on the stern of the boat, while a huge tropical moon rises above the sea.

Tahiti is still the land of double rainbows for me, the regal Queen of the Pacific, and the Diadème Mountain, which can best be viewed from the Fautaua bridge east of Papeete, is even shaped like a crown. A drive around the island of Tahiti will reveal seascapes that are reminiscent of all the island groups of Polynesia. Tahiti is an island that's alive with color, from the flamboyant flowers to the bright *pareo* clothing to the pink, yellow, orange, blue and green houses you'll see beside the circle island road. There are numerous waterfalls in the verdant valleys and you'll find challenging hikes in the mountains if you want to get off-track.

Tahiti is perhaps the most magical and beautiful island of all, but she will not reveal her treasures to you as readily as the smaller islands do. You have to get away from the mainstream of hotels and Papeete to feel the essence of this seductive island, which remains constant amidst the apparent changes of modern life. If you can appreciate the special beauty of a black sand beach of volcanic sand, or a quiet stroll through a forest of *mape* (Tahitian chestnut) trees, then you'll feel some of the spirit of old Tahiti.

Many of us who live on Polynesia's high islands dream of escaping to the **Tuamotu atolls**, where we can get lost between the immensity of sea and sky. Rangiroa, Manihi, Fakarava and Tikehau are the islands that may beckon to you, like a siren call. Here you can live on fish and lobster and coconuts, and scuba dive among an abundance of wild life in the wonderfully clear lagoons that attract professional underwater photographers from the world's top magazines.

The mysterious **Marquesas Islands** hold a fascination for an increasing number of voyagers, who seek the authenticity of lifestyle that is still lived in the isolated valleys of these distant islands of brooding beauty. The wood carvers on each island create magnificent sculptures for their churches, and to sell in the artisan centers. The young people dance the traditional *haka* and bird dance, and the herds of horses, goats and cattle watch the scenery from their pastures on the precipitous cliffs overlooking the bays.

Whenever I hear a *himene* group singing the old Polynesian hymns and chants, I am carried away in spirit to the **Austral Islands**, where the villagers gather in their Protestant meeting houses almost nightly to practice their songs for the Sunday church services. I can almost smell the *couronnes sauvages*, the necklaces of flowers and herbs that are placed around your shoulders when you arrive on the joyful island of Rurutu. And I can see the handsome, muscled young men who spend their days in the taro fields, while the women sit on *peue* mats on their terraces or in their living rooms, weaving hats, bags and mats from pandanus fronds.

The **Gambier Islands** represent another page from Polynesia's colorful and often tragic past. Under the severe staff of Father Honoré Laval, the docile, gentle people of Mangareva were converted to Catholicism and lost their lives under the forced labor of building churches. A neo-gothic city of 116 buildings of coral and stone and a cathedral for 2,000 people is a reminder of the priest who had a driving need to build.

Here's a quick preview of what Open Road's *Tahiti & French Polynesia Guide* offers you:

Society Islands

The **Society Islands** are the main tourist destinations in French Polynesia. They are the islands the furthest west in French Polynesia, and the home of more than 3/4 of the population. They are divided into the **Windward Islands** or *Iles du Vent* and the **Leeward Islands** or *Iles sous le Vent*, so named because of their position in relation to the prevailing wind.

The Windward Islands include the high islands of **Tahiti** and **Moorea**, and the uninhabited volcanic crater of **Mehetia**; plus the coral atoll of **Tetiaroa**, the late Marlon Brando's former retreat. The mostly flat island of **Maiao** still has its doors closed to the outside world, and visitors are not encouraged to spend the night ashore.

In the Leeward Islands the high islands of **Huahine, Raiatea, Taha'a, Bora Bora** and **Maupiti** lie 180 to 260 km. (112 to 161 mi.) northwest of Tahiti. The atolls of **Tupai, Mopelia, Scilly** and **Bellinghausen** are the westernmost islands of the Society group. These 4 atolls are either uninhabited or have no tourist facilities, but you can visit by sailboat from Bora Bora. Richard Postma's *Taravana*, which operates out of the Hotel Bora Bora, is frequently chartered by movie stars and other adventurous couples to explore this hidden paradise.

The high islands of the Leeward and Windward Society group are some of the most beautiful islands in the world, offering countless photogenic scenes of sawtooth mountain ranges, deep blue bays, green valleys and sparkling turquoise lagoons inside the fringing or barrier reefs. These are the names you've heard so much about: Tahiti, Moorea, Huahine, Raiatea, Taha'a, Bora Bora and Maupiti. On most of these islands you can explore the valleys, waterfalls and *marae* stone temples on a safari tour, or while hiking with a guide or on your own. In the opalescent lagoons you can swim, snorkel, scuba dive, water-ski, jet-ski, surf, kitesurf and windsurf, paddle an outrigger canoe, feed the rays, go sailing and picnic on the *motu*. And you can photograph the island, lagoon and reef while parasailing or taking a flight-seeing helicopter tour.

The airport and hotel on **Tetiaroa** were both closed in early 2004, but you can still explore this privately owned atoll during a day's sailing excursion from Tahiti. And you can make plans to stay at The Brando when this new hotel opens in 2010.

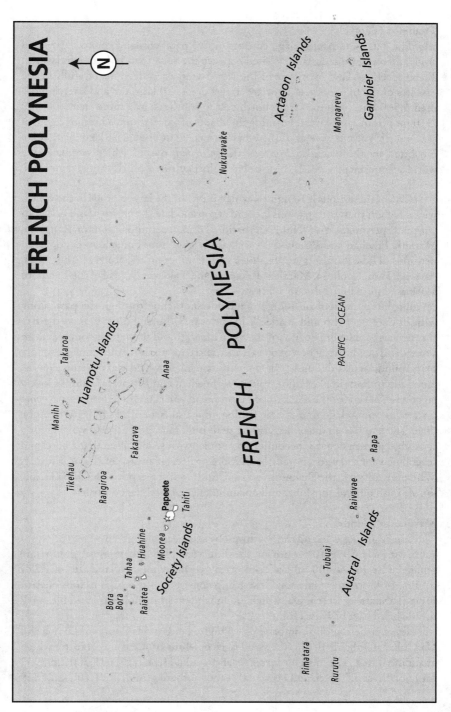

Tuamotu Islands

The **Tuamotu Archipelago** consists of two parallel island chains of 77 coral atolls and one upraised island, located between the Society and Marquesas Islands. These specks of land form one of the world's largest collections of atolls in the vastness of the blue Pacific. They are strewn across 10 latitudes and stretch more than 1,500 km. (930 mi.) from northwest to southeast and more than 500 km. (310 mi.) from east to west. Forming the shapes of a doughnut, a bean or cigar, an egg or a slice of pie, several of these half-drowned atolls enclose lagoons that are inhabited by the black-lip *Pinctada Margaritifera* oyster, which produces the world's finest quality pearls, now called Tahiti cultured pearls rather than black pearls.

One of these atolls is **Rangiroa**, which is one of the largest atolls in the world, with a lagoon that is so spacious it could accommodate the entire island of Tahiti within its perimeter. You'll find international class accommodations on Rangiroa, **Manihi, Tikehau** and **Fakarava**, as well as thatched roof bungalows or rooms in pensions. There are also guest facilities with families on the atolls of **Ahe, Anaa, Apataki, Hao, Kaukura, Mataiva, Takapoto** and **Takaroa**. Several of the Tuamotu atolls are uninhabited due to a lack of water.

Lagoon excursions on Rangiroa include snorkeling through the pass, along with hundreds of fish and sharks. You can watch the dolphins, look at the fish through a glass bottom boat, visit the *motu* islets around the vast lagoon, picnic on a *motu,* fish inside the lagoon or open ocean, and parasail above the immense watery playground. Scuba diving in the Tuamotus is rated world class by the experts, especially in Rangiroa, Manihi, Fakarava, Tikehau and Mataiva. Manihi's lovely lagoon is a haven for the black lipped oyster, and you can visit a pearl farm, picnic on a *motu*, snorkel, go line or drag fishing, join a sunset cruise and learn to scuba dive. Tikehau has an unspoiled lagoon with pink sand beaches just waiting for a footprint, and Fakarava is becoming so popular with scuba divers that a hotel and several pensions have been built, with more projects planned for the near future. Wherever you go in the Tuamotus you will find a warm reception, laughter, music, lots of fresh air and sunshine, and an abundance of fresh lagoon fish.

Marquesas Islands

The **Marquesas Islands** lie northwest by southeast along a 360-km. (223-mi.) submarine chain 7°-10° south of the Equator. Two geographical groups are separated by 96 km. (60 mi.) of open ocean, with a combined land area of 1,279 sq. km. (492 sq. mi.). The southern group consists of the 4 high islands of **Fatu Hiva, Tahuata** and **Hiva Oa**, which are inhabited, plus **Mohotani** and the small uninhabited islet of **Fatu Huku**.

The northern group comprises the 3 high islands of **Ua Pou, Nuku Hiva** and **Ua Huka**, all inhabited, plus the small islets of **Motu Iti, Eiao** and **Hatutu**, which are uninhabited. The most important island, Nuku Hiva, is about 1,500 km. (932 mi.) northeast of Tahiti, and Hiva Oa, in the southern group, lies 1,400 km. (868 mi.) northeast of Tahiti. The Marquesas Islands are younger than the Society Islands and do not have protective coral reefs. The wild ocean beats endlessly against the craggy, sculpted coasts, unbroken by any barriers for almost 6,400 km. (4,000 mi.).

Accommodations are available on all the inhabited islands, either in small hotels or in family pensions. Most of the rooms and meals are reasonably priced in the Marquesas, but the cost of land and sea transport is very expensive. Read the information on the *Aranui* in the chapter on *Planning Your Trip*. This is the best way to visit the Marquesas Islands, unless you want to stay a few days on one or more of the islands. You can also take an Air Tahiti flight to the Marquesas and board the *Aranui* there and fly back to Tahiti if you prefer.

In the Marquesas you can visit restored archaeological sites with giant stone tikis, hike to waterfalls and high plateaus and ride horses to remote villages. You can scuba dive among a wealth of wild sealife, charter a sailboat for a dive and sail outing through the islands, go deep sea fishing, and watch the wood carvers at work.

Austral Islands

The **Austral Islands** are the southernmost island chain in French Polynesia, lying on both sides of the Tropic of Capricorn and extending in a northwest-southeasterly direction across 1,280 km. (794 mi.) of ocean. They are part of a vast mountain range, an extension of the same submerged chain that comprises the Cook Islands.

The Austral Islands include the high islands of **Rurutu**, **Tubuai**, **Rimatara**, **Raivavae** and **Rapa**, plus the low, uninhabited islands of **Maria** (or Hull) and the **Marotiri** (or Bass) **Rocks**. These islands lie between 538-1,280 km. (334-794 mi.) south of Tahiti, and are separated from one another by a great distance of open ocean. These are French Polynesia's more temperate islands, where taro and potatoes, cabbages and carrots are grown for the market in Papeete.

TAHITI, WHERE LOVE LIVES

"Tahiti, where love lives" is one of the most popular slogans adopted by the Tahiti Tourist office to promote Tahiti and Her Islands to the American market. This campaign is aimed at busy executives from homes where both husband and wife work and have very little time to spend together.

When you choose the Islands of Tahiti for your vacation, you will find a complete change of scenery and a rhythm of life that is slow and relaxed, very conducive to romance. Tahiti is still the Island of Love. Here we take the time to enjoy one another. Time to simply be. One of Tahiti's favorite expressions is Haere Maru, which means "take it easy." That's what you'll learn to do when you get here.

You can fly to Rurutu, Rimatara, Raivavae and Tubuai, but you can get to Rapa only by boat, as the Rapan inhabitants have voted against this intrusion on their solitude. Raivavae and Rapa are the most beautiful of the Austral Islands and Rurutu is the most lively of all the group. You'll enjoy the communal spirit that exists here, in the taro fields, the artisan shops and in the churches of Rurutu. The people are enthusiastic in both work and play, and they keep their culture alive with annual tours to visit the religious and historic sites of the island.

You can explore Rurutu by horseback or 4WD vehicle, picnic on a white sand beach and hike to waterfalls and limestone grottoes with stalactites and stalagmites. Tubuai is noted for its sandy beaches of various shades, its *motu* islets and fish-filled lagoon. Raivavae has the most beautiful *motu* I have ever seen, but certain parts of its lovely lagoon are now contaminated with *ciguatera*, which prohibits the consumption of fish and *pahua (tridacna* reef clam).

3. The Best of French Polynesia

ITINERARIES

The Best One-Island Choice

If your ideal vacation is to fly to one island, check into a hotel, unpack and settle in, then I suggest that you choose a hotel on Tahiti, Moorea or Bora Bora if this is your first visit to French Polynesia. You will have more choices of restaurants and entertainment on the main islands and there is enough activity to keep you busy on land and in the lagoon for at least a week.

If you add Moorea to your itinerary, then I suggest that you fly direct from Tahiti to Moorea, providing you don't have to wait too long at the airport in Tahiti. Better yet, schedule an international flight that will allow you to connect from Tahiti to Moorea immediately after arrival at the Tahiti-Faa'a International Airport. The first Air Moorea flight from Tahiti to Moorea begins at 6am. If your overseas flight arrives in Tahiti in the middle of the night, as some of them do, you may want to pre-register in a hotel or family pension in Tahiti and continue your trip the next day.

The most important idea is for you to get settled into your hotel as quickly as possible, take a refreshing shower and nap, and go swimming in the lagoon when you awaken. As soon as you get out of your traveling clothes and into your swimsuit, shorts or *pareo*, you'll feel yourself starting to relax.

If you are staying on the island of Tahiti you owe it to yourself to visit Moorea at least for a day. You can hop aboard an inter-island fast catamaran for a 30-min. trip or you can take a 10-min. air shuttle flight to get to Moorea. And if you are staying on Moorea and want to go shopping and sightseeing in Tahiti, you can commute to Tahiti in the morning and return in the afternoon. Details for this inter-island connection are given in the *Moorea* chapter and the *Tahiti* chapter contains information on Day Tours to Moorea.

If you only want to stay on **Moorea** and **Tahiti**, I suggest you spend the first few nights on Moorea and the final part of your visit in Tahiti. One of the statements I hear the most often from visitors when they arrive in Moorea is: "Oh, how I wish I had come here first."

In Tahiti you "must" take a trip around the island, whether by guided tour or renting a car. The 4WD Safari Tour across the interior of the island is also very different and interesting. Be sure to visit the public market, the Marché Municipale, and watch the sunset behind Moorea.

The best things to do on Moorea are to take a 4WD Safari Tour to visit the Belvedere Lookout and the restored stone *marae* in Opunohu Valley. Go on a **dolphin watch** boat excursion to see the spinner dolphins that live in the open ocean. You can also enjoy some whale watching on this trip from July-Oct. If you want to swim with dolphins, then visit the Dolphin Park at ICH Moorea Resort.

The Best of the Leeward Society Islands
      Almost everyone yearns to see **Bora Bora**, yet there are some visitors who deny themselves this privilege, claiming that it is too expensive or that they don't have time. If you think you'll never pass this way again, then I urge you to indulge yourself and just go ahead and do it. I do not recommend a day tour to Bora Bora, because so much of your time is spent at airports and just getting there and back to Tahiti in one day. Do spend at least 1-2 nights, and be sure to take an outrigger tour to discover the incredibly beautiful lagoon and motu islets. Stops are made to feed the stingrays and sharks and to let you swim and snorkel in the clear warm lagoon. If your budget will stretch that far, then book yourself and your significant other into an overwater bungalow for the complete Bora Bora experience. **Huahine** and **Taha'a** are now counted among the main tourist islands, especially since the opening of luxurious international hotels. **Raiatea** still retains its flavor of old Polynesia, with accommodations in several guesthouses called pensions, as well as a 3-star international class hotel. **Maupiti** makes a good day trip by boat from Bora Bora, or you can fly there and stay in a family pension. There are no tourist hotels.
      The Leeward Islands provide the **best sailing area** for those who want to do some **bareboat cruising** or join a programmed **yacht charter** with captain and crew. These waters also provide some of **the best fishing grounds** for sportfishing, with prize-winning catches of blue marlin and swordfish. If you have dreams of taking a **helicopter flight** somewhere in the islands, then I suggest you do it in Bora Bora. Better yet, fly by helicopter from Bora Bora to Le Taha'a Island Resort & Spa and treat yourself to a real hedonistic experience by staying a few days in one of their magnificent villas. A word of advice: visit Moorea before you stay in one of the super luxurious hotel resorts in the Leeward Islands. The hotel facilities, beaches and views on Moorea may disappoint you by comparison to those in Bora Bora or Taha'a.

The Best Atolls
      Rangiroa, **Tikehau**, **Manihi** and **Fakarava** are now being added to the itineraries of travelers who wish to discover the quiet beauty of the unspoiled Tuamotu atolls. **Scuba divers** are especially thrilled to drift dive through the passes, surrounded by thousands of fish and sharks. There are deluxe hotels and family pensions on each of these 4 atolls and they are easy to get to by airplane. There are plenty of activities organized to visit the lagoon by boat, with a picnic on an uninhabited motu islet and visits to a pearl farm. The best way to discover the vast lagoon of Rangiroa is on board the *Haumana*, a 12-passenger cruising yacht that offers 3, 4, and 7-night packages. *Aquatiki* offers cruise and dive charters in the Tuamotu Archipelago. See information in chapter on *Rangiroa*.

The Best Islands Off Track

All 6 of the **Marquesas Islands** can best be visited by taking a 14-day cruise from Tahiti on board the *Aranui 3* passenger/cargo ship. The *Silver Dawn* (formerly *World Discoverer*) will cruise from Tahiti to the Austral Islands, the remote Tuamotu atolls and the Marquesas Islands from Apr.-Oct. 2009. See details in chapter on *Planning Your Trip*.

The Best Way to Visit the Islands

The wholesale tour operators who specialize in package programs to Tahiti and Her Islands offer several vacation choices that will allow you to visit 1-5 islands. Some of these programs will schedule you to fly direct from the airport in Tahiti to one of the outer islands, and they sometimes include an overnight stay in Tahiti on the way back home.

Air Tahiti offers an interesting choice of "air passes" that will allow you to island hop among the Societies, the Tuamotu, the Marquesas and the Austral Islands. Their "Island Adventures" packages include airfare, lodging and some meals in all 5 archipelagoes. See details on these programs in chapter on *Planning Your Trip*.

The Best Way to Spend Your Last Evening in Tahiti

One of the questions visitors most frequently ask me is where should they go on their last evening in Tahiti. They are usually flying into Tahiti from one of the outer islands sometime during the afternoon and they have to fly home that night. What to do with the hours in between flights if they have no hotel/pension room to go to? Many times this happens on a Sunday, when the shops are closed.

I tell them to check their luggage at the airport storage room and take *le truck* into Papeete. There they can walk around and have dinner on the roulottes. They can also have a good draft beer at Les Trois Brasseurs micro brewery, with dinner if desired. Then they take *le truck* back to the airport in time for check-in. Another suggestion I give them is to check their luggage and take *le truck* or a taxi to the nearby Intercontinental Tahiti Resort. They can hang around the hotel grounds and swimming pools and have a drink at Le Lotus swim-up bar while watching the sunset over Moorea. A third recommendation is to go to Le Belvedere restaurant for the sunset and an early dinner. They will pick you up at the airport or ferry dock and take you and your luggage up the mountain to the restaurant. Afterward, they will take you to the airport in plenty of time for your flight. See details in *Tahiti* chapter.

The Best of the Best Resorts: My Favorites

Hotel Bora Bora, Bora Bora Nui, Bora Bora Lagoon Resort, Bora Bora Pearl Beach, Tikehau Pearl Beach Resort, Manihi Pearl Beach Resort, Le Taha'a Island Resort & Spa.

Best Overwater Bungalows/Suites/Villas

Moorea: Hotel Sheraton Moorea.
Huahine: Te Tiare Resort.
Taha'a: Le Taha'a Island Resort & Spa.
Bora Bora: Bora Bora Nui Resort, Sofitel Motu, Bora Bora Lagoon Resort.
Tikehau: Tikehau Pearl Beach Resort. Their overwater suites are my favorite accommodations in all the islands.
Manihi: Manihi Pearl Beach Resort.

Best Beach Bungalows/Suites/Villas

Moorea: Sofitel Moorea Resort; ICH Moorea Resort.
Taha'a: Le Taha'a Island Resort & Spa. The beach villas here get my top rating.
Bora Bora: Bora Bora Pearl Beach Resort, Hotel Bora Bora.
Rangiroa: Hotel Kia Ora has nice beach bungalows with a Jacuzzi or pool.
Tikehau: Tikehau Pearl Beach Resort. The a/c bungalows are very popular.

Best Garden Bungalows

Moorea: Moorea Pearl Beach Resort has garden bungalows with or without pools.
Bora Bora: Hotel Bora Bora has spacious garden *fares* with small swimming pools. The garden suites at Bora Bora Pearl Beach have plunge pools.

Best Luxury Accommodations

Taha'a: Le Taha'a Island Resort & Spa's Royal Beach Villa.
Bora Bora: St. Regis Resort's 3-bedroom Royal Estate, Royal Beach Pool Villa, Royal Overwater Pool Villa; Four Seasons' Presidential Suite; ICH Thalasso's Poevai Overwater Suite; Bora Bora Nui's Royal Horizon Overwater Villa and Royal Hillside Villa; and Bora Bora Lagoon Resort's Presidential Villa with pool.

Best Honeymoon Resorts

Tahiti and Her Islands provide the ideal setting for a romantic honeymoon, and the deluxe hotels with overwater bungalows are a favorite destination for newlyweds and other lovers. All the tour operators have honeymoon programs, or they can create a personalized package according to your wishes. I suggest that you also contact the hotels of your choice for information on their honeymoon programs.

Stepping down into the lagoon from the steps of your overwater bungalow is an unforgettable sensual delight, and there are many other pleasures to be enjoyed in these units. Unfortunately, privacy is not one of them. Most of the overwater bungalows are built too close together to provide total discretion, and your neighbors may be sharing your passion, albeit unwittingly.

Tahiti: ICH Tahiti Resort, Radisson Plazza.

Moorea: ICH Moorea Resort, Sheraton Moorea Lagoon, Sofitel Moorea Resort.
Huahine: Te Tiare Beach Resort.
Taha'a: Le Taha'a Island Resort & Spa.
Bora Bora: St. Regis Resort, ICH Thalasso, Sofitel Motu, Bora Bora Nui, Bora Bora Lagoon Resort, Bora Bora Pearl Beach, Hotel Bora Bora.
Rangiroa: Hotel Kia Ora, Kia Ora Sauvage.
Manihi: Manihi Pearl Beach Resort.
Tikehau: Tikehau Pearl Beach Resort.
Fakarava: Hotel Maitai Dream.
Nuku Hiva: Nuku Hiva Keikahanui Pearl Lodge
Hiva Oa: Hanakee Hiva Oa Pearl Lodge.

Best Resort for Privacy
Rangiroa: Kia Ora Sauvage
Tikehau: Tikehau Pearl Beach Resort

Best Family Resorts
Tahiti: Radisson Plaza, ICH Tahiti Resort, Sofitel Tahiti Resort, Royal Tahitien.
Moorea: ICH Moorea Resort, Moorea Pearl Resort, Les Tipaniers, Hotel Hibiscus, Linareva, Fare Arana, Fare Hamara, Te Nunoa Bungalow.
Huahine: Relais Mahana, Villas Bougainville, Pension Mauarii.
Bora Bora: Le Méridien, St. Regis, Four Seasons, Bora Bora Pearl Beach Resort, Hotel Matira.

Best Beds
Bora Bora: Hotel Bora Bora, Bora Bora Nui, Sofitel Motu, Sofitel Bora Bora Beach Resort and Bora Bora Lagoon Resort all have wonderfully comfortable mattresses. The beds at St. Regis are also great except for the hard-to-see black base that juts out around the mattress, which can bruise your legs when you stumble against it.

Best Bathrooms
Huahine: Te Tiare Resort has a Jacuzzi bathtub and separate shower with powerful water pressure.
Bora Bora: St. Regis Resort has a deep bathtub, a separate shower with an oversize rain nozzle plus a hand held nozzle, and Acqua de Parma bath products. Bora Bora Nui has a huge well lit bathroom of pink marble with an oversize bathtub, a separate shower with rain nozzle and hand held jet nozzle, separate toilet and bidet, and Aveda personal toiletries. Hotel Bora Bora has claw footed bathtubs and a separate shower with oversize rain nozzle and their own range of bath products.

Best Resort Spas

Tahiti: Le Spa at the Radisson Resort.

Moorea: Hélène'Spa at ICH Moorea Resort; Mandara Spa at Hotel Sheraton Moorea.

Taha'a: Manea Spa at Le Taha'a Island Resort & Spa.

Bora Bora: Thalasso Deep Ocean Spa at ICH Bora Bora Resort; Manea Spa at Bora Bora Pearl Beach Resort, Mandara Spa at Bora Bora Nui, Marú Spa at Bora Bora Lagoon Resort, and Fare Taurumi at Hotel Bora Bora, where a Balinese masseuse gave me the best massage of all.

Manihi: Try the sensuous Monoi Poe massage at Manihi Pearl Beach Resort that involves a string of pearls.

Best Resort Wedding Chapels

Bora Bora: ICH Thalasso, Le Méridien, Bora Bora Nui, Bora Bora Pearl Beach.

Best Tahitian Wedding Ceremonies

Moorea: Tiki Village.

Bora Bora: Patrick Taurua of Patrick's Activities/Maohi Nui.

Best Resort Beaches

Moorea: Sofitel Moorea Resort

Huahine: Relais Mahana

Bora Bora: Hotel Bora Bora, Bora Bora Nui, Le Méridien, St. Regis.

Best Resorts for Snorkeling

Moorea: Hotel Sheraton Moorea.

Huahine: Relais Mahana.

Taha'a: Le Taha'a Island Resort & Spa.

Bora Bora: Hotel Bora Bora; Bora Bora Nui, Bora Bora Pearl Resort; Bora Bora Lagoon Resort.

Manihi: Manihi Pearl Beach Resort.

Best Resorts for Safe Swimming in Lagoon without much coral

Moorea: Sofitel Moorea Resort, ICH Moorea Resort, in inner lagoon.

Huahine: Te Tiare, Relais Mahana.

Bora Bora: Le Méridien's inner lagoon, lagoonarium at St. Regis Resort.

Tikehau: Tikehau Pearl Beach Resort, in front of beach bungalows.

Best Views

Tahiti: any hotel with a view of Moorea.

Moorea: Sheraton Moorea Lagoon Resort; Sofitel Moorea Resort.

Raiatea: Taha'a, Bora Bora and Huahine viewed from Mt. Tapioi.

Taha'a: Le Taha'a has an excellent view of Bora Bora.

Bora Bora: Otemanu Mountain viewed from Hotel Bora Bora, Bora Bora Lagoon Resort, Bora Bora Pearl Beach, ICH Le Moana Resort, Sofitel Motu, ICH Thalasso, Le Méridien, St. Regis and Four Seasons.

Best Landscaping & Gardens
Tahiti: Le Royal Tahitien
Moorea: Hotel Sheraton Moorea, ICH Moorea Resort.
Bora Bora: Hotel Bora Bora, Bora Bora Nui, Bora Bora Lagoon Resort.

Best Small Resorts
Moorea: Club Bali Hai, Les Tipaniers.
Huahine: Relais Mahana.
Taha'a: Hotel Vahine Island; Hotel La Pirogue.
Bora Bora: Novotel, Hotel Matira.
Rangiroa: Novotel.

Best Small Upscale Accommodations
Moorea: Dream Island, Villa Corallina, Fenua Mata'i'oa, La Baie de Nuarei, Te Nunoa Bungalow.
Huahine: Villas Bougainville
Taha'a: Fare Pea Iti, Tiare Breeze.
Bora Bora: Mai Moana Island.
Rangiroa: Motu Teta
Tikehau: Royal Tikehau
Fakarava: Raimiti

Best Restaurants
Tahiti: Restaurant Jimmy's for Thai, Vietnamese & Chinese food, Coco's for French gourmet cuisine; Pink Coconut for La Nouvelle Cuisine Française; Lotus Restaurant at ICH Tahiti for best fusion cuisine; Hotel Royal Tahitien for poisson cru and local style meals; Western Grill for BBQ ribs; Chez Loula et Remy in Taravao for fresh seafood and local dishes.

Moorea: Aito Restaurant for poisson cru, fresh lagoon fish and seafood; Le Mayflower for French gastronomic cuisine; Te Honu Iti for steaks and sauces.

Huahine: Restaurant Mauarii for Polynesian food, fish and seafood; Te Tiare Resort for mahi mahi burger.

Raiatea: Jade Garden for Chinese dishes; Moe Moea for local style food.

Taha'a: Chez Louise for Polynesian meals and seafood; Taravana Yacht Club for Continental and local dishes.

Bora Bora: Villa Mahana for French gastronomic cuisine; Fare Manuia for French dishes; Bloody Mary's for fish.

Rangiroa: Vaimario for best French cuisine.

Manihi: Manihi Pearl Beach Resort for best fresh lagoon fish.
Fakarava: Pension Raimiti for all their excellent photographic meals.
Nuku Hiva: Chez Yvonne Katupa in Hatiheu for best restaurant in the Marquesas Islands.

Best Snacks & Patisseries
    Tahiti: L'Oasis du Vaima, Patachoux
    Moorea: Le Rotui in Pao Pao, Le Motu in Haapiti
    Huahine: New Marara, Chez Guynette
    Bora Bora: Pofai Beach Bar at Hotel Bora Bora

Best Pizza
    Tahiti: Lou Pescadou
    Moorea: Daniel's Pizza
    Huahine: Haamene Pizza
    Bora Bora: La Bounty
    Rangiroa: Vaimario

Best Seafood Buffet
    Tahiti: La Soirée Merveilleuse at Intercontinental Tahiti Resort

Best Bars
    Tahiti: Tiki Bar at ICH Tahiti Resort has Happy Hour daily and live music Wed.-Sun. Best night to meet locals is on Thurs.
    Moorea: Eimeo Bar at Sheraton Moorea Lagoon has Happy Hour with 2-for-1 drinks daily except Thurs, with live music on Fri. and Sun.; Motu Iti Bar at ICH Moorea Resort, and Autera'a Bar at Moorea Pearl Resort have good selection of cocktails.
    Taha'a: Manuia Bar at Le Taha'a. Bartender Maurice makes great cocktails.
    Bora Bora: Pofai Beach Bar at Hotel Bora Bora; Bloody Mary's.

Best Polynesian Show
    Tahiti: ICH Tahiti Resort has live dance shows nightly. The best is on Sat. night when Les Grands Ballets de Tahiti perform.
    Moorea: Tiki Village Theatre 4 nights a week; Club Bali Hai on Wed. evening.
    Bora Bora: Maohi Nui dancers, led by Patrick Taurua, perform several nights a week in various hotels, including fire dancing.

Best Land Excursions and Best Guides
    Tahiti: Circle Island Tour with William Leeteg of Adventure Eagle Tours or Bernie's Circle Island Tour sold by Paradise Tours. A Full Day Cross the Island Tour by Patrick Cordier of Patrick Adventure.

Moorea: 4WD Safari Tour by Albert Tours (Blanc-Blanc, Tom or Sal).
Huahine: 4WD Island Echo Tour by Paul Atallah.
Raiatea: Circle Island Tours and Visits to Marae Taputapuatea
Taha'a: 4WD Safari Tours by Dave's Tours, Vai Poe Excursions or Vanilla Tours.
Bora Bora: Circle Island Tour with Simplet Taxi. 4WD Safari Tours with Patrick Taurua of Maohi Nui Private Excursions.

Best Lagoon Excursions and Best Guides
Moorea: Dolphin & Whale Watching Expedition by Dr. Michael Poole; Dolphin & Lagoonarium Tours by Harold Wright; Picnic on the Motu with Albert Tours or Hiro's Tours.
Huahine: Lagoon Excursions, Shark Feeding Excursions, and Picnics on the Motu with Marc Garnier of Huahine Nautique.
Raiatea: Lagoon & Motu Excursion by Faaroa Tours or West Coast Charters.
Taha'a: Lagoon Excursions and Visits to Pearl Farms with Vai Po'e Excursions.
Bora Bora: A Boat Trip Around the Island with Shark Observation and Ray Feeding, with Shark Boy of Bora Bora or Raanui Tours. Patrick Taurua of Maohi Nui Private Excursions is the best guide for private tours and picnics on the motu.

Best Diving
There is world class diving in the passes of **Rangiroa, Manihi, Tikehau, Fakarava, Ahe, Toau,** and most other atolls in the Tuamotu Archipelago that open to the ocean. The Society Islands also offer exciting dives. There are dive centers on 13 islands and atolls in French Polynesia. The best known are TOPdive, Bora Bora Blue Nui, Manihi Blue Nui, Tikehau Blue Nui and Raie Manta Club.

Best Surfing
Tahiti: Taapuna Pass near Fisherman's Point, Taharu'u in Papara, Hava'e Pass in Teahupoo on Tahiti-Iti, and Papenoo on the east coast.
Moorea: Haapiti, Temae
Huahine: Pass at Fare and Ara Ara Pass in Parea.
Rangiroa: Avatoru Pass
Tikehau: Tuheiava Pass

Best Sunrise
Tahiti: Between Tautira and Teahupoo on Tahiti Iti peninsula.
Huahine: Relais Mahana and Parea.
Rangiroa: Kia Ora Sauvage

Best Sunset

Tahiti: Sunset beside Moorea as seen from Point Venus, and sunset behind Moorea as seen from Tahiti's west coast, especially from ICH Tahiti Resort.

Moorea: Hotel Sheraton Moorea (Apr.-Sept.)

Raiatea: Sunset Beach Motel.

Taha'a: Taravana Yacht Club.

Bora Bora: From the terrace of the Matira Terrace bar at Hotel Bora Bora. Aboard the *Taravana* on a sunset cruise.

Fakarava: From the beach or pier at Pension Havaiki Nui.

At Sea as viewed from the *Aranui* between Tahiti and the Marquesas Islands.

Best Moonrise

Tahiti: Between Tautira and Teahupoo on Tahiti Iti peninsula.

Rangiroa: Ocean side of atoll.

Tikehau: Tikehau Pearl Beach Resort.

Manihi: Manihi Pearl Beach Resort.

Best Stargazing

Manihi Pearl Beach Resort on the airport runway, Kia Ora Sauvage on the beach, Tikehau Pearl Beach Resort on the beach, Pension Raimiti in Fakarava.

Best Budget Friendly Islands

Huahine, Raiatea, Maupiti, Marquesas and Austral Islands.

Best Service and Staff

Hotel Bora Bora, St. Regis, Bora Bora Nui.

4. Land & People

LAND

Tahiti and Her Islands, officially known as **French Polynesia**, are sprinkled over 5,030 million sq. km. (almost 2 million sq. mi.) of ocean in the eastern South Pacific. French Polynesia is east of the International Date Line. Tahiti is 6,200 km. (3,844 mi.) from Los Angeles; 3,900 km. (2,418 mi.) from Auckland, New Zealand; and 8,800 km. (5,456 mi.) from Tokyo. The most northerly island in the Marquesas archipelago, Eiao, also known as Hatutu, is more than 2,000 km. (1,240 mi.) from the Austral Island of Rapa, the most southerly island.

The word Polynesia means "many islands." The total land area of these 118 Polynesian islands and atolls adds up to only 3,500 sq. km. (1,365 sq. mi.). The territory is geographically and politically divided into five archipelagoes: the Society Islands, Austral Islands, Marquesas Islands, Tuamotu Islands and the Gambier Islands. These island groups differ in terrain, climate and, to a lesser degree, the people.

High Volcanic Islands & Low Coral Atolls

All the Polynesian islands are basically of volcanic origin that were formed millions of years ago when volcanoes erupted from a rising column of magma in the asthenosphere called a "hot spot." Five strips of islands correspond to a succession of hot spots along the Pacific seabed. The MacDonald hot spot, southeast of Rapa, is believed to have come to life 15 or 20 millions of years ago, and is still intermittently active. A 2006 geological study of the Society Islands stated that Mehetia is estimated at 1.16-2.03 milion years in age; Tahiti Iti at 0.45-0.78 million; Tahiti Nui at 0.19-1.37 million; Moorea at 1.36-1.72 million, Huahine at 2.91-3.08 million, Taha'a at 1.10-1.41/2.62-3.39 million; Raiatea at 2.44-2.75 million; Bora Bora at 3.21-3.48 million, and Maupiti seems to have come into existence 4.21-4.51 million years ago.

During **Charles Darwin's** visit to Tahiti in 1842 he climbed a mountain and discovered that the flat coral atoll is actually a high island that has sunk deeper into the ocean when the original volcano disappeared completely under the water. The old volcanic core still remains underneath the atoll, but all you see is the coral ring, which encircles the lagoon. The coral rim of the atoll indicates how big the island once was. A series of small coral islets, strung together by often-submerged coral reefs, are seldom more than a quarter of a mile wide and only a few feet above the sea. Inside this narrow strip of coral the lagoon can be the size of a salt-water pond or as big as an inland sea.

White beaches of coarse and fine coral sand create a border between the sea and the green oasis of coconut forests, flowering trees and scented bushes. The live coral gardens of the reefs and inner lagoons are filled with a fantastic variety of tropical fish, sharks, rays, turtles, crustaceans, and other marine fauna.

Flora

From the moment you step off your plane in Tahiti you become aware that you are surrounded by flowers. The first scent is the sweet perfume of the beautiful white **Tiare Tahiti** (*Gardenia taitensis*) that a smiling *vahine* offers to welcome you to this luxuriant land of flowers.

This traditional custom of the islands existed long before there were passenger ships and airplanes. Until recently, when the Tahitians were traveling between the islands, they were adorned with crowns and leis of flowers. This sign of the traveler is still a custom in some of the remote islands, but the health department now prohibits transporting food and plants from Tahiti to the outer islands because of the fruit fly and other destructive insects.

Walk through the public market in the heart of downtown Papeete and just watch for a few minutes as the vendors sell their brilliantly colored anthuriums, birds of paradise, asters, carnations, red and pink ginger flowers, delicate orchids, vivid roses, and myriads of varied bouquets. You won't be complaining about the

---

HOW TO WEAR YOUR FLOWERS

"They are very fond of flowers," wrote Captain Cook, when he first visited Tahiti in 1769. "Especially of the Cape Jasmine (Gardenia taitensis, known as the Tiare Tahiti), of which they have great plenty planted near their houses; these they stick into the holes of their ears and into their hair..."

Many of the visitors to Tahiti have noticed that there is a custom of conversing through the wearing of flowers, and this language of the flowers still exists. Learn to read what they are saying when you see a big, husky man digging a ditch and wearing his Tiare Tahiti bud behind his ear; or when you see a young lady with her long hair coifed so nicely for that special evening and laced with orchids; when you see the proud Tahitian grandmothers with their woven hats and a hibiscus behind an ear.

When you wear your flower behind your right ear—it means you are single, available and looking. When you wear your flower behind your left ear—it means you are married, engaged or otherwise taken. When you wear flowers behind both ears—it means you are married but are still available. When you wear your flower backward behind your ear—it means "follow me and you'll find out how available I am." When you wear a flower backward behind both ears—it means anything goes. And when you see the young vahine with flowers in her hair—it means she's desperate, you'd better hurry up!

prices here. A drive around the island will give you an opportunity to see the many varieties of flowers flourishing in the rich soil of Tahiti.

Here in the Polynesian islands, we incorporate flowers into our daily lives. Both men and women can be seen wearing a fragrant blossom behind their ears, even while performing the most humdrum tasks. Often you can hear them softly singing to themselves. Wearing flowers does make you want to sing.

Traditional Tahitian Food Plants

On all the islands and atolls of French Polynesia you will find the graceful coconut palm, the "tree of life" to the Polynesians, which can be used in dozens of ways. Other trees and plants that provide traditional Tahitian foods are breadfruit, bananas, *fei* plantains, taro, tarua, manioc, arrowroot, sweet potato and yams. Complimentary food plants include: sugarcane, pandanus, *mape* (Tahitian chestnut), ti or *auti* (*cordyline fruticosa*), *vi* Tahiti or Tahitian apple (*Spondias dulcis*), kava (*Pometia pinnata Forster*), *nono* (*Morinda citrifolia*), small ginger roots called *rea*, bamboo, the candlenut tree (*Aleurites molucanna*), the wild hibiscus called *purau (Hibiscus tiliaceus)*, the *hotu* fruit of the *Barringtonia asiatica*, and varieties of purslane and cress, as well as several types of ferns.

Imported Food Plants

The European explorers, botanists, sailors, missionaries, traders and civil servants brought many species of economic flora to Tahiti, which flourish on most

---

THE MYSTICAL-MAGICAL INTOXICATING TI PLANT

The ancient Tahitians had 13 varieties of the **ti plant** (Cordyline terminalis or fructicosa) that they called **auti**. The most sacred of all ti plants in old Tahiti was the Ti-'uti, which was a fine variety planted chiefly in the marae enclosures for the gods and religious uses. Beautiful varieties of ti have been introduced in recent years, but it is still the glossy green leaves that were worn by orators, warriors and enchanters that are worn today by dancers, high priests and firewalkers. This small tree of the Liliaceae family is believed to possess mystical-magical qualities that will protect the house from fire, and hedges of auti surround many of the homes in the islands. The broad leaves are used as food wrappers and to line the pits where breadfruit is preserved by fermentation.

The ti is also used in traditional healing for diarrhea, vomiting, abscesses or ear infections. The root can be cooked in the underground stone oven to replace the breadfruit and the taro, and the large fibrous tuber was formerly made into candy. This root is very rich in sugar, and during the reign of King Pomare II, natives from the Sandwich Islands (now Hawaii) taught the Tahitians how to build a still and produce a potent liqueur from the auti root.

of the islands today. Among these food plants you will find varieties of: avocado, bay rum tree, Brazilian plum, cantaloupe, cashew nut, cayenne pepper, citron, coffee, custard apple, grapefruit, guava, gooseberry tree, jackfruit, Java almond, lime, lychee, mamee apple, mandarin, mango, orange, pakai, Panama cherry, papaya, passion fruit, pineapple, pistachio, pomegranate, quenette, rambutan, sea grape, soursop, Spanish plum, Surinam cherry, star apple, sugar apple, tamarind, vanilla and watermelon.

Chinese Gardens

Chinese immigrants brought their garden vegetables with them, which they plant in the high valleys of Tahiti. These colorful vegetables can best be seen at the Papeete market, where you will recognize varieties of bok choy, cabbages, carrots, cilantro, cucumbers, eggplant, ginger root, green peppers, jicama, lettuce, long beans and snap beans, parsley, pumpkins, soy bean sprouts, spinach, squashes, tomatoes, watercress, white radishes and zucchini.

Sacred Trees of Old Polynesia

The sacred trees of old Polynesia were chosen for their medicinal value, and the quality of their wood, bark, leaves or roots. Some of these trees are still used for carving into furniture, *umete* bowls, platters, small canoes, tikis and ceremonial clubs. These precious trees are the *tamanu* or *ati* (*Calophyllum inophyllum*), the *tou* (*Cordia subcordata*), rosewood or *miro* (*Thespesia populnea*), banyan or *ora* (*Ficus prolixa*), *aito* or ironwood (*Casuarina equisetifolia*), *reva* or *hotureva* (*Cerbera odollam*) and the *pua* (*Fagraea berteriana*).

Land-Based Fauna

There are no snakes in Tahiti and Her Islands and there are no poisonous spiders or fearsome land animals, except for the centipede (*Scolopendra subspinipes*), which lives in dark, humid areas, under rocks and in palm frond structures. Its bite is venomous and very painful to humans. It is nocturnal by nature and its diet is made up exclusively of cockroaches, while the centipede itself is a delicacy for chickens. So don't strangle the roosters that crow outside your hotel window all night long!

Almost every home in the Polynesian islands has a few house pets in the form of the *mo'o*, a yellow lizard that lives on the ceilings, where they feed on mosquitoes and other flying insects and bananas if they're available. Sometimes these critters find their way into hotel rooms, which has been known to disrupt the tranquility of the human occupants. These geckos are harmless, but they do seem to occasionally take delight in dropping "whitewash" on inappropriate places, such as your bed or head. The reptile population includes four gecko species and three lizard species, none of which are to be feared.

Here you will find the yellowish-red Tahitian dog, some of whom are descendants of the barkless vegetarian dogs that crossed the ocean aboard the double-hulled voyaging canoes of the pioneer Polynesians. They eat meat these days and sometimes they bark all night, in tandem with the cocks.

Along with the dog, the pig was the only domestic animal known to the Polynesian before the arrival of the Europeans. Both animals were raised for food. The pig is still baked in the underground ovens for special feasts, and dogs are still served in a "special Chinese sauce" during big celebrations. Some of the pigs have taken to the bush and men on the high islands organize wild boar hunts.

Captain Wallis gave a cat to the high chiefess Purea in 1767, and it found a mate somewhere, because today cats abound in all the inhabited islands and atolls. The little Polynesian rat and its cousins, who arrived aboard ships and boats, are threats to coconut trees without the metal bands. The *Rattus norvegicus*, a large brown rat, carries Tahitian meningitis and other contagious diseases. They also steal birds' eggs and fruit, and love to make their nests in thatched roofs.

In the Marquesas Islands you will see wild goats, sheep and cattle grazing on the precipitous cliffs overlooking the sea. Wild and tamed horses roam the plains of Ua Huka. The ancestors of these small horses were brought from Chile by Dupetit-Thouars in 1842.

A land crab called *tupa* lives in holes in the ground close to the lagoon and as far as a mile inland. They're edible if you pen them up and feed them coconut for ten days. Some people feed the *tupa* crabs to their pigs, but few families eat them now.

The mosquito and *nono* (sandfly) are two obnoxious pests that can truly ruin your vacation if you don't protect yourself from their stings. They particularly favor visitors, so be sure to bring a good insect repellent with you.

Pesticides are used in massive quantities, especially on the island of Tahiti, which is a concern for the public because of the risks of pollution and toxic effects in rivers and lagoons. Fresh water shrimp and blue-eyed eels with long ears live in the rivers and streams.

Birds

The early Polynesians and European explorers brought birds (*manu*) into these islands and other species have been introduced from Asia, Africa, Australasia and the Americas. Habitat changes and introduced species of birds are believed to be accountable for the extinction of certain species that formerly inhabited the Windward Society Islands. There are presently 104 known species of birds found in Tahiti and Her Islands.

Of the 27 species of sea birds nesting here, Murphy's petrel (*Pterodroma ultima*) is the only species that lives in Polynesia all the time. The birds you may see include terns, boobies, noddies, frigatebirds, petrels and the graceful white tropicbirds (phaetons), identified by two long white plumes that form the tip of the tail as they soar high over the valleys from the rocky cavities where they nest. 21 species of migratory sea birds have been observed as they fly from the North to the South Pacific. The white sand beaches and the bushes on the *motus* inside the reef on Tetiaroa atoll are nesting grounds for several species of sea birds, and the Tuamotu atolls have numerous bird islands. Almost a million sooty terns (*kaveka*) live on a small island offshore Ua Huka in the Marquesas Islands.

At least 13 species of land-birds coming from North America and Siberia reach these islands on a regular basis. The main land bird you will see is the Indian Mynah (*Acridotheres Tristis*), which was imported to Tahiti around 1903 to eradicate a beetle that was destroying the young coconuts. The cheeky Mynah also wiped out several species of birds by robbing their nests. The turtledove (*geopelia striata)* was introduced in 1950, and the red-tailed bulbul (*Pyconotus cafer*), a native of Asia, was introduced more recently, brought in from Rarotonga in the Cook Islands. The Tahitians gave the name *vini* to several small finch-like birds, which include the chestnut-breasted mannikin (*Lonchura Castaneothorax*), common waxbill (*Estrilda Astrild*), red-browed waxbill (Estrilda Temporalis), crimson-backed tanager (*Ramphocelus dimidiatus*) and the gray-backed white-eye (*Zosterops Lateralis*).

The Tahiti Lorikeet (*Vini peruviana*) disappeared from Tahiti around the end of the last century, when the Swamp Harrier was introduced. This pretty little blue and white bird, also known as *lori-nonette*, is still found on some of the Tuamotu atolls, but is on the endangered species list, along with the *pihiti (Vini ultramarine-Kuhl)* of the Marquesas Islands and all the other lorikeets.

The *mo'a oviri* or wild cock is a jungle fowl of the *Gallus Gallus* family, which was introduced by the early Polynesians. The roosters are brightly colored with red, green and black feathers, and the hens are beige, brown or black. These birds can fly for several yards and they live in a free state, not really belonging to any family, but roost in trees and bushes close to a good source of food, such as my house. The roosters crow at all hours of the night, especially during the full moon, and of course, when you're trying to take a nap in the afternoon. I buy rice and bread for them and imported frozen chickens for myself. Their biggest enemies, apart from the Swamp Harrier, are little Tahitian boys, who catch the roosters and use them as fighting cocks.

Ocean, Reef & Lagoon Fauna

Scientists specializing in coral reefs have inventoried more than 800 species of shore fishes in Tahiti and Her Islands, with 633 species reported in the Society Islands. The oceanic slope is the richest part of a coral reef, and this is where you will have a better chance of finding crayfish or rock lobsters (*Panulirus penicillatus* called *oura miti*) and slipper lobsters (*Parribacus antarticus* called *tianee* in Tahitian). The near surface zones of the reef abound with surgeonfish, parrotfish, wrasses and red mullets. The external reef is also inhabited by various species of triggerfish, soldier-fish, squirrelfish, bass, perch, rock cod, angelfish, demoiselle-fish, mullet, and gray sharks and moray eels. You may also come across a green turtle (*Chelonia mydas*) or see a rare jellyfish or an occasional sea snake in this underwater zone.

Most of the mollusks and crustacea are found on the reef flats, which are also favored by pencil sea urchins and holothurians (sea cucumbers, called *rori* in Tahitian). The trigger-fish, puffer-fish, rock cods, box-fish, rascass and butterfly cod make their permanent homes here, and parrot-fish, surgeon-fish, angel-fish and small sharks, usually the harmless black-tipped and white-tipped variety, will visit the reef flats at high tide. Submerged coral plateaus act as passages between the oceanic slopes and the lagoons, and are the homes for echinoderms, particularly sea urchins, clam shells, octopus, small sponges and anemones, annelid worms and a variety of crabs. Lizardfish, puffer-fish and trumpet-fish are also common in this area. At high tide small schools of red mullet, jacks and parrotfish cross the zone on their way from the ocean to the lagoons.

On the lagoon slopes, as well as in the passes and the cracks in the reef (*hoa*), which have a sandy bottom sloping gradually to the center of the lagoon, is the favorite area of sponges, sand crabs, seashells (littorinids, nerites, ceriths), oysters, pearl oysters, cowries, strombs, spider shells, cones, all types of holothuria, *Ophiuridae*, starfish, *taramea*, some species of sea urchins (*vana*), soles, sand goby (*avaava*), leopard rays and some red mullets.

The coral outcrops and pinnacles are habitats of bivalve mollusks, including the colorful velvet-mantled reef clam (*Tridacna maxima*), called *pahua* locally. Numerous small species of fishes also gather here: surgeonfish, angelfish, butterfly fish, soldier-fish, harp-fish, butterfly cod, trumpet-fish, box-fish, porcupine-fish and trigger-fish.

There is almost no living coral or algae on the bottom of the lagoons, which are colonized by clamshells, pearl oysters, stony oysters and ark shells. Spider shells, a rare helmet shell or conch shell live on the softer sand bottom, but the majority of shells, including the pencil shells, miters, harp shells, olives, ceriths and several cones, remain hidden in the sand during the daytime.

The open lagoon waters are the habitat of roving fishes, including unicorn-fish (*ume*), *rotea*, *kukina*, coral trout (*tonu*), chameleon sea bass (*hoa*), lagoon sharks and stingrays. The (*lutjanus*) snappers, sweetlip, flying fish, garfish, great barracuda (*ono*), sea-pike barracuda (*tiatio*), jacks and mullets come and go between the lagoon and the ocean, and the silver scad (*ature*) also visit the lagoon for brief periods during certain seasons.

The flora of the fringing reefs is rich, and trochus are abundant in many parts of the fringing reef, but the fishes found here are usually in the juvenile stage. These may include moray eels, rock eels, rascasse, surgeonfish, wrasses, gobies, blennies and angelfish.

Three types of rays are found in Polynesian waters, and they are not aggressive unless threatened. The biggest danger is when a bather treads on a ray that is buried in the sand in shallow water. The most spectacular and famous member of the family is the giant manta ray (*Manta alfredi (Macleay), fafa piti),* that has a wingspan up to 25 feet across and may weigh almost two tons. The spotted eagle ray (*Aetobatis nari nari Euphrasen*) is the "bird ray" (*fai manu*) to the Tahitians because of its protruding head and narrow snout. They feed on mollusks and are one of the most important predators of the valuable pearl oysters in the lagoons of the Tuamotu and Gambier Islands. Several species of rays equipped with venomous spines on their tails are found in Polynesia. The stingray (*Himantura sp., fai iu*) lives near coral reefs or in the brackish water of some large bays around the high islands. The pectoral fins or wings of these species, as well as those of most other rays, are tasty and considered a delicacy, sometimes appearing on the menu in seafood restaurants in Tahiti and Moorea.

Sea turtles (*honu*) were once reserved for the high chiefs and priests of Tahiti, as this marine reptile was held *tapu* (sacred and forbidden). The three species living in Polynesian waters are the leathery turtle, the green turtle and the hawksbill turtle, which are on the list of endangered species and, therefore, *tapu*. However, these turtles are still massacred for their flesh and carapaces.

The most important commercial fishes found in the ocean depths surrounding French Polynesia include several species of the tuna family, principally, the yellow fin tuna (*Neothunnus albacora macropterus, aahi),* which are fished year round. Along with the tuna, the mahi mahi dolphinfish (*Coryphaena hippurus*) is the favorite fish served in restaurants. The great barracuda (*Sphyraena barracuda, ono*), the wahoo (*Acanthocybium solandri, paere*), the deep-water swordfish (*Xyphias gladius, haura or meka*), and the salmon of the gods (*Lampris Luna),* are also served in seafood restaurants. The bonito (*Katsuwonus pelamis, auhopu*) is the most commonly caught fish, and is preferred by most Tahitians to any other fish, but the taste is a bit too "fishy" for most visitors. Many other species of edible fish abound in this oceanic wonderland, which are taken home by the local fishermen for their own dinner.

Roughly one-third (or 25) of the species of dolphins and whales in the world are found in the waters of Tahiti and Her Islands. The spinner dolphins (*Stenella longirostris)* are the easiest to find around Tahiti and Moorea because they live the closest to shore. The humpback whales (*Megaptera novaeangliae*) can be seen and heard offshore Moorea between Jul.-Oct., when they come up from Antarctica to mate and give birth. They also escape the austral winters by visiting the Australs, Gambier and Tuamotu Islands, as well as the Leeward Society group and the Marquesas Islands. Black and white killer whales (*Orcinus Orca*) have been sighted numerous times in the Marquesas Islands, especially around Nuku Hiva, where there is a scuba diving center.

According to Richard H. Johnson, an American marine biologist and local shark specialist living in Tahiti, there are an estimated 35 species of sharks in French Polynesian waters. The sharks visitors normally see during a shark feeding or shark observation excursion inside the lagoon are the blackfin reef shark or *Carcharhinus Melanopterus*.

Natural Dangers

The ocean, coral reef, lagoons and coral gardens do have a few inhabitants that are not man's best friend. Sea snakes are rare in Polynesia and only one species

(*Pelamis platurus*) is occasionally seen and caught along the coasts of some of the islands. This bi-colored snake has a brownish back and yellow belly and its venom is dangerous to humans. The theory is that these serpents hitchhiked on the bottoms of ships arriving in Tahiti from islands to our west, where the snakes are prevalent.

The natural dangers you want to avoid in the lagoon are: the "crown of thorns" starfish, called *taramea* in Tahitian; the sting of the jellyfish; burns from the Holuthurian or sea cucumber, also called sea leech, *rori* in Tahitian, and its cousin with spaghetti-like sticky tubules; burns from the sea anemone; the sting of the stone fish, called *nohu* in Tahitian; the sting of the scorpion fish and fire coral; the sting of sea urchin spines, called *vana* in Tahitian; and the highly poisonous varieties of cone shells, members of the *Conidae* family. There are 60 species of cones in Polynesia, but the most dangerous are the geographic, textile, marbled, aulicus and tulip cones. The best way to protect yourself from any of these unpleasant encounters is to wear plastic reef sandals or other appropriate shoes when walking in the lagoon or on the reef, and to watch where you put your hands and body when snorkeling or scuba diving.

The moray eel rarely attacks humans, but it will bite when it is provoked and feels threatened. Keep your hands safely out of the crevices or cavities in the coral, where the moray eel may be lurking.

Shark attacks occur most frequently in the atolls, along the exterior of the barrier reefs and in the shallow fissures between the exterior reef and the interior lagoons. Some of these attacks happen when a spear fisherman is trailing a string of fish behind him. Several scuba diving and snorkeling excursions include feeding the sharks and moray eels, who have been "tamed" by repetitious feedings.

You can avoid any potential problems by swimming only in the areas where you see the locals swimming; do not swim in the ocean at night; leave your bright jewelry at your hotel when you go swimming, snorkeling or scuba diving, as it can reflect the sun and refracted light in the water, and attract the attention of moray eels and sharks; and wear protective footgear when you're swimming in the lagoons and walking on the reef.

PEOPLE

The census of September 2007 counted 259,596 residents of French Polynesia, an increase of 14,750 people (6%) since the last census of November 2002, for an average annual growth rate of 1.2%. Three-quarters of the population live in the Windward Society Islands; 13% in the Leeward Society Islands; and the rest in the Marquesas, Austral and Gambier Islands.

On the island of Tahiti, the commune of Faa'a remains the most populated, with 29,851 inhabitants, followed by Papeete with 26,017 residents. The Moorea-Maiao commune had an increase of 13% (now with 16,500 residents), while the commune of Bora Bora has 4% more people than in 2002 for a total population of 8,992.

Life expectancy in the islands is 73 years for men and 76.9 years for women, which means that people are living approximately 5 years longer than the numbers indicated just 3 years ago. However, the number of deaths due to road accidents was 3.5 times higher in French Polynesia in 2007 than in metropolitan France. There were 228 accidents with 42 dead and 325 injured people. Suicide by hanging or drinking herbicides also takes the lives of several young people each year.

The Polynesians

The majority of the people who live in the 5 island groups of French Polynesia are the **Maohi** people or Eastern Polynesians. Whether they live in the Society Islands, the Marquesas, Tuamotu-Gambier or Austral Islands, they are commonly referred to as **Tahitians**. The Polynesians refer to one another according to their island or archipelago, such as a Marquesan, a Paumotu (native of the Tuamotu Islands), a Rurutu or Rapa Iti, a Mangareva, and so forth.

Two distinct racial types settled the Marquesas Islands and some of the Marquesans have longer, narrow heads. Red hair was added by European sailors from exploration ships and whalers. There are striking differences in the Paumotu physical types, as well as their language and culture. Some of the men on the Tuamotu atolls are big strapping fellows, with wide flat noses, while others are more squat, with big heads, small button noses and dark brown skin. Still others have thin lips, aquiline features, slim bodies and light tan skin. The Austral Islanders resemble their neighbors in the Cook Islands, with almost blue-black hair, Spanish eyes and heavy beards. In Mangareva and the other Gambier Islands the earliest settlers appear to have been castaways from the Tuamotu archipelago, the Marquesas and Rarotonga.

The first European visitors to Tahiti were impressed by the personal cleanliness of the people. They may take 3-4 cold water showers a day. A group of dancers

---

POLYNESIAN ARISTOCRACY

The first Europeans to discover Tahiti found a highly evolved aristocratic society divided into three distinct groups. The first was the **Arii** or princely caste, whose king or Arii Rahi, was considered a sacred being. The **Raatira** were minor chiefs and landowners, and the **Manahune** were the common people. The **Arioi** were a kind of sect or religious fraternity that originated in Bora Bora. Their rank in the society was identified by their tattoos. They excelled in dancing and good manners and lived totally promiscuous lives, killing their children at birth. They traveled like troubadours from island to island, performing erotic ballets and political skits. The Manahune or *kaina* of today's Tahiti still forms the majority of the population. These Polynesians are the blue-collar workers, at the bottom end of the economic structure, with the least political power today.

or workers or spectators on a hot day smell only of soap, *monoi* or flowers. Being dirty or wearing dirty clothes was traditionally a matter of shame. There are, of course, many exceptions to this custom today.

The Chinese

The first Chinese were brought to Tahiti during the American Civil War to work for the Tahiti Cotton and Coffee Plantation Company in Atimaono, on Tahiti's south coast districts of Papara and Mataiea. A contingent of 329 Chinese laborers arrived in Tahiti from Hong Kong on February 28, 1865, coming from a district around Canton and the Kwangtung Province, who spoke the Hakka dialect. Eleven months later Atimaono had a total of 1,010 Chinese workers who planted cotton, coconut trees, coffee, sugar cane, fruit trees and vegetable gardens at Atimaono.

At the end of the war there was no money to send the Chinese home, so most of them took jobs to earn their return fare. About a hundred of these Chinese workers remained in Tahiti and began growing vegetables on rented land, opening small stores in Tahiti and several of the outer islands. A second wave of Chinese immigrants arrived in Tahiti in 1890, who had a higher social standing, and the first Chinese women arrived in 1907. Gradually these Chinese businessmen acquired wealth and today they are integrated in all the professions, but are primarily the merchants of French Polynesia. Many of the Chinese intermarried with the Tahitians and were eventually allowed to become French citizens, when several families changed their names to sound more "Frenchified." Today Mr. Wong has Chinese cousins who use the name of Vongue.

The French

French people from all walks of life began arriving in Tahiti as early as 1843, when the Protectorate was created in Tahiti, with Papeete as the government capital. French civil servants, lawyers, *notaires*, small businessmen, schoolteachers, medical professionals, missionaries and military men settled here, often intermarrying with the most important families of Tahiti.

Most of the French live on the island of Tahiti and her sister island of Moorea. There are small settlements of French *fonctionnaires* or retired civil servants living on Raiatea, Taha'a and Bora Bora, and in the Marquesas Islands of Hiva Oa and Nuku Hiva, with just a scattering of French on the more isolated islands.

The Expatriates

There are some 300 Americans living in French Polynesia, primarily in the Society Islands, where they are employed in tourism and the cultured pearl industry, or they have retired from business.

Even though the French and other Europeans have never settled in large numbers in French Polynesia, there has been a recent influx of French moving to these islands, as well as some other citizens of the European Union. The population also includes a few expatriates from Australia, New Zealand and other South Pacific Islands.

The Demi

A *demi* is a Polynesian with mixed blood. The first half-caste or *demi* was born about nine months after the Spanish caravel *San Lesmes* was wrecked on the reef of Amaru in the Tuamotu atolls in 1526. After that came more Spaniards, followed by the Dutch and then the British sailors, who arrived in Tahiti in 1767. The French followed and then Tahiti became a favored destination for sea rovers, merchants, lotus-eaters, writers, painters and wastrels.

Throughout the years the pure Polynesian stock has been diminished by contact with the French, English, Americans, Germans, Russian, Swedish, Norwegians, Spanish, South Americans, Japanese, Africans—you name it. The *demi* is often very attractive and reasonably intelligent, and usually has a pretty good education, and a good job with the local government, quite frequently obtained through family connections. The *demi* can also be one of the most confused people you'll ever meet, because they live between two cultures.

On one hand they want to be sophisticated and snobbish French, and on the other hand, they are happiest when they're slurping up the *ma'a* Tahiti with their fingers and singing *kaina* songs in Tahitian during a boozy *bringue*. Some of them are adept at combining the two contrasting cultures. There's a saying in Tahiti that describes the dilemma of the average Tahitian-European person: "When he wakes up the morning, the *demi* doesn't know which side of the bed to get out of."

THE VERY FRIENDLY PEOPLE OF TAHITI

During a 1981 interview on the *East-West Connection* television program in Los Angeles, the hostess asked Tahiti's Minister of Tourism: "What is the racial breakdown of the majority of the people?" He replied: "We used to say in Tahiti that the whole world slept with Tahiti."

---

5. A Short History

GENERAL HISTORY OF FRENCH POLYNESIA
The Polynesian Migrations

Archaeologists, ethnologists, anthropologists, linguists and other scholars have long debated the questions of when, why, and how the pioneer Polynesians crossed thousands of miles of open ocean to settle on these islands in the Eastern Pacific that are now called **French Polynesia.** New archaeological evidence and improved techniques of radiocarbon dating may refine the theories, but at present most of the experts who study this subject agree that the Australoid ancestors of the Melanesian, Micronesian and Polynesian people came from Southeast Asia. They walked across the landmass that existed in the final Ice Age to reach what are now the Indonesian islands of Sumatra, Java and Borneo, and on to Australia and New Guinea, which were then joined, settling in the Southwest Pacific around 30,000 BC. A group of dark-skinned people called the Papuans also came from Southeast Asia, arriving in the southwestern Pacific area between 7,000 and 3,500 BC.

Several thousands of years later, between 3,000 and 1,000 BC, a group of lighter-skinned Austronesians from Asia forced the Papuans to moved further inland in what is now Irian Jaya and Papua New Guinea. Some of these wanderers then set out to explore the more eastern South Pacific islands, eventually settling on every speck of land that could support life. They sailed eastward in their huge double ocean going canoes, using the sun, stars, wind, ocean currents, and the flight patterns of birds as their guides, referring to their crude stick charts to navigate to new islands. Carrying 100-500 people on board these canoes made of lashed planks with sails of pandanus matting, they brought with them their women and children, pigs and dogs, coconuts and taro, breadfruit tree seedlings and roots, shrubs and trees, as well as flowering plants, which were to be used for food, clothing, medicines, and other household needs. Historians believe this eastward progress occurred over 5,000 years, and departures from a settled island were necessitated due to overpopulation, food and water shortage or because of internal fighting.

The Polynesian culture is believed to have evolved in the central Pacific, in Tonga or Samoa, which they called Havaiki, their ancestral religious center. After a pause of 1,000 years, a migratory wave from this "cradle" of Polynesia brought the new explorers even farther eastward, and some archaeologists believe that as far back as 500 BC the first of these double-hulled canoes reached the Marquesas Islands. A tall and stately race of proud and cultured people settled on some of the 20 islands, which they called *Te Fenua Te Enata*, or *Te Henua Te Enana*, "The Land of the Men."

During the next migratory movement of the Polynesians, some 500 years after arriving in the Marquesas, the voyaging canoes sailed south and west to the Tuamotu Archipelago and Mangareva, north to the Hawaiian Islands, and even farther eastward to discover and populate Easter Island, all around 850 AD. The great Polynesian migrations then proceeded southwest, with canoes departing from the new religious and cultural center of Havaiki, Raiatea in the Leeward Society Islands, around 1,000 AD. These voyagers settled in Rarotonga in the Cook Islands and in New Zealand, completing a triangle of Polynesian colonization. The Polynesian people of French Polynesia, the Cook Islanders, Easter Islanders, native Hawaiians and the Maoris of New Zealand all speak variations of the Maohi language, the native tongue of their Marquesan ancestors.

European Exploration

In 1513 the Spanish explorer **Vasco Nuñez de Balboa** crossed the Isthmus of Panama and sighted the mighty Pacific Ocean. Seven years later, in 1520, **Ferdinand Magellan**, a Portuguese in the service of the Spanish, sailed to the Philippines, but the only island he sighted in Polynesia was the atoll of Puka Puka in the northeastern Tuamotu archipelago. The Spanish caravel *San Lesmes* was wrecked on the reef in Amaru in the Tuamotus around 1526 and the shipwrecked sailors supposedly married Polynesian women. In 1595 **Alvaro de Mendaña de Neira** was searching for the Solomon Islands, which he had discovered in 1567, and during this second voyage into the South Seas he discovered the southern group of the Marquesas Islands. In 1606, 80 years after the disappearance of the *San Lesmes*, **Pedro Fernández de Quiros**, who had been Mendaña's chief pilot, discovered a number of the Tuamotu Islands before continuing on to other island groups further west. This was the last of the Spanish explorations in the Pacific during that era.

In 1615-16 the Dutch explorers **Le Maire** and **Schouten** discovered several atolls in the Tuamotus, and in 1722 **Jacob Roggeveen**, another Dutch captain, sailed through the Tuamotus and passed the island of Makatea on his way to the Society Islands, where he sighted Maupiti in the Leeward Society Islands. But he failed to see Bora Bora, Raiatea or Taha'a, all high islands that are visible from Maupiti.

The Dutch were then followed by the British, with **Commodore John Byron**, grandfather of the famous poet, discovering more of the Tuamotu atolls aboard the *H.M.S. Dolphin* in 1765. If any of the European explorers found Tahiti, they left no record of their discovery.

The *Dolphin* returned to the South Seas in 1767 under the command of **Captain Samuel Wallis**, who discovered the island of Tahiti, and anchored in Matavai Bay on June 23, 1767. He was followed just 10 months later by French **Admiral Louis Antoine de Bougainville**, who also discovered Tahiti, and claimed the island for France during his visit in April 1768. In April 1769, Lieutenant **James Cook**, aboard the *H.M.S. Endeavour*, made his first trip to Tahiti. He returned again in 1773, 1774 and 1777. Cook visited Moorea and discovered the Leeward

Islands of Raiatea, Taha'a, Huahine, Bora Bora, Tupai and Maupiti, which he named the Society Islands, as they lay contiguous to each other.

In 1772 Spanish captain **Don Domingo de Boenechea** anchored his ship, the *Aguilla*, in the lagoon of Tautira on the Tahiti Iti peninsula. After claiming the island for his country and king, Boenechea sailed for Peru, but returned in 1774 to establish the first long-term European settlement on the island, with two missionaries and two military men. The Spanish rule ended in Tahiti following the death of Boenechea, when the missionaries returned to Peru.

"Breadfruit Bligh" & The Bounty

The story of **Captain William Bligh** and the mutinous crew aboard the *H.M.S. Bounty* provided a colorful chapter in Tahiti's history following their arrival at Point Venus in Matavai Bay on October 26, 1788. Once ashore, Bligh and his men had to wait five months before the breadfruit they sought would be at the right stage for transplanting. The sailors happily accepted this respite from Bligh's tight discipline, and willingly adapted to the Tahitian *aita pea pea* (no problem) philosophy of life, complete with all the pleasures any sailor could ever imagine.

When the *Bounty* weighed anchor on April 4, 1789, and headed toward the Leeward Islands of the Society group, Bligh was faced with a moody, belligerent crew. The punishments Bligh meted out for his men, and his insults to his officers were too harsh to endure after the idyllic life the men had enjoyed in Tahiti. Acting Lieutenant Fletcher Christian was especially disturbed, and his fury finally exploded into a dramatic mutiny, which is remembered as the most famous mutiny in history.

Bligh was hauled out of bed early on the morning of April 28, tied up and dragged on deck. He and 18 of his officers and men were put into an open launch with food and water, some wine and rum, a compass, a quadrant, some canvas, and lines and sails. Then the boat was set adrift in the open ocean, a few miles from Tofua in the Tongan Islands, whose inhabitants were extremely unfriendly in those days. Bligh's success in sailing the small open boat across 5,800 km. (3,600 mi.) of ocean to Timor and Batavia in the Dutch Indies, is one of the most remarkable voyages in history.

Twice Fletcher Christian sailed the *Bounty* to Tubuai, 568 km. (355 mi.) due south of Tahiti in the Austral Islands, but they were unable to stay there because the natives were so hostile. They returned to Tahiti for supplies, and when the *Bounty* left Matavai Bay for the last time, some of the British sailors remained ashore at Point Venus. Aboard the ship with Christian were 8 of his fellow mutineers, 6 Tahitian men, 12 Tahitian women and a little girl. This small group reached the uninhabited island of Pitcairn, where they burned the *Bounty* and began a new life ashore. There was no news of Christian and his party for 18 years.

The 16 men from the *Bounty* who chose to remain in Tahiti settled down with their wives and families. Two of them had died by the time the H.M.S. *Pandora* anchored in Matavai Bay in 1791, but **Captain Edward Edwards**, who had been sent from England in search of the mutineers, arrested the remaining 14 men. The *Pandora* was shipwrecked and 4 of the men were drowned before they could reach England for their trial. During a court martial inquiry in England, 3 of the men were condemned to death and hanged, and the remaining 7 were set free. **Peter Heywood** wrote the first Tahitian dictionary in prison while awaiting his trial.

Captain Bligh had also undergone a trial by the English court, which cleared his name for any guilt in the *Bounty* mutiny, and he sailed back to Tahiti, arriving in Matavai Bay on April 10, 1792, as commander of the *H.M.S. Providence* and her armed tender, the *Assistance*.

Bligh remained in Tahiti for three months, collecting 2,126 breadfruit trees and 500 other plants to take back to the West Indies. The breadfruit seedlings were planted in St. Vincent and in Port Royal, Jamaica. When the trees grew and began to bear fruit, the Negro slaves refused to eat the starchy breadfruit because they didn't like the taste.

The English Lose to the French

The English Protestant missionaries from the London Missionary Society (LMS) arrived aboard the *Duff* and landed at Point Venus on March 5, 1797, to convert the Tahitians to the Gospel. **George Pritchard** of the LMS gained the confidence of **Queen Pomare IV** and convinced her that Tahiti should be under the protection of England. Although **Queen Victoria** was unwilling to declare Tahiti a protectorate of England, a power struggle between the English Protestants and the French Catholic missionaries in Tahiti almost brought England and France to the brink of war.

The end result was that Queen Pomare IV and the LMS missionaries lost their battle with the French, under the guns of *La Reine Blanche*, a French warship commanded by **Admiral Dupetit-Thouars**. Tahiti became a French protectorate in 1842 and guerrilla rebellions on Tahiti and some of the other islands resisted the French invasion until 1846, when France gained control over Tahiti and Moorea.

French Colonialism

Tahiti and her dependencies became a full-fledged French colony on December 29, 1880, when the century-old reign of the Pomare family formally came to an end and French nationality and rights were bestowed on all Tahitians.

The Pomare's dominions included Tahiti, Moorea, Maiao, Mehetia, the Tuamotu islands and Tubuai and Raivavae in the Austral Islands. The French had already annexed the Marquesas Islands in 1842 and all the other islands were annexed by 1901.

In 1903 the *Etablissements Français de l'Océanie* (EFO), or French Territories of Oceania, were established, incorporating all of the French holdings in the Eastern Pacific into one colony. Copra, cotton, mother-of-pearl shell, phosphate, vanilla and fruits were exported in exchange for manufactured goods. By 1911 there were about 3,500 colonists, mostly French, living in Polynesia, plus the Chinese immigrants who had been brought to Tahiti in the 1860s to work in the cotton fields of Atimaono.

Although Tahiti was geographically far from the main theaters of the two world wars, the colony was politically involved because of its French connection. During World War I almost 1,000 Tahitian soldiers fought against the Germans in Europe, and the town of Papeete was bombarded by 2 German cruisers on Sept. 22, 1914, when they sank a French navy ship in the harbor.

During World War II young men from Tahiti joined the Pacific Battalion, were shipped to Europe, and fought side by side with the forces of the Free French. Bora Bora was used as a military supply base for the American forces, with 5,000 soldiers, sailors and Seabees arriving on the small island in 1942. Besides a few cannon in the hills and some old Quonset huts, the only reminders of the American presence in Bora Bora today are some blue-eyed Tahitians with light hair and skin.

French Polynesia

A 1957 statute changed the *Etablissements Français de l'Océanie* colony into a French Overseas Territory, with the official name of French Polynesia. In the early 1960s a large harbor was built in Papeete, an international airport was opened in Faaa, the French established the *Centre d'expérimentations du Pacifique* (CEP), the Pacific Experimentation Center in Tahiti, and MGM brought a big film crew to make another movie of *Mutiny on the Bounty*. All of these rapid changes brought French Polynesia into the modern age, accompanied by problems of inflation, unemployment, housing problems, pollution, emotional instability, juvenile delinquency and political discontent among an increasing number of the population.

French Nuclear Testing

French Polynesia entered the nuclear age in 1963 when the French chose the Tuamotu atolls of Moruroa, 1,200 km. (720 mi.) southeast of Tahiti, and Fangataufa, 40 km. (24 mi.) south of Moruroa, as sites for the *Centre d'expérimentations du Pacifique* (CEP), Pacific Experimentation Center. Although the local political parties protested the invasion, President Charles de Gaulle responded by outlawing political parties.

On Sept. 11, 1966, De Gaulle watched from an offshore French warship as the first nuclear test was carried out, exploding in the atmosphere almost 600 m. (2,000 ft.) above the turquoise lagoon of Moruroa. Between 1966-1974, the French made 41 atmospheric tests in Moruroa and Fangataufa, and between 1975-1991, some 134 underground tests were completed, by drilling a shaft deep into the coral foundation under the lagoons. President François Mitterand suspended the nuclear testing in April 1992 and most of the 7,750 employees of the CEP returned to France or to their islands in French Polynesia. In June 1995, France's newly elected president, Jacques Chirac, announced a new series of eight nuclear tests, to be completed by the end of May 1996.

The shock of this announcement reverberated around the world, and on Sept. 5, 1995, when a 20-kiloton explosion was carried out in Moruroa, the result was disastrous for France, and especially for French Polynesia's tourism and economy. Severe rioting broke out in Papeete, with several buildings burned, the Tahiti-Faaa International Airport terminal was partially burned, and the vehicles in the parking lot were damaged and burned. On Jan. 27, 1996, France made its 6th and final nuclear test at Fangataufa, and 2 days later President Chirac announced that the tests were finished forever.

Some of the 1,500 workers, technicians and scientists, brought from France and Tahiti for these tests, finished their work and studies and went home, while the French Army and Legionnaires dismantled the 2 nuclear bases.

Internal Autonomy Government

In 1977 the French government granted **administrative autonomy** to French Polynesia, and domestic or internal autonomy was given in 1984, consolidated in 1990 and extended in 1996. On February 12, 2004, the French government gave French Polynesia the status of a **French Overseas Community**, rather than a Territory, which means that the Assembly of French Polynesia can adopt "laws" in the most important areas, and not just "resolutions", or acts of an administrative nature. This revision of the Constitution also enlarges the field of responsibilities of French Polynesia, which can negotiate international agreements with foreign states, in matters relevant to its responsibility. It also may become a member of international organizations and have representation in foreign states.

The French Polynesian Government consists of a president, who is elected for a 5-year term by the Assembly and Council of Ministers whom he appoints before submitting the list to the Assembly's vote. The Assembly consists of 57 members, who are elected every 5 years by votes and who represent the 5 archipelagoes. The French Polynesian Government is represented in the French Parliament by 2 deputies and a senator, plus an advisor in the French Social and Economic Council.

A French High Commissioner represents the State in French Polynesia, and the Republic of France controls defense, law and order, justice, worldwide international responsibility and the currency. The French *gendarmes* have brigades on all the larger islands and each *commune* has one or more Tahitian *mutoi*, municipal policemen, whose duties may include directing school traffic and tracking down scooters or cars that were "borrowed" on a Saturday night. His job also includes keeping peace in his own neighborhood. There are also other branches of law enforcement in Tahiti, including the secret service police and the municipal police who patrol the "hot spots" of downtown Papeete on weekends, searching for drinking minors, drugs, fights and vehicles with boom boxes blaring at top volume, which are all illegal.

Today the Tahitian flag, white with red borders at top and bottom, with an emblem representing a double outrigger sailing canoe, flies side by side with the tri-color of the French flag. The archipelagoes also have their own emblems. The

Territorial anthem "Ia Ora 'O Tahiti Nui" is sung or played wherever French Polynesia participates in international meetings or sports events throughout the Pacific. You can listen to this anthem and learn all about the French Polynesian Government at *www.presidence.pf.*

Post-Nuclear Progress Pact for Self-Sufficiency

A **Progress Pact** between the French Polynesia and the Republic of France was signed in January 1993, to compensate for the loss of financial resources due to the ending of the CEP French nuclear tests in the Tuamotu Islands. A 10-year adjustment law and development contracts for 5-year periods were adopted in 1994, with the State providing assistance in the fields of education, training, research, health and transport infrastructures, agriculture, tourism and housing.

When French President Jacques Chirac decided in 1996 to halt all nuclear testing, France committed itself to maintaining the same amount of spending in CFP in French Polynesia. The spending level agreed to was 18 billion French Pacific francs (about US $1.8 million dollars) per year for 10 years, which was made possible by a reconversion fund. This agreement for strengthening the economic autonomy was signed between the French State and French Polynesia on July 26, 1996, and was valid until 2005. President Chirac then removed all boundaries on the reconversion fund payments so that French Polynesia is supposed to receive 18 billion CFP per year in perpetuity.

French Polynesia's main economic resources are **tourism** and **pearl farming**. In recent years, **deep-sea commercial fishing** has also shown promise, particularly with an increase in exports. **Agricultural products**, such as fruit, flowers and nono or noni (*Morinda citrifolia*), have also had some export success.

6. Planning Your Trip

WHEN TO GO

"When is the best time to go to Tahiti?" is a question I'll answer by asking you: "What do you want to do once you get here?" If you want to scuba dive, you'll have the best underwater visibility during the dry season. If you want to snorkel and swim in the limpid lagoons, then come between Oct.-June, when the water temperature is at least 80° Fahrenheit. If your goal is to photograph the most marvelous sunsets, complete with a "green flash", then come in Jul.-Aug., when the evening skies are more likely to be free of clouds. If you want to see Tahiti dressed in her most beautiful finery of flowering trees and ripening fruits, then come in the "springtime" months of Oct.-Dec. If you want to surf the huge rollers, make your reservations for Jan.-Mar.

If you intend to catch a record-setting marlin, then your guess is as good as the experts, who tell me they're now reeling in the big ones all year long, rather than just during the summer months. If you want to see the humpback whales, they come up from Antarctica between Jul.-Oct., and play around just offshore, in the passes and sometimes in the bays of the Society Islands. Whale-watching expeditions will take you just offshore Moorea or Tahiti to sight the gigantic visitors, and on the Austral Island of Rurutu a scuba diving company may let you swim with the whales.

If you want to charter a yacht and sail from island to island, the balmy trade winds blow most of the year, and are most pleasant from May-Sept. If your interest is outrigger canoe racing, the biggest competitions are in Jul.-Oct. And if you want to party with the Polynesians during the biggest celebration of the year, then reserve now for a room during the Heiva Festivals that begin in late June, reach a peak in Jul. and continue throughout most of Aug. with mini-Heiva programs in some of the larger hotels.

You may want to consult the *Calendar of Events* chapter before making your decision, as well as checking out the legal holidays in French Polynesia, which are listed in Chapter 7, *Basic Information*.

Another thing to keep in mind may be the school holidays, which can influence the availability of international and domestic flights, as well as accommodations in the small hotels and family operated hostels or pensions. The students in the Society Islands have a 2-week vacation in mid-Oct., a month's holiday from mid-Dec. to mid-Jan., another 2 weeks the first half of Mar., a week at the beginning of May, and a 7-week rest from early Jul. until the last week in Aug. Schools in the Marquesas, Australs and Tuamotu/Gambier Islands keep the same basic holiday schedule, except for Oct., when they have only a 3-day break during the 3rd week in Mar., when they get the entire month off, and their May break is taken during the 3rd week of the month. If you have any questions about the exact dates, the Tahiti Tourist office can answer them.

This means that from Christmas to the beginning of Jan., the end of Feb. or beginning of Mar., the Easter period, the beginning of May, the longer northern-summer holiday in Jul.-Aug. and the beginning of Oct. are likely to be busier.

Climate & Weather

The climate of these islands is usually benign, sunny and pleasant, and the cool, gentle breezes of the South Pacific Ocean and the northeasterly trade winds provide a natural a/c system. Meteorologists consider the months of Nov.-Mar. as the "rainy" season, when the climate is warmer and more humid, and Apr.-Oct. as the "dry" season, with a cooler drier climate. The yearly average ambient temperature is 27ºC (80.6ºF). Most of the rain falls during the warmer season (2,030 mm. or 81.2" in 2006), but there are also many days of sunshine during these months (average 2,648 hrs. in 2006), with refreshing trade winds.

The central and northern Tuamotus have warmer temperatures and less rainfall than in the Society Islands. There are no mountains to create cooling night breezes, as the elevation of these atolls ranges from 6-20 ft. above sea level. They can experience desert-like hot periods between Nov.-Apr., with devastating storms and cyclones.

The Marquesas Islands are closer to the equator, and temperatures and humidity tend to be slightly higher than in Tahiti, with more rainfall in verdant Fatu Hiva and more arid conditions in Ua Huka. The Marquesas archipelago lies in the midst of a trade wind belt from the northern latitudes, bringing northeasterly winds most of the year, with seasons that are reversed to those in the Society Islands. Although there is no real rainy season, trekking through the steep valleys to visit tikis and archaeological sites in the Marquesas can be a very steamy and often muddy hike at any time of the year.

The climate in the Australs is more temperate and less rainy than in Tahiti, and the seasons are more clearly defined. These islands lie at the southern boundary of the southeast trade winds, which blow from Nov.-Mar. In the cold season, from May- Sept., the winds are more variable and generally westerly, with temperatures of 50º-70º F.

French Polynesia is on the far eastern edge of the South Pacific cyclone (hurricane) belt, and has suffered serious damage from cyclones, tropical depressions, and other effects of El Niño.

Dry Season

From Jul.-Sept. the *mara'amu* trade winds can bring blustery, howling weather and rain from the south. But the rains don't always accompany these chilling winds. I lost the roof of my house one year in July during the *mara'amu* and I looked up to see a beautiful, bright sky filled with a moon and stars.

The dry seasons are sometimes too dry in many of the islands, when we suffer droughts and water rationing. This is especially true during June-Sept. We have also had a shortage of water in Jan., but our visitors enjoyed the bright, sunny days when they could work on their tans in the midst of Tahiti's so-called rainy season. Winter storms in the southern latitudes, down around the "Roaring 40s" south of the Austral Islands, can stir up some powerful waves, with 16-ft. swells damaging homes and hotels throughout the Society Islands.

These inclement weather conditions should not affect your vacation plans, as the months of July-Sept. or Oct. are especially beautiful in the islands, with day after day of glorious sunshine, and cool nights good for snuggling and gazing at the Southern Cross and other tropical stars. If your hotel is located on the southern coast of any of the Society Islands, just bring along a windbreaker or sweater, and throw an extra blanket on the bed.

Wet Season

"Is it going to rain during my vacation/honeymoon?" I get several e-mail inquiries on that subject every year. The answer is "it's highly possible". But don't let it stop you from coming. During the height of the rainy season, it can rain very heavily for days and days. During this time the trade winds stop and the temperature and humidity levels rise. When this happens the mugginess may make you feel hot, sticky and irritable if you stay indoors. The best thing to do is to take a walk in the refreshing rain or swim in the lagoon to cool off. It's true that you cannot work on your tan during this weather, but you can tour around the island and watch the double rainbows over the emerald green valley when the sun breaks through the clouds for a few minutes. This is also a great time to go shopping for your own special Tahiti cultured pearls!

Weather Report

You can get a 10-day weather report for Tahiti on the Internet at *www.weather.com, www.intellicast.com;* and at *www.tahitiplanet.com/webcam.htm* you can get the weather plus the sunrise, sunset, moon and star movements. Another site is *www.weatherunderground.com.*

WHAT TO PACK

Casual and cool are the keywords to packing for this tropical climate. Light, loose, wash and wear garments of cotton and other natural fabrics are best. Unless you are taking a cruise ship to Tahiti you can leave your formal dining clothes and coats and ties at home. Women should pack a few pairs of shorts and slacks, along with a couple of skirts and tops or comfortable dresses, plus 1-2 swimsuits. Men will be properly dressed in shorts and tee shirts almost everywhere, except for dinner in a few hotels, fancy restaurants and nightclubs, where you'll have to put on long pants, an open-neck shirt and shoes. You can both buy some colorful *pareos* once you are here to complement your wardrobes. Yes, men wear them too! But only around the hotel grounds or on the beach. Most Polynesians do not wear their *pareos* to town.

Both men and women will be in style in sandals or flip-flop rubber thongs, and be sure to include aqua socks or protective footgear, such as old tennis shoes, for walking on the coral reef and in the lagoons. Plastic sandals can be purchased in the islands for about $15, which can be worn in the lagoon and while walking in the valleys.

A lightweight sweater or windbreaker will feel good on cool evenings, especially during the months of Jul.-Sept., and anytime you are on the sea at night. Along with a hat or visor, don't forget to pack a good pair of sunglasses and your sun block or screen. A folding umbrella or a lightweight plastic rain coat or poncho that fits into a pocket or purse may also come in handy during tropical rain showers, which are refreshing rather than cold.

Some of the budget hotels and hostels or pensions do not supply face cloths, and in some of the backpacker's lodgings you will have to bring your own soap and towel. A universal sink plug is handy for most lavabos and bathtubs. Other useful items include an alarm clock, portable clothes line and pegs, small bags of soap powder, clothes hangers, beach towel, pocket flashlight, corkscrew, tin opener or Swiss Army knife, plastic fork and spoon, folding plastic insulated cup and zip-lock plastic bags to contain anything spillable. Bring a small first-aid kit containing your personal medicines, aspirin, indigestion tablets, vitamins, insect repellent, antiseptic cream, aloe gel, Band-Aids or other sticking plasters. Pack your toiletries and just a few cosmetics, and you may want to bring along your binoculars. Remember to put your sharp items in your luggage to be checked, rather than in your carry-on bag.

Don't forget to bring your camera, and make sure you know how to operate it before you get here, to prevent losing that perfect shot. Be sure to include lots of film and a waterproof bag to protect your camera from salt and spray during boat excursions. Also pack a small travel bag in which to carry your things when you're on tours and excursions.

Hair-dryers are provided in the luxury hotels, and if you bring a hair-dryer, make sure it can convert to 220 voltage, or bring a small adapter (transformer). Always ask at your hotel reception before plugging in your electrical appliances. You may want to bring your own supply of reading material. You can exchange books at most hotels. Some folks bring their own booze, which is expensive here. Last but not least—bring your passport, airline tickets, driver's license, traveler's checks, cash and all your international credit cards.

ENTRANCE REQUIREMENTS: PASSPORTS/VISAS

All U.S. citizens and nationals can apply for a passport by completing the application form DS-11, which is available in U.S. post offices. You can also obtain this form from the **U.S. Passport Agency** (*Tel. 202/647-0518*), which has offices in Aurora, Colorado, Boston, Chicago, Honolulu, Houston, Los Angeles, Miami,

New Orleans, New York, Norwalk, Connecticut, Philadelphia, San Francisco, Seattle, and Washington, D.C. You can also download a form from the website of the U.S. State Department at *www.travel.state.gov*. Complete the form and return it to the Passport Agency or to your nearest post office or federal courthouse.

All non-French citizens must have a valid passport to enter French Polynesia, as well as an airline ticket back to their resident country or to at least 2 more continuing destinations. Your passport or travel document must be valid for at least 3 months beyond your return date. Your first and last name on your passport must match your international air tickets.

Foreign nationals from the following countries are entitled to a 3-month stay without a visa:

European Union: Austria, Belgium, Cyprus, Denmark, Estonia, Finland, Germany, Greece, Hungary, Ireland, Italy, Latvia, Lithuania, Luxembourg, Malta, The Netherlands, Poland, Portugal, Czech Republic, United Kingdom, Slovakia, Slovenia, Sweden and Spain.

Other countries: Andorra, Australia, Iceland, Liechtenstein, Monaco, Norway, St. Martin, Switzerland and the Vatican.

Maximum stay of 3 months per semester: Brazil, China, and Chinese citizens holding a valid passport from Hong Kong, Macao and Bulgaria.

Refugees and stateless persons: If holding a travel authorization delivered by France.

Nationals from the following countries are entitled to a 1-month stay without visa:

North, Central and South America: Argentina, Bolivia, Canada, Costa Rica, Chile, El Salvador, Ecuador, Guatemala, Honduras, Mexico, Nicaragua, Panama, Paraguay, Uruguay, and the USA.

Asia-Pacific: Brunei, New Zealand, Japan, Malaysia, Singapore and South Korea.

Europe: Croatia.

Nationals from all other countries require visas, which may be obtained from the French Embassy or French Consulate in the country of residence. The visa must be endorsed "valid for French Polynesia", which applies also to aliens holding temporary visitor's permits (one year in metropolitan France). Aliens holding residence cards for metropolitan France are exempt from visa requirements. Except for nationals of the European Union and aliens holding a 10-year residence for metropolitan France, all foreigners entering French Polynesia must have a return ticket.

For further information please visit the website: *www.polynesie-francaise.pref.gouv.fr*

A foreigner with a residence card for the US is not exempt from having a visa for visiting French Polynesia. This visa exemption is subject to change at short notice. It is advisable to contact the nearest French Consulate or an airline serving Tahiti for specific information.

If you think you will want to extend your stay in French Polynesia beyond the 1-month visa exemption, you should apply for a 3-month visa at a French Consulate office prior to coming to Tahiti.

If there is some unforeseen reason why you will need to extend your visa once you are here, you can ask for another month or two at the Immigration office at the Tahiti-Faa'a airport, *Tel. 80.06.01.* This must be done at least one week before the exemption expires. The Police Air Frontière (PAF) who control this office have sometimes refused requests for visa extensions because they want you to get the visa before you arrive in Tahiti. All visitors must have a sufficient amount of resources to cover their planned stay in French Polynesia. Temporary residency visas for up to one year are more difficult to obtain, and have to be applied for at a French Consulate or Embassy before you arrive in French Polynesia.

French nationals require only a National Identity Card to stay in French Polynesia. However, the Delphine passport is necessary when transiting via the US.

In the US
- **Embassy of France:** 4101 Reservoir Rd., NW, Washington, DC 20007-2185, *Tel. 202/944-6200, Fax 202/944-6166; www.info-france-usa.org.*
- **French Consulates:** New York: 934 Fifth Avenue, New York, NY 10021, *Tel. 212/606-3600; Fax 212/606-3620; www.consulfrance-newyork.org.* San Francisco: 540 Bush St., San Francisco, CA 94108, *Tel. 415/397-4330, Fax 415/433-8357; www.consulfrance-sanfrancisco.org.* Los Angeles: 10390 Santa Monica Blvd., Suite 410, Los Angeles, CA 90025; *Fax 310/235-3200; Fax 310/479-4813; www.consulfrance-los angeles.org.*

Other French consulate offices are in Atlanta, Boston, Chicago, Houston, Los Angeles, Miami, New Orleans and Washington, DC. Residents of those cities are required to apply there. If there is no French consulate in your town, please contact the French Embassy in Washington, DC, listed above.

In Canada
- **Embassy of France:** 42 Sussex Drive, Ottawa, Ontario, KIM 2C9, *Tel. 613/789-1795, Fax 613/562-3735: www.ambafrance-ca.org.* The French Consulate in Ottawa is now closed.
- **French Consulates:** Montreal: 1501, McGill College, Bureau 1000, Montreal (QC) H30 3M8; *Tel. 514/878/4385; Fax 514/878-3981; www.consulfrance-montreal.org.* Toronto: 2 Bloor Street East, Suite 2200, Toronto (ON) M4W 1AB; *Tel. 416/847-1900; Fax 416/847-1901; www.consulfrance-toronto.org.* Vancouver: 1130 West Pender St., Suite 1100, Vancouver (BC), V6E 4A4 Canada; *Tel. 604/681-4345; Fax 604/681-4287; www.consulfrance-vancouver.org.*

U.S. CONSULATE IN TAHITI

A Consular Agency of the United States opened in Tahiti in 2004, after an absence of 38 years. This office is located in Punaauia on the upper level of the Tamanu Iti Center. Christopher Kozely, the vice consul, cannot issue or renew passports, but his services include helping Americans who have problems due to sickness or death or who have lost their passports. You can contact this office at B.P. 10765, Paea, Tahiti 98711, French Polynesia; *Tel. 689/42.65.35; Fax 689/50.80.96; E-mail: usconsul@mail.pf; or ckozely@mail.pf.* In US *917/464-7457.* For emergencies only *Tel. 21.93.19.*

MAKING RESERVATIONS

It is so much simpler to talk with your favorite travel agent to take care of all the reservations and details in planning your trip to Tahiti and Her Islands. Or you can arrange your entire trip by yourself, by contacting the airlines and hotels directly, going through one of the travel agencies in Tahiti, and checking the individual websites of the lodgings that interest you. The airlines have special fares and passes, which will cost you less if you reserve 2 weeks to a month in advance. The airfares also vary according to whether you go in the high or peak season, the shoulder season or the basic season. Check with the airline companies to learn which season will be in effect when you want to fly. If you are traveling on a tight budget, ask for their lowest fares, and be sure to learn what restrictions apply.

Some of the "discounter" travel agents buy airline seats and hotel rooms at wholesale prices. You may want to get a list of discounter travel agents, as well as worldwide discount air fares, from the Web site *www.etn.nl/discount.htm#disco.* Also check Internet specials at *www.discountairfares.com* and the Internet Travel Network at *www.itn.*

Some consolidators or "bucket shops" who buy and resell seats on the major international airlines, such as **Air Brokers International**, *Tel. 800/883-3273*; *www.airbrokers.com.* STA Travel, *Tel. 800/781-4040, www.statravel.com,* is the world's largest travel agency for students. The Internet websites offer some of the best deals you'll find on airfare, as well as hotels and car rentals. Two of the most popular travel sites are **Microsoft Expedia**, *www.expedia.com*, and **Travelocity**, *www.travelocity.com*. Before you shop for flights online, be sure to call the airlines or a travel agent to find out the lowest fare published.

Package Tours

The travel agencies listed in this chapter can suggest package tours that include international air travel to French Polynesia, accommodations, some meals, ground transfers, inter-island travel by airplane or boat, and some tours and excursions. Should you decide on a tour package, be sure to read the fine print so that you will understand what you are paying for. You don't want to limit yourself to eating all your meals in the same hotel when there are enticing restaurants to explore on the island.

Using Travel Specialists/Agents in USA and Canada

Contact the Tahiti Tourist Board for brochures, schedules and information. In the US, the contact is: **Tahiti Tourism North America**, 300 Continental Boulevard, Suite 160, El Segundo, CA 90245; *Tel 310/414-8484; Fax 310/414-8490; tahitilax@earthlink.net; www.GoToTahiti.com.*

The list below includes some of the wholesale travel companies, tour operators and travel agencies that have been approved by the Tahiti Tourist office in Los Angeles. Should your local travel agency need additional brochures and information, they can contact one of these companies, who are financially sound and have a well-trained staff with a good knowledge of Tahiti and Her Islands. Some of the wholesalers also work directly with the public. The list also includes some of the agents I can personally recommend for their vast knowledge of and love for these islands.

U.S.

• **Blue Pacific Vacations**, *Tel. 800/798-0590; www.bluepacificvacations.com* is a division of France Vacations. Owners John Biggerstaff and Ken Jordan are both very well seasoned in selling customized tours to Tahiti and Her Islands.

• **Brendan Worldwide Vacations**, *Tel. 800/421-8446 or 815/785-9696; www.brendanvacations.com.* This family owned business offers some interesting packages to Tahiti and French Polynesia. They also own Tahiti Vacations.

• **Crossroads Travel Advisors LLC**, *Tel. 800/322-0224; 804/794-7700; www.crttravel.com.* Uschi and David Helfrich own this full service travel company, which is the only independent American Express agency in Richmond, VA. Uschi visits Tahiti and Her Islands several times a year to gather information that helps in organizing the best programs for her clients. Her special interest is family travel, but you will see from their website that they cover every aspect of discovering these fabulous islands.

• **Fly Tahiti Vacations**, *Tel. 866/9Tahiti (866/982-4484), 714/274-0379; www.flytahiti.com.* Based in Huntington Beach, CA, this company specializes in personally tailored luxury travel packages exclusively to Tahiti and her Leeward Islands, the Tuamotus, and the Marquesas Islands. They can also plan family vacations in the smaller hotels and family pensions. Fly Tahiti's director, Jean-Louis Delezenne, is a Frenchman living in Los Angeles who also has a home in Moorea and a true passion for these islands. You can count on him for up-to-the minute information about special airline fares, hotel promotions, package deals and anything else concerning tourism and life in French Polynesia. (He is the Tahiti expert Meherio on the tripadvisor.com Tahiti forum). Jean Louis is a real go-getter who truly knows the meaning of personalized service, which he happily offers to each and every customer. Fly Tahiti Vacations also owns **Cruise Tahiti**, *Tel. 800/564-66.95; www.cruisetahiti.com.*

- **Islands in the Sun**, *Tel. 800/828-6877, 310/536-0051; www.islandsinthesun.com.* The late Ted Cook founded this company in 1965 and since then thousands of travelers have booked their South Pacific vacations through this well-informed and very helpful team.
- **Jetabout Island Vacations**, *Tel. 800/348-8145; www.jetabouttahitivacations.com.* This was formerly Qantas Vacations and they have some good packages for Tahiti.
- **Manuia Tours and Travel**, *Tel. 415/495-4500; manuiatravel@yahoo.com.* Owner Pascale Siu is from a big Chinese family in Tahiti and is the only French-Tahitian owned travel agency in San Francisco. They specialize in individual and personalized services, including Honeymoon packages and stays in Family Pensions.
- **Pleasant Holidays**, *Tel. 800/742-9244; www.pleasantholidays.com.* This big company is known for their packages to Hawaii and Mexico, but they also have interesting programs for Tahiti. They are a subsidiary of the Automobile Club of CA.
- **Sunspots International**, *Tel. 800/334-5623, 503/674-4325; www.sunspotsintl.com.* This is a good travel company based in Portland, OR.
- **Swain Tahiti Tours**, *Tel. 800/227-9246; 610/896-9595; www.swaintahiti.com.* They are based in Ardmore, PA, selling cruises, wedding packages and independent travel packages that also include Manihi and Tikehau. They have some good programs for families.
- **Tahiti Discount Travel**, *Tel. 877/426-7262; www.tahiti-discounttravel.com.* The owners formerly worked for Discover Wholesale Travel before they closed. See their website for low-priced packages to Tahiti and Her Islands.
- **Tahiti Legends**, *Tel. 800/200-1213, 714/374-5656; www.tahiti-legends.com; www.legendsluxurytravel.com.* This tour operator is based in Huntington Beach, CA. I highly recommended them for their brochures, packages and especially their well-trained staff, who are not only very familiar with Tahiti and Her Islands, but are truly in love with the islands, the people, and the hotels, cruise ships and tourist activities. You can download their 80-page Tahiti brochure and 16-page Lifestyles brochure.
- **Tahiti Travel**, *Tel. 800/747-9997, 323/655-2181, www.tahiti-explorer.com.* This is an online travel agency owned by Frenchman Yves Courbet in Los Angeles that has been in business since 1995, promoting discounted rates for customized vacations or honeymoons to all the Islands of Tahiti. His Tiare Tahiti specialists can also help you to choose from more than 30 packages listed on his website. See also *Website Forums and Bulletin Boards* in this chapter.

- **Tahiti Travel Planners**, (a Division of New Millennium Tours, Inc.), *Tel. 800/ 772-9231, 773/935-4707; www.gotahiti.com*. This Chicago based travel agency specializes solely in vacations to Tahiti and Her Islands and claim they are the world's leading experts for travel, vacation and honeymoon planning for the islands of French Polynesia. All their agents have received the Tiare Award distributed by the Tahiti Tourist office for outstanding knowledge about these islands. Their *www.gotahiti.com* website includes hundreds of travel packages. Their *www.tahitimoons.com* website includes honeymoon programs.
- **Tahiti Vacations**, *Tel. 800/553-3477; www.tahitivacation.com*. This is the wholesale tour operator for Air Tahiti, the domestic airline of French Polynesia. They offer some interesting packages to Tahiti and Moorea, as well as choices for all the other islands served by Air Tahiti.
- **The Adventure Travel Company**, *Tel. 212/397-9792; cnsmork@gmail.com; cnmork@inch.com*. Owner Camilla Mork is an adventure travel specialist agent in Manhattan, NY, who plans soft adventure tours for small groups. She and her husband Steve are escorts for an 18-day tour that includes Tahiti, Moorea, Bora Bora, Easter Island and Fakarava. She also organizes other customized tours.

Canada

- **Island Escapes by Goway**, *Tel. 800/387-8850, 604/264-8088; www.goway.com*. This company has an excellent reputation.
- **Fun Sun Vacations**, *Tel. 800/938-6786, 780/421-1272; www.funsunvacations.com*. This Canadian owned family business is one of Canada's top tour wholesalers and sells through retail travel agencies.

Diving

- **Dive Tahiti Blue**, *Tel. 689/56.25.33; (USA) 310/464-1490; www.divetahitiblue.com*. This company is owned by Laurel and James Samuela, who live on the island of Moorea. Laurel grew up in California and is a PADI certified dive master. James, who is Tahitian, grew up on Moorea and was once the youngest guide on the island, leading horse rides along the beach when he was 13. Now he is a diver and tattoo master. They know which scuba diving center is best suited to dealing with American clientele, and they provide full travel service, coordinating everything from airline tickets to transfers, lodging and scuba diving. They can even plan a live aboard scuba diving trip for you on board the *Aquatiki*. See also their website for *truetahitivacation.com*.
- **Diving in Tahiti and Her Islands**, *Tel. 689/53.34.96; www.diving-tahiti.com*. This is the Tahiti-based office representing all scuba diving centers in French Polynesia.
- **PADI Travel Network**, *Tel. 800/729-7234, 949/858-7234; www.padi.com*. They have packages for scuba divers.

• **World of Diving & Adventure Vacations**, *Tel. 800/Go-Diving (800/900-7657)* or *310/322-8100; www.worldofdiving.com.*

Using Inbound Travel Agents in Tahiti

You may want to contact one or more of these inbound agents when planning your trip. These are tourism professionals who live in Tahiti or Moorea and they can give you detailed information about every aspect of traveling in French Polynesia. The travel agencies can also arrange for you to be transferred from the international airport to your lodging, and handle any other land, sea or air transportation you may need.

• **Marama Tours**, B.P. 6266, Faa'a, Tahiti, 98702. *Tel. 689/50.74.74; Fax 689/ 82.16.75; maramatours@mail.pf; www.maramatours.com.* This company was founded in 1973 by Mata and Emile Cowan, a Polynesian family whose children also grew up in the tourist business and now take active roles in managing this popular agency. They are a full service travel agency with one of the largest transportation fleets. They also have travel desks in the big hotels.

• **Paradise Tours**, B.P. 2430, Papeete, Tahiti, 98713. *Tel. 689/42.49.36/ 77.07.63; Fax 689/42.48.62; paradise@mail.pf; www.paradisetourstahiti.com.* This is one of the oldest agencies in Tahiti handling inbound tours, founded in 1965.

• **South Pacific Tours**, B.P. 1588, Papeete, Tahiti 98713. *Tel. 689/80.35.00; Fax 689/80.35.12; in-bound@spt-tahiti.pf. www.south-pacific-tours.com.* In addition to being the biggest inbound agency in Tahiti for the Japanese market, they also handle clients from the U.S.A. and Europe.

• **Tahiti Nui Travel**, B.P. 718, Papeete, Tahiti 98713. *Tel. 689/46.41.41; Fax 689/ 46.41.30; marketing@tahitinuitravel.pf; www.tahitinuitravel.biz.* This is Tahiti's largest travel agency, and handles inbound tours for individuals and groups from all countries. They have a well-earned reputation for their professionalism. They have travel desks in the big hotels.

• **Tahiti Tours**, B.P. 627, Papeete, Tahiti 98713. *Tel. 689/46.40.46; Fax 689/ 42.50.50; sales@tahititours.pf; www.tahiti-tours.com.* This agency has been in business for more almost 50 years and is owned by Tahiti Nui Travel. They handle a lot of inbound tours and local excursions and day tours and they are the American Express representatives in Tahiti.

• **Tekura Tahiti Travel**, B.P. 2971, Papeete, Tahiti 98713. *Tel. 689/43.12.00, Fax 689/42.84.60, go@tahiti-tekuratravel.pf; www.tahiti-tekuratravel.com.* The knowledgeable English-speaking staff can book your hotel rooms, guest houses, villas, transfers, excursions, diving, cruises, yacht charters, sailboats, domestic flights, boat transportation to outer islands and car rentals.

• **True Tahiti Vacation**, *Tel. 689/56.25.33; (USA) 310/464-1490; www.truetahitivacation.com.* This is a full service travel company based in Moorea, providing expert guidance in the general, honeymoon and spa markets. American owner Laurel Samuela and her Tahitian husband, James Samuela, have a combined total of 20 years' experience in Tahiti tourism. They know every island first hand and have personally visited every hotel and pension. Their goal is to use their insider knowledge of the islands to make your vacation as extraordinary as possible. See their website on Dive Tahiti Blue listed under *Diving*.

Other Destination Management Companies in Tahiti
- **Haere Mai Federation**, B.P. 4517, Papeete, Tahiti 98713. *haere-mai@mail.pf; www.haere-mai.pf; www.haere-mai.com.* This association was created in 1997 and represents 160 family pensions and guesthouses on 21 islands in all 5 archipelagoes of French Polynesia. Contact them for online booking and information.
- **Islands Adventures Air Tahiti**, B.P. 314, Papeete, Tahiti 98713; *Tel. 689/86.43.68; Fax 689/86.42.67; islands.adventures@airtahiti.pf; www.air-tahiti-islands-adventures.com.* See information under Air Tahiti Island Stays in this chapter.
- **Dream Travel Tahiti**, B.P. 13409 Auae, Faa'a, Tahiti 98717. *Tel. 689/43.10.65; Fax 689/53.34.74; dreamtraveltahiti@mail.pf; www.dreamtraveltahiti.com.* This agency is headed by Didier Alpini, who also manages Aquatica, a 5-star PADI Dive Center based at the Intercontinental Tahiti Resort. They specialize in "green" tourism, with hiking, trekking, 4WD safaris, golf, participation in local sports such as marathons, as well as cruising and diving holidays. They also handle reservations for the outer islands of French Polynesia.
- **Website Forums** and **Bulletin Boards.** These are also a good source of information on deciding which islands to visit and where to stay. Not only do they have trip reports and photos of various hotels, pensions, activities and tourist sites in French Polynesia, but also you have access to an endless number of opinions on each subject. A very popular Tahiti Forum in English is *www.tahiti-explorer.com,* which is sponsored by Tahiti Travel in Los Angeles, with over 4,500 members. *www.tripadvisor.com* lists comments on hotels, restaurants and activities in French Polynesia, and even gives ratings on each establishment covered. One of the Tahiti experts on the Trip Advisor Tahiti Forum is Jean-Louis Delezenne, who lives part time in Moorea and is the director of Fly Tahiti Vacations in CA. His knowledgeable advice is given under the name of Meherio. The other Tahiti experts on this forum are also part-time residents of Moorea or come here often enough to consider themselves residents. *www.tahititalk.com* has a rather limited selection of posters, but most of them are very familiar with these islands and enjoy helping others to discover various aspects of Tahiti and Her Islands. If you're planning to visit the islands by cruise ship, then tune into the Cruise Critic forum, *www.cruisecritic.com*, and find out what former passengers have to say about the ship and shore excursions you'll be taking.

USEFUL WEBSITES IN TAHITI
Tahiti Guide, *www.tahitiguide.com*, has tourist information on all the islands,

hotels, pensions, and activities. **Tahiti Traveler,** *www.thetahititraveler.com,* has information on hotel resorts, small hotels and guesthouses, and it's partner, E-Tahiti Travel, *www.etahititravel,* can make the bookings for you.

TahitiWeb is the search engine to Tahiti's Websites: *www.tahitiweb.com.* If you want to find information about the **French Polynesia Government,** go to *www.presidence.pf.* **Tahiti Presse** is the government-owned press service with the news reported daily in French and English, *www.tahitipresse.pf.*

See *www.tahiti-realestate.com* if you want to rent or buy a house, bungalow or apartment in Tahiti and Her Islands. For information on the specific islands, most of them have their own website, which you can reach by typing the name of the island, preceded by *www. (moorea.com, raiatea.com, borabora.com, rangiroa.com, marquises.com, tahiti.com and papeete.com*), or you can type the name of the island plus the word «island» and you'll get another site, such as *mooreaisland.com, huahineisland.com* and so on. Some of these sites are owned by the Tahiti Travel Net and others belong to other travel agencies, who can help you plan your trip.

WHERE TO FIND MORE INFORMATION
• **Tahiti Tourisme,** B.P. 65 Papeete, Tahiti 98713, French Polynesia. *Tel. 689/ 50.57.00; Fax 689/43.66.19; tahiti-tourisme@mail.pf; www.tahiti-tourisme.pf.* This office is on the harbor side of the Papeete waterfront in Fare Manihini. English-speaking Polynesian hosts and hostesses are on duty to answer your questions in the visitors' center. Here you will find brochures and informational sheets on lodgings, activities, tours and excursions, le truck, taxis, rental cars, ferries, boats and air services to the outer islands, as well as maps and anything else related to tourism. The visitor's bureau is open Mon.-Fri. from 7am-5:30pm, on Sat. from 8am-4pm, and on Sun. from 8am-1pm. The offices for overseas promotion are located in the connecting buildings. Video and DVD films, posters, T-shirts, caps and sun visors can be purchased in the promotional materials department.
• **Tahiti Tourisme Overseas Representatives**
• **North America,** 300 Continental Boulevard, Suite 160, El Segundo, CA 90245; *Tel 310/414-8484; Fax 310/414-8490; E-mail address: info@tahiti-tourisme.com; www.tahiti-tourisme.com.*
• **Europe** (France, Benelux, Switzerland, Scandinavia, Russia), Tahiti Tourisme Paris, *28, Boulevard Saint-Germain, 75005 Paris; Tel. Consumers: 0.811.46/ 46/80 (France)/ +33.1.55.42.64.34 (other countries); Fax (33) 01.55.42.61.20; tahititourisme@tahiti-tourisme.fr; www.tahiti-tourisme.fr*
• **Central and Eastern Europe,** TMR International s.r.o, *Badeniho 1, Czech Republic, 16000 Prague 6; Tel. (420) 233 931 255; Fax (420) 233 931 254; tahiti@travel-marketing.cz*
• **Italy,** Aigo, *Plazza Caiazzo, 3, 20124 Milano – Italia; Tel. (39) 02.66.980.317; Fax (39) 02.66.92.648; E-mail: tahiti@tahiti-tourisme.it; www.tahiti-tourisme.it*
• **Spain/Portugal,** Connexions Aviación y Turismo, *Calle Serrano, 93, 2ºA28006-*

Madrid-Espagne, Tel. (34) 91.411.01.67; Fax (34) 91.563.80.62; info@tahititourisme.es; www.tahiti-tourisme.es

- **United Kingdom**, Hills Balfolur Synergy, Notcuff House, *36 Southwark Bridge Road, London SE 1 9EU United Kingdom; Switchboard: 44 (0) 20 7922 1100; Fax 44 (0) 20 7928 0722; Direct Line: 44 (0) 20 7202 6361; info@tahititourisme.co.uk; www.tahiti-tourisme.co.uk*
- **South America**, GIE Tahiti Tourisme, *Av. 11 de Septiembre 2214, Of.116, Providencia, Santiago, Chile; Tel. (562) 251.2826; Fax (562) 233.1787; E-mail: tahiti@cmet.net; www.entahiti.cl*
- **Australia**, The Unique Tourisme Collection, *362 Riley Street, Surry Hills NSW 2010, Sydney; Tel. (61) 2.9281.6020; Fax (61) 2.9211.6589; info@tahititourisme.com.au; www.tahiti-tourisme.com.au*
- **New Zealand**, Tahiti Tourism, *P.O. Box 106192, Auckland, NZ; Tel. (64) 9.368. 5262; Fax (64) 9.368.5263; info@tahiti-tourisme.co.nz; www.tahititourisme.co.nz*
- **Japan**, Kokusai Bldg. *1F 3-1-1 Marunouchi, Chiyoda-ku Tokyo, Japan 100-0005; Tel. 81-0(3)-5220-3877; Fax 81-0(3)-5220-3888; info@tahiti-tourisme.jp; www.tahiti-tourisme;jp*
- **Asia Regional Office** (Singapore, Taiwan, Thailand, Hong Kong and China), Tahiti Tourism Office c/o Pacific Leisure Group, 8/Floor, Maneeya Center Building, Lumpini, Patumwan 518/5 Ploenchit Road, Bangkok 10330 Thailand; *Tel. (66) 2.652. 05.07; Fax (66) 2.652.05.09; E-mail: eckard@plgroup.com*
- **Department of Tourism**, B.P. 4527, Papeete, Tahiti 98713, French Polynesia. *Tel. 689/47.62.00; Fax 689/47.62.02; sto@tourisme.gov.pf.* This office is in charge of the development and quality control of tourist accommodations, cruises and charter boats, land-based leisure activities and travel agencies.
- **Ministry of Tourism**, French Polynesia Government, The Presidency, *B.P. 2551, Papeete, Tahiti 98713. Tel. 689/48.40.00; Fax 689/48.40.14; www.tourisme.gov.pf.*
- **Chamber of Commerce, Industry, Services and Trade**, B.P. 118, Papeete, Tahiti 98713. *Tel. 689/47.27.00; Fax 689/54.07.01; cci.tahiti@mail.pf; www.ccism.pf.* Use this contact for questions regarding any business or trade in Tahiti.
- **Te Fare Tauhiti Nui Cultural Center (House of Culture)**, B.P. 1709, Papeete, Tahiti 98713, French Polynesia. *Tel. 689/54.45.44, www.maisondelaculture.pf.* The House of Culture is in charge of selected cultural events throughout the year. There is a library on the premises.
- **Oceanian Studies Society**, c/o Territorial Records, Tipaerui, B.P. 110, Papeete, Tahiti 98713, French Polynesia. *Tel./Fax 689/41.96.03; seo@archives.gov.pf.* Researchers may obtain permission to use the library and archives of the Société des Etudes Océaniennes.
- **Friends of Tahiti**, P.O. Box 2224, Newport Beach, CA 92659; *friendsoftahiti@yahoo.com.* Te Mau Hoa No Tahiti is the Tahitian name for

this cultural and charitable association, whose objectives include promoting friendship and cultural understanding between the people of French Polynesia and the United States through education, cultural arts exposure and travel. If you live in Southern California perhaps you can join them for their Tahitian galas and fundraiser programs, which include traditional Tahitian buffets and dance shows.

GETTING TO FRENCH POLYNESIA
Baggage Allowances and Storage

Airline regulations for international flights entitle each first-class or business-class passenger to a baggage limit of 30 kilograms (66 pounds). Economy-class passengers are allowed 20 kilograms (44 pounds). All passengers are allowed a carry-on bag that will fit under your seat, which means that it cannot exceed total measurements of 115 centimeters (45 inches). Only first-class or business-class passengers are allowed a second carry-on bag. All passengers may carry a small handbag on board, and most airlines will also allow you to board with one other accessory, such as a portable computer or camera bag, providing it does not weigh more than 7 kilograms (15 pounds).

Air Tahiti, the domestic inter-island company in Tahiti, has a baggage limit of 10 kilograms (22 pounds for each passenger). If you have a ticket connecting with an international flight within seven days, the baggage limit is 20 kilograms (44 pounds).

A baggage storage room at the Tahiti-Faa'a airport terminal, *Tel. 86.60.61*, is open daily from 5am-midnight on Tues.-Thurs, and on Sat.-Sun. They close at 7pm on Mon. night and at 11pm on Fri. night. On Sunday they close for lunch between 12-1:30pm. Their rates for 24-hr. storage start at 395 CFP for a small bag, and escalate to 950 CFP for the largest bags. The hotels and some family pensions offer free baggage storage for their guests.

Dangerous Goods

It is advisable to contact your airline representative for the latest information on what is allowed as carry-on baggage and what you'll have to pack in your checked luggage. The following items are prohibited in both hold and carry-on baggage: compressed gas or other explosives, inflammable liquids, corrosives, poisons, irritants, and substances or materials that are oxidizing, toxic, radioactive or magnetized. Safety regulations prohibit certain articles from being carried into the aircraft cabins. These include firearms, munitions, knives, scissors and other sharp or pointed instruments.

By Air From North America

All international flights arrive at the **Tahiti-Faa'a International Airport** on the island of Tahiti. The airline companies serving Tahiti from North America usually depart from the Los Angeles International Airport, for a 7 1/2-hour direct flight to

Tahiti. If you are flying to Los Angeles from another city or state, be sure to allow sufficient time between flights to make the connection. When your flight lands in Los Angeles it takes a while to transfer your bags from a domestic airline terminal to the international terminal. Due to increased safety measures, airport check-in time is now three hours before each international flight departure.

The following airline companies have one or more flights weekly between Los Angeles and Tahiti. Extra flights are added during the high seasons, which vary. The busiest seasons are generally the months of Jul.-Aug. and the Christmas-New Year's season. Once you arrive in Tahiti and want to check on arriving or departing flights you can contact the Tahiti-Faa'a International Airport at *Tel. 86.60.61.*

Airlines Serving Tahiti from Los Angeles

AIR FRANCE, in US *Tel. 800/321-4538 / 800/237-2747; in Canada 800/ 667-2747;* in Tahiti *Tel. 689/47.47.47; Fax 689/47.47.90. www.airfrance.com/pf.* France's international carrier has 4 Paris-Los Angeles-Papeete flights a week, flying 272-seat Airbus A340 aircraft. The Air France Tahiti office is on rue LaGarde in downtown Papeete.

AIR NEW ZEALAND, in US *Tel. 800/262-1234 / 310/615-1111, Fax 648-7017; in Canada Tel. 800/799-5494 (English) or 800/663-5494 (French); Fax 604/ 606-0155;* in Tahiti *Tel. 689/54.07.47, Fax 689/42.45.44; www.airnewzealand.com or www.airnz.co.nz.* In April 2007 Air New Zealand stopped flying from Los Angeles to Tahiti, but they have code sharing with Air Tahiti Nui for flights from New York-Los Angeles-Papeete. The Tahiti office is on the ground floor of the Vaima Center, on the corner of rue Jeanne d'Arc and rue du General du Gaulle.

AIR TAHITI NUI, in US, *Tel. 877/824-4846; Fax 310/640-3683; res@airtahitinui-usa.com;* in Tahiti *Tel. 689/46.03.03; Fax 689/46.02.20; res@airtahitinui.pf; www.airtahitinui.com or www.flyatn.com.* This is Tahiti's international airline company, and shouldn't be confused with Air Tahiti, which is the national carrier. Air Tahiti Nui has 5 flights a week from Paris to LAX and Papeete, 2 flights from New York to Los Angeles and Papeete, and 4 flights a week to Papeete that originate in Los Angeles. Qantas and Air New Zealand have code-sharing agreements for some of the US-Tahiti flights. Air Tahiti Nui have 5 Airbus 340-300 airplanes with 6 first class, 24 business class and 264 economy class seats. In 2007 Air Tahiti Nui won the Skytrax awards for the "Best Airline" and "Best Cabin Staff" in the Pacific region for the 5th consecutive year. Passengers are welcomed in traditional Tahitian style by smiling Polynesians who offer them a Tiare Tahiti flower when they board Air Tahiti Nui in Los Angeles and Paris. The airplanes provide individual movie screens in front of the seats, with a choice of 6 films, as well as telephones and music. The Air Tahiti Nui office in Papeete is located in Immeuble Dexter on rue Paul Gauguin at the Pont de l'Est.

QANTAS AIRWAYS, in US *Tel. 800/227-4500;* in Tahiti *Tel. 689/50.70.64; Fax 689/43.10.52; qantas@southpacificrepresentation.pf.* Their aircraft no longer flies to Tahiti, but Qantas maintains a code share agreement with Air Tahiti Nui for the New York to Los Angeles to Tahiti service. The GSA Tahiti office is located upstairs at the Vaima Center in Papeete.

By Other Air Routes

AIR CALEDONIE INTERNATIONAL, in US *Tel. 310/670-7302*; in Noumea *Tel. 687/26.4400*; in Tahiti *Tel. 689/85.09.04; Fax 689/85.09.05; E-mail: acippt@mail.pf; www.aircalin.nc.* Aircalin has a direct flight from Noumea, New Caledonia, to Tahiti each Sat., with an Airbus A320 airplane. The Tahiti office is on the first floor upstairs at the Tahiti-Faa'a International Airport.

AIR NEW ZEALAND, in US *Tel. 800/262-1234 or 310/615-1111;* in Tahiti *Tel. 689/54.07.47; Fax 689/42.45.44; www.airnewzealand.com* has 2 direct flights a week from Auckland to Papeete, code-sharing with Air Tahiti Nui. The Tahiti office is on the ground floor of the Vaima Center, on the corner of rue Jeanne d'Arc and rue du General du Gaulle.

AIR TAHITI, *Tel. 689/86.42.42; Fax 689/86.40.99; reservation@airtahiti.pf; www.airtahiti.aero.* Air Tahiti is French Polynesia's domestic airline that goes international once a week when it flies an ATR 42 airplane to Rarotonga in the Cook Islands. This service began in Apr. 2007 when Air New Zealand dropped Rarotonga from its Auckland-Papeete route. The twice-weekly flights have now been reduced to one flight each Tues. There are 3 airfare classes and baggage is limited to 20 kg. per passenger.

AIR TAHITI NUI, *Tel. 689/46.03.03* in Tahiti; *www.airtahitinui.co.jp or www.airtahitinui.com* has 2 direct flights from Tokyo to Papeete each week and 1 flight from Tokyo and Osaka to Papeete under a code-share agreement with Japan Airlines. You can also fly Air Tahiti Nui from Auckland to Papeete 2 times a week and from Sydney 3 times a week. They have code share programs with Qantas and Air New Zealand that provide connections from Australia to New Zealand and on to Tahiti and Los Angeles.

HAWAIIAN AIRLINES, in the continental US, Alaska and Canada *Tel. 800/367-5320; in Honolulu 808/838-1555; in Tahiti Tel. 689/42.15.00; Fax 689/45.14.51; ppt.admin@hawaiianair.pf; www.hawaiianair.com.* There is only one regular flight a week between Honolulu and Tahiti, departing Honolulu each Sat. The Tahiti office is located on the ground floor of the International Airport of Tahiti-Faa'a.

LAN AIRLINES, in US *Tel. 800/735-5526; in Tahiti Tel. 689/42.64.55; www.lan.com.* LAN (formerly LAN Chile) has 2 flights per week from Santiago, Chile and Easter Island. The Tahiti office is located upstairs at the Vaima Center in Papeete.

QANTAS AIRWAYS, in US *Tel. 800/227-4500;* in Tahiti *Tel. 689/50.70.64; Fax 689/43.10.52; E-mail: qantas@southpacificrepresentation.pf.* Qantas code shares 3 of Air Tahiti Nui's non-stop flights a week from Sydney to Papeete and on to the US.

By Passenger Ship

Tahiti's brief cruise ship season usually begins in Nov. and ends in Apr., with most of the passenger liners calling during the months of Jan.-Mar. The average number of cruise ships that call in Tahiti and Her Islands is only a dozen for the entire season. The 2007-2008 cruise season will welcome 19 different passenger ships between Sept. 2007 and June 2008.

These include Russian flag-carriers such as the *Bremen, Delphin Voyager,* and *Maxim Gorky,* whose passengers are primarily from Eastern Europe. The *Amsterdam, Astoria, Hanseatic, Mercury, Ryndam* and *Saga Rose* will bring English, German, French, and other European passengers who are cruising around the world. The *Topaz,* sailing under the colors of the Peace Boat, made 2 visits to Papeete. The *Queen Elizabeth 2* made her last port-of-call in Tahiti in Feb., before being delivered to her new owner, the Emir of Dubai, at the end of 2008, to become a floating hotel.

The *Regal Princess, Rhapsody of the Seas, Sun Princess, Crystal Serenity, Sapphire Princess* and Japan Cruise Line's *Pacific Venus* all included Tahiti in their cruise programs, and the *Pacific Princess* visited Tahiti 3 times during the season. The *Pacific Dawn* of P&O Cruises will close the cruise ship season on June 14, with a 28-night program called the "The Pearls of Tahiti". This is the first time in almost 25 years that P&O has made a round-trip cruise from Sydney to Tahiti. The ship will also visit Raiatea, Moorea and Bora Bora.

Ship day in Tahiti usually is limited to an early morning arrival in the harbor and a late afternoon departure, allowing enough time to make a tour of the island, perhaps to explore the coral gardens or tropical valleys and shop for post cards and souvenirs. South Pacific cruises also include Tahiti, Moorea, Raiatea and Bora Bora in their itineraries, and some of the ships are now calling at the Marquesas Islands, as well as Rangiroa and Fakarava in the Tuamotu Archipelago, in their shore programs.

By Private Boat

The best way to visit Tahiti and Her Islands is, of course, the leisurely way. Hundreds of cruising yachts from all over the world pass through the islands each year, with some boats stopping only long enough to get provisions for the next leg of the journey, while others linger until the authorities ask them to move on.

Their contact with the villagers in remote islands is often rewarding for all concerned, with the "yachties" often getting involved in the daily lives of the friendly Polynesians. Outgoing visitors are frequently invited to join in volleyball and soccer games and fishing expeditions. The young people will take you to hunt for tiny shells that are strung into pretty necklaces, and the women will teach you how to weave hats, mats, and baskets from palm fronds. You can also eat delicious seafood direct from the shell while standing on a Technicolor reef. In the evenings, you can sit on the pier under a starlit sky and watch the Southern Cross as you listen to the young men from the village playing melodic island tunes on their guitars and ukuleles.

There's a sailing adage that goes: "A month at sea can cure all the ills of the land." However, a month at sea with an incompatible crew can make you ill or want to kill. Sailing to Tahiti sounds so very romantic, and many people do realize their life-long dreams of anchoring inside an opalescent lagoon and tying a line around a coconut tree. It takes a month and sometimes much longer to sail from the US West Coast or Panama to the Marquesas Islands, the first landfall in French Polynesia. This long crossing is also disastrous for many relationships, so it is very important to know the dispositions of the other people on the yacht, and to be as easy-going and tolerant as you can be.

Valid passports and tourist visas are required for the captain and each crewmember. The Immigration Service in French Polynesia can issue a 3-month visa that is good for all of French Polynesia. In addition to the required visa, each crewmember must also deposit money into a special account at a local bank or at the Trésorerie Générale that is equal to the airfare from Tahiti back to their country of origin. Crew changes can only be made in harbors where there is a *gendarmerie*, and the Chief of Immigration must be advised of any crew changes.

CUSTOMS ALLOWANCES

In addition to your personal effects, when you come to French Polynesia you may legally bring in duty free: 200 cigarettes or 100 cigarillos or 50 cigars or 250 grams of smoking tobacco, 50 grams of perfume, 1/4 liter of *eau de toilette*, 500 grams of coffee, 100 grams of tea and 2 liters of spirits. Visitors under 17 years of age are not allowed to import tobacco or spirits. Each traveler over the age of 15 years can bring in other goods worth 30.000 CFP and under 15 years the limit is 15.000 CFP.

Prohibited items include narcotics, copyright infringements (pirated video and audiotapes), guns and weapons of all kinds, ammunition, dangerous drugs, counterfeit items or imitation brand names. Cultured pearls of non-French Polynesian origin are prohibited.

No domestic pets can be imported without authorization from the Food and Veterinary Department, *Tel. 689/42.81.47, Fax 689/42.08.31*. The importation of live animals, animal products and products of animal origin is subject to prior authorization. Plants and plant products are subject to phytosanitary control. In Dec. 2007 Tahiti's Service of Rural Development announced plans to open a quarantine station for animals and plants in the Tipaerui section of Papeete. For further information you can contact the Department of Agriculture, B.P. 100, Papeete, Tahiti, or at Tahiti-Faa'a Airport, *Tel. 689/82.49.99*, or at the Port of Papeete, *Tel. 689/54.45.85*. The Department of Customs and Indirect Duties also publishes information on the web site of the Ministry of Economics, Finance and Industry at: *www.finances.gouv.fr/douanes*.

Returning Home

US customs allows an exemption of $800 in goods for each US resident, including one liter of liquor, 200 cigarettes and 100 cigars. A *Know Before You Go* brochure is published by US customs, which you can read at *www.usacustoms.com*. US law allows the importation, duty-free, of original works of art. Because of concessions made to developing countries, jewelry made in Tahiti may qualify as original art, and thus be duty-free. The US customs has waived the import duty on Tahiti cultured pearls or pearl jewelry made in French Polynesia, so you will not be charged duty by the customs for these purchases. California residents will be charged a State tax on pearls if you declare them. If you purchase pearls or pearl jewelry, make sure to get a certificate from the place of purchase stating that the jewelry was made in the islands. See information on VAT Tax Refunds in *Basic Information* chapter.

Canadian residents have a personal exemption of Can$750 if they are absent from Canada for at least 7 days. You can learn all about their regulations at *www.canadaonline.com*.

TRAVELING ON YOUR OWN

Having the time to be flexible in your travels and being open to adventure and new experiences can bring you infinite rewards in discovering wonderful places and people. If you like to travel "by the seat of your pants" you can come to Tahiti without a hotel reservation and let serendipity be your guide. You can usually get a hotel room or a bed in a hostel or family pension on the most popular tourist islands without any advance notice if you are willing to settle for whatever accommodation is available. I have found spur-of-the-moment lodgings for friends who wanted to spend a couple of days in Bora Bora during the July Festival, which is normally overbooked at that time of year. Although Polynesians are now more discerning about inviting strangers into their homes, there are still numerous visitors who get "adopted" by a local Tahitian, French or Chinese family. One woman I know went to Huahine where she intended camping out, but she was invited to stay in the home of a Tahitian woman she met, who has a *roulotte* on the boat dock in Fare. The *Tahiti Beach Press* receives several letters each year, written by tourists who want to nominate a local resident for the "Mauruuru Award" because that local has been exceptionally kind to them. The hospitality extended to our visitors includes everything from giving a free ride and a tour around the island to inviting the tourist to their homes for a shower, a meal and quite often, free room and board for several days.

Tourism is very far from reaching the level of saturation in these islands, and the only long lines you'll find are at the buffet tables in the hotels during a special event. You can usually get a last-minute seat on an airplane, a cabin on an inter-island ship, a berth on a sailboat, or a place on any of the tours and excursions that are available on each island. However, it is certainly recommended to reserve in advance if you want to avoid delays, especially for airline flights.

GETTING AROUND TAHITI & HER ISLANDS BY AIR

AIR MOOREA, Tahiti-Faa'a International Airport, B.P. 6019, Papeete, Tahiti; (Papeete) *Tel. 689/86.41.41; Fax 689/86.42.99; (Moorea) Tel. 689/55.06.01; 55.06.09; reservation@airmoorea.pf; www.airmoorea.com.* The Air Moorea Terminal is in a separate building to the left of the main terminal as you exit Immigration and Customs in Tahiti. Just follow the arrows on the marked walkway. Air Moorea operates an air-shuttle service between Tahiti and Moorea, with a fleet of Twin-Otter aircraft, plus 2 Beechcraft Super King B200 planes. Most of the flights leave Tahiti every hour on the hour and depart from Moorea at 15 minutes past the hour, but there are exceptions during the busy period of the day when extra flights are added. There are up to 40 scheduled round-trips daily between Tahiti and Moorea, with the first Tahiti-Moorea flight at 6am. See information Arriving By Air and Departing by Air in *Moorea* chapter.

AIR TAHITI, Tahiti-Faa'a International Airport, B.P. 314, Papeete, Tahiti; reservations *Tel. 689/86.42.42;* information on flight arrivals *689/86.60.61/ 86.41.84; Fax 689/86.40.99; reservation@airtahiti.pf; www.airtahiti.aero.* The main ticket office, *Tel. 47.44.00,* is located on the corner of rue du Genéral de Gaulle and rue Edouard Ahnne, across the street from Fare Loto in downtown Papeete. Office hours are Mon.-Fri. 7am-5pm and on Sat. from 8-11am. The airport office, *Tel. 86.41.84,* is open daily from 5:30am-5pm, and the Moana Holidays office *Tel. 50.26.26,* at the Moana Nui Shopping Center in Punaauia, is open all day Mon.-Fri. 8am-6pm and on Sat. mornings from 8am-12pm. Tahiti Vacations is the Air Tahiti subsidiary in the US.

Air Tahiti Network

Air Tahiti operates domestic scheduled flights between the islands of French Polynesia, with a network of 44 islands, covering all 5 archipelagoes. A modern fleet of twin-turboprop aircraft comprises 4 ATR 42-500 planes with 48 seats, 5 ATR 72-500 planes with 66 seats, 1 Twin-Otter plane with 19 seats that is based in the Marquesas Islands, and 1 Beechcraft with 9 seats. All the aircraft have high wings, offering you great views of the beautiful islands if you are seated by the window. Air Tahiti also flies to Rarotonga in the Cook Islands each Tues. and Sat. See information for international flights *By Other Air Routes* in this chapter.

Air Passes

Air Tahiti offers 5 different **air passes** with 2 extension possibilities, which all begin in Papeete and are subject to special conditions. Your travel agent can arrange an air pass for you to visit several islands, which is the most popular and least expensive means of island hopping. Rates quoted here are for adults who buy their tickets outside French Polynesia, except for the Blue Pass and Discovery Blue Pass, which can be purchased only in French Polynesia. Contact an Air Tahiti sales office for more information or go to: *www.airtahiti.aero.*

Air Passes to the Society Islands

Pass MD230 is called the **Discovery Pass**, which will take you from Tahiti to Moorea and on to Huahine and Raiatea for 25.000 CFP. Pass MD 215 is called the **Bora Bora Pass**, which lets you visit all 6 of the major islands in the Society group: Tahiti, Moorea, Huahine, Raiatea, Bora Bora and Maupiti. You are not allowed to transit in Papeete within the pass nor to fly back to Papeete before the end of the pass, which is sold for 35.800 CFP from Jan. 1-May 31 and Nov. 1-Dec. 31, and 38.000 CFP from June 1-Oct. 31.

Air Passes to the Society Islands & Tuamotu Archipelago

Pass MD220 is the **Lagoon Pass**, which costs 40.000 CFP and combines a visit to Moorea with Rangiroa, Tikehau, Manihi, Fakarava and Ahe. One transit is allowed through Papeete between Moorea and the Tuamotu Archipelago. Pass MD213 (**Bora Bora-Tuamotu Pass**) is one of the most popular choices, especially for honeymooners and scuba divers. This pass costs 52.000 CFP and takes you from Tahiti to Moorea, Huahine, Raiatea, Bora Bora and Maupiti in the Society group, and on to Rangiroa, Tikehau, Manihi, Fakarava and Ahe in the Tuamotu atolls.

A **Blue Pass** (Code BD216) takes you from Tahiti direct to Huahine, Raiatea, Bora Bora, and then to Moorea. The Moorea-Tahiti flight can be made on board an Air Moorea or Air Tahiti flight during the day. This pass is sold in French Polynesia only and costs 26.200 CFP. It is subject to specific conditions and cannot be combined with the Austral or Marquesas Islands extensions. A **Discovery Blue Pass** (Code BD236) for 20.200 CFP is good for Huahine, Raiatea and Moorea.

Air Pass to the Marquesas Islands

You can also visit the islands of Nuku Hiva, Hiva Oa, Ua Pou and Ua Huka with an Air Tahiti **Marquesas Pass** (Code MLD240), which is priced at 64.900 CFP from Jan.1 to Mar. 31 and from Nov. 1 to Dec. 31. From Apr. 1 to Oct. 31 this same pass is 71.100 CFP.

Air Pass Extensions

Should you wish to discover some of the more remote archipelagoes you can take advantage of 2 Air Pass Extensions, which must be purchased with one of the four basic Air Passes available. The extensions to the Marquesas or Austral Islands can be used either before or after the pass, and you can buy both extensions if you so choose. A stopover in Tahiti is permitted before or after the extensions.

Code A is the **Austral Islands Extension**, which includes the islands of Rurutu, Tubuai, and Raivavae for an additional 27.100 CFP. Code M is a **Marquesas Extension** that will take you to the islands of Nuku Hiva and Hiva Oa for an additional 48.800 CFP.

Island Stays

Air Tahiti's **Island Adventures** specializes in off the beaten track stays in all 5 island groups, with ready made packages at preferential prices that include round-trip air fares between Tahiti and the outer island chosen, plus accommodations in a hotel, hostel or family pension, meeting and greeting with flower leis and travel documents, ground transfers and most of the government taxes. Depending on your package, you may also have 1-3 daily meals included, and an excursion thrown in. All the packages are detailed on *www.islandsadventures.com*, which is supposed to be in English. However, at publication time this website address automatically reverted to the French language site of *www.sejoursdanslesiles.pf.* Fax them at *689/ 86.40.99.*

Baggage
The normal baggage allowance of 10 kg. (22 lbs.) is raised to 20 kg. (44 lbs.) on most domestic destinations if you are connecting to/from an international flight. If you purchase your domestic flights locally then your limit is 10 kg. Divers are allowed an extra 5 kg. if proof is provided when checking in. Excess baggage fares vary according to destination. Rather than having to pay for excess baggage at each inter-island flight, you may choose the special "round-trip formula" available upon check-in at the Tahiti or Moorea airports. This will save you 30% off the normal round-trip rate.

Reconfirmations
You are not required to reconfirm your reservations with Air Tahiti, except in the following conditions. If Air Tahiti has no contact number for you then you should reconfirm 24 hrs. before your scheduled flight. If you take a flight for which you have no reservation or if you should choose to travel by other means, then you should reconfirm any subsequent reservations you've already made with Air Tahiti. If you are flying on board a Beechcraft or Twin Otter to the Eastern Tuamotu, the Gambier Islands or to Marquesas Islands you should reconfirm a week in advance. Air Tahiti advises that you verify the departure time of your flight in the event of a delay or flight cancellation, at *Tel. 86.42.42.*

Other Information
Check-in time for Air Tahiti flights is 1 hour in advance of your flight. If you haven't checked in by 20 min. before flight departure your reservation will be canceled. All Air Tahiti flights are non-smoking. Air Tahiti issues new timetables on Apr. 1 and Nov. 1, one for local distribution and the other for overseas markets. The rates quoted here were taken from the local distribution timetable that expired Mar. 31, 2008. Please check Air Tahiti's website for updated airfares and information at *www.airtahiti.aero.*

Charter Flights
AIR TAHITI, Tahiti-Faa'a Airport, B.P. 314, Papeete, Tahiti 98713. *Tel. 689/86.40.12/86.42.42; Fax 689/86.40.69; reservation@airtahiti.pf;*

www.airtahiti.aero. Aircraft available for charter within French Polynesia includes 4 ATR 42-500 planes with 48 seats, 5 ATR 72-500 planes with 66 seats, 1 Twin Otter with 19 seats and 1 Beechcraft with 9 seats.

AIR MOOREA, Tahiti-Faa'a Airport, B.P. 6019, Faa'a, Tahiti 98702. *Tel. 689/86.41.41 (Papeete), Tel. 689/86.42.42 (reservations); Tel. 689/55.06.01 (Moorea); Fax 689/86.42.99; reservation@airmoorea.pf; www.airmoorea.com*. Air Moorea has 30-min. flight-seeing tours over Moorea, and other charter flights can be arranged.

AIR ARCHIPELS, Tahiti-Faa'a Airport, B.P. 6019, Faa'a, Tahiti 98702. *Tel. 689/81.30.30; Fax 689/86.42.69; reservation@mail.pf; www.airarchipels.com*. This small airline is used for charters and emergency flight service. The fleet includes 2 Beechcraft Super King B200 aircraft, each with 7 VIP passenger seats or 9 high density seats.

By Helicopter

POLYNESIA HÉLICOPTÈRES, B.P. 424, Papeete, Tahiti 98713. *Tel. 689/ 54.87.20/78.65.05; Fax 689/54.87.21; helico-tahiti@mail.pf; www.polynesia-helicopter.com*. One AS 350 BA Ecureuil (Squirrel) 5-seat helicopter is based in Tahiti, providing sightseeing flights and charters on request to visit Tahiti and Moorea. There is also an AS 350 BA Ecureuil 5-passenger helicopter based in Bora Bora, and one 5-passenger Ecureuil based permanently in the Marquesas Islands, where they provide transfers from the Nuku Hiva airport to Taiohae village and other nearby islands, as well as photographic flights. A private charter is 173.100 CFP per hour. See further information in the destination chapters on *Tahiti, Moorea, Bora Bora* and *Nuku Hiva* in the Marquesas.

GETTING AROUND BY INTER-ISLAND PASSENGER BOATS & FREIGHTERS

Windward Society Islands

Tahiti and Moorea are connected by two fast catamarans that provide 30-min. crossings several times daily between Papeete and the Vaiare ferry dock in Moorea. **Aremiti V**, *Tel. 689/50.57.57* in Tahiti and *Tel. 689/56.31.10* in Moorea; *www.aremiti.pf*. This catamaran transports 700 passengers, 30 lightweight cars and 2-wheel vehicles. **Moorea Express Catamaran**, *Tel. 689/50.11.11* in Tahiti and *Tel. 689/56.34.34* in Moorea, has up to 8 trips per day from Tahiti to Moorea or from Moorea to Tahiti, carrying passengers and 2-wheel vehicles.

Passengers, cars and larger vehicles are transported on this route by the **Aremiti Ferry**, *Tel. 689/50.57.57/56.31.10*, and the **Moorea Ferry**, *Tel. 689/50.11.11/ 56.34.34*, for the 1-hr. trips across the Sea of Moons, as the channel is called. For rates and schedules see *Arriving by Boat* and *Departing by Boat* in the **Moorea** chapter.

Leeward Society Islands

HAWAIKI NUI, *B.P. 635, Papeete, Tahiti, Tel. 689/54.99.54, Fax 689/ 45.24.44; contact@stim.pf.*

The Hawaiki Nui is a cargo/passenger ship that provides twice-weekly inter-island service between Papeete and the Leeward Society Islands of Huahine, Raiatea, Taha'a and Bora Bora. Departures from Papeete are each Tues. and Thurs. See schedules and fares in each Island chapter. This ship carries only 12 passengers, who sleep on the deck or share cabins. Meals are available on board the ship. Note: All passengers must sleep in a cabin during the Thurs. trip because the ship is carrying fuel during that voyage.

VAEANU, operated by Société Coopérative Ouvrière de Production Ihitai Nui. *B.P. 9062, Motu Uta, Tahiti, Tel. 689/41.25.35; Fax 41.24.34, torehiatetu@mail.pf.*

This freighter is 79 m. (264 ft.) long and 12 m. (39 ft.) wide, with a draft of 6 m. (19 ft.). In 1981 this ship began its career in Polynesian waters as the *Aranui*, cruising to the Marquesas and Tuamotu Islands. It was sold and renamed in the early 1990s and now serves the Leeward Society Islands with 3 round-trips each week from Papeete. There are accommodations for 32 passengers in 2 triple cabins, 12 double cabins and one individual cabin, with deck space for 58 passengers. There is also a dining room on board.

This passenger/cargo ship departs from the Motu Uta quay in Papeete at 4pm on Mon., Wed. and Fri. See schedules and fares in chapters on *Huahine, Raiatea, Taha'a* and *Bora Bora*. Reservations for cabin space must be paid in full before 9am on the fixed date of departure from Papeete, and all passengers are boarded at 3pm. No alcohol or drugs are allowed on board.

MAUPITI EXPRESS II, B.P. 612, Bora Bora 98730. *Tel/Fax 689/67.66.69 (Bora Bora); Tel./Fax 689/66.37.81 (Raiatea); cell 78.27.22/72.30.48; www.maupitiexpress.com.* This 140-passenger launch transports passengers between Raiatea, Taha'a, Bora Bora and Maupiti. See each Island chapter for the schedules and rates. If you want to take a day-trip from Bora Bora to Maupiti, you should contact owner/captain Gérald Sachet by cell phone. He also has a small boat in Maupiti that is used for Maupiti Poe Iti Lagoon Tours and his wife runs Pension Poe Iti in Maupiti.

Marquesas Islands

ARANUI 3, operated by Compagnie Polynésienne de Transport Maritime, 2028 El Camino Real South, Suite B, San Mateo, California 94403; in US *Tel. 800/972-7268 or 650/574-2575; Fax 650/574-6221; cptm@aranui.com; www.aranui.com.* The Tahiti office is located at Motu Uta, across the harbor and bridge from Papeete, *Tel. 689/42.62.40; Fax 689/43.48.89.*

In my opinion the *Aranui* is the best way to visit French Polynesia if you have the time and interest to enjoy an authentic experience of ship-day in a small secluded valley in the Marquesas Islands. The *Aranui 3* was custom-built in

Rumania and began service in March 2003, replacing the *Aranui 2*, offering the same friendly atmosphere that has made the worldwide reputation of the Aranui ships and Polynesian crew. The *Aranui 3* is a working cargo/copra ship—not a cruise ship in the usual sense, where you put on your best finery to dine at the captain's table. You'll be more practically dressed in a cool shirt or blouse and shorts or pants that you don't mind getting wet and dirty when you get into the whaleboat for shore excursions. And don't forget your plastic sandals, protective hat, sunglasses, sunscreen and a good repellent against mosquitoes and *nonos* (sand fleas). The 200-passenger *Aranui 3* was specially designed with added space and the passengers' comfort in mind. The ship is 117.65 m. (386 ft.) long, 17.68 m. (58 ft.) wide and cruises at a speed of 15 knots. The ship has a/c in all passenger areas and indoor public spaces. There are accommodations for 208 passengers in 63 standard "A" cabins, 12 deluxe cabins, 10 suites with a balcony, and a dormitory with 30 bunk style beds. All the cabins and suites have a telephone and personal safe.

The 10 spacious suites all have picture windows and some suites even have a balcony. In addition to a queen-size bed with reading lights, there is a desk, chest of drawers, hanging closet, comfortable chairs and coffee table in the sitting space, a refrigerator, TV with video channel, private bathroom with bathtub/shower, and a selection of amenities. The suites cost 532.300-570.410 CFP per person, depending on location or whether it has a balcony.

The 12 deluxe cabins are large outside cabins with picture windows, a queen-size bed or 2 twin beds, refrigerator and private facilities with bathtub/shower, for 478.740 CFP per person. The 63 standard "A" class cabins, are all outside, with 2 lower berths and private facilities with showers, for 404.580 CFP per person. The class "C" dormitory style accommodations for 30 passengers are located on the restaurant deck. They have a/c and share the toilet facilities. These upper and lower berths are 232.570 CFP per person and are not accessible to children younger than 15 years.

The public facilities of the *Aranui 3* include a reception, colorful dining room with your choice of seating, a non-smoking lounge-library, boutique, video room, meeting rooms, elevator, gym, and infirmary with a doctor. There are 2 bars and lounges, a sun deck and salt-water swimming pool. Special marine facilities make it easy for you to fish, swim, snorkel and go scuba diving. There is daily maid service, twice-weekly laundry service and trained hostesses and guides. Organized shore excursions include picnics, Marquesan feasts, guided hikes to waterfalls, stone tikis and archaeological sites, visits to wood carvers and artisan workshops, plus inland and upland tours by 4WD vehicles.

The *Aranui 3* leaves Tahiti 17 times a year for 14-day round-trip voyages to the Marquesas Islands, with a brief stop at the Tuamotu atoll of Fakarava on the outbound trip, and in Rangiroa atoll on the return voyage. The *Aranui* means "The Great Highway" in the Tahitian language and it serves as a lifeline to the Marquesas Islanders, as the ship calls at each principal village and several remote valleys on the 6 inhabited islands. The big cargo holds contain food, fuel, cement and other building materials, trucks, fishing boats, beer, bedding and other necessities to offload in the distant Marquesas Islands. Copra, citrus fruit, fish and barrels of *noni* (*Morinda citrifolia*) are embarked to take back to Papeete.

Watching the *Aranui*'s muscular crew perform their tasks is part of the attraction and charm of this voyage. Even if hydraulics are not your favorite thing, you'll enjoy watching a pickup truck being loaded from the ship's hold onto a barge or double platform balanced on top of two whale boats lashed together. What's even more interesting is to see how the crew gets the truck safely ashore while the waves are bouncing the whaleboats up and down.

On-board guest lecturers are experts in their fields of Marquesan art, archaeology, history or customs, and they accompany the passengers ashore to enrich their visit by explaining the meaning of the designs in wood carvings, the stone tikis, the *paepae* platforms and *tohua* meeting grounds in the valleys. While you're watching the young people dance for you in the villages, tasting special Marquesan food and visiting the archaeological sites, the Marquesan men and boys are helping the *Aranui* crew to load burlap bags of copra in the whaleboats to be shipped to the copra processing plant in Papeete. A trip aboard the *Aranui* will give you many opportunities to meet the friendly and natural Polynesians, far removed from the normal tourist scene.

The 2008 rates quoted here are based on per person double occupancy and include 3 meals a day with wine at lunch and dinner, plus picnics and programmed meals on shore, as well as guided excursions. All taxes are included. Activities such as horseback riding, scuba diving and helicopter tours are optional. Add 50% for single occupancy. Children pay the adult fare. Adults sharing a cabin with 3 Pullman beds will have a 25% reduction from the full fare for the 3rd person.

For a sample itinerary of your voyage and other details, go to: *www.aranui.com/download/aranui-english.pdf.*

Tuamotu Islands

Before planning a trip to the Tuamotu Archipelago aboard any of the ships listed below, you should verify if the vessel is still in service. The treacherous reefs of the atolls are a graveyard for ships that have been wrecked on these coral shores. These distant atolls were named the Dangerous Archipelago for a good reason. During the past few years some of the older ships were destroyed by fire and/or sank at sea. Because these freighters are allowed to carry only 12 passengers, the owners have asked me not to list their ships anymore because they cannot even meet the needs of the inhabitants of the atolls. Other ships have been removed from this list because new rulings will not allow any passengers on board. The offices of these *goëlettes* (tramp boats) are located in the port area of Motu Uta, reached by bridge across the Papeete harbor.

ST. XAVIER MARIS STELLA III, operated by Société Navigation Tuamotu, B.P. 14160, Arue, Tahiti 98701; *Tel. 689/42.23.58; Fax 689/43.03.73; cell*

77.22.88; E-mail: maris-stella@mail.pf. The office is in a warehouse on the inter-island goëlette pier at Motu Uta.

This 207-ft. long red-hulled steel ship began its service to the Tuamotu atolls in June 2001. This ship carries only 12 passengers and priority is given to the people who live in the islands. They bring their woven mats and bedding and sleep on the deck or pay extra for a berth in a shared cabin. Meals are served. The ship reaches Rangiroa after 20 hours at sea, then continues on to all the western Tuamotu atolls: Ahe, Manihi, Takaroa, Takapoto, Arutua, Apataki, Kaukura, Toau, Fakarava, Kauehi, Raraka, Niau and Papeete. Only one day is spent in each port and the itinerary changes according to the freight on board. The ship leaves Papeete every 15 days and it takes 10 days to make the round-trip circuit. The one-way deck fares, with 3 meals per day included, are 7.070 CFP for Mataiva, Rangiroa and Tikehau, 8.484 CFP for Ahe and Manihi, and 11.830 CFP for Fakarava. The one-way fare for a berth in a cabin is 10.000 CFP for Mataiva, Rangiroa and Tikehau, 15.000 CFP for Ahe and Manihi, and 30.000 CFP for Fakarava.

MAREVA NUI, operated by Siméon Richmond, B.P. 1816, Papeete, Tahiti 98713. *Tel. 689/42.25.53, Fax 689/42.25.57.* The office is at the Motu Uta inter-island cargo ship pier.

This is a 181-ft. steel ship that transports passengers and cargo between Tahiti and the western Tuamotu atolls, with departures from Papeete every 15 days for the 8-day round trip voyage. There are 12 passenger berths and no cabins. The ship calls at Makatea, Mataiva, Tikehau, Rangiroa, Ahe, Manihi, Takaroa, Takapoto, Raraka, Kauehi, Apataki, Arutua, Kaukura, Niau, Fakarava, and then returns to Papeete. The one-way fares start at 3.800 CFP for deck passage to Makatea, Mataiva or Tikehau, and the most expensive fare is 8.200 CFP for a berth to the last stop on the itinerary, which may be Fakarava, Manihi or Takapoto. Three meals a day cost 2.200 CFP per person per day.

NUKU HAU, managed by Roland Paquier of S.T.I.M., B.P. 635, Papeete, Tahiti 98713, *Tel. 689/54.99.54/45.24.44*, is based at the Motu Uta quay.

This is a 210-ft. cargo ship that can take 12 passengers from Tahiti to the eastern Tuamotu and Gambier Islands during the 20-day round-trip voyages it makes once every 25 days. There is no cabin space but you will be served three meals a day on board. The itinerary includes Hao, Nego Nego, Tureia, Vanavana, Marutea Sud, Rikitea, Tematangi, Anuanuraro, Nukutepipi and Hereheretue, before returning to Papeete. The one-way fare is 7.950 CFP for deck space, plus 1.950 CFP per day for the meals.

Other ships serving the Tuamotus are **Cobia III**, *Tel./Fax 43.36.43*, **Dory III**, *Tel./Fax 42.30.55*; **Hotu Maru**, *Tel. 41.07.11, Fax 42.77.67*; and **Kura Ora III**, *Tel. 45.60.00; Fax 45.55.44.*

Austral Islands

TUHAA PAE II, operated by Société Anonyme d'Economie Mixte de

Navigation des Australes, B.P. 1890, Papeete, Tahiti, *Tel. 689/50.96.09; Fax 689/ 42.06.09; E-mail: snathp@mail.pf.*
     This is a steel hull ship, 59 m. (196 ft.) long that carries passengers and supplies to the Austral Islands. It makes 3 voyages a month from Tahiti to the Austral Islands, calling at Tubuai, Rimatara, Raivavae and Rurutu, then returning to Papeete. The itinerary may vary. The ship visits Rapa once every 2 months. The cabins are very basic, usually with 4 bunk beds, no portholes and no air. The showers and toilets are on a separate level from the cabins. The local passengers sleep in berths in a big open room up top, which is cooler but not private. Bring your own toilet paper, booze, towels, soap and electric fans (220 volts). The dining room serves simple but good food. There are no shore activities programmed. You can hitch a ride with some of the islanders who come to the ship to collect their merchandise from Tahiti or to load their taro and other vegetables that are being shipped to Papeete.
     The one-way fares from Tahiti to Rurutu, Rimatara and Tubuai are 3.817 CFP on the deck and 7.348 CFP for a berth in a cabin. The one-way fares to Raivavae are 5.502 CFP on the deck and 10.591 CFP for a berth in a cabin, and from Tahiti to Rapa the fare is 7.523 CFP on the deck, and 14.481 CFP for a berth in a cabin. Deck passengers can have a berth for 40% more. Meals are extra.

GETTING AROUND BY CRUISE SHIPS BASED IN TAHITI
     M/S PAUL GAUGUIN is owned by Apollo Management of Prestige Cruise Holdings, and is operated by Regent Seven Seas Cruises (RSSC), which is based in Fort Lauderdale, Florida, *Tel. 877/505-5370* (RSSC Expert), *Tel. 866/213-1272* (Travel Agent near you); *Tel. 954/776-6123, ext. 7306* (Charters & Incentive); *www.rssc.com.*
     Regent Seven Seas Cruises was voted the world's #1 small ship-operator in 2007 by readers of *Condé Naste Traveler*, and the *Paul Gauguin* has received awards as the "World's Best Cruise Ship," for the "Best Overall Cruise," "Best Food at Sea," and "Cruise Critic Editor's Pick."
     The 330-passenger *Paul Gauguin* was built in France to be based year-round in Tahiti, and in January 1998 it began regular 8 day/7 night cruises in the Society Islands. The ship is 156.5 m. (513 ft.) long, 21.6 m. (71 ft. wide), with a draft of 5.15 m. (16.9 ft.), and a gross tonnage of 19,200. All of the 160 staterooms and suites are outside, with sweeping ocean and lagoon views. Half of the staterooms have private balconies or verandas. The Owner's Suite has 457 sq. ft. of living space plus a veranda. The 3 largest of the Grand Suites each has 529 sq. ft., including a private balcony and veranda. There are deluxe suites with verandas, veranda suites, junior suites with balconies, and exterior cabins with windows or portholes in categories D, E and F. The smallest cabin is 205 sq. ft.
     The staterooms and suites have individual temperature control and are decorated in a contemporary motif, with exotic woods and warm colors. They each contain a queen-size bed or twin beds, white marble appointed bathroom with a

real bathtub and shower, hair dryer and terry cloth robes, closed circuit TV and video player, direct dial telephone, safe, numerous shelves and spacious closets. There is also a refrigerator stocked with soft drinks and mineral waters. Butler service and in-suite/stateroom bar setup are provided in higher categories. There is an international crew of 215, including a sufficient number of cabin stewards to provide individual service round-the-clock.

The 9-deck ship has 2 elegant restaurants and an outdoor grill, plus a 24-hr. room service menu. Passengers can choose single, open seating dining at their leisure to enjoy 6-star gastronomic meals featuring the menus created by Le Cordon Bleu Chefs of France. Fare Tahiti is an on-board museum, gallery and special information center with books, videos, and other materials on the ethnic art, history, geography and culture of Tahiti and Her Islands.

There is an Internet Café and Wireless access. In addition to 2 bars and lounges, there is a duty free boutique and Tahia Collins pearl shop, a panoramic nightclub and piano bar, a disco, casino, medical center and beauty salon. A full spa and fitness center is operated by **Carita of Paris**, and includes a steam room, as well as massages, body wraps, facials and full beauty services. In addition to the fully equipped Fitness Center and swimming pool, there is a nautical sports center with a retractable water sports platform. Water-skiing, windsurfing, sailing, kayaking and snorkeling are offered, as well as a full scuba dive program for novices and experts. Nightly entertainment is presented in the main lounge. The "Gauguines" or "Gauguin's Girls" are 12 pretty Tahitian *vahines* who sing and dance and act as gracious hostesses aboard the ship.

Rates include all meals, preselected wines with meals, non-alcoholic beverages and mineral waters, Captain's Welcome Cocktail, all nautical sports from the Marina nautical sports center except scuba diving, tips, welcome at the Tahiti-Faa'a International airport and transfer to a first-class hotel, use of hotel rooms for the morning on departure day, brunch at the hotel, transfers from the hotel to the *Paul Gauguin* in the afternoon, and transfers from the ship to the airport at the end of the cruise for international departure.

During the standard 7-night cruise the passengers board the *Paul Gauguin* each Saturday afternoon, with departure time at 10pm. The ship reaches Raiatea on Sunday morning, departing on Monday for Taha'a, where the passengers have use of a private islet between the barrier reef and the main island. The *Paul Gauguin* arrives in Bora Bora each Tuesday morning and remains inside the world-famous lagoon until Wednesday at 6pm, then it cruises to the island of Moorea, where it anchors in Cook's Bay or Opunohu Bay, allowing the passengers 2 days and a night to explore Moorea. On Friday evening at 5pm the ship leaves Moorea to return to Papeete for the final night, and the passengers disembark on Saturday morning. The 2008 fares for this program start at $2,195-$2,995, depending on the cruise date.

The 2008 itinerary also includes 9-night cruises through the Society Islands, 10 nights that include Rangiroa in the Tuamotu Islands, as well as the Society

Islands, and 11-night cruises that take you from Papeete to Rangiroa, Hiva Oa and Nuku Hiva in the Marquesas Island, then to Bora Bora, Taha'a, Moorea and back to Papeete. Some of the 14-night cruises include the Society Islands, Rangiroa and the Marquesan Islands of Fatu Hiva, Hiva Oa, Ua Huka and Nuku Hiva.

There is also a 14-day cruise departing on Sept. 27, 2008, that takes you from Papeete to Huahine in the Leeward Islands, on to Aitutaki and Rarotonga in the Cook Islands, then back to Tubuai in the Austral Islands, and from there to Taha'a, Bora Bora, Rangiroa, Moorea and Papeete. This cruise starts at $4,495 per person in double occupancy. Jean-Michel Cousteau will be the guest lecturer, speaking on the oceans and environment.

RSSC operates a charter flight service for the *Paul Gauguin* clients with round-trip add-on fares from several gateway cities in the USA. Free economy air specials and special cruise discounts are offered at various times of the year. Pre- and post-cruise packages are also available for those who wish to spend more time on their favorite islands. Although the original contract for the *M/S Paul Gauguin* to operate cruises in French Polynesia was for 10 years, that agreement has been extended for another year, ending in January 2010.

STAR FLYER is owned by Star Clippers Ltd. of Monaco. U.S.A. contact: Marketing, Sales & Reservations, 7200 NW 19th Street, Suite 206, Miami, FL 33126; *Tel. 305/442-0550; Fax 305/442-1611; Reservations 800/442-0551; info@starclippers.com; www.starclippers.com.*

The 170-passenger 4-masted sailing ship *Star Flyer* sailed from the Caribbean to Tahiti in Dec. 2007, and will be based year-round in Papeete for the next four years. The inaugural cruise began on Dec. 30, with a 7-night cruise program through the Society Islands. The ship also offers 10- and 11-night cruises, combining the Society Islands and the Tuamotu Atolls.

Star Flyer is a modern cruise ship that was created for comfort-loving passengers who also love the traditions and romance of the legendary era of sailing ships. She is 360 ft. long with a 50-ft. beam, a 16-ft. draft, a tonnage of 2,298 ft., and a crew of 72. The masts are 226 ft. tall and the 21 sails have a total of 36,000 sq. ft. of sail area. The guest cabins are located on all 4 decks. The deluxe Owner's suite has a dimension of 226 sq. ft., and the other cabins range from 97-150 sq. ft. All cabins have en suite shower and toilet facilities. The decor is reminiscent of the grand age of sail, with teak, polished brass, gleaming mahogany rails, antique prints and paintings of famous sailing ships.

There is open seating in the elegantly appointed dining room and no need for formal gowns and black tie. The chef's international cuisine is complimented by a selection of equally fine wines and the service is friendly and gracious. You will also find a convivial atmosphere at the indoor-outdoor Tropical Bar or while singing a few old favorites with friends around the piano bar. In certain ports local performers are brought on board to give passengers an authentic taste of Polynesian music and dance. Quieter pleasures can be found in the Edwardian style library with its Belle Epoque fireplace. For the health-minded there is also a gym, sauna and spa, as well as a swimming pool on board.

The 7-night program leaves Papeete on Sun. for Huahine, Raiatea, Taha'a and Bora Bora, then arrives in Moorea's Cook's Bay on Fri., sails over to Opunohu Bay for the night and returns to Papeete on Sat. evening. Guests disembark the ship on Sun. morning. The 2007-2009 economy rates for this cruise start at $1,845 for a Category 6 cabin and escalate to $3,965 for the Owner's cabin, based on per person double occupancy. Port charges are $210 per person.

A 10-night voyage leaves Papeete and sails to Fakarava in the Tuamotu Atolls, continuing to Rangiroa and on to Bora Bora, Raiatea, Taha'a, Huahine, Moorea and back to Papeete. The economy rates range from $2,735-$5,825, plus $300 port charges per person. The 11-night trip adds an overnight stay in Huahine and sells for $2,915-6,205, plus $330 for port charges for the economy fare. Value rates for each cruise program are more.

TAHITIAN PRINCESS, *24305 Town Center Dr., Santa Clarita, CA 91355, Tel. 800/PRINCESS or 661/753.0000; Fax 661/753.0136; www.princess.com.*

The 670-passenger *Tahitian Princess* has offered year-round cruises in Tahiti and the South Pacific since December 2002. For 5 consecutive years the 592-ft. long ship has started and ended its sailing programs in Tahiti, with 10-day cruises to the Leeward Society Islands and Rangiroa in the Tuamotu Islands or to Rarotonga in the Cook Islands, and an occasional cruise to the Marquesas Islands.

In 2008 the *Tahitian Princess* will continue its 10-day itinerary in the Society Islands and the Cook Islands for the first 4 months, then it will sail to Honolulu on May 8, and on to Vancouver, B.C. on May 19. Starting on May 29 the ship will make 8 roundtrip cruises of 14 days each between Vancouver and Alaska, before returning to Honolulu on Sept. 18 and embarking for Tahiti on Sept. 28. On Oct. 10 the *Tahitian Princess* will resume its 10-day cruises from Papeete to the Leeward Society Islands and Rangiroa, making 7 round-trip cruises before leaving Tahiti on Dec. 19 for a world cruise. Princess Cruises has not announced whether the ship will return to Polynesian waters after its circumnavigation.

The old world decor on board the ship features elegant cherry-colored wood finishes, lush window treatments, and upholstered furnishings in a design scheme that evokes a British country house hotel feeling. The 342 cabins give you a choice of 8 accommodation categories, with the size varying from the spacious owners' suites, with 786-962 sq. ft., to the "G" class ocean view double cabin, with 146 sq. ft. More than 200 of the staterooms feature balconies, and all the cabins have twin or queen-sized beds, sofa or sofa bed, telephone, TV, desk, refrigerator, and bathroom with shower, or a tub and shower. The owner's suites have a large bathroom with a whirlpool tub, an entertainment center, two TV's and a separate sitting room with dining area. There are individual temperature controls, ample closet and drawer space, a personal safe, vanity with mirror, hair dryer and full-length mirror. There is also 24-hour room service.

The ship's restaurants give you a choice of traditional dining, anytime dining, specialty dining and casual dining. The specialty restaurants include the Sterling Steakhouse and Sabatini's for Italian cuisine. Nighttime entertainment features seasoned professionals and the ship's hot spots include the Cabaret Lounge, Casino, Tahitian Lounge and the Movies Under the Stars outdoor theater. The Club Bar, Pool Bar and Casino Bar are also cozy lounges.

The *Tahitian Princess* also has an Internet café, library and card room, swimming pool and 2 hot tubs, golf practice cage, shuffleboard, jogging track, full-service Lotus Spa with fitness center, beauty salon, and gift shops. There are two formal nights per 10-day cruise, when the passengers dress in "resort casual formal" clothes. The rest of the time the cruise is resort casual.

The **Pacific Princess** is an identical sister-ship to the *Tahitian Princess*. It is no longer based year-round in Tahiti, but does visit on occasion. On Dec. 15, 2007 this ship left Papeete for Fort Lauderdale, and on Jan. 10, 2008, the Pacific Princess began a 102-day voyage around the world.

SILVER DAWN is the former 6,072 gross ton expedition ship *World Discoverer*, now owned by Silversea Cruises Group Ltd., *www.silverseaships.com*, which was voted the World's Best Cruise Line during a *Condé Naste Traveler* poll. Following a multi-million dollar refurbishment in Trieste, the *Silver Dawn* will accommodate 132 passengers in 5- and 6-star luxury standards, catered to by a crew of 106. From April-Oct. 2009, the *Silver Dawn* will cruise the non-traditional routes of French Polynesia, taking tourists to discover the southernmost Austral Islands, the widespread Tuamotu Archipelago and the northernmost Marquesas Islands. The rest of the year the ship is expected to cruise in Antarctica waters.

TU MOANA and **TI'A MOANA** are sister ships owned by Bora Bora Cruises, *P.O. Box 40186, Fare Tony, Papeete, Tahiti 98713; Tel. 689/54.45.07; resa@boraboracruises.com; www.boraboracruises.com*. North America: *Tel. 949/ 487-0522; joann@kurtzahlers.com*.

These two luxury yachts were built in Australia to the specifications of Bora Bora Cruises (BBC) and the interior design is Swedish. Since their delivery in 2003 the yachts are based year-round in the Leeward Society Islands. If you are looking for a quiet, intimate, low-key cruise, their programs offer refinement in a relaxed atmosphere. Former passengers have described their cruise on board the *Tu Moana* and *Ti'a Moana* "like being a guest on a billionaire's mega yacht."

Each yacht is 69 m. (226.7 ft.) long, with a beam of 13.8 m. (45.3 ft.) and a draft of 2.3 m. (7.5 ft.). There are 20 ocean view cabins for 40 guests on 3 of the 5 decks, with a choice of queen size, double or twin beds. Each guestroom has large windows, individually controlled a/c, a writing desk with stationery, flat screen LCD television, individual DVD/CD player, telephone, mini-bar refrigerator, personal combination lock safe, under-bed baggage storage area, bathroom with adjustable shower-head with temperature control, fitted hairdryer, and bathroom amenities.

The public facilities in the fully a/c ships include a panoramic restaurant, lounge, reading room and Internet area, library of books, DVD movies and CD music, a gallery showcasing local artists, a boutique, fitness spa, 2 Jacuzzis, shaded outdoor lounges and sundecks, reception and concierge, excursion office, and watersports platform for tenders, kayaks, swimming and fishing. An open seating dining room serves gourmet meals with special diet and kosher meals available on request. The ship's 41 personnel include Europeans, who are recruited by a specialized agency in Monaco, and trained Polynesians.

The 7-day/6-night Nomade Yachting Cruise itinerary begins each Mon. in Bora Bora, with a visit to Taha'a on Tues., to Huahine on Wed. and Thurs., to Raiatea on Fri. and Sat., and back to Bora Bora on Sun. During this memorable week, in addition to having the pleasure of cruising among the beautiful Leeward Islands in a unique, exclusive and exotic manner, you will also be treated to some innovative experiences. These include: a champagne breakfast served in the lagoon; a moon light dinner on the beach while watching a South Seas movie, which is screened under the stars on a *motu* islet; cruising around the island of Taha'a at sunset time; visiting Taputapuatea, the most important religious and political center of the Polynesian culture; paddling up the Faaroa River by kayak or joining a motorized outrigger canoe tour; visiting a vanilla plantation, a tropical botanical garden, and photographing the children of Raiatea as they dance for you on board the ship. Optional activities and excursions include daily massages on board the ship or on the *motu*, taking a 4x4 safari tour, visiting the lagoon aquarium, taking a tour by outrigger speed canoe, Waverunner or Quad bike, helicopter flights, deep-sea fishing and scuba diving.

The 2008 rates for this 7-day/6 night cruise are €5,800 per person. All Bora Bora Cruises include all meals, light meals and beverages, complimentary mini-bar, champagne and fresh fruit welcome at the Bora Bora airport, transfers to/from the yacht for embarkment/disembarkment, local taxes and gratuities, plus a number of unique events and activities. Port charges of €150 per person are compulsory.

GETTING AROUND BY CHARTER BOAT

If your romantic spirit is stirred at the sight of a white-sailed ship beating out to the wide sea, you can put yourself aboard your dream by chartering a sailboat in Tahiti. Comfortable modern yachts of every description are available for chartering by the day or week, with bases in Tahiti, Moorea, Raiatea, Taha'a, Bora Bora, Rangiroa and Fakarava. Please check each island section for details on chartering a sailboat.

Billowing sails, white against the horizon, beckon you to "come aboard" one of the sleek yachts you see gliding gracefully across the lagoon, within the protective embrace of the barrier reef that encloses Raiatea and Taha'a. Sailing conditions are ideal in the Leeward Islands and a large variety of yachts can be chartered in Raiatea for bare-boating, day sailing or for longer excursions with skipper and crew.

ARCHIPELS, *B.P. 1160, Papetoai, Moorea 98729. Tel. 689/56.36.39, Fax 689/56.35.87; www.archipels.com; Skype: archipels.*

Archipels Croisières is based in Opunohu Bay on the island of Moorea. Their fleet for 2008 includes 4 new 5-cabin Eleuthera 60' catamarans and 2 Marquises 57' deep-sea Fontaine Pajot 57 sailing catamarans with 4 cabins. Their fixed sailing programs can take you to the Leeward Society Islands or to the Tuamotu atolls of Rangiroa, Toau and Fakarava. Individuals can choose a "by the cabin" shared-boat cruise, paying €1880 per person during the low season and €2,090 in the high season for a 7 day/6 night Leeward Islands cruise. A 7 day/6 night Tuamotu cruise from Fakarava to Toau and Rangiroa is €1,880/2,090 during the low/high seasons. It costs €1,092/1,207 per person for a 4 day/3 night Tuamotu cruise inside the atoll of Rangiroa, or €820/935 per person for a 3 day/2 night cruise inside the immense lagoon of Rangiroa. The rates include meals, hotel services aboard in double occupancy cabins, and organized shore activities such as 4x4 excursions.

Three yachts are kept in Raiatea for sailing the Leeward Islands. You can charter the entire yacht for €11,280/12,540 for 2-4 passengers, €13,160/14,630 for 5-8 passengers, or €16,920/18,810 for 10 passengers for a 7 day/6 night private Leeward Island Cruise. You start in Bora Bora, sail to Taha'a and Raiatea and end the cruise in Huahine, or you can begin in Huahine and end in Bora Bora.

Another yacht is based year-round in Rangiroa for cruising the Tuamotu Islands. A 7 day/6 night private cruise from Fakarava to Toau and Rangiroa starts at €11,280 for 2-4 passengers. A 3 day/2 night private cruise inside the atoll of Rangiroa is €4,920 for 2-4 passengers during the low season, and a 4 day/3 night private cruise inside the Rangiroa lagoon is €6,550 for 2-4 passengers. Please see information in the *Moorea, Raiatea, Rangiroa* and *Fakarava* chapters.

THE MOORINGS, *B.P. 165, Uturoa, Raiatea 98735. Tel. 689/66.35.93/cell 78.35.93; Fax 689/66.20.94. www.moorings.com. North American reservations: Tel. 800/669-6529, outside US and Canada Tel. 727/535-1446.* The nautical base was taken over by First Choice Holidays in 2007, along with Sunsail. It is located at Apooiti Marina in Raiatea and has an average fleet of 25 yachts. Please see further information in *Raiatea* chapter.

SUNSAIL, *B.P. 331, Uturoa, Raiatea 98735. Tel. 689/60.04.85; Fax 689/ 66.23.19; www.sunsail.com.* This nautical base has been moved to Apooiti Marina and is now owned by First Choice Holidays. They have a fleet of 25 sailing yachts. Please see further information in *Raiatea* chapter.

TAHITI YACHT CHARTER, *Tahiti office: Monette Aline, B.P. 364, Papeete, Tahiti 98713; Tel. 689/45.04.00; Fax 689/42.76.00; www.tahitiyachtcharter.com. Raiatea base: Tel. 689/66.28.86; Fax 689/66.28.85.*

The office is located in Tahiti and the yacht base is at the Apooiti Marina in Raiatea. You can charter a catamaran bareboat or with provisions and captain and hostess/cook. The whole fleet has been renewed and most catamarans are less than 2 years old. Some of them, the "Tropiques" models, have generator and a/c; the "Grande Croisière" models have generator, water maker, a/c and kayaks on board.

Charter rates start at 408.000 CFP for an 8-day/7 night cruise aboard a Lagoon 380 with 4 cabins during the low seasons (Jan. 1-Mar. 30 and Sept. 29-Dec. 31), which is 7.300 CFP per night for 8 passengers.

A crewed Lagoon 440 "Grande Croisière", with fly bridge and forward cockpit can accommodate 8 passengers for a week's cruise, starting at 1.444.000 CFP for the boat, crew and all meals, which breaks down to 25.700 CFP per night per person for 8 people, with all meals included and 4 islands visited.

The "Tahiti twosome" program has been specially created for honeymooners searching for privacy and romance. They are the only passengers on board. This 7-day/6-night program in the Leeward Islands starts at 600.000 CFP for 2, including the skipper/guide/cook, and all meals except 2 dinners. A complimentary Polynesian massage is offered.

In 2008 the Iti Iti Pearl Cruise has been added, in partnership with Pearl Resorts. This 4 day/3 night program starts from 156.000 CFP per person including a dinner at Le Taha'a Private Island & Spa with a possible start from the Hawaiki Nui Hotel in Raiatea and a stop at the Bora Bora Pearl Beach Resort. Please see more information in the *Tahiti* and *Raiatea* chapters.

Other Charter Yachts described in the Island chapters include: **Atara Royal**, based in Raiatea; **Catamaran Tane**, based in Raiatea; **Bisou Futé** and **Fai Manu**, based in Taha'a; **Eden Martin**, based in Huahine; and **Haumana**, based in Rangiroa.

GETTING AROUND BY FISHING BOAT & SPORT CHARTERS

TARAVANA ISLAND SPORT CHARTERS BORA BORA, B.P. 186, Bora Bora. *Tel. 67.77.79 (evening) or cell 689/72.30.99 (day); Fax 689/60.59.31; www.taravana.com.* Based at the Hotel Bora Bora.

Captain Richard Postma is an American who has 35 years of sailing experience in French Polynesia and for most of that time he has lived in Bora Bora. *Taravana*, his 50-ft. state-of-the-art custom Lock Crowther-design ocean cruising catamaran, is equipped for comfort, stability and sportfishing. *Taravana* is the first sailboat in the world designed to be competitive in international big game tournaments. Each of her spacious double cabins offers queen-size bunks and semi-private facilities and the boat is well designed for both day, overnight and extended charters. On a day cruise you can explore Bora Bora's beautiful protected lagoon or ocean sail and sportfish near the atoll of Tupai, the island closest to Bora Bora. It takes 1 1/2 hrs. to cross the 10-mi. channel and you can sportfish on the way to the reef, enjoy superb snorkeling and have lunch on the calm side of the lagoon.

Famous Hollywood stars who want to get away from it all find the privacy and tranquility they seek when they charter the *Taravana* for an overnight sail. Some movie stars have even gotten married aboard Richard's famous catamaran. A 2-day cruise can easily include visits to the nearby islands of Taha'a and Raiatea. Richard also owns the Taravana Yacht Club on Taha'a, which is managed by his son Maui. Contact Richard direct for the best rates. See information in *Bora Bora* chapter on *Deep Sea Fishing*, and *Day Sailing Excursions and Sunset Cruises*.

GETTING AROUND BY LIVE ABOARD DIVE BOATS, CRUISE & DIVE CHARTERS

AQUA TIKI. *Contact Patrice Poiry at Aqua Polynésie, Tel. 00 33 1 64 90 50 10; www.aquatiki.com.*

Aqua Tiki is a 46-ft. Bahia deep-sea catamaran that provides dive cruises. Six passengers/divers can sleep in the 3 double guest cabins, each with its own bathroom. There is a TV and VCR player on board, as well as full scuba diving equipment. Divers or non-divers can charter a cabin or the whole boat for a choice of cruises in the Leeward Islands or the Tuamotus. A 9-day/8-night cruise takes you from Fakarava to Kauehi and Toau and back to Fakarava, and the low season rate starts at €2,560 for divers and €2,160 for non-divers, including taxes. Please see information under *Fakarava* in the *Tuamotu* chapter. *Aqua Tiki* will also offer cruises in the Marquesas Islands of 10-, 15-, or 17-days, sailing out of Nuku Hiva. A 10-day/9-night cruise for divers is €3,080 and for non-divers it is €2,630. You can charter the whole boat for €15,780. Contact them directly for sailing program and details.

Scuba Diving Conditions & Requirements

The clear, tropical waters of Tahiti and Her Islands are ideal for year-round diving, providing a diversity of magnificent dive sites in the lagoons, passes and outer coral reefs. Because French Polynesia covers such a vast area, with varying degrees of latitude and longitude, the underwater scenery is different from archipelago to archipelago, from island to island. The average water temperature is 29 ºC/85ºF during the summer months of Nov.-Mar., and 25ºC/79ºF during the Austral winter months of Apr.-Oct. Underwater visibility is normally good up to distances of 30 m. (100 ft.).

All non-certified scuba divers must have a certificate from a doctor indicating that you are in good health. A medical exam can be taken in Tahiti for the necessary papers, and examinations are available to obtain diving diplomas.

Around the island of Tahiti you will find some of the best scuba diving conditions for the beginner or the veteran diver who needs a reorientation. Due to the location of dive centers on the west coast of the island, in the lee of the prevailing easterly winds, you will find minimal currents and calm surface conditions. There is good visibility, with colorful small reef fish, friendly moray eels, eagle rays, small white-tip sharks and nurse sharks. Dive attractions also include a sunken inter-island schooner and a seaplane, and a vertical cliff on the outer reef that descends to infinity from a plateau 4.5 m. (15 ft.) deep. Moorea's special diving features are the feeding of moray eels, barracuda and large lemon sharks, plus a friendly encounter with leopard rays and large Napoleon fish. A sunken ship is clearly seen in the translucent waters of Papetoai.

Bora Bora is famous for its multihued lagoon, but also for the abundance of large-species marine life that inhabit this environment, especially the graceful manta rays that are sometimes found in groups of 10 or more, swimming inside the lagoon and in the pass. In the lagoon surrounding Huahine Nui and Huahine Iti you can feed sharks and see large schools of barracudas, big red snappers, tuna, turtles, rays and Napoleons. The lagoon that is shared by Raiatea and Taha'a attracts large schools of pelagic fish, leopard rays and a few manta rays. Divers can watch or join in the feeding of the large blue-green Napoleon fish, pet moray eels, and observe white-tip, black-tip and gray sharks.

In the Tuamotu atolls you will find world-class diving in luminescent waters with very good visibility inside the lagoons and passes. Rangiroa is one of the top diving destinations in the world. This is the largest atoll in the Southern Hemisphere and one of the largest in the world. Rangiroa's two most famous diving spots are the Avatoru and Tiputa passes through the coral reef. Schools of sharks, squadrons of eagle rays, jacks, tuna, barracuda, manta rays, turtles and dolphins swim through these passes when the very strong currents from the ocean flow into the lagoon or rush back out to sea.

Manihi is famous for the **pearl farms** inside its crystal clear lagoon. Excellent diving conditions are favorable for beginners and experienced divers. The sites include a beautiful variety of coral gardens, big Napoleon fish, black-tip reef sharks, gray sharks, eagle and manta rays, schools of snappers and big tuna fish. One favorite site is a breathtaking wall that drops 3 to 1,350 m. (10-4,500 ft.). When the famous French diver Jacques Cousteau explored the lagoon in Tikehau he said that it contained more fish than any of the other lagoons in this part of the Pacific. The inhabitants ship parrotfish and other lagoon fish from the Tikehau lagoon to Tahiti by airplane and fishing ships. Fakarava is the second largest atoll in the

---

SCUBA DIVING TERMS

For the uninitiated in the vernacular of scuba diving, **PADI** is the **Professional Association of Diving Instructors**. An OWDI is an overwater diving instructor. The PADI system of training divers is used in North America. The techniques differ from those of the French system of **CMAS** (**Conféderation Mondiale des Activités Subaquatiques**), which is the World Underwater Federation. Most of the diving monitors and instructors in Tahiti and Her Islands are qualified to teach both PADI and CMAS.

The **FFESSM** is the **Fèderation Française des Activités Subaquatiques**, or French Underwater Federation. A level of B.E. training in the FFESSM equals a CMAS one star rating; the first echelon or level equals a two-star rating in CMAS; and autonomous diver equals a three-star rating in CMAS. In France a monitor (moniteur) is more qualified than an instructor. A moniteur d'Etat is the equivalent of a State instructor, with levels of BEES 1, 2 or 3. BEES 3 is the highest level you can reach, except for a moniteur federal, who is not supposed to accept money for giving lessons. All the instructors and monitors in Tahiti are paid for their services.

Tuamotu archipelago, where scuba diving is the most spectacular in the Garuae Pass, which is one km. (.62 mi.) wide and 16 m. (52 ft.) deep.

Experienced divers will be treated to a panorama of underwater life that includes manta rays, dolphins, barracudas, tiger sharks, hammerhead sharks and whale sharks. A dive center is now open on the atoll of Makemo, where a virtually unexplored scuba diver's paradise awaits discovery. Some of the dive boats include Toau, Kauehi, Tahanea and Aratika on their itinerary.

The northern group of the Marquesas Islands offers underwater caves with large fauna, recommended for adventurous, experienced divers only. Some of the world's most famous underwater photographers come here to dive and photograph the dozens of manta rays, leopard rays, stingrays, friendly hammerhead sharks and pigmy killer whales that inhabit the open waters surrounding the islands.

In the southern latitudes of the Austral Islands the humpback whales are a big attraction for scuba divers just offshore the island of Rurutu. These mammals, which are 14-18 m. (46-59 ft.) in length, are seen during the months of July-Oct., when they come up from Antarctica to mate and give birth, while escaping the austral winters. Several humpbacks also visit Moorea, Tahiti and the Tuamotu atolls.

There are more than 30 scuba diving clubs in French Polynesia, located on the islands of Tahiti, Moorea, Huahine, Raiatea, Taha'a and Bora Bora in the Society Islands, the atolls of Rangiroa, Tikehau, Manihi, Fakarava, Makemo and Hao in the Tuamotu archipelago, on Nuku Hiva in the Marquesas Islands, and on Rurutu and Tubuai in the Austral Islands. Please check each destination chapter for information on the most popular diving clubs used by tourists.

GETTING AROUND BY CAR

In the Society Islands most of the roads that circle the islands are paved. There are a few places in Raiatea and Taha'a where the road is not sealed but they are pretty well graded. Following heavy rains there are frequently holes in the road that can be very dangerous, especially if you are driving a scooter or bicycle. In most of the Marquesas Islands the 4-wheel drive vehicles (called 4x4, pronounced "cat-cat") are usually rented with driver, because the roads are abominable. You can rent a self-drive 4WD in Atuona on the island of Hiva Oa. Rangiroa has a paved road between the two passes and there's nowhere else to go by car. The Austral Islands have mostly concrete or unpaved roads, which you can drive in a normal car, except for some places in Rurutu, where a 4WD is required.

You will drive on the right side of the road in French Polynesia, just as you do in North America and continental Europe. A valid diver's license from your State or home country will be honored here. Should you buy an international driver's license, which is not at all necessary, you will still need to show your normal driver's license in order to rent a car or scooter. The minimum age is 21 years to rent a 4WD vehicle and to rent 2-wheel vehicles the driver must be 18 or 19 years old, depending on the island.

Speed limits are 40 km. per hour (24 mi. per hour) in the towns and villages, 60 km. (37 mi. per hour) on the winding roads of most of the islands and 80-110 km. (50-68 mi. per hour) on a short stretch of freeway leading from Tahiti's west coast to downtown Papeete. Seat belts are mandatory for the driver and passenger in the front seats of vehicles on all islands, and helmets are required for anyone riding a motorcycle or scooter.

Anyone driving a 2-wheel vehicle should remember to go single file. There are no bicycle paths in these islands and some of the local drivers are in a mighty big hurry to get somewhere, even with nowhere to go. After all, they take their driver's lessons from the French!

You should also be alert for drunk drivers, especially late at night, and young boys doing "wheelies" on bicycles or scooters, often with no lights at night. You also have to look out for children and dogs when you pass through the villages around the island.

Liability Insurance

Vehicle insurance includes third party liability insurance. It is possible, depending on the conditions of the driving license and age, to take a comprehensive insurance that covers collision, damage and waiver.

Automobile Rental

Europcar and **Avis-Pacificar** are the biggest names for rental cars in French Polynesia, although **Hertz** also has offices in the more popular tourist islands. There are also a few individuals who rent cars, scooters and bicycles. See information for each island in the *Getting Around Town* section.

ACCOMMODATIONS

By the end of 2008 Tahiti and Her Islands will have 48 international class hotels on 12 islands, offering 2,853 rooms in the 4- and 5-star categories. These up-market hotel accommodations include deluxe rooms, suites and villas with a/c, direct dial international telephones, Internet access, individual safes, satellite TV and room service. Some of these accommodations are similar to American hotel or motel rooms, usually in concrete buildings of 2 or more levels. Most of the newer hotels also offer these conveniences in their deluxe Polynesian style bungalows.

Mid-range accommodations are also available in small hotels, which may be an air-conditioned room in downtown Papeete, a self-contained, totally equipped villa on Moorea or Huahine, or an attractive bungalow on a motu in Taha'a or Bora Bora, with a ceiling fan, cooking facilities and TV. On each island there are also non-classified guesthouses, bed and breakfast lodgings, hostels and home stays, locally referred to as *family pensions*.

The typical Polynesian style bungalows can be very elegant, especially when they are built overwater, with a glass panel or table in the floor, allowing you to have a peek at what the fish are doing in the coral gardens below. These bungalows often have thatched roofs of woven pandanus leaves and woven bamboo walls. The interior walls are sometimes covered with pandanus matting from Indonesia, and a chic Polynesian decor incorporates all the flamboyant colors you'll find in the tropical gardens, or it reflects the softer colors of the lagoon. The most deluxe hotels have replaced the Polynesian furnishings with a neutral decor of off-white, cream and beige, adding accent colors with cushions. Most of the newer bungalows have air-conditioning, large bathrooms with a bathtub/shower, bathtub and separate shower, or Jacuzzi and separate shower. They also have lighted dressing tables and living areas, plus a terrace or veranda, and the overwater bungalows have steps leading into the lagoon, with a shower on the landing. To answer the demands of their American guests, the hotel rooms most frequently chosen by honeymooners are also equipped with a satellite TV, plus a DVD and CD player. Some even have 2 TV's and an espresso machine. Most of these hotels have also added a spa whose services include a relaxing massage for two, sometimes at the edge of the lagoon at sunset time or under the starry sky.

The small *fare* (FAH-rey) often has a thatched roof, overhead fan and colorful linens and curtains. Some are screened, and most have a porch or terrace. In the family-operated guesthouses and *pensions* you usually have a private room or bungalow. In some *pensions* you have cooking facilities and in others you eat what your hosts prepare. You may have a bathroom to yourself with a hot water shower, or share the outdoor facilities, which may have a cold water shower. On some of the more arid islands your water supply may be limited. Backpackers' lodgings and campgrounds are available on several islands. Check the accommodation information for the individual islands.

Hotel projects under way at publication time include the 3-star Hotel Tahiti Nui on Ave. Prince Hinoi in Papeete, which will open in Dec. 2008 with 91 rooms. Also on the island of Tahiti is the Manava Suite Resort under construction on Tahiti's west coast community of Punaauia, which will open in April 2009 with 114 apartments, duplex suites, lagoon and garden suites and superior rooms. This is on the site of the former Iaorana Villa that was originally built as a French military offers' retreat. It was later operated as a hotel. This new resort will be managed by South Pacific Management, French Polynesia's largest hotel chain, which includes the Pearl Resorts collection of 9 hotels on 9 islands.

The Legends Resort Moorea will open in July 2008 with 49 deluxe villas on the hillside overlooking the Intercontinental Resort Moorea and 3 motu islets inside the lagoon. Warwick International has signed a contract to manage a 5-star 150-room deluxe hotel that will soon begin construction on the property of the Moorea Green Pearl Golf Course. A 3-star hotel with 130 rooms will also be built next to the lagoon adjacent to the golf course, and a complex of residential villas will be built by the same group of investors from French Polynesia and New Caledonia. No date has been announced for the completion of these 3 projects.

The Four Seasons Resort will open on Bora Bora in June 2008 with 100 overwater suites and 7 beachside villas located on Motu Tofari, adjacent to the St.

Regis Resort. Also announced for construction are 15 Four Seasons Private Residence villas to be built on the same motu.

A French-Canadian investor has approved plans to build a 40-unit hotel in the Faanui commune of Bora Bora, which is supposed to open in 2010. He has also bought the atoll of Nukutepipi in the Tuamotu Archipelago and plans to build a vacation village for 25-4o people.

Also scheduled for a 2010 opening is The Brando, a deluxe eco-friendly hotel to be built on Tetiaroa, the private atoll belonging to the family of the late Marlon Brando. This 30-40 bungalow resort will be built and managed by Tahiti Beachcomber SA, a Tahiti company, the majority owner and management company of the 4 Intercontinental Resorts in Tahiti, Moorea and Bora Bora, plus Le Maitai Polynesia Bora Bora.

International Hotel Chains

The eventual opening of the **Warwick International** on Moorea will give French Polynesia 23 hotels operated by international hotel chains. **Starwood Hotels and Resorts** has 4 chains: 2 Sheraton hotels, 2 Le Meridiens, 1 St. Regis and 1 Luxury Collection. The French group **Accor** has 2 chains: 4 Sofitel hotels and 2 Novotel hotels. The **Intercontinental** chain has 4 hotels, **Radisson** has 1 hotel, **Amanresorts** has the Hotel Bora Bora, **Orient Express Hotels** owns the Bora Bora Lagoon Resort, there is a **Club Méditerranée** in Bora Bora, and a **Four Seasons Resort** is also in Bora Bora.

Locally Owned Hotel Chains

Financière Hôtelière Polynésienne (FHP) is a Tahiti company comprised primarily of Air Tahiti and Banque Socredo, along with private investors. They own the 5-star Le Taha'a Island Resort & Spa, which is a member of the prestigious **Le Relais et Chateaux** association, and the 5-star Bora Bora Pearl Beach Resort. Their 4-star hotels are the Manihi Pearl Beach Resort, Tikehau Pearl Beach Resort, Moorea Pearl Resort, Nuku Hiva Keikahanui Pearl Lodge, and the Hiva Oa Hanakee Pearl Lodge. **South Pacific Management** (SPM) is a locally owned company that manages all the properties marketed as Pearl Hotels, which also include Te Tiare Resort in Huahine and the Hotel Hawaiki Nui in Raiatea. SPM will also manage the Manava Suite Resort Tahiti.

Hotel Management & Services (HMS) is owned by Dick Bailey, an American resident of Tahiti, who also heads Tahiti Beachcomber SA, the company that owns the Intercontinental hotels in French Polynesia, and Le Maitai Polynesia in Bora Bora. They also manage the Hotel Maitai Dream Fakarava, and will own and manage The Brando in Tetiaroa, once it is built.

7. Basic Information

Listed here, in alphabetical order by topic, are practical information and recommendations for your trip to Tahiti and Her Islands.

BUSINESS HOURS

Several of the small restaurant/snacks and the Papeete Municipal Market, **le Marché**, open around 5am, and between 7:30-8am the post office, government offices, banks, airline offices, travel agencies and boutiques open. Many of the shops and offices still close for lunch between 12pm and 1:30 or 2pm, while others are now remaining open through the lunch period. Except for the restaurants and sidewalk cafés and bars, most of Papeete is closed down by 6pm.

The suburban shopping centers remain open until 7-8pm. Most businesses close at noon on Sat. and all day Sun. and holidays. The food stores are open on Sat. afternoon and usually open on Sun. and holidays from 6-8am, with a few *magasins* remaining open until noon and then reopening between 5-7pm.

COST OF LIVING & TRAVEL

French Polynesia can be very expensive and it can also be affordable, depending on how you choose to go. I've been living in Tahiti and Moorea since 1971 and I have never ceased to be amazed at the costs. We pay the same prices as you will when we go to the restaurants and grocery stores, take a taxi or buy gas for our automobiles. Only recently have the residents begun to benefit from reductions on inter-island airfares, hotel rates and some of the excursions. Many Americans spend their entire vacation complaining about the cost of Coca-Cola, beer, water and food. Some of these tourists are so concerned with how much money they're spending that they cannot even enjoy their vacations.

Even though some of the prices here are still astronomical compared to what you'll pay in the United States, Canada or wherever you are, they are actually lower for many items than we paid a few years ago. I remember when a package of celery, or a head of cauliflower or broccoli cost 1.300 CFP! Today, in Moorea I pay 645-1.075 CFP a kilo for broccoli imported from Australia or the USA, and it is only 495 CFP a kilo at a big super market in Tahiti. I pay 360 CFP for a head of cauliflower imported from the USA. Imported celery is 425 CFP for 16 oz. Locally grown frisée lettuce is 570 CFP a kilo, green peppers are 785 CFP per kilo, cucumbers are 355 CFP a kilo and locally grown tomatoes are 470-620 CFP a kilo, depending on the season. Watermelons from Maupiti or Huahine sell for 230 CFP a kilo in Tahiti and cantaloupe from those islands are 331 CFP per kilo, depending on the type of melon. The same fruit would cost double the price in Moorea.

With the opening of the "mega" markets (Carrefour, Hyper-U Tropic Import, Cash and Carry, Price Club, Hyper Champion and Casino) in Tahiti, competition brought the prices down a little. Larger supermarkets have also opened in the outer islands, providing a wider choice of goodies at slightly lower prices. But then, the value added tax brings them up again.

Hotel Rates

Most of the rack rates for the international class resorts change according to the times of year when the rooms are most in demand. The seasons may vary a little for the different hotels, but generally, the **High Season** is June 1-Nov. 15, and Dec. 22-31. **Low Season** is Jan. 1-May 31 and Nov. 16-Dec. 21. Some of the hotels also add a mandatory charge for New Year's Eve dinner for any room booked on Dec. 31. Check with the hotels of your choice to get the details.

You won't find many real bargains for a hotel room in Tahiti and Her Islands, unless you get way off the tourist track or stay at a hotel with a construction project underway. However, some of the top resorts are now offering breakfast and even all meals during the slow seasons. Check out the promotions on their websites.

Here is a general idea of what it will cost for an accommodation in Tahiti and Her Islands. Have a look at the prices listed in the *Where to Stay* sections of each island chapter and you will see that the cost of a standard room in a deluxe hotel in Tahiti is 30.000-35.000 CFP double (at the current exchange rate, about $366-$427). The exception is the Sofitel Tahiti Resort, where the year-round rate for a mountain view room is 21.681 CFP (about $264).

Overwater bungalows are the most popular accommodations with honeymooners. At the Intercontinental Tahiti Resort an overwater bungalow on the motu costs 50.030 CFP and the newer units over the lagoon are 72.870 CFP. Le Méridien Tahiti sells their overwater bungalows for 65.000 CFP. The lowest priced overwater units in Moorea are 53.000-78.000 CFP, except for Club Bali Hai, which has a special rate in 2008 of €175 (20.883 CFP) for an overwater bungalow and breakfast. On Raiatea an overwater bungalow starts at 33.000 CFP, on Rangiroa they are priced at 68.000 CFP, on Tikehau the lowest price is 49.000 CFP, on Manihi the rates start at 52.000 CFP, and on Rangiroa the overwater bungalows are 68.000 CFP. On Huahine the rack rates are 78.000 CFP for an overwater bungalow, on Taha'a an overwater unit at Vahine Island is 57.995 CFP, and at Le Taha'a Island Resort & Spa the lowest priced overwater unit is 95.000 CFP.

Bora Bora's 12 hotels with overwater bungalows start at 48.450 CFP at Le Maitai. Sofitel Resort Bora Bora and Sofitel Motu price their overwater units at 66.372 CFP, Bora Bora Pearl Resort charges 69.000 CFP during the low season, ICH Le Moana charges 70.220 CFP, Le Méridien Bora Bora starts at 80.000 CFP, Bora Bora Lagoon Resort charges 82.935 CFP, ICH-Thalasso starts at 88.190 CFP, Bora Bora Nui has overwater units for 89.000 CFP, the Hotel Bora Bora's overwater bungalows start at 95.500 CFP, and the St. Regis has priced their cheapest overwater units at 98.000 CFP. The Four Seasons rates will start at 97.500 CFP.

The rates for a standard double room in a medium-priced classified hotel start at 13.620 CFP in Tahiti, 11.500 CFP in Moorea, 21.500 CFP in Huahine, 12.000 CFP in Raiatea, 15.487 CFP in Bora Bora, 19.469 CFP in Rangiroa, and 8.000 CFP in Rurutu.

You will find some of the least expensive accommodations in the pensions, bed and breakfast guesthouses, backpacker's lodgings and family homes. Some of their rates, however, are higher than you would pay in a moderate priced hotel. The economy lodgings on Tahiti are usually priced between 6.500-9.600 CFP for a room and shared bath for 2 with no meals. A room or bungalow with private bath is 8.500-16.000 CFP, and sometimes breakfast is included or a kitchen is available. On Moorea you can get a room or bungalow with no meals for 4.800-24.000 CFP double; or a small backpacker's cabin for 2.500-3.800 CFP a day. Rooms or bungalows in Raiatea start at 7.700 CFP double, usually with private bath and shared kitchen facilities, and on Huahine you can find a room or bungalow for 2 from 5.000-20.000 CFP. Bora Bora's pensions charge 6.000-10.500 CFP per couple for a room and 15.000-21.000 for a garden bungalow. On Maupiti you will have breakfast and dinner included with the cost of your bungalow, from 10.000-25.000 CFP double. In Rangiroa the room or bungalow with a modified American plan (MAP), called *demi-pension*, ranges from 11.000-31.500 CFP double, and many of these pensions will serve you lunch on request. In the more remote Tuamotu atolls you are usually served 3 meals a day (*pension complete*), but you can also rent a bungalow or room with no meals or just breakfast and dinner.

The cost of a room or bungalow in Tikehau with full-board or American Plan (AP) meals is 14.000-21.000 CFP double, and in Fakarava you will pay 16.000-21.900 CFP per night with a bungalow and MAP meals, and 29.760 CFP double for accommodations and all meals. Some of these facilities require a 2-3 night minimum stay.

A bed in a dormitory costs 2.050-2.500 CFP per person on Tahiti, 1.200-2.000 CFP per person on Moorea, 1.750-2.000 CFP on Huahine, and 3.400 CFP on Bora Bora. If you bring your tent you can rent camping space for 1.500 CFP per person per day on Tahiti, 1.100-1.500 CFP a day on Moorea, 1.250 CFP a day on Huahine, 1.100 CFP a day on Raiatea, 2.000 CFP a day on Maupiti, 2.000-2.500 CFP on Bora Bora, 1.050 CFP a day on Rangiroa, and 2.000 CFP a day on Fakarava. The rates for dormitories and camping are higher for 1-night stays.

Transportation Costs

See each Island chapter for details and costs on how to get around. You can rent a car on all the Society Islands, in Rangiroa, on most of the Marquesas Islands and on some of the Austral Islands. Gasoline is sold by the liter (4 liters = 1.06 gallons), and in Moorea you'll pay 148 CFP per liter for unleaded gas, or 592 CFP per gallon, which is used by most of the rental cars. Diesel fuel is 125 CFP a liter or 500 CFP per gallon. Most service stations sell Total and Mobil products, and Shell has a few stations on the island of Tahiti and Moorea.

ELECTRICITY

The current is 220 volts, 50 cycles in most hotels and family homes. Some of the newer upscale hotels have outlets for both 220 and 110 volts. Most hotels provide 110-volt outlets for shavers, and hair dryers are usually provided. It's best to ask the management before you plug in hair dryers, battery chargers and computers. Adapters are usually necessary for American appliances, as the French plugs have two round prongs. You can bring your adapters with you or buy them at a general store in Tahiti. The hotels sometimes, but not always, have a transformer or converter for your electrical appliance.

FESTIVALS & HOLIDAYS

All the islands in French Polynesia celebrate New Year's Day, Missionaries Day (March 5), Good Friday, Easter Sunday, Easter Monday, May Day (May 1, which is Labor Day), May 8, which was also Victory Day 1945, Pentecost (7th Sunday after Easter), Pentecost Monday, Ascension Day (June 1), Bastille Day (July 14), Assumption (August 15), All Saints Day (November 1), Armistice Day 1918 (November 11), and Christmas Day.

Internal Autonomy Day is celebrated on June 29 if the autonomist party is in power at that time. The independence party ignores this date.

All government offices, banks, airline offices, travel agencies and most private offices are closed on official holidays, and if it falls on a Thurs. or Tues., quite often the businesses will make a bridge, giving their employees an extra day off to enjoy a long weekend. See *Calendar of Events* chapter.

GETTING MARRIED

Tahiti, the Island of Love, has long been a favorite honeymoon destination for lovers of all ages. Getting married in Paradise has also become a popular activity for some of our visitors. In Tahiti, Moorea, Huahine, Taha'a and Bora Bora couples from around the world are now saying "Oui" at the Mairie (Town Hall), "Hai" in the wedding chapels at the hotels, and "Eh" while standing in front of a Tahitian high priest.

Young Japanese couples choose to get married in French Polynesia to avoid the exorbitant costs of a wedding "correctly" done in Japan, which costs $50,000 or more for some 80 guests. Travel agencies and hotels in Tahiti take care of all the details, and the prospective newlyweds are already legally married according to Japanese law before they leave home. Along with their rented wedding clothes and rings, they bring a certificate of marriage, which has been completed and officially stamped at their own town hall. This paper must be translated and stamped at the French Embassy in Japan before a wedding can be performed in Tahiti.

Tying the knot in French Polynesia requires several steps and official stamps. For non-French applicants each person needs to furnish a birth certificate, must be of legal age, and must present a certificate of celibacy to prove that they have never been married. If they are divorced or widowed they must have the legal papers to prove that too. Birth certificates are required for any children of either party, and all these papers must be translated into French by a legal translator who has been granted an official stamp. All birth certificates must have been issued or translated in French within 3 months prior to application.

In addition, each spouse has to provide a pre-marriage medical certificate issued within the last 2 months. In order to verify if the projected marriage is not contrary to public order, the municipal authority has the right to demand a customary certificate from the foreign authorities, which can be either the ministry or consulate of your country. A certificate of residency is necessary to prove that one or both of the future spouses has an address or has established residency in one of the communes of French Polynesia for a minimum of one month's continued residency prior to the marriage date. The wedding will be performed at the Mairie in that commune.

The marriage bans will be posted for 10 days in the commune where the wedding will take place and in the last place of residence of the future spouse not residing in French Polynesia. If one of the applicants has neither address nor residence in French Polynesia, the wedding bans must be published in his/her place of residence and must be verified by a certificate of publication.

Tiki Village in Moorea specializes in creating authentic Polynesian weddings. Most lovers, however, get married back home and splurge for a fun-filled colorful wedding ceremony in the authentic tradition of old Polynesia. And it's not just newlyweds who are getting married in the Tahitian style, but also loving couples who are celebrating their anniversaries, who wish to renew their vows to one another. Non-binding Polynesian weddings are also being performed at some of the international class hotels in Tahiti, Moorea, Huahine, Taha'a and Bora Bora.

HEALTH CONCERNS

On the island of Tahiti you will have access to a large government hospital (a new hospital is under construction), 2 private clinics, and numerous specialists who provide good medical and dental services. In addition to the allopathic doctors, you have alternative health care in the form of homeopathic medicine, acupuncturists, Chinese herbalists, traditional Tahitian healers, massage therapy, magnetizers and thalassotherapy. Many of these specialists speak English. Moorea, Raiatea, Nuku Hiva and Tubuai have small hospitals, and all the other islands have medical centers, infirmaries or dispensaries. The more populous islands also have pharmacies and dentists. In Tahiti and Moorea there are optical services, where you can have minor repairs made to your eyeglasses or new glasses made, and should you need emergency attention for your hearing aid, that is also available in Papeete.

All the islands maintain hygienic controls to combat potential epidemics of tropical diseases, such as the dengue fever, which is also known as "breakbone" fever, because of the intense pain in the head and muscles. This viral disease is carried by the *Aëdes aegypti* mosquito, which also lives indoors and bites during the daytime. In addition to a high fever, excruciating headache, pain in the joints and back, and a general feeling of weakness, the victims also develop an itchy body rash. Unfortunately, there is no vaccine, and you cannot take aspirin for the pains, as it may cause the stomach to bleed. The doctors can treat this disease with a *dengue cocktail*, which is an injection of Vitamin C and other vitamins, but the symptoms can last from 7-10 days. There are several forms of *dengue*, and the most severe type can cause death in children, although this is very rare in French Polynesia.

Leptospirosis or Weil's disease has some of the same symptoms as the dengue: high fever, severe headaches, chills, muscle aches, vomiting, jaundice, red eyes, abdominal pain, diarrhea or a rash. This is caused by bacteria of the genus *Leptospira* and affects humans and animals. Most of the cases reported in French Polynesia are caused by dried rat urine that is mixed with the food, water or soil. You can also get this disease from swimming downriver from pigpens. In addition to causing kidney damage, meningitis, liver failure and respiratory distress, the disease is usually fatal. Be sure to wipe off the tops of all bottles and cans before drinking, because rats live in all the storerooms in the tropics. Better yet, drink from a clean glass.

Malaria is not present in the islands of French Polynesia, and the inhabitants generally have a high standard of health. There is an occasional outbreak of conjunctivitis, and some of the long time residents have suffered from filariasis or elephantiasis, an insect-borne disease that attacks the lymphatic system. Preventive medicine is distributed free every 6 months in all the islands, which keeps this disease well under control, and it is not a threat to the short-term visitor.

Pests & Pets

Mosquitoes are tropical pests, and in addition to the high cost of living and the noise of the roosters, the biggest complaints in French Polynesia are about the hungry mosquitoes that just love fresh blood from our visitors. There's not much you can do about the inflated prices and the crowing rooster you'd love to throttle at 2-3-4-5am, but you can avoid being bitten. In the high-end hotels, you will find an electric diffuser or mosquito destroyer that uses a bottle of liquid or blue pastilles, treated with Allethrin, to ward off mosquitoes. Other lodgings usually provide mosquito coils that you can burn, or you can buy them at any food store.

Bring a good mosquito repellent with you or go to the pharmacy once you're here and buy your defense products. I have found Dolmix Pic cream to be effective, which is sold in pharmacies. Aerogard spray or lotion is a good Australian product and can be purchased in the supermarkets. Tourists have also reported satisfactory results with *monoi* oil mixed with citronella, and this is available in most supermarkets, small *magasins* and hotel gift shops. My favorite anti-mosquito cream is Rid, which is made in Australia, but it is not sold in Tahiti. It is available in other Pacific Island groups, however. Be aware that mosquitoes will bite you day and night, and are most active when the weather is hot and sticky, which means during our rainy seasons. You have to remember to reapply your mosquito protection throughout the day or evening, especially if you are perspiring or swimming, as the water and sweat wash the product away.

On some of the islands you may encounter the *nono*, which is a minuscule "no-see-um" sand fly with a nasty sting. They are most prevalent at daybreak and late in the afternoon, when they come to chew on your ankles. You might not even know you've been bitten until hours later, when the itching starts. Do not scratch it, however, as that will only aggravate the pain and cause an infected sore. Slathering yourself in oil is the best way to keep these little buggers at bay, as they just slide off your skin. Any kind of oil will do, although Avon's Skin So Soft from the States, or *monoi* oil, which is sold all over French Polynesia, will certainly smell better than cooking oil. Daily doses of 500 milligrams of vitamin B1 will help to ward off the pesky nonos.

If you do get stung by a mosquito, nono, wasp or bee, or cut yourself on coral, a good first aid treatment is to squeeze fresh lime juice on the wound to avoid infection. Cuts and scratches infect easily and take a long time to heal, so it is important to prevent any problems. Creams are also sold to take away pain from stings. Just remember to include an antibacterial cream in your traveling first aid kit, which you should definitely pack for your trip. The ingredients of such a kit will vary according to your own needs. The most important items to include would be any prescription drugs you take. Bring an extra pair of eyeglasses if you use them.

Ciguatera

More than 400 species of lagoon and reef fish are potential carriers of **ciguatera**, a poisoning from eating infected fish. This phenomenon existed in some of the coral islands before the arrival of the first Europeans, and is caused by a microscopic marine organism that lives on or near the coral reef, especially reefs that have been disturbed by shipwrecks, port construction and other developments.

The larger carnivorous fish, such as the parrot fish, surgeon fish, coral bass, sea perch, snappers and jack fish are all potential carriers of ciguatera, as well as the big barracuda, as they tend to store the toxins found in the smaller coral fish on which they feed. The open ocean fish, such as mahi mahi, tuna, swordfish, salmon of the gods and marlin and other pelagics do not carry the ciguatera toxin.

If you catch your own fish, it is best to get the advice of the local people before you cook it. They know which spots are more likely to be affected by ciguatera. The seafood served in the restaurants of French Polynesia is as safe as you'll find anywhere. Just avoid eating the head, gonads, liver and viscera of the fish.

Drinking Water

The Department of Health in French Polynesia reports that the tap water in Papeete has been treated with chlorine and is potable, and the water on the islands of Bora Bora, Taha'a and Tubuai is drinkable. For the rest of the island of Tahiti and on all the other islands, it is advisable to drink bottled water. Eau Royale and Vaimato are two of the companies in Tahiti that sell bottled water, and the lab tests have given a higher rating to Vaimato for purity and cleanliness. There are also several brands of bottled water imported from France. Some of the hotels have water filter systems.

Too Much Sunshine!

More vacations have been ruined from an overdose of sun than from any other factor. So many of the elderly tourists, who come ashore from their air-conditioned cruise ships, walk along the road in the heat and humidity of the noonday sun. Back home they drive round and round the parking lot, hoping to find a parking place close to the entrance to the shopping center or super market. When they come here they decide to walk the equivalent of several blocks or even kilometers, with the sun blazing on their heads.

I have escorted groups of American doctors to Marlon Brando's atoll of Tetiaroa for a day tour. No matter how much they were warned about the dangers of the sun, when it was time to fly back to Tahiti in the afternoon, every doctor in the group, including the dermatologists, was red as a boiled lobster. The Tahitian name for white people is *popa'a*, which is derived from the Tahitian word for "red lobster."

Fair-skinned people have to be especially careful in the tropics. Do your jogging, take your walk and work on your tan at the beginning of the morning or in the late afternoon, when distant clouds low on the horizon filter the ultra violet rays. During your picnic on the *motu* or while riding in any open boat, make sure you apply a sufficiently strong sunscreen or sunblock (containing 25 to 50 sunburn protection factor) on all the exposed parts of your body. Wrap up like a mummy if there is no sun protector on the boat. Don't forget to rub the lotion on your feet and reapply the sunblock throughout the day, as you sweat and swim. Always wear a hat when exposed to the sun, and protect your nose and lips with zinc or a similar barrier cream.

Should you forget this advice and get yourself "cooked" while vacationing in Tahiti and Her Islands, there are several remedies to ease the pain and help the healing process. These include applying tomato juice or vinegar to the sunburned parts, as well as Calamine lotion, aloe vera gel, tamanu oil, and a range of other products, which are available at the pharmacies in your country and in Tahiti.

Diarrhea

The abundance of tropical fruits you'll find so tempting in Tahiti are also very good for you if you exercise moderation. If you go overboard on the tropical fruit, you may regret it. Your system is not accustomed to so much Vitamin C, which can have a cataclysmic effect on your bowels.

The change of water, food and climate are the primary reasons for an upset digestive system. Drink bottled mineral water, eat in balanced proportions and get plenty of rest, and you will most likely avoid any disruptive problems. When you're packing for your trip to Tahiti be sure to include a remedy for treating diarrhea. There are many products on the market from which to choose, such as Imodium and Lomotil.

Should symptoms of diarrhea manifest, it would be best to avoid the consumption of raw vegetables and chilled beverages. Eat steamed white rice and boiled eggs and yogurt, and drink lots of bottled water to restore body fluids lost through dehydration.

Sex in the South Seas

Exercise the same precautions you would apply back home. Since the arrival of the first European ships in 1767, Tahiti has earned a worldwide reputation as a sexually permissive port-of-call. Even with the strong influence of all the missionaries and church groups that have worked for over 200 years to change the sexual mores of the Polynesians, the promiscuous practices have not been completely eliminated.

Papeete is a hot spot of very young female prostitutes and *mahu* (male transvestites), who frequent the nightclubs and bars and hang out on the corner of Boulevard Pomare and Avenue Prince Hinoi, looking for a pick-up. Safe sex in Tahiti often means that when boy meets girl for a clandestine rendezvous, they are both reasonably sure that his wives and girlfriends and her husband and/or boyfriends are not going to catch them in the act—this time. Even though there is an on-going educational program on the dangers of unprotected sexual encounters, there is still a reticence to put the knowledge into action. Thankfully, French Polynesia today has one of the world's lowest rates of the Acquired Immune Deficiency Syndrome (AIDS) virus, known as SIDA in French. This terrible disease has already claimed several lives in Tahiti, however, and all the other sexually transmitted diseases are prevalent here as well.

Vaccinations

No immunizations are required for entry into French Polynesia unless you are arriving from an infected area. The U.S. State Department has a 24-hour **Travel Advisory**, *Toll Free 888/407-4747; www.travel.state.gov/travel/warnings.html.* Check their website for up-to-date overseas health information, as well as crime and politics in foreign countries, and information on medical insurance overseas. The US Center for Disease Control in Atlanta, Georgia, gives travel advisories on an **International Traveler's Hotline**, *Toll Free 877/FYI-TRIP (877/394-8747); www.cdc.gov/travel/default.aspx.*

MAPS

Free maps are available at the Tahiti Tourist Bureau, including a map of downtown Papeete. The *Tahiti Beach Press* includes maps of Papeete and the islands of Tahiti, Moorea and Bora Bora. You'll also find maps in the bookstores and newsstands. Pacific Promotion's *39 Tourist Maps of Tahiti and Her Islands* sells for about 1.500 CFP and includes the locations of all hotels and pensions. **Librairie Klima**, *Tel. 42.00.63*, at Place Notre Dame in Papeete, sells oceanographic charts of the islands. **Nauti-Sport**, *Tel. 50.59.59*, in Fare Ute, also sells French nautical charts of Polynesia.

The Topographic Section of the **Service de l'Urbanisme**, *Tel. 46.82.18*, is located on the 4th floor of the Administrative Building at 11 Rue du Commandant Destremeau, where you can find topographical maps of the islands. **Pacific Image**, *Tel. 50.34.34/77.17.75; infos@pacific-image.pf; www.pacific-image.com; www.tahitiphotos.com* has CD-Rom maps, photos and posters of French Polynesia.

MONEY & BANKING

The **French Pacific franc**, written as **CFP**, or **XPF** in banking circles, is the official currency of French Polynesia. One of the banks in Tahiti told me that CFP stands for *cour de franc Pacifique*, and in the currency exchanges on the Internet XPF means *comptoirs français du Pacifique franc*. The colorful CFP notes, which may look like play money to you, are issued in denominations of 500, 1.000, 5.000 and 10.000 francs (CFP); and coins are 1, 2, 5, 10, 20, 50 and 100 francs (CFP).

The CFP franc has been anchored to the euro since January 1, 1999, on a fixed parity basis. With 1.000 CFP you have 8.38 Euros (**1 euro = 119.33 CFP**). Even though the French franc was replaced by the Euro starting January 1, 2002, the French Pacific franc (CFP) will continue, for the time being, to exist as a separate monetary entity. This currency is valid only in the French Overseas Communities and Territories of the Pacific: French Polynesia, New Caledonia and Wallis and Fetuna.

The 7 Euro bills are in denominations of 500, 200, 100, 50, 20, 10 and 5. The 8 coins are the 2 Euro coin, the 1 Euro coin, and cents—50, 20, 10, 5, 2 and 1 Euro cents. The local banks will accept Euro bills, just as they accept American dollars, but they will not accept Euro coins or American coins. Some of the stores, shops, boutiques and other small vendors will not accept even the Euro bills. Most shops will accept American dollars, but you probably won't get good exchange rates in the process.

The exchange rate for the US dollar fluctuates daily in the banks and by the second on the Internet. The average yearly US dollar exchange rate has steadily dropped from 105.7 CFP in 2003 to 96.1 CFP for 2004 and 2005, to 95.1 CFP for 2006, and finally to 87.1 CFP for 2007. **At press time, the rate is about 81.5 CFP for one US dollar.**

If you have access to the Internet you can get currency conversions on *www.xe.com/ucc/full.shtml.*

Ready Cash

Banque de Polynésie and Socredo Banque have offices at the International Airport of Tahiti Faa'a, where you can buy French Pacific francs as soon as you arrive in Tahiti, and exchange your leftover francs for US dollars just before you leave.

Banque de Polynésie, Banque de Tahiti and Banque Socredo have offices on most of the main islands. All the banks accept and issue travelers checks and have a currency exchange counter. Be prepared to pay the bank charge of 500-600 CFP per transaction.

The automatic teller machine (**ATM**) is called a *distributeur*. All the banks are now equipped with this handy service, even in most of the outer islands. Socredo and Banque de Polynésie also have ATM windows at the Tahiti Faa'a Airport, and there is an ATM at the Moorea Airport. Some of the post offices also have ATM windows. Most, but not all, of these machines will accept your Visa and Mastercard transactions, as well as Eurocard, but they do not accept American Express or Diner's. Although you may see the Cirrus logo on the ATM, these machines will process only Cirrus from France.

You can get cash advances with your Visa and Mastercard inside the banks, which are limited according to the type of credit card you have. American Express cash advances can be transacted at Tahiti Tours in Papeete and some of the banks are now able to handle American Express transactions as well.

Currency Exchanges

Banque de Polynésie has a currency exchange booth *in the baggage area* that is open for international flight arrivals, as well as a bank *in the main terminal* that is open for international arrivals and departures. It would be advisable to exchange some dollars for CFP (francs) before leaving the airport.

All the main banks have a currency exchange window and most of the branch offices will also exchange currency. You can also exchange your dollars for CFP at your hotel, which is sometimes necessary, but you will not receive as good a rate as you'll get at the banks.

Credit Cards & Personal Checks

Visa is the most widely accepted credit card in the tourist islands of French Polynesia. The international class hotels, airlines, car rental agencies and some of the pearl shops will accept all major credit cards. Some restaurants and shops accept American Express, Mastercard and Diner's Club.

All the banks in Tahiti can help you with any questions regarding Visa and Mastercard. **Tahiti Tours**, *Tel. 54.02.55*, is the local representative for American Express services; **Socredo Bank**, *Tel. 41.51.23*, handles JCB; and **Banque de Polynésie**, *Tel. 46.66.66*, is the representative for Diner's Club. Some of the small hostels and pensions do not accept credit cards.

To secure a reservation in a hotel or hostel, you may send a personal check for the required deposit, but once you arrive, most businesses will not accept personal checks unless they are written on a local bank account. Some of the owners of art galleries and pearl shops will occasionally accept a personal account on a foreign bank if you are making a big purchase.

To get the best exchange rate for your dollar I recommend charging your hotel bill, restaurants, activities, pearls, gifts and all other purchases on your credit cards. You will need some local cash in your pocket for incidentals, and if you have CFP left over at the end of your stay, then apply it to your hotel bill.

MOVIES & VIDEOS

The impact of movies showing the South Sea Islands has been so motivating that several people moved down here to live forever after seeing films such as *Tabu*, *Sadie Thompson* (also known as *Rain*), *Return to Paradise*, one or more versions of *Mutiny on the Bounty*, and the 1958 release of *South Pacific*, starring Mitzi Gaynor, John Kerr and Rosanno Brazzi.

I was once the tour guide for a group of Japanese tourists, who sang "Bali Hai," "Bloody Mary," "Happy Talk" and other songs from *South Pacific* all day, as we drove around the island of Tahiti. This movie was not made in Tahiti, nor did the book or film ever indicate that Tahiti, Moorea or Bora Bora was the setting, yet many people still assume otherwise. The former Bali Hai hotels on Moorea, Huahine and Raiatea, as well as the Club Bali Hai on Moorea, were named for the movie, not the other way round. The "Bali Hai" mountain on Moorea (Mou'a Roa or 'long mountain' in Tahitian) does not even resemble the "Bali-ha'i" of the original movie. Still, escapist dreams are very good for tourism and for the well being of the dreamer.

ABC Productions made a remake of *South Pacific* in 2000, which was shown on American TV and is now available in VHS and DVD. Although most of the movie was filmed at Port Douglas in Queensland, Australia, ABC Productions chose Opunohu Bay in Moorea for the scenes that include the spectacular beauty of the island of Bali-ha'i and the Mou'a Roa mountain. Thus, the legend became reality and the mountain named Bali Hai by the Hotel Bali Hai "boys" is now immortalized on film as the famous Bali-ha'i peak that beckons to the sailors across the sea.

Movies to Set the Mood

Here is an abbreviated list of movies that were either filmed in Tahiti, or supposedly used stories or settings from Tahiti. Perhaps you can locate a few of these in your local video rental stores. And you, too, can dream of Tahiti and Her Islands.

White Shadows in the South Seas (1927), *The Pagan* (1928), *Tabu* (1931), *Never the Twain Shall Meet* (1931), *Bird of Paradise* (1932), *Mutiny on the Bounty* (1935) with Charles Laughton and Clark Gable, *Hurricane* (1937), *Aloma of the*

South Seas (1941), *Son of Fury* (1942), *The Moon and Sixpence* (1941), *South of Tahiti* (1941), *The Tuttles of Tahiti* (1942), *Bird of Paradise* (1951), *Drums of Tahiti* (1953), *Cinerama South Sea Adventure* (1958), *Enchanted Island* (1958), *Mutiny on the Bounty* (1962), Trevor Howard, Marlon Brando and Tarita Teriipaia, *Tiko and the Shark* (1963), *Donavan's Reef* (1963), *Hurricane* (1978). *Beyond the Reef*, also known as *The Boy and The Shark*, was filmed on Bora Bora by Dino de Laurentiis, immediately following the *Hurricane*, using some of the same decor. *The Bounty* (1984) was filmed in Moorea with Mel Gibson as Fletcher Christian and Anthony Hopkins as a more sympathetic Captain Bligh. *A Love Affair* (1994) was a Warner Brothers movie filmed in Moorea, starring Warren Beatty and Annette Bening.

The Stone Cutter is a 35-mm. film written, narrated and produced in 2001 by Moorea resident Aad van der Heyde. The 72-min. movie, based on a fairy tale, has an all-Tahitian cast and no dialogue and was filmed on Moorea. The DVD is now available at Tower Records, Blockbuster, Walmart and other video stores in the USA and Canada.

Tahiti's government-owned audiovisual company, Institut de la Communication Audiovisuelle (ICA), has a good selection of video films and TNTV programs. These include performances by Tahiti's best professional dance troupes, Heiva festivals, old movies made in Tahiti, and video films featuring various islands of French Polynesia. Contact them at *dca@mail.pf* or *www.ica.pf.*

Tahiti has several private companies that produce video films on all the islands, from the land, sea and sky. The most notable is Teva Sylvain's Pacific Promotion. The quality of the color is excellent and most, but not all, of these films are compatible with the American video systems. The Tahiti Tourisme office has a selection of promotional films for sale. Tahiti Music, in front of the Notre Dame Cathedral in Papeete, has a large choice of commercial films, as well as Odyssey, a big new bookstore-music shop behind the Cathedral.

POST OFFICE & COURIER SERVICES

You can leave your American stamps at home because they won't be acceptable for mailing your postcards overseas from any of the islands in French Polynesia. I say this because I've met several Americans who do bring their stamps to Tahiti, thinking they'll be saving money on postage. Each country has its own postal system, and in Tahiti this is an important source of revenue for the country.

The cost of mailing letters weighing less than 20 grams is 140 CFP to all international destinations except France and French Overseas Departments and Territories.

The main post office is on Boulevard Pomare in downtown Papeete. Services include stamps for letters and parcels, express delivery service, international telephone calls, telegrams, telex, fax, phone cards, and a philatelic center. Some post offices also have Internet service for the public. There are post offices on all the inhabited islands of French Polynesia.

ADDRESSING A LETTER TO FRENCH POLYNESIA

When addressing a letter or package to anyone living in French Polynesia, it is necessary to include the name of the person, hotel or business, the B.P. (boite postale) number, the town or village where the post office is located, the island, the zip code if known, and the country. Example: **Jan Prince, B.P. 298, Maharepa, Moorea, 98728 French Polynesia.** On some of the islands the PK number is used instead of a B.P., which should always be followed by the name of the village and any other specifics you may have, then the name of the island and country. Example: **Jan Prince, Chez Wilder, PK 12.5, côté montagne, Pihaena, Moorea, French Polynesia.**

Zip codes are a relatively recent addition to our postal services and many people still don't know what their zip code is. I haven't included the name of the country in the addresses given in this book, but each address should always include the name of the island, followed by French Polynesia.

General Delivery mail service is available at all the post offices. On the envelope you should write the person's name, c/o Poste Restante, and the name of the island, and make sure that this is followed by French Polynesia.

B.P. = *bôite postale* or post office box

You will note that most of the addresses listed in this book show the initials B.P., which stand for *bôite postale*, the equivalent of post office box in the US. You can write P.O. Box or B.P. and your letter to French Polynesia will be processed with no problem.

PK = *poste kilometre*, the number of kilometers from the *mairie* or post office

Should you be given an address with a PK number instead of B.P., on the island of Tahiti, this indicates how many kilometers that person lives from the *mairie* (town hall) in Papeete. On other islands, such as Moorea, the 0-kilometer can be at the post office. PK stands for *poste kilometre*, and when you're driving around the Society Islands you will see the kilometer markers on the mountainside of the road. Look for the red-capped white painted stone or concrete markers with the kilometer number painted in black on two sides.

For Stamp Collectors

The **Philatelic Center** of the Offices Des Postes et Télécommunications (OPT) in Tahiti is located in the main post office, where you can buy sets of collector stamps, along with a stamped "first day" envelope. The themes for these beautiful stamps include the fruits, flowers, fishes and fauna of Polynesia, along with pictures of pretty *vahines*, fancy hats, outrigger sailing canoes, old *goelette* schooners and lovely seascapes. All the major post offices in the islands also carry selections of these collectors' items. You can also order stamps from home: Centre Philatélique de Polynésie Française, Office des Postes et Télécommunications, Mahina 98709 Tahiti, French Polynesia, *Tel. 689/41.43.35; Fax 689/45.25.86;* or through the Internet, *E-mail: phila@mail.opt.pf, www.tahiti-postoffice.com.*

Courier Services

DHL Worldwide Express, B.P. 62255, Faa'a, Tahiti, *Tel. 83.73.73, Fax 83.73.74,* is located in the Immeuble Tavararo, at PK 4.8 in Faa'a, a building on the right just before you reach the entrance leading to the Tahiti-Faa'a International Airport. Open Mon.-Thurs. 7:30am-4pm and on Fri. until 3pm. They do not close at lunch. They provide 4-day delivery service from Tahiti to the USA. They charge 5.670 CFP to ship documents weighing less than 1 kg. from Tahiti to NY, and 7.324 CFP for a package.

Federal Express (Fedex), *Tel. 45.36.45,* has an office in the Immeuble Polyfix building in Faaa. Open Mon.-Fri. from 7:30am-5pm. They charge 5.555 CFP for shipping documents and 6.709 CFP for a package weighing less than 1 kg. to the United States.

PUBLICATIONS ABOUT TAHITI
Newspapers & Magazines

Tahiti Beach Press is a 20-page English language magazine that is published monthly and distributed weekly for visitors. You will find it in hotels in Tahiti, Moorea, Huahine, Raiatea, Bora Bora and Rangiroa. You can also pick up a copy at Tahiti Tourist Bureau, the airports, ferry docks, car-rental agencies, and in the restaurants and businesses that advertise in the *Tahiti Beach Press*. A one-year subscription to this publication is $37 for airmail postage to the U.S. Address your subscription request to *Tahiti Beach Press,* B.P. 887, Papeete, Tahiti 98713, French Polynesia. *Tel. 689/42.68.50; tahitibeachpres@mail.pf; www.tahitibeachpress.com.*

La Dépêche de Tahiti and *Les Nouvelles* are Tahiti's daily French-language newspapers. The *International Herald Tribune, USA Today, Time* and *Newsweek* are sold at Le Kiosk in front of the Vaima Center on Boulevard Pomare and at La Maison de la Presse on Boulevard Pomare in Papeete. The copies you can find in Tahiti will not be the most current editions. You can also find newspapers and magazines on Moorea at Kina Booksellers, adjacent to the post office in Maharepa, at Supersonics in Le Petit Village, and in the boutiques of the larger hotels. La Maison de la Presse in Bora Bora also carries magazines and newspapers.

Books

You may still find some of the reference books and novels in public libraries, specialized bookstores and secondhand shops. Free catalogs of publications may be requested from: **Bishop Museum Press**, P.O. Box 19000-A, Honolulu, HI 96817-0916, *Tel. 808/848-4135;* **University of Hawaii Press**, 2840 Kolowalu Street,

Honolulu, HI 96822; **The Book Bin**, 351 NW Jackson Street, Corvallis, OR 97330; **Mutual Publishing**, 2055 N. King Street, Suite 201, Honolulu, HI 96819; **Colin Hinchcliffe**, 12 Queens Staith Mews, York, Y01 1HH, England; and **Société des Océanistes Catalogue**, Musée de l'Homme, 75116, Paris, France. You can also buy books about Tahiti and Her Islands, including this travel guide, online at *www.amazon.com* and *www.bn.com*.

Reference Books

Ancient Tahiti (Bulletin 48 Bernice P. Bishop Museum, Honolulu) by Teuira Henry, is based on material recorded by her grandfather, the Reverend J. M. Orsmond, who came to Moorea as a Protestant missionary in 1817. This is my primary reference book for the plants, flowers, trees, religion, culture and legends of the Society Islands. *Ancient Tahitian Society* (The University Press of Hawaii, Honolulu, 1974) is a 3-dome collection by Douglas L. Oliver. These scholarly studies are an excellent reference for the history and culture of the Tahitians.

Bengt Danielsson, a Swedish anthropologist and historian, who crossed the Pacific from Peru to the Tuamotus with Thor Heyerdahl aboard the *Kon-Tiki* raft in 1947, settled in Tahiti until his death in 1997, and published a wide variety of books. They include: *The Happy Island* (London, 1952), *Work and Life on Raroia* (Stockholm, 1955), *From Raft to Raft* (London, 1960), *Forgotten Islands of the South Seas, Love in the South Seas* (Mutual, 1986), *Tahiti-Circle Island Tour Guide* (Les Editions du Pacifique, 1976), and *Moruroa Mon Amour—the French Nuclear Tests in the Pacific* (1977), by Bengt & Marie-Thérèse Danielsson.

Fatu-Hiva—Back to Nature (Penguin Books, 1976) is Thor Heyerdahl's account of the sojourn he and his wife undertook for more than a year on this lonely island in the Marquesas Archipelago, just before the outbreak of World War II. *History and Culture in the Society Islands* (Honolulu, 1930), *Marquesan Legends* (Honolulu, 1930), *Polynesian Religion* (Honolulu, 1927), and *The Native Culture in the Marquesas*, Honolulu, 1923), all by Craighill Handy.

Polynesian Researches (1829) by William Ellis, is a 2-volume work by a missionary who spent nearly 6 years in the South Sea Islands. *Polynesia's Sacred Isle* (Dodd, Mead & Company, New York, 1976), by Edward Dodd, is part of a 3-volume *Ring of Fire* set about the island of Raiatea.

Ra'ivavae—An expedition to the most fascinating and mysterious island in Polynesia (Doubleday & Company, Inc., New York, 1961). Author-anthropologist Donald Marshall describes life on Ra'ivavae, one of the Austral islands south of Tahiti.

Return to the Sea (John deGraff, Inc., New York, 1972), by William Albert Robinson, is the story of Robinson's 70-ft. brigantine *Varua*, in which he sailed to Tahiti in 1945, to settle in Paea, where his house still stands. Robinson used *Varua* as a floating laboratory to travel throughout the Pacific Islands, helping to eradicate the filariasis parasite transmitted by mosquitoes that causes elephantiasis.

Robert Suggs, an American archaeologist who did seminal work for the American Museum of Natural History of New York in the Marquesas Islands during the 1950s and 1960s, has written *The Island Civilizations of Polynesia* (New American Library, Mentor Books, New York, 1960), *Hidden Worlds of Polynesia* (Harcourt, Brace and World, New York, 1963) and *Marquesan Sexual Behavior* (Harcourt, Brace and World, New York, 1966), which are interesting reading and good reference books for anyone interested in the Marquesas Islands. His latest book is *Manuiota'a, Journal of a Voyage to the Marquesas Islands,* which was written with Burgl Lichtenstein and published by Pa'eke Press in 2001.

Many archaeologists and historians who specialize in the South Seas consider Patrick V. Kirch the expert authority on Polynesian pre-history. His works include *On the Road of the Winds: An Archaeological History of the Pacific Islands Before European Contact,* (University of California Press, May 2000), *The Lapita Peoples: Ancestors of the Oceanic World (The Peoples of South-East Asia and the Pacific),* (Blackwell Publishers, December 1996), *The Evolution of the Polynesian Chiefdoms* (Cambridge University Press, reprint edition August 1989), and *Historical Ecology in the Pacific Islands: Prehistoric Environment and Landscape Change* (co-authored with Terry L Hunt, Yale University Press, March 1997).

Tahiti, Island of Love by Robert Langdon is a popular account of Tahiti's history, and it's easy reading. *Tahitian Journal* (University of Minnesota Press, 1968) is a diary written by George Biddle between 1917 and 1922, along with paintings and drawings by the author. The setting is Tautira on the Tahiti-Iti peninsula, where Biddle lived among the Tahitians. *Tahitians—Mind & Experience in the Society Islands* (University of Chicago Press, 1973) by Robert I. Levy is an anthropologist's reference book for anthropologists, containing a wealth of cultural information. *The Journals of Captain James Cook* (Cambridge University, 1955, 1961, 1967), edited by J. C. Beaglehole, were published in 3 volumes.

Mystic Isles of the South Seas (Garden City Publishing Company, Inc., New York, 1921) by Frederick O'Brien, is based on his visit to Tahiti during one of three journeys he made to the South Seas. His story of Lovina Gooding, the colorful character who owned the Tiare Hotel in Papeete, is classic. O'Brien's *White Shadows in the South Seas* are about the Marquesas Islands, and *Atolls of the Sun* feature the Tuamotu Archipelago.

South Sea Idylls (James R. Osgood & Co., Boston – 1873), was written by Charles Warren Stoddard, about life in the Marquesas Islands during his visit in the 1800s. This is one you may have to search for in specialized shops. *Tahiti* (Grant Richards Ltd., London) by Tihoti, the Tahitianized name of George Calderon, who visited Tahiti in 1906. He was killed in the war in Gallipoli in 1915, and the book was completed from his notes. This is truly a collector's item and is illustrated with Calderon's drawings of the people he met while wandering around the island of Tahiti.

Tales of the South Pacific (1947) and *Return to Paradise* by James A. Michener are all-time classics by a very descriptive writer. *The Bounty Trilogy* (1932) by

Charles Nordhoff and James Norman Hall comprises the three volumes of *Mutiny on the Bounty*, *Men Against the Sea* and *Pitcairn's Island*. *The Dark River* (1946) by Charles Nordhoff and James Norman Hall, is set in the wild and natural *fenua 'aihere*—the Land of Forests—of the Taiarapu peninsula on Tahiti-Iti. The descriptions of this savage beauty transport us right onto the scene of this lonely land. *The Hurricane* (1935) by Charles Nordhoff and James Norman Hall is an exciting story set in the Dangerous Archipelago of the Tuamotus. *Typee: a Real Romance of the South Seas; Omoo; a Narrative of Adventures in the South Seas, a Sequel to Typee and Marquesas Islands* by Herman Melville are all based on Melville's experiences in the islands.

A Tahitian and English Dictionary (Haere Po No Tahiti, 1985) with introductory remarks on the Polynesian language and a short grammar of the Tahitian dialect. This was first printed in 1851 at the London Missionary Society's Press. *Fa'atoro Parau* is a 684-page illustrated Tahitian/English-English/Tahitian dictionary written by Sven Wahlroos, Ph.D., also known as Taote Tivini.

Recent Novels, Island Tales & Modern Accounts

All of the following books can be ordered from *www.amazon.com*.

To Live in Paradise is an autobiography by Renée Roosevelt Denis, a long-time resident of Tahiti and Moorea. It takes us from Bali to Haiti to Tahiti and is filled with tales of adventure with her grandfather, André Roosevelt, her famous parents, her Tahitian husband and children, her years with Club Med in Moorea and her meetings with Marlon Brando on his private atoll in Tetiaroa.

Together Alone is a 2004 publication written by Ron Falconer, my former Scottish neighbor in Moorea. Ron tells the true story of his experiences sailing around the world and settling on Caroline Island, an uninhabited atoll in Kiribati, now known as Millennium Island. He spent almost 4 years on this desert island, along with his French wife and their 2 children who were under the age of 5 years. In this book you will meet some of the characters that still live on Moorea, Tahiti and Ahe, in the Tuamotu Islands. If you're going to be in Moorea on a Thurs. or Sun. night, then you can buy an autographed copy of the book from Ron while he is singing at Alfredo's Restaurant in Cook's Bay during dinner.

Tahiti Blue by Alex W. duPrel, who lives in Moorea and publishes *Tahiti Pacifique Magazine*. *Breadfruit, Frangipani, and Tiare in Bloom,* 3 books by Célestine Hitiura Vaite, a young Tahitian woman who lives in Australia. *Varua Tupu*, a collection of stories and poems written by residents of French Polynesia that are translated into English. *The Old Broom Road Tahiti* edited by Fran Dieudonne and Ann Kuhns. *Omai, The Prince Who Never Was,* by Richard Connaughton. *Cocktails in Tahiti* by Richard Bondurant. *Teahupoo: Tahiti's Mythic Wave*, by Tim McKenna. *Tahiti: Polynesian Peasants and Proletarians*, by Ben R. Finney. *Tahiti of Yesteryear*, black and white photos by Stafford-Ames Morse. *Polynesian Interconnections: Samoa to Tahiti to Hawaii*, a scientific education book for young adults, by Peter Leiataua AhChing. *Ra'ivavae*, by Edmundo Edwards; and *Runaway to Tahiti*, a sailing story by Harry F. McIntyre.

Books Available in English in Tahiti
   Librarie du Vaima in the Vaima Center in Papeete carries some books and pamphlets about Tahiti printed in English. **Odyssey**, behind the Cathedral, and **Archipels**, on rue des Remparts, also stock some Polynesian books in English. The **Paul Gauguin Museum** in Papeari sells a few books and booklets in English.
   Paperback editions of books by James Norman Hall can be purchased at the James Norman Hall House and Library on the mountainside at PK 5.5 in Arue, *Tel. 50.01.61/50.01.60; www.jamesnormanhallhome.pf.*

RADIO
   Radio Television Française d'Outre-Mer (RFO), also known as Radio Tahiti or Radio Polynésie, (FM 89), is the official station, which operates with French and Tahitian broadcasts on 89 FM and 91.8 FM, plus several other frequencies. There are also several other stations that broadcast in French and Tahitian. Just turn the dial from 88.6 to 106, until you find music to your liking. Don't rely on your radio for soft music for dreaming while you contemplate the clouds or classical music for a superb sunset. You'll have a hard time finding it. More than half the population here is under 20 years old, and the music is played primarily for that audience.

RETIRING IN TAHITI, BUYING LAND OR HOUSES IN FRENCH POLYNESIA
   If you have a dream of living in Tahiti and Her Islands, then I suggest that you come here on a visit first and get a feel of the place before you take the next step. Spending a relaxing vacation on a small island in the middle of the South Pacific is quite different from living so far removed from the choices and conveniences of life in a big modern country. The complexities are even more magnified if you do not speak or read and write French, which is the official language of French Polynesia.
   In the past it was possible, although not easy, for foreigners to buy land or houses here, and some American couples have retired quite happily in these islands. Others divide their time between their homes in the States and their "fares" on Tahiti, Moorea, Huahine or wherever in the islands. They can have the best of both worlds. During the past few years, however, it has become increasingly difficult for non-Polynesians to buy property here. The government's approvals or denials are made on an individual basis.
   Another option to actually buying the land is to take a long-term rental or a lease for 30 years or more. There are about 3 dozen real estate agencies in Tahiti that can answer your questions regarding the purchase of land, houses, villas, condos and apartments. Please do not contact me with questions about real estate.

I have no experience with realtors and cannot tell you the correct price of land or houses.

SHOPPING

All the main tourist islands have souvenir shops and arts and crafts centers, where you can find hand-painted *pareos*, locally made T-shirts, carved Marquesan bowls, ceremonial spears, drums, ukuleles, tables and tikis, plus tapa bark paintings, Tahitian dancing costumes, basketry and woven hats, shell jewelry, mother-of-pearl creations, *tifaifai* bed covers, vanilla beans, Tahitian music and video films, *monoi* oil, soaps and perfumes, and beautiful Tahiti cultured pearls. See information in each Island chapter.

Tahiti Cultured Pearls

The emerald and turquoise lagoons of the Tuamotu and Gambier Islands of French Polynesia are a natural haven for the black-lipped oyster, the *Pinctada Margaritifera* (*Cumingi variety*), which produces the world's finest black pearls. At the beginning of the 19th century the lagoons of Polynesia were filled with pearl oysters, also called *nacres*. From 1802-1940 the smoky gray mother-of-pearl shell was sought after as material for buttons. With the introduction of watertight diving glasses the divers could go deeper and deeper to find oysters of an acceptable size, as they exhausted the ready supply. With the advent of synthetic buttons and the depletion of accessible oysters in the lagoons, the adventurous days of the famous South Seas pearl divers ended after World War II, with controlled diving seasons continuing into the 1960s.

During the highlight of the pearl diving days there was an average of one pearl found among 15,000 oysters killed. The *Pinctada margaritifera* came very close to extinction, until researchers experimented with techniques to harvest the spawn of the *nacre* to collect the baby spats that would grow into oysters.

The first trials were made at culturing black pearls in the lagoon of Hikueru in 1962 and in Bora Bora in 1964, using the grafting technique that was invented in Japan in 1893, and refined by Mikimoto in the early 1900s. The first undersea pearl farm was established in the lagoon of Manihi in the 1970s, and the culturing of black pearls slowly grew from an isolated experiment into an industry. In 1976 the Gemological Institute of America (G.I.A.) gave formal recognition to the authentic character of the cultured pearls of Tahiti, and in 1989 the official designation of this gem became "Perle de Culture de Tahiti," the label decided upon by the *Confederation Internationale de la Bijouterie Joaillerie et Orféverie* (CINJO). Just a few years ago there were about 900 more or less functioning pearl farms, essentially in the Tuamotu and Gambier atolls, with a few small pearl farms in the Society Islands of Huahine, Taha'a, Raiatea and Maupiti. That number has been greatly reduced today as the government has imposed more restrictions to improve the quality of the pearls.

The Tahiti cultured pearl is French Polynesia's biggest export item and the most sought after souvenir purchase made by visitors to Tahiti and Her Islands. Just a few years ago this pearl was virtually unknown in the United States, and today you can buy Tahitian pearl jewelry through the Home Shopper's Channel on TV, as well as on E-bay and several other websites on the Internet. Some of the pearl merchants in French Polynesia also have their own shopping websites.

When you shop for your pearls you can make a better choice if you know what to look for in choosing a quality pearl. The main criteria are size, shape, surface quality, luster and color.

Size: Although you can find a few Tahiti cultured pearls with a diameter of 7 or 7.5 millimeters, they usually start at 8 millimeters. The average size is 9.5-11.5 millimeters, and anything over 16.5 millimeters is very rare and often valuable. The bigger the pearl, the more it costs. The largest round Tahiti pearl on record is the Robert Wan, which measures 20.92 millimeters (over 13/16 of an inch) and weighs 12.5 grams. This beauty is on display at Robert Wan Pearl Museum in Papeete.

Shape: The shape or form of the pearl is judged by roundness and symmetry. They are graded as round, semi-round, semi-baroque, baroque and circle. The round pearls are rare, therefore more expensive, but a drop or pear-shaped pearl that is perfectly symmetrical can be as expensive as a round pearl.

Surface quality: In 2001 the French Polynesia Assembly adopted measures that revised the classification of Tahiti's cultured pearls. The pearls are graded Gem, A, B, C, and D quality according to the number of flaws, pits, scratches and rays that blemish the surface.

A "Gem" quality pearl is extremely rare, as it is perfect, with no blemishes. "A" category pearls have no more than one imperfection or a group of localized imperfections concentrated over less than 10% of a pearl's surface. These pearls also have a very beautiful luster. "B" category pearls are defined as those with some imperfections "concentrated" over less than a third of their surface and with a beautiful or average luster. Instead of just having imperfections over less than a third of their surface, the imperfections must now be concentrated. The majority of pearls are "C" quality, those with "light concentrations" of imperfections over less than two-thirds of their surface and an average luster. Before the new ruling in 2001, the imperfections did not have to be lightly concentrated over less than two-thirds of a pearl's surface. "D" category pearls are pearls with "light" imperfections over more than two-thirds of their surface and "no deep imperfections;" or "D Category" pearls are those with deep concentrations "over less than half of their surface" and with "a soft luster." When I sold pearls I used to tell people that a "D" quality pearl looks like your dog has been chewing on it, leaving lots of tooth marks. Some pearl shops have started grading their pearls as AAA, AA, B+, B-, C+, C-, and so on.

Luster or orient: The most important criteria in judging the quality of a Tahiti cultured pearl are its luster or orient. Luster is the reflective quality or mirror-like shine on the pearl's surface. Orient is the iridescence or radiance from the inner-layer quality of the pearl. The thicker the mother-of-pearl (nacre) covering the nucleus inside the pearl, the more light it reflects. From the grafting to the harvesting of a pearl, a period of 18 to 24 months is necessary to achieve the desirable thickness that produces a fine quality pearl with a good luster and orient. The minimum nacre thickness required was formerly set at 0.6 millimeters, but the Tahitian government increased the minimum thickness to 0.8 millimeters, effective July 1, 2002. Reputable pearl dealers sell only those pearls with a nacre thickness of 1.5 to 2 millimeters, which can be determined by knowing the size of the nucleus that was grafted into the oyster and measuring the diameter of the finished pearl. No x-rays are needed for this information, but some of the more aggressive pearl dealers use gimmick advertising, claiming that you will receive an x-ray of the pearl you buy.

Color: After years of publicity campaigns to promote black pearls in overseas markets, including Elizabeth Taylor's "Black Pearl Perfume", the marketing experts decided to change the name from Tahitian black pearl to Tahiti cultured pearl. They feel this better describes the product and helps to eliminate confusion when people see that the pearls come in many colors. Black pearls are rarely black, which may come as a surprise to you, but they are called black pearls because they come from the black-lipped oyster.

The color of a Tahiti cultured pearl may range from white to lunar gray, with gradations of cream, peacock green, rainbow tints, aubergine (eggplant), blue, pink and golden. The color of the pearl depends on the color of the mantle or lip of the donor oyster used to graft into the producing oysters during the cultivating process. The grafter trims the outer mantle, the epithelium, of a donor oyster and cuts it into about 50 small pieces. Then he takes one tiny sliver of this living cell and transplants it into the gonad gland of a three-year old oyster, along with a nucleus, a small white round ball that is made from the shell of the Mississippi River mussel. The grafted oysters are then placed in wire nets and suspended from platforms under the lagoon, where they live for 18 to 24 months while the oyster is covering the nucleus with up to 16,000 micron-thin layers of mother-of-pearl, which is comprised of aragonite. The pearls that are produced from the slivers of mantle from one oyster will all be different, as there are no two pearls exactly alike.

Color is also affected by the mineral salts present in the water, the degree of salinity, the plankton that the oysters feed on, and the water temperature. Although some pearl sales people will tell you that the nuances of color do not affect the price of a pearl, they actually do. Pearls with a prevalence of white or gray are priced lower and pearls with rare hues, such as rainbow, aubergine, fly-wing green and shiny black, are more expensive.

Pacific Pearl Colors has a website, *www.pacificpearlcolors.pf,* which may answer your questions concerning the colors of Tahiti's pearls.

Where to Buy Your Pearls

I have covered this subject in the individual Island chapters. My recommendation for choosing your pearl is to find a sales person you like and a pearl that "winks" at you. I sold pearls on a part-time basis in Moorea for five years, and I learned that certain pearls naturally attract the attention of the person who should be wearing them. They have their own magic, you know. In the outer islands, such as Moorea and Bora Bora, some of the pearl shops are owned by people who have their own pearl farms and jewelers, or they own the shop, so there's no middle man to pay. Therefore, they can sell the pearls at a lower price than in Papeete. Plus you have the advantage of being able to walk outside the boutique and look at the pearls in the natural light, which truly brings out the beauty of this living jewel, especially in the early morning, at sunset time and on cloudy days. The same tactic won't work on a bright sunny day at noon.

People often ask if a pearl costs less when you buy it from a pearl farm, such as on Manihi, Rangiroa and Fakarava. The answer is yes, but the best pearls are usually shipped to Tahiti to be set into jewelry, or sold at auction to the big name buyers from overseas. Most of the smaller pearl farms belong to a co-operative that sells their pearls at an international auction held twice a year.

Get a receipt and a certificate of origin and authenticity for each pearl you buy. You can claim a tax refund (Value added Tax or VAT) for pearl jewelry you purchase in French Polynesia, but this exemption does not cover unset pearls or precious stones. See information under *Taxes* in this chapter. Keep in mind there is no import duty on Tahiti cultured pearls when you pass through US Customs on your way home.

You will probably be warned against buying pearls from street vendors. This notice is to protect you against the possibility of receiving stolen goods and buying inferior merchandise. Customs officials at the international airport in Tahiti now have three powerful x-ray machines that can see everything in your suitcases, carry-on bags and containers. Some people have been caught trying to leave Tahiti with quantities of inferior quality black pearls that haven't been claimed as export items. Normally, these reject pearls are dumped into the ocean under controlled conditions.

Smuggling Tahiti cultured pearls out of the country will get you into a lot of expensive trouble. An American tourist heading for Honolulu was caught by the x-ray machine with 220 reject pearls. Another person with a ticket to Easter Island had a cooler filled with pork ribs and two raw ducks. The x-ray machine revealed two sacks of mediocre quality pearls stuffed inside the ducks. If you buy pearls in quantity you will have to present your pearls to the Service de la Perliculture to receive an export certificate, once they have determined the quality of the pearls you have purchased.

STAYING OUT OF TROUBLE

When you're packing your bags for a trip to Tahiti please do not include any drugs that are illegal in your country. They are also illegal here and the French Immigration and Customs authorities do not consider the importation of any stupifiants as a light matter. "Dope dogs" are trained to sniff out anything suspicious in your luggage when it's unloaded from the plane, and x-ray machines make it possible for the officials to see everything inside your suitcases. Heavy fines and jail sentences are a sure way to ruin a good vacation. Should you decide to risk it anyway, then please use discretion and do not give or sell any illegal drugs to a local person. This is a very small place and news travels amazingly fast via the "Coconut Radio."

When I first came from Houston, Texas, to Tahiti as a tourist in 1968 I remember that I was so afraid of theft that I took my handbag with me when I took a ride across the beautiful Bora Bora lagoon aboard an outrigger sailing canoe. Inside the bag were my passport, return plane tickets, traveler's checks, money, driver's license and other important papers. After I moved to Tahiti I learned to relax more and to leave the watch and handbag in my hotel room when I went out in a boat. Many times there were no doors to lock and no windows to close.

Due to the increasing hotel room thefts, most of the rooms are now more protected. Experience has taught me to lock the valuable papers inside the safe provided in some of the hotels, or at least to lock the door to the hotel room or bungalow, and to close the windows.

For police, dial 17.

The shops, boutiques and especially the *roulottes* (mobile diners) in Papeete have their share of thefts, and you should watch out for purse-snatchers in the city, which also includes pre-teenage girls. The delinquency problems are not so pronounced that you have to be afraid to take your eyes off your suitcase at the airport. Please don't let fear ruin your vacation, when you should be relaxed and carefree, but just be cautious and use the same common sense that you would use when traveling anywhere.

If you want to discover Papeete-by-night, stay in the main stream of lighted streets, sidewalk cafés and bars, where lots of people are on the streets. Avoid drunk Tahitians and you'll enjoy yourself more. A municipal police station is close to Papeete's municipal market, adjacent to the Loto (lottery) building on rue Edouard Ahnne. You can also dial 17 at any telephone booth without having to deposit coins and you will be connected to the *gendarmerie*, the French national police station.

Women Traveling Alone

If you're a woman traveling alone or with a girlfriend, then you should be aware that the crime rate in Tahiti is low compared to most cities anywhere in the world, but you should still use caution. Back in the 1970s and 1980s, in my pub-crawling days, I used to feel totally at ease running around in Papeete at any time of the night, popping into a nightclub here and there to see what was going on and to dance the night away. Experience has since taught me to heed my own advice and avoid drunk men and dark streets.

Another word to the wise for women alone: do not sunbathe in the nude or even topless on secluded beaches. Some of the Tahitian males see this as an open invitation, and they will pursue you, even if it takes all day. This warning needs to be heeded in the remote islands as well as in the more popular tourist islands.

A form of rape called *mafera* existed in these islands long before the Europeans arrived, not to be confused with *motoro*, the traditional courtship practice of a fellow slipping into his girlfriend's bed or onto her *peue* mat for consensual sex. The difference between the two customs depends on whether or not the girl agrees. If she does, then they are simply making love. If she objects and he does it anyway, then it is *mafera* or rape. Older Tahitian men on various islands claim that neither custom is practiced on their island today because the young people are better educated now. Others say that the *tane haere po* (guy who creeps around in the dark) is more interested in smoking his *pakalolo* (marijuana) than peeking or crawling through windows.

Tahitian men can be very charming and are always ready for sexual encounters. Many of them have told me that they do not notice whether a woman is young or old, fat or skinny, pretty or not. What they see is a woman. One of their favorite expressions is: "Age makes no difference. It's love that counts." What woman would want to argue with that philosophy? Should you succumb to the erotic mist that covers these tropical isles, then be sure that you provide your own protection against sexually transmitted diseases, which exist in Tahiti and Her Islands just as they do back home. Do not rely on your partner for anything except a brief moment of pleasure, which is not even guaranteed.

A woman visiting the islands by herself is often open to all kinds of experiences, which may include being invited to stay in the home of a Tahitian family. Should this happen to you, then chances are you'll create a lifelong friendship and wonderful memories. Just use your female intuition in making your decision.

TAXES – WHAT YOU WILL PAY

Add **5% government hotel tax** to room rates in the international classified hotels and cabins of cruise ships based in French Polynesia. The pensions and guesthouses are not subject to this tax.

Add **6% value added tax** (VAT in English, TVA in French) to all room rates in international classified hotels, as well as non-classified hotels, family pensions, campgrounds and ships. This 6% VAT is also added to prepaid meal plans and all transfers the hotel or pension provides between the airport or boat dock and the hotel or pension or ship. Meal plans are: MAP (American Modified Plan, with breakfast and dinner, also called *demi-pension*); AP (American Plan, with breakfast, lunch and dinner, also called *pension complete*).

Add **2% service charge** on accommodations, food and beverage costs in the international classified hotels and cabins of cruise ships based in French Polynesia.

Add **150 CFP municipal tax** (also called sojourn tax, visitors tax, city tax or tourist tax) per person per day to your bill at the international classified hotels, international cruises or any other establishment of equal characteristics.

Add **50 CFP sojourn tax** per person per day on non-classified hotels, family pensions or campgrounds on the following islands: Tahiti, Moorea, Huahine, Taha'a, Raiatea, Bora Bora, Rangiroa, Tikehau and Mataiva. The tax on Fakarava is **40 CFP**. There is no sojourn tax in Manihi and Maupiti. Children under the age of 12 staying with their parents are exempt from the municipal tax.

A 10% VAT is added to tourist services such as transfers made by a taxi or transfer service, all restaurants and snacks, all tours and excursions. A 6% VAT is added to all inter-island transportation by air and boat, including charter flights and chartered boat trips. The 6% VAT also applies to non-alcoholic beverages, medicines, books, newspapers and magazines. Alcoholic beverages are taxed 16%.

Passengers on international cruises are charged 200 CFP per day for Tourist Development Tax while the ship is visiting French Polynesia. They are also charged 500 CFP per person per day on cruising activity (T.A.C.) for any tours or excursions they take.

Unless specified, most of the rates quoted in this guide do not include taxes, which are subject to change at any time.

VAT Tax Refunds

If you are visiting French Polynesia for less than 6 months you can claim a tax refund (Value Added Tax or VAT) for eligible goods you take home. The value of purchases from any single store, tax included, must total at least 5.000 CFP. All the goods must be taken back with you, in your carry-on or checked luggage, when you leave French Polynesia. All tax refunds must be claimed within 6 months of purchasing the goods. Not all stores are participating in the tax-free program; therefore, prior to your purchase, verify this with the store concerned. If they do participate, you will have to prove that you are not a resident of French Polynesia and that you are 15 years old or over. Most people who apply for this tax refund have bought Tahiti cultured pearl jewelry of some value.

At the Tahiti-Faa'a International Airport you should present the 3 copies of the Retail Export Form, as well as the goods purchased under the tax-free program. Customs will retain the pink copy #3 and will stamp the other two copies. You need to return the stamped pink copy #2 to the store for your refund. The green copy #4 is for your records.

Do not forget to keep the goods with you at all times when you apply for Customs endorsement of the Retail Export Form at Tahiti-Faa'a International Airport. Customs officers may want to check them. Within a reasonable period of time, once you are back home, you should receive the amount of refunded tax from the store, credited directly to you credit card. Once you are back home, you may still claim the tax refund if the Retail Export Form has not been endorsed by Customs upon leaving French Polynesia. However, the process is time consuming and may be more expensive than the amount of tax refund that you are claiming.

There is no refund for tax you pay on food products and beverages, tobacco products, medicine, firearms, unset precious stones and pearls, cultural property, automobiles, motorcycles, boats, planes, as well as their parts and accessories. Nor is there a refund on taxes for purchases of a commercial nature (in such quantities that it is reasonable to believe they are not intended for your personal use).

TELEPHONES & TELECOMMUNICATIONS

Dial 19 to reach a long-distance operator in Tahiti from any of the islands of French Polynesia. They all speak good English and are very efficient and courteous. Dial 3612 for information on telephone numbers within French Polynesia, and 3600 for international information. The telephone numbers for government offices, hotels and other private businesses, as well as all home phone numbers, contain only 6 digits.

Public pay phones are easily identifiable booths of metal and glass, with black letters on a yellow background. There are several phone booths in the most populous islands, and you will probably even find a public phone in the most remote village of the Marquesas Islands, the Gambier, or Rapa in the Austral Islands.

The pay phones require a *télécarte*, a phone card that you can buy at any post office and in many shops and newsstands. These plastic cards are often decorated with some of the same scenes as the postage stamps, and are collectors' items as well. A 30-unit card is 1.000 CFP, a 40-unit card is 1.550 CFP, a 60-unit card is 2.000 CFP and a 150-unit card is 5.000 CFP. A digital readout on the phone states how many units remain on your card as you talk with your party.

You can also go to an Internet café and call home via Yahoo Messenger or Skype.

Calling Tahiti

When dialing direct to Tahiti and Her Islands, dial the proper International Access Code + 689 (Country Code) + the local number. The International Access Code if calling from the US is 011. Therefore, if you were calling me at the *Tahiti Beach Press*, you would dial 011+689+42.68.50. Some businesses and individuals are now listing their phone numbers as 426-850, rather than 42.68.50.

The same codes apply when sending faxes. When transmitting telex messages from the US, the code 702 or 711 + FP must precede the telex number. You can look up telephone or fax numbers in French Polynesia online at *www.annuaireopt.pf.*

Calling Home from Tahiti

To call overseas from anywhere in Tahiti and Her Islands, dial 00, then the country code (1 for the US and Canada), followed by the area code and phone number. You can dial direct from your hotel room or by going to the nearest post office or phone booth. In the post offices you give the postal clerk the number you are calling and she will direct you to one of the booths when your call is placed.

Automatic direct dial calls to Hawaii, the US mainland or Canada from Tahiti at any time during the day or night, Sun. and holidays included, cost 102 CFP per min. This rate also applies to metropolitan France, New Zealand, New Caledonia,

Australia, Japan and the Cook Islands. The cost of calling most European countries is 170 CFP per min. from 6am-12am and 102 CFP per min. from 12am-6am. To call Mexico, South America, Asia or Eastern Europe, you will pay 204 CFP per min. day or night.

At the post office you can pay directly for the call, place a collect call or charge the call to your AT&T, MCI or similar long-distance calling card if you live in the US or Canada. If you live in Hawaii and have a Hawaiian Telephone Company GTE card, that is also acceptable. Canadians with a Teleglobe Canada card can also use it in Tahiti. You can now dial 1-800 numbers direct from French Polynesia, but these calls are billed at the normal rate of 102 CFP per min.

Calling Within Tahiti and Her Islands

When calling from a fixed phone to a fixed phone, intra-island calls (on the same island) cost 34 CFP for every 4 min. Inter-island calls (such as from Tahiti to Huahine or Rangiroa to Nuku Hiva) cost 34 CFP for every 2 min. and 30 seconds between 6am-10pm, and 34 CFP for 5 min. between 10pm-6am. Just dial the 6-digit telephone number, as there are no area codes within the territory.

Most individuals and business people now carry their cell phones wherever they go. These numbers have a prefix of 7 or 2. If you are calling from a fixed telephone to a mobile vini (cell) phone, the local cost is 60 CFP per min. from 6am-6pm during the week, from Mon.-Fri. The price is reduced to 34 CFP per min. between 6pm-6am Mon.-Fri., and the 34 CFP per min. rate applies day and night on weekends and holidays. These rates include taxes.

Calling from Hotels

Whether you dial direct from your hotel room or go through the hotel switchboard, the surcharge can often double the cost of your international call.

Cellular or Mobile Phones

If you want to bring your own cell phone with you when you visit French Polynesia, make sure that it is an unblocked phone that can operate on a 900-megahertz system. If you have a Global System for Mobiles (GSM) phone you should buy a prepaid SIM card for French Polynesia. (Cellular Abroad in Santa Monica, CA., *Tel. 800/287-3020; www.cellularabroad.com* has these).

Or you can wait until you get to Tahiti and have a new Vini chip inserted in your cell phone at a post office or at one of the many shops that sell Vini phones. (Vini is the name of a small finch that lives in these islands and it is also the name used by the Tikiphone department of the telephone company). Save your original chip to put back in once you are on your way home. You will also be given a local phone number. This number can be reached from overseas by dialing 011+689+your 6-digit mobile phone number. This phone number is valid for 180 days unless you replace it with your original chip.

The cost of this prepaid Vinicard is 4.400 CFP, which gives you a calling credit of 30 min. of local calls. The amount of credit for international calls depends on the destination and duration of the call. If you want to continue the service, make sure you buy a replacement card before the credit is used up. The recharge cards cost 500 CFP for 7 min., 1.000 CFP for 14 min., and 3.000 CFP for 42 min., valid for 15, 30, and 60 days, respectively.

You will also have voice mail service when you buy the Vini card. Be sure you specify that you want an English-speaking version; so that you will understand when she tells you how much credit you have left. Because your credit can be used up very quickly, it is best if you buy a phone card (*télécarte*) for long conversations. If you're on a yacht or somewhere else where a phone isn't available, then quickly call your family and friends on your cell phone and ask them to call you back.

For further information, contact the Tikiphone Vini Network at *www.opt.pf,* or *www.vini.pf.* Details of how to use the Vinicard and prices for international visitors are listed in English, and you can also check their map of network coverage. Once you arrive you can also get information at the Tikiphone Customer Service in Papeete in the OPT (*Office Postes Télécommunications*) building at the Pont de l'Est, *Tel. 689/48.13.13; Fax 689/48.72.48; www.vini.pf.* The Travel Insider, *www.thetravelinsider.info,* is also a good source for understanding the intricacies of preparing your cell phone for a trip to Tahiti.

Other options are to rent a cell phone in the US from InTouch USA, *Tel. 800/872-7626; www.intouch-global.com,* or from RoadPost, *Tel. 888/290-1606 or 905/272-5665; www.roadpost.com.* In Tahiti you can buy a cell phone for 9.900 CFP or you can pay up to 70.000 CFP for a more deluxe model.

TELEVISION

Télé Polynésie and **Tempo** are 2 free channels televised by Radio Television Française d'Outre-Mer, RFO Tahiti, the French government-owned station. **Tahiti Nui Satellite** (TNS) provides 22 channels of cable service, including CNN and TCM in English, **Tahiti Nui Television** (TNTV), with local news and other programs in French and Tahitian, and **Canal+**, another cable service. Most hotels in the Society Islands have access to the TNS satellite programs, especially CNN, which is the version made for the Asia-Pacific region rather than the United States programs you are used to seeing.

TIME

The island of Tahiti, as well as all the rest of the Society Islands, the Tuamotu Archipelago and the Austral Islands, is **10 hours behind Greenwich Mean Time.** These islands are in the same time zone as Hawaii, and are 2 hours behind US Pacific Standard Time and 5 hours behind US Eastern Standard Time. You'll add one-hour difference in time between Tahiti and the US when daylight saving time is in effect in the US. This means that between the first Sunday in April and the last Sunday in October, when it is noon in Tahiti, it is 6pm in New York and 3pm in Los Angeles; and between the last Sunday in October and the first Sunday in

April, when it is noon in Tahiti, it is 5pm in New York and 2pm in Los Angeles.

The Gambier Islands, which form the most eastern archipelago in the territory, are an hour ahead of the rest of French Polynesia, and a half-hour ahead of the Marquesas Islands, which are a half-hour ahead of the Tuamotus, Societies and Australs. Therefore, when it is noon in Tahiti, it is 12:30pm in the Marquesas and 1pm in the Gambier Islands.

French Polynesia is east of the International Date Line, with the same date as the US. These islands are one day behind Tonga, Fiji, New Zealand and Australia. Tahiti is 20 hours behind Australian Eastern Standard Time.

TIPPING

The brochures published by the Tahiti Tourist office state that tipping is not expected in Tahiti and Her Islands. In tour guides and tour operator brochures you will read that tipping is considered contrary to the Polynesian custom of hospitality, or that a Tahitian will be offended if you try to tip them.

At this writing (Jan. 2008) it is still true that tipping is not the official custom here, but that may change very soon if the Assembly of French Polynesia approves an obligatory 4% service charge to be paid by consumers. Tahiti's economic, social and cultural council (CESC) has proposed adding 4% to all customer bills in restaurants, snacks, bars, cafés, hotels, family pensions, etc. The Ministry of Tourism also agrees that it is time to get away from this "taboo" that was invented. This will probably be one of the priority issues to decide on when a new government is elected in Feb. This service charge will be a means of increasing the salaries of hotel and restaurant employees, including those who have no direct contact with the public.

Most of the international class hotels and some restaurants in the tourist islands already have a printed form that includes a place to add tips when you sign to your room or pay your bill. At the bottom of the menu in some restaurants you'll occasionally see a notice that tips are appreciated. There may also be a "Tips Accepted" sign posted in some obvious place inside the restaurant.

I have been tipping wait staff, bellmen and even polite and helpful taxi drivers for years. If you want to tip someone, you will make him or her happy and you'll feel good about it yourself, because you are probably accustomed to tipping back home.

WEIGHTS & MEASURES

French Polynesia is on the metric system, but for your convenience, I have converted kilometers to miles, meters to feet, kilos to pounds, liters to gallons, and Celsius to Fahrenheit, where appropriate. To facilitate your own conversions, here are the equations:

1 meter = 3.28 feet
1 meter = 1.09 yards

1 foot = 0.30 meters
1 yard = 0.91 meters

1 square meter = 10.7639 square feet 1 square foot = 0.09 square meter
1 square meter = 1,1960 square yards 1 square yard = .08 square meter
1 hectare = 2.4710 acres 1 acre = .04 hectares
1 kilometer = .62 miles 1 mile = 1.61 kilometers
1 liter = 1.06 quarts 1 quart = 0.95 liters
4 liters = 1.06 gallons 1 gallon = 3.79 liters
1 kilogram = 2.20 pounds 1 pound = 0.45 kilograms

Temperature Guide

0° Celsius = 32° Fahrenheit =	Freezing point of water
10° Celsius = 50° Fahrenheit =	Winter in the Austral Islands
20° Celsius = 68° Fahrenheit =	Comfortable for you, chilly for some of Tahiti's residents
30° Celsius = 86° Fahrenheit =	Quite warm-almost hot
37° Celsius = 98.6 Fahrenheit =	Normal body temperature
40° Celsius = 104° Fahrenheit =	Heat wave conditions
100° Celsius = 212° Fahrenheit =	Boiling point of water

8. Calendar of Events

For further information and specific dates of programmed events in this chapter, you can contact the following organizations. For sporting events on Moorea, *moorea@sjs.pf; www.sjs.pf; or www.mooreaevents.org.* For surf events; *fedesurf@mail.pf; www.surf.pf.* For other events contact: *com@heivanui.pf.* You can also contact the Tahiti Tourist Bureau in Tahiti, *Tel. 689/50.57.00*; or Los Angeles, *Tel. 310/414-8484.*

January
Tahiti "Tere Fa'ati". This celebration is held every other year on the first Sunday of the New Year. Following a tradition in Tahiti you will ride around the island in a flower decorated *le truck,* complete with a band of musicians playing the guitar, ukulele and "gut-bucket" bass, and singing "kaina" style Tahitian songs, while you rattle 2 spoons in a beer bottle and sing along until you're hoarse. There are normally about 10 *le trucks* and 300 people on this tour and you stop at several of the most beautiful natural sites to visit waterfalls, public gardens, parks and beaches, with a traditional Tahitian feast served on the beach in Tautira. This 12-hr. tour ends on the beach at Point Venus, with the election of a King and Queen and a fire dance is performed against the golden rays of the setting sun.

February
Chinese New Year. Tahiti's Chinese community welcomes in the New Year of the Chinese horoscope, which takes place the end of Jan. or the first part of Feb. Celebrations include parades, the Dance of the Lion and Dragon, and open house on Cultural Day at the Chinese temple in the Mamao suburb of Papeete. There are traditional dances, martial arts demonstrations, food tasting, calligraphy, paintings and fortune telling. A Grand Ball with dinner and entertainment is also a highlight of this celebration. The colorful events end two weeks later with a Parade of Lanterns and a fireworks show over Papeete harbor. The Year of the Rat began on Feb. 7, 2008.
Tahiti Nui Marathon on Moorea. A 42.195 km. scenic marathon is held each year on the island of Moorea on the second Sat. of Feb., with some 700 runners participating. A 21 km. Half-Marathon and a 6 km. Fun Run are also held in conjunction with the international event. First aid, refreshment and sponge stations are located every 2.5 km. and Tahitian music along the route helps to keep the pace lively. A Pasta Party and Tahitian Feast with a dance show are organized each year as part of the activities. The 20th edition was held on Feb. 9, 2008.

Moorea "Tere Fa'ati". This island tour around Moorea by "le truck" is similar to the circle island tour organized in Tahiti at the beginning of Jan., complete with Tahitian musicians, singers and dancers. The Moorea outing takes place in mid-Feb. on the Sun. following the Moorea Marathon. The tour stops at all the best sights and sites on the island.

March

Missionaries Day. Mar. 5 is a public holiday each year to commemorate the arrival of the first English Protestant Missionaries on Mar. 5, 1797. Reenactment ceremonies are held in the Evangelical churches and at some of the stadiums in the Society Islands and special celebrations are sometimes held in the Austral Islands.

National Women's Day. The women's associations from throughout French Polynesia meet in Papeete on Mar. 8 to discuss the Women's Condition. Songs, dances and skits punctuate these well-attended colorful meetings.

Raiatea International Billfish Tournament (RIBT) is held every year during Mar. The 2008 edition took place Mar. 3-10 in the Leeward Islands. Blue marlins weighing more than 500 kilos (1,010 pounds) have been caught by Polynesian fishermen ever since Zane Grey discovered the Tahitian waters in the 1930s. The best-recorded catch so far was the 707 kilo (1,560-pound) blue marlin caught by the Bonnet/Tavanae team in 1986. For information contact Dominique Goche at *Tel. 689/60.05.45; raiateabillfish@mail.pf; www.worldbillfishseries.com,* or *www.fishwbs.com.*

April

Air Tahiti Nui Von Zipper Surfing Trials. This is a qualifying surf competition in Teahupoo on Tahiti Iti, prior to the famous Billabong Pro that brings together foreign and local surfing pros. This takes place April 20-26, 2008.

May

Billabong Tahiti Pro. Each year during the month of May the top 44 professional surfers in the world face the impressive rollers offshore Teahupoo on Tahiti-Iti. This event is part of the World Cup Tournament (WCT) of international surfing. Surfers and spectators enjoy the friendliness, warmth and local color provided by the residents of Teahupoo, the little village at the end of the road on the Tahiti-Iti peninsula, closest to the surfing action. May 8-18 is the date set for 2008. Contact *www.billabong.com* for dates of future surfing competitions.

Tahiti Pearl Regatta. This international yachting regatta is held in the Leeward Islands, starting from Raiatea and sailing to Taha'a and Bora Bora. Trophies for each leg are awarded to the winners of various categories and each day ends with a Polynesian dinner and a dance show. Activities include diving, snorkeling, Polynesian games, outrigger canoes and Hobie cats. Participants usually fly to Tahiti and charter yachts in Raiatea. The 5th edition of the Tahiti Pearl Regatta is set for May 8-12, 2008, and the international press has been invited.

"Me" is celebrated during the month of May in each Maohi Protestant (Evangelical) parish throughout the islands. This religious festival is also a fundraising event and the money collected not only finances the churches' projects but is also given as aid to the underprivileged. At the end of the ceremony a huge feast is prepared by the church members to thank everyone for their generosity.

Miss Dragon is elected in Tahiti each year in May or June. The winner then represents Tahiti's Chinese community in the Miss Asia Pacific beauty pageant.

Raid Moorea. This event is divided into individual and team categories. Competitors ride a mountain bike for 20 km., run for 8 km. in the mountains and paddle a kayak for 5 km. The 5th edition of this race is May 25, 2008.

Commemoration of the Arrival of the *Bounty*. This re-enactment ceremony takes places every two years on the island of Tubuai, where Fletcher Christian and the *Bounty* mutineers tried to settle in 1789.

Arii Mata Tini Race. Individual outrigger canoe races are held in the lagoon of Rangiroa and other atolls in the Tuamotu Archipelago. This event takes place on May 31, 2008.

Festivities of the Pleiades "Matarii I Raro"
This is a cultural commemoration for the end of the cycle of abundance, and the beginning of the dry period when the land stops producing. The program is set for May 18, 2008, when the star group Pleiades disappears from sight for six months.

June

Tama Hiti Rau. Performances by the traditional dance schools are presented during the month of June at Place Vaiete in Papeete at the beginning of the Heiva i Tahiti Festival.

Annual Tahiti International Pro/Am Golf Open. This popular event is sponsored by the Australasia Pro Golf Association Tour (PGAT) and it attracts golfers from many parts of the world, who compete for the cash prizes at the Olivier Breaud International Golf Course in Atimaono, on Tahiti's south coast of Papara. Contact *www.pgatour.com*.

Tahiti-Moorea Sailing Rendez-Vous. This is an annual sailing rally from the island of Tahiti (Marina Taina) to the island of Moorea (Vaiare Bay), organized by Tahiti Tourisme. This voyage is meant to welcome and create a gathering of charter boat passengers, crews of the Transpacific race stopping over in French Polynesia, sailing fans from the islands, the local population, as well as marine sport and tourism professionals. It takes place June 27-28, 2008.

Heemoana Outrigger Canoe Race. A 56 km. outrigger canoe race between the ocean passes of Teahupoo (Hava'e) and Punaauia (Taapuna), featuring local athletes and competitors for other Pacific countries.

Miss Tahiti Contest. Lovely and talented young *vahines* compete for the coveted title of Miss Tahiti during the first part of the month. The winner then goes to Paris to vie for the title of Miss France in December.

Anniversary of Internal Autonomy Day with a Hiva Vaevae Parade in Papeete. If an autonomist government is in power at the time, then on June 29 the biggest folkloric parade of the year is held along Blvd. Pomare in downtown Papeete. This celebration is to commemorate the anniversary of a French parliamentary statue that was adopted in 1984, giving French Polynesia increased self-governing powers. In Tahiti you will see all the dance groups, youth groups, church groups, sports groups and special interest groups parading on foot, roller blades, bicycles, motorcycles, horses, in pirogues, cars and trucks and aboard decorated floats.

July

Heiva i Tahiti. The Heiva Festival is the biggest event of the year. It begins in late June and continues for almost a month. There are daily activities, but the main events are scheduled at Place To'ata for Thurs.-Sun. each week, as well as in some of the other communes around the island. In addition to traditional Polynesian sports such as stone lifting, fruit carrier races, copra preparation and javelin throwing, Tahiti's competitions also include outrigger sailing canoe races, bicycle races and a beer race of restaurant and bar waiters. Outrigger paddle canoe races are held inside the lagoon and in the open ocean. The program includes a fire walking ceremony, song and dance competitions and all-night balls. Carnival type rides and fairground booths called *baraques* are set up in two locations, where the kids of all ages can munch popcorn and cotton candy and jump on the Ferris wheel, merry-go-round and other thrilling rides.

Heiva of the Artisans. The Rima'i Crafts Festival is a star attraction during the Heiva activities in Tahiti, with dozens of exhibits of handcrafts from all the island groups. Live concerts, song and dance competitions, Polynesian meals and various games accompany daily demonstrations of traditional arts and crafts. The Crafts Festival is a 3-week event and includes 100 or more arts and crafts stands.

Heiva Festivals on all the Islands. The schedules vary, but these festivals usually begin during the month of July. Each island has traditional sports competitions, including fruit carriers' races, javelin throwing, copra chopping contests and outrigger canoe races, arts and crafts stands and games for children. The singing and dancing contests are the highlight of each festival, which usually lasts from 4-6 weeks. The most popular outer island festivals take place on Bora Bora, Raiatea, Taha'a and Huahine.

French Bastille Day Parade. France's National Holiday of July 14th is celebrated throughout French Polynesia with parades, parties and all night balls. Large hotels also organize special evenings for this event. A military parade is staged on Blvd. Pomare along the Papeete waterfront, followed by a champagne party at the residence of the French High Commissioner. Horse races and bicycle races are usually scheduled for that afternoon.

Te Aito Va'a. Almost 300 individual outrigger canoe racers compete in this 20-km. course in Tahiti's Matavai Bay, which is from mid to late July. The Aito

(Polynesian warrior) winners of this race qualify to compete in the Super Aito competitions.

August

Mini Heiva Festivals. The Intercontinental Tahiti Resort and Le Méridien invite the winners of the Heiva i Tahiti song and dance competitions to perform during a Mini Heiva Festival that is held over a period of 3 or more evenings. Gastronomic feasts are followed by first class entertainment.

Super Aito Individual Outrigger Canoe Channel Race. Along with the local paddlers who qualify for this most important individual va'a competition, foreign paddlers are invited to join the 4-leg race that is held over a 4-day period in mid-Aug. The first 3 legs take place in Tahiti and the 4th leg is a distance of 21.5 km. (13.3 mi.) starting at Moorea's Temae Beach and ending at Place To'ata in Tahiti. Women's competitions are also held. The winners receive cash prizes.

Tahiti Agricultural Fair. Farmers from all 5 archipelagoes of the territory gather in Tahiti for this big event, which is held in late Aug. or early Sept. Along with stands of fruits, vegetables and flowers, there are displays of arts and crafts, Tahiti cultured pearls and other local products, as well as *ahima'a* (earth ovens) with Polynesian food.

September

World Tourism Day. All the tourist islands participate in this annual celebration in honor of our visitors. World Tourism Day is Sept. 27, and that entire week is filled with traditional singing and dancing shows, arts and crafts exhibits, and Polynesian bands playing music in the streets while hostesses distribute flowers to tourists. The airports, hotels, tourist offices, banks and other offices are decorated with flowers for the occasion.

Raid Painapo. This annual event is held on the island of Moorea, with teams of 3 making a trail run of 25 km. across the Opunohu Valley, where pineapple (painapo) plantations slope down the mountainside. The 7th edition will be held on Sept. 21, 2008.

Taapuna Master Surfing Competition. The 2008 6-day competition for amateur surfers will take place Sept. 11-27, 2008 at the Taapuna Pass (Punaauia), featuring several disciplines and categories.

Taapuna Pro/Am Surfing Competition. Surf competition in the Taapuna Pass with the best amateur and professional surfers and body-boarders. The 6th edition will be held Sept. 29-Oct. 3, 2008.

October

Hawaiki Nui Va'a. This is a 4-day outrigger canoe race between the Leeward Islands of Huahine, Raiatea, Taha'a and Bora Bora, with more than 100 canoes and hundreds of paddlers. This is the ultimate va'a competition, which is held each year

in Oct. The dates for 2008 are Oct.29-31. Contact: *ftvaa@ifrance.com; www.hawaikinuivaa.pf.*
Rotui's Tour. A 15 km. foot race around Moorea's Mount Rotui.

November

All Saints Day. The graves in the cemeteries and in the yards of private homes are weeded and cleaned in preparation for this annual event. Flower stands are set up all around the island of Tahiti on this public holiday, which takes place on Nov. 1, when families decorate the graves with dozens of fresh and plastic flowers. That night the cemeteries are lighted with candles as the families sing hymns and recite prayers for their departed loved ones.

Tattoonesia. This is a 4-day gathering of tattoo artists from all the archipelagoes of Tahiti and Her Islands, as well as overseas participants. Contests are held in Tahiti for the best tribal tattoos and the best modern designs. This event is usually held in the early part of Nov. Contact: *info@tahitievent.com; www.eventseye.com.*

Festivities of the Pleiades "Matari'i I Nia". This cultural celebration has become an annual event that lasts for a month in Tahiti, from mid-Nov. to mid-Dec. The highlight of the festivities takes place on Nov. 20, when the star group Pleiades reappears in the sky, marking the return of the season of abundance, when the produce of the earth and sea abound. Cultural re-enactments, songs and dances are performed during this month of welcoming.

December

Tiare Tahiti Days. Tahiti's national flower, the fragrant white Tiare Tahiti (*gardenia taitensis*), is honored during this 3-day annual event that usually takes place during the first week of Dec. On the major tourist islands the airports, hotels, some restaurants, tourist offices, post offices and banks are decorated with garlands of Tiare Tahiti blossoms, and Tiare Tahiti flowers are presented to tourists on the streets. A public ball is also held to pay tribute to this lovely flower.

Rotui Green Triathlon. The 6th edition of this event will be held on Moorea on Dec. 30, when athletes will swim 400 m. or 800 m., cycle 8 or 20 km., and run 4 or 6 km., according to their category.

Christmas in Tahiti. Santa Claus or "Papa Noel" arrives in Tahiti by outrigger canoe, jet ski, helicopter or horse, accompanied by Polynesian musicians as he distributes candies to the children in Papeete. The streets and city halls of each commune are decorated and Christmas villages in Papeete and Faa'a have rides and games for the children. The major hotels in the tourist islands and several restaurants offer special menus and entertainment on Christmas Eve and Christmas Day, which also include roast turkey with chestnut dressing. And the perfect French wine to accompany the meal, of course!

9. Taking the Kids

Tahiti and Her Islands are a haven for the young! So bring your kids and let them enjoy the attention they'll receive from the friendly Polynesians, who adore babies and little children. If they're still young enough to be picked up easily, that will be even more fun for the child and the Tahitians, who love to kiss and hug little people, little puppies and anything that is still a baby. When they get older and bigger, that's another story for the animals and local kids, but the Tahitians will still treat visiting children with genuine warmth and patience.

International airline companies and Air Tahiti give preferential seating to families traveling with children. Kids generally pay only half the adult fare on international airline routings. **Air Tahiti gives at least a 50% discount to children between 2-11 years** and the fare for babies less than 2 years is 10% of the adult fare. Most of the hotels, hostels, guest houses and pensions will let the kids younger than 11-12 years stay for free if sharing a room with their parents, or they only charge for an extra bed.

Your travel agent can make all the reservations for you, securing spacious bulkhead seats on airlines and determining which flights are least crowded. They can also seek out the best deals on lodging and meals.

When traveling with children of any age, make sure their vaccinations are up to date and bring their health records and any special medications they made need. In the event of an emergency, there are medical facilities on all the islands. **Mamao Hospital in Tahiti has a modern pediatric department.** Make sure that your repatriation insurance also covers your child.

Don't show up hungry at the airport. Feed yourself and all the family before you go so that you are not waiting in line at the limited number of airport eateries. Also, bring food for you and your family to eat on the plane should you be stuck on the tarmac.

Traveling with Babies

Hopefully, you'll be at least two people to bring a baby on a long airplane flight to Tahiti. Bring a suitcase filled with baby supplies, including a sufficient supply of disposable diapers, food, light clothes that cover the whole body, a sun hat, favorite toys, Q-Tips, baby wipes, a first aid kit with sun block, mosquito repellent, baby aspirin, thermometer and a treatment for diarrhea. The supermarkets and small *magasin* stores carry fresh or powdered whole milk, bottled mineral water, dry cereals that must be cooked, canned fruits and jars of baby food, but you'll pay much more for these items in Tahiti than you will back home. Bring a stroller with sunshade or cloth carrier for your baby, or a car seat-sleeper combination. Only a few of the hotels can provide cribs and high chairs for babies.

Toddlers & Little Tykes

Along with the shorts, T-shirts, sweater, waterproof shoes and sun hat you pack for your small children, you should also include some of their favorite snacks, books and toys. If they're big enough to snorkel, pack their own snorkel gear, plus a bucket and shovel and inflatable beach ball. In their first-aid kit be sure to include some preventive drops for swimmer's ear. Cleanse and treat any minor cuts or abrasions immediately to prevent staph infection. Make sure they're protected from the hot tropical sun and mosquitoes and that they drink a sufficient amount of water throughout the day.

Juniors & Adolescents

The warm climate, natural setting, aquatic games and lack of poisonous creatures make Tahiti and Her Islands a paradise for children of all ages. Many of the hotels have swimming pools and beach activities, such as outrigger paddle canoes, pedal boats and windsurf boards. Swimming or playing in the reef-protected lagoon waters is also relatively safe, as long as you keep an eye on the little ones, because there are no lifeguards. Children enjoy lagoon excursions, picnics on the *motu*, feeding the fish, rays and sharks, sailing and other water activities. Some of the scuba diving centers will accept divers as young as four years. Some of the hotels and guesthouses provide bicycles for their guests, or you can rent them on most of the islands.

McDonald's is located in downtown Papeete and there is another outlet next to the Marina Taina in Punaauia, which has a pool and playground equipment for children. A new McDonald's outlet will open in mid-2008 in the Arue commune of Tahiti, and yet another one is planned for Taravao on the isthmus of Tahiti Nui and Tahiti Iti. On several of the islands you'll find hamburgers, sandwiches, pizzas, tacos, pancakes and crêpes. All the food stores carry some American snacks and good ice cream. Most of the hotels have children's menus and give special discount rates for buffets and Tahitian feasts for children under 12 years of age. The more luxurious hotels have room service, which can be convenient for families, and several of the moderate range hotels and family pensions provide kitchen facilities.

Babysitters

Hotels that welcome children generally have no problem arranging babysitters. If you're staying in a pension or guesthouse, ask your hostess to find a babysitter for you. Make sure they speak some English.

Travel Agents Specializing in Family Travel

RASCALS IN PARADISE, 500 Sansome St., Suite 601, San Francisco, CA 94111, *Tel. 415/921-7000; Fax 415/433-3354; www.rascalsinparadise.com.* They specialize in customized vacations for parents and/or grandparents who want to travel with their children or grandchildren. Their South Pacific tours for families with kids can include accommodations at a carefully selected resort, so that you can relax and enjoy some "down time" with the little ones. After your trip you can post your photos and comments online at: *kids@rascalsinparadise.com*.

CROSSROADS TRAVEL ADVISORS LLC, *Tel. 800/322-0224; 804/794-7700; www.crttravel.com.* This full service travel company is located in Richmond, VA. Owner Uschi Helfrich has a special interest in family travel. She visits Tahiti and Her Islands several times a year to gather information that helps in organizing the best programs for her clients, and she knows which resort hotels are the most "kid friendly."

Check the website for **Tahiti Tourism North America,** *www.gototahiti.com.* They list the travel agents and tour operators who promote Family Vacation Deals. These include: **Tahiti Legends** "Kids Fly Free–Moorea Family Special" from $4,170; **Pacific Holidays** "Tahiti Family Vacations" from $4,387; **Springboard Vacations** "Cool Capers for Kids" from $9,480, **Sunspots International** "French Polynesia Family Vacation Tahiti and Moorea" from $9,115; and **Swain Tahiti Tours** has a choice of "Family Getaway", "Family Adventure;" and "Family Vacation" packages, from $6,315-$22,890. In some of these programs children under 15 stay free at the hotel resorts, and the "Kids Fly Free" package with Tahiti Legends also includes 1 free child airfare, free kid's menu and free Dolphin program at the Intercontinental Moorea Resort & Spa.

Special Family Activities at Hotels

INTERCONTINENTAL MOOREA RESORT & SPA . The Moorea Dolphin Center is located at the Intercontinental Moorea Resort & Spa. This is a big attraction for children, who delight in their interactive sessions with the trained bottlenose dolphins that live inside a lagoon park. There are programs designed for children in different age groups. The whole family will also enjoy a visit to the Sea Turtle Care Center and Nursery on the IC Moorea Resort property.

LE MÉRIDIEN BORA BORA. This family friendly resort has added a fully equipped children's playground. They provide small snorkeling gear for kids from 2 years old, small cha-cha sailboats and a small windsurf board that an 8-year old can handle. An exclusive treat for guests of all ages at Le Méridien is to visit the turtle nursery on the hotel property and watch dozens of baby sea turtles being fed each morning. You can even swim with the turtles inside the clear waters of a *hoa* channel that flows from the ocean into the protected lagoon. The turtle eggs are hatched on the hotel's beach and the turtles are released from the nursery into the ocean a year later, then tracked by satellite as part of an environmental program. You can even become a godparent to one of the turtles and receive news of its progress. A special Le Méridien Tahiti family package is advertised on their website, which includes a 15% discount off the 2nd room, a free breakfast buffet for parents, and 50% off the meals for children under 12 years.

PEARL RESORTS. The Pearl Resorts are especially attentive to the needs of children, providing cribs, rollaway beds and baby-sitting services in all their hotels. The Pearl Resorts in Moorea, Tahaa, Bora Bora, Manihi and Tikehau also provide a welcome basket of candies, plus beach toys (rake, spade, bucket) for the 3-8 year olds, and board games for the 8-12 year olds. They have life jackets and snorkeling gear for children, DVD with cartoons for kids, special children's menus or child's portions of food. In Manihi and Tikehau children are also given drawing kits at the dining table. At the Bora Bora Pearl Beach Resort and at Le Taha'a Island Resort & Spa, there are bathroom amenities for kids, including slippers and bathrobe. Le Taha'a also offers ukulele, palm frond weaving and Tahitian dance classes for their young guests. The Bora Bora Pearl Beach Resort and Manihi Pearl Resort have a mini-golf course, and there is even a movie theatre at the Pearl Resort in Bora Bora.

In all the Pearl Resorts, the accommodations, transfers and meals (except beverages) are free of charge for children less than 3 years old if they are sharing a room with parents. For children less than 15 years old the accommodation is free of charge if they are sharing a room with parents, and they pay 50% on meals and transfers, except for helicopter flights.

ST REGIS RESORT BORA BORA CREATIVITY CLUB. St. Regis Resort, Bora Bora has a Kids Creativity Club, with facilities built especially for their littlest guests. These include a secluded beach and an indoor play area for children between 5-12 years of age. Activities include coconut painting, making flower leis, pandanus weaving, Tahitian dancing, and scavenger hunts.

Kids can also participate in the complimentary Resort activities, such as swimming with the marine life in the protected lagoonarium, snorkeling (free equipment), paddling a kayak or outrigger canoe, playing tennis (complimentary equipment), riding an all terrain bike on the Resort's private island, building sand castles, and joining a crab hunt and race. They can also go Hobie cat sailing, windsurfing and paddle boating.

With a responsible adult, children can participate in paid activities such as Aqua Safari, a Bora Bora lagoon cruise, deep sea fishing, jeep safari, jet ski lagoon circle, Lagoonarium, motu picnic, motu private barbecue, submarine, *Taravana* sailing, water-skiing and wakeboarding.

For guests with children the St. Regis Resort provides cribs and child-sized bathrobes in the rooms, and in the restaurants there are high chairs and special dishes for children. A selection of children-friendly movies and in-room toys are at your disposal by simply calling your St. Regis Butler.

With 24 hour's notice, they can arrange reliable babysitting services for your little ones. A fee applies to babysitting, and this service is available only for children one year old and over.

House, Boat & Car Packages

Another good idea for family travel in Tahiti and Her Islands is to rent a self-contained house or villa where you can do your own cooking. I have listed several lodgings on most of the islands that include kitchen facilities. Have a look at the *Huahine* chapter and see the choices for renting a villa with a boat and car included in the package price. Some of the facilities even include a washing machine on the premises.

10. Food & Drink

I've listened to big beefy American men comparing prices while standing in a hotel swimming pool beside Moorea's Cook's Bay, totally ignoring the incredible beauty of the mountains and lagoon, as they talked about how they managed to cut costs on their trip to Moorea. One of them bragged that he had collected free packages of coffee, tea, sugar, cream, mustard, ketchup, mayonnaise, crackers and other condiments from the fast food outlets in his town, and had brought them along.

Others described all the snacks, soft drinks and alcohol they had packed into a cooler for the trip. These people were not eating in the hotel or nearby restaurants. They spent their week surviving on processed snack foods they brought with them, plus the crusty French *baguette* bread, luncheon meats, cheese and crackers bought at the nearest food store. Although the hotel had (it is now closed) a no-food-in-the-room policy, it was usually ignored, and some of the guests were unwilling to spend 200 CFP for a cup of coffee in the hotel restaurant.

If you decide to travel on a very tight budget, try not to let the high prices occupy so much of your attention that you cannot even enjoy these magnificent islands. You may want to have a look in the larger supermarkets in Tahiti, where there are deli counters with a varied selection of prepared foods. The smaller *magasins* in Tahiti and the outer islands sell tasty take-away meals of rice with chicken, meat or fish, and containers of *poisson cru* for about 700-800 CFP. The mobile diners, *les roulottes*, are found in all the Society Islands, where you can have a good meal for about 1.200 CFP. There are also small, inexpensive restaurant/snacks, which are listed under *Where to Eat* for each island.

You can buy a soft drink for 135 CFP in the supermarket and you'll pay around 180-200 CFP at a few of the *roulottes* and snack bars, but this same canned drink will cost you up to 500 CFP in a hotel bar. Tahiti's favorite locally brewed beer is Hinano, which sells for 170-190 CFP for a 33 cl. can in grocery stores, and from 400-600 CFP in restaurants and bars. Some restaurants serve *vin ordinaire* (table wine) by the carafe, and an acceptable quality of Bordeaux can be purchased at the grocery stores for around 1.300-1.500 CFP a bottle.

For most of us, one of the greatest pleasures of traveling to a foreign country is to sample the local cuisine. If your budget allows a few meals in a restaurant while you're visiting Tahiti, Moorea, Bora Bora or any of the other islands in French Polynesia, then chances are you will have a superb meal.

La Nouvelle Cuisine Tahitienne

The hotels and restaurants in Tahiti have earned a reputation among gourmet

ORDERING FROM A FRENCH MENU

Helpful hints in ordering from a French menu should include a translation of how you want your steak cooked.

- **Bleu** = rare
- **Saignant** = medium-rare
- **à Point** = medium
- **Bien Cuit** = well done.

If you have the audacity to order a steak bien cuit, however, most French chefs will send it out to you when it is about half-cooked.

visitors for serving choice cuisine. The chefs have united the flavors of Europe and the Orient, spiked with a fresh tropical island accent. Whether he came from France, Switzerland, Italy, South America or Asia, each newcomer brought his little sprig of thyme, his chili pepper, soybean or ginger, perhaps to ward off the effects of home sickness in a foreign land.

Culinary choices feature French *haute cuisine*, 7-course Imperial dinners from the provinces of China, Vietnamese *nems*, Italian pasta, Algerian *couscous*, Spanish *paella*, spicy West Indian specialties and Alsatian *choucroute*. These imaginative and creative chefs have also introduced a *nouvelle cuisine Tahitienne* that is a combination of the traditional recipes of their own home countries and the fresh bounty of the Polynesian waters and fruit orchards. Dishes may include fresh local snapper infused with vanilla sauce, a lagoon *bouillabaisse*, reef clams in garlic butter, sautéed crab with ginger, *varo* with champagne and cream, roast duck with papaya or chicken drumsticks with *fafa* and taro.

To accompany these memorable meals are fine French wines and champagnes, locally brewed beer, or a selection of imported beers and wines. Most of the bars bill themselves as a "Bar Americaine" and serve mixed cocktails. Freshly squeezed orange, grapefruit or pineapple juices are sometimes available, or you will be served fruit juices from the cartons of the Moorea Fruit Juice Factory and Distillery. Perrier and a wide variety of boutique carbonated waters are stocked, as well as the most popular soda pops, sometimes including carbonated diet drinks. Bottled waters from Tahiti and France are also served, and can cost as much as 850 CFP for a bottle of sparkling water such as San Benedetto, while in the supermarkets it is only 155 CFP.

Snack Bars, Fast Food, Salons de Thè & Patisseries

You'll find an abundance of small restaurants in Tahiti and Her Islands that are advertised as Snacks or Restaurant/Snacks. Most of these places are clean and serve daily specials of local style home cooking. The food is usually delicious and inexpensive. The choices often include *poisson cru* with coconut milk, beef or lamb stew, an assortment of curry dishes, fresh lagoon fish, chicken and vegetables, prawns in garlic sauce, pork and taro, chow mein, or *ma'a tinito haricots rouge*, which is a Chinese dish of red beans, macaroni, pork or chicken, Chinese vermicelli noodles and a few more good things.

Fast foods have definitely arrived on the scene in Tahiti, with international and local style hamburger stands popping up all over the island. McDonald's has a prime site in downtown Papeete. There is also a McDonald's adjacent to Marina Taina in Punaauia on Tahiti's west coast, which replaced a Kentucky Fried Chicken site that closed soon after opening. A new McDonald's in Arue is planned to open in mid-2008, and another McDonald's is on the drawing board for Taravao. The McDonald's counter at the Tahiti-Faa'a Airport sells only muffins, soft drinks and ice cream. These days you hardly have to pause at all in your shopping to have a bite to eat. You can walk up to a sidewalk food stand and order a *casse-croûte*, a ham and cheese *croissant*, a small pizza or a *panini* sandwich. Or you can beat the heat of the Papeete streets while enjoying some of the world's best ice cream.

Salons de thè serve a variety of teas and *infusions*, as well as *espressos* and vanilla flavored coffee from Pacific plantations. *Patisseries* provide people watching in air-conditioned comfort while nibbling on your choice of flaky pastries.

Les Roulottes

Les roulottes (not roulettes) are mobile diners (roach coaches) that set up shop each evening near the cruise ship dock at Place Vaiete on the Papeete waterfront. They serve hot meals until the wee hours of the morning. These colorful food vans provide good, fast food at reasonable prices, as well as a barstool or a table with chairs, where you can sit and watch the waterfront scene of Papeete-by-night.

You can order barbecue steaks, chicken and *brochettes* (shish kabob), served with French fries, *poisson cru*, or *salade russe*, which is potato salad with beets. Specialty diners serve pizza cooked in a wood-burning stove, *couscous*, grilled fish and chips, Tahitian food, barbecue veal and freshly wokked hot delicacies from the provinces of China. Your dinner can be a veritable moveable feast, with a tempting choice of *crêpes* for dessert. No alcohol is served here, but the bars and nightclubs are just across the street.

Place Vaiete has been modernized and is now an attractive, well-lit and popular gathering place at night because of the 30 roulottes that rent space here and also because of the free music concerts frequently presented in the music gazebo. In addition to public restrooms there is also a special place where the *roulotte* owners can wash dishes and pots and pans. These facilities and all of Place Vaiete are kept clean at all times by a special group of women who are government employees.

Tahitian Feasts

Several hotels and individually owned restaurants in Tahiti and the other tourist islands feature regular Tahitian feasts. The *tamaara'a* (tah-mah-AH-rah-ah) is Tahiti's equivalent to the luau served in Hawaii, only much more authentic. This feast features *ma'a Tahiti* (MAH-ah), foods that are cooked for several hours in an underground *ahima'a* (ah-HEE-mah-ah) oven. These usually include roast pig, *taro* root, *tarua* root, breadfruit, yams, bananas, *fei* (fey-ee) plantains, *fafa* (taro leaves cooked with chicken and coconut milk that tastes like spinach), and accompanied by coconut sauces. Dessert is a gooey pudding called *po'e*, (PO-eh), which is made with bananas, papaya, pumpkin or other fruits and flavored with coconut milk.

The national dish of Tahiti is *ei'a ota* (ee-ah OH-ta), which the French call *poisson cru*. It is made with small cubes of fresh tuna or bonito fish that have been marinated in lime juice and mixed with chopped tomatoes, grated carrots, thinly sliced onions and cucumbers and coconut milk. It's delicious and even better with a French *baguette*. If you have an adventurous palate then you'll want to try *fafaru*, slices of fish marinated in a stinky sauce that most Tahitians just adore. The traditional manner of eating *ma'a Tahiti* is with your fingers, although forks are normally supplied. Most hotel restaurants also serve a buffet of Continental foods along with the Tahitian dishes. In hotels the *tamaara'a* is normally accompanied by Tahitian music and an hour-long folkloric dance show. The colorfully costumed entertainers perform the traditional dances of Tahiti and the musicians play exciting music on their drums, guitars and ukuleles. The dancers may even invite you to dance the *tamure*.

Meals for the Health-Conscious, Vegetarians, & Vegans

Tahiti is not a paradise for dieters or vegetarians, and even less so for vegans. Most of the restaurants serve rich dishes made with real butter, knowing that few people go out to diet. It is difficult to get a piece of grilled fish or steak without having a generous serving of parsley butter on the top. French chefs are also very

---

DRINKING LAWS

Beer, wine and all other alcoholic beverages are sold in the larger supermarkets and *magasins* in Tahiti and most of the outer islands. The legal age for buying alcohol is 18 years. You can buy beer and booze on Sun. mornings and public holidays before 10am in some of the shops and in others not at all. A new law went into effect in Jan. 2008 stating that no drinking is allowed in public places. This means no drinking in front of the *magasin* stores (a favorite place for groups of Tahitian men), in public parks, on the quays and beaches or beside the road. Offenders will be charged 4.534 CFP, the price of a case of the big bottles of Hinano beer.

partial to crême fraiche, a thickened fresh cream that is served on most meals you order in a French restaurant. Vegetarians probably won't mind this unless they are pure vegans. Lagoon fish and prawns are sometimes served with the heads intact, so if you're squeamish about having your dinner looking at you, order a fish filet or something else. Vegetarians usually have a choice of rice, potatoes, carrots, green beans and salads, plus fresh fruits, French cheeses and tempting desserts. A few restaurants do have vegetarian plates and sandwiches. These are indicated in the *Where to Eat* section of each island.

Health conscious visitors will find whole grains, breads, cereals, crackers, dried legumes, nuts and fruits at La Vie Pacifique, a health food store located on rue Jean Gilbert in the Quartier du Commerce in downtown Papeete. They also carry vitamins, soya milk and vegetable juices. Another source for these items is at La Vie et Sante, *Tel. 50.82.56*, a health food shop operated by the Seventh Day Adventist Church, located on Cours de l'Union Sacrée in Fautaua. Take Avenue Prince Hinoi from downtown Papeete towards Pirae and turn right at the Seventh Day Adventist Church. Most of their products come from France and New Zealand. The large supermarkets in Tahiti, such as Carrefour in Punaauia and Arue, Champion in Papeete and Hyper U in Pirae, carry a line of health food products, including soya milk and tofu. You can buy fresh tofu, as well as fresh fruits, vegetables and herbs, at Le Marché, the public market in the center of Papeete.

On Moorea you can usually find soya milk and tofu at Champion Fare Toa in Afareaitu and at Supermarché Are in Pao Pao. Champion Fare Toa has a special organic (bio) section that contains a small selection of Swedish (Björg) products of whole grain pastas, breads, cereals, galettes, lentils, soup, bouillon, herbal salt and a few bottled or packaged sauces with low sodium and sugar. I even found polenta there, but never have I found corn meal in these islands, except at Supermarché Cecile (years ago) and at the Adventist store. Most of the supermarkets on Moorea carry a very small selection of fresh and dried fruits and nuts, fresh vegetables and supplies for spring rolls. I also checked the supermarkets in Bora Bora and Raiatea and found that they had long life soya milk and tofu on the shelves. Most of the supermarkets have yogurt, including the low sugar and added bifidus Nature yogurt.

If you have lodgings with access to a kitchen, you should have no problems finding enough nutritious food to eat while visiting Tahiti and Her Islands. Otherwise, you'll have to pick and choose carefully from the hotel menu, or have a heart to heart talk with the chef de cuisine.

11. Tahiti

QUEEN OF THE PACIFIC

Polynesian mythology tells of a lovely *vahine* named Terehe, who defied the gods of great Havai'i on the island of Raiatea by swimming in the river during a period of sacred restriction. The angry gods caused the young maiden to be overcome by a feeling of numbness and she sank to the bottom of the river and was swallowed by a giant eel. Terehe's spirit then possessed the eel, who thrashed about, tearing away the earth between Raiatea and Taha'a. The eel's body was magically transformed into a fish, which swam away from Havai'i toward the East. Tu-rahu-nui, artisan of Ta'aroa, the supreme god, guided the fish in its course, and the warrior Tafai used a powerful ax to cut the sinews of the fish, to stabilize the new land. Thus were formed lofty mountain ranges, winding gulfs, an isthmus, bluffs and caves. The insouciant soul of Terehe lives today in this transplanted land called **Tahiti**.

Tahiti Nui Mare'are'a, Great Tahiti of the Golden Haze, the Polynesians sang. This is Tahiti of many shaded waters; various are the songs of the birds. Great Tahiti, the mounting place of the sun. The Tahitian people of old had to boast, because the people of Raiatea, the sacred island of Havai'i, regarded Tahiti as a plebeian island with no gods.

When the Europeans discovered Tahiti, beginning with the arrival of English Captain Samuel Wallis in 1767, followed by Frenchman de Bougainville, Captain James Cook, Captain Bligh and the famous *Bounty* crew, they too shouted the praises of this seductive island, where dreams are lived. Explorers, artists, writers and poets, sea-weary sailors and beachcombers of all makes spread the word. The myth of Tahiti as an earthly paradise was born.

Throughout the years Tahiti has become known as the Land of the Double Rainbows, the Romantic Isle, Beloved Island, Isle of Illusion, Island of Love, the Amorous Isle and the World's Most Glamorous Tropic Isle. Tahiti, the living Spirit of Terehe, is hailed as the most famous island in the South Seas—Queen of the Pacific.

ARRIVALS & DEPARTURES

Arriving By Air

If you are flying from a cold country to Tahiti, then make sure you can take off heavy garments once you arrive here, especially if you are continuing on to Moorea, Bora Bora or any of the other outer islands. You'll probably arrive in the cooler hours of the dawn, but once the sun rises you'll be sweltering in sweaters, woolens and polyesters. So layer your traveling clothes.

If you are on a package tour you will be met inside the baggage room or

> ### A TAHITIAN PROPHECY
>
> The ancient Tahitian seer named Pau'e prophesied: "There are coming children of the glorious princess, by a canoe without an outrigger, who are covered from head to foot." **King Pomare I**, hearing him say so, inquired how a canoe without an outrigger could hold its balance and not upset; so to illustrate his subject, Pau'e took an 'umete (wooden trough) and set it afloat with a few stones placed in it in a pool of water close by; then turning to the King he said: "What will upset that 'umete without an outrigger. It is balanced by its breadth, and so also is the canoe without an outrigger that is coming."
>
> Pau'e also said: "There will come a new king to whom this government will be given, and new manners will be adopted in this land; the tapa and the cloth-beating mallet will go out of use in Tahiti, and the people will wear different, foreign clothes."
>
> Three days afterwards Pau'e died, and a little later the Dolphin arrived with Captain Wallis, when the people exclaimed: "There is the canoe without the outrigger of Pau'e, and there are the children of the glorious princess!" When the Dolphin coasted the Taiarapu peninsula of Tahiti Iti, the natives approached the ship, headed by a man who held up a banana shoot, which to them was an effigy of their own persons, and after a welcome speech, he dropped it into the sea, signifying that their intentions were friendly and that the sea was sacred to all, for the Tahitians regarded it as a great moving marae or temple.
>
> — Extract from *Ancient Tahiti* by Teuira Henry

immediately outside the Customs area of the **International Airport of Tahiti-Faaa**. The tour operators hold signs listing the names of their arriving guests. Banque de Polynésie has a currency exchange booth in the baggage area, and another branch with an ATM machine in the main terminal, and Banque Socredo has an ATM and currency exchange machine in the terminal. If you need to make a phone call, book a room or continuing flight, rent a car, pick up a map, post a letter, go to the restroom, eat or drink, shop for a gift or check your e-mail, you can do it all inside the modern airport terminal.

The airport is located at PK 5.5 (3.4 mi.), west of downtown Papeete. If you arrive between 8pm and 6am be prepared to pay the night rates for a taxi. See details under *Taxi & Limousine Service* in this chapter. If you arrive in the daytime and want to save money, you can walk out to the main road and catch *le truck*. When you leave the airport you'll turn right on the main road (Route 1) to go to the west coast hotels and turn left to go downtown and to the east coast. You have a choice of the old coastal route or the freeway, (Route 5), which is called the RDO. You'll see the freeway entry almost in front of the airport.

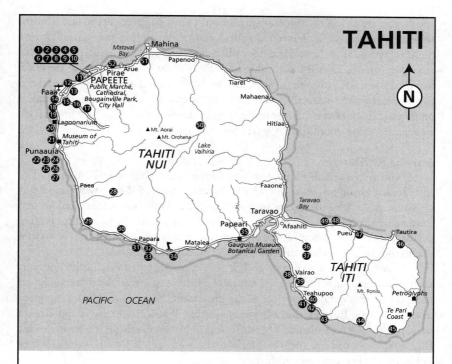

TAHITI

1. Hotel Kon Tiki Pacific
2. Le Mandarin
3. Hotel Tahiti Nui
4. Ahitea Lodge
5. Pension Puea
6. Teamo Hostel-Pension
7. Hotel Tiare Tahiti
8. Fare Suisse
9. Mahina Tea
10. Chez Myrna
11. Sheraton Hotel Tahiti
12. Heitiare Inn
13. Tahiti Airport Lodge
14. Tahiti-Faa'a Airport
15. Tahiti Airport Motel
16. Chez Lola
17. Pension Damyr
18. Intercontinental Tahiti
    Resort
19. Sofitel Tahiti Resort
20. Manava Suite Resort
    Tahiti
21. Hotel Le Meridien Tahiti
22. Pension de la Plage
23. Pension Te Nahe ToeToe
24. Pension Otaha
25. Taaroa Lodge
26. Relais Fenua
27. Te Miti
28. Marae Arahurahu
29. Maraa Grottos
30. Hiti Moana Villa
31. Papara Village
32. Fare Ratere
33. Papara Surfing Beach
34. Atimaono Golf Course
35. Vaipahi Garden &
    Waterfall
36. Taravao Plateau
37. Chez Jeannine
38. Meherio Iti
39. Pension Chayan
40. Vanira Lodge
41. La Vague Bleue
    (Tauhanihani)
42. Pension Vaiani
43. Teahupoo Surfing Site
44. Pension Te Pari Village
45. Pension Le Bonjouir
46. Pension Te Hihi o Te Ra
47. Pueu Village
48. Punatea Village
49. Fare Maithe
50. Relais de la Maroto
51. Radisson Plaza Resort
    Tahiti
52. Hotel Royal Tahitien

If you are flying to Moorea you can push your baggage cart to the Moorea terminal, which is to the left of the main terminal. Just follow the signs. The first flight to Moorea is at 5:30-6am, depending on the day. If you are flying to any of the other outer islands the Air Tahiti counter is at the extreme right of the main terminal when you come out of the Customs area. There is a baggage storage room next to the flower/shell stands in front of the terminal building. See information on *Baggage Allowances & Storage* in chapter on *Planning Your Trip*. The hotels have a baggage storage room, which is free for their guests.

Arriving By Boat

If you arrive in Tahiti on board a passenger cruise ship you will disembark at the **Quai d'Honneur** or at one of the concrete piers in downtown Papeete. A currency exchange office is located on the dock. Tour buses, taxis, guides and tourism representatives meet each ship's arrival, and a Tahitian dance show is often performed for the visitors. A covered reception area with public restrooms and telephones has been built adjacent to the Tahiti Tourist office.

Before arriving in the port of Papeete by yacht you must notify the port authorities via channel 12 of HF 26 or 38 KHz of your arrival. You can anchor at the quay or beside the beach close to the Protestant church, and you are supposed to check in with Immigration as soon as possible. If you arrive on a Fri. afternoon then you'll have to wait until Mon. morning before checking in, as offices for Immigration, Customs and the Harbormaster are all closed on weekends and holidays. Their offices are on the cruise ship dock.

The Harbormaster's office, *Tel. 50.54.51*, is open Mon.-Thurs. from 7-11:30am and from 12:30-4pm, and on Fri. to 3pm. The office hours for Immigration, *Tel. 43.94.90*, are Mon.-Fri. from 7:30am-12pm and from 2-5pm. The Customs office, *Tel. 42.01.22*, is open Mon.-Thurs. from 7am-2:45pm, and on Fri. from 7am-1:30pm.

You will have to complete a Port Documentation form at the Port Captain's office, *Tel. 50.54.62*. This paper contains information for boats that are entering, moving or leaving the port. It also includes port fees for docking, electricity, water and garbage pick-up if you want to tie up at the yacht quay along the waterfront.

Anchorages are available at the Yacht Club in Arue, at the Marina Taina in Punaauia, and at the Tahiti Nautic Center at Port Phaeton in Taravao. Yachts are no longer allowed to anchor at the Sofitel Tahiti Resort. This practice is tolerated by the harbormaster only during a 4-month period each May-Aug., in the height of the cruising season. Each crewmember is required to have a return air ticket or pay a repatriation bond to your home country. See more information in Chapter 6, *Planning Your Trip*.

Departing By Air

You should reconfirm your international flight no later than 72 hours before your departure date. Check-in time for departing international flights is 3 hours prior to departure. You can exchange your francs for dollars at the Banque Socredo or Banque de Polynésie offices inside the terminal, if they are still open when you leave. Once you pass Immigration and go into the international departure lounge, you will find a few duty free shops that sell cigarettes, liquors, French perfumes, Tahitian music, Tahitian cultured pearls and various gift items.

Departing By Boat

The cruise ship company or travel agency arranging your cruise will give you details of what you will do when you arrive in Tahiti to board a passenger ship. Groups are met at the airport and transferred to a hotel until time to board the ship, when they will be transferred by boat to the Quai d'Honneur in Papeete, where the ship is moored.

If you are departing by private yacht you must advise the Immigration office in Papeete of your final departure, and the Police Air Frontière (PAF) who run this office will issue a release from the bond that you were required to post upon arrival. This document must be presented to the *gendarmes* on the last island you visit before leaving French Polynesia, and your bond will be refunded.

ORIENTATION

Tahiti is located in the Windward Islands of the Society archipelago of French Polynesia. This is the largest of the 118 islands and atolls, with a population of around 179,892 people living in 12 *communes* on Tahiti Nui (big Tahiti) and Tahiti Iti (little Tahiti), also known as the Taiarapu peninsula.

Tahiti Nui and **Tahiti Iti** are shaped as a turtle, a lady's hand mirror or a reclining figure 8. Geologists say that these two majestic green islands emerged from the sea in separate volcanic births millions of years apart. Comprising a total of 1,042 sq. km. (402 sq. mi.) of land, Tahiti Nui and Tahiti Iti are joined by the narrow isthmus of **Taravao**, 60 km. (37 mi.) from the noise of **Papeete** by the south coast and 54 km. (34 mi.) by the north coast.

The circle island tour around the coastal road of Tahiti Nui is 114 km. (71 mi.). Away from the metropolitan area close to Papeete the paved roads are 2 lanes, with very few straight stretches, and there are usually no streetlights and very few guardrails at the edge of the seaside cliffs. The east coast is less developed, with numerous waterfalls and deep verdant valleys, modest homes and beautiful flower gardens beside the road. Here you will find the golden-brown sands of the volcanic beaches and cool streams ferrying tiny boats of flower blossoms to the sea. A fringing reef borders the shoreline in a few places, but most of the coast is battered by the waves of the frequently turbulent open ocean.

The west coast is much more congested, with houses and traffic, and high fences around the luxurious homes that often conceal ocean views to the motorists. A few white sand beaches border the shoreline and the shimmering turquoise lagoon is protected by a coral reef. Beyond the reef, across the Sea of Moons, is the island of Moorea.

Tahiti Iti has 18 km. (11 mi.) of paved road on the eastern and western coasts and a 7 km. (4 mi.) interior road that leads past dairy farms and citrus groves to a panoramic view of the Plateau of Taravao. Beyond the road's end of the peninsula's southern tip lies the *fenua 'aihere*, the magnificent bush land, and the steep sea cliffs known as Te Pari. You can explore this coast by boat or hike across the rivers and volcanic bluffs.

PAPEETE & ENVIRONS

The busy, bustling town of **Papeete**, on Tahiti's north coast, is the capital of French Polynesia. This is the administrative center for the 259,596 people (census of Sept. 2007) who live in the 5 archipelagoes that comprise this French Overseas Community.

Papeete (Pah-pay-eh-tay) is a Tahitian word meaning «a basket of water». The town is spread along the waterfront on Tahiti's north coast, 5 km. (3 mi.) east of the airport, facing the island of Moorea across the channel. Papeete harbor is an international port, as well as home base for the *Paul Gauguin* and *Tahitian Princess* cruise ships, the *Star Flyer* sailing cruise ship, the *Aranui 3* passenger/cargo ship, and other inter-island ships, copra freighters, fishing boats, ferries and a small fleet of French naval ships.

Among the winding streets of Papeete and its environs you will find the government operated medical center and hospital (a new government hospital is under construction in the Taaone section of Pirae), 2 private clinics, pharmacies, French and Tahitian government offices, tribunal courts, *gendarmerie*, municipal police, port authorities and post office with international communications. Services also include the tourist bureau, banks, airline offices, shipping and travel agencies, TV and radio stations, newspapers in French, English and Tahitian, hotel and technical schools, lycée and university, cathedrals and temples, sports centers and stadiums, health clubs and gyms, a cultural center, museums, art galleries, movie theaters, shopping centers, boutiques, crafts centers and a public market.

Dreams for a Better Tomorrow

Papeete's waterfront has been improved during the past few years, with the addition of 2 concrete piers for cruise ships and the extension of the boardwalk along the waterfront, which will eventually go all the way to the Olympic swimming pool adjacent to the cultural center (Te Fare Tauhiti Nui). The cultural center will be torn down and a new one built a block inland, in the space formerly occupied by the Vaiami Hospital. A branch of the Museum of Tahiti and Her Islands is also planned as part of the future cultural center.

A big landfill project between the yacht quay and Place To'ata has added a space that is used for beach games, and the carnival rides and *baraques* (stands) for the Heiva Festival were placed here in 2007. Future plans include building the 12.3-acre (5 ha.) Hokule'a Park in this area, which will add 3 green sections with 500 trees, 2 waterfalls, a playground, 2 volley ball courts, 2 carrousels, 4 big pergolas, 2 *fare pote'e* shelters, racks for 108 outrigger paddle canoes, a police station, toilets and dressing rooms, and a suspended white sand beach. Swimming in this area is currently prohibited due to pollution, so that problem will have to be solved first of all.

A long-term project for Papeete includes tearing down some of the old buildings along Blvd. Pomare and creating a vast esplanade so that the public Marché will open onto the quay. The buildings on rue Colette and Leboucher will be destroyed, thereby providing a direct view of Papeete harbor and the cruise ship docks. New office and apartment buildings of 10-stories or more will be built on the mountainside in Paofai, Vaiami and the Bambridge stadium, and a second phase will add buildings in the To'ata and Aroa Nui Ave. Pouvanaa a Oopa (formerly Ave. Bruat) areas.

Today's Reality

These are just a few of the changes envisioned by Tahiti's leaders for years to come. In the meantime, the security forces have their hands full with more unpleasant changes that are taking place in the capital.

The crime rate for purse snatching and other petty thefts comprise 50% of infractions reported, representing an increase of 26% in 2007, even though there are more security personnel patrolling the streets. A municipal police station is now located near the public *marché*, which is the center of town. Juvenile delinquency increased by 20% in 2007 over the 2006 rate. Security authorities report that this is due to alcohol and drugs. The French gendarmerie confiscated 70,000 marijuana plants in 2007 compared to 53,000 in 2006. The consumption of cocaine and ice and other hard drugs has also increased during the past few years.

Prostitutes of all sexes (including Polynesia's third sex, the *mahu*) are rampant. You'll find them in the bars, sidewalk cafés and nightclubs on Rue des Ecoles and near Avenue Prince Hinoi, and some of them are glamorously attired in satins, sequins, feathers, makeup and wigs when they patrol the streets at night. The street surveillance teams also keep an eye on their behavior. A new anti-noise law was passed in 2004 to eliminate the loud music booming from cars and 4WD vehicles in downtown Papeete or anywhere on the island. Few revelers, however, pay any attention to this law.

GETTING AROUND TOWN
Car Rentals

Note: The minimum age for renting a 4-wheel vehicle is 21 years and for 2-wheel vehicles it is 18 or 19 years, depending on the island. The driver must have a valid driver's license of one-year minimum from his country of residence or an international driver's license corresponding to the class of vehicle rented. You will have to pay a guarantee deposit when renting cars, scooters and bicycles. When you rent a car, do not leave anything at all inside the car when you're not in it. All major credit cards are accepted.

- **Avis**, *in US Tel. 800/230-4898; in Tahiti, Tel. 689/54.10.10/ Fax 689/42.19.11; avis.tahiti@mail.pf; www.avis-tahiti.com.* The main office for **Avis-Pacificar** is at 56 Rue des Remparts at the Pont de l'Est in Papeete, and there are also sales offices at the Tahiti-Faaa International Airport, *Tel. 85.02.84* and in Taravao, *Tel. 85.02.84.* A 3-door Citroen rents for a package price of 9.600 CFP per day, with unlimited mileage and insurance. An a/c Citroen or Peugeot 107 is 11.500 CFP per day. A Suzuki Jimmy 4WD vehicle costs 12.700 CFP per day. Rentals are available for several days and by the week or month.
- **Europcar**, *in US Tel. 800/227-7368; in Tahiti, Tel. 689/45.24.24; Fax 689/ 41.93.41; tahiti@europcar.pf; www.eurocar.com.* The main sales office is on Avenue Prince Hinoi in Papeete, and there are branch offices at the Tahiti-Faaa International Airport, *Tel. 86.61.96;* at all the major hotels and in Taravao. A 3-door Twingo or Punto rents for 2.190 CFP per day and 44 CFP per min. or a forfeit price of 9.400 CFP with unlimited mileage and insurance. You can also rent an automatic drive a/c Mazda 6 Sedan for 19.500 CFP per day, and Europcar offers a variety of other choices, including an a/c Kia minibus for 21.542 CFP per day.
- **Hertz**, *in US Tel. 800/654.3001; in Tahiti, Tel. 689/42.04.71 (Office), Tel. 689/ 82.55.86 (Airport); Fax 689/43.49.03; hertz@mail.pf.* They have a sales counter at the Tahiti-Faaa International Airport and sales desks at the major hotels. A 3-door a/c Peugeot 107 is 7.610 CFP and an a/c Peugeot 107 with automatic transmission is 11.800 CFP. A 9-passenger Hyundai van with a/c is 19.630 CFP. All rates include unlimited mileage and insurance, and 3-day packages are available.
- **Tahiti Rent A Car**, *Tel. 689/81.94.00,* has an office at the airport. A 3-door Hyundai-Getz is 8.976 CFP for a one-day package, and a 5-passenger a/c Peugeot 206 is 12.113 CFP, including insurance and unlimited mileage.
- **Daniel Rent-A-Car**, *Tel. 689/81.96.32/ 82.30.04; Fax 689/85.62.64; daniel.location@mail.pf.* They have a sales counter at the airport. A 4-seat Peugeot 106 rents for 8.019 CFP per day with unlimited mileage and a 5-place Peugeot 206 with air-conditioning is 10.794 CFP per day. Other choices are available.
- **Tahiti Auto Center**, *Tel. 689/82.33.33; Fax 689/83.33.34; tahitiautocenter@mail.pf; www.tahitiautocenter.pf.* This car rental agency offers the lowest rates. They are located at PK 20.200 in Paea on Tahiti's west coast. Open Mon.-Fri. 7am-5pm and on Sat. 8-11:30am. A Fiat Punto is 5.500 CFP a day, a 5-door a/c Peugeot 107 is 6.500 CFP, and a 9-seat Hyundai minibus is 15.000 CFP. Weekly and monthly rates available. Rates include insurance and unlimited mileage. They also rent scooters and motorcycles.

Taxi & Limousine Service

A taxi stand is located at the Tahiti-Faaa International Airport, *Tel. 86.60.66,* at the Vaima Center, *Tel. 43.72.47,* at the Papeete Market, *Tel. 43.19.62,* and at

Mana Rock Cafe, *Tel. 41.23.42.* Your hotel reception can also call a taxi for you. The taxi fares quoted here have been in effect since Dec. 1989, and the president of the taxi drivers association said that the rates will change sometime in 2008.

A taxi ride between the airport and downtown Papeete is 1.500 CFP during the day and 2.500 CFP between 8pm and 6am. The taxi fare between the airport and the west coast hotels, as far as Sofitel Maeva Beach, is 1.000 CFP during the day and 1.500 CFP at night. The daytime fare from the airport to Le Méridien is 2.000 CFP and 3.500 CFP at night. Between the Intercontinental Resort Tahiti and downtown Papeete you will pay 1.800 CFP in the daytime and 3.000 CFP at night, and from Le Méridien Tahiti to Papeete the fare is 2.500 CFP during the day and 4.500 CFP at night. From the airport to the Royal Tahitien the taxi fare is 2.000 CFP during the day and 3.500 CFP at night, and to the Radisson Plaza Resort the daytime fare is 2.240 CFP and 4.000 CFP at night. The official cost of a circle island tour by taxi is 21.000 CFP, but you usually can make an agreement with the taxi chauffeur and pay between 15.000-20.000 CFP. The hourly rate for a taxi is 4.000 CFP. Drivers charge 100 CFP for each big bag transported.

Carl's Taxi, *Tel. 77.13.69/82.22.72*, is operated by Carl Emery, who grew up in Australia and speaks excellent 'Aussie' English. He has an 8-passenger a/c Toyota High Ace mini-van that he uses for private taxi service and tours, and he charges 15.000 CFP for a half-day circle island tour and 25.000 CFP for a full-day tour, which can be divided among the passengers.

Mami Elisa Taxi, *Tel. 72.46.31*, is available 24-hrs. a day to drive you wherever you want to go. I have used her on several occasions and she is very reliable as well as friendly.

Taxi Mike, Tel. 24.29.20; Fax 83.77.89, is owned by Michael from the Cook Islands, who speaks excellent English. He drives a luxurious Logan Break.

Tour & Transport Companies

When you book your visit to Tahiti through a travel agent, your ground transportation is normally part of the package. If you are traveling on your own, you can save money by contacting a local tour and transport company to drive you between your hotel and the airport or ferry dock. Be sure to reserve at least one day in advance. See the list of Tahiti's inbound travel agencies in Chapter 6, *Planning Your Trip*.

Le Truck & "Busscar" Transportation System

Tahiti's public transport system was traditionally provided by *le truck*, which is a brightly painted wooden cabin mounted on the rear of a flatbed truck. Some of these colorful vehicles still operate during the daylight hours, with night transportation provided from downtown Papeete only to the airport and hotels on the west coast, as far as Sofitel Resort. The last run depends on what is happening in Papeete. Each *le truck* has a specific route, with the destination usually painted on the top or sides of the vehicle.

Except for some urban routes, Tahiti's famous *le truck* has been replaced with modern buses, which are locally called "**Busscar**." The buses are painted according to the zone they serve. The red buses are for the urban zone from Pirae to Punaauia; orange is for the West coast, from Punaauia to Taravao and Teahupoo, and green is for the East coast, between Tautira and Papeete. The name and number of the zone served is also shown on the front of the bus, just like buses in the United States.

The minimum fare is 130 CFP, which is valid between the Sofitel Resort and downtown, and you'll have to pay 200 CFP at night. The one-way fare to the end of the road in Teahupoo or Tautira on the Tahiti Iti peninsula is 400 CFP. The Tahiti Tourist office can give you specific details on where to catch the bus to your destination.

So, with all this modernization program, what will happen to the beloved *le truck*? Some of them have been kept in Tahiti to transport groups of tourists who arrive aboard the passenger liners or for "Kaina Island" tours around Tahiti. Other *le trucks* have been shipped to the outer islands.

WHERE TO STAY
Downtown Papeete – Superior to Moderate
HOTEL TAHITI NUI, *B.P. 302, Papeete, Tahiti 98713. Tel. 689/50.33.50; Fax 689/42.16.32; chris.beaumont@mail.pf; www.hotelmandarin.com.* On Ave. Prince Hinoi. This 3-star 7-story contemporary style hotel will open in Dec. 2008 with 91 rooms, some with kitchenettes. A standard room is 30 sq. m. (323 sq. ft.), a junior suite is 56 sq. m. (603 sq. ft.), and a deluxe suite is 80-90 sq. m. (861-969 sq. ft.). There will be a 92-seat restaurant, a cafeteria for 90, a conference room, swimming pool, massage and fitness rooms, and a 2-level underground parking garage. Because it is located on a busy street with traffic noises, the rooms overlooking the road will have double-glassed windows. The hotel will be built around an interior garden and patio where street noises will not be heard. The contact numbers will change once the hotel is open.

Moderate
HOTEL LE MANDARIN, *B.P. 302, Papeete, Tahiti 98713. Tel. 689/ 50.33.50; Fax 689/42.16.32; chris.beaumont@mail.pf; www.hotelmandarin.com. 2008 EP Rates: Standard room 13.500 CFP sgl, 15.000 CFP double; mini-suite 15.500 CFP sgl, 17.500 CFP dbl; third person 2.000 CFP. Add taxes. All major credit cards.*

On Rue Colette in downtown Papeete, 2 blocks inland from the waterfront and across the street from the Mairie of Papeete (City Hall). 38 a/c rooms on 5 floors, with elevator. Each room has a queen size bed or twin beds, private bathroom with shower, refrigerator, tea and coffee facilities, TV and IDD telephone. Restaurant Le Plaza, in the same building, and Restaurant Le Mandarin, around the corner, are 2 first-rate a/c Chinese restaurants and bars, and there is also a coffee shop in the hotel. This Chinese-owned hotel offers a convenient location for downtown activities, and rates second for quality of the accommodations. Rental cars and island tours and excursions can be reserved at the reception desk.

HOTEL TIARE TAHITI, *B.P. 2359, Papeete, Tahiti 98713. Tel. 689/ 50.01.00; Fax 689/43.68.47; hotltiaretahiti@mail.pf; www.hoteltiaretahiti.info. Blvd. Pomare, on waterfront adjacent to Papeete Post Office. EP Rates: Standard room 15.285 CFP sgl/dbl; harbor view room 16.950 CFP sgl/dbl; panoramic view 18.615 CFP sgl/dbl; panoramic suite #502 is 20.280 CFP. Third person 2.925 CFP. Continental breakfast 1.100 CFP per person. Rates include all taxes. All major credit cards.*

This hotel is near the Papeete Post Office, overlooking Boulevard Pomare and the yacht quay on the waterfront. It is the best choice for the downtown area and reservations have to be made well in advance. The 38 rooms are located in a five-story building with an elevator. They have a/c, private bathrooms with showers, telephone, cable television and a hair dryer on request. Most of them have balconies. Breakfast is served in the cafeteria above the reception. Several restaurants, bars and boutiques are less than a block away.

HOTEL KON TIKI PACIFIC, *B.P. 111, Papeete, Tahiti 98713. Tel. 689/ 54.16.16; cell 78.45.69; Fax 689/42.11.66; kontiki@mail.pf. 2008 EP Rates: Standard room 12.360 CFP sgl; 13.620 CFP dbl; Twin bed room 14.730 CFP. Extra person 2.150 CFP. Continental breakfast 850 CFP per person. Taxes included. All major credit cards.*

This 7-story hotel is popular with the French military men, as it is located at the lower end of Boulevard Pomare, opposite a naval base in the Papeete harbor. It is only 2-3 blocks from the downtown center. 20 of the 36 a/c rooms have deep balconies facing the waterfront, where you can watch the Moorea ferries coming and going. You may hear some noise coming from the nearby discos on the street level when they are in full swing on weekends, but the a/c in the rooms drown out a lot of exterior sounds. The rooms on the back facing the mountains are quieter. The TV sets are more or less functional. Each room is equipped with a telephone and small refrigerator, and there is a bathtub/shower in the tiled bathroom. There is no restaurant, but breakfast will be brought to your room if you order it from reception in advance.

Economy

AHITEA LODGE, *B.P. 5597, Pirae, Tahiti 98716. Tel. 689/53.13.53/ 76.63.88; Fax 689/42.09.35; pension.ahitea@mail.pf; www.ahitea-lodge.com. In Fariipiti, 15 min. from airport and 900 m. (3,000 ft.) from ferry dock. 2008 EP Rates: Room with shared bathroom 8.500 CFP; Family room with shared bath 10.800 CFP; Room with private bath 9.500 CFP; Room with private bath, TV, ceiling fan and mini-refrigerator 13.500 CFP; add 2.000 CFP per day for a/c. Breakfast included in all rates. AE, MC, V.*

This renovated 2-story bed and breakfast is in an alley between Ave. Chef Vairaatoa and Ave. Prince Hinoi, facing the Plomberie and Suzanna Shop in the

Fariipiti neighborhood of Papeete. This is a working class neighborhood of Tahitian families, complete with children and dogs. The 10 comfortable standard guest rooms give you a choice of a room for 2 people or 2 adults and 2 children, with private or shared bathrooms and hot water showers. Each room has a ceiling fan, and 1 room has a/c, TV and a mini-refrigerator. You have to reserve this room months in advance. The best bedrooms are in the main house, and the upstairs rooms open onto a balcony. The least expensive rooms are in an adjacent building. A tropical breakfast is served in the dining room or on the terrace, and guests share a kitchen with refrigerator and microwave oven. There is a charge for laundry, ironing and locker storage room. There is also a pond with tropical fish and a swimming pool in the garden, which is surrounded by a high fence. You can walk about 5 blocks to downtown restaurants, snacks and the roulotte food wagons. Owners Ado and Michel Moevai also own Puea Pension.

FARE SUISSE, *B.P. 20255, Papeete, Tahiti 98713. Tel./Fax 689/42.00.30; info@fare-suisse.com; www.fare-suisse.com. Rue des Poilus Tahitiens in Quartier Buillard in Paofai, 10 min. from airport and 3 blocks inland from Papeete waterfront. Free airport transfers. 2008 EP Rates: Maupiti and Tahiti double rooms 9.600 CFP; Moorea twin room 4.800 CFP per person; Bora Bora family room 15.000 CFP. Breakfast 1.200 CFP. MC, V.*

This is a one-story white concrete house operating as a bed and breakfast. Since its opening in Sept. 2006 the Fare Suisse has quickly become very popular with European visitors as well as guests from many other countries. Owner Beni and his wife Therese are highly praised by former clients for their friendly, helpful and reliable service, as well as the immaculately clean, comfortable and spacious rooms they provide. Some say that this is the best place they have ever stayed anywhere in the world! This 4-bedroom house is located in a quiet, safe, secluded gated community up the hill from Champion Supermarket on rue du Commandant Destremeau, a 10-min. walk from the center of downtown Papeete. The Maupiti Room has a double bed with a private shower, the Tahiti Room has a double bed, and the Moorea Room has 2 single beds. Guests in these rooms share the well equipped kitchen, the terrace and BBQ grill. The Bora Bora Room has a double bed and a single bed, with a private living area and kitchen, terrace and BBQ grill. The well-appointed rooms are airy, bright, clean and cozy. The bathrooms have been described by some guests as luxurious, with a basket of towels and little soaps for guests to use. Breakfast is served on the terrace. A washing machine is available for guest use and Beni will also store your luggage while you visit the outer islands. He will drive you to the ferry or to the airport and pick you up when you return, at no extra charge.

CHEZ MYRNA, *B.P. 790, Papeete, Tahiti 98713. Tel./Fax 689/42.64.11; cell 689/77.09.75; dammeyer.family@mail.pf. In Tipaerui valley, a five minute walk inland from Rue du Commandant Destremeau. One-way transfers 1.600 CFP. EP with breakfast, room 4.450-6.100 CFP sgl 6.150-7.855 CFP dbl; dormitory 2.050 CFP sgl. Add municipal tax. No credit cards.*

Myrna and her husband Walter Dahmmeyer have a concrete 5-bedroom house with a double bed in each room, with a private or shared bathroom. There is also a dormitory and kitchen. Only breakfast is served. You can walk to nearby restaurants, snack bars and *magasins*. Luggage storage available.

Northeast Coast: Arue/Pirae – Deluxe
RADISSON PLAZA RESORT TAHITI, *B.P. 14170, Arue, Tahiti 98701. Tel. 689/48.88.88; Fax 689/48.88.89. Reservations: Tel. 689/48.88.00; sales-tahiti@radisson.com; www.radisson.com/aruefp. On Lafayette Beach in Arue Commune, 7 km (4.3 mi) northeast of Papeete. 2008 EP Rates: Ocean View room 33.500 CFP sgl/dbl; Ocean View room with Jacuzzi 39.900 CFP sgl/dbl; Ocean View suite 44.500 CFP 3 adults + 1 child; Ocean View duplex suite 47.200 CFP 3 adults + 1 child; extra person 7.000 CFP. Rates include 1 breakfast buffet. Transfer charge from airport is 3.000 CFP. Add taxes. All major credit cards.*

The Radisson Plaza Resort was originally planned as a residence hotel with kitchens and large balconies overlooking 2,600 ft. (792 m) of black sand beside the lagoon at Lafayette Beach on Tahiti's northern coast of Arue. The 7 concrete buildings that are spread out around an 8,611 sq. ft. (800 sq. m) swimming pool were already under construction when the owner decided to upgrade his project to that of a 5-star hotel. Units with kitchens are no longer rented to guests.

All the 165 guest rooms and suites are located on 4 levels and there are elevators and underground parking for 50 cars. Each unit overlooks the ocean and they all have a 140 sq. ft. (13 sq. m) balcony or lanai, thus creating an external living room. There are 42 standard rooms, 44 rooms with a dbl. Jacuzzi on the covered balcony, 52 suites and 27 duplex suites. There are 140 inter-connecting rooms. All the suites are furnished with a king size bed or 2 double beds and a sofa bed and can accommodate 3 adults and a baby bed. Each of the rooms has a king size bed or 2 twin beds. All units have individually controlled a/c, color TV with satellite, radio, local and IDD telephones with 2 lines, voice mail, broadband Internet access, bathroom with shower and bathtub or shower and Jacuzzi, bathrobes, bathroom scale, personal safe, minibar, coffee and tea making facilities, hair dryer and daily housekeeping service. The suites also have an iron and ironing board, and guests staying in the rooms also have access to iron and board on request. There are no CD or DVD players. Room service is available.

The guest rooms and suites, as well as the restaurant, bar, lounge, reception and all other public areas are decorated in a mixture of trendy modern and exotic Polynesian, with furnishings from all over the world. Hiti Mahana, the resort's signature restaurant, overlooks Lafayette Beach and historic Matavai Bay. See further information under *Where to Eat* in this chapter.

The resort's Lafayette Bar is named for the (in-)famous Lafayette after hours nightclub that was located here from the 1940s through the early 1970s. This upmarket bar is a gathering place for Tahiti's young international set of beautiful people who come to listen to music played by local bands. The James Norman Hall

Lounge, located to the right of the reception, is the perfect place to relax with a cup of coffee or tea while waiting to meet a friend or business associate.

Le Spa is a full-service spa on the resort's 3rd floor and is reached by elevator. A trained staff welcomes hotel and non-hotel guests for treatments on appointment. Hotel guests can use their room key for access to the a/c Fitness Center, which is adjacent to Le Spa. In addition to the Star Trac Pro equipment, there are locker rooms, 2 showers, a sauna and a steam room There is extensive cardio fitness and free-weight equipment, and professional yoga and aquagym classes are available. See more information under *Massages and Spas* in this chapter.

At the entrance to the Radisson you will find a Perlissima Tahiti Eden Store displaying Tahitian cultured pearls, a boutique featuring original pottery and jewelry from Antipodes Gallery, and an interesting arts and crafts shop with colorful displays of *tifaifai* quilts, pareos, woven hats and bags, mother-of-pearl jewelry and drums. There is Jacques Dessanges Coiffure and Tahiti Holidays travel agency is also located here, where you can book your excursions and rent a car. The hotel's meeting rooms and events spaces are named after some of the famous European explorers and ships that visited Tahiti and especially Matavai Bay in the latter half of the 1700s. These include the Endeavour Room, Captain Samuel Wallis Room, Captain James Cook Room, Captain Louis A. Bougainville Room, the Dolphin Meeting Room, the Restaurant Hiti Mahana, the Lafayette Bar, the Endeavour patio and Endeavour garden.

Like all the favorite Honeymoon Hotels in Polynesia, Radisson Plaza Resort Tahiti also has special packages for newlywed guests and other loving couples. A Starlight Dinner is 30.430 CFP for two, and a "Delicious Sunset" private lanai dinner is 36.590 CFP. Please contact the hotel directly for all details on the Romantic Packages and Polynesian Weddings.

Moderate

HOTEL ROYAL TAHITIEN, *B.P. 5001, Pirae, Tahiti 98716. Tel. 689/ 50.40.40; Fax 689/50.40.41; Reservations Tel. 689/50.40.45; royalres@mail.pf; www.hotelroyaltahitien.com. On the beach in Pirae, on Tahiti's north shore, 4 km (2.5 mi) east of Papeete. 2008 EP Rates: Standard room 18.000 CFP sgl/dbl; 21.000 CFP tpl. Add taxes. All major credit cards.*

Although this is an old hotel that was built in the 1960s, it is still very popular with travelers who want to be close to Papeete but away from the noise and dirt of the city. They also appreciate the moderate rates and beautiful grounds. The 40 a/c rooms are located in 2-story motel-type structures beside a spacious garden with flowering trees and a small river meandering toward the sea. The carpeted rooms have a telephone, refrigerator and tea/coffee facilities, bathtub/shower and a private balcony or terrace overlooking the tropical gardens. Tahiti's royal family once owned this land. You can swim in the lagoon beside a black sand beach, relax in a Jacuzzi spa and sunbathe on the adjacent wooden deck, or you can cool off under the waterfall in the tropical swimming pool in the garden. Meals are served in the thatched roof Tahitian style dining room or under the shade of huge almond trees on the terrace. There is also a snack *fare* adjacent to the swimming pool. This is a favorite destination for local diners and the Happy Hour crowd who come to the spacious bar on Fri. evenings to dance to tunes played by Tahiti's favorite musicians. For more information see *Where to Eat* in this chapter.

Airport Area: Faaa/Punaauia – Deluxe
  SHERATON HOTEL TAHITI, *B.P. 416, Papeete, Tahiti 98713. Tel. 689/ 86.48.48; Fax 689/86.48.40; Reservations Tel. 689/47.88.00, Fax 689/47.88.01; reservations.tahiti@sheraton.pf; www.sheratonsintahiti.com. 190 guest rooms and 10 suites beside the lagoon in Auae, 1.6 km (1 mi) from downtown and 3.5 km (2.2 mi) from the airport. 2008 Year-Round EP Rates sgl./dbl: Lagoon View Room 34.000 CFP; Superior Lagoon View Room 36.000 CFP; Deluxe Lagoon View Room 42.000 CFP; Spa-Room Lagoon View 51.000 CFP (minimum stay 2 nights, including 1 free massage during 2nd night stay); One-Bedroom Suite 75.000 CFP; Two-Bedroom Suite 88.000 CFP; 3rd person 6.000 CFP. Add 9.075 CFP per person for MAP and 12.685 CFP for AP. Add taxes. All major credit cards.*

  This deluxe hotel opened in July 1999 on the site that was occupied by the famous Hotel Tahiti from the early 1960s until March 1997, when it was closed to make way for the new 200-unit structure. Ten of the rooms have been turned into apartments and there are now 190 soundproof rooms and suites located in 5 concrete buildings with low-rise wings of 4-5 floors. The upstairs rooms are reached by 3 elevators and long winding passageways that are decorated with paintings by local artists and an enviable collection of *tifaifai* (Tahitian patchwork quilts).

  The rooms have all been updated, replacing the carpet with polished wood floors and new tile in the bathrooms. The Sweet Sleeper beds are covered with white sheets and duvets, and the Feng-Shui environment includes dark woods, colonial style furniture with contemporary design, and Tahitian touches. The rooms are categorized according to their view and they all have private balconies that overlook the lagoon. Each unit has central a/c, a king size bed or 2 double beds, computer data ports, phone with voicemail, TV with satellite cable, iron and board, alarm clock radio, electronic door locks, in-room safe, refrigerator, coffee & tea makers, full tub with shower, makeup mirror and hairdryer. There are cribs and connecting rooms available, as well as 5 rooms equipped for the disabled, and there are also non-smoking floors. Some of the higher-priced rooms have an extra terrace, a larger bathroom with a bidet, and a solarium. The 1-bedroom junior suites have a 180-degree view from the 2 balconies overlooking Papeete harbor and the island of Moorea, and there are 2 lavabos in the bathrooms. All rooms have daily maid service and next day laundry and dry cleaning service on request. Room service is available from 6am to 10pm.

  The public areas of the hotel include a reception area with 24-hour front desk service, valet service, a currency exchange, multilingual concierge service, a

Kaimana Boutique, a Robert Wan Tahiti Pearls shop, beauty salon, travel desks, and car rental agency. The business center includes computers for guest use and Wifi Internet connections are available in the public areas and around the pool. The fitness center has Star Trac exercise equipment, and even includes a special spring floor for aerobics. The Mandara Spa, next to the fitness center, has a sauna and steam room, which guests may use free of charge. See details under *Massages & Spas* in this chapter.

The Restaurant Moevai is built over the water, where breakfast, lunch and dinner are served. La Terrasse serves light meals, and poolside food and beverage service is also available. Drinks are served in Quinn's Bar from 10am-11pm, and there is live entertainment on weekends. Four a/c meeting and banquet facilities can accommodate up to 500 people and outdoor functions for up to 1,500 people can be held in the garden or on the beach. For further information see *Where to Eat* in this chapter.

An infinity swimming pool with a grotto and waterfalls faces the lagoon and the spacious green lawns of the Sheraton Hotel Tahiti. You can climb the steps above the pool to the 16-person whirlpool spa, and relax your body while gazing at the sunset and the island of Moorea. A white sand beach has been added and you can dive from the pier built over the lagoon. There is also a nautical center on the premises, including the TOPdive Tahiti scuba dive center. During the Tahitian arts and crafts demonstrations that are held at the hotel several times a week, you can learn how to make floral garlands, weave coconut leaf plates, baskets and seasonal ornaments.

The hotel has a list of suggested "Romantic Touches" for lovers, and you can even order a traditional Tahitian Wedding Ceremony to be performed in the hotel gardens. Contact the hotel directly for details.

INTERCONTINENTAL TAHITI RESORT (formerly Tahiti Beachcomber Inter-Continental), *B.P. 6014, Faaa, Tahiti. 98702. Tel. 689/86.51.10; Fax 689/ 86.51.78; reservationspf@interconti.com; www.tahiti.interconti.com. Beside the lagoon at the border of Faaa and Punaauia, 7 km. (4.3 mi.) west of Papeete and 2 km. (1.2 mi.) west of the airport. 260 units. 2008 Low/High season EP Rates sgl/dbl: Standard Room 26.450/29.380 CGP; Garden View Room 29.380/32.640 CFP; Lagoon View Room 34.500/38.330 CFP; Panoramic Room 39.870/44.290 CFP; Panoramic Suite 79.730/88.580 CFP; Overwater Bungalow on Motu 50.030/ 55.580 CFP; Overwater Bungalow on Lagoon 72.870/80.960 CFP; Overwater Villa on Motu 95.770/106.410 CFP; extra person add 8.000 CFP. Add 8.820 CFP per person for MAP and 12.650 CFP for AP. Canoe breakfast 6.090 CFP per person. Add taxes. All major credit cards.*

The Intercontinental Resort Tahiti opened as the Travelodge in 1974 and was later known as the Beachcomber, Beachcomber Parkroyal and Beachcomber Inter-Continental. Although the Beachcomber name was dropped at the beginning of 2005, local residents, as well as many tour operators and tourists, continue to call it the Tahiti Beachcomber. It is located on 30 acres (12 ha.) of lush tropical gardens on the western shore of Tahiti, facing the island of Moorea, built among palm trees and grassy lawns, and has its own white sand beaches and inner lagoon. The 260 accommodation units include fully renovated garden and lagoon view rooms, each with 307 sq. ft. (28.5 sq. m.) of floor space plus a balcony. These rooms give you a choice of a king size bed or two twin beds. An extension of 60 panoramic view rooms is located in 2 additional 3-story buildings. These units offer 414 sq. ft. (38.5 sq. m.) of living space, plus a wide terrace overlooking the sandy bottom swimming pool adjacent to the Lotus Restaurant, and the island of Moorea across the Sea of Moons. The decor is tropical colonial, with bamboo, wood and wicker furniture, wooden floors, and a canopy and padded headboard for the 2 queen size beds or 1 king size bed. A shuttered window between the bedroom and bathroom can be opened if you want to gaze at the lagoon while soaking in the big oval bathtub. There is also a separate shower with 2 adjustable showerheads, and there are 2 lavabos of black marble. The panoramic suite is also in this section.

On a private motu across a bridge from the main hotel property are 16 overwater bungalows with 30.5 sq. m. (328 sq. ft.) of living space. The overwater bungalows are built in the Polynesian style, with thatched roofs and natural woods. In addition to a/c they also have a ceiling fan, screened windows and sliding glass doors, as well as private balconies and sun decks with steps leading into the lagoon. They are equipped with a king size bed and a double sofa bed. There are 15 beautifully appointed overwater junior suites at the Restaurant Lotus end of the property. These units have 38.5 sq. m. (414 sq. ft.) of living space, excluding the terrace and deck. You can reach these bungalows by taking the hotel's *le truck* or electric cart, or by a leisurely stroll through the hotel gardens. The water is deeper here and the current is sometimes too choppy for good swimming, but these units provide the most intimacy. On request, guests staying in the overwater bungalows can be served breakfast by outrigger canoe.

All rooms and bungalows have adjustable a/c, separate bathrooms with bathtubs and courtesy soaps, *monoi*, bath gel, shampoo, conditioner, body lotion, shaving set, toothbrush and lots of other amenities. Each room has blackout curtains, a stocked mini-bar, coffee and tea making facilities, personal safe, hair-dryer, make-up mirror, satellite cable TV, video access on demand, IDD telephone and Internet connections. There is twice-a-day maid service, 3 guest laundry rooms, and same-day laundry and dry-cleaning service. Room service is available round-the-clock.

The Bora Bora Villa is also built over the water on the private motu. This unit is a model of the 80 overwater villas that were built for the Intercontinental Resort & Thalasso Spa Bora Bora. This villa has a king size bed and 2 sofa beds and can sleep 4 adults or 3 adults and 2 children.

In the reception area of the main building is a lobby with comfortable sofas and easy chairs. In addition to 24-hour reception, there is a concierge service and public relations counter. There are desks for guest activities, rental cars, excursions, and day trips to outer islands. Also on this level you will find a duty free gift shop and newsstand, a Tahiti Pearls boutique, and function rooms that are used for conferences, seminars and art shows. One of the hotel's 3 bars is in the corner of the lobby, and is open from 10pm-5:30am, serving drinks and snacks for late arrivals. You can take the elevators or the stairways to the ground level, where you will find the spacious Tiki Bar and open-air Tiare Restaurant, which has all-day dining. The a/c Hibiscus Restaurant is on the second floor and is used for special occasions. Le Lotus Restaurant is built over the lagoon and offers the most romantic setting of any restaurant on the island, with a lovely view of Moorea. See information under *Where to Eat* in this chapter.

The landscaped tropical gardens surrounding the hotel include a 1-mile jogging track and exercise area. Guests can use the snorkel equipment, tennis racks, balls and 2 floodlit tennis courts free for 1 hour. They have free access to 2 large fresh water swimming pools, an outdoor Jacuzzi and 2 white sand beaches. Aquagym classes are held daily except Sun. and you can also help feed the fish in the interior lagoon twice a day. At the Aquatica Nautical Center on the hotel premises you can join a free excursion to feed the Moray eels. See information on paid activities under *Nautical Centers & Clubs* in this chapter. There is also a helipad on the hotel grounds, and a Fitness center and Spa are due to open in July 2008. The hotel also has an a/c shuttle van that makes 4 trips to Papeete a day, for 400 CFP per passenger.

A daily program of cultural activities takes place at the Tiare swimming pool or Tiki Bar, which includes an arts and crafts exhibit, pareo dying and tying demonstrations, dance lessons, and lessons on how to create floral crowns, tifaifai patchwork bed covers, or how to make the famous Tahitian fish salad called *poisson cru*. Happy Hour is held in the Tiki Bar from 4:30-5:30pm every afternoon, and Thursday nights are especially lively, when Happy Hour is extended from 4:30-6:30pm. The bar is very active each evening from Wed.-Sun. when popular local musicians entertain the crowds of young people who come to meet their friends and enjoy the ambience. Hotel guests and other tourists can also safely mix with the friendly locals in this secure environment. This is the only hotel on the island to offer a Tahitian dance show each night of the week.

When newlyweds mention "Honeymoon" on their reservations at the Intercontinental Resort Tahiti they will receive special gifts and treats on their arrival at the hotel. A catalog of 'Romantic Ideas' has been prepared for honeymooners and other lovers, which tells you all about the Romantic Touches that can be added. These even include a choice of Traditional Tahitian Wedding Ceremonies. Contact the hotel directly for details.

Superior
   HOTEL LE MERIDIEN TAHITI, *B.P. 380595, Tamanu, Punaauia, Tahiti 98718. Tel. 689/47.07.07; Fax 689/47.07.08; Reservations Tel. 689/47.07.26, Fax 689/47.07.28; in North America 800/543-4300; rez@lemeridien-tahiti.pf; www.lemeridien-tahiti.com. Beside the lagoon in Punaauia, 15 km (9.3 mi) from*

downtown Papeete and 9 km (6 mi) west of the international airport. 150 units. 2008 EP Rates sgl/dbl: Garden View Room 35.000 CFP; Lagoon View Room 40.000 CFP; Deluxe Lagoon View Room 45.000 CFP; Junior Suite 60.000 CFP; Overwater Bungalow 65.000 CFP; Senior Suite 75.000 CFP; Presidential Suite 90.000 CFP. Third person 5.000 CFP. American Buffet Breakfast 2.910 CFP; add 6.910 CFP per person for MAP at La Plantation Restaurant and 10.910 CFP for AP. Add taxes. All major credit cards.

Le Méridien Tahiti opened in June 1998, on 11.12 acres (4.5 ha.) of land close to the Museum of Tahiti and Her Islands and just 20 min. from the Atimaono International Golf Course. Facilities include 12 a/c overwater bungalows with thatched roofs, and 130 a/c guestrooms and 8 suites in 4-story concrete buildings. The overwater bungalows are 60 sq. m. (646 sq. ft.) in size and feature a spacious living area opening onto an outdoor deck over the lagoon. The suites include 5 junior suites, 2 deluxe suites and 1 presidential suite. From each room you can see the lagoon and the island of Moorea across the Sea of Moons. All the rooms and bungalows are decorated in a brightly colored tropical French contemporary motif, with tiled floors. Amenities include IDD telephones, Internet Wifi connections, satellite cable TV, mini-bars, personal safes, coffee and tea facilities, hair dryers, Le Méridien toiletries, separate bathtubs and showers and handy makeup mirrors. Room service is provided round-the-clock and same day laundry service and ironing are also available.

There is also a transit room for guests who need somewhere to stay or put their luggage after they have checked out of their room. In addition to a business center, a gift shop and O'Poe pearl jewelry boutique, travel agency and car rental desk in the main building, there are 5 conference and banquet rooms accommodating from 20-500 people. La Plantation is the main restaurant, which offers specialties combining the subtleties of French cuisine and the original, exotic savors of Polynesian cuisine. Le Carré is a beachside restaurant serving gastronomic cuisine for lunch and dinner and it is best to reserve. The main bar, L'Astrolabe, serves exotic cocktails while you listen to the rhythms of piano jazz. You can get panini sandwiches and burgers at the Pool Bar during the day. A Polynesian Night is presented in La Plantation restaurant each Fri. evening, with fire dancing around the pool. A cold buffet is served at noon each Sat. and Sun. Please see further information under *Where to Eat* in this chapter.

The 2,500 sq. m. (26,910 sq. ft.) sand bottom swimming pool is prolonged by a stream, providing a vast watery playground in the hotel gardens close to the beach. Free activities also include snorkeling equipment, kayaks, aquagym classes, yoga classes, ping-pong, badminton, beach volley, bacci ball, and tennis on the hotel's court. Optional activities include scuba diving with Eleuthera Plongée, joining a snorkeling safari, sailing cruise, or a dolphin/whale watch expedition. You can go deep sea fishing, charter a private boat for a half-day's outing, play golf or discover Tahiti's charms on a circle island tour. You can also opt for a relaxing massage in your room. The travel desk in the lobby can book your tours and excursions or rent you a car for your own personal explorations. Le Méridien operates a shuttle bus service aboard a «le truck' that will take you to Papeete and back for 1.000 CFP per person. This shuttle leaves the hotel morning and afternoon on Mon., Tues., and Thurs., in the morning only on Wed., 3 times a day on Fri., and 4 times on Sat. It does not operate on Sun. Or you can walk out to the circle island road and catch a local bus and pay the one-way fare of 130 CFP.

A new activity at Le Méridien is an atelier (artist's workshop) located on the 6th floor for painters, sculptors and photographers. Visiting artists can exhibit their works here and some of them even give lessons to hotel guests or other students who are interested in learning their craft. Le Méridien also has a program for Honeymooners, including a non-binding Polynesian wedding ceremony and honeymoon dinner. Contact the hotel directly for details.

Note: During my last visit in Aug. 2007, I was told that the rooms were renovated in 2003-2004 and that the furniture would soon be changed. I do hope this includes the tables in La Plantation restaurant, which are very scarred, with all the finish scraped off. The light posts around the terrace were leaning, and the terrace of Le Carré is also looking worn. The fruit served on the breakfast buffet at La Plantation was old and some of it was too ripe for consumption. The shower in my room #657 smelled very strongly of mold, the toilet flush button kept sticking, and the 2 beds pushed together had very hard mattresses. However, as always, the hotel staff was very friendly and helpful.

SOFITEL TAHITI RESORT (formerly Maeva Beach), *B.P. 60008, Faaa, Tahiti 98702. Tel. 689/86.66.00; Fax 689/43.84.70; Reservations 689/86.66.66; Fax 689/41.05.05; reservation.tahiti@accor.com; www.sofitel.com. Beside the lagoon in Punaauia, 7.5 km (4.6 mi) west of Papeete and 2.5 km (1.5 mi) west of the airport. 2008 EP Rates sgl./dbl: Mountain View Room 21.681 CFP; Lagoon View Room 24.336 CFP; Suite 37.168 CFP. Add taxes. All major credit cards.*

The Sofitel Maeva Beach closed for major renovations in Apr. 2005 and reopened in Sept. 2005 as the Sofitel Tahiti Resort. This rebranded hotel is the flagship of the 6 hotels operated by the French group Accor in French Polynesia. It opened in 1969, offering a fabulous view of the island of Moorea across the Sea of Moons. Accommodations include 216 a/c rooms and suites in a 7-story pyramid shaped building. Each room is tiled and has a terrace or balcony, bathtub/shower, separate toilet, IDD telephone, plasma TV with satellite cable, Wifi Internet connections, personal safe, mini refrigerator, tea and coffee facilities, hair-dryers and makeup mirrors. The rooms also include Sofitel's patented My Bed, which are covered with bougainvillea-inspired bedspreads. The interior design of the Sofitel Tahiti's rooms uses vibrant colors and striking contrasts reminiscent of Paul Gauguin's paintings.

In addition to the renovation work done in the rooms and bathrooms, the reception and lobby were also updated in 2005. There are desks for car rentals, tours and activities, plus a gift and sundries shop. Seminars and banquets can be held in the 3 meeting rooms, which can seat up to 200 people. A business center and secretarial service are provided, as well as fax, copy/print facilities, Internet connections, translators and interpreters.

Breakfast, lunch and dinner are served in the open-air Bougainville restaurant on the ground level. Live music and Polynesian dance shows accompany some of the special evenings and luncheon feasts. The Sakura is a Japanese teppanyaki restaurant adjacent to the hotel lobby that is open for dinner. See *Where to Eat* in this chapter. The Moorea Bar is open from 9am-11pm, serving light snacks and your favorite cocktails beside the renovated swimming pool and its new deck. Happy Hour is held here daily from 5-6pm, with live music starting at 6pm on Thurs. and Fri. evenings.

Aquagym classes are held at 8:30am on Mon.-Sat. in the big swimming pool, and yoga classes are held on Mon. and Wed. There are 2 lighted tennis courts and a golf driving range on the hotel premises, as well as an outlet of the Eleuthera Scuba Diving Club. Each day's activities are printed on individual sheets in French and English and displayed in the lobby or placed in the rooms.

MANAVA SUITE RESORT TAHITI, c/o South Pacific Management, *Tel. 689/50.84.45; Fax 689/43.17.86; res@spmhotels.pf; www.pearlresorts.com.* Beside the lagoon at PK 10.8 in Punaauia, between the airport and Le Méridien. This new hotel is under construction on the site of the former Iaorana Villa, and will comprise 114 rooms and suites that will open to the public in April 2009. It is owned by 3 local businessmen and will be managed by South Pacific Management (SPM), the same company that represents the 9 Pearl Resorts in the Society Islands, Tuamotu and Marquesas Islands.

The size of the rooms will range from 41 sq. m. (441 sq. ft.) in the garden and lagoon studios to 139 sq. m. (1,496 sq. ft.) for the duplex suites, plus a terrace. All rooms will have a/c and most of the units will have kitchens. The hotel will also have 2 restaurants, including one built on stilts overwater, 3 bars, a fitness center, a conference room of 180 sq. m. (1,938 sq. ft.), and an underground parking garage. The project also includes the largest swimming pool on the island of Tahiti.

Moderate

TAHITI AIRPORT MOTEL, *B.P. 60113, Faaa, Tahiti 98702. Tel. 689/50.40.00; Fax 689/50.40.01; www.tahitiairportmotel.com. On mountainside facing Tahiti Faaa airport. 2008 EP Rates: Double/Twin Room 12.876 CFP; Family Room 21.845 CFP; Adapted Reduced Mobility Room 16.317 CFP; extra bed 3.885 CFP; breakfast 1.500 CFP. Add city tax. All major credit cards.*

This new 2-star lodging has a/c 46 rooms, including 1 room for guests with reduced mobility, just across the road from the airport. You'll have to take a taxi from the airport or pull your suitcases up the airport access road or stairs to get to the main road, then up an incline to get to the entrance of the motel. The 3-story motel has no elevators, but luggage service is normally available. The rooms are equipped with a double bed or 2 twin beds, refrigerator, TV, Wifi Internet, coffee/tea machines, safe, a closet and bathroom with hot water shower. An iron and board are available on request. There is parking for 14 vehicles and they have a baggage storage service. There is no restaurant here, but there are drink and snack machines, plus a coffee machine in the lobby. No smoking allowed in the motel.

Economy

CHEZ LOLA, *B.P. 6102, Faaa, Tahiti 98702. Tel./Fax 689/81.91.75; cell 78.08.52; holozet.lola@mail.pf. PK 4.5 mountainside in the Sainte-Hilaire neighborhood in Faaa Commune, 1 km inland from airport. Free round-trip transfers in the daytime and 1.500 CFP per car at night. EP room 5.000 CFP sgl, 7.000 CFP dbl/tpl, taxes included. Reduced rates starting on 3rd night. Free breakfast. Dinner on request. No credit cards.*

Lola rents out 2 bedrooms in her family home, which is a modern concrete house above the airport. Each room has a double bed and a fan. There's hot water in the bathroom, which you'll share with the other guests. House linens are provided. You'll also have use of the living room, dining room, TV and terrace. Not only does Lola meet you at the airport upon arrival, but she will also drive you to the main road to catch *le truck* to Papeete, and come to fetch you at the airport after you've finished your sightseeing and shopping.

PENSION DAMYR, *B.P. 6492, Faa'a, Tahiti 98702. Tel./Fax 689/83.69.13; cell 70.81.31. On the mountainside at PK 5 in the Aubry quartier of Faa'a, overlooking the airport and the island of Moorea. Free round-trip transfers provided. 2008 EP Rates: Room with communal bathroom 6.000 CFP sgl; 7.000 CFP dbl, breakfast included. 1.500 CFP for third person. Studio with private bathroom 8.500 CFP sgl/ dbl, 10.000 CFP tpl, 11.000 CFP for 4 people. Breakfast included first day. 7th night free. Add taxes. No credit cards.*

Daniel and Myrtille Duquenne have a large property with 2 rooms for guests in the house, who share a bathroom with hot water, as well as the dining room and terrace. Each room has a double bed, large closet and electric fan. There is also a completely equipped studio with a private bathroom and hot water, kitchen, dining room and terrace, plus cable television, a ceiling fan in the bedroom and an electric fan in the living room. A *magasin* store is about 650 ft. away. I have booked several American and Australian friends here and they were all very impressed with the cleanliness of the house, as well as the friendliness and efficiency of the hosts.

Southwest Coast: Punaauia to Mataiea – Economy to Moderate

PENSION DE LA PLAGE, *B. P. 381593, Tamanu, Punaauia, Tahiti 98718. Tel. 689/45.56.12; Fax 689/82.85.48; laplage@mail.pf; www.pensiondelaplage.com. PK 15.4 on mountainside in Punaauia Commune, 9.5 mi from downtown. Look for the sign beside the road. One-way transfer from airport 1.000 CFP per person during day and 2.000 CFP min. at night, plus 1.000 CFP for each extra person. 2008 EP Rates: Room without kitchen 7.900 CFP sgl, 8.800 CFP dbl; extra bed 2.000 CFP. Room with kitchen 9.100 CFP sgl, 10.300 CFP dbl; extra bed 2.000. Breakfast 900 CFP; lunch 1.500 CFP; dinner 2.500 CFP per person. Add taxes. MC, V.*

This pension is close to the Tamanu shopping center, the Museum of Tahiti and Her Islands and several restaurants, including those at Le Méridien hotel. Even though the name indicates that it is a guesthouse on the beach, it is actually on the mountainside, with access to the beach, which is only 100 m. away. There are 12 rooms located in 2 one-story concrete buildings, each with a double bed or sgl beds, and private bathroom with hot water. The bright, cheerful rooms have bamboo furniture, a refrigerator, ceiling fan and TV, and they open onto a terrace facing the swimming pool and flower gardens. Some of the units have a kitchenette. You can also have owner Anne-Marie Moreels cook your meals for you. She is a French woman who uses fresh local products.

PENSION TE NAHE TOETOE (formerly Chez Armelle) *B.P. 380640, Tamanu, Tahiti 98718. Tel. 689/58.42.43/77.79.99; Fax 689/58.42.81; armelle@mail.pf; www.pension-tenahetoetoe.net. PK 15.2 on seaside in Punaauia Commune, 9.6 mi from downtown. Look for the sign on the road shortly after the Mobil Station and Plage de Toaroto sign. One-way daytime transfers 1.500 CFP per person and 2.500 CFP at night. EP room with breakfast 5.980 CFP sgl; 7.620 CFP dbl; triple room 9.120 CFP. Add 2.000 CFP per day for A/C. Meals on request. Special long-term rates. Taxes included. MC, V.*

This pension/snack is located beside the coral sand beach, close to the Museum of Tahiti and Her Islands and to Taapuna, one of Tahiti's most popular surfing spots. Six rooms have a double bed, ceiling fan and a private bathroom with hot water, and 2 rooms can sleep 3 people, also with fans and private bathrooms. A/C on request. Outrigger paddle canoes are provided and cars can be rented. Manager Raimana Riviere will arrange island tours and excursions for you. The snack is open daily, serving dinner specials for 1.500 CFP.

PENSION OTAHA, *B.P. 380231, Tamanu 98718 Punaauia, Tahiti; Tel. 689/58.24.52/71.55.54; paemiti@hotmail.com; www.otaha-lodge.com. PK 17.3 on seaside in Punaauia Commune, 17.3 km (10.7 mi) from downtown and 14 km (8.7 mi) from the airport. 2008 EP Rates: 2-bedroom Garden Bungalow with kitchen 15.000 CFP for 4 people; Garden Studio with private bathroom, terrace and kitchenette 9.000 CFP sgl/dbl plus a child; 4 Beach Studios with local style kitchenette 11.000 CFP sgl/dbl plus a child; Beach Bungalow with kitchen 18.000 CFP for 4 adults. Add taxes. No credit cards. 2-night stay required.*

Titaua Schenck runs this popular pension beside the white sand beach in Punaauia, and she speaks English. There's a big sign beside the road and you get off Le Truck right at the driveway to the pension. All guests have access to a washing machine, kayaks and snorkeling gear. There are restaurants, snack bars and roulottes, as well as various Chinese *magasin* stores selling food in this area.

TAAROA LODGE, *B.P. 498, Papeete, Tahiti 98713. Tel/Fax 689/58.39.21; Cell 689/78.84.86; taaroalodge@mail.pf; www.taaroalodge.com. PK 18.2, beside the beach in Punaauia behind Snack PK 18. One-way transfer 2.000 CFP for one/1.500 CFP each for 2 or more. EP room 6.000 CFP sgl/dbl; bungalow for 1-3 people 10.000*

CFP per day; bungalow-chalet 16.000 CFP per day for 1-5, 20.000 CFP for 6-10 people; dormitory 2.500 CFP per person per day; plus taxes. MC, V.

Ralph Sanford welcomes surfers, backpackers and anyone else who wants to stay beside one of Tahiti's nicest beaches. He has a large chalet style wooden bungalow with a bedroom and double bed on the ground floor, complete with a private bathroom and hot water. On the mezzanine is a 7-mattress dormitory, whose occupants share a bathroom with hot water. All guests have use of the kitchen, dining room and big terrace. Two wooden bungalows overlooking the lagoon have a double bed and a single bed in each, as well as a refrigerator, microwave oven and facilities for coffee and tea. They also have a small covered terrace, where you can sit and watch Moorea and the sunset. No meals are served, but the Sanfords will bring you fresh bread and fruit in the mornings, and there is a restaurant/snack in front of the house. Mahana Park is less than 500 ft. down the road, where you'll find a restaurant and a snack bar. You can catch *le truck* to the airport or town in front of the house.

RELAIS FENUA, *B.P. 381585, Tamanu, Punaauia, Tahiti 98718. Tel. 689/ 45.01.98/77.25.45; Fax 689/45.30.03; relais.fenua@mail.pf; www.relais-fenua.pf. PK 18.25 on mountainside in Punaauia, right across the road from Taaroa Lodge and 150 m from the public beach of Mahana Park. One-way transfers 1.250 CFP per person (min. 2). 2008 EP Rates: Room 8.500 CFP sgl, 8.900 CFP dbl; 9.300 tpl; Room with a/c 9.500 CFP sgl/dbl; 10.900 CFP for 4 people. Reduced rates after 3 days. Breakfast 900 CFP per person. Taxes included. MC, V.*

This pension has been awarded a 3-Tiare rating by Tahiti Tourisme. The modern white concrete house contains 7 neo-colonial style rooms for singles, doubles and families, and one room can accommodate handicapped guests. Some of the rooms have a/c and all of them have ceiling fans, TV, personal safes and a private bathroom with hot water. There is a boutique of local arts and crafts on the premises, and a small swimming pool and whirlpool are located in the tropical garden. Le Truck passes along the coastal road just 150 m. in front of the property. This guesthouse is convenient to scuba diving centers, marinas, the Museum of Tahiti and Her Islands, the Lagoonarium and the big hotels on Tahiti's west coast. A restaurant-bar and food store are also close by.

TE MITI, *B.P. 130088, Moana Nui, Punaauia, Tahiti 98717. Tel./Fax 689/ 58.48.61; Cell 689/78.60.80; pensiontemiti@mail.pf; www.pensiontemiti.com PK 18.6, mountainside, 11.5 mi from Papeete in Lotissement Papehue, in Paea Com-mune, 100 m (328 ft.) after the Paea sign, across road from Mahana Park public beach. Round-trip transfers 1.500 CFP per person 24/24. EP room with breakfast 6.500-7.500 CFP sgl/dbl; dormitory 2.500 CFP per person. Reduced rates start at 7 nights. Taxes included. MC, V.*

A "Bed and Breakfast" sign on the mountainside of the circle island road points the way to this hostel, which is located on 1/4-acre of land with lots of fruit trees. This pension is a good choice for surfers and backpackers, as it is just 200 m (218 yds.) from Tahiti's prettiest white sand beach at Mahana Park. Three clean, modern houses provide 5 bedrooms with ceiling fans, mosquito nets and plenty of storage space. Two dorms have 4 beds each. Guests share 2 fully equipped kitchens, 3 bathrooms with hot water, a TV corner, a washing machine and several spacious patios. Other services include telephone, fax and Internet access at 500 CFP for 30 min. Snorkeling gear is provided and all arrangements can be made for 4WD excursions, scuba diving and surf schools. Nearby are car and scooter rentals, restaurants, snacks and *magasin* food stores. This is a highly rated hostel according to the tourist feedback at the Tahiti Tourisme Bureau. Frédèric and Christelle are a young, dynamic couple who treat their guests very well.

HITI MOANA VILLA, *B.P. 10865, Paea, Tahiti 98711. Tel. 689/57.93.93; Fax 57.94.44; cell 74.16.67; hitimoanavilla@mail.pf; www.papeete.com/moanavilla. At PK 32, 19.8 mi from Papeete beside the lagoon in Papara Commune, 10 min. from golf course and surfing beach. One-way transfers from airport 5.000 CFP per person and 2.500 CFP each for 2 passengers. 2008 EP Rates: Garden View Bungalow without kitchen 10.000 CFP sgl/dbl; Lagoon View Bungalow without kitchen, 10.500 CFP sgl/dbl; Lagoon View Bungalow with kitchen 13.000 CFP for 1-4 people; Mara Bungalow beside pool with lagoon view and kitchen 14.500 CFP for 1-4 people. Extra bed 1.000 CFP. Breakfast 900 CFP per person. All taxes included. AE, MC, V.*

This is a clean, modern pension built in a lovely flower garden between the road and the lagoon in Papara, just 10 min. by car from the international golf course and the international surfing beach of Taharuu. There are 4 concrete studios with tiled floors, each with a double bed in the separate bedroom and 2 single beds in the living room, plus a private kitchen, private bathroom with hot water, TV, ceiling fans and a covered narrow terrace facing the lagoon. Paved walkways also lead to the 4 newer bungalows that are built in the local government subsidized style with wood shake roofs, a double bed in the sleeping/living room, a private bathroom with hot water, ceiling fan, TV and a terrace overlooking the flower garden and lagoon.

All the rooms are very attractively decorated in bright Polynesian motifs. In addition to a swimming pool, you'll also have the advantage of a private pontoon. Owner Steeve Brotherson can arrange a circle island tour by minivan, fishing, and outings on a barge for you, and help you organize other activities. A washing machine is available for guest use at a charge, and there is a public telephone booth beside the road in front of the pension. The Restaurant Nuutere is across the street and supermarkets and snack bars are close by. Former guests have had problems with thieves coming into their rooms, so take extra precaution here.

East Coast: Papenoo Valley – Moderate

RELAIS DE LA MAROTO, *B.P. 20687, Papeete, Tahiti 98713. Tel. 689/ 57.90.29/72.98.21; Fax 689/57.90.30; maroto@mail.pf. In the mountains of Papenoo Valley on the cross-island road between the communes of Mataiea and Papenoo. Round-trip 4WD transfers provided from bottom of valley to hotel for 4.250 CFP per adult and 2.500 CFP for child. 2008 EP Rates dbl: Standard room 7.800-10.600 CFP;*

Bungalow 19.000 CFP; Suite 25.000 CFP. Continental breakfast 1.300 CFP; American breakfast 1.700 CFP. Lunch and dinner à la carte. MAP package from Sat. afternoon to Sun. morning with room, dinner and breakfast 12.450 CFP per person. All taxes included. AE, MC, V.

If your preferences include quiet mountain retreats in a cool, peaceful setting of tree ferns, waterfalls, archaeological sites and wild beauty in every imaginable shade of green, then you'll be happy at Maroto. This is Tahiti's only mountain lodging, located in the center of the island in the historic Papenoo Valley, at the convergence of Vaituoru and Vainavenave rivers. In pre-Christian days this valley was formerly inhabited by thousands of Maohi people. Several of the basaltic house platforms, petroglyphs, meeting sites and *marae* temples of stone have been restored, and you can hike from the hotel to explore the interior of the island, where you'll find tunnels, grottos, caves and lava tubes.

The hotel buildings were originally used to house construction crews who built several hydroelectric dams in the Papenoo Valley. Although the interiors were completely renovated a couple of times, the rooms are still very basic and reminiscent of summer camp. There are now 15 standard rooms, 3 bungalows and 2 suites, all containing a queen size bed, and there are also single beds in the bungalows and suites. Each accommodation has a private bathroom with hot water and a terrace overlooking the mountain peaks and lush valley. Another large building houses the reception area, living room, convention room, dining room, bar, kitchen and game room. The restaurant serves à la carte French cuisine and Te Ana, their wine cellar, is supposed to be the most prestigious in all of the South Pacific, with impressive prices and *crus*, including Napa Valley's best labels.

You can get to La Maroto by 4-wheel drive vehicle from Mataiea or through the Papenoo Valley. If you decide to drive up this tortuous mountain road make sure you have a strong 4x4, and be especially careful during the frequent rains, as the roads can be very slippery. You can also drive from the circle island road to the Fare Hape site in the Papenoo Valley and the Relais de la Maroto will send someone to transfer you to the small family hotel. You can also join a full-day Across the Island Tour with Tahiti Safari Expedition (See information under *Mountain & Waterfall Tours*), which stops at the restaurant here for lunch. You can walk from the hotel to the restored *marae* in the Papenoo Valley.

Other Family Pensions, Guest Houses, Surf Lodges, & Dormitories on Tahiti Nui (Big Tahiti)

PENSION PUEA, *Tel. 85.43.43; pension.puea@mail.pf,* at 87 Rue Octave Moreau in Fariipiti, has 8 rooms for 4.820 CFP sgl, 6.990 CFP dbl, and 9.500 CFP for a family of 2 adults and 2 children. Rates include breakfast.

TEAMO HOSTEL-PENSION, *Tel. 42.00.35/42.47.26; teamohostel@mail.pf.* This is a wooden house at 8, rue du Pont Neuf in the Mission neighborhood of downtown Papeete, a few blocks inland. There are 5 private rooms, including some with a/c, and 3 dormitories with 4-6 beds. Guests share kitchen, library and TV.

MC and V accepted. Rates are 5.800-7.000 CFP for a room (max. 3 people). Transfers provided.

MAHINA TEA, *Tel. 42.00.97*. This old 2-story wooden pension has 16 rooms for 6.000-7.000 CFP a night, and 15 studios with kitchenettes for 10.000 CFP per night in St. Amelie valley behind the French Gendarmerie. Monthly rentals available.

HEITIARE INN, Tel. 83.33.52, PK 5, Faa'a, near airport, has 6 rooms (5 have a/c) with private bathrooms from 8.500-10.000 CFP sgl/dbl. Free transfers.

TAHITI AIRPORT LODGE, *Tel. 82.23.68/79.30.84*. PK 5.5 Cité de l'Air in Faaa, overlooking airport. 6 rooms in 2-story colonial style house, from 5.000 CFP sgl, 6.000-8.000 CFP dbl. Owners are an old couple who have received great praises and several complaints from former guests. Do not confuse this pension with Tahiti Airport Motel.

PAPARA VILLAGE, *Tel. 57.41.41; pacificresort@paparavillage.com*; at PK 38 on the mountainside in Papara. 1 family house with kitchen and 2 bungalows with kitchenette. Swimming pool and *Fare Pote'e* shelter. No restaurant services.

FARE RATERE, *Tel. 57.54.04; www.frenchpolynesialodging.com*. Beside the Taharuu surfing beach at PK 39.2 in Papara. 2 Beach Bungalows and 3 duplex Garden Studios, with kitchens, TV, and hot water showers, plus a dormitory for surfers.

Tahiti Iti Peninsula (Little Tahiti)

Transfer service by mini-bus is available from Papeete or the airport to Tahiti Iti. Contact: **Verofredo Transports**, *Tel. 78.77.65/78.86.32; verofredo@mail.pf*. They charge 5.700-7.000 CFP for 1-2 passengers. You can rent a car at the airport, your hotel or in Taravao to drive yourself to the Tahiti Iti peninsula. You can also take a public bus for 400 CFP each way.

Te Reva Nei, *Tel. 56.20.01/71.81.24; terevanei@hotmail.com*. This small company has a special tour to visit Tahiti Iti for the day. They take you to visit the Taravao Plateau, the famous surf spot of Teahupoo, and swimming from a black sand beach. Lunch is served at Beach Kaikai, the restaurant terrace at Pension La Vague Bleue, also known as Tauhanihani Village Lodge. This 9am-4pm excursion costs US$135 per person for 4-6 passengers.

Tahiti Iti – Economy to Moderate

PENSION CHAYAN, *B.P. 8836, Taravao, Tahiti 98719. Tel./Fax 689/ 57.46.00; cell 72.28.40; pensionchayan@mail.pf; www.pensionchayantahiti.pf. On mountainside at PK 14 in Vairao, on west coast of Tahiti Iti. 2008 EP Rates: bungalow 14.150 CFP sgl/dbl; extra bed 3.000 CFP; 1.500 CFP for child 4-12 years. Add taxes. MC, V.*

This pension has been awarded a 3-Tiare rating by Tahiti Tourisme. Chayan is a contraction of Chantal and Yannick Salmon, the owners of this 4-bungalow pension they opened in Dec. 2002, between the mountain and the lagoon of

Vairao. Although they are on the mountain side of the road, their guests have access to a small beach and a pier built over the lagoon. Their own verdant property has a waterfall and basin in the back yard, and in the middle flows a stream where fresh water eels swim and feed. The 4 concrete bungalows are far enough apart to insure privacy. Each unit has an attractively decorated bedroom with a queen size bed, louvered windows, a fully equipped kitchen, a tiled bathroom with hot water shower, and a terrace. Kayaks are available for guest use, and your hosts can help you arrange all boating excursions and other activities.

VANIRA LODGE, *B.P. 8458, Teahupoo, Tahiti 98719. Tel./689/72.69.92; Fax 689/57.70.18; vaniralodge@mail.pf; www.vaniralodge.com; Skype: vaniralodge. On the mountainside at PK 15.6 in Teahupoo, 75.6 km. (46.9 mi.) from the airport. One-way transfer 7.500 CFP for 1-2 people. 2008 EP Rates: 16.000 CFP for 1-4 people; extra bed 1.200 CFP; breakfast 1.200 CFP per person. Taxes included. MC, V.*

Tahiti Tourisme has awarded this pension with the top rating of 3 Tiares. The 4 artistically designed bungalows are built in a 5 acre (2 ha.) park on a plateau 164 ft. (50 m.) above sea level, offering a magnificent 180° view of the lagoon, the surfing waves of Teahupoo, and the tropical sunset. The grounds include fruit trees, a swimming pool, a small waterfall and a pond for goldfish and ducks.

Anyone who ever saw the bungalows at the now defunct Fare Nana'o in Taravao and the former Hana Iti in Huahine (destroyed by a cyclone in the 1990's) will recognize the creative touch of French builder Jean-Claude Michel in the bungalows at Vanira Lodge. Three of the naturalistic style units are made of wood, stone, bamboo and thatch, and the 4th bungalow is more modern, but decorated with a traditional Polynesian motif. Each bungalow is 538 sq. ft. (50 sq. m.) and can sleep 3-5 people. There is a bedroom or mezzanine with a double bed, a lounge with 2 single beds, a kitchenette, bathroom with hot water shower, and roofed terrace. There are fans and mosquito nets in the rooms, and they are cleaned every other day.

French owner Karine Lavalle can help you arrange your activities to go surfing, discovering the Tahiti Iti peninsula by boat or car, tramping to Te Pari, riding horses at the Rauvau Ranch on the Taravao plateau, or finding good restaurants and snacks nearby. Vanira Lodge provides bicycles for their guests. The steep track from the road to the lodge can be slippery when wet. The kayaks are also free of charge and are located at the marina some 984 ft. (300 m.) from the lodge. Karine also knows the person who can give you a good massage in your room.

LA VAGUE BLEUE *(Tauhanihani Village Lodge), B.P. 66, Taravao, Tahiti 98719. Tel./Fax 689/57.23.23; cell 74.81.82; kotyvaguebleue@mail.pf; www.infinitysurfboards.com. Beside the lagoon at PK 16 in Teahupoo village, 76 km. (47 mi) from the airport. One-way transfers 5.700 CFP for 1-2 people. 2008 EP Rates: Garden Bungalow 14.000 CFP sgl/dbl; Beach Bungalow 16.000 CFP sgl/dbl; extra bed 2.000 CFP. Breakfast 500-800 CFP, lunch or dinner 800-1.600 CFP. Special package for 4-5 surfers in bungalow, 3.500 CFP per person. Rates include all taxes. AE, MC, V.*

Koty and Réné Manuireva have 5 local style FEI (government subsidized) bungalows on their property at the edge of the lagoon in the middle of Teahupoo village facing the famous Hava'e Pass. They have two sons who surf and take care of the family pension. Everyone here speaks English. Each bungalow has a king size bed and two single beds (or 5 single beds for surfers), a ceiling fan or electric fan, color TV, a private bathroom with hot water shower, and a covered terrace. The beach units also have a refrigerator and coffee maker. There is a small beach here and kayaks for the guests. They also have a 12-passenger boat they use for excursions to explore the wild coast of Te Pari at the south end of Tahiti Iti for picnics, visits to Vaipoiri grotto and to shuttle the surfers out to the big waves. Beach Kaikai is the name of the on-site restaurant, where Koty serves family style meals.

TE PARI VILLAGE, *B.P. 697, Papeete, Tahiti 98713. Tel. 689/42.59.12/ 42.01.49/78.91.12; Fax 689/42.59.12; teparivillage@yahoo.fr. 2 km (1.2 mi) beyond the end of the road in the Fenua Aihere (wild land), a 30-min. walk or a 10-min. boat ride from the Teahupoo dock on the south coast of Tahiti Iti. One-way mini-bus transfer from airport to boat dock in Teahupoo 2.700 CFP. Free round-trip boat transfers between boat dock and pension. AP bungalow and excursion 10.450 CFP per person; day tour excursion with lunch 5.500 CFP. Add taxes. No credit cards. Minimum stay of 2 nights during week and 1 night on weekends.*

Vanina Teamotuaitau and Désirée Liant have 4 bungalows in a big grassy area beside the lagoon in a tropical paradise of coconut groves, fruit trees, coffee and vanilla plantations and flowers. Units contain 1 or 2 double beds, private bathroom with hot water, and a terrace. The bungalows are spacious, clean and attractively decorated with Tahitian fabrics and a mosquito net. All guests share the living room and dining area. A 5-min. boat ride takes you to the most fabulous surfing spot in Polynesia and you can hike to the waterfalls and tropical jungle of Te Pari cliffs. Canoes and kayaks are provided and you can swim, dive and visit the grotto of Vaipoiri. Most of the clientele are French people who live in Tahiti and want to get away for the weekend or a few days in a quiet, peaceful environment.

LE BONJOUIR, *B.P. 8255, Taravao, Tahiti 98719. Tel. 689/77.89.69/ 57.02.15; bonjouir@mail.pf; www.bonjouir.com. Beside the lagoon on the south coast of Tahiti Iti in an area called Te Pari, a 12-min. boat ride beyond the end of the road and the Teahupoo boat dock. A one-way car transfer between airport and Teahupoo boat dock 3.000 CFP per person. Round-trip boat transfers between Teahupoo dock and pension 2.000 CFP per person. Private parking 500 CFP per day. 2008 EP Rates: bungalow and private bathroom for 2-6 people 9.500-15.000 CFP; studio for 2-6 people 5.000-7.000 CFP; ocean view room for 2-3 people with communal bathroom 7.000-8.000 CFP. MAP meal plan 4.500 CFP. Surfer packages available. No credit cards.*

Owner Annick Paofai calls her pension the 'Eden of Tahiti', as the lush green property is located between the mountains and the lagoon and a river flows through it. The 6 simply furnished bungalows, 6 *fares*, 2 studios and 3 rooms offer a variety of accommodations, including private bathrooms with hot water showers, and mosquito nets over the beds. 2 bungalows are equipped with private kitchens. You can take a 4 km. (2.5-mi.) hike along the seashore to buy food at the *magasin* store in Teahupoo. The pension also operates a shuttle boat service daily at 12pm and 5pm that will take you to Teahupoo and back for 2.000 CFP per person. Meals are served in the pension's main restaurant. Breakfast costs 1.250 CFP and dinner is 3.250 CFP. Beer, wine and cocktails are also available.

Kayaks are free for guest use, but you should bring your own snorkeling gear. There is a TV in the restaurant/bar area, and there are facilities for soccer, volleyball and bacci ball. You can also swim, hike, go fishing in the river or lagoon or chill out in a hammock under the big Fare Pote'e gazebo.

A shuttle boat is available to transfer surfers to the famous spots of Hava'e, Te Ava Iti and to the Vairao pass, for 2.000-3.500 CFP per person for the first 3 hours; add another 1.000 CFP per person after that, depending on which pass you choose. The mornings here are especially magnificent, as you can see the sun rising from behind the horizon of the sea. A special sunset cruise or moon cruise can be arranged, as well as picnics on the motu.

PUNATEA VILLAGE, *B.P. 20756, Punaauia, Tahiti 98713. Tel. 689/ 77.20.31/72.17.01; punatea-village@mail.pf; www.punatea.com. On seaside at PK 4.7 in Afaahiti on the east coast of the Tahiti Iti peninsula, 64.7 km (40 mi) from Papeete. 2008 EP Rates sgl/dbl: Bungalow 9.000 CFP sgl/dbl; Room 5.500 CFP sgl/ dbl; extra bed 2.000 CFP. Breakfast is 800 CFP. Add taxes. MC, V.*

This pension is built on 18.5 acres of land beside the lagoon in Afaahiti between Taravao and Pueu. There are 4 separate bungalows and a block of 5 rooms, all built of wood and cedar shake roofs in the style that has become the "norm" for pensions that receive special financial support from the local government. Each of the bungalows contains a double bed and a convertible sofa, a private bathroom with hot water, plus a kitchen and covered porch. There are ceiling fans and electric mosquito repellants. People staying in the rooms share the bath facilities. Owner/ manager Titaua Bordes speaks English and is very helpful with her guests. Meals are served à la carte in 2 dining *fares* by the sea. Free activities for guests include a fresh water swimming pool, swings for kids, volleyball net, kayaks and bicycles. Paid activities include horseback riding, trips to visit a private waterfall, picnics on Motu Nono and boat excursions to Te Pari on the end of the peninsula. Punatea Village also has a massage chair and Japanese sauna.

Other Family Pensions, Guest Houses, Surf Lodges & Dormitories on Tahiti Iti (Little Tahiti)

CHEZ JEANNINE, *Tel./Fax 57.07.49/77.27.37*, PK 4, Taravao Plateau on Tahiti Iti, has 5 rooms and 4 bungalows, plus Vietnamese Restaurant on premises.

FARE MAITHE, *Tel./Fax. 57.18.24; www.chez-maithe.com.* A 2-room guesthouse with kitchen beside the sea at PK 4.5 in Afaahiti, on the east coast of the Tahiti Iti peninsula. Room 7.500 CFP dbl. Private transfer in minibus available.

PENSION TE HIHI O TE RA, *Tel. 72.85.24; Fax 57.92.78.* Tino Haro has 3 rooms with a communal kitchen and bathroom in Tautira, at the start of the hiking trail to the Fenua Aihere on the Tahiti Iti Peninsula. Boat transfer from the marina in Tautira is 1.000 CFP per person. 2008 Rates: Room with breakfast is 2.500 CFP per person, MAP is 4.500 CFP and AP is 8.500 CFP.

MEHERIO ITI, *Tel. 72.45.50, Fax 57.68.49,* on the seaside at PK 11.9 in Vairao, has 6 simple bungalows.

PENSION VAIANI, *Tel./Fax 57.96.16,* on the seaside at PK 16.9 in Teahupoo, has 3 rooms with 7 dormitory beds and communal bathroom, for 6.500 CFP per person MAP. This no frills lodging is designed for surfers.

PUEU VILLAGE, *Tel./Fax 57.57.87,* on the seaside at PK 9.8 in Pueu on the east coast of the Tahiti Iti peninsula. Owner Victor Van Cam has 4 bungalows for 10.000 CFP without a/c or 12.000 CFP with a/c sgl/dbl. He is still planning to build 6 rooms in a concrete building. Swimming pool on premises, which used to be the Hotel Te Anuanua.

WHERE TO EAT
Tahiti Nui (Big Tahiti) – Hotel Restaurants
INTERCONTINENTAL TAHITI RESORT, *Tel. 86.51.10. PK 7, Faaa. Open daily for BLD. All credit cards. Add 10% tax.*

Tiare Restaurant is the main restaurant, offering all day dining from 5:30am-10pm. The Continental breakfast buffet for 2.440 CFP and the American breakfast buffet for 2.970 CFP is served from 7-10:30am. This buffet also includes Japanese breakfast foods such as miso soup, rice and pickled vegetables. Burgers, salads and other light meals are served for lunch and a 3-course *table d'hôte* menu is 4.400 CFP. Between 11:30am-2:30pm during the week you can also choose your own combinations to be stir-fried in a Chinese wok, for 2.350 CFP. Dinner features local dishes and international cuisine. Hot or cold appetizers are 1.250-2.100 CFP, and Tahitian specialties are 1.860-2.850 CFP, which include shrimp curry, chicken and taro leaves, and grilled mahi mahi. A 3-course set dinner menu is 6.560 CFP.

A Rotisserie Barbecue Dinner is featured on Wed. night, followed by a Tahitian dance show, for 6.810 CFP per person. The *Soiree Merveilleuse* (Marvelous Evening) costs 8.400 CFP and is held on Fri. night, with a seafood buffet and entertainment provided by one of the best professional dance groups of Tahiti. A Bounty Dinner and Show is held on Sat. nights, with a special buffet of imaginative dishes prepared with local products and a musical re-enactment of the "Mutiny on the Bounty" story of Captain Bligh and Fletcher Christian performed by Les Grands Ballet de Tahiti, the premier dance group of Tahiti. This costs 7.790 CFP per person. A Tahitian brunch for 4.350 CFP is served in the Tiare restaurant every Sun. morning, which gives you the opportunity of tasting some very unusual treats such as *taioro, firi firi* and vanilla coffee laced with coconut milk. The Mahana Buffet is served at noon on Sun. and costs 3.690 CFP.

Le Lotus is an overwater restaurant adjacent to a sandy bottom swimming pool with an outdoor Jacuzzi and swim-up bar. From 10am to 6pm you can sip a tropical cocktail from your underwater barstool as you gaze at the beautiful island of Moorea across the Sea of Moons, and watch the outrigger canoe paddlers glide past in the opalescent lagoon. This is one of Tahiti's most beautiful and romantic restaurants and you'll think you're in a movie setting of the South Seas.

Le Lotus is open daily 11am-2:30pm and 6:30-10pm, serving a trendy alliance inspired by world foods and European culinary traditions. The hotel management signed a partnership agreement in 2001 with Paul Haeberlin of Alsace and his restaurant, l'Auberge de l'Ill, one of the grand names of French gastronomy, who has a 3-star Michelan rating. A Haeberlin chef now collaborates with the Lotus' own chef to combine Tahiti's fresh products with the recipes from l'Auberge de l'Ill. You should reserve.

Luncheon choices range from a Lotus Express one-plate meal for 3.950 CFP to a 3-course gourmand selection for 5.145 CFP. The main courses include a fusion of Mexican, Oriental, Asian and Mediterranean cuisine. Desserts for 1.500 CFP include a raspberry and coconut sundae and a white mint sorbet with chocolate and vanilla ice cream. A glass of wine or a tropical cocktail costs 1.300 CFP.

Dinner can be a 2-course Fine Bouche meal for 7.220 CFP, a 3-course Gourmet meal for 8.950 CFP, or a 4-course Degustation (Tasting) selection for 10.290 CFP. Appetizers on the à la carte menu are 3.100-4.100 CFP; fish dishes are 4.350-5.400 CFP, and meats are 5.400 CFP. The menu changes frequently, but the last time I ate here the main courses included boned pigeon with fois gras, pan-fried scallops, caramelized quail and guinea fowl supreme. You can choose your wines and champagnes from an extensive menu, and toast one another to the musical accompaniment of your old favorites that are played softly on the piano as you dine.

Tiki Bar is the name of the main bar, which is open daily from 10am-midnight. This is one of the most popular gathering places in Tahiti for young professionals looking for entertainment. Happy Hour starts at 4:30pm daily and lasts for 2 hours on Thurs., with live music from 5-9pm. Musical groups also perform each Wed., Sat. and Sun., starting at 5pm. The Lobby Bar is open daily from 10pm-5:30am, with light meals served on request.

LE MERIDIEN, Tel. 47.07.07. PK 15, Punaauia. Open daily for BLD. All credit cards.

La Plantation is the hotel's main restaurant, where you can serve yourself from the American Breakfast Buffet for 2.910 CFP. Lunch is served here on Sat. and Sun. only, with an à la carte menu from 12-3pm. Appetizers are priced from 1.350-1.900 CFP, and the main courses from 2.400-2.700 CFP. The restaurant is closed on Mon. and Tues. Dinner is à la carte except on Fri. evening when a seafood buffet is served for 6.624 CFP. This price also includes a Polynesian dance show.

Le Carré is a gastronomic restaurant beside the beach, where you can sit on the sundeck under a big umbrella at lunchtime or under the stars at night while dining by candlelight. Inside the square restaurant are square tables and chairs, square place settings, napkins and dishes, all designed to carry out the theme of Le Carré—the square. Luncheon choices offer an appetizer for 2.020 CFP, one main course for 2.725 CFP, an appetizer and one main course for 4.340 CFP, a main course and dessert for 4.240 CFP, or a 3-course meal for 4.945 CFP. Some of the suggestions include eggplant fritters with fresh goat cheese on a green salad, carpaccio of venison, tender poultry stuffed with shrimp and ginger, and crème brûlée with pineapple and crystallized ginger.

Dinner at Le Carré gives you choices of Formula dining. You can opt for the Cold Discoveries appetizers, which give you either salmon, lobster, crab, rabbit or pork starter courses. The Tasting Menu is 9.990 CFP, and Le Carré Salé is 5.960 CFP, which gives you a hot or cold starter and main course of your choice, or Le Carré Sucré for 5.150 CFP, which is the main course and dessert. Le Grand Carré for 7.670 CFP includes the starter, main course and dessert. There are also à la carte selections, including vegetarian dishes starting at 1.815 CFP, sea bass for 3.530 CFP, or the chef's cassoulet for 3.835 CFP.

The wine cabinet is filled with select choices of wine from Spain, Chile, Argentina, Australia, California, South Africa, France, New Zealand and Tahiti.

The **Pool Bar** serves light snacks, drinks and ice cream. **L'Astrolabe** is the main bar just above La Plantation Restaurant. Here you can order your favorite exotic cocktails and other libations from a prize-winning barman. A local band entertains here on Thurs. and Sat. evenings.

RADISSON PLAZA RESORT TAHITI, *Tel. 48.88.88. Open daily for BLD. All credit cards.*

Restaurant Hiti Mahana is the resort's signature restaurant, overlooking Lafayette Beach and Matavai Bay. An American buffet breakfast is 2.950 CFP and a la carte choices are available. A Sun. morning brunch is 3.950 CFP and a Sun. luncheon brunch is 4.550 CFP.

A luncheon buffet of raw vegetables is served Mon.-Fri. for 1.580 CFP, or you can order burgers for 1.800-1.900 CFP, salads for 2.050-2.270 CFP, or fish and meat dishes for 2.000-2.600 CFP. A 2-course set luncheon menu is 3.150 CFP, and a 3-course set dinner menu is 4.350 CFP. The dinner menu offers a mix of Tahitian, Southeast Asian and international cuisine. The starter courses are 1.600-2.650 CFP and main courses are 2.250-3.350 CFP. A 3-course set menu is 4.350 CFP. A buffet of Tahitian foods is served on Fri. nights, accompanied by a Tahitian dance show for 6.000 CFP.

Lafayette Bar is on the hotel's upper level and is open from 4pm until late at night. The resort's signature drink is the Pisco Sour, and an extensive variety of cocktails, beers, spirits, wines and champagnes can be served on request.

SHERATON HOTEL TAHITI, *Tel. 86.48.48. Open daily. All credit cards.*

Restaurant Moevai is built over the water, serving BLD. You have a choice of a Baker's Basket for 700 CFP, a Parisian breakfast for 1.100 CFP, a Yankee breakfast for 1.500 CFP, a Continental breakfast for 2.250 CFP, or the American breakfast buffet for 2.780 CFP. Lunch consists of carpaccios and tartares for 1.650-2.200 CFP, salads for 1.450-1.950 CFP, pizza or pasta for 1.400-1.900 CFP, and a hot dish for 2.550-3.750 CFP. A 2-course luncheon menu is 3.980 CFP, and a 3-course dinner menu is 6.480 CFP. The à la carte dinner menu lists appetizers from 1.400-2.650 CFP, fish and seafood from 2.550-3.100 CFP and meat and poultry dishes for 2.400-3.450 CFP. Desserts are 300-1.200 CFP. Special theme dinners may include specialties from the various regions of France, Italy, Spain or Asia. A Lobster Beach Party is held each Sat. evening, with a large choice of lobster specialties for 7.800 CFP per person.

La Terrasse is open daily 11am-5:30pm, serving burgers, salads and light meals. Poolside food and beverage service is also available from 10am-6pm. Drinks are served in **Quinn's Bar** from 10am-midnight, and tapas are available at 5pm. There is live entertainment on weekends and for other special occasions.

SOFITEL TAHITI RESORT, *Tel. 86.66.00. PK 7.5 Punaauia. Open daily for BLD. All credit cards.*

Restaurant Bougainville, on the ground level, is an open-air restaurant for 200 people. The American breakfast buffet is 2.901 CFP. Lunch includes a salad bar for 2.300 CFP and burgers from 1.600 CFP. A set luncheon menu is 3.148 CFP and a set dinner menu is 5.340 CFP. The dinner menu lists salads and appetizers from 1.200-2.200 CFP, and main courses from 2.600-5.000 CFP. A 3-course tourist menu is 4.500 CFP. A Barbecue buffet is presented each Wed., with live jazz and local music; a Mediterranean buffet is featured on Fri., with a Polynesian dance show; and a Tahitian buffet is held each Sun. noon, accompanied by a Polynesian dance show. Each buffet costs 5.200 CFP. Sandwiches, hamburgers and salads are available during the daytime at the **Moorea Bar** beside the swimming pool, and you can also enjoy your favorite cocktails at this outdoor bar.

Sakura is a Japanese restaurant located adjacent to the lobby of the Sofitel Tahiti Resort. Open daily 6:30pm-9:30pm. Teppanyaki cooking is featured, with main dishes of fish, chicken, steak, shrimp and scallops from 2.500-4.000 CFP, and combinations from 4.500-6.000 CFP. The vegetables do not include mushrooms and bean sprouts, as you normally find in this type of cooking. Nonetheless, all the chefs (no Japanese) are kept busy and reservations are a must.

ROYAL TAHITIEN, *Tel. 50.40.40. On waterfront in Pirae at the Hotel Royal Tahitien. All credit cards. Open daily for B,L,D.*

This is one of Tahiti's most popular restaurants with local residents. You can dine on an open deck overlooking the black sand beach and lagoon, or inside the Polynesian style restaurant, which has an intricately woven pandanus ceiling that is reminiscent of Tahiti's "la belle epoch" of the good old days. Breakfast includes choices of French, Continental, American or Tahitian foods.

The lunch or dinner menu offers so many of my favorite foods that it is difficult to choose, and most of the prices have not changed in several years. I usually get the excellent poisson cru or the nems and sashimi combo for lunch, and the breaded veal cutlet Cordon Bleu for dinner, or you can order the mahi mahi Cordon Bleu.

Soups include gazpacho for 850 CFP or onion soup for 1.050 CFP and salads start at 1.600 CFP. Special Island dishes are 1.980-2.850 CFP and include chicken and fafa (taro leaves) or breaded mahi mahi in coconut. American style BBQ ribs are 2.700 CFP. A *plat du jour* daily special is served at lunch for 1.950-2.250 CFP. A 3-course tourist menu is 3.850 CFP. Cheeseburgers, mahi mahi burgers or steak burgers are served with fries for around 1.400 CFP. Desserts are 750-1.200 CFP and include coconut pie or a banana split.

The bar and terrace become a hot spot for cool jazz played by a local band each Wed. evening, and on Fri. nights there is live music for dancing, accompanied by a special BBQ dinner. This is a good place to meet the friendly people of Tahiti.

Downtown Papeete – Deluxe
   CORBEILLE D'EAU, *Tel. 43.77.14. Blvd. Pomare, Paofai. AE, MC, V. Open for L,D. except for Sat. noon, all day Sun. and holidays. Reserve.*
   The name of this small elegant restaurant is the French version of Papeete, which means, "water basket" and it's located in the block just west of the Protestant Church in Paofai across from the waterfront. If you're walking from downtown it is worth the few extra steps to experience the gastronomic French cuisine that is served in a very intimate A/C setting. The menu changes very frequently, featuring 4-6 modern and inventive selections according to the market. You may not understand what you're reading on the menu, but the *maître d'hotel* will graciously explain it all to you, as well as suggesting the appropriate wines for your meal.

Superior
   L'O A LA BOUCHE, *Tel. 45.29.76. Passage Cardella. AE, MC, V. Open for L,D. Closed Sat. noon and all day Sun. Reserve.*
   This is one of the best-rated restaurants in Tahiti, right in the heart of Papeete. The name indicates that you'll be salivating when you order the original specialties of fusion cuisine. The menu changes every 6 months, offering fish and seafood dishes for 2.950-3.700 CFP, and meats for 2.950-3.750 CFP. The suggestions are priced from 1.950-3.150 CFP. Vegetarian platters are also served. You can order a glass of good Bordeaux wine for 850 CFP or a bottle for 2.800-6.600 CFP for white wine and 3.100-14.150 CFP for red wine. This a/c restaurant has a modern French décor and a faithful clientele.
   LA PETITE AUBERGE, *Tel. 42.86.13. Rue des Remparts at the Pont de l'Est. All major credit cards. Open Mon.-Sun. 11:30am-1:30pm, and Mon.-Sat. 7-9:30pm. Closed Sun. night.*
   This small, intimate A/C restaurant is one of the rare non-smoking eateries in Tahiti as well as a favorite gathering place for cognizant gourmets of gastronomic French cuisine. There is also outdoor dining beside a busy street. The traditional menu includes starter courses for 1.550-2.950 CFP, fish and shellfish dishes for 2.350-2.800 CFP and meats for 2.550-3.250 CFP. A specialty is Tournedos Rossini for 3.150 CFP.

ROYAL KIKIRIRI, *Tel. 43.58.64. Rue Colette, between Rue Paul Gauguin and Rue des Ecoles. AE, MC, V. Open Mon.-Sat. 11:30am-2pm, and Wed.-Sat. 7-9:30pm. Closed all day Sun. and at night on Mon. and Tues.*

This small, simply decorated restaurant is A/C and is located above the Kikiriri nightclub, serving very good Chinese and local style food as well as French cuisine. Fresh lagoon fish is frequently imported from the Tuamotu atolls. Appetizers are 890-2.600 CFP and may include New Zealand oysters. Fish dishes are 1.950-3.100 CFP, seafood is 1.700-3.900 CFP, and meats and poultry are 1.750-3.580 CFP. Chinese dishes start with appetizers for 980 CFP, chow mein special for 1.450 CFP, and main courses for 1.300-3.680 CFP, and include a spicy tofu dish with minced pork and chicken for 1.450 CFP. Desserts, from 650-1.200 CFP, include fresh local fruits such as papaya baked with citron. Wines range from 1.865-14.300 CFP.

They offer a 3-course tourist menu for 3.500 CFP, and every Tues. they serve *ma'a tinito haricots rouge* (Chinese food with red beans) for 1.600 CFP. On Fri. they alternate between prime rib for 4.000 CFP and *ma'a Tahiti* (Tahitian food), also for 4.000 CFP. A big buffet for gourmands is presented on the last Sat. night of each month, and the price of 5.800 CFP includes a Tahitian dance show. Afterwards, you can go downstairs and dance in the A/C Kikiriri nightclub, one of the most popular discos in Papeete.

Moderate to Superior

LA ROMANA, *Tel. 41.33.64. 3 Rue du Commandant Destremeau. AE, MC, V. Open for lunch Mon.-Fri. 11am-2pm and for dinner Mon.-Sat. 6-10pm. Closed for lunch on Sat. and all day Sun.*

This A/C restaurant has an active lunchtime business as it is located near the complex of government offices. The décor is supposed to be reminiscent of Tuscany, with a restful, old world decor and soft lighting, along with plastic trees and flowers. The starter courses are 950-2.550 CFP, salads are 1.350-1.500 CFP, fish and seafood are priced from 2.200-2.800 CFP, meats are 2.550-3.200 CFP, and the chef's specialties are 2.100-2.600 CFP. On Thurs., Fri. and Sat. nights fish and meats are grilled on a wood fire, and include smoked sausage, salmon filet, lobster, T-bone steak, beef ribs and lamb chops, priced from 2.200-4.500 CFP. Desserts, priced from 750-1.200 CFP, include floating island, crêpes Romana and fondant au chocolat. Cocktails, beers, wines and champagnes are also available.

LA SAIGONNAISE, *Tel. 42.05.35. Ave. Prince Hinoi. V. Open for lunch and dinner. Closed Sun. MC, V.*

To reach this Vietnamese restaurant if you're walking from downtown Papeete, follow Avenue Prince Hinoi from the waterfront to the first traffic light, and continue straight ahead, walking on the left side of the street until you see the restaurant in the next block. You can relax in the small, A/C dining room while choosing your meal from a varied menu, which hasn't changed in 30 years. In addition to the soups and salads, which are light and pleasing to the palate, you'll want to try some of Jeannot's house specialties, such as the *nems*, a Vietnamese omelet or the very light and tender fried balls of pork, which are priced from about 1.200 to 4.500 CFP.

LE CAFE DES NEGOCIANTS, *Tel. 48.08.48; www.lecafédesnégociants.pf; 10 Rue Jean-Gilbert, Quartier du Commerce. MC, V. Meals served 8am-1am Mon.-Fri. and Sat. night. Closed Sat. noon and all day Sun.*

You will find this small French bistro from the waterfront street of Boulevard Pomare by following the side street behind *La Maison de la Presse*. There are also tables outside, beside the pedestrian street. The menu includes a creative selection of salads, carpaccios, poisson cru and tartares, as well as French specialties such as Couscous Royale. Tapas are available at night when a live band performs. A Tahitian "bringue" (party) is held on Fri. and Sat. nights from 8pm-2am.

LE GALLEINI, *Tel. 42.01.29. Hotel Royal Papeete, Blvd. Pomare. All major credit cards. Open for lunch daily except Sun. and for dinner nightly except Tues. and Sun.*

This a/c restaurant may be a bit run down at the heels, but it is one of Papeete's hidden culinary treasures, and you will be happily surprised with the food, service and prices. The menu offers several mouth-watering selections of French and local style cuisine. Fish and seafood dishes range from 1.650-2.350 CFP, meat choices are 1.700- 2.560 CFP, and daily suggestions are 1.450-2.060 CFP. The specialty of the house is the tender California style prime rib *au jus*, served with baked potatoes and horseradish sauce, for 2.160-3.880 CFP. This is available each Thurs., Fri. and Sat. for both lunch and dinner. The dessert trolley is also very tempting.

LE MANDARIN, *Tel. 50.33.50. 26, Rue des Ecoles. All major credit cards. Open daily 11am-1:30pm and 6-9:30pm except Sat. and Sun. noon.*

If you're in downtown Papeete and are in the mood for good Chinese food, this a/c restaurant just around the corner from the Hotel Mandarin is one of the better restaurants. The upstairs dining room is decorated in an elaborate Chinese Mandarin motif and serves authentic Cantonese specialties, using local seafood and fresh produce. The soups are priced 780-1.300 CFP, appetizers are 840-2.650 CFP, fish courses are 1.750-1.990 CFP, meat dishes are 1.600-2.150 CFP, seafood is 1.300-3.950 CFP, and poultry is 1.600-2.550 CFP. Specialties, such as beignets of taro stuffed with pork are 1.950 CFP, and Peking duck is 7.700-9.700 CFP. A tourist menu is 2.050-3.400 CFP per person. The menu changes weekly, featuring unusual dishes such as soup made from chicken and *bêche de mer* (sea cucumber), *cigale de mer* (slipper lobster) and steamed *limande* (flounder). The talented chef will also prepare you an unforgettable dinner of *ta pen lou* (Chinese seafood fondue) if you give him a day's advance notice. The wine cellar contains a varied selection of the best of Bordeaux. Live music is performed during lunch on Fri. and in the evenings on weekends.

MORRISON'S CAFE, *Tel. 42.78.61. On fourth level of the Vaima Center. MC, V. Open 11:30am-2pm Mon.-Fri., and 7-10pm Tues.-Sat. Open to midnight on Fri. Closed Sat. noon and Sun.*

Take the private outside elevator between L'Oasis and Air New Zealand to reach this rooftop restaurant with A/C dining or a table on the garden terrace. Workers from the travel agencies and airline offices in Papeete meet here for lunch to gossip while feasting on low calorie salads or specialties from the garden menu. The *plat du jour* is 2.350 CFP and includes a drink and coffee. There are several salad choices for 1.950-2.250 CFP, fish dishes are 2.150-2.950 CFP, and meats are 2.050-2.950 CFP. A wine cellar carries a large selection of wines from the vineyards of France. As a very young man, owner "Pasha" Allouch used to wash dishes in a restaurant in Houston, Texas, where Jim Morrison and The Doors rock band were playing. He became such a Jim Morrison fan that he named his restaurant after the famous singer. Live music begins each Thurs. at 8pm.

RESTAURANT JIMMY, *Tel. 43.63.32. 31, Rue des Ecoles (behind the Papeete Mairie). MC, V. Open Mon.-Sat. 11am-2pm; Mon.-Thurs. 6-9:30pm; and Fri. and Sat. 6-10pm. Open holidays 6-9pm. Closed Sun. Reserve.*

This is my favorite restaurant in Tahiti and it is absolutely a "must try" recommendation if you like Thai, Vietnamese or Chinese food. President Jacques Chirac ate here when he visited Tahiti in 2003 and he reportedly enjoyed his dinner just as much as I do when I have the occasion to eat some of the excellent food here. Teresa and Feye Sisengehanh bought this restaurant in Jan. 2001 and have turned it into an ideal place to meet for lunch or dinner. The a/c restaurant has seating for 100 people on two levels and there is a very pretty aquarium on the ground floor. Teresa, who is from Vancouver, takes care of the front part, and the waitresses are well trained, friendly and very efficient. Feye, who is originally from Laos, performs magic in the kitchen, preparing each wonderful dish on order. They receive the necessary spices from family and friends in Thailand and France and they grow their own cilantro and other herbs or know where to find them year-round in Tahiti.

The Thai section of the menu lists starter courses that include fish beignets with lemon grass, and shrimp salad with lemon grass. There are soups, sautéed noodles, delicious beef filet mignon with Thai curry and other curry dishes. Vietnamese dishes include shrimp spring rolls, nems, rice and noodle dishes, and chicken with caramel. One dish you really have to try is the steamed Vietnamese raviolis. Feye makes these by hand and they are flavored with cilantro and other marvelous and mysterious flavors. Order them as one of your starter courses. I always want more because they are so good.

Chinese specialties include all my favorites, such as lemon chicken, Chinese poisson cru, aubergine (eggplant) satay, pork with oyster sauce, and Cantonese rice. They also have vegetarian dishes, including tofu with spicy sauce or cooked with black mushrooms, sautéed vegetables and eggplant sautéed with garlic. Beignets of bananas, pineapple, taro or apples are served for dessert. Wine is sold by the half bottle or full bottle.

Moderate

MANGO TAHITI, *Tel. 43.25.55/78.95.90. Ground floor of Vaima Center on*

Rue Jeanne d'Arc. AE, MC, V. Open 11am-10pm or later with nonstop service Mon.-Fri. Open Sat. night. Closed Sat. lunch and all day Sun. Reserve for lunch Mon.-Fri. This glass-walled restaurant opened in Jan. 2007 on the site where Le Rubys formerly stood. The decor looks like an upscale ice-cream parlor, with white walls and splashes of bright sorbet colors—yellow, orange, lime and mango. The menus were created by artists who are passionate about culinary arts, then corrected and approved by dieticians and nutritionists. Although I have had only a glass of fresh mango juice here, friends who have eaten their food have warned me not to even include it in my book, while other friends have raved about the great food they serve.

The lunch menu suggests six combinations, which give you a choice of an appetizer, dessert and coffee for 2.850 CFP, a fish or meat dish with dessert and coffee or with an appetizer and no dessert, ranging from 3.350-4.250 CFP. An appetizer, main course, dessert and coffee is 5.350 CFP. The dinner menu has soup and starter courses for 900-2.750 CFP, which include Mango's platter of fried shrimp, chicken and beef for 1.950 CFP. Pasta dishes include raviolis of crab and shrimp with orange sauce for 900 CFP. Fish choices start at 1.850 CFP and the fish of the day is 2.450 CFP. Meats are 2.200-3.950 CFP, offering grilled T-bone steak, venison chops and Osso bucco. Desserts, from 800 to 1.250 CFP, include Napoleon of caramel biscuit with strawberries and cream. Mango's wine list contains a lengthy selection of Cabernet Sauvignon and Merlots from France and Chile, as well as white and rosé and eight kinds of champagne. The cocktail menu gives you a choice of margaritas, including the Mango Acapulco Gold Margarita made with mango purée, for 1.600 CFP. They can also make a Cosmopolitan and Mojito for 1.000 CFP.

L'APIZZERIA, *Tel. 42.98.30. Blvd. Pomare. AE, MC, V. Open 11:30am-10pm with nonstop service. Closed Sun.*

This garden restaurant has been serving Italian specialties and French food on the waterfront since 1968. In addition to a choice of 16 pizzas and mini pizzas cooked in a wood-burning oven, you may also want to try the lasagna for 1.750 CFP, or one of the 12 salads priced from 890-2.480 CFP. Mahi mahi dishes start at 2.450 CFP, a barbecued steak is 1.680 CFP, and veal Marsala is 2.480 CFP. Italian wines start at 1.580 CFP. Parking is available on the mountain side of the restaurant.

LA TERRASSE API, *Tel. 43.01.98. Rue du General de Gaulle. MC, V. Open 6am to 7pm. Closed Sun.*

This indoor-outdoor restaurant is located on the corner of Fare Tony, across the street from the Vaima Center. The tendency here is to linger over a meal or a draft beer (*pression*), while sitting on the covered terrace and people watching. The menu includes a choice of burgers from 650 CFP and a hotdog costs 600 CFP, but there's a lot more besides. You can order an American breakfast with bacon and eggs for 1.000 CFP. Their selection of fresh salads includes a very generous portion of *salade Niçoise* (Mediterranean salad) for 1.350 CFP. Their daily luncheon specials are plentiful and cost 1.350-2.150 CFP. These may be filet of mahi mahi, veal, chicken, duck or beef dishes. Desserts are 650-700 CFP.

LE MANAVA, *Tel. 42.02.91. Corner of Ave. Pouvanaa a Oopa and Ave. Commandant Destremeau. Lunch and dinner Mon.-Fri. Closed Sat. and Sun. No credit cards.*

Specialties from the Southwest region of France are featured in this A/C restaurant, and in the outdoors dining gazebo, located near the government buildings downtown. The luncheon crowd includes politicians, judges and business people, who may order the *plat du jour* of salmon and tuna tartare, veal kidneys or *confit de lapin*. Starters are 700-2.350 CFP, salads are 1.100-2.350 CFP, the fish courses range from 1.300- 2.550 CFP, and the meats cost 2.150-3.150 CFP.

LES TROIS BRASSEURS, *Tel. 50.60.25. Blvd. Pomare, across street from Moorea ferryboats. MC, V. Open daily 7am-1am with continuous food service.*

This sidewalk restaurant and microbrewery continues to be one of the most frequented spots in Tahiti. The name means the three brewers, and it is Tahiti's first and only boutique brewery, serving beer fresh from the copper holding tank into your glass. Choices include blond, amber, white and brown beer, which you can order by the glass, mug or pitcher.

They also offer all the services of a classic restaurant and bar, with a snack menu, daily luncheon specials, and French brasserie choices such as grilled pork and lentils for 2.100 CFP, or *choucroute* (sauerkraut, heaping portions of pork, and boiled potatoes) for 2.100-2.600 CFP. Their homemade 'Flammekeuches', or flambé tarts, are made with cheese, onions, mushrooms, bacon, white cheese, fresh cream and other ingredients, which you slice like a quiche and eat with your fingers to accompany your brew.

LOU PESCADOU, *Tel. 43.74.26. Rue Anne-Marie Javouhey. MC, V. Open 11am-2:30pm and 6:30-11pm. Closed Sun.*

This lively Italian restaurant is Tahiti's most popular pizza parlor, offering 12 choices for 980-1750 CFP. Italian or French Provençal specialties range from 980-2.650 CFP. Mario, the owner-chef, sets the ambiance with good cheer, good smells and good food. Even the decor is boisterous and happy, with murals of waterfront scenes from the Mediterranean coast, Chianti wine bottles tied to the support posts, with checkered tablecloths and bottles of spicy olive oil on the tables. There is a well-stocked bar, where you can order *kir* or *pastis* or your favorite cocktail. The friendly waitresses are mostly big Tahitian "mamas" who have been with Mario for many years, and they all wear ample sized tee-shirts sporting Mario's face with a grizzled beard. Behind the Cathedral of Notre Dame, on the same street as the Clinique Cardella. He closes every year from Dec. 15-Jan. 15, and May 1-10.

SUSHI BAR, *Tel. 45.35.25. On second level of Vaima Center. All major credit cards. Open Mon.-Sat. 11:15am-2pm and 6:15-10pm on Wed., Thurs., Fri. and Sat. Closed Sun.*

Plates of tempting sushi are 310 CFP-810 CFP. They also serve miso soup, poisson cru, tuna sashimi, tartare or carpaccio, California rolls and vegetarian sushi. Tempura is available on Fri. only. You can eat in the small restaurant or order take away.

Economy to Moderate

LE MARCHE, *(Papeete Public Market), Tel. 42.25.37. Rue Edouard Ahnne, one block inland from Blvd. Pomare. V. Open 5am-4pm. Closed Sun.*

On the ground floor of the public market are take-out counters where you can get a selection of very good Chinese pastry, sandwiches, *casse-croûtes* and fries. Coffee and soft drinks are also available here, but you have to eat and drink standing up.

Go up the escalator to the second floor of the public market and you will find a cafeteria-style restaurant where you can eat breakfast, lunch or a snack, and you can order a freshly squeezed pineapple juice or orange juice. *Couscous* is served each Thurs. for 1.480 CFP and Fri. is *ma'a Tahiti* day, for 2.000 CFP. A live band keeps you entertained while you eat, playing music from 11am-1:30pm. (You are not allowed to take food from the first floor to eat upstairs).

LE RETRO, *Tel. 42.86.83. Street level of Vaima Center, Blvd. Pomare. All major credit cards. Open daily with non-stop service until 11pm.*

This is an all-purpose restaurant for breakfast, lunch and dinner, a snack, *salon de thé* and bar. It is a great place to people watch as it is on the waterfront street across from the boat docks. The menu changes daily, and includes salads, *poisson cru*, burgers, pizza, pasta and daily specials, which are priced just under 2.000 CFP.

MARKET COFFEE, *Tel. 45.60.70. 4 Rue Edouard Ahnne. Open Mon.-Sat. from 5:30am-2:30pm, and Fri. and Sat. nights from 5:30-10:30pm. Closed Sun. AE, M, V.*

Their breakfast formula includes a choice of a fresh fruit plate, croissant or pain au chocolat, grilled fish, poisson cru and omelets, bacon and eggs, fried chicken, or sautéed beef with vegetables. Each item is served with coffee, tea, chocolate, bread, butter and jam, and costs 1.200 CFP. On Sat. they also have roast pork, poisson cru and firi firi for 1.700 CFP. Lunch and dinner choices include salads for 1.000-1.600 CFP, appetizers for 1.300-2.000 CFP, fish and seafood dishes for 1.500-2.400 CFP, and meat dishes for 1.500-2.000 CFP. Desserts are 500 CFP. You can also order beer, cocktails, or bottled wines.

PATACHOUX, *Tel. 83.72.82/78.95.90. In Fare Tony Center between Snack Hollywood and La Terrasse Api on Rue LaGarde. No credit cards.*

This is a very popular pastry and chocolate shop, as well as a bakery, take-away service and snack restaurant with tables on a covered terrace beside a pedestrian street in the heart of Papeete. Choices include a slice of pizza, guacamole, vegetable tacos, sandwiches, salads, poisson cru, and luncheon daily specials of fresh fish and vegetables, priced from 300-1.600 CFP. You can also get chocolates, pastries, cakes and breads to take with you. If you have a car you may want to stop at their **Pastryland** shop *on the seaside at PK 12.5 in Punaauia, Tel. 45.03.33.*

Economy

LA MARQUISIENNE, *Tel. 42.83.52. Rue Colette. No credit cards. Open Tues.-Fri. 5am-5pm, on Sat. 5am until 2pm and on Sun. until 8:30am. Closed Mon.*

The smell of the coffee will lure you into this a/c pastry shop, but you won't regret following your nose, because you'll discover a wonderful selection of French pastries, cakes, pies, quiches, slices of pizza and sandwiches that will make you glad you came.

LE MOTU, *street level of Vaima Center, on the corner of Rue General de Gaulle and rue Georges LaGarde. No credit cards.*

This kiosk on the back side of the Vaima block serves a good selection of takeout sandwiches, cheese *croissants* and crusty *casse-croûtes*, as well as soft drinks and ice cream A Tahitian hotdog is 360 CFP and a Parisian hotdog with cheese is 460 CFP.

L'OASIS DU VAIMA, *Tel. 45.45.01. Street level of Vaima Center, on corner of rue Jeanne d'Arc and Ave. General de Gaulle. No credit cards. Open 6am-6pm. Closed Sun.*

You can buy a sandwich or choose from 10 panini selections at the kiosk counter and eat as you go, or you can sit on the covered dining terrace and watch the daily drama of people passing, while sipping a cold *pression*. You can serve yourself from the salad bar and dine on the daily specials of French food in the a/c restaurant a few steps up.

McDONALD'S TAHITI, *Tel. 53.37.37. Rue General de Gaulle. No credit cards. Open daily 6am-10:30 or 11pm.*

McDonald's has been firmly established in Tahiti since 1996 and this was the first location to open. School kids, government officials and visiting South Pacific dignitaries all stand in line to order their Big Macs, fries and soft drink. You won't find the bargains here that you are used to back home - a double cheeseburger meal is 690 CFP. But that doesn't keep the people of Tahiti from flocking here on a regular basis. There is also a big McDonald's in Punaauia and a new one in Pirae, plus a small kiosk at the Tahiti-Faa'a airport that doesn't sell burgers. Another outlet is planned for Taravao.

East of Papeete to Mahina – Deluxe

LE BELVEDERE, *Tel. 42.73.44. Fare Rau Ape Valley, Pirae. AE, MC, V. Open daily for lunch and dinner.*

You will feel on top of the world in this rustic setting, 600 m (1,800 ft.) above the sea, overlooking Point Venus and Moorea. Tetiaroa atoll is visible some 42 km. (26 mi.) to the north. The mountains of Huahine, an island 150 km. (93.2 mi.) from Tahiti, can be seen on a clear evening at sunset, with the help of the telescope on the terrace.

Le Belvedere's bright yellow *le truck* provides unforgettable transportation from your hotel, and you will feel and smell the change of air as *le truck* winds up the one lane road with some 70 hairpin curves, climbing through the Fare Rau Ape Valley.

The restaurant is a combination of a wooden Swiss chalet and Polynesian decor. There are 4 dining areas, but you will probably want to sit on the terrace for the best view, if the air isn't too chilly. During the "winter" months of June, July and Aug., the manager sometimes has to close the windows of the restaurant and light a fire in the fireplace, just like in a real Swiss chalet!

The *fondue bourguignonne* (beef fondue) is the house specialty, with tender slices of New Zealand beef that you cook to your own taste. This is accompanied by a salad bar, hot French fries, tasty sauces and carafes of white or red wine, with ice cream and coffee served afterward. The cheese fondue and seafood fondue are also great favorites, as well as French onion soup, mahi-mahi, *couscous* and pepper steak.

The tourist menu, which includes transportation, a choice of beef or cheese fondue, fish or steak, is 5.600 CFP per person. The seafood fondue is 4.250 CFP. Reserve for your transportation. Pick-up at the hotels on the west coast begins at 11:30am for lunch, 4:30pm for sunset and dinner, and 7pm for the last service. If you have a plane to catch during the night and are looking for a place to spend your last evening in Tahiti, why not take advantage of the Belvedere's free *le truck*, who will pick you up at 4:30pm somewhere near the airport, ferry dock, tourist office or at your hotel, and after dinner they will drop you off at the airport around 8pm. You can also bring your luggage with you to the restaurant.

Superior

LE LION D'OR, *Tel. 42.66.50. Rue Afareii, Pirae. All major credit cards. Open Mon.-Fri. 9am-2pm and 6-10pm, Sat. 6-10pm. Closed Sat. noon and all day Sun. Reserve.*

This is a gastronomic restaurant specializing in seafood and French cuisine, a 5-10 minute drive from Papeete via Ave. Prince Hinoi to Pirae. The A/C restaurant is upstairs behind the Banque de Tahiti and a pharmacy on the right side of the road in a small shopping center. Seafood choices include a dozen fresh oysters for 1.600 CFP, escargots for 1.900 CFP, grilled fish for 2.700 CFP, grilled lobster for 4.200 CFP, and their special seafood platter for 5.950 CFP. A 3-course tourist menu is 3.000 CFP.

Moderate to Superior

DAHLIA, *Tel. 42.59.87. PK 4.2, Arue. MC,V. Open 10:45am-1pm and 6-9pm. Closed Sun.*

This A/C Chinese restaurant is located on the seaside, across the road from the French military base in Arue. Soups are 1.190-1.300 CFP and the prices range from 1.470 CFP for chicken dishes to 6.900 CFP for a whole Peking duck. You can even order a whole turbot fish for 12.500 CFP and abalones with oyster sauce for 8.600 CFP. The sizzling platters are very popular and cost 1.740-3.050 CFP. Seasonal additions are algae, crab, lobster, cuttlefish and river shrimp.

LE CHEVAL D'OR, *Tel. 42.98.89. Fariipiti, Taunoa. V. Open Mon.-Sat. for L, D. Closed Sun.*

Whenever I eat here I always order the *riz Cantonnais Cheval D'or*, which is fried rice with bits of shrimp and fish, the house specialty of the "Golden Horse" for 1.200 CFP. Some of my other choices are the eggplant stuffed with fish paste, and shrimp cooked in a spicy sauce and served on a sizzling platter. The prices are 1.200-2.000 CFP per dish and the roast suckling pig in coconut sauce, which is served only on weekends, is 2.400 CFP. This A/C restaurant is almost always packed with Chinese, French, Tahitian and American residents, which gives me the impression that it's a popular restaurant with everyone who knows how to find it. You'll need transportation and a map to get here from downtown. The simplest way is to turn right from Boulevard Pomare at the first street past the Hotel Royal Papeete, and follow Avenue du Chef Vairaatoa about 12 blocks until you come to Cours de l'Union Sacrée. Turn left and head toward the sea, where you'll find the restaurant in front of you where the inland road ends.

Economy

SNACK MAMA ELIZA, *Tel. 45.06.21. This popular snack is located at Point Venus, beside the parking lot. Open daily 8am-5pm, with meals served 8:30am-3:30pm. No credit cards.*

A breakfast of 2 eggs costs 300 CFP and a special Tahitian breakfast with poisson cru is 800-1.600 CFP. Casse-croute sandwiches are 300-1.000 CFP, Chinese dishes are 1.200-1.600 CFP, and a daily special hot plate is 2.000 CFP. Wine and beer are served.

West of Papeete to Paea – Deluxe

COCO'S, *Tel. 58.21.08. PK 13.5, (seaside) Punaauia. AE, MC, V. Open daily and on holidays for L, D. Reserve.*

This is where you want to go to celebrate romance or that special occasion. You will be enchanted from the moment you walk through the entrance and feel, as well as see, the magnificent tropical setting of casual elegance, with orchids and ferns, a gentle or booming surf on the shore and romance in the air. This is old Tahiti at its best—a thatched roof and woven bamboo covering the walls, the soft glow of gas lamps, colorful paintings by resident artists, pink tablecloths and gentle music wafting through the air. You begin your evening with a glass of champagne on the lawn beside the lagoon, watching the last rays of the sunset fade into mauve and purple behind the peaks of Moorea. Then you adjourn to your table inside the open sided dining room, to enjoy your gastronomic meal.

Appetizers begin at 2.450 CFP and feature foie gras in terrine with stewed figs for 3.200 CFP. Fish dishes start at 2.850 CFP and include grilled sea bass, or a lobster tail in Navarin sauce perfumed with vanilla and caramelized mango, for 4.450 CFP. Meats are 2.950-3.800 CFP and desserts are 1.550 CFP. Set menus are suggested for 5.850-12.400 CFP to allow you to sample up to five courses. The wine cellar includes prestige *grands crus* from Saint Emilion, Pomerol, Medoc, Margaux and Saint-Estephe, as well as dessert wines. An American style bar is separate from the dining room and serves all your favorite beverages.

Superior

CAPTAIN BLIGH, *Tel. 43.62.90. PK 11.4 (seaside), Punaauia. AE, MC, V. Open for L, D. Closed Sun. night and all day Mon.*

Just 7 miles from Papeete, on Tahiti's "Gold Coast" overlooking Moorea, this overwater restaurant can seat more than 300 diners. A deluxe seafood buffet is served each Fri. and Sat. night for 5.000 CFP, which includes a Tahitian dance show. Live music is played each Sun. during the noon buffet of *ma'a Tahiti* (a Tahitian feast) for 3.950 CFP. The à la carte menu lists salads for 600-900 CFP, *poisson cru* for 1.350 CFP, shrimp cocktail for 1.600 CFP, a seafood plate for 1.800 CFP, filet mignon for 2.500 CFP and steak and lobster for 3.800 CFP. A pier beside the restaurant leads to the Lagoonarium, and admission is free when you dine in the restaurant.

PINK COCONUT, *Tel. 41.22.23, Marina Taina, PK 9 (seaside) Punaauia. Open Mon.-Sat. 11am-2:30pm and Tues.-Sat. 6:30-10:30pm. Open holidays. Closed all day Sun. and Mon. night. AE, MC, V.*

Painted palm branches and coconuts create the decor in this open sided restaurant at the water's edge. Beyond the luxury yachts berthed at the marina, the island of Moorea beckons across the Sea of Moons. The menu here features French *nouvelle cuisine* that is very pleasing to the eye as well as the palate. Starter courses and a selection of carpaccios are 1.750-2.600 CFP. Fish and seafood are 2.600-3.200 CFP and meat dishes are 2.500-3.400 CFP. Desserts are 900-1.000 CFP and a cheese plate is 2.300 CFP. This is definitely a place to come back to, especially on a Thurs., Fri. or Sat. evening when local musicians entertain for guests at the Pink Coconut and the neighboring restaurant, Quai des Îles. A daily Happy Hour from 5:30-6:30pm features special drinks from the cocktail menu.

QUAI DES ÎLES, *Tel. 81.02.38, Marina Taina, PK 9 (seaside), Punaauia. Open 11:30am-2:30pm Tues.-Sun., 7-9:30pm Tues.-Thurs., and on Fri.-Sat. from 7-10:30pm. Closed Sun. night and all day Mon. AE, MC, V.*

This popular restaurant at Marina Taina is adjacent to the Pink Coconut, and you can gaze at the yachts while enjoying a meal in open-air splendor. Exotic cuisine from the Caribbean or Madras dishes from the Indian Ocean are featured, such as Colombo d'Agneau for 2.100 CFP, beef curry for 2.200 CFP, or a Creole plate for 2.450 CFP. BBQ ribs are 1.850 CFP and a seafood plate is 4.200 CFP. I especially like the way they prepare fish dishes from the Polynesian lagoons, such as parrotfish and ature, which are available in season. Happy Hour is held from 5-7pm each Thurs.-Fri.-Sat. Live or recorded music Thurs.-Sat. nights.

CHEZ REMY, *Tel. 58.21.61, PK 15, (seaside) Tamanu Iti Center, Punaauia.. Open daily for L, D except Sat. noon, all day Sun. and holidays. AE, MC, V.*

This manager of this small restaurant and bar describes the cuisine as semi-gastronomic, meaning that it has quantity as well as quality. The menu features French specialties such as kidneys and sweetbreads. Starters are 1.200-2.950 CFP, salads are 1.100-2.500 CFP, fish dishes are 2.300-3.100 CFP, and meats are 2.200-3.900 CFP. Chateaubriand steak for two is 6.600 CFP, and desserts are 700-1.100

CFP. Wine prices are government regulated. The smoke that hangs heavy during meals will disappear in Apr. 2008 when a new law goes into effect, banning smoking in all restaurants, bars and discos.

Moderate to Superior

LE CIGALON, *Tel. 42.40.84. PK 15, (seaside) Punaauia between Tamanu Iti Center and Hotel Le Méridien. Open Tues.-Sun. for lunch and Tues.-Sat. for dinner. Closed Sun. noon and all day Mon. AE, MC, V.*

You can eat in the non-smoking a/c restaurant or on the smokers' terrace beside a small pool. The French cuisine includes appetizers for 950-2.850 CFP, fish and seafood for 2.250-2.850 CFP, and meats and poultry for 2.180-2.880 CFP. Desserts are 880 CFP and you can order draft beer, imported beers and a variety of wines. Daily specials, such as Hungarian goulash, are 2.380 CFP. A snack-bar counter on the terrace serves hot dogs for 420 CFP, burgers from 450-850 CFP, 6 chicken nuggets for 370 CFP, and 3 dozen choices of pizzas and calzones for 970-1.900 CFP.

WESTERN GRILL, *Tel. 41.30.56. On seaside at PK 12.6 in Punaauia, near school 2+2=4. Open daily for lunch and dinner. V. Reservations advised.*

If the name doesn't prepare you for this experience, then you'll certainly get the idea when you walk through the swinging saloon doors into this frontier scene right out of the old Wild West. Cowhide rugs, longhorn chairs, wagon wheels, gunny sacks, horseshoes, guitars, serapes, sombreros, leather saddles, Native American pictures, dream catchers and woven art, gold mining pans, lassos, miniature covered wagons, and a ceiling covered with old flags all provide the rustic décor for this most unusual restaurant. Of course there's a long wooden bar and country music, and it's only natural that the waiters are dressed in western gear, complete with big cowboy hats.

The place mat menus list a mouth-watering choice of good grub described as Tex-Mex, but the dishes are named after several states and there's also a touch of New Orleans, complete with Cajun spices. You can start off with nachos or potato skins for 990 CFP, move on to gazpacho for 890 CFP or ceviche for 1.050 CFP, then pig out on the barbecue ribs for 1.890 CFP, or a Nebraska filet (400 g) for 2.890 CFP. Fish and seafood dishes are 1.490-1990 CFP, grilled foods are 1.590-2.890 CFP, and specials, such as fajitas, jambalaya, or a hunk of kangaroo are priced from 1.500-2.790 CFP. Desserts are 550-890 CFP, with such treats as homemade brownies, floating island, and apple pie. Saloon Desserts with an alcoholic kick are 890 CFP. The excellent draft beer is brewed at Les Trois Brasseurs in Papeete (my favorite watering hole). There are also cocktails and wines, so you can wet your whistle while you gnaw away on your smoked ribs, which are served with a tasty BBQ sauce. A Western show is performed every Wed., Thurs. and Sat. Be sure to reserve well in advance for these nights.

Moderate

CASA BIANCA, *Tel. 43.91.35, Marina Taina, PK 9 (seaside), Punaauia. All credit cards. Open daily for L, D.*

This new Italian restaurant has replaced the Casablanca, and features pizzas and calzones for 1.100-1.800 CFP. The house specialty is pizza by the meter for 3.300 CFP for 1/2m and 6.000 CFP for 1m (for 6 people). They also have pasta for 1.400-1.800 CFP, meats for 1.950-2.400 CFP, and veal on a spit for 1.500 CFP. Spanish evening is held on Thurs., when you can order a giant paella Valenciane for 2.400 CFP, including a glass of sangria. An Italian singer performs on Fri. evenings and Sat. is jazz night. The **Dinghy Bar** has Italian wine tasting for 1.200 CFP, or grappa for 700 CFP. You can also order a draft beer brewed by Les Trois Brasseurs in Papeete, who have now added this new bar and restaurant to their growing list of restaurants and bars.

CÔTÉ JARDIN, *Tel. 43.26.19, Moana Nui Shopping Center, PK 8.3, Punaauia. MC, V. Open daily 8am-8pm.*

This is a handy place to rest and people watch while you're shopping at Carrefour or waiting for someone who is browsing around the mall. You can sit at a table on the mall level or go upstairs to the a/c dining room, where you can order from an interesting menu that includes 10 kinds of pizza from 1.195-1.695 CFP. Salads start at 695 CFP, pasta dishes at 1.195 CFP, *poisson cru* is 1.395 CFP, and Japanese sashimi is 1.895 CFP. The main courses of fish, poultry and grilled meats are between 1.495 and 2.050 CFP. You can order wine by the glass, carafe or bottle. They also have fresh fruit juices, Hinano on draft, and a list of Belgian beers. You can order pancakes for breakfast for 300 CFP, bacon and eggs for 750 CFP, or an omelet for 795 CFP.

Economy

CHOCOLATINE, *Tel. 43.26.31. Moana Nui Shopping Center, PK 8.3, Punaauia. No credit cards. Open daily 7am-7pm.*

This busy snack stand is located at the exit doors of Carrefour super market. They sell casse-croûtes for 230-320 CFP, panini sandwiches for 350 CFP, hamburgers for 550 CFP, salads for 690-990 CFP, sashimi for 1.200 CFP, and a daily lunch special for 1.500 CFP. Service is cafeteria style. Italian ice cream is 300 CFP and there is a good selection of soft drinks and fresh juices.

McDONALD'S TAHITI, *Tel. 48.07.07. Taina Beach, PK 9, Punaauia. No credit cards. Open daily 9:30am-10pm.*

This is the second McDonald's outlet in Tahiti. You'll find all the familiar burgers and fries and fast service here and there is also a drive-through window and games for the kids in the parking lot. There is a white sand beach behind the restaurant with an entry into the lagoon.

Elsewhere Around Tahiti Nui (Big Tahiti) – Moderate to Superior
NUUTERE, *Tel. 57.41.15. PK 32.5, Papara (mountainside). Open for L, D. Closed Tues. AE, MC, V.*

The menu here is exceedingly extensive for a fairly small restaurant, even if they do advertise their cuisine as gastronomic French. It would be better to order from the chef's suggestions to avoid frozen fish and other microwave foods as much as possible. These may include a dozen fresh oysters for 4.500 CFP, duck with olives for 2.200 CFP, foie gras poêlé for 3.100 CFP, or filet of kangaroo for 3.200 CFP. A 3-course tourist menu is 2.800 CFP. They also carry 20 different beers from Belgium and France and their wines are from the best vineyards in France and other countries.

GAUGUIN MUSEUM RESTAURANT, *Tel. 57.13.80. PK 50.5, Papeari. AE, MC, V. Open daily for lunch.*

This popular restaurant is built over the lagoon in Papeari, 50.5 km (31 mi.) west of Papeete and just 364 m. (400 yds.) west of the Paul Gauguin Museum and Harrison Smith Botanical gardens. Chances are you'll be able to admire a double rainbow over Tahiti-Iti while dining on stuffed crab, grilled mahi mahi, shrimp dishes and Continental cuisine, complete with yummy homemade coconut, papaya or lime pie. Or you may prefer the buffet of salads and Tahitian food, with fresh fruits and coconut for dessert. The maitai rum drinks are a house specialty, and after a few of these, you'll be happier if you're not driving.

Englishman Roger Gowan and his Chinese wife, Juliette, opened the restaurant in 1968, and are still on the job, greeting guests and running back and forth between the kitchen or bar and the dining rooms, making sure that the service is smooth and efficient. The staff includes people from the neighborhood in Papeari, some of whom have worked in the kitchen right from the beginning. Be sure to look at the fish and sharks in the enclosures beside the restaurant.

Moderate
CLUB HOUSE, *Tel. 57.40.32. PK 40,2 in Papara, at the Atimaono Golf Course. Open daily 11:30am-3pm and on weekends until 4pm. AE, MC, V.*

This is the Golf Course restaurant and is open to the public. The menu includes salads from 450 CFP, poisson cru and other raw tuna dishes for 1.350-1.450 CFP, fish and shellfish for 1.850-2.350 CFP, including pan-fried mahi mahi with tartar sauce. Charbroiled steaks and other meats are 1.750-2.700 CFP.

RESTAURANT SNACK MOTU OVINI, *Tel. 57.17.59. PK 51.5, Papeari. Open daily 9:30am-5pm. MC, V.*

After you have visited the Paul Gauguin Museum and strolled through the Harrison Smith Botanical gardens, you'll be able to quench your thirst or enjoy a full meal in the restaurant beside the parking lot. You can sit beside the lagoon or dine in the open sided building, where there is usually a good breeze. The menu includes poisson cru, burgers and fries, daily specials of fish, shrimp and meat dishes, desserts and fresh juice, beer and wine. Ma'a Tahiti (Tahitian food) is served each Sun. for 3.000 CFP, complete with local music.

Economy to Moderate
BEACH BURGER, *Tel. 57.41.03. PK39, Papara. Open Sun.-Thurs. 8:30am-9pm and Fri-Sat. 8:30am-9:30pm. MC, V.*
This restaurant-snack is located near the surfing beach in Papara and is a convenient roadside stop when you're driving around the island. Hot dogs are 350 CFP, burgers start at 450 CFP, and a combo of hamburger, fries and Coke is 850 CFP. Pizzas are 1.290-1.690 CFP and steaks are 1.420-2.190 CFP. There are also daily specials, milk shakes, chocolate sundaes, wine and beer. American owner Skip Anderson has added an a/c room for more comfortable dining.

Tahiti Iti (Little Tahiti)
AUBERGE DU PARI, *Tel. 57.13.44. PK 17.8, Teahupoo, Tahiti-Iti. Open 12-3pm on Sat., Sun. and holidays, and at night by reserving a day in advance. MC, V.*
This simple open-air restaurant is located beside the lagoon in Teahupoo village, almost at the end of the road on the west coast of the Tahiti-Iti peninsula, with a good view of the famous international surfer's spot of Hava'e Pass. This is a nice place to linger over a long lunch of shrimp, crab, or lobster while sharing a bottle of wine. The menu depends on seasons and what the fishermen catch. Spicy prawns are 2.600 CFP, and a seafood platter for two is 8.800 CFP.
CHEZ LOULA ET REMY, *Tel. 57.74.99. Turn off from circle island road onto Tautira road and drive to Taravao center. Take first road to right after post office. Open daily for L, D. except Sun. night. All major credit cards.*
It is worth a drive from Papeete to Taravao just to eat at this excellent restaurant. Remy, a rotund Frenchman, wears a baseball cap as he circulates among the various sections of his restaurant, which include an a/c room for 15 people, and he creates a noisy, lively atmosphere with his *joie de vivre*. This is not a fancy place, but the customers don't seem to mind the plastic flowers on the tables. They come here again and again for the superb choices and quality of the food.
I highly recommend the shrimp and ginger for 2.480 CFP. It is heavenly—what more need I say? A Neptune Royal plate for 2.850 CFP consists of sashimi, carpaccio, tuna tartare, seared tuna and raw shrimp. A Reef plate for 4.500 CFP contains grilled shrimp, gambas, *cigales* (slipper lobster) and rock lobster. Grilled lobster Maori, flambéed with Armagnac, is 3.850 CFP, and grilled meats are 1.850-2.850 CFP. Specials may include frog legs for 1.990 CFP, fresh local rabbit for 2.480 CFP, cassoulet of stuffed crab Antillais style for 2.350 CFP, two filets of sole meunieres for 1.980 CFP, or seafood paella for 3.500 CFP. A truly rare treat you can sometimes find here is varo (sea centipede), priced at 4.500 CFP for two varo. Desserts include apple pie for 790 CFP and profiteroles for 950 CFP. A 3-course tourist menu is 3.150 CFP. The wine list is also good and reasonably priced.

CHEZ MYRIAM, *Tel. 57.71.01. PK 60, Taravao. Open Mon.-Sat. 7am-11pm and Sun. 9am-3pm. MC, V.*

This friendly restaurant and open terrace snack bar is on the mountainside at the crossroads of Tahiti-Nui and Tahiti-Iti. Myriam is a Chinese-Tahitian lady who speaks English and likes to meet people, and she serves traditional French cuisine and quality Chinese food. You can order a *poisson cru* with coconut milk for 1.500 CFP or shrimp curry with coconut milk for 2.100 CFP. She serves *ma'a Tahiti* (Tahitian food) on weekends for 2.500 CFP a plate, which is complete with all the traditional foods, including roast pig.

Other Restaurants & Snacks on Tahiti Iti

Restaurant Taumatai, *Tel. 57.13.59,* is on the left side of the road leading from Taravao to Tautira, catty-cornered to Chez Loula et Remy. I have heard several reports that this is the best restaurant on Tahiti Iti, but unfortunately, it was closed when I went to check it out. A young couple from Taravao from the Jamet family are said to serve food that is even better than Chez Loula et Remy. **Chez L'Eurasienne,** *Tel. 57.07.49,* is a Vientamese Restaurant at Pension Jeannine on the Taravao Plateau. **Chez Romeo,** in Teahupoo, provides good take-out meals.

La Plage de Maui (Maui Beach) in Toahotu has a small strip of white sand beach and a good snack bar. The kitchen was destroyed in an explosion by vandals in Jan. 2008, and owner Rose Wilkinson said it would take several months to rebuild, but she will do it.

SEEING THE SIGHTS

Papeete Highlights

The best way to visit Papeete is to take a walking tour, which you can do on your own or with a guide. You will enjoy the walk more if you do it in the cool of the morning. Everyone gets going early around here, so you shouldn't have any problems with closed shops if you begin your stroll around 7:30am

Start your tour at the **Tahiti Tourisme Bureau** on the waterfront side of Boulevard Pomare, at the corner of Rue Paul Gauguin. This building is called **Fare Manihini,** which is the Tahitian word for "Visitor's House." The helpful hosts speak good English and will give you brochures and a map of the city and they will answer any questions you may have. You can also follow the map printed on pages 8-9 of the *Tahiti Beach Press,* which is available at the Tourist Bureau.

On the right, just outside Fare Manihini, is the **Captain Tamarii a Teai Square,** named in honor of a former Tahitian merchant marine officer. This is an attractive place with benches and shade trees, where you can relax and enjoy watching the activity on the waterfront after your stroll. Some of the phone numbers on the informational panels may be out of date, but they also show maps, and give information on the birds and fish that are found around Tahiti.

Across the road is the **Vaima Center,** a 4-story mall of boutiques, pearl shops, restaurants, a bookstore, travel and airline agencies, and business offices. It was

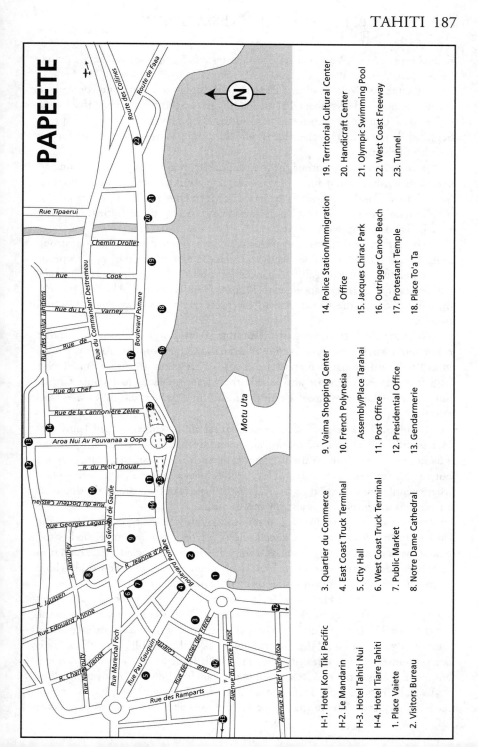

PAPEETE

Rue Tipaerui
Chemin Drollet
Rue
Cook
Rue du Lt.
Varney
Rue des Poilus Tahitiens
Rue du Commandant Destremeau
Rue de
Boulevard Pomare
Rue du Chef
Rue de la Cannoniere Zelee
Aroa Nui Av Pouvanaa a Oopa
R. du Petit Thouar
Rue du Docteur Cassiau
Rue Georges Lagarde
Rue Général de Gaulle
R. Javouhey
R. Jaussen
Rue Edouard Ahnne
R. Charles Vienot
R. Nansouty
Rue Marechal Foch
Rue Pau Gauguin
Collette
Rue des Ecoles des Freres
Rue des Remparts
Avenue du Chef Vairaatoa
Avenue du Prince Hinot
R. Jeanne d'Arc
Boulevard Pomare

Route des Collines
Route de Faaa

Motu Uta

H-1. Hotel Kon Tiki Pacific
H-2. Le Mandarin
H-3. Hotel Tahiti Nui
H-4. Hotel Tiare Tahiti
1. Place Vaiete
2. Visitors Bureau
3. Quartier du Commerce
4. East Coast Truck Terminal
5. City Hall
6. West Coast Truck Terminal
7. Public Market
8. Notre Dame Cathedral
9. Vaima Shopping Center
10. French Polynesia
    Assembly/Place Tarahai
11. Post Office
12. Presidential Office
13. Gendarmerie
14. Police Station/Immigration
    Office
15. Jacques Chirac Park
16. Outrigger Canoe Beach
17. Protestant Temple
18. Place To'a Ta
19. Territorial Cultural Center
20. Handicraft Center
21. Olympic Swimming Pool
22. West Coast Freeway
23. Tunnel

named for the Snack Vaima, a very popular restaurant and sidewalk café that has been replaced by Le Retro.

All set to go? Walk westward along the renovated **yacht quay** and you will see the catamarans and dive boats that are loading passengers for a day sail to Moorea or Tetiaroa. Cruising yachts tie up here during the peak sailing months of Apr. to Sept., while the owners make necessary repairs and provision their boats for the next leg of their journey.

Across the Papeete harbor the international container ships dock to unload cars, lumber, household furnishings, food, fuel, and numerous other supplies. Several inter-island cargo vessels are based at **Motu Uta**, Tahiti's shipping port of wharves and warehouses, which is connected by a bridge to the industrial area of Fare Ute and downtown Papeete.

This little motu used to be a quiet islet that was reached only by boat or strong swimmers. It was formerly owned by the Pomare family, whom the first Europeans considered the royalty of Tahiti. Chances are you will also see the fast catamarans and ferries that connect Papeete with Moorea. This is one of the busiest French-owned harbors in the world, due to the passenger traffic between Tahiti and Moorea.

Walking along the quay past the **Bounty Tunnel** you will come to a traffic roundabout where **Aroa Nui Avenue Pouvanaa a Oopa** (formerly **Avenue Bruat**) joins **Boulevard Pomare**, the waterfront road. This grassy area is decorated with flags from several countries and a pedestrian walkway leads to **Jacques Chirac Square**, a pleasant semicircular-shaped landfill in a garden setting of trees and flowers.

In this park is a stele of 5 stones representing the 5 archipelagoes of Tahiti and Her Islands, where most of the workers came from who were stationed on the Tuamotu atolls of Moruroa and Fangataufa during the 30 years that France carried out 181 nuclear tests in that area. These stones form a "paepae", a gathering place where people can come and go freely, and the history of their origin is printed on a tableau stand in French, Tahitian and English.

Several stairways lead down to the underground parking garage below the garden, and a new extended boardwalk allows you to continue your leisurely stroll beside the harbor. Docking facilities, complete with water and electrical hookups, have been added for the sailboats from many countries around the world, whose owners are living their dreams of cruising the South Pacific.

In the area called **Hokule'a Beach**, you will see several outrigger canoes on supports. You may even be able to watch some of Tahiti's canoe teams practicing for the next big race, which is a national passion. The Hokule'a stele has been temporarily removed until the construction work of the landfill is completed. This is a monument in the form of twin canoe hulls imbedded in stone, which was erected in honor of the *Hokule'a*, a replica of an ancient Polynesian voyaging canoe that was built in Hawaii. It is sponsored by the Hawaiian Voyaging Society to retrace the sailing routes of the Polynesian pioneers who settled the tiny specks of land that make up the Polynesian triangle. The *Hokule'a* made its first voyage to Tahiti in 1976, navigating by the winds, stars and sea currents, and arrived in Tahiti to an overwhelming welcome by thousands of Tahitians.

Your destination on this side of the street is **Place To'ata**, also called **Tahua To'ata**, which is an immense outdoor theater, concert arena and meeting place, complete with public restrooms and showers and exhibit space. Visitors enjoy coming here to sit on a bench among the flower gardens and watch the activity in the harbor, as well as the families who bring their children to skate or ride their scooters in the fresh air. All the restaurants here were recently rebuilt and back in business at the beginning of 2007.

The **Maison de la Culture** at Fare Tauhiti Nui, adjacent to Place To'ata, is Tahiti's cultural center, library and theater/concert hall. Here you will find a snack bar and public toilets, but those at Place To'ata are better. The **Olympic swimming pool** is just beyond the cultural center, and beyond that is the **Artisan Center**, where you can buy arts and crafts made in Tahiti and Her Islands.

When you get ready to head back toward the center of town, perhaps you will prefer to go up the stairs to the crossover bridge in front of the Artisan Center to get to the other side of the road. Or you can use the designated crossing in front of Place To'ata. Trying to get across the five lanes of traffic can be quite tricky and even dangerous in Papeete, even though there are pedestrian zones.

Once you have negotiated getting across Boulevard Pomare, you will soon come to the **Clinique Paofai**, then the **Protestant Temple**, which used to be part of the Evangelical Society of French Polynesia. In mid-2004 all the former Evangelical churches changed their name to Maohi Protestant Church and all the preachers are Tahitian. The missionaries from the London Missionary Society brought the Gospel to Tahiti in 1797 and the Protestant religion was predominant in the Windward Society Islands until the year 2000, when a poll revealed that 45 percent of the population is Catholic and 34 percent is Protestant.

The new **Robert Wan Pearl Museum** is also located in this area of Paofai, on the same side of the street as the Maohi Protestant Church. This is the only pearl museum in the world and is definitely worth a visit. It is open Mon.-Sat. from 9 a.m-5pm, but it is best to get there at least by 4:30pm.

Continue down Boulevard Pomare and turn right on Aroa Nui Avenue Pouvanaa a Oopa (still called Avenue Bruat by most residents). Walk a block and cross the street on Rue du Commandant Destremeau, which changes to Rue du General de Gaulle at this corner. Walk under the shady trees up Avenue Pouvanaa A Oopa and see the government buildings and war memorials.

Here you will find the French court or *tribunal*, the Police station, the *gendarmerie*, and the **Presidential Palace**, the impressive building that houses the offices of the President of French Polynesia. More than 500 employees work in this showcase. Across the street is the **Ministry of Culture** and its lovely flower gardens. In front of these colonial buildings are the memorials for the Polynesian soldiers who were killed during the First World War of 1914-1918, as well as plaques for the men killed in Korea, Indochina, Madagascar, North Africa and in other war battles.

Go back to Rue du General de Gaulle and continue toward the center of town, passing more government buildings. On your right is **Place Tarahoi**, where Queen Pomare IV lived in an elaborate mansion before the French took control in 1842, and used Tarahoi as their headquarters. The offices and home of the **French High Commissioner** are located in the building on the right. The roof has 5 points, representing the archipelagoes of French Polynesia. Against the fence in the parking lot is the **Pacific Battalion Monument**, a tribute to the French Polynesians who fought with General Charles de Gaulle's Free French forces during World War II.

To the left of the French High Commissioner's office is the French Polynesia **Assembly** building, where the local politicians have a good go at one another during their hot debates. In front of the building is a monument to **Pouvanaa a Oopa** (1895-1977), a man from the island of Huahine who was a decorated hero fighting for France during World War I. He became an even bigger hero to the Tahitian people when he was sentenced to prison in France while seeking independence for his own country. After spending 15 years behind bars during the 1960s and 1970s, Pouvanaa returned to Tahiti, but was sent back to France again, this time as Tahiti's representative in the French Senate.

Cross Rue du General de Gaulle again in the crosswalk between Place Tarahoi and the rear of the **Papeete Post Office**, just before you get to McDonald's, Tahiti's favorite fast-food joint. (One of Tahiti's local newspapers recently reported that a McDonald's cheeseburger in Tahiti costs more than 10 full meals in China).

Double back toward the west for a few yards until you see the green oasis of **Bougainville Park** on your right, adjacent to the post office. A gurgling stream meanders through the tree-shaded gardens. This was Queen Pomare's favorite bathing pool when she lived at Place Tarahoi, and it was from this little river that Papeete received its name: *Pape* (pah-pey) means water in the Tahitian language; and *ete* (eh-tey) means basket; therefore, Papeete means water basket. Before the houses were equipped with water pipes, the people used to come to this spring with their gourds wrapped in woven leaves and take the *pape* home in their *ete*.

Although this park was named for the French explorer, Louis Antoine de Bougainville, he never laid eyes on this site, because he spent his entire brief visit to Tahiti on the east coast of Hitiaa. However, he was the first French discoverer, and his statue stands between the **two cannons** that are adjacent to the sidewalk on the Boulevard Pomare side of the park.

The cannon nearest the post office was taken from the *Seeadler*, a World War I German raider that belonged to the luckless Count Felix von Luckner. His ship ran aground on Mopelia atoll, in the Leeward Society Islands in 1917, after having captured 14 British, French and American ships in the South Pacific. The other gun comes from the *Zélée*, a small French navy vessel that was sunk in Papeete harbor in 1914 when the German raiders *Scharnhorst* and *Gneisenau* bombarded Papeete.

After you have walked around the cannons, continue toward the center of Papeete on Boulevard Pomare. Turn right on Rue Jeanne d'Arc beside the Vaima Center and you'll see the **Cathédrale de l'Immaculée Conception**, which is usually called the **Cathedral of Notre Dame**. This cathedral was built in 1875 and has been restored a few times. If the door is unlocked go inside, where it is quiet and cool, and look at the paintings of the Crucifixion.

Cross over to the left side of the street at the Pharmacie de la Cathedrale, which is on the corner opposite Place Notre Dame. Walk past Tahiti Voyages travel agency and Tahiti Music and turn left at the end of the block. The sidewalk here is usually quite crowded with Tahitians who are shopping or hanging out, talking with friends. Walk past the police station and you will see the public market, the **Marché Municipale**, which is the heart and breadbasket of Papeete. The Tahitian "mamas" and even young men sell orchids, anthuriums, ginger flowers, roses, and other flowers of every imaginable hue.

Past the flower vendors inside *le Marché* you will see traditional Tahitian fruits and tubers on the left of the aisle and vegetables sold by the Chinese are on the right. The fish and meat markets are off to the right and upstairs you'll find all kinds of locally made products, including some nice *tifaifai* bed covers or wall hangings and lots of seashells. Outside *le Marché* are hundreds of colorful *pareos*. The cotton ones were made in Tahiti and the rayon *pareos* with fringe are imported from Indonesia.

Leave *le Marché* and go out the door closest to the counters selling woven hats, bags and grass skirts. Walk straight ahead on Rue Colette for one block until you come to Rue Paul Gauguin. Turn right at the corner and you will see the **Mairie of Papeete on** the left. This impressive building is the town hall, called *Hôtel de Ville* in French and *Fare Oire* in Tahitian; it is a replica of Queen Pomare's royal palace that once stood at Place Tarahoi. The elaborate building, with crystal chandeliers and pink marble imported from Italy, was inaugurated in 1990. Former French President **François Mitterand** was the guest of honor for the dedication ceremonies. Walk up the steps into the building and take the elevator to the third floor. There are frequent art exhibits on display in the room to the left as you get off the elevator. Walk around the building and admire the decor, and be sure to see the stone carvings in the gardens all around the outside of the building. They were made by sculptors living in Tahiti, the Marquesas and Easter Island.

Following your tour of the town hall, walk back toward the waterfront and the Tahiti Tourime Bureau. Cross Boulevard Pomare to the harbor side, and as you approach Fare Manihini, take a little detour to the right to have a look at **Place Vaiete**, also called **Tahua Vaiete**. This square was the site of the first territorial parliament in 1945. It was also the place where the 4th Festival of Pacific Arts was held in 1985. For many years the traditional song and dance competitions took place here during the July *fête* celebrations, and the carnival type stalls, carousel, Ferris wheel and *papio* rides for children were built next to the amphitheater.

In 2001 this square was enlarged to a tiled area of 1,200 sq. m (129 sq. ft.). A low stone wall encloses Place Vaiete and there are benches and a waterfall, public toilets, and round-the-clock security guards. The roulottes (mobile diners) still set up shop here in the evenings, but they are now limited to 30, and there is even a washroom where they can clean their dishes and pots and pans. Many of the roulottes bring their own linoleum to spread under their vans to protect the tile from grease spots, and some of them place tables and chairs beside the roulotte for more comfortable dining. Local musicians give free concerts in the bandstand and the audience sits on the low wall, the benches and the tiled floor of the square.

If this 2-hour walk is too long for you, it can be shortened by crossing Boulevard Pomare at Avenue Pouvanaa Oopa, after you have visited the waterfront and had a look at the yachts. You can head inland to see the government buildings and continue the above itinerary from there. You will eliminate the extra walk to Place To'ata, the Cultural Center, Artisan Center, Protestant Temple, and Robert Wan's Tahitian Pearl Museum, which you will certainly want to visit another time.

Around the Island

Most tour drivers follow the northeast coast through Papeete's neighboring *communes* of Pirae, Arue and Mahina. Ask your driver to stop at the **James Norman Hall House and Library**, at PK 5.5 in Arue. It is well worth a visit. See information under *Museums & Special Sightseeing Stops* in this chapter. From the **Tahara'a Lookout Point** at PK (poste kilometre) 8.1 in Arue you can see historic Matavai Bay. When **Captain James Cook** sailed the *Endeavour* into this bay in 1769, he sighted a single tree (*Erythrina indica*) with bright red-orange flowers growing on the promontory above the bay. He used the tree as a navigational landmark and named this reference point "One Tree Hill." Although the gnarled old tree has disappeared, this lookout provides a spectacular panoramic view of the island of Moorea, the Sea of Moons, the coral reef and lagoon, and Tahiti's majestic fern-softened mountains.

The next stop will be at **Point Venus** at PK 10 in Mahina. This historic site beside Matavai Bay is where English **Captain Samuel Wallis** of the *H.MS. Dolphin* came ashore in 1767, to become the first European to discover Tahiti. When Captain Cook led an expedition of scientists to Tahiti to observe the transit of the planet Venus across the sun on June 3, 1769, he named the site Point Venus. **Captain William Bligh** and the *Bounty* crew came here in 1788 to collect breadfruit plants, and representatives of the **London Missionary Society** waded ashore in 1797, in search of souls to save.

In addition to the monuments in honor of Captain Cook and the missionaries, you'll see a lighthouse, snack bar with picnic tables, an arts and crafts center, toilet facilities, tropical gardens and a black sand beach, usually decorated with topless sunbathers, mostly French women. Raise your gaze from the bare twin peaks on the beach and look up at the double summit of Tahiti's highest mountain, Mt. Orohena, reaching 2,241 m (7,353 ft.) high into a crown of clouds. Point Venus is a lovely spot to photograph the bathing beauties as well as the tropical sunset, with a magnificent view of the nearby island of Moorea.

Continuing along the east coast you'll see the surfers riding the waves offshore Papenoo, before coming to the **Blow Hole of Arahoho** and the **Three Cascades of Fa'arumai** in Tiarei at PK 22. The Vaimahuta waterfall is easily reached by a 5-min. walk across the bridge over the Vaipuu river, following a well defined path under a cool canopy of wild chestnut (*mape*) trees and *Barringtonia asiatica (hutu)* trees. Countless waterfalls cascade in misty plumes and broken curtains down the mountainside to tumble into a crisp, refreshing pool. This is a good swimming hole, but don't forget your mosquito repellent.

Back on the circle island road you will pass country villages, modern concrete homes and modest little *fare* huts brightly painted in yellow, pink and blue. Flowers and hedges of every shape and hue border the road and breadfruit, mangoes, papaya and banana trees fill the luxuriant gardens. Birdhouse-shaped boxes stand by the road in front of each home, ready to receive the daily delivery of fresh French *baguettes* that are baked by the Chinese and eaten by the Tahitians as their staple food.

At PK 37.6 in Hitiaa your guide may point out a plaque beside the bridge. The French explorer, **Louis Antoine de Bougainville**, made a deed of annexation in Apr. 1768, when his ships *Boudeuse* and *Etoile* dropped anchor just inside 2 islets offshore the village. Bougainville proclaimed French sovereignty over the island, which he named New Cytherea. He placed the deed in a bottle and buried it in the ground between the river and the beach. Bougainville's ships lost 6 anchors during his 10-day visit.

At PK 60 you'll be in the village of Taravao, the isthmus that connects Tahiti Nui with Tahiti Iti, the Taiarapu peninsula. If you're saving your discovery of Tahiti Iti for another delightful day, then continue on to **Papeari**, where you'll find the **Paul Gauguin Museum** and the **Harrison Smith Botanical Gardens** (see information under *Museums* and also under *Gardens* in this chapter.

Most tour buses stop for lunch in the vicinity of Taravao or Papeari, where you have a good selection of restaurants and snack bars. The most popular luncheon choice is the **Gauguin Museum Restaurant**, *Tel. 57.13.80,* at PK 50.5 in Papeari. This very spacious restaurant and bar is built over the lagoon, just 400 yd west of the Paul Gauguin Museum and Harrison Smith Botanical gardens. (See description in the *Where to Eat* section).

LAND OF THE DOUBLE RAINBOW
When you stop at the **Vaipahi Gardens and Cascade** in Mataiea, look out over the lagoon and perhaps you'll catch sight of a double rainbow arching over the peninsula of Tahiti Iti. This is where I fell in love with Tahiti during my first visit to the island in 1968. There's magic in the air here, a haunting beauty that touches the soul.

The latter half of your tour will take you to the **Vaipahi Gardens and Cascade**, at PK 49 in Mataiea. If you are making the island tour on your own, then stop at the **Vaima River**, PK 48.5 in Mataiea, very close to the public gardens. This is one of Tahiti's favorite watering holes, complete with underground springs that bubble up like a cold Jacuzzi. Leave your car in the parking lot and wade waist-deep through the clear, refreshing river. Wild hibiscus (*purau*) trees lend their shade and purple water hyacinths add their color to the scene. This is a welcome treat on a hot sunny day.

On the southwest coast you'll pass the **Atimaono Golf Course**, *Tel. 57.40.32*, at PK 40.2, where international championship tournaments are played each July. A little further on you'll see the black sand beach of **Papara**, where world-class surfers compete. Several of the tour guides will stop at the **Ava Tea Distillery and Tasting Room**, *Tel. 53.32.43*, on the mountainside at PK 26.2 in Paea. You can learn how the liqueurs and *eau de vie* are made from coconuts, gingerroot, *pamplemousse* grapefruit, mangoes and other tropical fruits. You are welcome to taste all the flavors, and if you imbibe too much and drowse on the bus, then you can take the **West Coast Tour** another day to see what you missed. If you are touring on your own, keep in mind that they close at 5:30pm and are not open at all on Sun.

The side road leading into the valley to the **Marae of Arahurahu** is at PK 22.5 in Paea. Follow the road to the parking area and walk a few steps to the 2 restored open-air stone temples, which were used in pre-Christian days for religious ceremonies, meetings, cultural rites, sacrifices and burials. There is no entry fee to visit the *marae* except during special performances that take place during the **Heiva I Tahiti Festival** in July and Aug. These colorful reenactment ceremonies choose various themes, such as the crowning of a king and royal weddings, with a cast of dozens of beautifully costumed Tahitian dancers, musicians, warriors and *tahua* priests. No performances have been held here during the past 3-4 years, however.

The **Grottos of Mara'a** at PK 28.5 in Paea, are joined by a flower-bordered walkway. The **Paroa cave** is the largest of 3 natural grottos, where overhead springs drip through wild ferns and moss, forming a pool where children play. **Queen Pomare** used to bathe here and **Paul Gauguin** wrote of swimming inside this cave. Drops of water from the overhead ferns reflect rainbow hues in the rays of the afternoon sun. No entry fee.

On the west coast of the island you'll see a sign on the seaside at PK 15.7 in Punaauia, directing you to the **Museum of Tahiti and Her Islands (Musée des Iles)**. Some of the tour guides stop here. See information under *Museums*.

In the communes of Paea and Punaauia, you will catch only glimpses of Tahiti's lovely beachfront properties behind the walls and thick hedge fences that protect them from the road. You may even see some old Polynesian style homes that are built of pandanus and woven bamboo. The millionaires' modern villas are up in the mountains, overlooking the island of Moorea. Here suburbia Tahiti blends the past with today. The thatched roof *fare*, colonial mansions and concrete homes are neighbors with schools, shopping malls, used car lots and video shops. Supermarkets sell foods for all tastes and boutiques sell surfboards and beachwear from California and Hawaii.

From 1897 to 1901, the artist **Paul Gauguin** lived in a comfortable villa at PK 12.6 in Punaauia, before he left for the Marquesas Islands in search of a wild and savage beauty. Your guide may point out the **2+2=4 school** that was built adjacent to Gauguin's former property.

Museums & Special Sightseeing Stops

Robert Wan Pearl Museum (Musée de la Perle), On Blvd. Pomare in the Paofai section west of downtown Papeete near Protestant Church. Open Mon.-Sat. 9:30am-5pm. Last entry at 4:45pm. This is the only museum in the world dedicated to pearls. Several promenades and themes teach you many lessons about the history and culture of the pearl, a gem that has been regarded as a wonder and a mystery to man and woman since time immemorial. No entry fee. For information or private visits contact Jeanne Lecourt, *Tel. 46.15.55; 46.15.62; Fax 45.15.53; jlecourt@robertwan.com; www.robertwan.com.*

James Norman Hall House and Library, *Tel. 50.01.61/50.01.60; www.jamesnormanhall.pf.* On mountainside at PK 5.5 in Arue. Open Tues.-Sat. 9am-4pm. Entry 600 CFP. This colonial style green house is a replica of the famous author's original home, and his library of more than 3,000 books is displayed in numerous bookshelves. James Norman Hall and Charles Nordhoff, both American heroes of World War I, moved to Tahiti in 1920. Hall wrote 17 books by himself and co-authored 12 books with Nordhoff. Their most famous works included *Mutiny on the Bounty, Men Against the Sea, Pitcairn's Island, The Hurricane,* and *The High Barbaree.* Hall's office library contains his original writing desk and typewriter and is arranged exactly as it was on the day he died in 1951. The house is filled with antique wooden furniture, family pictures, Hall's poems written to his family, his favorite paintings, gramophone and other personal effects. One of the 3 Oscars awarded to his son, the late Conrad L. Hall, for his achievements as a cinematographer in Hollywood films, is also on display. Be sure to visit Mama Lala's Tea Room, named in memory of Hall's wife, Sarah Winchester Hall.

Paul Gauguin Museum, *Tel. 57.10.58.* Beside the lagoon at PK 51.2 in Papeari, adjacent to the Harrison Smith Botanical Gardens. Open daily 9am-5pm. Entry 600 CFP. This is a memorial to the late French artist, with only a few original carvings and wood blocks located in the Salle Henri Bing. Reproductions of Gauguin's paintings and carvings are exhibited in 3 buildings beside the sea. In the 2nd building you can see where the originals of Gauguin's works of art are located today. 3 ancient stone *tiki*s from Raivavae in the Austral Islands stand in the gardens surrounding the museum, and now the people of Raivavae want them returned to their original sites.

Museum of Tahiti and Her Islands (Te Fare Iamanaha), *Tel. 54.84.35,* on the sea side at PK 15.7 in Punaauia, at Fisherman's Point (Pointe des Pêcheurs).

Open Tues.-Sun. 9:30am-5:30pm. Entry 600 CFP. This museum presents the natural environment; Polynesian migrations, history, culture and ethnology in 4 exhibit halls. On display are stone and wooden tiki, hand-hewn canoes, intricate sculptures, tapa bark, seashells and other traditional Polynesian objects and tools. Walk out to the beach and watch the surfers before you continue your tour. Breathe deeply and smell the fresh salty air.

If you plan to visit the museum by public transportation, you should know that the last bus for Papeete passes in front of the Tamanu shopping center at 4pm, except during the Heiva Festival in July, when they run a little later.

Lagoonarium, *Tel. 43.62.90*, at PK 11.4 in Punaauia at the Captain Bligh Restaurant. Open daily 9am-5:30pm. Entry 500 CFP for adults and 300 CFP for children 3-12 years old. No entry charge if you eat in the restaurant. 4 big fish parks are built into the lagoon, filled with thousands of fish, sharks, rays, turtles and moray eels. If you arrive at noon you can watch the daily shark feeding show.

Parks & Gardens

Mahana Park is beside the lagoon at PK 18.2 in Paea. Open daily. No entry fee. This public park covers a 1-acre grassy lawn and parking area and borders a beach facing the island of Moorea. The tranquil lagoon is good for swimming. There are public toilets and showers and you can picnic at one of the tables under the trees. The Manu Ura (red bird in Tahitian) Café is a small snack beside the road that is open all day except Mon. and Tues. The restaurant beside the beach may be open, but it changes ownership quite frequently.

Harrison W. Smith Botanical Gardens, *Tel. 57.11.07/57.10.58*, at PK 51.2 in Papeari, adjacent to the Paul Gauguin Museum. Open daily 9am5pm. Entry is 500 CFP. Protect yourself from mosquitoes and stroll through the 137 ha. (340 acres) of tropical gardens, streams and water lily ponds. You will see hundreds of trees, shrubs, plants and flowers gathered from tropical regions throughout the world by Smith, who was an American physics teacher who escaped to the South Seas in 1919 and created his own Garden of Eden in Tahiti. The most impressive part of this park is a natural forest of Tahitian *mape* trees, with their convoluted roots above the ground. This grove provides a cool and pleasant walk, with a small stream meandering through the shaded garden. Main attractions in the gardens are two huge land turtles, which were brought to Tahiti in the 1930's from the Galapagos Islands. These pets placidly pose for photographs and will stop eating to raise their long wrinkled necks and stare at the cameras.

Vaipahi Gardens and Cascade, on the mountainside at PK 49 in Mataiea. Open daily. Free entry. Take a pleasant stroll through these public gardens and discover a sparkling waterfall at the end of a short path. Huge tree ferns and giant leaves of elephant ear plants provide a natural setting for the cascade, which is a popular photographic choice for travel brochures on Tahiti. The gardens are filled with luxuriant vegetation, including *rambutan* fruit, fragrant *pua* flowers, ground orchids and the exotic jade vine. Crotons and hibiscus add to the flamboyance in these gardens of dancing color. You can enjoy a picnic at a table on the seaside if you are touring the island by private car.

Guided Island Tours

You can book your sightseeing tours through the travel desk at your hotel in Tahiti and see the island with a knowledgeable guide aboard an a/c bus, minivan or Mercedes luxury car.

A **Half Day Circle Island Tour** starts at 4.200 CFP plus entrance fees to the museums and gardens visited. These tours operate daily between 8:30am and 12:30pm, or between 1:30 and 5:30pm. A **Full Day Circle Island Tour** starts at 4.600 CFP plus entrance fees and lunch, with a pickup at your hotel at 9:30am, returning around 3:30 to 4pm. Entrance fees to the Gauguin Museum and Botanical Garden are 600 CFP each.

A knowledgeable guide who speaks good English is essential for your introduction to the sights and stories of Tahiti. For 17 years I worked as a tour guide in Tahiti, in addition to my journalistic endeavors, and I will recommend the best guides so that you'll be able to make an agreeable choice when you book a tour.

Adventure Eagle Tours, *Tel. 77.20.03*. William Leeteg is the son of Edgar Leeteg, the famous black velvet painter who lived in Moorea until he died in a motorcycle accident in 1953. William has a great sense of humor and knowledge of Tahiti's history as well as current events. He may even sing for you as he drives you around the island in his a/c 9-seat minibus. He has a half-day West Coast Tour, and Grand Circle Island Tour of Tahiti, with morning or afternoon departures.

Bernie's Circle Island Tour, sold by Paradise Tours, *Tel. 42.49.36*. Bernie Kamalamalama is part Hawaiian and one of the sweetest and most helpful people you'll meet anywhere. He is also a very good guide.

Dave's VIP Tours, *Tel. 79.75.65; tahiti1viptours@yahoo.com*. Dave Ellard is an English-speaking guide who will take you on a half-day tour of Tahiti in his 10-seat a/c minibus.

Marama Tours Tahiti, *Tel. 50.74.74*, has a number of guides who do a good job of telling Tahiti's tales. Mata and Emile Cowan, both Polynesians, are owners of the company. Emile taught me to be a guide way back in the early 1970s.

Tahiti Nui Travel, *Tel. 46.41.41*, has a travel desk in all the hotels, a variety of interesting tours and multi-lingual guides.

You can also go to the Tahiti Tourist Bureau and ask for a booklet entitled *Tahiti-Moorea Historic Circle Island Tour by Jean-Louis Sacquet*, or try to find a copy of the late Bengt Danielsson's *Circle Island Tour Guide*, and rent a car for a do-it-yourself excursion. If you have the time and the inclination, I suggest that you take a guided tour around Tahiti Nui (big Tahiti) and on another day rent a car and drive around the island, stopping where you choose and exploring both coasts of Tahiti Iti (little Tahiti), as well as driving up the Plateau of Taravao, where you will see horses and cattle grazing in rolling green pastures bordered by eucalyptus trees and orange groves. Or better yet, spend a few days in a bed and breakfast or family pension on Tahiti Iti and get a totally different perspective of life on this island.

Mountain & Waterfall Safari Tours

Excursions by four-wheel drive vehicle (4x4) are designed for you to get off the beaten track and up into the mountains and valleys of Tahiti. The "Queen of the Pacific" will disclose a few of her mysteries and magic as you are driven in A/C or open-air Land Rovers or other 4WDs through the tropical forests of giant ferns, centuries old Tahitian *mape* chestnut trees, wild mango and guava trees, and more waterfalls than you can count.

A **Half-Day Mountain Tour** can be made in the morning or afternoon. This excursion takes you to a height of 4,500 ft. up **Mount Marau** via the **Tamanu Canyon**. Or you can choose a **Half Day East Coast Tour**, which also takes you to Mount Marau and the Tamanu Canyon, plus you will see the **Blowhole of Arahoho** and the **Fa'arumai Cascades of Tiarei**. This tour is noted for the numerous waterfalls you will see.

A **Full Day Across the Island Tour** takes you from Mataiea in the south to the **Papenoo Valley** in the north, crossing the main crater of Tahiti. You leave the circle island road at PK 47.5 in Mataiea and follow the winding track that leads 11.2 km (7.4 mi.) up to **Lake Vaihiria**. At an altitude of 465 m (1,550 ft.) above the sea, this is Tahiti's only fresh water lake. The scenery along the way seems almost vertical, with a saw-tooth mountain range, deep ravines and tumbling cascades above and below you. As you snake to dizzying heights around the curves you will pass small catchment lakes, dams and hydroelectric substations.

After you traverse the **Urufau Tunnel**, which is 110 m. (361 ft.) long, your guide will probably stop to let you look out over the Papenoo Valley. It is believed that from 10,000 to 20,000 Maohi people once inhabited this area, and the valley was totally deserted by 1850. At this height of (780 m.) 2,558 ft. you will have an impressive view of Tahiti Nui's great extinct volcano. A junction in the road near the tunnel leads to the **Relais de la Maroto** (Maroto Inn), where some tours stop to have lunch. If you have brought your own lunch, then your driver will usually continue on to a site in the Papenoo Valley that is known as **Fare Hape**. This is an area rich in archaeological sites, and some 190 *marae* and sanctuaries have been found in the high valley since the road was built. After a refreshing swim under a sparkling waterfall and a satisfying picnic lunch eaten at a table under a big covered shelter, you can walk with your guide to visit the Fare Hape site. Several of the *marae* temples have been restored and there are archery sites, house foundations and a huge boulder carved with petroglyphs.

Note: due to frequent landslides portions of the road may be closed for months at a time, making it impossible to reach Lake Vaihiria and the Papenoo Valley from the Mataiea side. 4WD excursions are still possible from Papenoo.

Tahiti Safari Expedition, *Tel. 42.14.15/77.80.76; tahiti.safari@mail.pf; www.tahiti-safari.com.* Patrice Bordes has 5 Land Rovers with English-speaking guides. He offers mountain tours of the Papenoo Valley, with discounted rates if you book through his website. A half-day mountain tour of Papenoo Valley is 4.000 CFP and a full-day tour is 6.500 CFP. You can bring your own picnic lunch or eat at Le Relais de la Maroto, where an excursion plate costs 1.250 CFP in their restaurant. Patrice's tours were recommended by *Géo Magazine* for their efficiency and expertise. He was the pioneer of the inner island tours in 1990, and he's still the leader. These excursions are not for pregnant women or anyone who is frail, as the unpaved roads can be quite bumpy, and most uncomfortable if you are sitting on the bench in the back. These lush green valleys get a lot of rain and you will also get wet unless the side flaps are closed, creating a hothouse effect for the passengers, who can no longer see the misty beauty of the rainforest. Patrice advises his passengers not to wear the color blue as it attracts mosquitoes.

Patrick Adventure, *Tel. 83.29.29/79.08.09; patrickaventure@mail.pf; www.papeete.com.* Patrick Cordier has a 9-passenger Mazda 4WD and he is a very knowledgeable guide who covers the entire range of subjects concerning Tahiti: the history, culture, legends, geology, archaeology, agriculture, botany, religion, foods, modern life and everything else any visitor would want to know about an island and its people. His full day tour is 6.500 CFP and also takes you around the island of Tahiti Nui. Bring your own lunch to eat at a picnic table in the covered shelter at **Fare Hape** in the Papenoo Valley, and then swim in the pool under the waterfall just behind the picnic area. Patrick takes you to visit the restored *marae* temples on the premises. He also has a half-day mountain tour to visit Tahiti's east coast for 4.500 CFP. Children pay half-price on all his tours.

Natura Excursions, *Tel. 43.03.83/79.31.21; natura.explo@mail.pf; www.natura-exploration.com.* Owner Arnaud Luccioni leads half-day Landrover tours for 8 passengers to Mount Marau or to the Papenoo Valley for 5.000 CFP. His full-day exploration costs 7.500 CFP with a picnic or 6.500 CFP without, and includes the fee to visit a restored *marae*. He takes you across the central crater of Tahiti Nui to follow the tracks of the *Bounty* mutineers who hid out in this valley when their ship was leaving Tahiti. Private group rates available.

Marama Tours Tahiti, *Tel. 45.40.44/78.40.11,* and **Tahiti Nui Travel,** *Tel. 46.41.41,* offer half-day morning or afternoon tours to visit Mount Marau, for 5.500 CFP. The full-day Tahiti Inland Expedition or Inner Island Safari by 4WD with a picnic is 10.200 CFP.

Maima Tours Safari, *Tel. 48.35.85/78.68.69;* **Mato-Nui Excursions,** *Tel. 78.95.47;* and **Tahitian Safari,** *Tel. 82.69.96/72.24.18,* also lead 4WD safari tours.

Helicopter Tours

A helicopter tour offers the best of Tahiti's scenic sights, giving you a close-up look at the tallest mountains, dipping into the lush green valleys to hover like a hummingbird in front of a sparkling waterfall, and soaring over the lagoon, reef and sea. Go early in the morning before the clouds veil the view.

Polynesia Hélicoptères, *Tel. 689/54.87.20/78.65.05; Fax 689/54.87.21; helico-tahiti@mail.pf; www.polynesia-helicopter.com.* A 5-seat "Squirrel" AS 350 BA helicopter is based at the Tahiti-Faa'a airport and is available for tourist flights around Tahiti, transfers to Moorea and specific charters on request. A 20-min. flightseeing tour of Tahiti is 16.300 CFP and a 35-min. "Moorea Discovery" tour for a minimum of 4 passengers costs 26.300 CFP per person with a departure from the Faa'a Airport in Tahiti. Private transfers from a hotel in Tahiti to a hotel in Moorea are 56.000 CFP, and a private charter is 173.100 CFP per hour.

NIGHTLIFE & ENTERTAINMENT

Reputed as the South Seas heart of hedonism, Papeete by night is prowl-about time. The shops are closed and nightclubs swing. Sounds of techno, disco, zouk, beguine, reggae, calypso, rock, rap, waltz and jazz compete with the pulsating rhythm of the *tamure*, Tahiti's tantalizing national dance.

Some of Tahiti's larger hotels feature folkloric dance shows and Tahitian orchestras for dancing, and there are frequent all-night balls presented by the various sports clubs and friendship organizations on the island. These events always include live music and entertainment and the Tahitians never tire of seeing their professional or amateur dance groups performing the *ori Tahiti*. After the show the beautifully dressed Tahitians, Chinese and French diners fill the dance floor, where they glide so gracefully to the upbeat tunes of the fox trot and Tahitian waltz. When the tempo suddenly erupts into the sensual *toere* drumbeat of the hip-swiveling, rubber-legging *tamure*, the floor is suddenly packed with Tahitians, who involve their whole being—body, mind and soul—into vigorously performing their favorite dance.

Most of the bars, nightclubs and cafés are located in the heart of Papeete, along the waterfront street of Blvd. Pomare and rarely no more than a block inland. The nightclubs and casinos require proper attire. This means that the women cannot wear shorts and the men should wear a shirt, rather than a tank top, plus shoes, rather than rubber thongs or going barefoot. The nightclubs usually charge an entry fee for men, which includes a drink, and unescorted ladies get in free most of the time, sometimes with the bonus of a complimentary first drink. Some of these nightclubs change ownership and names frequently, so don't be surprised if you don't find the place you're looking for. Just ask a few people at your hotel to give you the new name, and you'll probably get mixed answers.

Local Style

LE ROYAL KIKIRIRI, *Tel. 43.58.64, on Rue Colette between Avenue Prince Hinoi and the Mairie of Papeete (town hall).* This place started out as a true Tahitian bar, where the musicians tuned up for an evening of *kaina* music, playing the songs of the islands on their guitars and ukuleles, strumming the chords of a gut bucket bass or rattling 2 spoons together in a beer bottle. The revelers enthusiastically sang and danced as they got happy on Hinano beer or Johnny Walker whisky, and the chairs had a hard time staying upright in the general melee. This bar has now been transformed into a chic a/c nightclub that attracts a completely different type of clientele. For several years it has been one of the choice nightspots in Papeete, where good-looking, well-dressed young people gather to dance to live and recorded Tahitian and disco type music.

LE ROYAL TAHITIEN, *Tel. 50.40.40,* in Pirae, is the Happy Hour gathering place for many of Tahiti's office workers each Fri. afternoon, when local residents come to dance at the bar and on the terrace to the tunes of Polynesian music played by a live band. A special barbecue dinner is also served for those who feel like diluting their booze with some veal cooked on a spit. The security is good here and no fights take place, according to manager Lionel Kennedy, an expatriate Aussie, who is also a musician. He plays jazz with other musicians each Wed. evening at the bar.

Discos & Jazz

LE PIANO BAR, *Tel. 42.88.24,* on Rue des Ecoles, the street behind Mana Rock Café. If you want to see a female impersonator strip show Tahitian style, this is the place to go. The transvestite *mahu* dancers, Polynesia's "third sex," are friendly. This can be a fun place and is quite harmless, unless you try to make out with someone else's boyfriend.

LE PARADISE, *Tel. 42.73.05,* on Blvd. Pomare, across from the French naval station. Le Paradise normally has a European ambiance, but it can also resonate to an Afro-Caribbean rhythm. This is a complex of Le Night restaurant, Le Paradise nightclub and Le Chaplin's brasserie, cocktail and video lounge. This is the second choice of "best" nightclubs chosen by some of my swinging friends in Tahiti, while others tell me it's awful.

MORRISON'S CAFÉ, *Tel. 42.78.61,* in the Vaima Center, with a private elevator located on Rue General de Gaulle, adjacent to the Air New Zealand office. This is an indoor/outdoor restaurant and café, where the sounds of sweet jazz sing out over the rooftops of Papeete, played by American or French musicians who are frequently imported to liven up the scene. This café is named after Jim Morrison (of The Doors), and the musical ambiance is a combination of American rock music, jazz and modern Tahitian rock bands.

CLUB 106, *Tel. 42.72.92,* on Boulevard Pomare adjacent to the Moana Iti restaurant. This is one of the oldest private dance clubs in Papeete. There's no entry charge, but you must take care of your "look" to be permitted. Simply ring the bell at the front door downstairs and then join Papeete's "in crowd" and dance to taped music for all tastes.

LE GRENIER DE MONTMARTRE, *Tel. 79.59.29/76.64.31,* is on Rue Gauguin facing the Papeete City Hall. Music includes live rock, live Hawaiian, soul, funk & disco music from the 1980s, or techno and electro.

LET THE MUSIC PLAY

The Tahitian custom of inviting someone to dance is rather subtle. You are sitting at the bar or a table, alone or with friends. A young man begins to stare at you, trying to get your attention, or perhaps returning your own flirtatious glance. When he catches your eye, he just lifts his eyebrows and nods his head toward the dance floor. You can ignore him, shake your head negatively, or raise your own eyebrows in a positive reply and meet him on the dance floor. Tahitian men assume that if a woman isn't dancing with anyone, she is available to dance with him, even if she is sitting with a man.

Dancing with a Tahitian **tane** involves little or no conversation. Normally there is no desire for introductions before or during the first few dances. People are there to dance, and grab a feel, perhaps, but not to talk. Each trip to the floor lasts for the duration of two songs, played to similar tempos. This gives you a good opportunity to get to know one another, with little or no conversation transpiring between you. But there is definitely a communication going on.

If you continue to dance with the same man, for the first hour or so of the evening he is very polite and dances beautifully, as he holds you at a respectful distance. He smells divine, wearing the best perfume of his sister, wife or live-in vahine, the mother of some of his children. After he has drunk a few bottles of Hinano beer he becomes more relaxed and informal. Also much more intimate. He squeezes you close and his hands become freer in their wanderings around your body. He might ask you to leave with him after the dance, as he nuzzles your neck and presses his body close to yours. The next hour after that is when you have to start holding him up, if you are still on the scene by that time.

Here are some of the other night spots: **Be Angel** is an "in" disco for the very young chic crowd, located above Le Newport Restaurant on the corner of Blvd. Pomare and Ave. Aroa Nui Pouvanaa a Oopa. If you like techno sounds, this is the place to go. **Le Manhattan** is a nightclub next to the Hotel Kon Tiki on Blvd. Pomare. **Metropolis** (ex-Shark, ex-Zizou), across from the ferry dock on Blvd. Pomare, combines a local ambience with recorded disco tunes. **Café des Négociants**, in the Quartier du Commerce, and **Les Trois Brasseurs** on Blvd. Pomare, have live rock bands on Fri. and Sat. nights. **Dao**, above the Piano Bar, has karaoke. **Bar Taina** is in the same block as Les Trois Brasseurs, and is a bar preferred by Tahitians and French military men. Couples or women without escorts may find the atmosphere a little too rough, but men in search of meeting a friendly Tahitian *vahine* or *mahu* may find it to their liking. Hervé, the French manager, speaks

English. You can drink on the covered terrace outside and dance to recorded music inside the bar. There's a live Tahitian band every Fri. night.

New "cool" night spots include the **Ute Ute Restaurant** and **Le Gaia**. **Place Vaiete** on the waterfront near the ferry dock has free concerts and dance performances on some weekends. Outside of town on the West Coast the **Western Grill** at PK 12.6 in Punaauia presents a Western Show or Drag Show during dinner on Wed., Thurs., and Sat. nights. Reservations are required. The **Pink Coconut, Quai des Iles** and **Casa Bianca** are 3 restaurants at the Marina Taina that have live entertainment on weekends.

SPORTS & RECREATION
ATV-Quad Excursions

Tahiti Aventures, *Tel. 29.01.60,* is based at the Intercontinental Resort Tahiti, offering you another way to discover the island. You will have an unforgettable experience when you join a guided ATV outing into the Papenoo Valley, up to the heights of Mount Marau or the Belvedere in the Fare Rau Ape Valley. Protective goggles and head gear provided and closed shoes are obligatory. The hotel travel desks charge 13.200-18.000 CFP for 2-hr. excursions, 16.500-24.000 CFP for a half-day trip to Mount Marau, and 22.000-35.000 CFP for a full-day trip to the Papenoo Valley with picnic included.

Golf

If golf is your game you can tee off at the **Olivier Breaud International Golf Course of Atimaono,** at PK 40.2 in Papara, *Tel. 57.40.32; Fax 57.49.68.* Located between the mountains and the sea 25 miles from Papeete on Tahiti's southwest coast, you'll find an 18-hole course 6,900 yd. long, par 72, mostly flat, and well known for some of the world's toughest par 3's. The greens are planted with hybrid Bermuda grass from Hawaii. Two artificial lakes and wide, hilly fairways surrounded by fruit trees add to the beauty and pleasure of this course, which attracts professional and amateur golfers from overseas, who compete in the annual Tahiti International Pro/Am Open, held each July or Aug. This event is now part of the Australian PGA circuit.

Plans are to rebuild the Club House and add 9 more holes. The Club House presently has locker rooms and showers for men and women, a full bar and a restaurant serving French and local foods with service to 4pm. There is a swimming pool, spa pool and a driving range, plus a pro shop and boutique for sales and rentals. The course is open daily from 8am to 4pm and the Club House stays open to 6pm. The green fees are 5.500 CFP for 18 holes and 3.300 CFP for 9 holes, which include all taxes. You can rent a sack of clubs for 2.500 CFP, a pull cart for 650 CFP, and an electric car is 4.600 CFP for 18 holes and 2.900 CFP for 9 holes.

Hui Popo Golf Tours, *Tel. 57.40.32; Fax 57.49.68; skiptahiti@yahoo.com,* is managed by Skip Anderson, an American expatriate resident who is also in charge of the Club House. He provides round-trip transfers by a/c mini-bus from the Port of Papeete or any hotel to the golf course and back, for 10.000 CFP for 2 people. Skip offers 7 golf packages that can include a set of clubs, golf car, golfer's lunch, green fee, round trip transfers, free practice balls and a souvenir & play package. Contact him for details.

Tahiti Nui Travel, Tekura Tahiti Travel and Marama Tours travel desks located in the hotel lobbies sell a golf package for 23.900 CFP for one person and 29.900-34.900 CFP per couple, which includes round-trip transportation between your hotel or ship and the golf course, the green fee, a set of clubs, practice balls, a motorized golf car, golfer's lunch and the souvenir and play package.

Hiking

Feel like taking a hike? Tahiti's mountains and valleys and rugged Te Pari coast offer an interesting choice of treks. Even though you may be tempted to set out on your own to discover the lava tubes, burial caves and hidden grottos, my advice is to go with a guide and the proper equipment. The weather can be variable in the heights, and sudden downpours can suddenly swell the rivers, making them impassable for several days.

Polynesian Adventure, *Tel./Fax 43.25.95, cell 77.24.37; polynesianadv@mail.pf; http://www.polynesianadv.fr.st.* Vincent Dubousquet is a professional guide who specializes in 30 different hikes on Tahiti and Moorea, including exploring the lava tubes. Following are some of his most popular hikes.

The **Fautaua Valley** is one of the easiest walks, which most people accomplish in four to seven hours. The waterfall here was the romantic setting described in *The Marriage of Loti*, a novel written by a French sailor named Louis Marie Julien Viaud, who came to Tahiti in the 1880s. A minimum of two people is required for this half-day outing, or to visit other valleys on Tahiti's east coast, including **Le Belvedere, Tuauru** or **Faananu**. The cost for a half-day hike is 5.400 CFP per person, plus there is an access fee of 700 CFP per person to visit the Fautaua Valley and another 700 CFP to get to the Diademe Pass.

Half-day hikes to the west coast valleys of **Vaipohe** or **Mateoro** are rated easy to sportive and also cost 5.400 CFP per person for a minimum of two people. All-day easy to medium level hikes can be made to the **Fautaua Valley**, the **Hamuta** Pass 900 m (2,952 ft.) high on the **Aorai** trail, to the basaltic organs of **Tuauru Valley** in Mahina, to **Te Faaiti Valley** in Papenoo, which is a park with natural Jacuzzis, or to **Faananu Valley** in Tiare, all on the east coast. The west coast hikes can take you to the canyon of **Vaipohe Valley** in Paea, or to **Mateoro Valley** in Papara, where there is a small canyon and lots of flowers. All these hikes require a minimum of two people and cost 7.200 CFP per person, plus an access fee of 600 CFP per person to enter the Fautaua Valley.

You should be in good physical condition and not subject to vertigo to climb to **Fare Ata**, the second refuge, at a height of 1,810 m (5,937 ft.) on **Mount Aorai**, which at 2,066 m (6,776 ft.), is the second highest peak on Tahiti. Vincent includes this one-day hike in his "sportive" level, which requires a minimum of two people.

Other rugged hikes are to the **Teovere** Pass in Papeete, which gives you a good view of the Fautaua Valley and **Le Diadème**, the crown mountain; to the high waterfalls of **Te Faaiti Valley** in Papenoo; and to **Vaihi Valley** in Hitia'a with lovely waterfalls and a view of the east coast. You'll need at least four hikers to go to the **Lava Tubes**, river and tunnels in Hitia'a; up to the refuge of Faaroa and the rugged cliffs of **Te Pari** in Teahupoo; or to **Vaipoiri Grotto** on Tahiti Iti. Each of these tougher treks costs 9.300 CFP per person and you will have to pay an access fee of 700 CFP to get to Teovere Pass.

Two or three hikers can divide the total cost and still make the treks that normally require a minimum of four. All material is provided for the hikes in Tahiti Iti and Hitiaa. Boat transfers are also provided on the Tahiti Iti treks. Ground transfers are free up to 35 km from pick-up point to the trail entrance. Cold meals and a drink are furnished for 1.200 CFP per person. Minimum age for these hikes is 12 years. Polynesian Adventure also has two-day camping hikes into the valleys of Tahiti Nui and Tahiti Iti, for 17.700 CFP a person, including meals. Vincent Dubousquet also leads all-day treks in Moorea.

Tahiti Evasion, *Tel. 74.67.13/56.48.77; tahitievasion@mail.pf; www.tahitievasion.com.* Eric LeNoble leads day hikes into Fautaua Valley and Orofero Valley, which are rated as family outings without difficulty. He will take confirmed hikers up to a height of 1,400 m (4,522 ft.) on Mount Aorai. He also leads 3-day hikes to the Pari and Fenua Aihere wild lands of Tahiti Iti, including a 2-night bivouac on the beach. You need to be in good physical condition and able to walk on varied terrain for this trek. His rates start at 4.000 CFP per person.

Tiare Mato Excursions, *Tel. 43.92.76/77.48.11; tiaremat@mail.pf.* Guillaume Dor specializes in canyoning trips that take you to the lava tubes of Hitia'a, to the heights of Orofero or to Maroto in the Papenoo Valley. He also leads hikes and all level trekking for one or two days, ranging from the first category for easy walks to the fifth category for confirmed mountain climbers, using ropes and rappel techniques. He furnishes all equipment except your shoes, personal clothing and sandwich.

Other well-known guides include: Mataa'e Rangimakea of **Presqu'ile Loisirs**, *Tel. 57.00.57*, Hervé Maraetaata of **Mato-Nui Excursions**, *Tel. 78.95.47*; Serge Pihatarioe of **Puarai Excursions**, *Tel. 42.41.65*; Noella Tutavae of **Hina Trekking**, *Tel. 78.36.31*; Zena Angelin, *Tel. 57.22.67*, of **Le Circuit Vert**; and Fabien Tetaz of **Tahiti Rando-Trek**, *Tel. 73.04.69*.

Horseback Riding

Most of the horses in Tahiti are from the Marquesas Islands, descendants of Chilean stock. The equestrian clubs now have thoroughbreds from New Zealand as well. You can ride by the sea or in the mountains with a guide, who will take along a picnic lunch upon request. The **Club Equestre de Tahiti**, at the Pirae Hippodrome race track, *Tel. 42.70.41*, and **L'Eperon de Pirae**, *Tel. 42.79.87*, in a nearby stable, have both races of steeds for your riding pleasure.

Ranch Rauvau, *Tel 73.84.43*, is located at PK 2.5 on the Taravao Plateau of Tahiti Iti. You'll need to reserve in advance if you wish to explore "little Tahiti" by horseback, but the magnificent views are worth the effort. There are 16 horses available for riding for 2.000 CFP per hour, 6.000 CFP for a half-day outing with picnic, and 8.000 CFP for an all-day ride with picnic. The basic tourist ride costs 3.000 CFP for 1.5 hours in the saddle. This ranch is also called L'Amour de la Nature A Cheval (Love of Nature by Horseback).

Tennis

Tahiti's climate is ideal for playing tennis year-round, by scheduling a match in the early morning or at sunset time, to avoid the hottest hours of a tropical day. Tennis courts are located at the following hotels: **Le Méridien, Intercontinental Tahiti Resort** and **Sofitel Tahiti Resort**. Sports clubs and private tennis clubs also have their own courts, where you can play for a nominal fee and meet some of the local resident players. These include the **Tennis Club of Fautaua**, just to the west of downtown Papeete, *Tel. 42.00.59*; **Fei Pi Tennis Club** at PK 3.2 in Arue, *Tel. 42.53.87*; and the **Excelsior Tennis Club** in the Mission Quarter of Papeete, *Tel. 43.91.46*.

Deep Sea Fishing

Zane Grey put Tahiti on the world map of outstanding deep-sea fishing spots in the 1930s, when the American novelist had his own fishing camp in Vairao on the Tahiti Iti peninsula. Game fishing has become a year-round sport in Tahiti, and your chances are very good of reeling in a big blue marlin, sailfish, swordfish, yellow fin tuna, mahi mahi, wahoo, ocean bonito or tiger shark. You may also catch jack crevally, blue crevally, rainbow runner, dogtooth tuna and barracuda just outside the reef.

You have a choice of several professional fishing boats throughout the islands, whose crews compete in local tournaments in preparation for the **Tahiti International Billfish Tournament**, which is held every two years, usually in Raiatea and the Leeward Islands. Alban Ellacott is the president of this association, *Tel. 54.41.54/42.37.14; Fax 43.28.45; tibt@mail.pf, tiba@mail.pf.*

Haura Club of Tahiti, *Tel. 42.37.14/77.09.29; pat.four@mail.pf,* presided by Georges Poroi, is based at Marina Taina in Punaauia. This is the game fishing club or marlin club of Tahiti. They can also give you the names of other sports fishing boats for charter.

Ahavini, *Tel. 43.81.41/77.13.06,* is a 4-passenger 31-ft. Bertram Sportfisherman owned by Jean Tellier, based at the Marina Taina in Punaauia.

Toohi II, *Tel. 50.11.00/70.45.14/72.12.55; Fax 50.11.01; toohicharter@mail.pf; www.toohicharter.atahiti.com.* Willy and Pascale Maufay own a 30-ft. Arcoa 900 motorboat with two 135 HP diesel engines. They can take up to 4 passengers for half- or full-day fishing outings around the islands of Tahiti, Moorea and Tetiaroa.

Nautical Centers & Clubs

Aquatica Diving Center and Nautical Activities, *Tel. 53.34.96; aquatica@mail.pf; www.aquatica-dive.com*, is located at the **Intercontinental Tahiti Resort**. Guests of the hotel can use the snorkeling equipment free for one hour. Otherwise, the cost is 1.000 CFP for the mask & snorkel and 1.000 CFP for fins, with a 5.000 CFP deposit. The same rules apply for tennis rackets and balls and use of tennis courts. You can rent a kayak for 1.800 CFP or a pedal boat for 1.500 CFP for one hour (the first hour is free for the kayak and a 10.000 CFP deposit is required). You can sunbathe and swim from a floating pontoon in the lagoon for 1.000 CFP. A non-guided snorkel trip is 4.000 CFP. You can join a Dolphin Cruise for 10.000 CFP, wakeboard initiation for 11.000 CFP, or sign up for a Sunset Sailing Cruise aboard the *Enjoy* for 10.000 CFP. You can rent the boat with skipper for an hour for 20.000 CFP, or for the day for 100.000 CFP. You can hire a Jet-Ski for 15.000 CFP an hour, or an ATV Quad for a 2-hour guided excursion, for 15.000 CFP. A half-day deep-sea fishing charter is 65.000 CFP and 80.000 CFP for the whole day. Aquatica Diving Center charges 6.500 CFP for an exploration dive, 7.000 CFP for an initial dive, 8.000 CFP for night diving, and 12.000 CFP for a 2-tank dive. Even if you are not staying at the hotel, you can take part in the activities by making reservations. See more information under *Scuba Diving* in this chapter.

Le Méridien Tahiti Watersports Activities Center, *Tel. 47.07.07*, is open daily from 8am to 6pm. Snorkeling equipment and kayaks are free for Le Méridien hotel guests, as well as the Aquagym classes that are held in the sandy bottom swimming pool. Snorkeling excursions cost 6.500 CFP, the Dolphin Watch is 7.500 CFP, a Lagoon Safari is 8.000 CFP, a 3-hour Whale Watch (Aug.-Oct.) is 12.000 CFP, and a 4-hour excursion by private boat is 60.000 CFP for a maximum of 4 passengers. The Eleuthera scuba dive center is based here, offering all levels of diving and lessons. They charge 7.000 CFP for the first dive or fun dive, and 8.500 CFP for a Nitrox dive.

Water-Skiing Club of Tahiti, (Ski Nautique Club de Tahiti), *Tel. 45.39.36/ 77.22.62; Fax 41.26.09; www.tahitiskiclub.com*. This club is located beside the lagoon between the Intercontinental Resort Tahiti and Sofitel Tahiti Resort. Patrick Pluviaud, the fully qualified monitor will help you perfect your water-skiing techniques on the wakeboard, ski-tubes, by mono-ski or barefoot. A floating pontoon in the lagoon is available for sunbathing and swimming.

Marinas

Marina Taina, *B.P. 13003-98717, Punaauia, Tahiti; Tel. 689/41.02.25; Fax 689/45.27.58; marinataina@mail.pf.* This modern marina is located at PK 9 in Punaauia, on Tahiti's west coast, facing the island of Moorea. Whether you want information on chartering a sports fishing boat, a luxury motor yacht or a safe mooring for your own sailboat, you can contact manager Eric Malmezac and his efficient staff. There are berths and moorings for about 550 local boats and 50 visiting yachts. The dock can handle up to six units at a time (stern to). The fees are 100-200 CFP per foot per day, which includes water. Their services also include electricity, fuel, mail handling, office communication, on-board telephones, cable TV, car rental, laundry service and much more. The Eleuthera Dive Center, Haura Fishing Club and 3 restaurants and a computer center are on the premises, as well as a ship chandler, repair shop and a marine gas station.

Tahiti Nautic Center Marina, *B.P. 7305-98719, Taravao, Tahiti; Tel. 689/ 54.76.16; Fax 689/57.05.07; tnc@mail.pf; www.tahitinauticcenter.pf.* Located at PK 56 in Taravao, beside Phaeton Bay, with berths for 40 boats up to 50 ft. long catamarans and a maximum draft of 2 m. On the premises are a restaurant, clubhouse, laundry service, naval shipyard, superstructure store and mechanical workshop.

For information on anchoring in the **Port of Papeete** see information in this chapter under *Arrivals & Departures, By Boat.*

Sailing Charters

Tahiti Yacht Charter, *Tahiti office: Monette Aline, B.P. 364, Papeete, Tahiti 98713; Tel. 689/45.04.00; Fax 689/42.76.00; tyc@mail.pf; www.tahitiyachtcharter.com. Raiatea base: Tel. 689/66.28.86; Fax 689/66.28.85.*

Tahiti Yacht Charter is a 100% locally owned company. They have been established in French Polynesia for 20 years, chartering bareboats or crewed boats. They have a fleet of 20 catamarans, most of them less than 2 years old, all based at the Apooiti Marina in Raiatea, with Papeete as a possible departure point. Rates and details are listed in the chapter on *Planning Your Trip* and in the *Raiatea* chapter under *Sailing Charter Yachts.*

Day Sailing & Boat Excursions

You'll find day sailing and other boat excursions easy to arrange once you're here, simply by booking with your hotel activities desk or walking along the quay at the Papeete waterfront, across from the post office, and talking with the captain of the boat you choose to fulfill your dream

Intercontinental Tahiti Resort, *Tel. 53.34.96; aquatica@mail.pf,* is a 12 m (40 ft.) Fontaine Pajot sailing catamaran based at the Intercontinental Resort Tahiti. This yacht with skipper charters for 50.000 CFP for a half-day or 100.000 CFP for all-day private day-sailing excursions for a maximum of 10 passengers. A sunset cruise, including a drink, costs 10.000 CFP, and a Dolphin Cruise is 10.000 CFP per person.

Jet France, *Tel./Fax 56.15.62,* is the name of a company that provides day cruise charters to Tetiaroa. Jean-Jacques Besson keeps his 15-m. (49-ft.) yacht *Vehia* tied up at the yacht quay on the Papeete waterfront. The boat sails to Tetiaroa each Wed., Sat. and Sun. at 7am and returns to the quay at 6-7pm. You will have about five hours ashore at Tetiaroa, and they will guide you to visit Bird Island. Bring your own lunch and drinks. The captain takes 10-16 passengers for 13.000 CFP each.

L'Escapade, *Tel. 72.85.31, Satellite Tel. 00.872.76.25.24.382; escapade@mail.pf; www.escapade-voile.pf.* This 46-ft. aluminum Sea Breeze sailboat is owned by Anne-Marie and Paul Gasparini, who have 20 years' experience in sailing, spent cruising around the world with their family, and chartering in the Caribbean. You can join them for a relaxing day in Tetiaroa, with departures from the Papeete waterfront quay at 6am on request. You will arrive in Tetiaroa at 10:15am and visit the motu islets, the seabird sanctuary and swim in the clear warm lagoon. Lunch is served on board and the boat leaves Tetiaroa at 3:15pm, arriving in Tahiti at 7:30pm. Breakfast, lunch and drinks included for the price of 13.000 CFP per person. They also do long cruises on request.

Tahiti Cruise/Margouillat, *Tel. 72.23.45; mahi@mail.pf; www.tahiticruise.pf.* Margouillat is a 43-ft. catamaran based at Marina Taina in Punaauia that can accommodate 8 passengers in 4 double cabins for a long cruise and 14 people for a day sail. Daily cruises with or without meals will take you around Tahiti, Moorea or Tetiaroa, on outings to discover the dolphins and whales, or for sunset cruises for groups. A half-day sailing & snorkeling lagoon cruise is 9.000 CFP, a full day cruise with lunch on board is 14.500 CFP and a sunset cruise with cocktail is 6.500 CFP. A weekend in Moorea cruise of two days and one night departs from Papeete on Sat. morning and returns on Sun. evening, or you can arrange cruises of 3 days to 3 weeks or more. A skipper and hostess will accompany you. Contact Jean-Marie Libeau.

Scuba Diving

The protected lagoons, passes and outer coral reefs offer ideal conditions for scuba diving year-round and you'll discover an abundance of dive clubs on the island of Tahiti. The diving instructors are highly qualified and speak English to varying degrees. Safe, dependable boats are used to take you to discover several beautiful locations, which may include "**The Aquarium,**" a calm, clear, fish feeding site; "**The Wrecks,**" a ship and aircraft on the same dive; and "**The Tahiti Wall & Shark Cave,**" an outer reef drop-off with canyons, crevices and shark cave. The small reef sharks and moray eels are fed by hand.

Intercontinental Tahiti Resort, *Tel. 689/53.34.96; aquatica@mail.pf; www.aquatica-dive.com.* This is a 5-star PADI Center "Gold Palm IDC" #6313, Scubapro SEA center and NITROX scuba diving center based at the Nautical Activities Center at Intercontinental Resort Tahiti. Manager Didier Alpini is a CMAS** certified monitor and a PADI master instructor. See diving rates under *Nautical Centers & Clubs* in this chapter.

Eleuthera, *Tel. 689/42.49.29/77.65.68; Fax 689/48.04.04; info@dive-tahiti.com; www.tahiti-dive.com.* This 5-star PADI center is located at Marina Taina in Punaauia. Managers Nicolas Castel and Joshua Rouger are International CMAS ** and *** instructors, BEES 1 federal instructors, Sea-Guides and PADI, OWSI and ANMP certified instructors. They provide 4 outings per day, including ocean dives at 9am and 2pm. They offer programs from beginners to certified divers, specifically adapted to each level.

Fluid Dive Center, *Tel./Fax 689/85.41.46; Cell 70.83.75; fluid@mail.pf; www.fluidtahiti.com.* Yannis Saint-Pé is a scuba dive instructor who provides personalized service aboard his boat **Fluid** for up to 6 divers or snorkelers, including the diving equipment. He has 2-tank dives and half-day dolphin and whale (in season) watching excursions. All levels of PADI and CMAS/ANMP courses available. Refreshments served on board.

Tahiti Plongée, *Tel. 689/41.00.62/43.62.51; Fax 689/42.26.06; plongée.tahiti@mail.pf; www.tahitiplongee.pf.* This dive center is based on the grounds of the ex-Hotel Bel Air between the Intercontinental Tahiti Resort and Sofitel Tahiti Resort. Henri Pouliquen has been teaching children and first time divers the necessary basics of scuba diving since 1979 and has a very good reputation in Tahiti for his success and his gentle personality. He holds a CMAS *** international rating and can deliver all levels of CMAS certification.

TOPdive Tahiti, *Tel. 86.49.06/70.55.55/77.13.07; Fax 83.51.26; topdivetahiti@mail.pf; tahiti@topdive.com; www.topdive.com.* Bernard Begliomini heads this PADI 5 star and Scubapro S.E.A. center at the Sheraton Hotel Tahiti, assisted by personal dive trainers. They provide snorkeling tours, scuba diving, open water training, wall dives, wreck dives and night dives. Public rates for scuba diving start at 7.000 CFP for an introductory dive, fun dive or night dive; an open water certification course is 65.000 CFP, and a package of 10 dives is 63.000 CFP. The diving rates include taxes and all equipment. This package can be used at TOPdive centers in Bora Bora, Moorea, Rangiroa, Fakarava and Tahiti. Nitrox scuba diving is available in Bora Bora, Moorea and Rangiroa at the same rate as air.

Surfing

The Tahitians claim that their Maohi ancestors invented surfing, and the chiefs of Tahiti used to compete with one another on long wooden boards. Surfers come to Tahiti from all around the world to surf the edges of the passes, and international surfing champions have found challenging waves offshore Teahupoo at the end of the Tahiti Iti peninsula. Between Oct. and March strong swells from the north bring sizable waves, and from Apr. to Sept. the Antarctic winds from the south produce powerful waves that are great for riding the tube.

Prime surf spots include the break at the mouth of the **Papenoo River** at PK 17 on Tahiti's northeast coast. Southwest of Papeete the **Taapuna pass** at PK 15, close to Fisherman's Point in Punaauia, is a favorite reef break spot for local surfers. Further along the coast you'll find the **Taharuu black sand beach** at PK 36 in Papara, where the waves are good enough for the popular **Horue open**, an international competition held each July. The **Billabong Pro Tahiti** is part of the World Championship Tour (W.C.T.). This competition takes place in May, and is reserved exclusively for the 44 best surfers in the world. Accompanying the big name surfers are the international press and crowds of spectators who flock to the beautiful untamed coastline of **Te Pari**, at the southern tip of Tahiti Iti. The passes

WHAT TO DO ON TAHITI ITI

Tahiti Iti Tour and Surf, *Tel./Fax 57.42.04, cell 75.55.66, riou@mail.pf* is owned by Alain Clemendot, whose nautical sports base is at PK 10.100 in Vairao. He operates a taxi boat service to take passengers to the surf spots, to visit the Vaipoiri Grotto, Te Pari cliffs, the coral garden, and to look for dolphins and whales during the season of July-Oct. He can also take you waterskiing, wakeboarding and fishing.

Teahupoo Excursions, *Tel. 75.11.98; teahupooexcursions@mail.pf* belongs to a young Frenchman named Michaël, whose boat can take up to 6 passengers to visit Motu Fenua Aino, to swim in the Vaipoiri River and to photograph the rugged Te Pari coastline. A half-day excursion is 15.000 CFP and an all day outing is 28.000 CFP. He will also take surfers out to the best waves for 1.000 CFP round/trip for a drop-off in Teahupoo or 1.500 CFP to surf the waves of Vairao.

Moana Paofai's Eden Day Adventure Boat Trip, *Tel. 57.02.15/ 77.89.69,* to explore the Fenua Aihere and Te Pari is an outrigger excursion for 8 or more passengers that takes you to visit the southern coast of Tahiti Iti, exploring a hidden tributary, hiking through a rain forest to enter a cave and swimming in the refreshing clear waters of the underground grotto of Vaipoiri. Guests staying at his wife's Pension Le Bonjouir pay 4.500 CFP per person. All others pay 9.000 CFP per person, which includes lunch for a minimum of 8 adults. If you come to Teahupoo for an Eden Day Tour Moana will meet you at the Eden boat beside the lagoon just before the end of the road in Teahupoo. If you rent a car to get here then you can leave it in his private parking area. You can also get a round-trip mini-bus or car transfer.

Iti Nui Surf School, *Tel. 73.14.21, doumeitinui@yahoo.fr,* information center at Magasin Z'Spot in Taravao. Doumé is a qualified surfing instructor who also has the surfboards and boogieboards to teach his students the skills and techniques required to master the impressive waves on the Tahiti Iti peninsula. He charges 3.500 CFP a lesson and 14.000 CFP for 5 lessons.

Valentin, *Tel. 70.49.82,* is a trained mountain guide who knows all the secrets of Te Pari. She charges 7.000 CFP for a half-day outing, which includes the boat transfers and a picnic, as well as a hike adapted to the level of the walkers. She also organizes 2-day hikes for 15.000 CFP per person. (More guides and treks are listed under *Hiking* in this chapter).

Prisca, *Tel. 70.38.14,* is a masseuse who will come to your room to help you relax with a Polynesian, Californian, or hot-stone massage.

of Hava'e, Te Ava Ino and Tapueraha are good for riding the waves to the left, and Te Ava Piti pass sends you to the right.

Tura'i Mata'are Surf School, *Tel. 77.27.69; surfschool@mail.pf; www.tahitisurfschool.info* is operated by Olivier Napias (contact him through the Kelly Surf Shop in the Fare Tony Center in Papeete). Half-day classes in surfing or bodyboarding are given by a certified surf instructors, and all material, transportation and insurance is included for 4.800 CFP. Surfboard rentals cost 1.500 CFP per hour, 3.000 CFP for a half-day and 4.000 CFP for a full-day.

Moanareva, *Tel./Fax 42.45.28, cell 72.11.72; moanareva@mail.pf; www.moanareva.com*. Gerald Fournier operates this surf school at Point Venus in Mahina, with introductory classes in surfing or bodyboarding. Boards, transfers and insurance included. Kayaks, bodyboards, paddleboards, wakeboards and surfboards available for rent.

Spectator Sports

Soccer is Tahiti's favorite sport, and during the *futbol* season enthusiastic crowds gather at the **Fautaua Stadium** near Papeete on weeknights and during weekends to cheer their team to victory.

Outrigger canoe racing is the top traditional sport. At almost any time of the year you will see the muscled young men practicing for the next big *pirogue* race. The racing season begins around May, and the best teams of male and female paddlers compete in the Heiva Festival races in July, which are held inside the lagoon and in the open ocean. More races are held in Aug. and Sept. to select the teams who will compete in the **Hawaiki Nui Pirogue Race** that is held each Nov. During this 3-day event, the paddlers race from Huahine to Raiatea, then to Taha'a and on to Bora Bora. Tahitian-style **horse racing** is held on special occasions at the **Pirae Hippodrome**, where jockeys used to ride bareback, wearing only a brightly colored *pareo* and a crown of flowers. Safety regulations now require saddles and helmets. You can place your bets, but the payoffs are very small. **Cockfighting** is another Sun. afternoon event. Although it is officially illegal, everyone seems to know where the fights will take place on a certain day. Ask at your hotel for specific details.

Almost every weekend in Tahiti or Moorea you will find a marathon or triathlon or bicycle-racing event going on. Other competitions are held for Hobie Cats, wind surfers and jet-skiers, as well as tennis, golf, *petanque* or bacci-ball, volleyball, basketball, boxing, archery, rugby and track.

Astronomy Club

The **Astronomers Club of Tahiti** (SAT) has frequent open house visits at their observatory in the Cité de l'Air overlooking the International Airport of Tahiti-Faa'a. You can come alone or with a group to gaze at the celestial lights above the island through their powerful telescopes. To find out exact dates of observation, call Stephane at *Tel. 79.30.82* (he speaks English), or leave a message at *Tel.*

82.17.83; *sat@mail,pf*; *www.astrosurf.com/sat*. Also check out the English language website of Roland Santallo, who has a privately owned observatory in Faa'a, *www.southernstars-observatory.org*.

SHOPPING

Tahiti is not a shopper's paradise, but some of the merchandise is different from what you're used to seeing back home. Made-in-Tahiti items can be good souvenir purchases, but be aware that some of the wooden masks, clothing and pearly shells that are sold in boutiques and curio shops were imported from Indonesia or the Philippines. The *pareu* or *pareo*, which is called a sarong or lava lava in other countries, is Tahiti's national garment. It is made from a piece of cotton fabric approximately 2 yards long and 1 yard wide and tie-dyed, airbrushed or hand painted. You will find these in shops along the Papeete waterfront, at sidewalk stands, in arts and crafts centers all around the island, in hotel boutiques, and displayed at the colorful kiosks set up permanently outside and upstairs at **le Marché**, the municipal market in the heart of Papeete.

One of the nicest selections of hand painted pareos, shirts, caftans (boubou) and beach cover-ups is at **Le Tiare de Tahiti** boutique on the second level of the Vaima Center. Fabrics to make your own *pareos* or brightly patterned shirts and dresses are sold by the meter at **Tahiti Art**, **Tahiti Beach**, the **Venus** fabric stores and other Chinese-owned shops in the vicinity of the public market.

Polynesian style bikinis, beachwear and ball gowns are fabricated by local factories and couturiers in attractive hand-blocked materials. You'll find the choicest selections in the hotel boutiques, and in dozens of shops in Papeete, including **Tahiti Art**, **Marie Ah You**, **Celina** and **Tiare Shop** on Boulevard Pomare, **Anémone** on Rue Marechal Foch, **Shop Gauguin Curios** on Rue Gauguin, **Tamara Curios** in Fare Tony Center, **Vaima Shirts**, **Bikini Boutique** and several other shops in the Vaima Center. **Tahiti Shirts**, on Boulevard Pomare, carries several lines of quality shirts that are designed by young artists in Tahiti. **Tahiti Art** also sells wall hangings, tapestries, lampshades, candles, jewelry boxes, paintings and engravings, all with Polynesian designs. Sports and Surf clothes are sold all over town, as well as in the Moana Nui (Carrefour) center in Punaauia, where you will find **Kelly Surf**, **Tahiti Sport** and **Graffity**. **Hinano Boutique**, beside the Cathedral, sells tee shirts, dresses, swimsuits, caps, cups, glasses, ashtrays and all sorts of gift items bearing the famous Hinano beer label.

Look upstairs at **le Marché** for carved Marquesan bowls, ceremonial spears, drums, ukuleles, tables and tikis, plus many other gift items. You can also shop upstairs and downstairs at the market for Tahitian dancing costumes, basketry and woven hats, plus shell jewelry, mother-of-pearl creations, *tifaifai* bed covers or wall hangings, embroidered cushion covers and wood carvings. The **Artisan Village** adjacent to Tahiti's Maison de la Culture (cultural center) on the Papeete waterfront in Tipaerui should have some interesting carvings. Handcrafts stand or artisan centers are located in almost every village around the island, and the major hotels have arts and crafts demonstrations several times a week. You can buy very pleasing souvenir gifts directly from the person who created them

Monoi oil is an especially nice and inexpensive purchase, and is made from coconut oil and the essence of flowers. The most popular fragrance is that of the Tiare Tahiti, the white gardenia. Other floral choices of *monoi* are made with Pitate, Ylang Ylang, Tipanie (Frangipani or Plumeria), and you can also buy vanilla, coconut and sandalwood scented *monoi* products. *Monoi* oil can be used as a moisturizing lotion, a perfume, suntan lotion, mosquito repellent, hairdressing and a massage lotion. This can be purchased, along with *monoi* soaps, shampoos, bath gels and balms, in pharmacies, super markets, hotel boutiques and in many shops in Papeete and all around the island. Tamanu oil and creams are also popular, as well as beauty and health products made from the Tahitian noni fruit and tamanu fruit.

Tahitian vanilla beans make an unusual souvenir item, and are found in **le Marché** and in souvenir shops and grocery stores. Candies, cookies, *confitures* and coconut toddy, all Tahiti products, are good for gifts. And don't forget the Tahitian musical choices, in cassettes, compact disks and on video and DVD films of the islands. There are French perfumes, French fashions, crystal ware and French *patés* and cheeses. Duty Free Shops are found in Papeete and at the International Airport of Tahiti-Faaa. Very French-y style lingerie is on display in several of the shop windows. **Vahine's Secret**, beside the Cathedral, carries name brands of lace bras and thongs or strings, such as Calvin Klein, Aubade, Morgan, Simone Pérèle, Diesel and the Rien Collection.

Gastronomic gift items can be found at **Boutique Comtess du Barry** on Rue Edouard Ahnne in Papeete. In addition to a large selection of French wines, champagnes, apéritifs and digestifs, you'll find bamboo platters and wicker baskets filled with fois gras, confit de canard, jars of baba au rhum, fruit confitures, gourmet nuts and French chocolates. The shops at Tahiti-Faa'a International Airport carry a wide selection of gift items, including Tahitian calendars, mouse pads, music, glasses and cups, T-shirts, pareos, and locally made soaps and lotions. Once you pass Immigration you can buy Duty Free items, including Tahitian pearl jewelry, at the shops inside the waiting area.

Art Galleries

Galerie Winkler, *Tel. 42.81.77*, is located on Rue Jeanne d'Arc in Papeete, where you will find a variety of paintings, pottery, sculptures and other art works. **Galerie Les Tropiques**, *Tel. 41.05.00*, is on the corner of Boulevard Pomare and Rue Cook, a few blocks west of the Vaima Center. Frequent exhibits feature the works of resident artists. **Galerie Olivier Creations**, *Tel. 50.71.71*. Rue Paul Gauguin, facing Air Tahiti Nui office, between the Papeete Mairie and the Pont de l'Est. The paintings of Joannis and Thierry Fiérin are among the exhibits of paintings by contemporary resident artists you'll find in this interesting gallery. **Au Chevalet**, *Tel. 42.12.55*, is at 158 Boulevard Pomare in Fariipiti. **Ganesha**, *Tel.*

43.04.18, is on the second level of the Vaima Center, with paintings, tapa bark cloth, wood and stone carvings, traditional culture and contemporary art. **Galerie Antipodes**, *Tel. 54.05.05*, is in the Fare Tony Building in Papeete.

Where to Buy Tahitian Cultured Pearls

Tahiti's biggest export item is the Tahitian cultured pearl, which is also the most sought-after souvenir item. Exquisite jewelry, fashioned of pearls, 18-karat gold and diamonds, can be purchased in Tahiti, as well as pearls set in crystallized Pyrex and pure crystal, or braided coconut fibers, plus unset pearls of all sizes, shapes, quality and prices. Shops selling these jewels of the sea are found on practically every block in downtown Papeete, in addition to all the hotel boutiques.

I like the creative settings, quality and colors of the pearls sold at **Tahia Collins Pearls**, *Tel. 54.06.00*, on the corner of Avenue Prince Hinoi and Boulevard Pomare, as well as the friendliness and knowledge of the sales staff. Their main showroom is in Moorea, and they also have 2 pearl shops in Bora Bora and a boutique on board the *Paul Gauguin* ship.

The biggest name in the pearl business here is **Robert Wan Tahiti Perles**, who specializes in long rope necklaces of big pearls from his own pearl farms. He also owns Tahiti Pearl Museum. **Vaima Perles**, *Tel. 42.55.57*, upstairs in the Vaima Center, is another good shop for creative designs, and **Dany's Black Pearl**, *Tel. 54.58.89*, on Blvd. Pomare, has nice selections of pearl jewelry. **Tahiti Pearl Market**, *Tel. 54.30.60*, at 25 Rue Colette, between the Papeete Marché and Mairie, has 150,000 pearls direct from the producer's pearl farm, from which you can make your selections. They will even help you to drill your pearls and create you own jewelry. **Orau Pearls**, *Tel. 58.21.25*, is a wholesaler-retailer upstairs in a building on the corner of Rue Paul Gauguin and Rue Colette, between the Papeete City Hall and Le Marche.

Tua at **Ariihau Nui Pearls & Handicrafts**, *Tel. 42.66.12*, is my contact for inexpensive pearls. Her shop is upstairs at Le Marche (the Papeete Market). Take the escalator and walk through the restaurant and you will find Tua at the 4th or 5th shop on the left. You'll see the pearls in a showcase, as well as jillions of tie-dyed pareos, mother-of-pearl jewelry, carved artifacts and many more items. Tua and her children keep busy making all these items, which they also sell to boutiques and shops throughout the islands. She takes credit cards, including American Express and she speaks English. The photographs on the wall are of her great-great-grandmother, Teha'apapa, known as the warrior queen, who was the last queen of Huahine. See more information on pearls under Shopping section of *Basic Information* chapter.

MASSAGES & SPAS

Mandara Spa, *Tel. 86.48.68*; *www.mandaraspa.com* is located at the Sheraton Hotel Tahiti, and is open Mon.-Fri. from 9am-8pm, and on weekends and holidays from 9am-6pm. Mandara Spa is part of a chain of more than 60 spas located throughout the world. Qualified technicians offer a range of services, such as facials, manicures, pedicures, floral Jacuzzi baths, body scrubs and wraps, a choice of relaxing massages, essential oil treatments and other pampering touches. A Heaven & Earth Massage is 11.500 CFP for 50 min. and a Volcanic Aroma Stone Massage is 22.500 CFP for 75 min. Elimis facial elixirs start at 12.500 CFP, and a South Pacific Indulgence last 2 hrs. and 50 min. and costs 39.500 CFP. Hotel guests may use the sauna and steam room free of charge.

The Fitness Center is adjacent to Mandara Spa, and is open from 7am-8pm during the week and from 9am-6pm on weekends and holidays. Cardio-training, circuit training, free weight fitness, stretching, yoga, and body sculpting are some of the classes led by professional trainers.

Le Spa, *Tel. 48.88.88*, is on the upper level of the Radisson Plaza Resort in Arue. They even carry their own clothing line and products created exclusively for Le Spa. There are two single and two double treatment rooms with jet baths, saunas, steam rooms, a rainfall shower and a full-service salon for facial care, makeup, manicure and pedicure. Signature treatments feature black sand and volcanic stones as well as indigenous fruits such as mango, guava, papaya, coconut and vanilla. Massages are priced from 11.000 CFP for 50 min. to 17.000 CFP for 80 min., and there are also duo massages. A selection of baths followed by an 80-min. massage starts at 18.000 CFP, and body scrubs and body packs are 8.500 to 17.000 CFP. An 80-min. papaya mask facial is 17.000 CFP. Body care packages include treatments priced from 26.000 to 45.000 CFP. You can also get a manicure, pedicure, facial care or make up. A 24-hour fitness center with cardio and strength training equipment as well as a yoga center is located next to Le Spa.

Intercontinental Tahiti Resort, *Tel. 86.51.10*, plans to open a Spa and Fitness Center in July 2008, located behind the main swimming pool. There will be 4 massage areas, a steam room, lockers and showers, with steam perfumes like they use at the Thalasso Spa in Bora Bora. Aquagym classes are held in the main pool daily except Sun.

Rikardo "The Relaxer," *Tel. 73.18.18*, is a one-man massage service operated by Richard Hammill, an American expatriate resident of Tahiti. He is located in the Tiniouru Medical Building, behind the Cathedral, across the road from Odyssey bookstore. He's on the first level, which Americans know as the second floor.

Philippe Girodeau, *Tel./Fax 689/56.40.42, cell phone 77.54.79*, will bring his massage table to your room and make you feel like a new person after he works on your body, mind and soul. He opens your chakra energy centers and heals your aches and pains with magnetism and a pair of very strong hands. He charges 10.000 CFP, but the massage usually lasts more than an hour. He lives in Moorea and goes to Papeete a couple of times a week on request. This is my preferred massage therapist

Frederic Precloux, *Tel. 42.23.30*, is a chiropractor who studied at the Los Angeles College of Chiropractic. He speaks very good English and his office is located behind the Cathedral in Papeete, in the Tiniouru Medical Building, facing the Odyssey bookstore. He's on the second floor, just above the street level.

TATTOOS

Aroma Tattoo Art, *Tel. 78.06.73; demonaroma@yahoo.com.* Aroma Salmon is located upstairs at the Papeete public market, along with his brother, Manu Salmon of **Manu Tattoo Art.** They are both professional tattoo artists. Their parents, Manihi and Tila Salmon, own Pension Motu Aito Paradise in Fakarava. Both brothers speak English and work in hygienic conditions. You'll also find some good tattoo artists from the Marquesas Islands on this level of the Papeete market. Tattoo rates start at 5.000 CFP and average 10.000 CFP.

DAY TOUR TO MOOREA

Moorea is only 17 km. (11 mi.) across the channel from Tahiti, and the rugged profile of her mountains beckon you to cross the Sea of Moons, so named by the ancient Polynesians, and come on over to have some fun. This is where the residents of Tahiti go when they need to "escape" for a day or weekend. If your plans do not include a stay on Moorea, then a day tour is certainly on the "must do" list.

You can book your excursion at the Tahiti Nui Travel or Marama Tours travel desk in your hotel lobby. They will make all the arrangements so that you can be totally carefree. Following are some of the standard tours, which require a minimum of 2 people and are not available on Sun. and public holidays.

A **Moorea Island Tour** with lunch at the Intercontinental Moorea Resort & Spa includes all transfers in Tahiti and Moorea, the round-trip by fast catamaran, a full circle island tour of Moorea, plus a drive up the mountain to the **Belvedere** lookout point and a stop at the *marae* stone temples in Opunohu Valley. The hotel travel desks sell this Moorea Day Tour for 14.900 CFP, which includes lunch and round-trip boat fare. Should you wish to go by boat and return to Tahiti by plane, the cost is 18.700 CFP, and if you prefer to fly both ways you will pay 19.200 CFP. The cost of the Moorea Day Tour by boat and without lunch starts at 10.500 CFP. A **Dolphin Experience** can be combined with a **Moorea Day Tour** at the Intercontinental Moorea. The cost of round-trip boat fare and the Dolphin Center starts at 28.500 CFP without lunch, which is 4.000 CFP for a 2-course meal. You can also go by boat and return by air, have the Dolphin Experience and a Circle Island Tour and lunch for 37.100 CFP, or have a 4x4 Safari Tour instead of a Circle Island Tour, which costs 36.900 CFP for the package. A Snorkeling and Ray Watching Excursion can be substituted for the land tours for a total cost of 38.200 CFP. You can also opt for a **Moorea Spa Day Tour**, which includes lunch and a massage at Helene'Spa at the ICH Moorea. This excursion with round-trip boat fare starts at 22.600 CFP.

A **Moorea Tiki Day Tour**, available from Tues.-Sat., includes a visit to the Tiki Village. The cost of 14.300 CFP covers all transfers, round-trip fare on the fast catamaran, lunch and a bus tour from the boat dock in Moorea through **Cook's**

Bay to the **Moorea Distillery and Fruit Juice Factory** and the **Belvedere** lookout point, and on around the island. The beach at Tiki Village is not as pretty as some others on the island, and the lagoon is very shallow and warm close to the shore. But you will certainly find all the entertainment you want. Here in this typical **Polynesian village**, you'll see Tahitians weaving palm fronds, dying *pareos*, making floral crowns, sculpting wood or stone, tattooing and creating jewelry from Tahitian cultured pearls. You can paddle a canoe and go snorkeling in the coral gardens. You can eat lunch in the **Papayer Restaurant** and watch a mini-show of **Polynesian dances** performed in the white sand. Should you choose to go to Moorea by boat and return to Tahiti by air, your cost will be 18.000 CFP, and air/air has a special cost of 18.600 CFP.

You can also visit Moorea quite easily on your own. The least expensive way will cost you a minimum of 2.660 CFP for land and sea transportation. You can catch le *truck* from your hotel to downtown Papeete for 130 CFP, get off on Boulevard Pomare by the Banque de Polynésie, cross the street to Fare Manihini, the Tahiti Tourist Bureau, and walk along the wharf a couple of blocks until you come to the dock for the Moorea ferries. You'll see the ticket office for *Aremiti* catamaran *(Tel. 50.57.57)* inside the building on the waterfront that sells ferryboat tickets to Moorea. A one-way fare is 900 CFP for adults. The *Aremiti* is a/c and comfortable. The service from Papeete to Moorea starts at 6:05am Mon.-Fri., and at 7:30am on Sat.-Sun., respectively. Visitors usually like to take the boat that leaves Papeete at 9am daily. You will arrive in Moorea just 30 min. later, which gives you time for a full day of discovering this lovely island.

You can reserve a guided tour of Moorea through your travel desk in Tahiti, or you can rent a car in the main terminal at the **Vaiare** boat dock in Moorea. Both **Avis** and **Europcar** have sales counters here.

Should you decide on the least expensive way to visit Moorea for the day, just walk to the parking lot in front of the ferry terminal, where you will see at least 2 buses loading passengers. The first bus in line usually serves the **North Coast** of Moorea, passing by the hotels Sofitel Moorea Resort & Spa, Moorea Pearl Resort & Spa, Hotel Kaveka, Club Bali Hai, Sheraton Moorea Lagoon, Intercontinental Moorea Resort & Spa, Hotel Les Tipaniers, Hotel Hibiscus, and Hotel Vaimoana (not visible from the road). The second bus goes around the **South Coast** of Moorea, passing by Hotel Linareva, the Tiki Village, Hotel Hibiscus and Vaimoana, stopping at Le Petit Village, which is within easy walking distance of the hotels in that vicinity. Be sure to ask the bus driver which direction he's headed, and you pay him 300 CFP before boarding the bus. There's just one standard fare.

The **best public beach** on the island is adjacent to the Sofitel Moorea Resort (whose facilities are off-limits to all but hotel guests), which is a short walk from the circle island road. Ask the driver to let you off at the turn-off for the *plage publique de Temae* and follow the dirt road for a couple of blocks. There are changing rooms, toilets and showers here, as well as *roulotte* food vans that sell snacks, soft drinks and bottled water.

If you want to see the coastal sights of Moorea, then take one of the buses to **Haapiti**, and get off at the end of the line, which is at the **Moorea Visitors Center** in Le Petit Village. From there you can walk across the street to the island's **second best white sand beach**. You can also choose one of the hotels in the vicinity as your home for the day. They have public showers and toilets and you'll find several restaurants, snack bars, boutiques and pearl shops within easy walking distance of Le Petit Village.

If you visit Moorea on a Sun., you may want to go to the **Painapo Beach**, where you can swim, snorkel, and have lunch under the shade of an almond tree beside the lagoon. They have a Tahitian feast on certain Sundays. To get here you should take the South Coast bus from the ferry dock.

The buses depart from **Le Petit Village** one hour before each arrival and departure of the ferries. Therefore, if you are taking the last *Aremiti* from Moorea to Tahiti, which leaves at 4:45pm Mon.-Sat. and at 5:40pm on Sun., just stand beside the road an hour before departure time and wave for the driver to stop.

When you get back to Papeete you'll have to walk back to the stop for *le truck*, where you'll find a *le truck* that will take you to the hotels on the west coast, but there will be fewer of them running on weekends.

DAY TOURS TO BORA BORA

The travel desks in your hotel lobby can sell you a Day Tour to Bora Bora, starting at 40.100 CFP per person. I personally do not recommend anyone going to Bora Bora just for the day, because so much time is spent just getting there and back that you have very little time left to see the island. If it is at all possible to do so, I suggest you try to spend at least one night on Bora Bora, so that you can enjoy the overwhelming beauty of the lagoon. Some of the family pensions have good rates for budget travelers.

PRACTICAL INFORMATION
Books, Newspapers and Magazines

La Maison de la Presse, *Tel. 50.93.93*, is on Blvd. Pomare across the street from Place Vaiete. **Librairie du Vaima**, *Tel. 45.57.57*, is on the top level of the Vaima Center in Papeete. **Librairie Archipels**, *Tel. 42.47.30*, is on Rue des Remparts, across from the Mairie of Papeete (town hall). **Odyssey**, *Tel. 54.25.25*, is behind the Cathedral, adjacent to the Aorai building. They have books, CD's, DVD's and office supplies.

Churches & Religious Services

Many religions and denominations are represented in French Polynesia. Following are the main numbers for the religious offices on the island of Tahiti:
• **Protestant Evangelical Church**, (**Maohi Protestant Church**) Tel. 46.06.00
• **Catholic Church**, Tel. 50.30.00 (Cathedrale parish), Tel. 50.23.51 (Archdiocese)
•**Mormon Church**, Tel. 50.55.05

- **Seventh Day Adventists**, Tel. 50/82.50/50.55.05 (regional office)
- **Sanito**, Tel. 42.22.58
- **Jehovah's Witnesses**, Tel. 54.70.00
- **Alleluia Church**, Tel. 42.95.88
- **Assembly of God Pentecostal Church**, Tel. 45.36.61
- **Neo-Apostolic**, Tel. 57.93.02
- **Israelite Synagogue**, Tel. 41.03.92, cell 72.66.17

Church services on Sun. morning will offer you an insight into the Tahitian culture away from the hotel scene. You'll enjoy the singing, which is best in the Protestant churches or temples, formerly called **Eglise Evangelique**. This name was changed in 2004 to **Eglise Maohi Protestant**. The missionaries taught the Tahitians to sing the old time hymns in the early 1800s, and over the years the people have transformed the old religious songs into their own versions called himene. The singing is a capella, with the men sitting behind the women and the kids running around everywhere. Be prepared to sit on the side up front, where you can look at the parishioners and they can smile back at you. They are used to visitors and will warmly welcome you.

Consulates
- **Consular Agency of the United States**, *B.P. 10765, Paea, Tahiti 98711, Tamanu Iti Center, (1st floor), Punaauia. Tel. 689/42.65.35, Fax 689/50.80.96; usconsul@mail.pf / ckozely@mail.pf. Fax in USA 917/464-7457.* Consular sessions are held each Tues. between 10am-12pm. You can contact Christopher Kozely 24 hours a day for emergencies only at *cell 21.93.19.*
- **Australia and Canada**, *Tel. 689/46.88.06; Fax 689/46.88.54*
- **Great Britain**, *Tel. 689/42.05.00/70.63.82*

Currency Exchange
Banque de Polynésie, Boulevard Pomare, *Tel. 46.66.66*; **Banque de Tahiti**, Rue Cardella, *Tel. 41.70.00*; **Banque Socredo**, Rue Dumont d'Urville, *Tel. 41.51.23;* client relations *Tel. 47.00.00.* There are several branch offices of these banks in downtown Papeete and around the island of Tahiti, with various business hours, and all the major locations have an ATM See sections on *Ready Cash and Currency Exchanges* in Chapter on *Basic Information.*

Hospitals & Doctors
You can find English-speaking doctors, dentists, nurses and other medical personnel in Tahiti, but they are not common. The Mamao Hospital and the two private clinics are open 24 hrs. There is also a hospital in Taravao. See Health Concerns in *Basic Information* chapter for further details.
Mamao Hospital, *Tel. 46.62.62* (switchboard), *Tel. 42.01.01* or 15 (emergency), is the government operated medical center on Avenue Georges Clemenceau

in Mamao, a suburb just east of Papeete. Taravao Hospital, *Tel. 54.77.77* (switchboard), *Tel. 57.76.76* (emergency). **Clinique Cardella**, *Tel. 46.04.00* (switchboard), *Tel. 46.04.25* (emergency), and **Clinique Paofai**, *Tel. 46.18.18*, are privately owned clinics in Papeete. **S.O.S. Medecins**, *Tel. 42.34.56*, is an emergency unit of doctors and other medical personnel, who will come to the hotel to attend to your needs.

Optika Vaima, also called **Krys Vaima**, is in the Vaima Center, Tel. *50.11.85*, and **Pacific Optic Nguyen**, Rue Yves Martin in the Quartier du Commerce, 1 block inland from Boulevard Pomare, *Tel. 42.70.78*, will repair your glasses while you wait. **Surdité de Polynésie**, *Tel. 43.33.04*, in the Quartier du Commerce close to the Tracqui store will solve your hearing aid problems while you're in Tahiti.

Internet Service – Cyber Cafés

Tahiti's Internet service provider is **Mana**, which has installed WiFi "surfing spots" around the islands of Tahiti and Moorea. This service will be extended to the outer islands during the first few months of 2008, providing high-speed wireless Internet access for portable computers and Vini cell phones in all 5 archipelagoes. They have issued "ManaSpot" WiFi cards that sell for 990 CFP for 1 hr., or 5.280 CFP for a 10-hr. card. Monthly rates with unlimited volume are available for professionals. You can buy these cards at any post office.

Cyber Marina, *Tel. 50.05.99*. This a/c room is located at Marina Taina for the convenience of people who are on yachts here. They have 4 PC's with French keyboards, plus a printer. Wifi available. Rates start at 1.000 CFP for 1 hr. and 40 min. Open 7:30am-4pm Mon.-Fri. Closed weekends.

Cybernesia, *Tel. 85.43.67; cybernesia@mail.pf; www.cybernesia.pf*. This cyberspace is on the third level of the Vaima Center above the Concorde Cinema in the heart of Papeete. There are 8 last generation computers with Internet access (you can plug your laptop into the network). Other services include color printing, copies and CD engraving. Open Mon.-Fri. 8am to 6pm and on Sat. 9am-4pm.

Dpi @ Business Center, *Tel. 50.84.95; digital@mail.pf; www.dpi.pf*. This business center and cyber café is located at the Tahiti-Faa'a Airport at the entrance to the domestic terminal. Services include Internet access, e-mail, color copying, scanning, documents copied to digital files, digital photo cards transferred and CD-Rom engraving.

La Maison de la Presse, *Tel. 50.93.93*, is on Blvd. Pomare facing Place Vaiete. There are 9 computers upstairs, all with flat monitors. The rates are 250 CFP for 15 min., 500 CFP for 30 min. and 1.000 CFP per hour. Open Mon. and Tues. from 7am-7pm and on Wed.-Sat. until 10pm.

Mana Rock Café, *Tel. 50.02.40*, is on the corner of Blvd. Pomare and Rue des Ecoles. There are 2 computers, with the Internet rates starting at 250 CFP for 15 min. Access to this service is available daily from 11 am-10pm.

Tiki Soft C@fe, *Tel. 88.93.98; contact@tikisoftcafe.com; www.tikisoftcafe.com*. *Rue des Remparts at the Pont de l'Est.* AE, M, V. Open Mon.-Fri. 10am-8pm. Closed weekends. Nina is the half-American lady who owns this popular cyber café, which is gay-friendly but not a gay hangout. Bring your laptop or use the on-site PC. Rates start at 250 CFP for 15 minutes for a fixed line and 350 CFP for 15 minutes on Wifi. Sandwiches and salads served. Special cocktails featured on Thurs.

Tahiti Tourisme Cyber Center, *Tel. 50.57.12* is located in the welcome center of the Visitors Bureau on the Papeete waterfront. Open Mon.-Fri. 7:30am-5:30pm, Sat. 8am-4pm, and Sun. 8am-1pm. Rates are 300 CFP for 15 min, 550 CFP for 30 min., and 1.000 CFP for 1 hr. There are 2 computers and a printer.

Laundry Service

All the larger hotels provide laundry service, and can arrange to have your dry cleaning done. **Lavex Sa M'Plaix**, *Tel. 41.26.65*, is the name of an automatic laundry on Boulevard Pomare in downtown Papeete, close to Broadway Tobacco shop between Avenue Prince Hinoi and Rue Clappier. They're open Mon. to Fri. 6am to 5pm, and Sat. on request. Closed Sun. They will wash, dry and fold up to 4 kg. (8.8 lbs.) of laundry for 1.000 CFP, and you can pick it up at the Broadway. They charge 4.000 CFP to iron a basket of clothes. There is also a self-service laundromat called **Laverie**, *Tel. 43.71.59*, which is located at 64 Rue Gauguin, facing the Papeete Mairie (town hall) near the Pont de l'Est. They charge 950 CFP to wash 8 kg. of clothes and 1.100 CFP for the dryer, plus 100 CFP for the soap powder. They will wash, dry and fold your clothes for 1.950 CFP. Ironing is also available.

Pharmacies / Drugstores

There are half a dozen pharmacies in the Papeete area, and several around the island. One of the easiest to find in Papeete is the **Pharmacie du Vaima**, *Tel. 42.97.73*, on Rue de Général de Gaulle at Rue Georges La Garde, behind the Vaima Center close to McDonald's Hamburgers. The pharmacist is Nguyen Ngoc-Tran, who speaks English.

Pharmacie Moana Nui, *Tel. 43.16.98*, is in the Carrefour shopping mall in Punaauia, convenient to the Intercontinental Tahiti Resort and Sofitel Tahiti Resort. **Pharmacie Tamanu**, *Tel. 58.20.34*, is located in the Tamanu shopping center in Punaauia, next door to Le Méridien. The pharmacies rotate night and weekend/holiday duty, so it is best to check with your hotel to find out which one is available should you need medical supplies after hours. The medicines sold in French Polynesia are French brands.

Police

The main headquarters of the French gendarmerie, *Tel. 46.73.67* or *17*, is located on Avenue Bruat in Papeete. There are also brigades in Faaa, Punaauia, Paea, Papara, Taravao, Tiarei and Arue.

Post Office

The main post office is on Blvd. Pomare in downtown Papeete, *Tel. 41.42.42.* There are also several branches all around the island.

Restrooms

There are public toilets on the Papeete waterfront at the passenger ship dock, just outside the **Tahiti Tourisme Bureau.** The public facilities at **Tahua Vaiete** (Place Vaiete) and **Tahua To'ata** (Place To'ata), on opposite ends of the waterfront, are kept clean 24-hours a day by a team of Tahitian government employees. You'll also find public toilets in the building that houses the **Moorea Ferry** freight bureau, at the ferry dock on the Papeete waterfront. Bring your own paper just in case, and do not be surprised if some of the public facilities are not clean. You can also use the restrooms in the restaurants downtown.

Around the island, you'll find public restrooms at the main tourist stops, such as Point Venus, the Blowhole of Arahoho and the Three Cascades of Tiarei, the Paul Gauguin Museum, the Vaipahi Gardens and Waterfall, and at the Grottoes of Mara'a.

Yacht Services

Polynesia Yacht Services, *Tel. 77.12.30 (Laurent); 70.71.41 (Mike); Fax 689/56.18.79; pys@mail.pf; www.polynesiayachtservices.com.* Laurent Bernaert and Mike Raoult are both young Frenchmen whose efficient and friendly "no hassle attitude" will make your visit to French Polynesia smooth and pleasant.

Their services include: all official formalities with Customs, Immigration and Port; visa extension, bond exemption for non EEC crew members, duty free fuel formalities; advanced port and marina berth reservation, security arrangements, agency discounts for parts and ship's chandlery, Customs brokerage service for import/export orders; express courier shipments; coordination of all kinds of repairs and maintenance; shipyard and refit consultancy; dry docking storage in Tahiti or Raiatea; absentee yacht management; domestic services (laundry, dry cleaning, etc.); dive guides, PADI certifications, underwater yacht services; cruise programs, books and charts for all of Pacific Ocean; gas bottle refills, waste oil removal; international and local travel arrangements; hotel accommodations; rental cars, taxis, VIP services (private plane, helicopter); food and beverage provisioning; medical and dental assistance; mail drop, phone, fax WiFi connection; mobile phone and local SIM cards rental; monthly payment; banking services.

12. Moorea

Scientists say that **Moorea** (Mo-oh-RAY-ah) is shaped like an isosceles triangle, and romantics believe the island is in the form of a heart. I think it looks like a swimming turtle. Geologists say that Moorea is twice as old as Tahiti and once contained a volcano that reached 3,300 m (11,000 ft.) into the sky. Polynesian legend tells us that Moorea was created when a magical fish swam from the lagoon of Raiatea and Taha'a to become the island of Tahiti; and the second dorsal fin of this enormous fish grew into land that was called "Aimeo i te rara varu" for the eight mountain ridges that separate the island. The traditional shortened name of this island was Aimeho, Aimeo or Eimeo. Following a vision by one of the Polynesian high priests, the name was later changed to Moorea, which means, "yellow lizard."

Moorea offers you the tropical South Seas island that you expect to find when you fly to Tahiti, just 17 km (11 mi.) across the Sea of Moons. Some people say it's worth the airfare to Tahiti just to see Moorea. Others say that Moorea was created so that people on Tahiti would have something to stare at across the sea.

Moorea's magnificent beauty covers an area of 136 sq. km (53 sq. mi.), which is the south rim of a crater that was formed following cataclysmic explosions eons ago. The lofty cathedral-shaped peaks and jade velvet spires that you will see reflected in the lapis lazuli waters of **Cook's Bay** and **Opunohu** (belly-of-the-stone-fish) **Bay** are the basaltic remains of the crater's interior wall.

The volcanic peaks of the mountain range resemble a fairy castle or a serrated shark's jaw, dominated by **Tohive'a** (hot spade) at 1,207 m (3,983 ft.). **Mou'a Roa** (long mountain), with an altitude of 880 m (2,904 ft.), resembles a shark's tooth. This is the most photographed of the spectacular wonders, and it is often pointed out to visitors as "Bali Ha'i." **Mou'a Puta** (split rock), the 830 m- (2,739 ft.-) high mountain with a hole in its top, is a tempting challenge for hikers. The hole is said to have been made by the spear of Pai, a favorite son of the gods of old Polynesia, who was warned that Hiro, god of thieves, wanted to steal the sacred **Rotui** Mountain and take it home to Raiatea. The warrior Pai threw a spear from Tahiti that pierced the top of Mou'a Puta and the noise woke up all the roosters on Moorea, who crowed so loudly that the thieves were forced to flee. But Hiro did manage to take a piece of Rotui's crest and this stolen land can be seen on top of a mountain in Raiatea, covered with the *toa* (ironwood) trees similar to those that grow on **Mou'a Rotui**.

Moorea's crystalline lagoons, filled with gardens of fanciful coral and exotic sea creatures, are said to have been a gift from Ruahatu, king of the ocean. This benevolent god specially created the azure waters of the fjord-like bays. Tane, the Polynesian god of beauty, bordered the lagoons with white sand beaches and

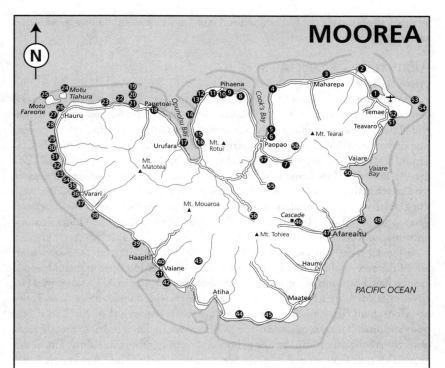

MOOREA

1. Temae Airport
2. Golf Course
3. Moorea Pearl Resort
4. Hotel Kaveka
5. Club Bali Hai
6. Motel Albert
7. Village Temanoha
8. Fruit Juice Factory
9. Pension/Restaurant Aito
10. Pension Motu Iti
11. Sheraton Moorea Lagoon Resort & Spa
12. Fare Nani
13. Village Faimano
14. Mareto Public Beach
15. Fare Vaihere
16. Fare Hamara
17. Les Tipaniers Iti
18. Papetoai Temple
19. Intercontinental Moorea Resort & Spa
20. Dolphin Center
21. Legends Resort Moorea
22. Fenua Mata'i'oa
23. Hotel Les Tipaniers
24. Dream Island
25. Villa Corallina
26. Le Petit Village
27. Hotel Hibiscus
28. Fare Vaimoana
29. Camping Nelson
30. Moorea Camping
31. Moorea Fare Miti
32. Fare Tapu Lodge
33. Fare Matotea
34. Fare Manuia
35. Tiki Village
36. Te Nunoa Bungalow
37. Fare Edith
38. Painapo Beach
39. Residence Linareva
40. Mark's Place Moorea
41. Haapiti Surf Lodge
42. Tarariki Village
43. Nature House of Mou'a Roa
44. Fare Arana
45. Fare Aute
46. Atiraa Waterfall
47. Chez Pauline
48. Pension Te Ora Hau
49. Motu Ahi
50. Vaiare Ferry Dock
51. Sofitel Moorea Beach Resort
52. Temae Public Beach
53. La Baie De Nuarei
54. Fare Maeva
55. Marae Titiroa
56. Belvedere Lookout
57. Opunohu Valley Ranch
58. Pineapple Fields

planted an abundance of fragrant white Tiare Tahiti blossoms among the majestic coconut palms.

ARRIVALS & DEPARTURES
Arriving By Air
Air Moorea, *Tel. 86.41.41 in Tahiti; Tel. 55.06.01 in Moorea; Fax 86.42.99; reservation@airmoorea.pf; www.airmoorea.com.* 10-minute air taxi service is provided daily between Tahiti and Moorea with up to 40 round-trip flights between the sister islands. The Air Moorea terminal in Tahiti is located 300 m. (984 ft.) from the **International Airport of Tahiti-Faaa** and the domestic terminal. You have to pay 100 CFP to use the luggage carts and you can retrieve your money when you attach it to the luggage rack, just like in other airport terminals. You can push the carts from one terminal to another, following a sidewalk with arrows. There are restrooms, a public telephone, a snack and bar counter, and a Moorea tourist information counter in the small Air Moorea terminal in Tahiti.

The 19-passenger Twin Otter DHC6/300 planes depart from the Faaa airport in Tahiti every hour on the hour from 6am to 6pm. Additional flights are added on the half-hour during peak times. Reservations are required. The one-way fare for non-residents is 3.500 CFP. Air Moorea also provides night service from Tahiti to Moorea on Sat. and Sun., corresponding with the arrival of Air Tahiti Nui international flights from Los Angeles. This service makes it possible for you to go directly to Moorea without having to book an overnight room in Tahiti. The flights leave Tahiti at 8:30pm and 9pm on Sat. and Sun. and the one-way cost is 5.100 CFP. You must reserve in advance and check-in closes 15 min. before each departure.

Air Tahiti, *Tel. 86.42.42.* There is an ATR flight daily from Bora Bora to Huahine to Moorea.

You can also charter an airplane to Moorea with **Air Moorea,** *Tel. 86.41.41* or **Air Tahiti,** *Tel. 86.42.42,* and **Air Archipels,** *Tel. 81.30.30.* Helicopter flights can be organized with **Polynesia Hélicoptères,** *Tel. 54.87.20.*

The modern **Temae Airport** terminal in Moorea has restrooms, a pearl shop, boutiques, ATM, car rental agencies, and information counters for tour and excursion companies. Taxi service is usually available for all arriving flights, and there is a taxi phone at the main entrance. There is no bus or *le truck* service provided directly to the airport. If you are not carrying heavy bags and wish to walk about 4 blocks to the main road to catch *le truck*, you want to be sure that you schedule your arrival with that of the ferries from Tahiti, when the public transportation service will be operating. During the day you can stand beside the Total Station and wave down the first bus that passes, which will be going from the Vaiare ferry dock toward Cook's Bay. **Torea Nui Transport** provides land transfer service for 600 CFP per person during the day and 1.100 CFP at night. See details under *Tour & Transport Companies* in this chapter.

Arriving By Boat

The **Moorea Boat Dock** (Gallieni Wharf) in Papeete, a couple of blocks east of the Tahiti Tourist Bureau on the waterfront, is where you will find the two fast catamarans and two ferries that transport passengers between Tahiti and Moorea. You can buy tickets in the building adjacent to the ferry dock. Be sure to verify the schedules before or when you get to the ticket window, because they are subject to change at any time without much advance notice.

Aremiti V, *Tel.50.57.57* in Tahiti and *Tel. 56.43.24* in Moorea. The air-conditioned fast catamaran *Aremiti V* is 56 m. (184 ft.) long and 14.4 m. (47 ft.) wide, with 2 bridges and 3 passenger salons, a snack bar with tables in the rear, clean toilets, TV screens, comfortable seating for 700 passengers, including 70 places on the upper sundeck, and space for 30 passenger cars and scooters. The crossings from quay to quay take 30 minutes. Promotional fares at press time included a one-way adult fare for 900 CFP and 450 CFP for anyone between 4-23 years.

The *Aremiti V* leaves Papeete each Mon.-Thurs. at 6:05am, 7:30am and 9am, 12pm, 4:05pm and 5:30pm, with the exception of Wed., when the 12pm departure actually leaves at 12:15pm. The Wed. schedule of 12:15pm also applies for Fri., with the addition of an extra crossing leaving Papeete at 2:40pm. The Sat. departures from Papeete to Moorea are at 7:30am and 9am, 12:15pm, 2:40pm, 4:05pm and 5:30pm. On Sun. the boat leaves Papeete at 7:30am and 9am, and at 3:30pm, 4:50pm and 6:20pm. See further information on the **Aremiti** boats under *Inter-Island Cruise Ships, Passenger Boats & Freighters* in the chapter on *Planning Your Trip*.

Aremiti Ferry, *Tel. 50.57.57* in Tahiti and *Tel. 56.31.10* in Moorea. This is a 272-ft. long steel hull catamaran that transports cars, big trucks and construction equipment, and up to 500 passengers between the two islands. A one-way crossing takes 50 minutes. There are toilets, an A/C lounge and a snack bar on board. This boat is not recommended for people who have difficulty climbing steep stairs. The *Aremiti Ferry* leaves Papeete for Moorea on Mon.-Fri. at 6am, 9:15am and 11:45am. On Mon.-Thurs. afternoons the ship leaves Tahiti at 3:10pm, and on Fri. the ship leaves Tahiti at 2:30pm and 5pm. On Sat. the *Aremiti Ferry* leaves Papeete at 6:45am and 9am, and 11:45apm. The hours on Sun. are 7:45am, 3:30pm and 6pm. The one-way passenger fares are 900 CFP per adult and 450 CFP anyone between 4-23 years. Occupants of vehicles being transported round-trip on board the *Aremiti Ferry* benefit from reduced rates: the round-trip fare for adults is 1.484 CFP and 848 CFP for people between 4-23 years of age. The round-trip cost to transport a passenger car starts at 4.505 CFP.

Moorea Express Catamaran, *Tel. 50.11.11* in Tahiti, *Tel. 56.34.34* in Moorea. This fast catamaran is 41.60 m (136 ft.) long, has a/c, and can transport 306 passengers, as well as scooters and bicycles, from dock to dock in 30 minutes. There is a snack bar on board but no meals are served. One-way fares are 900 CFP per adult and 450 CFP per child. The one-way fare for a bicycle is 200 CFP and 750 CFP for scooters and motorcycles. On Mon.-Thurs. *Moorea Express* leaves

Tahiti for Moorea at 6am, 7:25am, 9:05am, *12:05pm, 4:05pm and 5:20pm. *The Wed. departure is at 12:30pm. Each Fri. the *Moorea Express* leaves Papeete at 6am, 7:25am, 9:05am, 12:05pm, 2:40pm, 4:05pm and 5:20pm. The Sat. departures from Papeete are at 7:05am, 9:05am, 12:05pm, 1:45pm, 3:45pm and 5:30pm. The Sun. schedule is 7am, 8:30am, 10am, 3:30pm, 5:15pm and 7:20pm.

Moorea Ferry, *Tel. 50.11.11* in Tahiti, *Tel. 56.34.34* in Moorea. This is a 190-ft. long steel hull ship that can transport 300 passengers, cars, heavy trucks and freight during the 1-hour crossings between Tahiti and Moorea. On board are a lounge, snack bar and toilets. The one-way adult fare is 900 CFP and half-price for children 4 to 12 years. Lightweight cars are 2.650 CFP one-way, 4WD vehicles are 3.180 CFP and bicycles are 200 CFP. The Papeete-Moorea schedule for Mon.-Fri. has departures at 6am, 10:15am, 2pm and 4:45pm. The *Moorea Ferry* leaves Papeete each Sat. at 6:30am, 9:30am, 12pm and 5:15pm. On Sun. it leaves Papeete at 9:30am, 5:15pm and 7:45pm.

You will find public telephones, car and scooter rental agencies, taxi service, toilets, fruit stands and snack bars at the two terminal buildings on the **Vaiare Ferry dock or quay.**

Public ground transportation in Moorea is provided by buses or *le truck*, with vehicles waiting in front of the terminal upon the arrival of the catamarans and ferries from Tahiti. Give the driver the name of your destination and verify that you're getting onto the right bus, as one goes on the north coast to **Cook's Bay** and onward to the **former Club Med** area, and the other bus heads in the opposite direction, towards **Afareaitu** and on to **Haapiti** and the **Club Med** area, by way of the south coast. You pay the driver 300 CFP before boarding, and pull the cord, ring the bell or holler "stop" when you want to get off.

Departing By Air

Air Moorea, *Tel. 55.06.01.* The first flight from Moorea to Tahiti is at 6:15am daily, and the last flight is at 6:15pm Mon.-Fri. and at 6:45pm on Sat. The hourly flights leave Moorea at a quarter past the hour (7:15am, 8:15am, 9:15am, etc.) and extra flights are added at a quarter to the hour (6:45am, 10:45am,) during the peak times. It is best to pick up an Air Moorea schedule when you arrive or check out their flights by Internet, as they are subject to change without notice. Reservations are necessary. Check-in no later than 15 min. before the flight.

The regular fare from Moorea to Tahiti is 3.500 CFP and the night fare is 5.100 CFP. This latter rate applies to the Air Moorea flights on Sat. and Sun. nights that connect with Air Tahiti Nui's international departures. The scheduled night flights from Moorea are at 8:45pm, and 9:15pm on Sat. and Sun. This service can be used to catch your Hawaiian Airlines flight to Honolulu, or any other flights leaving Tahiti during the middle of the night or early morning hours. This Air Moorea flight from Moorea to Tahiti is also subject to an earlier departure; therefore, be sure to check in at the airport one hour in advance.

Air Tahiti, *Tel. 86.42.42/86.41.84* on weekends in Tahiti or *Tel. 55.06.00* in

Moorea, provides ATR service from Moorea to the Leeward Islands. You can fly direct from Moorea to Huahine once a day. There are 3 flights a day between Moorea and Bora Bora, including direct service or with a stop in Huahine or Raiatea. There are direct flights from Moorea to Raiatea on Mon., Tues., Wed. and Sun., and the Fri. flight and one Sun. flight stops first in Bora Bora. One-way fares to Huahine or Raiatea are 13.000 CFP and 18.400 CFP to Bora Bora.

Departing By Boat
Aremiti V Catamaran, *Tel. 56.31.10/50.57.57,* leaves Moorea for Papeete Mon.-Fri. at 5:25, 6:50, and 8:10am. A 10:50am departure is made on Mon., Tues. and Thurs., and on Wed. and Fri. at 11:30am, to coincide with the school program. The afternoon boats leave Moorea at 3pm and 4:45pm Mon.-Thurs., and at 1:50pm, 3:20pm and 4:45pm on Fri. On Sat. the boat leaves Moorea at 6am, 8:10am and 10:50am, and at 1:50pm, 3:20pm, and 4:45pm. The Sun. schedule is at 6:30am, 8:10am, 2:50pm, 4:10pm and 5:40pm. Ticket counters for the *Aremiti* catamaran and ferry are located at the new terminal of the Vaiare Ferry dock in Moorea. One-way fare is 900 CFP for adults and 450 CFP for 4-23 years old.
Aremiti Ferry, *Tel. 56.31.10/50.57.57,* leaves Moorea for Papeete Mon.-Thurs. at 7:30am, 10:30am, 1:15pm and 4:20pm, and on Fri. at 7:30am, 10:30am, 1pm, 3:45pm and 6pm. The Sat. departures from Vaiare are at 7:45am, 10:15am and at 4:45pm. The Sun. ferry leaves Vaiare at 2:30, 5pm and 7pm. One-way fare is 900 CFP for adults and 450 CFP for 4-23 years old.
Moorea Express Catamaran, *Tel. 56.34.34/50.11.11,* provides fast catamaran service from Moorea to Tahiti with departures each Mon.-Thurs. at 5:20am, 6:40am, 8:10am, 10:50am, 2:50pm and 4:40pm. The Wed. departure is at 11:30am instead of 10:50am. Each Fri. the *Moorea Express* leaves Vaiare dock at 5:20am, 6:40am, 8:10am, 10:50am, 1:50pm, 3:20pm and 4:40pm. On Sat. the departures are at 6am, 7:45am, 11am, 12:45pm, 2:50pm and 4:50pm. The Sun. departures are at 6:15am, 7:45am, 9:15am, 2:50pm, 4:15pm and 6:45pm. One-way fares are 900 CFP per adult, and 450 CFP for a child. The one-way fare for a bicycle is 200CFP and 750 CFP for scooters and motorcycles.
Moorea Ferry, *Tel. 56.34.34/50.11.11,* provides passenger and car service between Moorea and Papeete Mon.-Thurs. at 4:45am, 8am, 12:30pm and 3:30pm, and on Fri. at 4:45am, 8am, 12:30pm and 3:15pm. The Sat. departures from Moorea are at 5am, 8am, 10:45am, and at 4pm. The *Moorea Ferry* leaves Vaiare on Sun. at 8am, 4pm and 6:30pm. The ticket window is in the old terminal and the one-way fare is 900 CFP per adult and 450 children. One-way fares to transport cars starts at 3.180 CFP, a bicycle is 200 CFP and other 2-wheel vehicles are 750 CFP.

ORIENTATION
A paved road hugs the coast for 60 km (37 mi.) around Moorea, where you'll see thatched roof *fares* with bamboo walls, little shacks with tin roofs and lovely

villas with stone walls. The census of Sept. 2007 counted 16,329 inhabitants and most of them live on the mountainside of the road, with a sprinkling of homes along the white sand beaches. Gardens of fruit and flowers border the road and during the summer months (Nov.-Mar.) you will see the flamboyant red or yellow Royal Poinciana trees in bloom.

You can happily take pictures on this beautiful island without having electric lines mar the photograph. All the cables are underground. However, you now have to shoot the scenery while trying to avoid the streetlights that have been placed beside the road in the tourist sections of the island. Although there has been a lot of grumbling about these lights, they are helpful for visitors who wish to walk beside the road at night when searching for a place to eat, and they also help drivers to better negotiate the twists and curves along the coastal road at night, while trying to avoid the kids on bikes, people walking in the road and dogs lying or just standing on the pavement.

Moorea doesn't have a town and until recently there was no central shopping area on the island. The administrative center is in the village of **Afareaitu**, which most visitors never see except from a tour bus. Located on the eastern coast facing Tahiti, this sleepy little settlement contains the principal *mairie* (town hall), local government offices and hospital. Most of the churches, schools, supermarkets, small *magasin* stores, banks, boutiques and restaurants are located in the villages of **Maharepa, Pao Pao, Papetoai** and **Haapiti**. Most of the hotels, hostels, family pensions and campgrounds are found beside **Cook's Bay** or beside a white sand beach in **Haapiti**, although you can now find accommodations all around the island. The **Raihau Center** in Maharepa is adjacent to the **Socredo Center** that includes a bank, post office, newsstand, snack stand and a few other shops. The **Centre Noha** is across the road. This area is slowly building up with new boutiques and pearl shops opening here and there. At PK 2.7 in Tiaia, **Centre Tumai** is a shopping area located on both sides of the road between Maharepa and the airport in Temae. You will find interesting clothing and souvenir shops here, as well as a snack shop and a computer store with Internet service. The **Maeva Center** in Pao Pao has 6 small shops operated by resident artisans, plus a museum of artifacts from Moorea's Maohi culture.

An environmental impact study will determine if the **Quesnot Commercial Center** at PK 24 in Tiahura will be built beside the road adjacent to the Intercontinental Moorea Resort & Spa, which also faces the Legends Resort Moorea. This shopping center will contain 21 boutiques, a restaurant with 6 food courts, a pharmacy, 4 medical offices, a bank, 6 professional offices, and 5 lofts for residency.

There are many enjoyable ways to spend your vacation on this special island. You can now tee off at the 18-hole Moorea Green Pearl Golf Course near the airport, which opened in 2007. The beautiful clear lagoon invites you to come on in for a swim, or you can snorkel, scuba dive, water-ski and jet-ski. You can view the fish and coral through a glass bottom boat, wear a Jules Verne type helmet to walk on the sandy bottom of the lagoon gardens with Aqua Blue, or grab onto a motorized Sea Trailer and snorkel to the reef. You can zoom across the lagoon in a motorboat, kayak, pirogue or lagoon jet, and you can let the trade winds propel you on a flysurf or windsurf board. There are sailing excursions, beach barbecues and fishing trips. You can take a Dolphin & Whale Watching Expedition, sunset cruise or moonlight cruise. Professional lessons are available for all water sports, as well as for tennis at various hotel courts, and for horseback riding in Opunohu Valley. You can take your aerial photos during a helicopter ride or airplane tour of Moorea, and you can soar above the lagoon on a parasail.

You can also discover the island by rental car, scooter, bicycle or on foot. Guided tours will show you Moorea's most breathtaking scenery, around the coastal road, in the interior valleys, up the mountains and to the Atiraa waterfalls of Afareaitu. You can visit a fruit juice factory and distillery, and sample a tall cool drink at a lively Happy Hour. At the hotels and at Tiki Theatre Village you can photograph traditional dance shows, learn to tie a *pareo*, grate a coconut and dance Tahitian style. You can even "get married" in a traditional non-binding Polynesian ceremony.

Moorea's excellent restaurants and snack bars have menu selections for all tastes and prices for all budgets. The highlight of your culinary explorations in Moorea should include a *tamaara'a*, an authentic Tahitian feast.

GETTING AROUND MOOREA
Car, Scooter & Bicycle Rentals
- **Albert Rent-a-Car**, facing Club Bali Hai, *Tel. 56.19.28*, facing Moorea Pearl Resort, *Tel. 56.30.58*, facing Intercontinental Moorea, *Tel. 56.33.75*. You can rent a 3-door Hyundai Getz for 6.000 CFP for 4 hrs., 7.500 CFP for 8 hrs., and 8.500 CFP for 24 hrs. A 5-door a/c Hyundai Getz with automatic drive starts at 8.000 CFP for 4 hrs. Longer rentals available. 50cc scooters rent for 4.500 CFP for 4 hrs., 5.000 CFP for 8 hrs., and 5.500 CFP for 24 hrs. Insurance and free mileage are included in all rentals.
- **Avis-Pacificar** has a sales office at the Moorea Airport, *Tel. 56.32.61*, the Vaiare Ferry Dock, *Tel. 56.32.68*, and at Club Bali Hai, *Tel. 56.52.04*. A 3-door Ford Ka rents for 5.555 CFP for 4 hrs., 7.579 CFP for 8 hrs., and 9.600 CFP for 24 hrs. A 5-door a/c Ford Fiesta starts at 7.260 CFP for 4 hrs. A 5-door Ford Fiesta with a/c starts at 9.922 CFP for 4 hrs. You can also rent a 2-seat Suzuki 4WD vehicle starting at 7.678 CFP for 4 hrs. Rates include taxes, unlimited mileage and insurance. Rentals are available for several days and by the week or month.
- **Europcar** has a main office adjacent to Pai Moana Pearls in Haapiti, *Tel. 56.34.00*; sales offices at the Moorea Airport, *Tel. 56.41.08*; Vaiare Ferry Dock, *Tel. 56.28.64*; and at the 4 big hotels on Moorea. A 4-place a/c Fiat Uno rents for 7.700 CFP for 4 hrs., 8.800 CFP for 8 hrs. and 9.900 CFP for 24 hrs. You can also rent an a/c 5-door Kia Picanto with automatic drive starting at

9.350 CFP for 4 hrs. An a/c Suzuki mini-bus starts at 15.400 CFP for 4 hrs. A 2-place PGO Bugxter is 6.600 CFP for 4 hrs. and a 2-place Buggymax starts at 8.800 CFP. A 3-wheel Scooter starts at 3.850 CFP for 4 hrs. Europcar also has a special overnight rate of 4.400 CFP if you rent a car at 5pm and return it the next morning by 8am. These rates include taxes, unlimited mileage and insurance. Fuel and flat tires are not included. You can rent a beach bike for 880 CFP for 4 hrs., 1.760 CFP for 8 hrs. and 1.870 CFP for 24 hrs.

- **Moorea Fun Bike**, *Tel. 70.96.95*. Single, 21 speed, tandem and trail bikes, plus Les Rosalies covered bikes for up to six people. Delivered to your holiday place anywhere between Haapiti and Pao Pao.
- **Rent A Bike/Rent a Scoot**, *Tel. 71.11.09*, is beside the road adjacent to Le Petit Village in Haapiti. Free pick-up service is available. They rent bicycles for 1.000 CFP for 4 hrs., 1.400 CFP for 8 hrs. and 1.500 CFP for 24 hrs. They also rent motorbikes or scooters for 4.500 CFP for 4 hrs. up to 5.500 CFP for 24 hrs. Gas is not included.
- **Tehotu Location Scooter**, Tel. 56.52.96/78.42.48, has an office at the Vaiare ferry dock, where you can rent a scooter for 5.000 CFP for 4 hours, 5.500 CFP for 8 hours, 6.000 CFP for 24 hours. The scooter is insured and you will be required to wear a helmet, which is included.

Some of the hotels and pensions rent bicycles to their guests. Check with your hotel activities desk for details.

Taxis

You'll find a taxi stand at the airport, *Tel. 56.10.18*, from 6am to 6:30pm. You can also call: Albert Transport, *Tel. 77.47.21*; D'esli Grand, *Tel. 73.37.19*; Taxi Justin, *Tel. 77.48.26*; John Teamo, *Tel. 77.57.56*; Edgar Ienfa, *Tel. 78.52.69*; Elizabeth Teraiharoa, *Tel. 27.30.85*; and Taxi Nadette, *Tel. 70.37.45*. All the taxis are equipped with taximeters, and charge 5.000 CFP per hour. The flag fall rate is 800 CFP plus 120 CFP per kilometer. The following rates are just to give you an idea of how much you will be paying, and the actual fare may be a little more or a little less than listed here. The fare between the airport and ferry dock is 1.500 CFP for a distance of 2.4 mi. (3.9 km). It will cost you about 1.000 CFP from the airport to the Sofitel Moorea Beach Resort, 1.500 CFP from the airport to the Moorea Pearl Resort, 1.800 CFP to the Hotel Kaveka in Cook's Bay, 2.000 CFP to the Club Bali Hai in Pao Pao, 2.500 CFP to the Sheraton, 3.800 CFP to the Intercontinental Moorea, and 4.000 CFP to the area of Le Petit Village in Haapiti.

Tour & Transport Companies

Some of the Tour and Transport Companies handle round-trip transfers between the airport or ferry dock and your hotel. They will also provide taxi service if you want to dine out in the evening or arrange a special shopping tour. The best deal you can get is with Loulou and Mate at Torea Nui Transport, *Tel. 56.12.48/ 77.01.52*. They have an office at the Moorea Airport and they provide a transfer service from the airport to any hotel on the island for 600 CFP. When you buy your Tahiti-Moorea airline ticket at the Air Moorea counter in Tahiti, ask for a land transfer. Once you arrive at the airport in Moorea, go to the Torea Nui Transport counter and show them your transfer ticket and they will drive you to your destination on Moorea.

While you are on Moorea you can also use their transfer services in the day time hours to get from one hotel to another, to one side of the island to the other, to go shopping, or whatever, as long as it is on the main road, for just 600 CFP one way. You have to reserve in advance. Their last transfer is at 5:15pm except on Sat. and Sun. nights, when Air Moorea has flights that coordinate with the arrival of Air Tahiti Nui international flight service from Los Angeles. On these nights Torea Nui will pick you up at the Moorea airport and drive you to your hotel or pension for 1.200 CFP.

Buses & Le Truck

Public transportation is provided by eight companies who rotate the service, using various kinds of buses and a couple of the traditional wooden bodied *les trucks*. Some of these vehicles are hand-me-downs from the big transport companies in Tahiti. All these vehicles operate schedules that coincide with the arrivals and departures of the fast catamarans and ferries from Tahiti, and with the school programs.

The **bus terminals** are located beside the Moorea Visitors Bureau at Le Petit Village in Haapiti, and at the Vaiare Ferry dock. The buses leave Le Petit Village Mon.-Sat. at 4:30am, 5:30am, 6:30am, 9:30am, 1:30pm and 3:30pm. The Sun. and holiday schedule is 6:30am, 1:30pm, 2:30pm and 4:30pm. It is best to be at the Moorea Visitors Bureau 15 min. in advance of departure time. From Le Petit Village terminal the buses and *le truck* head in both directions around the island to get to the Vaiare Ferry dock. You just stand beside the road and wave to the driver to stop, and you pay 300 CFP when you get off.

You can use this service for other purposes in addition to your arrival and departure transfers, and you can even go around the island for 600 CFP, as long as you coordinate your plans with the bus schedules, which the drivers normally adhere to.

WHERE TO STAY
Airport & Motu Temae – Deluxe
SOFITEL MOOREA BEACH RESORT, *B.P. 28, Maharepa, Moorea, 98728. Tel. 689/55.12.12, Fax 689/55.12.00; HO566@accor.com; Reservations 689/86.66.66, Fax 689/41.05.05; reservation.tahiti@accor.com; www.sofitel.com. Beside the lagoon at PK 2 in Temae, on northeast coast facing Tahiti, 2 km (1.2 mi.) from the airport and 2 km from the ferry dock. 114 bungalows. 2008 Low/High Season EP Rates sgl/dbl: Deluxe Garden Bungalow 36.726/41.593 CFP; Superior Beach Bungalow 49.115/53.097 CFP; Deluxe Beach Bungalow 60.177/65.044 CFP;*

Overwater Bungalow 69.027/74.779 CFP; Deluxe Overwater Bungalow 76.549/ 84.956 CFP. Add taxes. All major credit cards.

In November 2006, following a US$40 million overhaul of the former Sofitel Ia Ora Moorea, the upgraded 5-star Sofitel Moorea Beach Resort opened its doors to in-house guests, but not to the general public. Along with a new name and new look, a new policy requires anyone not staying at the hotel to ask permission and make an appointment to visit the premises, whether it is for a site inspection, to dine in one of the restaurants, or to have a spa treatment. Forget the idea of going to the beach here, which is the best on the island, and don't even think of sneaking past the security guard at the gate—there are hidden cameras at all possible entrances.

The 35-acre resort now has 114 beach, garden and overwater bungalows, ranging in size from 41 to 75 sq. m. (441-807 sq. ft.). The exterior of each bungalow is traditional Polynesian, with a thatched pandanus roof and walls of Kohu wood. The interior decoration is modern, featuring wooden floors, Sofitel's famous "My Bed" with white bed covers and mosquito netting, and orange tables that are supposed to resemble the color of the Tahitian fe'i (plantain) when it is cooked. All rooms have a/c, ceiling fans, a bathroom with a rain shower, separate toilet, hair dryer and make-up mirrors, a mini-bar, individual safe, direct dial phone, coffee and tea making facilities, and a plasma TV with satellite cable. Bathrobes and toiletries are furnished. The overwater bungalows have a window floor for fish watching and there is also a covered terrace, plus steps leading into the lagoon and a shower to rinse off when you come out of the water. The 19 new deluxe overwater units also have an outside shower that is an extension of the tiled shower in the bathroom. They have a walk-in closet, as well as a larger terrace furnished with two lounge chairs. The 20 older overwater units are classified superior and have 2 sitting chairs on a smaller terrace. Some of the overwater bungalows face the beach, some face the horizon, and some units face other bungalows. The deluxe beach bungalows also have a walk-in closet and a private garden where you can shower. Three bungalows are equipped to accommodate disabled guests.

In addition to two restaurants and a bar, room service is available from 6am-10pm. Dance shows are performed each evening during dinner. See information under *Where to Eat* in this chapter. The business center has Internet service and Wifi access is available at the Spa, the pool, the bar and in the restaurants. There are modern meeting rooms, a conference room, gift shop and Pearl Romance shop on the property. An activities desk and car rental desk are located in the lobby.

Among the spacious grounds are a nautical activities center, and an enlarged infinity swimming pool beside the white sandy beach. The new luxurious Le Spa offers 7 treatment rooms. See information under *Massages & Spas* in this chapter. There is no longer a wedding chapel and Gilles' Tattoo fare has also disappeared. The two tennis courts were closed for needed repair when I visited the Sofitel Moorea in November 2007.

Superior
   LA BAIE DE NUAREI, *B.P. 605, Maharepa, Moorea 98728. Tel./Fax 689/ 56.41.81, cell 23.80.69; labaiedenuarei@mail.pf; www.labaiedenuarei.com. Adjacent to the public beach on Motu Temae, 5 minutes from the airport and 10 minutes from the ferry dock. 2008 EP Rates: Bungalow Sakura 24.000 CFP sgl/dbl, 27.500 CFP tpl and 30.700 CFP for 4 people; Bungalows Vaiki and Vahia 19.800 CFP sgl/ dbl, 22.600 CFP tpl. Continental breakfast and all taxes included. No credit cards.*
   There are 3 rental bungalows in this secluded beachfront property owned by Tamara Kindynis-Tamagna. Each unit is different and very tastefully decorated in a Mediterranean style to reflect her Polynesian and Greek origins. The Sakura deluxe beach bungalow with a mezzanine and kitchen is a/c and sleeps 2-4 people in 2 bedrooms. The Vaiki and Vahia garden bungalows each have one bedroom that will accommodate 2-3 people, plus a kitchen and dining room in traditional Tahitian style. Each of the 3 bungalows has king size beds, TV, a security box, tea and coffee facilities, a private spacious bathroom and toilet, plus bathroom amenities. There is daily maid service, and guests have free use of bicycles, snorkeling equipment and a kayak. A nice white sand beach and lagoon are just outside the pension. There is a grocery story nearby and some restaurants provide free pick-up to go out for dinner. Tamara will be happy to assist you in arranging your activities on Moorea.
   There are also 2 additional bungalows that are available on occasion. The Tamara unit is a deluxe beachfront bungalow with a bedroom and bathroom, an electric fan and refrigerator, which sleeps two and rents for 17.800 CFP per night. The Vanessa unit is a garden bungalow with bedroom, bathroom, a/c and refrigerator, which costs 16.500 CFP for 2 and 18.500 CFP for 3 people.

Moderate
   FARE MAEVA, *B.P. 3170 Temae, Moorea 98728. Tel. 689/56.18.10; faremaevamoorea@mail.pf; www.faremaevamoorea.com. On the ocean side on Motu Temae, 4.5 km (2.8 mi.) from the ferry dock and 2 km (1.2 mi.) from the airport. EP Rates: bungalow 8.500 CFP sgl/dbl. 3rd person add 1.500 CFP for adult and 1.000 for child under 12 years. Continental breakfast on request 1.000 CFP per person (min. 2). Add taxes. No credit cards.*
   This modern and clean family pension is located just after Kerebel Jeweler on Temae motu, which is really a peninsula connected to the main island. Follow the dusty road beside the airport landing strip and look for the sign. There are 3 garden bungalows, each with a double bed, well-equipped kitchen and private bathroom with hot water. The sheets and towels are changed every 3 days. There is also a small terrace plus a *fare pote'e* shelter for each unit, complete with a table and chairs. The trees and plants here are similar to those found on an atoll and the beachy scene is accented by a yard filled with white sand. You also have access to a nice white sand beach, but there is no lagoon here, just the reef and open ocean. The public beach, which does have a nice lagoon, is very close by and one of Moorea's most popular

surfing spots is also in this vicinity. Your hostess, Maeva Jacquemin, is a young Polynesian-French woman who specializes in arts and crafts. She teaches her guests how to make *poisson cru*, dye and tie a *pareo*, and how to open and grate a coconut. Guests have free use of bicycles. Free pick-up by some restaurants for dinner. Food store 500 m (1.650 ft.) from pension.

Cook's Bay Area: Maharepa to Paopao – Deluxe
   MOOREA PEARL RESORT & SPA, *B.P. 3410, Temae, Moorea 98728. Tel. 689/55.17.50; Fax 689/55.17.51; www.pearlresorts.com. Reservations: Tel. 689/ 50.84.45; Fax 689/43.17.86; sales@spmhotels.pf. Beside lagoon at PK 5, between Moorea airport and Cook's Bay, 5 km (3 mi.) from the airport and 9 km (5.5 mi.) from the Vaiare ferry dock. 94 units. 2008 Low/High Season EP Rates sgl/dbl: Garden View Room 27.000/30.000 CFP; Garden View Duplex 33.000/36.000 CFP; Beach Bungalow 36.000/39.000 CFP; Garden Pool Bungalow 43.000/46.000 CFP; Premium Beach Bungalow 51.000/56.000 CFP; Overwater Bungalow 53.000/59.000 CFP; Premium Overwater Bungalow 65.000/69.000 CFP; third person 8.000 CFP. Add 8.250 CFP per person for MAP and 11.500 CFP for AP. Canoe breakfast for two 9.900 CFP. Add taxes. All major credit cards.*
   The 4-star Moorea Pearl Resort is situated on 7.5 acres of land just 2 miles from Cook's Bay. This traditional Polynesian style hotel offers 28 overwater bungalows, 8 beach bungalows, 28 garden bungalows with private pool, and 30 garden rooms, single or duplex. All units are a/c and the bungalows also have a ceiling fan. The garden view rooms and duplexes have a king size bed or two twin beds plus a sofa, and all the other units have a king-size bed and sofa. All units feature a sundeck, coffee/tea making facilities, mini bar, hair dryer, safety box, satellite television with 26" flat screen plus DVD/CD player, IDD telephone and an Internet outlet/fax line. In addition, the overwater bungalows have bathtubs and separate showers, glass tables to view the aquatic life of the lagoon, a large sundeck and sitting area with direct access by steps to the water. Two garden bungalows are specially equipped for guests in wheelchairs, and public areas and the pool are easily accessible. There are wide cement paths, ramps and an elevator.
   The hotel has 2 restaurants, a bar, boutique/pearl shop, and an activities desk. A 108-person conference room can be used as 3 separate rooms, complete with all the audio-visual equipment for meetings. The Manea Spa offers a full range of relaxing and esthetic treatments. See more information under *Massages & Spas* in this chapter. Room service, laundry service, secretarial services, currency exchange, public Internet service, and a daily newsletter are all available. There is a 7,500 sq. ft. infinity edge swimming pool, which you can see by Webcam on the hotel's website. Beside the hotel's overwater bungalows is a coral nursery called To'a Nui, where 700 fish have settled and developed in this unique environment. Although the water here is not ideally clear, snorkelers can observe the colony of coral that is regenerating in ecological conditions.
   There is an in-house photographer, Polynesian tattooer and the Moorea Blue

Diving scuba center. Guests have free use of snorkeling gear, outrigger paddle canoes and kayaks, and they can also play beach volleyball, badminton, ping-pong and petanque (French bowls). Beach toys and child size life jackets and snorkeling gear are also available, as well as a child's menu in the restaurant and babysitting service.

The Autera'a Bar and Terrace becomes a lively place around sunset, when there is often a trio of Tahitian musicians playing island songs. A buffet dinner and dance show takes place each Wed. night at the Mahanai Restaurant, and a seafood buffet and Polynesian dance show is held on Sat. nights. See more information under *Where to Eat* in this chapter.

Honeymooners and all other lovers have a choice of Romantic Rendez-vous programs. These include Romantic Welcomes, Romantic Interludes, Romantic Escapades, and Polynesian Wedding Ceremonies, complete with champagne and photos. Contact the hotel directly for details.

Moderate

KAVEKA, *B.P. 373, Maharepa, Moorea 98728. Tel. 689/56.50.50; Fax 689/ 56.52.63; kaveka@mail.pf; www.hotelkaveka.com Beside lagoon at PK 7 on east side of Cook's Bay, 7 km (4.3 mi.) from the airport and 11 km (7 mi.) from the ferry dock. 2008 EP Rates sgl/dbl: Lanai Bungalow (no a/c) 11.500 CFP; Garden Bungalow (a/ c) 15.500 CFP; Garden Family Bungalow (a/c) 17.500 CFP; Lagoon View Bungalow (a/c) 18.500 CFP; Lagoon Family Bungalow (a/c) 20.500 CFP; Beachfront Bungalow (a/c) 19.500 CFP. Add 5.500 CFP for 3rd person. Add 5.500 CFP for MAP and 8.500 CFP for AP. All taxes included. Deposit required. AE, MC, V.*

There are 25 wooden bungalows in the gardens, at the edge of the lagoon and beside a small white sand beach that slopes into the warm water of Cook's Bay. This 2-star hotel offers a multi-millionaire's view of the postcard scenery of mountains, coral reef, sea and sky. Some of the bungalows have a/c and all units have a ceiling fan. Most of the rooms have a TV, refrigerator, bathroom with hot water shower, a tiled floor and a large covered terrace with two lounge chairs. Beds are either king size or double, with 1-2 single beds in room. The lanai rooms are sold as a bare bones, no frills package deal, but you can rent refrigerators, TV's, and cell phones on request. There are no coffee/tea makers in any of the bungalows, but they all have a private safe in the closet and they are also furnished with blackout curtains. A high rock wall helps to eliminate noises from the road while giving the hotel more privacy.

This hotel has full service, including a restaurant, bar, laundry, beach, activities, tour desk, free transportation to the shopping center and church, staff with expert local knowledge, on site owners, security, and thousands of satisfied customers around the world for more than 25 years.

Restaurant Kaveka is built overwater, providing indoor or outdoor dining and a truly breathtaking view of Cook's Bay. Please see more information under *Where to Eat* in this chapter.

CLUB BALI HAI, *B.P. 8, Maharepa, Moorea 98728. Tel. 689/56.13.68, Fax 689/56.13.27; reservations@clubbalihai.pf; www.clubbalihai.com Beside the lagoon at PK 8 in Cook's Bay, near Pao Pao village, 8 km (5 mi.) from the airport and 12 km (7.5 mi.) from the ferry dock. 44 a/c rooms and bungalows. 2008 EP Rates sgl/dbl: Beachfront Bungalow with breakfast €160; Overwater Bungalow with breakfast €175; Diver's special US$150 per night for Bayview Room. Add taxes. All major credit cards.*

Club Bali Hai overlooks the panoramic beauty of Cook's Bay and the surrounding mountains of cathedral peaks and spires. The 44 A/C units include 13 overwater bungalows, 6 beachfront bungalows, 5 garden rooms with no kitchen, and 20 rooms in a two-story colonial style building. Most of the rooms in the 2-story building have kitchenettes and they all have coffee machines. A bayview room will be quieter as the road traffic can be quite noisy, but the advantage of the mountain view rooms is the lower price plus a kitchenette. The overwater and beach bungalows are Polynesian in decor, with a bedroom, separate kitchen/dining area and terrace facing the spectacular scenery. The floors and bathrooms are tiled and there are plenty of mirrors in the bedroom and bathroom. These units are furnished with a ceiling fan, a queen size bed in the bedroom and a twin bed in the living room, with a door in between for a little privacy, although the wall does not extend all the way to the ceiling. The kitchen contains a stove and oven, as well as a microwave and coffee/tea making facilities. The windows are screened, but not the sliding door leading to the sundeck. All the bathrooms have hot water showers. Club Bali Hai is a hotel with a Vacation Time-Share program, which is affiliated with Resort & Condominium International (RCI).

The Blue Pineapple (l'Ananas Bleu) is a snack bar located on the hotel premises beside the bay. Matahi Hunter and his wife Virginia and their crew serve breakfast and lunch daily from 7am to 3pm, which you can enjoy while gazing at the magnificent view of the mountains overlooking Cook's Bay. They also serve wine and beer, but there are no other alcoholic beverages available, unless you bring your own booze to the poolside in the afternoon and listen to Muk McCallum, one of the three "Bali Hai Boys", talk story about the old days at Hotel Bali Hai. Muk is there every day at 5:30pm except on Wed. and he brings the ice and the entertaining answers to your questions. The other two founders of a chain of Bali Hai Hotels were Hugh Kelley, who died a few years ago, and Jay Carlisle, whom you will probably meet around the snack bar.

The hotel staff are all Tahitians who have worked for the Hotel Bali Hai and/ or Club Bali Hai for many years. There is a big boutique at the hotel entrance next to the reception area and you can watch CNN on a TV in the lounge beside the reception desk. A public phone is on the wall near the reception and you can buy a phone card from Rosalie in the boutique. Internet service is just half a mile from the hotel. There are a few good restaurants near the hotel and most restaurants in the Cook's Bay area provide free transportation for dinner.

Club Bali Hai offers their guests a free tennis court, a fresh water swimming pool and a small white sand beach with good swimming in Cook's Bay. Free activities also include *tupa* crab races on Mon. evening, a *pareo*-tying demonstration on Tues. evening and a Tahitian dance show on Wed. evening. Hiro Kelley of **Hiro's Tours/What to Do on Moorea Tours** has an activities desk at the hotel and he also has rental kayaks. Avis has a desk in the lobby and other rental cars, scooters and bikes can be rented across the street. For more information on optional activities, see *Lagoon Excursions, Snorkeling & Picnics on the Motu* in this chapter.

Check the Internet on the Club Bali Hai website, as they often have specials that can mean big savings for your next vacation on Moorea. They offer the lowest prices in French Polynesia on overwater bungalows.

VILLAGE TEMANOHA, *B.P. 94, Maharepa, Moorea 98728. Tel./Fax 689/ 55.25.00, cell 77.17.00; Fax 689/55.25.01; temanoha@mail.pf; www.temanoha.com. In Pao Pao Valley behind school, 10 km (6 mi.) from the airport, 14 km (9 mi.) from the ferry dock, and 1.2 km from the belt road. One-way transfer 1.000 CFP per person. 2008 EP rates: Fare Tiare bungalows 13.500 CFP sgl/dbl; 16.700 CFP tpl; Fare Rotui bungalows 15.000 CFP sgl/dbl; 18.200 CFP tpl. No charge for child under 5 years. Continental breakfast 1.500 CFP. Add taxes. No credit cards.*

There are 6 high quality wooden bungalows with 40 or 50 sq. m (431 or 538 sq. ft.) of living space built around a swimming pool in a tropical garden of 5,000 sq. m (53,820 sq. ft.) at the foot of Mount Rotui and Moua Puta. You'll have cooler temperatures and a wonderful view of the cathedral shaped mountains from this elevation, and the quiet setting is ideal for those who enjoy meditating, taking long walks, lying beside the pool with a book and simply being. Each bungalow contains a double bed and a single bed with mosquito nets, a small living room, equipped kitchen, 1 free bottle of water, private bathroom of wood and river stone paving and a solar hot water shower, plus a covered terrace. There is a ceiling fan in the living room, split bamboo wall coverings, natural tapa on the doors, teak furniture and TV and electric mosquito repellent in each bungalow. Housekeeping service is provided and breakfast is served to your bungalow on request. Free Internet access for messages. Bicycles are available for 1.500 CFP per day. The rocky road from Pao Pao to the pension is recommended for 4WD vehicles only, but once you arrive you will want to stay. Hosts Christa and Mathieu Castellani will help you arrange your island tours.

Economy

MOTEL ALBERT, *B.P. 27, Pao Pao, Moorea 98728. Tel. 689/56.12.76; Fax 689/56.58.58; motel.albert@laposte.net; http://motelalbert.free.fr. Mountainside at PK 8 in Pao Pao, across from Club Bali Hai, 8 km (5 mi.) from the airport and 12 km (8 mi.) from the ferry dock. EP Rates: room 5.000-7.000 CFP sgl/dbl; bungalow 9.000 CFP for 4 people; additional person 1.000 CFP per day. Minimum 2 nights or add 1.000 CFP to rates. Add taxes. No credit cards.*

This is a good choice if you are traveling on a tight budget and want to be in the Cook's Bay area, where you can see the famous mountains surrounding the bay.

You'll also be within easy walking distance of supermarkets, restaurants and snacks. There are 2 small rooms and 4 larger rooms, plus 8 big bungalows available to rent by the night, week, month or year. The wooden bungalows are on stilts, each with two bedrooms, living room, a spacious kitchen with regular stove and big refrigerator, large screened in terrace, screened windows and sliding glass doors, and private bathroom with hot water shower. The decor is old Polynesia with pareo cloth bedspreads and curtains. There are one or two double beds in the rooms, as well as a kitchen and private bathroom with hot water shower. The Polynesian owners told me years ago they were going to renovate these rooms, but they still have not been done because they are in constant use.

Opunohu-Papetoai Area – Deluxe

SHERATON MOOREA LAGOON RESORT & SPA, *B.P. 1005, Papetoai, Moorea 98729. Tel. 689/55.11.11; Fax 689/55.11.55; reservations.tahiti@sheraton.pf; www.sheraton.com. Beside the lagoon at PK 14 between Cook's Bay and Opunohu Bay, 14 km (8.7 mi.) from the airport and 18 km (11 mi.) from the ferry dock. 106 bungalows. 2008 Low/High Season EP Rates sgl/dbl: Garden Bungalow 36.000/ 40.000 CFP; Superior Garden Bungalow 42.000/47.000 CFP; Beach Bungalow 58.000/65.000 CFP; Spa Bungalow 84.000/93.000 CFP; Overwater Bungalow 78.000/87.000 CFP; Horizon Overwater Bungalow 84.000/93.000 CFP; Premium Horizon Overwater Bungalow 90.000/99.000 CFP; Extra person 10.000 CFP. Add 9.075 CFP per person for MAP and 12.685 CFP for AP. Outrigger canoe breakfast 4.630 CFP. Add taxes. All major credit cards.*

Most guests love this thatched roof Polynesian style hotel, which is located in 12 acres of tropical gardens, coconut palms and gnarled old tamanu trees, along a white sandy beach. Upon arrival at the Sheraton Moorea Lagoon you will be greeted with a flower lei, a cold face cloth and a glass of fruit punch. After completing your registration one of the friendly Tahitian valets will drive you and your luggage to your room in an electric golf cart.

The 106 units consist of 52 garden and beach bungalows and 54 bungalows over the water. There are double bungalows for families, smoking and non-smoking rooms and units for handicapped guests in wheelchairs. All the bungalows are equipped with individually controlled a/c, ceiling fan, smoke detector system, blackout drapes, They contain a king-size bed or two double beds and there is a sofa bed and writing table. The furniture is made of local semi-precious woods, and includes tables and padded lounge chairs on the partially shaded terraces. Amenities include direct-dial phones, color TV with satellite/cable, Internet access, alarm clock/radio, CD player, individual safe, mini-bar, coffee/tea making facilities, and ironing board with an iron. The bathroom features a claw-footed bathtub and a separate shower with degree-controlled faucets. There are separate toilets with telephones, and the overwater bathrooms also have bidets. All units have an extendible lighted makeup mirror and full-length mirror and hairdryer. A nice selection of Mandara Spa soaps, shampoos, bath gel and other toiletries is replenished daily. A pillow menu offers you a choice of various sizes and shapes of head rests, from feather soft to firm.

If you have booked an overwater bungalow be prepared for a wonderful surprise when you enter your room. The golden-orange walls provide a warm setting for the rich-grained wood furniture. Your eyes are immediately drawn to the picture postcard scenery of the shimmering turquoise lagoon and velvet green mountains visible beyond your terrace. You have a feeling of being suspended in space above the water, which indeed you are. It's simply stunning!

The overwater bungalows have a two-level terrace with steps that let you shimmy down into the warm lagoon, which is about 4 feet deep, and there is an outdoor shower on a landing above the water. The overwater units also have a long glass floor and a glass table for fish watching, and you are guaranteed an interesting performance of jewel-colored fish in these coral-rich waters. You'll find some of the best snorkeling on Moorea in the vicinity of the overwater bungalows.

The resort's public buildings carry out the theme of Polynesian architecture with enormous thatched roofs, local woods, and shell lamps hanging from the ceiling. The gardens are carefully landscaped with basaltic boulders and huge hibiscus flowers of every hue. Walkways take you from the spacious reception area and activities desk past gardens of white ginger, ixora and other lush tropical plants. Waterfalls cascade into fern-rimmed pools where golden carp frolic and swim. Robert Wan's Tahiti Perles shop displays chokers and earrings of high quality Tahitian cultured pearls. Kaimana Boutique is a shopper's dream of tropical clothing, *tifaifai* wall hangings and unusual gift items.

In addition to the Arii Vahine Restaurant, Rotui Beach Grill & Bar, Toatea Bar on the pier, and the Eimeo Bar, there is also room service available from 6am to 10:15pm. The Manager's Cocktail Party takes place each Thurs. from 5-6pm, and there are special theme evenings with Tahitian dance shows and live entertainment in the main bar, which offers half-price drinks during Happy Hour. See more information under *Where to Eat* in this chapter.

Hotel services include 24-hour front desk service, 24-hour security, laundry and dry cleaning service, valet service, guest ice machines, multilingual concierge service, pre-registration service, currency exchange, banquet and meeting facilities, daily newsletters and a business center. Guests can buy an Internet card to use the four computers and printer in the lounge section of the Eimeo Bar, where there is also a wide-screen TV. In the lobby you will find a guest relations desk, excursions and activities desk and a car rental agency.

At the Nautical Fare on the beach you can check out a kayak, outrigger paddle canoe or snorkeling gear at no charge. Or you can sign up for boat excursions, guided jet-ski tours, deep-sea fishing, scuba diving, parasailing, picnics on the motu, waterskiing and other water activities. Across the road from the hotel is a Fitness Center with Technogym equipment, two changing rooms, lockers and showers. There are also two lighted tennis courts that are open 24/24 and are free to in-house guests.

There is a fantasy swimming pool and a Jacuzzi adjacent to the beach, as well as a Pool Fare, where you can get beach towels. Mandara Spa, also on the beach level, has a sauna and steam room, which hotel guests can use at no extra charge. There is also a Jacuzzi and rain shower, and the trained massage therapists suggest an interesting choice of relaxation treatments. You can even get the kinks of a long plane flight massaged out of your neck, shoulders and back while relaxing beside the pool. A French *coiffeuse* provides hair care in the Spa. See more information under *Nautical Activities Centers*, *Scuba Diving*, and *Massages & Spas* in this chapter.

Moderate

PENSION MOTU ITI, *B.P. 189, Paopao, Moorea 98728. Tel. 689/55.05.20/ 74.43.38; Fax 689/55.05.21; pensionmotuiti@mail.pf; www.pensionmotuiti.com Beside lagoon at PK 13.2 between Cook's Bay and Opunohu Bay, 13 km (8 mi.) from the airport and 17 km (11 mi.) from the Vaiare ferry dock. 2008 Rates: EP bungalow sgl/dbl, 10.500 CFP in garden and 12.000 CFP on beachfront; dormitory 1.650 CFP per person, including taxes. AE, MC, V. Reserve.*

Each of the 5 modern Polynesian style bungalows has a wood shingle roof and the interior walls are covered with pandanus matting. The big bamboo furniture includes a king-size bed and desk. Each unit has a ceiling fan, TV and a bathroom with tiled shower and hot water. The windows and sliding glass door are unscreened, but each room is equipped with an electric machine for mosquito repellent. There are chairs on the terrace and a faucet is placed beside the steps at the front entrance to rinse off sandy feet. You can have room service on your terrace for breakfast, lunch or your favorite drinks.

A 15-cot dormitory over the reception area is cooled by a large opening on the lagoon side, as well as a series of fans. There are two clean bathrooms downstairs. A high stone wall on the roadside helps to keep traffic noises to a minimum. An overwater *fare* provides shelter as well as a sundeck for guests who want to spend a few quiet hours reading, napping in a lounge chair or gazing at the sea and sky. Kayaks are provided free of charge and owner Auguste Ienfa will drive you to the Sheraton to join a tour or excursion. There are computers in the reception with Internet service. The Motu Iti restaurant is on a covered terrace facing the lagoon, and the excellent Aito Restaurant is just next door.

FARE NANI, *B.P. 61572, Faaa, Tahiti 98702. Tel./Fax 689/56.19.99; Cell 79.89.73. Beside the lagoon in Pihaena at PK 14.1, between the Sheraton Moorea Lagoon Resort and Village Faimano, 14 km (8.7 mi.) from the airport and 18 km (11 mi.) from the ferry dock. EP Rates: Tahitian fare 10.000 CFP for two adults and two children under 12 years. Third person 1.000 CFP. All taxes are included. No credit cards.*

Maeva Bougues, one of Tahiti's best songwriters, operates this little pension. She speaks good English and Spanish in addition to French and Tahitian, her native language. Each of the 3 little thatched roof *fares* has a double bed with mosquito net and small electric fan, a lounge with sofa and mattresses, a kitchen and outside bathroom with cold water. 3 paddle canoes and 2 kayaks are available for exploring the lagoon and there is a small white sand beach, with shade provided by gnarled old wild hibiscus (*purau*) trees. You have to walk past the trees to get into the lagoon or watch the sunset, but they add a feeling of privacy, which the guests appreciate. Maeva also has houses in Maatea for rent on a short-term basis.

VILLAGE FAIMANO, *B.P. 588, Maharepa, Moorea 98728. Tel. 689/ 56.10.20, Fax 689/56.36.47; faimanodenis@mail.pf; www.faimanovillage.com Beside the lagoon at PK 14.1 in Pihaena, near the Sheraton Moorea Lagoon Resort, 14 km (8.7 mi.) from the airport and 18 km (11 mi.) from the ferry dock. 2008 EP Rates: Garden Bungalow 10.000 CFP 1-3 people; Beach Bungalow 10.000 CFP sgl/dbl; 11.500 CFP tpl; family bungalow 14.000 CFP 4-6 people per day. Add taxes. MC, V.*

This little seaside pension offers good value for money. The location is very pretty, with a white sand beach and clear lagoon for easy swimming. This is a very popular weekend destination for Tahiti residents, and the ambiance is often local, which means Tahitian music and songs. Your choice of 7 Polynesian style bungalows includes 2 family size *fares*, each with 2 rooms with a double bed, 1-2 single beds in the living room, plus a kitchen and private bathroom with solar hot water. Or you can rent one of the 5 smaller *fares*, each with a bedroom and double bed, single beds in the living room, kitchen and private bathroom with solar hot water. Each bungalow has a barbecue grill and television. Bikes, outrigger paddle canoes and kayaks are free of charge for guest use and you can sunbathe on a floating dock within a few laps from the shore. The reception is also a communal room with books and games. Faimano, who is Tahitian, and her French husband, Denis Feildel, who own the pension, have now retired to Taha'a, and Faimano's niece Valerie takes care of the guests. She speaks a little English.

FARE HAMARA, *Tel. 689/56.25.65. On mountainside at PK 16.4 overlooking Opunohu Bay. Reservations: Bob Hammar, Tel. 253/564-0180; hamara@harbornet.com; www.farehamara.com. Private home US$1,600 per week.*

Fare Hamara is a Lindal cedar home with 2 bedrooms: 1 king, 1 queen. A twin trundle in the great room and 2 sleeping mats afford sleep space for 8. The large bathroom has a double shower and twin sinks. The American style kitchen is fully equipped. The house is a well-planned octagon shape with a wrap-around deck. Features: personal safe, screened windows & doors, linens, washer & dryer, BBQ on deck. Fantastic views of Opunohu Bay.

FARE VAIHERE, *B.P. 1806, Papetoai, Moorea 98729. Tel./Fax 689/56.19.19; cell 79.00.97; farevaihere@mail.pf; www.farevaihere.com. Beside the lagoon at PK 15.5 in Opunohu Bay, 15.5 km (9.6 mi.) from the airport and 19.5 km (12 mi.) from the ferry dock. 2008 EP Rates sgl/dbl: bungalow plus Continental breakfast 17.800 CFP; add 1.650 CFP per day for extra bed. Add visitor tax. Dinner 3.500 CFP per person. MC, V.*

This quiet family pension offers a taste of old Moorea, with local style architecture, thatched roofs and woven bamboo walls, on the verdant east coast of Opunohu Bay. Look for a sign with the design of a breadfruit leaf at the entrance, and ring the bell at the gate. There are 4 bungalows for a maximum of 3 people, each one named for the tree that grows beside it, and each unit has a different color scheme. The honeymoon bungalow beside the beach is Badamier (almond tree) and the bed covers and mosquito net are orange. Letchi (Lychee) is decorated in yellow and pink, Manguier (mango tree) in blue, and Uru (breadfruit tree) in green. Each unit has a double bed and a single bed, a tiled bathroom with hot water shower, and a covered porch. They are furnished with a ceiling fan, desk, small refrigerator, a kettle with supplies of coffee and tea, and a bottle of water to welcome you. A complimentary Continental breakfast is served in the dining room furnished with teak, and dinner is also available on request. Or you can eat at the big table outside. This communal *fare* has a mezzanine lounge with a small library, TV and DVD player. Guests can also check their email on the pension's computer.

Guests have free use of the bicycles, snorkeling gear and kayaks, and you can swim off the end of the long pier in front of the property. Smaller kids can play in the shallow water beside a narrow beach. Owner/manager Jean Marc provides lagoon excursions in his 24-ft. boat for up to 8 passengers, which are also available to people not staying in his pension. Rates are 6.000-8.000 CFP for à la carte tours.

Economy

PENSION AITO, *B.P. 648, Maharepa, Moorea 98728. Tel./Fax 689/56.45.52, cell 23.27.63; aito12@mail.pf; www.aitomoorea.com. Beside the lagoon at PK 13 in Pihaena, between Cook's Bay and Opunohu Bay. 2008 EP rates sgl/dbl; 3 rooms 6.500, 7.500, 10.450 CFP including taxes. Weekly and monthly rates available. MC, V.*

Jean-Baptiste and Vanina Cipriani, who own the now famous Restaurant Aito, also have accommodations for guests who want to linger for a night, a week, a month or longer. Two budget-priced rooms adjacent to the parking area have a double bed, kitchenette, refrigerator, TV, and bathroom with hot water. The honeymoon room, with a big bed and TV, is upstairs over the restaurant, and the exotic bathroom, complete with bathtub and hot water, is on the ground level.

Guests have free use of bicycles and snorkel gear. A Continental breakfast is 900 CFP, an American breakfast is 1.500 CFP, and a Sunday morning Polynesian breakfast is 3.500 CFP. You will definitely want to eat all your meals in the restaurant, because the food is so good. I know a couple from Richmond, VA who own a travel agency. They chose to stay here rather than getting a free room in a deluxe hotel, simply because they thought it would be more fun. And it was.

West Coast: Papetoai to Haapiti – Deluxe

INTERCONTINENTAL MOOREA RESORT & SPA, *B.P. 1019, Tiahura, Moorea 98729. Tel. 689/55.19.19, Fax 689/55.19.55; reservationspf@interconti.com; www.moorea.interconti.com. Beside the lagoon at PK 24 between Papetoai and Haapiti, 24 km (14.8 mi.) from the airport and 28 km (17.3 mi.) from the ferry dock.*

144 rooms and bungalows. 2008 Low/High Season EP Rates sgl/dbl: Lanai Room 28.890/32.090 CFP; Garden Suite Bungalow 39.910/44.340 CFP; Beach Suite Bungalow 47.550/52.830 CFP; Premium Beach Bungalow Suite 53.300/59.220 CFP; Overwater Suite Bungalow 65.920/73.240 CFP; Premium Overwater Bungalow Suite 69.790/77.540 CFP; Teremoana Lanai Suite 69.790/77.540 CFP. 3rd person 15 years or over 8.000 CFP. Canoe Breakfast 6.090 CFP per person; Add 8.820 CFP per person for MAP and 12.650 CFP for AP. Add taxes. All major credit cards.

This property covers 17 acres of beautiful gardens and manmade beaches on a mini-peninsula on the northwestern side of Moorea, between Opunohu Bay and the tourist hotels and shops in the former Club Med area of Haapiti.

There are 48 a/c lanai rooms, including 2 handicapped rooms, and 1 suite located in colonial style 2-story concrete buildings, each with a king-size bed or two twin beds and a balcony or lanai overlooking the lagoon. The 17 garden bungalows, 28 beach bungalows and 50 overwater bungalows are all built in the traditional Polynesian design with thatched roofs. These units have a separate sitting area with a writing desk, a king-size bed and a sofa bed. All the bungalows have a/c and ceiling fans in the living room and bedroom, and in the bathrooms there are separate bathtubs and showers and a private toilet section. Standard amenities in all rooms and bungalows include international direct dial telephones with 2 sets, satellite color TV, in-house video movies, radio and music. There is a fully stocked self-service mini-bar/refrigerator in each room and bungalow, as well as complimentary tea and coffee making facilities, a personal electronic safety box, a hair dryer, 240/110-volt electrical outlets and complimentary grooming items. All the bungalows have a private balcony with table and two armchairs and 2 snorkeling masks. The overwater bungalows are just at the edge of the lagoon and have steps leading into the water and mats for sunbathing.

An enormous thatched roof building houses the reception, Fare Nui restaurant for 250 diners, Fare Hana poolside restaurant for 80 people, Motu Iti bar with seating for 70 people, a conference room for 80-100 diners or 150 theater-style seats, a concierge service and public relations activities desk, taxi, car and bike rental desk, gift shop and pearl shop. Guest services include twice a day maid service, next day laundry and dry cleaning service (Mon.-Fri.), iron and ironing board on request, currency exchange, and mail and postal service. In-room dining is available 24 hours a day and a special romantic touch for guests staying in most of the overwater bungalows is to order breakfast served to their balcony by flower decorated outrigger canoe.

Guests have free use of the hotel's fresh water swimming pool, two tennis courts and white sand beaches, and snorkeling equipment and outrigger paddle canoes are also provided. There is an on-site nautical sports center and New Bathy's Club has a scuba dive center here. The Moorea Dolphin Center is a big attraction for people who want to play with the dolphins in an enclosed environment and there is also a turtle sanctuary. Helicopter rides are available with a landing pad on the hotel grounds. In addition to a daily program of activities presented at the hotel, you will also have an interesting choice of excursions to discover the romantic beauty of Moorea's seashore and interior valleys. Should you feel in the mood to just relax and be pampered, you can treat yourself to a fresh floral bath and massage at Héléne'Spa, located on the hotel grounds. See more information under *Massages & Spas* in this chapter.

Musicians play songs from the islands around the bar at sunset, and various activities are organized in the lobby or at the Motu Iti bar. These include pareo-tying demonstrations, tamure lessons, learning how to prepare Tahitian marinated fish and watching video films on the Tahitian cultured pearl. The weekly entertainment program begins on Mon. evening with Polynesian Night, when a buffet of Tahitian and seafood specialties is served, followed by a dance show. The dinner and show costs 6.560 CFP. Barbecue Night is held each Wed. beside the swimming pool, accompanied by a Polynesian show, and it is also 6.560 CFP. The *Soirée Merveilleuse* held each Sat. evening is a gastronomic buffet featuring a variety of fresh seafood, usually served on the beach under the stars and tropical moon. A Tahitian dance group performs on a stage set between two graceful coconut trees. This costs 8.400 CFP. A Sun. Buffet lunch is served in the Fare Hana beside the pool, to the tune of a musical trio.

The ICH Moorea has a catalog of "Romantic Ideas," "Celebrations of Romance" and "Romantic Touches" for honeymooners and other lovers. You can also exchange vows in a non-binding Polynesian wedding ceremony.

LEGENDS RESORT MOOREA, *B.P. 4546, Papeete, Tahiti 98713. Tel. 689/83.19.09; Fax 689/83.19.01; www.legendsresort.fr. On the mountainside at PK 24 between Papetoai and Haapiti, 24 km (14.8 mi.) from the airport and 28 km (17.3 mi.) from the ferry dock. EP Rates: Garden Villa 33.000 CFP per night, 140.000-175.000 CFP per week; Premium Sea View Villa 55.000 CFP per night, 295.000-365.000 CFP per week. 15% surcharge during high seasons. Add taxes.*

Legends Resort is located on a 17.3-acre (7 ha.) hillside on Moorea's northeast coast, overlooking the Intercontinental Moorea Resort & Spa, the lagoon and 3 motu islets inside the lagoon. Scheduled to open in July 2008, Legends Resort will offer 49 private 2- and 3-bedroom contemporary style villas, plus a 50th villa that will serve as the reception and lounge areas. There is also a boutique, a delicatessen and breakfast café. A gourmet restaurant and bar are located at the entrance to the resort, and Legends Resort offers catering or room service. The resort also has a horizon swimming pool and a tennis court, as well as its own private motu with a snack house. A free shuttle boat will transfer guests to the motu.

The villas are built of wood and stone and stand on tall stilts on a sloping hillside. They are classified as "Nui" (big) or "Iti" (little). The big villas for 2-6 people are 1,883 sq. ft. (175 sq. m), and the little villas for 2-4 people have 1,292 sq. ft. (120 sq. m). Each elegantly furnished villa has spacious a/c bedrooms, en suite bathrooms, lounge with a flat screen TV and DVD player, a fully equipped kitchen, linen/laundry room, a deck and a large terrace with a Jacuzzi and small shelter, and a shower in the garden. Guests have a choice between maximum privacy and intimacy or the use of such hotel services as the changing of household linen, daily villa cleaning and daily breakfast.

These units will be managed collectively as a residence resort, which is different from the time-sharing or condominium concepts. It is a fractional ownership, which is similar to time-sharing. Each owner is entitled to use of his/her villa five weeks every year, and non-owners staying in a villa will pay a rental fee representing 5.45% net of the villa's purchase price.

DREAM ISLAND, *B. P. 1175, Papetoai, Moorea 98729. Tel. 689/77.84.70; Fax 689/56.38.81; darmin@mail.pf; www.dream-island.com. 3 deluxe houses on a private motu facing former Club Med property in Haapiti. Taxes included. No credit cards.*

Kolka and Josy Muller say that this is the private island everybody dreams about without believing it could really exist...yet it does. Their 3 deluxe houses are surrounded by unspoiled beauty on a white sand beach just a 5-minute boat ride from the main island. Fare Polynésie is a 3 bedroom, 2 bath house with a private apartment, large lounge, kitchen, dining room and 2 terraces, for US$500 a night, $2,950 a week or $9,500 a month. Fare Pacifique has 2 bedrooms, 2 bathrooms, a lounge, kitchen and 2 terraces and rents for US$450 a night, $2,550 a week or $8,500 a month. Fare Gauguin has 2 bedrooms, a master bathroom and another bathroom, a lounge, kitchen and dining room, for $350 a night, $1,050 a week or $6,900 a month. These rates are for 4 people maximum per house. Each additional person will be charged $340 extra per week. Each house is equipped with a TV, telephone, lovely furnishings and homey touches. Check out the photos on their website.

VILLA CORALLINA, *B.P. 19, Maharepa, Moorea 98728. Tel. 689/77.05.90; Fax 689/56.36.65; manager@villacorallina.com; www.villacorallina.com. A 2-bedroom villa on the west side of Motu Fareone, across the channel from the former Club Med in Haapiti, 27 km (16.7 mi.) from the airport and 5 minutes by boat from main island. 2008 EP Rates sgl/dbl: US$490 per night and US$3,150 per week. Add taxes. No credit cards. Minimum stay 4 nights.*

The main house of Marco Ciucci's Villa Corallina offers a 3,000 sq. ft. residence with 2 double bedrooms, 2 bathrooms, a living room, dining room, breakfast area, fully equipped kitchen, beach terrace with barbecue, a private white sand beach with lounge chairs and 6,000 sq. m (64,583 sq. feet) of private grounds on a quiet motu islet, providing panoramic views of the lagoon, coral reef, deep ocean and open skies. Amenities include ceiling fans, 2 TV's, a video player and VCR library, a CD player in the rooms and in the living room, cellular phone, fax, books, refrigerator, freezer and house linens. There is also an extra bungalow for a young couple or 2 children, with a ceiling fan but no bathroom. This is free if you rent the villa for more than 4 people. Guests have free use of snorkeling equipment, 2 kayaks and outrigger paddle canoe. The housekeeping and beach maintenance are assured daily by the staff. A courtesy shuttle will transfer you to the main island.

There is also a one-bedroom self-contained garden cottage on the interior of the property, which can be rented for US$290 a night or US$1,950 per week, with a 3-night minimum. This can only be rented when the main villa is not in use. See the website for details.

Superior
FENUA MATA'I'OA, *B. P. 1192, Papetoai, Moorea, 98729. Tel. 689/55/00.25; Fax 689/55.00.26; eileenb@mail.pf; www.fenua-mataioa.com. Beside the lagoon in Tiahura Village, between the Intercontinental Moorea Resort and Hotel Les Tipaniers. EP Rates: Room for two people 30.000 CFP; Princesse Maimiti Royal Suite 50.000 CFP; additional person is 5.000 CFP per day, including taxes. MC, V.*

This unique lodging is an exclusive, elegant *residence* located in a gated community. Eileen Bossuot, the hostess, is a former designer for the Relais et Chateaux properties in France, and she and her husband Serge have filled their lagoon-side home with all the treasures of their many voyages throughout the world, including Eileen's collection of 2,500 owls. The décor is a blend of Tahitian, French Provincial, European and Asian, and each item has its own story. Along with the mirrors, lamps, sconces, and objets d'art, there are many colorful tableaux that were painted by Moorea's resident artists. Fenua Mata'i'oa offers a choice of 6 rooms for 2-3 guests or a 2-level duplex suite with beds for 4 guests. All the rooms are a/c and furnished with a king-size bed, large sleeping sofa, color satellite TV, music system, DDD telephone with modem data port, mini-bar and large terrace, all lovingly decorated. Each of the rooms also has a private bathroom with a large shower, 2 lavabos, toilet, hair-dryer and tasteful decor. In the suite the upstairs bedroom has a private safety box, and the bathroom contains a Jacuzzi bathtub and shower.

Guests can enjoy their refined meals in the privacy of their rooms, on the pier or in the small interior or exterior dining rooms. There is no beach here, but lounge chairs and palapa type thatched roof umbrellas line the wooden deck beside the lagoon and there is a Jacuzzi pool in the garden. Snorkeling equipment is provided at no extra charge, as well as kayaks and bicycles.

Moderate
HOTEL LES TIPANIERS, *B.P. 1002, Papetoai, Moorea 98729. Tel. 689/56.12.67, Fax 689/56.29.25; tipaniersresa@mail.pf; www.lestipaniers.com. Beside the lagoon at PK 25 in Haapiti, 25 km (15.5 mi.) from the airport and 29 km (18 mi.) from the ferry dock. 22 bungalows. 2008 EP Rates: Standard Bungalow 14.250 CFP sgl/dbl, 15.550-16.850 CFP 3-4 people; Local Garden Bungalow with kitchen 14.250 CFP sgl/dbl, 16.600 CFP 3-4; Local Beach Bungalow with kitchen 16.250 CFP sgl/dbl, 17.100 CFP 3-4; Vanilla Garden Bungalow with kitchen 15.400 CFP 1-3 people, 17.400 CFP 4-6 people. Add 2.000 CFP for extra person in kitchen bungalows. Add 4.947 CFP per person for MAP and 8.568 CFP for AP. Continental breakfast 1.326 CFP, American breakfast 1.785 CFP, Dinner 3.621 CFP. Add taxes. All major credit cards.*

"Les Tipaniers" means frangipani or plumeria, the trees of white, pink, orange and yellow flowers you will see and smell throughout the gardens of this very Polynesian style hotel. The local style bungalows have a thatched roof and can sleep 3 or 4 people, with or without a kitchen. The vanilla style units are built in the French colonial architecture with gingerbread trim and have kitchens, accommodating up to 6 people. Each bungalow has a porch or terrace, as well as screens on the windows but not on the sliding glass doors. All the bungalows were renovated in 2003, and this popular hotel enjoys 80 percent occupancy year-round.

The beachside restaurant-bar is open for breakfast, lunch and sunset cocktails, and the main restaurant is open for dinner. See information under *Where to Eat* in this chapter. You can easily walk from this hotel to several restaurants, shops, boutiques and pearl shops.

Free activities include outrigger paddle canoes, volleyball, ping-pong, French bowls and bicycles. Facing the hotel's white sand beach are three *motu* islets, which you can reach by canoe or boat. Tip'Nautic activities center is on the premises and will arrange your outings on the lagoon. See more information under *Nautical Activities* in this chapter. Scubapiti is a dive center based at the hotel, with a qualified instructor. See more information under *Scuba Diving* in this chapter. The reception staff will help you to arrange your vehicle rentals and paid activities, which can include hiking with Tahiti Evasion. See more information under *Hiking* in this chapter.

LES TIPANIERS ITI, *an annex to the main hotel, is located beside the lagoon at PK 20 in Papetoai, 4 km (2.5 mi.) from Hotel Les Tipaniers, 20 km (12.4 mi.) from the airport and 24 km (14.8 mi.) from the ferry dock. 5 local style bungalows with kitchens can accommodate up to 4 people. 2008 EP rates start at 8.200 CFP sgl/dbl and 8.950 CFP for 3-4 people per night, plus taxes. Special rates starting 7th night. Add 4.947 CFP per person for MAP and 8.568 CFP for AP meals at the main hotel. All major credit cards.*

"Little Tipaniers" has 5 thatched-roof bungalows with kitchenettes and beds for 3-4 people. A sun deck type wharf overlooks the entrance to magnificent Opunohu Bay. You have access to all the activities available at Les Tipaniers. A complimentary shuttle van will transfer you to the main hotel for dinner on request.

HOTEL HIBISCUS, *B.P. 1009, Papetoai, Moorea 98729. Tel. 689/56.12.20, Fax 689/56.20.69; hibiscus@mail.pf; www.hotel-hibiscus.pf. Beside the lagoon at PK 27 in Haapiti, next door to the former Club Med, 27 km (16.7 mi.) from the airport and 31 km (19.2 mi.) from the ferry dock. 2008 EP Rates: Garden Bungalow with fan 14.000 CFP 1-3; Lagoon View Bungalow with fan 16.400 CFP 1-3; A/C Room 16.000 CFP dbl; A/C Studio 27.000 CFP 4-5 people; extra bed 1.800 CFP. Add visitor and service tax. Add 5.250 CFP per person for MAP meals and 8.250 CFP for AP. All major credit cards.*

The 29 thatched roof bungalows are compact but comfortable, with beds for 3-4 people, tiled bathrooms with hot water showers, a separate toilet compartment, double sinks, a kitchen corner with a mini-refrigerator and 3-burner hot plate, plus cooking and eating utensils, wardrobe closet, ceiling fan, and a covered terrace with table and chairs. There are also 10 a/c rooms and 2 a/c studios in a 2-story building beside the swimming pool that can sleep 3-4 people. These units also have a kitchenette and a balcony or private garden. Le Sunset Restaurant is beside the white sand beach in front of Hotel Hibiscus, serving pizza and French, Italian and local cuisine. In addition to a fresh water swimming pool in the spacious gardens, and a white sand beach, you can rent a bicycle at the reception desk, sign up for island tours or check your e-mail with the Internet service provided.

This hotel attracts a mid-range clientele and is favored by Europeans, as well as New Zealanders. Owners Sylvette and Jean-Claude Perelli, who bought Hotel Hibiscus in 1993, are very helpful and friendly, and will make sure that your visit is a happy event.

FARE VAIMOANA, *B.P. 1181, Papetoai, Moorea 98729. Tel. 689/56.17.14; Fax 689/56.28.78; farevaimoana@mail.pf; www.fare-vaimoana.com. Beside the lagoon at PK 27 in Haapiti, west of Club Med, 27 km (16.7 mi.) from the airport and 31 km (19.2 mi.) from the ferry dock. 14 bungalows. 2008 EP Rates: Bungalow 15.000-21.000 CFP; Continental breakfast 1.300 CFP; American breakfast 1.800 CFP; Tahitian breakfast 2.200 CFP; MAP meals 7.200 CFP. Add visitor tax. All major credit cards.*

This small hotel is built beside a white sand beach, close to other hotels, restaurants, boutiques and pearl shops. The white concrete bungalows with pandanus thatch roofs offer beachfront, ocean view and garden accommodations. Each unit has a mezzanine and can sleep up to 5 people. They contain a refrigerator, safety box, bathroom, and a small terrace facing the lagoon. The windows are not screened and some of the units have no fans or hot water.

The small restaurant, bar and dining terrace are open to the sea, with a Polynesian flavor that includes posts carved as Marquesan tikis. Tahitian feasts are frequent events, as well as Saturday night (loud) music for dancing until 4 am. See more information under *Where to Eat* in this chapter.

FARE TAPU LODGE, *B.P. 2025, Papetoai, Moorea 98729. Tel. 689/ 55.20.55; Fax 689/56.32.79; tapulodge@mail.pf; www.tapulodge.com. On mountainside at PK 28.2 in Haapiti, 1 km. (0.62) miles from Le Petit Village. EP Rates: Small fare 15.900 CFP; large fare 26.500 CFP; add 1.500 CFP for extra bed. Add taxes.*

Six modern guest houses are built on stilts on the mountain slope overlooking Moorea's sunset coast of Haapiti. The smaller units are 70 sq. m. and have a king size bed plus a mezzanine with a single bed. The large *fares* are 120 sq. m, with 2 bedrooms, each furnished with a king size bed. There are also 2 single beds in the living room. All units have TV, a fully equipped kitchen, bathroom with hot water, and a balcony. A white sand beach is just 50 m. away. All land and lagoon activities are provided by Moorea Mahana Tours, and include a free boat transfer to the nearby motu.

MOOREA FARE MITI, *B.P. 1074, Papetoai, Moorea 98729. Tel. 689/ 21.65.59; mooreafaremiti@yahoo.fr; www.mooreafaremiti.com. Beside the lagoon at PK 27.5 in Haapiti, 27 km. (16.7 mi.) from the airport and 32 km. (19.2 mi.) from the ferry dock by the north coast. 2008 EP Rates 1-4 people: Garden Bungalow 13.000 CFP, Beach Bungalow 15.000 CFP. Extra person 2.000 CFP. Add taxes. No credit cards.*

There are 7 garden bungalows and 1 beach bungalow for rent on the property that was formerly part of the Hotel Moorea Village before it closed in Oct. 2005. These Polynesian style bungalows have a thatched roof, woven bamboo walls, screened windows and sliding glass doors with screens. Each unit has a bedroom with a queen size bed, living room with 2 day beds, floor fan, equipped kitchen with 2-burner electric stove, small refrigerator, pots and pans and dishes and utensils, bathroom with hot water shower, covered veranda with a big table and 4 chairs. A mattress can be added for a 5th person. A long white sand beach extends to the former Club Med and you can swim to the little motu in front of the pension. Sunset watching is magnificent from the beach. Rental bikes and scooters on premises and this is only a 10-minute walk to a food store, restaurants, snacks and shopping.

TE NUNOA BUNGALOW, *PK 32, Côté Montagne, Haapiti-Varari, Moorea 98729. Tel. 689/56.25.33; US 310/464-1490; stay@mooreabungalow.com; www.mooreabungalow.com. On the mountainside of the road, 32 km. (19.8 mi.) from the airport and 37 km. (22.9 mi.) from the ferry dock by the north coast. 2008 EP Rate: 154 Euro (approximately US$200) per night for 1-4 people. AE, MC, V.*

This brand-new all equipped Polynesian style bungalow is owned by Laurel and James Samuela. She is American and he is Tahitian and they live next door with their 2 children. Laurel owns 2 online travel companies: *wwwtruetahitivacation.com*, and *www.divetahitiblue.com*. James has a tattoo studio on the premises.

Te Nunoa, which means red sky or "that particular sunset when everything is red" is a true gem and an ideal choice for those who long to experience the Tahiti that exists outside of the hotels, without sacrificing luxury and comfort. The bungalow and its lush tropical garden are surrounded by a protective wall of bamboo and stone. Complete with a thatched roof and bamboo walls, the bungalow is lovingly furnished with a very comfy king size bed with a Memory Foam mattress, covered by a mosquito net. There is also a twin day bed with a twin trundle bed underneath that can slide out to accommodate a child. The furniture is teak, including 2 steamer lounge chairs. There are 2 ceiling fans, lamps, an electronic wall safe, satellite TV, CD player, telephone and high speed Internet access. The stainless steel kitchenette is on one wall of the big room, with nice wood cabinets, a 2-burner stove, toaster oven, and a big refrigerator with a freezer. The bathroom has tile from Spain, a hot water shower with a rain nozzle, a hair dryer and specially made fluffy bath and beach towels. There is original art on the walls, including black and white photos by Laurel and tattoo designs by James. Maid service is provided daily and laundry facilities are available, as well as a port-a-crib and high chair. Sliding doors lead to the private garden, where there is a *fare pote'e* shelter, a hammock and BBQ grill. Bicycles, snorkeling equipment and kayaks are available for guest use, and you will also have access to a pretty white sand beach across the road. The nearest food store is just a 5-min. walk and Le Petit Village is a 15-min. bike ride. Free transportation is provided to take you to a nearby dive center.

RESIDENCE LINAREVA, *B.P. 1 H, Haapiti, Moorea 98729. Tel. 689/ 55.05.65; Fax 689/55.05.67; linareva@mail.pf; www.linareva.com. Beside the lagoon at PK 34 in Haapiti, 21 km (13 mi.) from the ferry dock and 25 km (15.5 mi.) from the airport around the south coast. 2008 EP Rates: A/C Garden Studio with kitchenette 12.500 CFP sgl, 14.500 CFP dbl; A/C Garden Bungalow with kitchenette 11.500 CFP sgl, 13.500 CFP dbl; A/C Beachfront Studio with kitchenette 14.500 CFP sgl, 16.500 CFP dbl; 17.500 CFP triple; Beach Bungalow with kitchenette 15.500 CFP sgl, 17.500 CFP dbl; 18.500 CFP triple; A/C Beachfront Bungalow with kitchenette 21.500 CFP sgl/dbl, 27.500 CFP up to 6 people; Lagoon view Villa with kitchen 25.500 CFP up to 4 people, 28.500 CFP for 7 people. Extra bed 1.300 CFP. Add 50 CFP per adult for visitor tax. Minimum of 2 night stay required. AE, MC, V.*

This small family hotel overlooks a small beach and Moorea's sunset sea and has a 3-tiare rating from the Tahiti Tourist office. Each of the 8 units is lovingly and tastefully decorated with a refined Polynesian touch. You have a choice of king size, double or single beds, according to the unit chosen. All the kitchens are well equipped with stove and refrigerator, toaster and coffee maker, and cleaning products are provided daily. Five of the units have a/c and they all have a ceiling fan, TV, safety box, library of books, private tiled bathroom with hot water shower, and a covered terrace. Daily maid service is provided, and you can even have breakfast delivered to your room for 1.550 CFP. Bicycles, snorkeling gear, outrigger canoes, kayaks and barbecue grills are free for guest use, and there's a sunbathing deck on the long pier. There is a public phone in the garden and an Internet service in the reception/boutique area, which you can pay for with a local phone card. Free Wifi service is available in all the bungalows. There is no longer any restaurant on the premises, as the floating restaurant, Le Bateau, was closed at the end of 2006. The reception has a list of restaurants that will provide free pick-up service. Linareva's owners, Eric and Florian, also own the popular Raimiti family pension on a private motu in Fakarava. Read about it in the *Tuamotu* chapter.

HAAPITI SURF LODGE, *Haapiti, Moorea 98729. Tel./Fax 689/56.40.36; cell 72.64.84; haapitisurf@mail.pf. On the mountainside at PK 22.5 in Haapiti. Round-trip transfers included. EP Rates: 8.500 CFP sgl/dbl for first night, with digressive rates for longer stays. Add 1.500 CFP per day for a/c and 1.500 CFP per day for extra bed. No charge for child under 12 years. Add taxes. No credit cards.*

There are 4 modern white concrete bungalows on the mountainside overlook-ing the surfing pass of Haapiti, where the spinner dolphins play inside the lagoon year round and the humpback whales swim just beyond the reef between July and early November. Petero Tehuritaua, the young Tahitian owner, built his surfing lodge in 2001 and has everything well organized for his guests. Each clean and attractively furnished bungalow has a double bed, TV, ceiling fan, (a/c on request), equipped kitchen and a bathroom with hot water and a bathtub/shower, as well as a terrace with a dining table and individual barbecue grills. One of the units is a Honeymoon bungalow, built a little higher than the other three, offering a better view of the lagoon, the pass and the romantic tropical sunsets. Guests with children can put up a tent in the yard beside their bungalow. There is also an outdoor shower.

Petero provides his guests with kayaks and bicycles at no charge, and he will also take you on a tour of the island in his 4WD. There is a long pier on the beach side of his property, where you can fish and swim You can buy fish from vendors on the road or bike to the nearest magasin store for food supplies, which is only a kilometer away. Meals can be provided on request for charter groups of 8-10 people. They will even provide laundry service for long-stay guests.

MARK'S PLACE MOOREA BUNGALOWS, *B.P. 41, Maharepa, Moorea 98728. Tel./Fax 689/56.43.02; cell 78.93.65; www.marksplacemoorea.com. On mountainside at PK 23.5 in Haapiti, in front of the surfing pass, 25 min. from Vaiare ferry dock and 35 min. from Temae airport. Pick-up at ferry dock 1.000 CFP per person; from airport 1.500 CFP. 2008 EP Low/High Season Rates: Fare Aute Private bedroom 5.000/6.000 CFP sgl./dbl; Fare Miti 7.000/9.000 CFP sgl./dbl; Fare Fetia 8.000/10.000 CFP sgl./dbl.; Fare Tiare, Fare Manu and Fare Mahana 8.000/10.000 CFP sgl./dbl, 10.000/12.500 CFP 3-4 people, 12.500/15.000 CFP 5-6 people; Fare Manu and Fare Mahana 7-8 people 2.500/3.000 CFP per person. Fare Reva 2.000/ 2.500 CFP sgl; Fare Ie camping space 1.050 CFP per person. Add taxes. MC, V.*

Look for the Mark's Place Moorea Bungalows sign beside the circle island road just past the Eglise de la Sainte Famille, the Catholic Church with twin towers. Follow the dirt road into the valley until you see the bungalow complex on the right. Owner Mark Walker, an American expatriate builder and wood worker who has lived in French Polynesia for many years, has built 7 quality bungalows on his grassy property, and he still has more plans in the works for improving his accommodations. These include wooden studios and bungalows that are perfect for couples, families or groups, with sleeping accommodations for 2, 6 or 8 people. All units are equipped with a kitchen, bathroom, satellite TV and stereo. Some of the studios and bungalows also have a living room, deck and barbecue grill. Check Mark's website to choose the accommodation you prefer.

Bicycle and kayak rentals are available for 1.000 CFP per day, and a snorkeling mask and fins are 500 CFP per day. A load of washing is 1.000 CFP and there is a public phone on the premises. In addition to surfing the pass in Haapiti, Mark's guests enjoy hiking over the mountains and participating in the other activities that are available on Moorea.

FARE ARANA, *B.P. 3351, Temae, Moorea 98729. Tel./Fax 689/56.44.03; gautierfabienne@mail.pf; www.farearana.com. On mountainside at PK 19.5 in*

Atiha, 15 min. from the ferry dock and 20 min. from the airport. 2008 EP Rates sgl/ dbl.; Small bungalow 9.900, large bungalow 11.900 CFP. Add 2.500 for 3rd person. Taxes included. No credit cards.

High on a hillside overlooking Avarapa Bay, Fare Arana offers panoramic views of the ever-changing colors of the lagoon and ocean. The verdant gardens are filled with fruit trees and flowers, providing the perfect setting for 4 thatched roof bungalows of high quality and craftsmanship. Three of the concrete bungalows have a/c and 70 sq. m. (753 sq. ft.) of living space. On the mezzanine there are 2 double beds and 1 single bed, all with mosquito nets. The ground floor has a living/ dining area with TV and ceiling fan, a well-equipped kitchen, and a bathroom with hot water shower. The furniture is teak and bamboo and the windows and doors are screened. Steps from the covered terrace and open sundeck lead down to the gardens and pool area, where you can relax in an elegant hammock.

There is also a smaller bungalow with a double bed and a folding settee, a ceiling fan, kitchen, bathroom with hot water, and an iron. A BBQ grill is available on request and guests can use the washing machine. Owners Nicolas and Fabienne Gautier are offering Internet packages of 2-4 days that include hikes, 4WD excursions, boat tours, deep-sea fishing, hovercraft and quad excursions, and a visit to Tiki Village.

Economy

CAMPING NELSON, *B.P.1309, Papetoai, Moorea 98729. Tel./Fax 689/ 56.15.18; campingnelson@mail.pf; www.camping-nelson.pf. Beside the lagoon at PK 27.1 in Haapiti, 27.1 km (17 mi.) from the airport and 31.1 km (19.5 mi.) from the ferry dock. EP room 4.800-6.300 CFP sgl/dbl; Tahitian fare 5.000 CFP sgl/dbl; dormitory 2.000 CFP per person; camping 1.300 CFP per person per day. Discounts starting second night. Taxes included. MC, V.*

In addition to a spacious campground by the sea, this backpacker's hostel offers 10 dormitory rooms for 2 people, plus a variety of rooms and *fares*. Everyone shares the 7 toilets, 7 showers with cold water and the lavabos and there is also a toilet and shower for handicapped guests. The communal kitchen and dining room are adjacent to the reception area, or you can order take away dishes in the snack bar. They also own Restaurant Tumoana next door, which serves Chinese and Polynesian food. Information on activities and rental vehicles and kayaks is available at reception. There are several restaurants, snacks, food stores, pearl shops and souvenir shops in the immediate neighborhood.

MOOREA CAMPING, *Haapiti, Moorea 98729. Tel. 689/56.14.47; Fax 689/56.30.22; einui@hotmail.com Beside lagoon at PK 27.5 in Haapiti, 500 m from ex-Club Med, 27.5 km (16.7 mi.) from the airport and 31.5 km (19.2 mi.) from the ferry dock. 2008 EP Rates: room 2.500-3.800 CFP sgl/dbl; bungalow 4.800–5.800 CFP sgl/dbl, 6.000-7.000 CFP triple, 6.500-7.500 CFP 4 people; bed in dormitory 1.200-1.800 CFP per day, camping 1.100-1.500 CFP person per day. Rates include all taxes. No credit cards.*

This is a gathering place for backpackers and campers and adventurers from all parts of the globe. There is a pretty white sand beach here and some organized activities are available at reduced rates. There are four bungalows for two people, one bungalow for 3 people, and one bungalow for four people. Nine rooms have double or single beds, and there are two dormitories with 3 or 5 berths. A communal kitchen and dining room is built beside the beach, and the communal bathrooms have cold water. House linens are furnished but you bring your own soap and towel. You can camp in the gardens, under the trees or beside the beach. Bikes and kayaks can be rented at reception. Check-in is at 11am and checkout is at 9am.

Afareaitu to Vaiare – Moderate

TE ORA HAU, *B.P. 4005, Maharepa, Moorea 98728. Tel./Fax 689/56.35.35; cell 77.48.22; pensionteorahau@mail.pf; www.teorahau.com. Beside lagoon at PK 8.2 in Afareaitu, facing Motu Ahi, 4.2 km (2.6 mi.) from the Vaiare ferry dock and 8.2 km (5 mi.) from the airport. EP fare 13.500 CFP dbl, 6-person fare 22.000 CFP, plus visitor tax. No credit cards.*

You'll sleep to the sounds of the ocean in this environment that resembles that of the Tuamotu Islands, complete with a white sand beach, sea breezes blowing through the pandanus trees, and a motu islet right in front of you. In the distance, however, you can clearly see the island of Tahiti with its mountains and houses. Your Polynesian hostess, Heipua Bordes, has 3 large wooden bungalows or *fares* that are completely equipped with a kitchen, washing machine and bathroom with hot water shower. The bungalows are clean, modern and very tastefully decorated and the bed linens are changed every 3 days. BBQ grills and kayaks are provided. Heipua is well versed in the culture and legends of Polynesia and she has taught her cleaning staff to speak a little English. You can shop for groceries at Champion Fare Toa, which is 1.7 mi. from the pension. Cars, scooters and bicycles can be rented at the nearby ferry dock in Vaiare.

Other Family Pensions, Guest Houses, Surf Lodges, Dormitories & Camp Sites

Island Rainbow Pension, *Tel. 689/56.35.10/73.98.43; claudine@tahiti-experience.com.* 5 screened bedrooms, big kitchen and 2 bathrooms with hot water for rent by day, week or month in big house on mountainside at PK 5 in Maharepa. Small refrigerator and coffee/tea facilities in each room. EP room 5.000 CFP dbl; a/c room and breakfast 8.000 CFP dbl. Weekly package with activities for 10-12 people. Owner Claudine Ro'ometua speaks good English.

Fare Oa Oa, *Tel./Fax 689/56.25.17; fareoaoa@magicmoorea.com.* 4 rooms and dormitory with shared bathroom and kitchen on mountainside at PK 13 in Pihaena, 4.000 CFP sgl., 6.500 CFP dbl., 3.000 CFP dorm., including breakfast. English spoken.

Moorea Fare Auti Ura, *Tel. 689/56.14.47.* 6 bungalows with kitchens on mountainside at PK 27, across road from Moorea Camping, for 5.800 CFP. MC, V.

Pension Teataura, *Tel. 689/56.22.01*. 5 simply furnished studios with kitchenettes on seaside in Haapiti, for 9.000 CFP sgl/dbl 1st night and 7.000 CFP 2nd night. Monthly rentals.

Fare Matotea, *Tel. 689/56.14.36; Fax 689/56.32.54; mtt@mail.pf; www.farematotea.com*. 9 bungalows on a spacious property beside the lagoon at PK 28.7 in Haapiti, with one bedroom for 9.540 CFP and 2 rooms for 11.130 CFP. All units have a living room, equipped kitchen, bathroom with hot water and a terrace.

Fare Manuia, *Tel. 689/56.26.17; Fax 689/56.10.30; kinarei@hotmail.com*. 6 *fares* at PK 30 in Haapiti. Standard bungalow 11.200 CFP for 1-4; garden bungalow 14.000 CFP for 1-6; and beach bungalow 17.000 CFP for 1-6. All units have kitchens, terrace and hot water showers. English spoken.

Fare Edith, *Tel. 689/56.35.34/75.01.05; fareedith@mail.pf*. 2 garden bungalows and 2 beach bungalows beside lagoon at PK 32.5 in Varari. One or two bedrooms, living room, kitchen, covered terrace, private bathroom with hot water, laundry, garage, a/c in one bedroom in family unit, ceiling fans, TV, mosquito nets. EP rates: 8.000 sgl, 11.500 CFP dbl, up to 17.000 CFP for 5-6 people.

Tarariki Village, *Tel. 689/55.21.05; pensiontarariki@mail.pf*. 6 rustic bungalows, tree houses and 2 dormitories beside beach in Vaianae, near surfing pass. Dorm 1.600-2.300 CFP, bungalow 5.500-7.520 CFP sgl/dbl.

Fare Aute, Tel. 689/56.45.19/78.23.34; pension.aute@mail.pf; www.pensionaute.com. 5 well-equipped bungalows for 4-6 people include kitchens, ceiling fans, mosquito nets, hot water, TV and washing machine, on the white sand beach at PK 16.2 in Atiha, for 11.700-16.000 CFP per night. No English.

Chez Pauline, *Tel. 689/56.11.26; Fax 689/83.71.21*. 7 rooms in an old colonial style wooden house (opened in 1918) at PK 9.8 in Afareaitu village. Room and breakfast 4.000 CFP sgl/5.500 CFP dbl. Restaurant on premises.

Nature House of Mou'a Roa, *Tel. 689/56.58.62/72.62.58; Fax 689/56.40.47; mouaroa@mail.pf; www.lamaisondelanature.com*. 8 rooms in a big colonial style house on an agricultural farm in Vaianae valley at PK 21 between Haapiti and Atiha. Experience a "green" vacation and biologic meals. MAP room 8.700 CFP; AP room 9.700 CFP. Guided hikes.

WHERE TO EAT
Airport & Motu Temae – Deluxe

SOFITEL MOOREA BEACH RESORT, *Tel. 55.12.12. Restaurant Pure is open daily for B, L, D and snacks. Restaurant K serves D only. Bar Vue on the beach is open daily 10am-10:30pm. All credit cards.*

Restaurant Pure is the main dining room, which serves an American breakfast for 2.901 CFP, a set luncheon menu for 3.148 CFP, and a set dinner menu for 6.451 CFP. Luncheon fare is 1.820-2.980 CFP for starter courses and 1.720-2.930 CFP for the main dishes. Snacks are served from 2:30-6pm, offering salads for 1.920 CFP, a Club sandwich for 2.330 CFP and a cheeseburger for 2.530 CFP.

The *a la carte* dinner menu lists appetizers for 1.320-2.520 CFP, main courses for 1.720-3.130 CFP, lobster for 6.870 CFP, and desserts for 1.320-1.730 CFP. You can order wines from Argentina, Chile, Italy, France, New Zealand and Tahiti. Theme nights include a Round the World buffet on Tues. for 7.200 CFP; a Polynesian buffet on Thurs. for 8.400 CFP, serving traditional Tahitian food cooked in the underground oven; and a Pacific buffet on Sat., featuring seafood for 7.800 CFP. There is a dance show each night during dinner in Restaurant Pure.

Restaurant K (for Kahaia tree) is the resort's gourmet restaurant, where you are required to dress elegantly for dining with your feet in the sand floor. The beachy atmosphere becomes a romantic setting with candlelight. The menu lists choices from 1.900-6.500 CFP, which include parrotfish, gambas, roast pig, veal chops, beef filet and lobster. Diners are entertained by the Te Vahine show on Tues. and Sat. evenings.

Bar Vue serves all your favorite drinks plus some exotic cocktails. You can sit on the terrace and watch the lights of Tahiti across the Sea of Moons.

Cook's Bay Area: Maharepa to Paopao – Deluxe

MOOREA PEARL RESORT & SPA, *Tel. 55.17.50. Mahanai Restaurant is open daily for B,L,D. Matiehani Restaurant is open for D. Autera'a Bar & Terrasse serves L and cocktails. All credit cards.*

The **Mahanai Restaurant** opens onto the view of the swimming pool, lagoon and overwater bungalows. An American breakfast is 2.750 CFP, a set luncheon menu is 3.500 CFP and the set dinner menu is 5.950 CFP. The Polynesian buffet is held each Wed. night for 6.600 CFP, followed by a Polynesian dance show, and a Seafood buffet and dance show takes place each Sat. night, for 7.900 CFP per person.

You can also eat your lunch while sitting at the spacious **Autera'a Bar & Terrasse** facing the pool. A choice of menus allows you to eat between 12 and 2pm or between 12 and 4:30pm. Interesting selections include a panini for 1.500 CFP, a Caesar salad with grilled chicken for 1.600 CFP, a club sandwich for 1.800 CFP, a Moorea salad with shrimp and pineapple for 1.850 CFP, burgers and fries for 1.700 CFP up, and a Polynesian plate for 2.200 CFP, which includes sashimi, tuna tartare, poisson cru and Nems (spring rolls).

Matiehani is the name of the a/c gourmet restaurant that serves dinner nightly except on Wed. and Sun. Seating for maximum of 12 people. Gastronomic French cuisine includes appetizers for 2.700-3.200 CFP, fish and seafood for 3.950-4.950 CFP, and meat choices for 3.900-4.500 CFP. Sweet Temptations are 1.550-1.900 CFP. Candlelight dining is also available on the terrace overlooking the lagoon.

HONU ITI, *Tel. 56.19.84, PK 8, beside Cook's Bay, Pao Pao. MC, V. Open L, D. except Sun. noon and all day Wed. Courtesy shuttles between Sofitel and Intercontinental Moorea Resort.*

In 1974 Roger Igual won France's most prestigious diploma for chefs—the Concours National de la Poêle d'Or. That same year he brought his cooking skills to Tahiti, and since 1991 Roger has been serving his gourmet specialties to Moorea diners. The overwater terrace of his Honu Iti restaurant provides a privileged setting, where you can gaze at the romantic scenery of Cook's Bay, bordered by pineapple fields and fairy castle mountains, while enjoying some of the island's finest French cuisine. In the evening you can feed the rays and fish that swim close to the terrace, hoping for handouts.

Appetizers are 1.500-2.200 CFP, which include a tasty French onion soup and a sea snail pie in a casserole. Fish and seafood specialties are 3.200-4.700 CFP, featuring mahi mahi with vanilla sauce and scallops served with leeks. Roger's famous Tournedos Rossini at 3.800 CFP is the very best, which is beef tenderloin with goose liver in Madeira sauce. His meat and poultry dishes are priced from 2.900-3.800 CFP. My favorite meat choice is the very tender beef Bourguignon, marinated in red wine for 2.900 CFP, and his osso bucco Milanese is 3.800 CFP. Desserts are 1.200-1.400 CFP and include the chef's special apple pie with ice cream, as well as homemade chocolate cake or Crêpes Suzette. Wines feature some tempting *grands crus* from France's best vineyards.

Superior

LE MAHOGANY, *Tel. 56.39.73, PK 5, mountainside, Maharepa. MC, V. Open 11am-2:30pm and 6-9:30pm. Closed Wed. Reserve for dinner. Pick-up service available.*

This popular indoor-outdoor restaurant is the first restaurant on the mountainside you will see when coming from the airport or ferry dock toward Cook's Bay. A street-side chalkboard lists the daily specials, which may be veal Marengo for 2.150 CFP, cassoulet for 2.750 CFP, or gambas for 2.850 CFP. In addition to a varied menu of French cuisine, they also serve a few Chinese dishes, including good chow mein from 1.450-2.250 CFP. The shrimp curry with coconut sauce is 2.250 CFP and highly recommended. The soups and salads are 980-2.250 CFP; seafood dishes are 1.950 to 2.650 CFP and meat dishes are 2.150-3.150 CFP. Burgers and fries are served at lunchtime, along with a selection of salads and grilled rib eye steak.

LE COCOTIER, *Tel. 56.12.10, PK 4.7, mountainside, Maharepa. Diners, V. Open Mon.-Fri. B., L, D. Closed Sat. noon, and all day Sun. Free pick-up service between Sofitel and Sheraton resorts.*

Pascal Mathieu, the manager and chef, presents a varied menu of well-prepared dishes that are served in the open-air restaurant, on the terrace or inside the a/c dining room. The menu of classic French cuisine lists starter courses for 750-2.100 CFP, fish choices at 2.150-2.350 CFP, meats from 2.050-2.950 CFP, and desserts at 850-1.450 CFP. A chalkboard on the wall lists the chef's suggestions of the day, which may be a bouillabaisse for 2.850 CFP, stuffed crab for 2.950 CFP, or *St. Jacques au calvados* for 2.850 CFP. A 3-course tourist menu is 4.200 CFP. You can order wine by the glass or bottle, and choices include some of the *grands crus* from the best vineyards of France.

LE SUD, *Tel. 56.42.95, Pizzeria, Tel. 76.42.40. PK 5.5, seaside on Cook's Bay, Maharepa. MC, V. Open L, D. Tues.-Sat., and D. on Sun. Closed Sun. noon and all day Mon. Free pick-up service from Sofitel to Sheraton Resort.*

You can order thin-crust pizzas for 1.150-1.600 CFP to eat here or take away. The open sided restaurant also serves French cuisine, such as fish and seafood couscous for 2.850 CFP, paella for 2.950 CFP each (min. 2 people), kangaroo steak for 2.490 CFP, ostrich steak for 2.690 CFP, or tournedos Rossini for 3.490 CFP. A tourist's menu is 4.950 CFP and a child's menu is 1.490 CFP.

ALFREDO'S, *Tel. 56.17.71, VHF Channel 69; chrismar@mail.pf; www.alfredosofmoorea.com, PK 8.5, mountainside, Cook's Bay, Pao Pao MC, V. Open daily 11am-2:30pm and 5:30-9:30pm. Pick-up service available. Reserve on Thurs. and Sun. evenings.*

This indoor-outdoor restaurant can seat 100 and on Thurs. and Sun. evenings it is often filled with American tourists and other lively people who come for "party night". This is when Ron Falconer, a Scottish musician, plays his body harp and harmonica and sings songs from the 1960s and 1970s. As the evening progresses the show really gets "Rollin' on the River" and you can also get up and sing with Ron if you feel in the mood. Or you can dance the jitterbug, twist or rock 'n roll. Some people enjoy themselves so much that they come back for dinner almost every night during their week's stay.

I take most of my houseguests here to enjoy the fun, ambiance and music and to have a good giggle with owner Christian Boucheron, a Frenchman who lived in the States for 21 years, where he owned several restaurants. Christian's dedicated team offers friendly, attentive service. Some people find the food very expensive and only so-so, but they enjoy the music and atmosphere. The menu gives you a varied choice of Italian or French cuisine. For 600 CFP you can order garlic bread to nibble on while you sip your cocktail, beer or glass of wine. Appetizers are 1.550-2.450 CFP, pasta dishes are 2.350-3.750 CFP, and pizza is 1.650 CFP. You'll pay 3.500 CFP for osso bucco or Fettuccine Alfredo, and 3.950 CFP for shrimp and lobster profiterole. Meats and poultry are 2.450-3.850 CFP including my favorite, escalope de veau Milanaise for 3.250 CFP. The wine list includes half-bottles and bottles of Bordeaux, or wine by the glass. Alfredo's has an interesting cocktail menu, which includes virgin cocktails for 1.150 CFP, exotic cocktails for 1.450 CFP, and erotic cocktails with naughty names for 1.550 CFP.

RUDY'S, *Tel. 56.58.00/70.47.47. On mountainside at PK 6 in Maharepa. MC, V. Open daily for L,D. Free pick-up service.*

This a/c Spanish hacienda style restaurant opened in early 2007 featuring fine steaks and seafood, with seating for 50-60 people. Owner Syd Pollock has successfully owned or managed several hotels and restaurants in Moorea and Tahiti since 1968, and is known for his hospitality in receiving and pleasing his guests. Although he is training his son Rodolphe (Rudy) to take over the reigns of the business, Syd is usually on hand to lend a hand and say hello.

Starter courses are 950-2.300 CFP and include breaded seafood, snails in puff pastry and fois gras poelé. Fish dishes are 1.900-2.450 CFP and rock lobster medallions flamed in pastis are served on a bed of pasta for 3.450 CFP. Meats are a specialty at Rudy's, priced at 2.100-3.250 CFP. Choices include beef tartare, tournedos Rossini, tenderloin of lamb, spare ribs, T-bone and rib of beef. The desserts are 850-950 CFP and Rudy's has just the right wine to accompany your meal. There is usually live music during dinner on Wed., Fri., and Sat. nights.

Moderate

MARIA TAPAS, *Tel. 55.01.70, is in the Kikipa Center at PK 6 in Maharepa. MC, V. Open 11am-2pm and 6-9pm on Mon., Wed., Thurs. and Fri. Open Sat. 5pm-1am. Closed all day Sun. and Tues. They pay half of taxi fare from hotels if you come for dinner.*

This combination restaurant, snack, bar and cybercafé serves salads for 450-1.700 CFP and burgers for 1.200-1.600 CFP. Tex-Mex specialties are 950-2.200 CFP, a Greek salad is 1.600 CFP, and the main course is 1.900-2.400 CFP. A *plat du jour* (daily special) is 1.200 CFP and tapas are 550-650 CFP. The beer menu includes 30 choices from all over the world. Salsa music is played for dancing on Wed. night and live or recorded dance music is played on weekends. Half-price beer is served during Happy Hour on Thurs. (6-7pm) and Fri. (6-8pm). One or two computers can be used to connect to the Internet.

HOTEL KAVEKA RESTAURANT, *Tel. 56.50.50, PK 7, Maharepa. All credit cards. Open daily for breakfast, lunch and dinner. Courtesy shuttle available.*

This spacious overwater restaurant has a fantastic view of Cook's Bay and the peaked mountains that fringe the mirror-like waters of the bay and lagoon. This is an especially agreeable place to cool off during the hot tropical summers, while enjoying a glass of cold beer or a good meal.

A Parisian breakfast is 1.000 CFP, the buffet breakfast is 1.800 CFP and the American breakfast is 2.500 CFP, including taxes. The luncheon and dinner menu includes an appealing list of appetizers, priced from 950-1.450 CFP, and salad plates for 1.950 CFP. Burgers and fries are 1.350-1.550 CFP and sandwiches are 850 CFP. Pizzas are 1.650 CFP, fish and seafood dishes are 1.600-2.850 CFP, and beef dishes are 2.100-2.500 CFP. Chinese dishes are 1.000-2.300 CFP per plate. Desserts are 750-1.200 CFP and a kid's menu is 1.500 CFP with dessert. Cocktails are 1.300 CFP and wine is served by the carafe or bottle.

ALLO-PIZZA, *Tel. 56.18.22, is on the mountainside at PK 7.8 in Pao Pao, across the road from the French gendarmerie (police station). Open 11am-2:30pm and 5-9pm Tues.-Sat. Closed all day Sun. and Mon. noon. No credit cards.*

You have a choice of 43 thin crust pizzas cooked in a wood burning pizza oven, which includes salmon pizza and banana pizza, priced from 1.200-1.900 CFP. A grilled steak, baked potato and green salad cost 1.950 CFP. Be sure to try the homemade chocolate mousse and freshly baked bread. You can eat at the counter or take it to your room. They will deliver a minimum of 2 pizzas to your hotel within the limits of Sofitel Moorea and Sheraton Moorea.

BLUE PINEAPPLE (l'ananas bleu), *Tel. 56.12.06. Club Bali Hai Bar, Pao Pao. MC, V. Open daily 7am-3pm and for dinner on Wed. nights.*

This waterside restaurant offers an incomparable view of Cook's Bay, yachts in the harbor and pineapple fields on the jagged mountain slopes across the bay. Burgers with fries start at 860 CFP, *poisson cru* is 1.250 CFP, grilled fish is 1.950 CFP and beef curry is 1.850 CFP. You can order soft drinks, juice, a milkshake and even a banana split, as well as beer and wine.

The Wed. night BBQ follows the free Tahitian dance show presented by Club Bali Hai. You can order chicken, steak, or seafood kabobs for 1.800-2.400 CFP. I also like to eat here on Sunday mornings or holidays, when owner Matahai Hunter prepares a typical Tahitian breakfast of marinated fish with coconut milk, grilled fish, *taioro* (sour coconut sauce with onions), *firi firi* (a figure 8 donut), and coffee flavored with vanilla and sweetened with coconut milk and sugar. If that sounds too heavy for your appetite, perhaps you'll prefer a glass of fresh pineapple juice for 500 CFP. You can also order pancakes for 650 CFP, eggs with ham or bacon or a Spanish omelets for 850 CFP, or steak and eggs for 1.650 CFP.

CHEZ JEAN-PIERRE, *Tel. 56.18.51, PK 9, beside the quay in Cook's Bay, Pao Pao. MC, V. Open 11am-2:30pm and 6-9:30pm. Closed Mon. night, all day Wed. and Sun. noon.*

The specialty here is family style Chinese food, but they also have some French dishes, which are quickly prepared and served in their two dining rooms adjacent to the fishing boat dock at Cook's Bay. Soups and appetizers start at 1.150 CFP. The seafood dishes are 1.650-2.150 CFP, chicken and duck are 1.450-1.650 CFP and beef and pork choices are 1.550-1.750 CFP. Specials include tofu, mahi mahi with citron sauce and braised beef.

Economy to Moderate

CARAMÉLINE, *Tel. 56.15.88, PK 5, Maharepa, in shopping center on mountain side, along with Socredo Banque and the post office. MC, V. Open daily 7am-5pm.*

Here is the ideal place to sit and write your post cards while enjoying something good to eat and drink. You can exchange your dollars at the bank, buy post cards at Kina newsstand, write them at Caraméline and mail them at the post office, all in the same small center.

Breakfast is available all day at this popular snack and pastry shop. A Continental breakfast is 990 CFP, an American breakfast is 1.550 CFP, and a Tahitian breakfast that includes fish and coconut milk is 2.100 CFP. They serve ham and cheese croissants, quiches and pizzas, hot dogs, burgers, crêpes, and good salads at affordable prices. Poisson cru with coconut milk is 1.380 CFP and the daily luncheon specials are 1.300-1.600 CFP, which may be steak and fries, veal in a white sauce, garlic shrimp or mahi mahi with rice or fries. Along with fresh fruit juices, fresh limeade and Hinano beer, you will also have a good choice of ice creams, 25 flavors of milkshakes for 490 CFP, and a banana split or pineapple split for 770 CFP. Don't forget to check out the pastry counter inside. Service may be slow when the place gets crowded.

Economy
   SNACK ROTUI, *Tel. 56.18.16, PK 9.5, beside Cook's Bay, just after Are's Supermarket in Pao Pao. No credit cards. Closed Mon.*
   This is the best snack bar on the island, with very fresh food at budget prices. You can sit on a stool at the counter, eat at one of the tables in back or take away a sandwich and soft drink, a *poisson cru*, lemon chicken, or other prepared Chinese dishes served with rice for 700 CFP. Don't resist having a piece of yummy chocolate cake. For 180-200 CFP you can get a *casse-croûte* (omelet, chow mein, ham and cheese, tuna or ground beef), and the big nems or spring rolls and fried chicken are also good here.

Paopao to Haapiti – Deluxe
   SHERATON MOOREA LAGOON RESORT & SPA, *Tel. 55.11.11. Arii Vahine Restaurant serves B,L, D daily and L & D are also served at Rotui Pool Bar & Grill. Toatea Bar on the pier serves crêpes in the evening. Snacks and cocktails are available in the Eimeo Lounge Bar. All major credit cards.*
   In the **Arii Vahine Restaurant** the breakfast buffet is 2.780 CFP. A 2-course lunch is 3.980 CFP and a 3-course dinner is 6.480 CFP. The à la carte dinner menu includes French onion soup or pumpkin soup for 1.000 CFP, starter courses from 1.500-2.650 CFP, vegetarian dishes for 1.500-1.900 CFP; fish and seafood dishes for 3.350-4.250 CFP, and meats from 3.200-4.200 CFP. Grilled lobster is 5.500 CFP. A Mediterranean buffet is presented each Tues. evening for 7.200 CFP, which includes a Polynesian dance show. A special Seafood Buffet on Sat. night is 8.200 CFP per person, and also includes a traditional dance show.
   Rotui Pool Bar & Grill, beside the white sand beach, is open daily from 10am-9pm. The lunch menu includes salad choices for 1.800-2.200 CFP, including Cobb Salad and a delicious Chinese salad with sliced chicken breast, rice noodles, cabbage, onions, almonds and crispy wanton. Sandwiches are 1.800-1.900 CFP, including a Polynesian cheese steak sandwich. Paninis are 1.400 CFP, burgers start at 1.600 CFP and desserts are 350-1.150 CFP, including a banana split and a strawberry sundae. The dinner menu includes 6 pizzas priced 1.400-1.600 CFP, and 3 main courses starting at 2.500 CFP. The grilled mahi mahi with vanilla sauce is divine! This is one of my favorite restaurants on Moorea. Wine is sold by the glass or bottle and they have Hinano on draft.
   Toatea Bar is on the overwater pier nearest the main buildings of the hotel. They serve your favorite crêpes for 800-1.600 CFP nightly except Tues. and Sat., when there are special buffets and a dance show in the Arii Vahine Restaurant.
   Eimeo Bar serves your favorite libation at sunset, and you get two drinks for the price of one during Happy Hour, which takes place between 5:30-6:30pm daily except Thurs., when the Manager's Cocktail Party is held. Short drinks (Margaritas,

Cosmopolitan, whisky sour) are 1.200 CFP, long drinks (mojito, pisco sour, Long Island Ice Tea) are 1.350 CFP, and Polynesian cocktails are 1.500 CFP. You can also order dry snacks (mini quiches, spicy buffalo wings, Asiatic plate or shrimp cocktail) for 1.000-1.400 CFP. Live music is played at the bar on Fri. and Sun. evening.

INTERCONTINENTAL MOOREA RESORT & SPA, *Tel. 55.19.19. Fare Nui Restaurant is open daily for B., D., and Fare Hana Restaurant is open daily for L. All credit cards.*

Fare Nui Restaurant presents an Express breakfast for 1.332 CFP, a Continental breakfast from the cold buffet for 2.625 CFP, and the full buffet or American breakfast is 3.197 CFP. Breakfast delivered by outrigger canoe to guests in overwater bungalows is 6.090 CFP per person. The dinner menu features gourmet *à la carte* dining, with soups for 960-1.240 CFP, starter courses from 1.960-2.610 CFP, meats at 3.020-4.180 CFP, and fish and seafood dishes from 3.020-4.180 CFP. Grilled lobster is 5.140 CFP, and desserts are 940-1.445 CFP. A fixed 3-course dinner menu is 6.560 CFP. Barbecue Night is held each Wed. beside the swimming pool, accompanied by a Tahitian dance show, for 7.065 CFP. The *Soirée Merveilleuse* on Sat. evening is a gastronomic buffet featuring a variety of fresh seafood, usually served on the beach under the stars, accompanied by A Tahitian dance group. This costs 9.052 CFP.

Fare Hana Restaurant beside the pool serves a luncheon of salads for 1.330-2.200 CFP, Polynesian dishes such as shrimp, tuna, sashimi, and smoked fish, from 1.600-1.985 CFP. Club, mahi mahi, or steak sandwiches are 1.295-1.920 CFP, and burgers start at 1.440 CFP. A 3-course set luncheon menu is 4.400 CFP. A Sunday Buffet lunch is served to the tune of a musical trio.

Motu Iti Bar is an attractive, spacious lounge and sit-down bar in the main building, overlooking the pool and beach. The drink menu lists non-alcoholic cocktails for 1.050 CFP, classic cocktails for 1.250 CFP and their own cocktails for 1.350 CFP. Here you can order a Sea Breeze, Cucumber Martini, Balsamic Martini, Frozen Mango Margarita or a Strawberry Daiquiri. They also have Hinano beer on tap. A jazz group entertains on Sat. from 5-7pm.

Moderate to Superior

AITO RESTAURANT, *Tel. 56.45.52/23.27.63. Beside lagoon at PK 13.1 between Cook's Bay and Opunohu Bay. Closed all day Tues. and at noon on Wed. MC, V. Free pick-up service to some hotels.*

In a previous edition of this book I wrote that every island needs a funky beach-shack restaurant where you can eat deliciously prepared fish served by a "boozy" Corsican, and that Jean-Baptiste Cipriani and his Aito Restaurant play this role in Moorea. Since then the restaurant has been cleaned up, improved, and enlarged to seat 70 people in the overwater restaurant, on a covered terrace and under the sky on the beach. Jean-Baptiste also cleaned up his act, replacing his daily intake of 10 glasses of scotch and Coke with a shandy or panaché of beer and soda. This restaurant is still my favorite hangout, and everyone I have ever taken here just loved the setting, the food and Jean-Baptiste, who is a real character.

Aito Restaurant is a thatch-covered terrace at the edge of the lagoon. Tall Australian pines (*aito* in Tahitian) shade the small beach and three big *aito* trees grow right through the floor and sagging palm-frond ceiling of the restaurant. A series of Plexiglas windows can be propped open with a stick so you can enjoy the fresh ocean breezes. This is a most delightful place to be on a hot summer's day, when you can feel the trade winds blowing, gaze across the sparkling lagoon to the white line of spume on the reef and watch the gray herons and white fairy terns as they fish nearby.

Vanina, Jean-Baptiste's Tahitian wife, is in charge of the kitchen and makes superb poisson cru, tuna carpaccio and local style fish dishes. The daily specials are listed on a chalk board, which may be Antillaise style stuffed crab for 2.600 CFP, shrimp flambéed with pastis for 2.800 CFP, meka with ginger and soy sauce for 2.800 CFP, or flambéed slipper lobster (cigale de mer) for 4.500 CFP. The printed menu lists appetizers for 1.280-2.200 CFP, fish for 1.980-3.800 CFP, mako shark with a choice of sauces for 1.900-2.500 CFP, meats for 1.950-2.550 CFP, and bouillabaisse for 3.950-5.450 CFP for a minimum of 2 people. It takes Jean-Baptiste 10 hours to make the special sauce for his Corsican dishes such as Tagliatelle à la Cargesienne, Chicken Sartenaise, Red tuna à la Bonifacienne, or Corsican style steak. These dishes are 1.850-2.600 CFP.

Jean-Baptiste grows his own hot peppers and puts small bowls of pepper sauce on each table, which he says goes well with the food he serves, accompanied by crunchy baguette bread and butter. It's even better when you wash it down with a spicy Bloody Mary or a bottle of wine. Desserts are 780-1.350 CFP and may include coconut or banana pie, tarte tatin or a pineapple surprise. The house specialty is the Crêpe Aito for 1.050 CFP.

A musical duo performs every Friday night, featuring a country and blues singer and Hawaiian tunes played on a lap steel guitar. Jean-Baptiste provides free transfers for lunch or dinner guests staying at the Intercontinental Moorea Resort, Sheraton Moorea Lagoon, Club Bali Hai, Kaveka, Moorea Pearl Resort or in family pensions in those areas. Transfers to the Sofitel Moorea Beach Resort are free for a minimum of 4 people.

Jean-Baptiste also operates **Aito Pension**, which is on the same premises. He has 3 rooms on the ground level, each with a private bathroom and kitchen. A new honeymoon suite has the bedroom upstairs and the coral floor bathroom with bathtub is on the ground level. They are priced from 5.500 CFP to 12.500 CFP, with special discounts after the third night. He serves breakfast, lunch and dinner to his pension guests, provides them with free snorkeling gear and even has rental bikes.

West Coast: Haapiti – Superior
   LA PLANTATION, *Tel. 56.45.10, www.laplantationmoorea.com, PK 27, on*

*mountain side just past Le Petit Village in Haapiti. AE, MC, V. Open 11:30am-
9:30pm, non-stop service. Closed all day Tues. and Wed. noon. Free pick-up service
to certain hotels.*

This large open-air restaurant has seating for 70 inside and on the covered
terrace near the street, which can be quite noisy in the daytime. Refined French
cuisine features pan-fried fois gras, as well as crab, lobster, shrimp and other local
products prepared with lots of spices. You will also find the Cajun flavor of
Louisiana in the crabcake, jambalaya, and roasted crawfish dishes. Appetizers are
1.400-2.950 CFP and include Creole Gazpacho and crab gratin with Cajun spices.
Fish dishes are 2.400-3.200 CFP, shellfish are 2.800-4.500 CFP, and meats are
2.700-3.600 CFP. A Discovery Menu is 4.500 CFP and a Cajun Menu is 5.100
CFP. Desserts are 950-1.300 CFP and include chocolate brownies with vanilla ice
cream and maple syrup caramel, or a Plantation Cup with praline vanilla,
chocolate, whipped cream and Donatella sauce. Cocktails for 1.300 CFP include
drinks with such names as Cajun Bloody Mary, Blue Suede Shoes, Hit the Road
Jack, and Soul Man. Tax-free wines are 2.420-69.270 CFP.

The luncheon menu suggests soup and salads for 950-1.300 CFP, main
courses for 1.900 CFP and desserts for 750 CFP. A simple light menu of salads,
poisson cru and sashimi is served in between lunch and dinner for afternoon diners.
You can also come to La Plantation for drinks without having to order food. They
have a stage and a piano and every other week they feature live entertainment. The
music for dancing includes jazz, rock and roll, rhythm and blues and soul music.
There is no reggae, techno or local music played here. Free pick-up service is
provided for a minimum of 2 people staying at the Intercontinental Moorea and
for 4 people staying at the Sheraton. A special treat available at lunch time only is
a helicopter transfer from the airport in Tahiti to the back yard of La Plantation.
You will be flown around one side of Moorea when arriving and on the other side
of the island when returning to Tahiti.

Moderate to Superior
   LE MAYFLOWER, *Tel. 56.53.59, PK 27, Haapiti, seaside. Open Tues.-Sun.
11:30am-2:30pm and 6:30-10:30pm. Closed all day Mon. and Sat. noon. AE, MC
and V.*

This is the best restaurant in the Haapiti section of Moorea, and perhaps the
choice place to dine out on the island. It is located beside the road next door to Hotel
Hibiscus. Laurence and Bertrand Papin are the French owners who chose the name
Le Mayflower because Americans identify with that name. The nautical décor
includes an old oak barrel, photos of ships, wooden ceiling, walls and floor, brass
lights, oil lamps and thick cords of rope. An intimate ambience is added by soft
lighting and soft music, live plants, pink tablecloths and fresh flowers on the table.

Bertrand is a young chef from the Loire region of France, whose impressive
haute-cuisine française has pleased Moorea diners for years, first at Le Cocotier, then
at Le Pitcairn restaurant, before he opened his own restaurant. Appetizers are

priced at 950-2.300 CFP, fish and seafood dishes are 1.850-2.900 CFP, and meat and poultry choices are 1.950-3.250 CFP. His specialties change nightly, and may include beef Bourguignon for 2.300 CFP, osso bucco Milanaise for 2.300 CFP, or scallops sautéed with Calvados sauce for 2.900 CFP. The *piece de resistance* is lobster ravioli, which is usually available as an appetizer or main dish for 1.900-2.850 CFP. There are also vegetarian dishes for 1.500-1.950 CFP. A child's menu of chicken nuggets and ice cream is 1.200 CFP, and a 3-course tourist menu is 4.200 CFP. Desserts may include crème brûlée for 950 CFP, and profiteroles with hot melted chocolate sauce and whipped cream for 1.050 CFP. Wines are priced from 2.240-27.370 CFP. This is definitely a restaurant worth trying and returning to again and again.

FARE VAIMOANA, *Tel. 56.17.14, PK 27, Haapiti, seaside. Open daily for B,L,D. All major credit cards.*

This hotel restaurant is not visible from the road, but it is well worth a little detour toward the lagoon at the same lane that leads to Camping Nelson. You can watch the action on the beach and lagoon while eating in the attractive little restaurant or on a covered terrace beside the sea. A Continental breakfast is 1.300 CFP, and an American breakfast is 1.800 CFP. The luncheon menu includes burgers for 700-900 CFP. Appetizers are 1.750-2.650 CFP, seafood is 2.200-3.550 CFP, and meat dishes are 2.250-3.650 CFP. Desserts are 800-1.200 CFP and a tourist menu is 5.750 CFP.

PAINAPO BEACH, *Tel. 55.07.90, painapo@mail.pf; is on the seaside at Painapo Beach, PK 33 in Haapiti. Open for lunch Thurs.-Mon. 9am-3pm. Closed Tues.-Wed. No credit cards.*

This is a good place to spend the day, swimming in the lagoon, sunbathing on the white sand beach and enjoying a delicious lunch under the shade of almond trees overlooking the lagoon. Or you can eat inside the big thatched roof dining room with a white sand floor. A platter of *poisson cru*, red tuna sashimi, carpaccio of tuna and tuna tartare makes a nice lunch for two and costs 4.200 CFP. This is served with taro and breadfruit chips and rice. Add a few slices of fresh French baguette and a nice bottle of wine, and you might not even have room for dessert. Other specials include a selection of cooked fish, shrimp, fresh *pahua* (tridacna clams) from the reef or crab with garlic or ginger sauce. You can also order sandwiches, salads and other light meals, as well as drinks, at the thatched roof snack bar beside the road. Ma'a Tahiti (Tahitian food) is served on some Sundays for 3.500 CFP. Thursday is Tahitian Day, when you can watch demonstrations of traditional activities, such as weaving palm fronds and making floral crowns and heis. See more information under *Tahitian Feasts* in this chapter.

Moderate

LES TIPANIERS, *Tel. 56.12.67, PK 25, seaside, Haapiti. All credit cards. Beach Bar Restaurant open daily 7-9:30am and 12-2 p.m. Main restaurant open daily for dinner 6:30-9:15pm. All major credit cards. Best to reserve.*

Although the beach space is limited here, you will usually find groups of French people sunbathing, swimming in the lagoon, participating in a variety of water sports, or reading in the shade. Breakfast and lunch are served in the beachside restaurant. You can order burgers and sandwiches for 980-1.380 CFP, salads from 650 CFP, and pasta from 980 CFP. Fish and grilled meats are 1.800 CFP. Take-away sandwiches are less than 500 CFP. Live Tahitian music at the beach bar each Fri. from 5:45-6:45pm.

Dinner is served in the main restaurant beside the road, featuring pasta and fine Italian specialties from 980-1.580 CFP, and French dishes such as fish soup for 1.050 CFP and lamb sirloin with goat cheese for 1.980 CFP. Ron Falconer plays the body harp and harmonica and sings Scottish and folk songs, blues and old favorites from the 1970s every other Sat. night, starting at 7pm in the main restaurant.

RESTAURANT IRENE, *Tel. 56.15.93, PK 25.5 on mountainside, between Les Tipaniers and Le Petit Village in Haapiti. Open for Sun. breakfast and for L., D. Tues.-Sun. noon. Closed Sun. night and all day Mon. MC, V. Pick-up service to some hotels.*

This is a very popular and friendly local style restaurant featuring seafood and Polynesian cooking. Meals are served on the open-air terrace and inside the restaurant, which may be rather hot during the daytime as this restaurant does not benefit from ocean breezes. Starter courses are 500-1.200 CFP, chicken is 1.200-1.500 CFP, meats are 1.500-1.700 CFP and shrimp dishes are 1.800 CFP. Specialties include poisson cru for 900 CFP, pahua (reef clam) curry with coconut milk for 1.800 CFP, a duo of shrimp and chicken for 2.000 CFP, and a duo of shrimp and octopus for 2.500 CFP. Desserts are 400 to 700 CFP, with such delights as fried bananas and ice cream or baked papaya with ice cream.

IGUANE ROCK CAFÉ, *Tel. 56.17.16, PK 26 in Le Petit Village in Haapiti. Open daily with non-stop service from 7am to midnight. Closed Sun. night. MC, V.*

This is an ice cream parlor, bar, snack, pizza parlor and a full service restaurant, with a menu offering French, Tahitian and Chinese foods. The dining rooms can seat 150 people and a special area is provided for children, where they play in security while the parents dine in tranquility. Burgers start at 1.350 CFP and pizzas are 1.500 CFP. There is a cybercafé with Internet connections in the back corner.

BUS STOP, *Tel. 56.41.19, PK 27 in Haapiti, across street from Le Mayflower. Open 11am-3pm and 6:30-9:30pm. Closed Wed. MC, V.*

Owner Cédric Brocard is a young French chef who cooked at some of Moorea's top hotels before opening his own restaurant-snack and pastry shop. His specialties include homemade bread, macaroons and cakes, as well as spring rolls and innovative French dishes priced from 1.500-2.750 CFP.

PK 0, *Tel. 56.55.46/28.06.70, PK 27.3, Haapiti. MC, V. Open for L., D. Closed all day Mon. and at noon on Tues.*

Isabelle, the friendly and vivacious young French owner of this restaurant/ lounge, chose the name PK 0 because she said it is the beginning, the meeting place.

Local musical groups from Tahiti or Moorea play here on Thurs., Fri., and Sat. nights. You can order tapas for 700 CFP, Chinese dishes for 1.000 CFP and special dishes of shrimp or tuna for 1.200-2.300 CFP.

LE SUNSET, *Tel. 56.26.00, PK 27, on the beach at Hotel Hibiscus, Haapiti. MC, V. Open daily for B,L. D.*

You'll pay 1.200 CFP for a Continental breakfast, 1.950 CFP for an American breakfast, or you can order a la carte. You can eat pizzas, grilled meats and homemade pastas or sip a cold beer while sitting at a picnic table on the open deck overlooking the white sand beach, the lagoon and the nearby *motu* islets. Or you can sit inside the restaurant and look at the enormous rubber trees that grow at the edge of the hotel's spacious lawn. Sandwiches are 700 CFP, burgers with fries are 1.300 CFP, salads are 1.300-1.500 CFP, sashimi or poisson cru are 1.600 CFP, a choice of 11 thin crust pizzas are 1.400 CFP, fish dishes are 1.850-2.200 CFP, steaks are 2.100-3.200 CFP, the plat du jour is 2.000 CFP, a 3-course tourist menu is 3.300 CFP and the kids' menu offers several choices for 1.500 CFP. Desserts are 800-1.200 CFP and wines are 2.200-7.500 CFP per bottle. Draft beer is 450 and 700 CFP.

TUMOANA PLAGE, *Tel. 56.37.60, PK 27.1, Haapiti, on seaside adjacent to Fare Vaimoana. Open Sun. for B, L., D. and Tues.-Sun. for L., D., closed Mon. MC, V.*

You'll be caressed by ocean breezes while dining on the covered terrace overlooking the white sand beach and lagoon. They serve Chinese dishes for 900-1.800 CFP, fish and seafood dishes for 1.500-1.950 CFP, and steak for 1.900 CFP. A Tahitian breakfast is available on Sun. morning and good *ma'a* Tahiti (Tahitian food) is served buffet style at lunch on Sun. for 4.000 CFP. A Tahitian trio plays music on Fri. night and Sun. afternoon. The Tahitian servers are very friendly and efficient. See more information under *Tahitian Feasts* in this chapter.

LE PAPAYER, *Tel. 55.02.50, PK 30, at Tiki Village in Haapiti. AE, MC, V. Open Tues.-Sat. 12-3pm. and 6-10pm. Closed Sun. and Mon.*

This is a good luncheon choice while you are visiting the traditional Tahitian style Tiki Village. The thatched roof open-air restaurant overlooks the lagoon and coral reef, providing a beautiful view as well as good food, served *a la carte*. A mini-show is provided at 1pm by the young dancers and musicians from the Tiki Theatre Village. If you feel like becoming a Tahitian Chief and wining and dining your Princess in tropical splendor, then reserve the Royal Floating Fare, a private houseboat, where your lunch will be served by canoe and set upon a glass bottom table on the terrace. You can enjoy your meal and admire the beautiful multicolored fish while taking in the spectacular surroundings.

A big buffet of Tahitian food and international dishes is served in Le Papayer restaurant each Tues., Wed., Fri. and Sat. evening, when the Tiki Theatre Village dancers and musicians present a spectacular Polynesian show. Please see further information under *Tahitian Feasts* and the *Nightlife & Entertainment* sections of this chapter.

Economy to Moderate

LE MOTU, *Tel. 56.16.70, PK 26, Haapiti, in St. Jacques Center, right across street from ex-Club Med. MC, V. Non-stop service Tues.-Sun. 9:30am-8pm. Closed Sun. night and Mon. night.*

This is a good choice for salads from 600 to 1.400 CFP, crêpes for 800 to 1.000 CFP, 15 choices of pizzas from 1.050 to 1.300 CFP. Sashimi, carpaccio of tuna and poisson cru are 1.300 CFP. You can choose from 13 kinds of burgers for 470 to 800 CFP and a plate of fries is 450 CFP. Steaks are 1.500 to 1.800 CFP and daily specials are 1.400 to 1.600 CFP. They have an unusual selection of sandwiches that are served on half a loaf of the crusty French *baguette*. My favorite is the ground beef sandwich, which is grilled hamburger meat, with lettuce, tomatoes, onions and mayonnaise spread on a *baguette*. It is much bigger and better than the hamburgers on buns and costs 450 CFP. It's not on the menu they give you at the tables because most people get it to go. The bar is well stocked and there are several imported beers and soft drinks in the cooler.

Economy

DANIEL'S PIZZA, *Tel. 56.39.95.* PK 34.1 seaside, close to Linareva in Haapiti. No credit cards. Open 11am-9pm. Closed Thurs.

This is where you'll find the best pizza on the island. Daniel has built a wood-fired pizza oven in his garage and you can sit on a stool and eat at the wooden counter or take it with you. He offers 13 choices of pizza priced from 1.300 to 1.500 CFP. No alcohol is served. Look for his sign beside the road on the seaside just before you get to Hotel Linareva.

Other Restaurants, Snacks & Roulottes

La Petite Maison, *Tel. 56.34.80.* Small restaurant adjacent to bridge in Pao Pao, open daily for L, D. Tahitian, Chinese and French food, paella and seafood couscous at economy prices. **Jules et Claudine**, a stationary roulotte beside the quay and fish market in Cook's Bay, Pao Pao. Quality of food varies but is usually good. **Motu Iti**, *Tel. 55.05.20*, Restaurant for Pension Motu Iti at PK 13.2 in Pihaena. B., L., D. Salads, pizzas and local style meals. **Le Patio**, *Tel. 56.12.70*. A restaurant and café with non-stop service in Le Petit Village in Haapiti, serving pizza and Mediterranean specialties. **A l'Heure du Sud Roulotte**, a stationary roulotte on mountainside between Le Petit Village and La Plantation restaurant. **Snack Coco d'Isle**, *Tel. 56.59.07.* On lagoon side at PK 27.5, Haapiti. Good food, good prices. Closed Sun. Pizza, chow mein, special Backpacker, Globetrotter or Surf plates. **Royal Chicken**, *Tel. 78.53.53.* A stationary roulotte next to Magasin Aimeo in Haapiti. Open L, D., closed Mon. Provençale style rotisserie chicken and rosemary herbed potatoes to go. **Chez Teina**, *Tel. 56.29.29.* Restaurant/snack at PK 13,200 on seaside in Maatea. Open L.D. Closed Mon. Best Chinese food on the island. Eat here or takeout. **Pauline Restaurant**, *Tel. 56.11.26*, on mountainside in center of Afareaitu village. Open daily for L.,D, serving local style meals.

Tahitian Feasts

PAINAPO BEACH, *Tel. 55.07.90, on the seaside at Painapo Beach Village, PK 33 in Haapiti. No credit cards.*

A Tahitian feast is served buffet style at noon on certain Sundays, according to the tourist season, so it is best to telephone in advance. All the traditional favorites are included: *poisson cru* with coconut milk, *pua'a chou* (a pork stew with cabbage and carrots), *poulet fafa* (chicken and taro leaves with coconut milk), roast breadfruit, *fei*, (mountain plantains), cooked bananas, sweet potatoes, taro and tarua (root vegetables), baked fish, roast pig, *po'e* (a sweet dish with coconut milk and bananas, papaya or pumpkin), and both fresh and fermented coconut milk sauces to dip your food into. *Fafaru* (a stinky but good marinated fish once you've acquired the taste for it) is also on the buffet table, covered with a plate to hold the smell inside. This excellent food costs 3.500 CFP per person, and you can eat outdoors under the shade of almond trees or inside the thatched roof dining area with a sand floor.

SOFITEL MOOREA BEACH RESORT, *Tel. 55.12.12, PK 2, Temae. All major credit cards. Reserve.*

The Tahitian underground oven is opened at 6:30pm each Thurs. evening and a Polynesian buffet of Tahitian food is served in Restaurant Pure, followed by a Polynesian dance show at 8pm, which may also include fire dancing. The cost of 8.400 CFP per person is for the food and show only. Drinks and wine are extra.

TIKI THEATRE VILLAGE, *Tel. 55.02.50, PK 30, Haapiti, AE, MC, V.*

A big buffet of Tahitian food, as well as grilled meats and fish, is served in Le Papayer Restaurant each Tues., Wed., Fri. and Sat. evening, when the Tiki Theatre Village dancers and musicians present a spectacular Polynesian show, complete with fire dancing. The *ahima'a* underground oven is opened as part of the cultural visit through the village. Even if you don't like the looks or tastes of Tahitian food, there are other, more familiar choices of foods served. The total price for unlimited welcome punch, the dinner buffet with all the house wine you want, a guided visit through the Tiki Village and a dance show with 60 performers is 8.700 CFP. Round trip bus transfers from the airport, the boat dock or any hotel on the island is 1.150 CFP.

TUMOANA PLAGE, *Tel. 56.37.60, PK 27.1, Haapiti, on seaside adjacent to Fare Vaimoana.. MC, V.*

A Tahitian breakfast of vanilla flavored coffee, fried fish, firi firi doughnuts, taioro coconut and other traditional foods is available on Sun. morning. A full buffet of *ma'a* Tahiti is served at lunch on Sun. for 4.000 CFP, to the tunes played by a trio of Tahitian musicians. The atmosphere is reminiscent of Tahiti some 20 years ago—happily laid-back island style.

SEEING THE SIGHTS

Look for the **PK** (*poste kilometre*) markers on the mountainside of the road, which are placed one km (.62 mi.) apart. The signs are in concrete in the shape of Moorea, which resembles a heart. PK 0 is located at the old post office in **Temae**, close to the airport road. If you're coming from the airport and turn right onto the circle island road, you'll soon see the PK 1 marker opposite Lake Temae, which was actually a swamp filled with nonos (stinging flies) before the golf course was built. You can see the Moorea Green Pearl Golf Course on both sides of the newly repaved road.

The distance markers continue on around the northwest coast to the village of **Haapiti** to PK 35, and then there's a gap in the numbering system. Here you'll want to photograph the **Mou'a Roa** and **Tohivea mountains** that rise in the distance behind the soccer field. On the seaside is a Protestant Church. The next marker you'll see will be PK 24, where another lovely landscape of the mountains is visible from the courtyard of the Catholic Church, **Eglise de la Saint Famille**. The PK numbers then descend from PK 24 to PK 4, where you'll find the Ferry dock at **Vaiare Bay**, and then on down to PK 0, where you'll see the old Temae post office again. The newer post office is in the commercial center of **Maharepa** at PK 5.

At the end of Opunohu Bay at PK 18 you can leave the circle island road and turn left onto a partially paved inland road that passes through the **Opunohu Valley**. Here you will see horses, cows, sheep and goats grazing in verdant green pastures under the shadow of Moorea's sacred **Rotui Mountain**. There is an agricultural school in this valley and the students look after the livestock. Beside this road, in a forest of *mape* Tahitian chestnut trees, are restored *marae* temples of stone and ancient archery platforms, where the Maohi chiefs and priests used to worship and play. **Le Belvedere** is a popular destination at the top of a steep and winding road, and from the **Lookout Point**, at the end of a torturous road, you have the visual pleasure of **Cook's Bay** and **Opunohu Bay** far below, which are separated by Mt. Rotui. You continue on along the *route des ananas* (the pineapple road), where you'll see the mountain slopes of Pao Pao valley covered with pineapple plantations. Forests of mahogany, teak, acacia and mangoes border the rutted red dirt road, which leads you back to the circle island road at PK 9 in the village of **Pao Pao**.

Land Tours

The **Circle Island Tour** takes you by minivan or large bus on a 3.5 to 4-hr. voyage along the coastal road, winding around Cook's Bay and Opunohu Bay and inland to the Opunohu Valley, with stops at the *marae* of Titiroa and the other Polynesian stone temples and archery platforms in this area, the Belvedere Lookout, pineapple fields, vanilla plantation, and to the Moorea Fruit Juice Factory & Distillery, where you can taste different liqueurs made with the fruits of Moorea. This tour sells for 3.000 CFP up.

The **Mountain Safari Tours** and **Photo Safari Excursions** are also usually half-day tours, varying according to the guides, which sell for 4.000-5.000 CFP. In addition to the sights and sites mentioned above, these 4WD excursions also take you off the main road to discover groves of oranges and pamplemousse (grapefruit), gardens of lush tropical fruits, medicinal plants, rosewood, tamanu, coffee plantations, soft green meadows and a jungle undergrowth of ferns and bamboo. The highlight of this excursion is a visit to the waterfalls of Afareaitu, which includes a 15-min. hike uphill and a refreshing splash under the cascade of water. You will discover Moorea from the mountain to the sea and learn all about the history, culture and daily lives of the people of Moorea.

Here are some of the companies and guides who will be happy to show you Moorea:

Albert Transport & Activities, *Tel. 55.21.10/55.21.11/78.46.60; Fax 56.40.58; www.albert-transport.net.* This family business was established in 1962 and is the oldest operating tour company on Moorea. Albert Haring's guides are usually his sons, who grew up in the tour business. They provide a combined circle island tour and interior island tour by a/c bus with shopping at the Haring's family-owned pearl boutiques, Heivai and Moorea Black Pearl. Private VIP tours and taxi service are also available.

Hiro's Tours/What To Do On Moorea, *Tel. 78.70.10/56.57.66.* Hiro Kelley has an activity desk in the reception area of Club Bali. His 4WD Safari Tour operates daily departing at 8:15am and 1:15pm for a 4-hr. tour, for 4.000 CFP per person. Hiro's guides speak English and know the history and legends of Moorea.

Inner Island Safari Tours, *Tel. 56.20.09/78.70.88/72.84.87; Fax 56.34.43; www.innerislandsafari.com.* Alex and Ghislaine Mahotu operate half-day inner island photo tours in a/c and open jeeps. They also take you to "Magic Mountain," where you will climb the side of a crater for a 360-degree view. Be sure to bring your camera. These are very well informed guides, who speak good English.

Moorea Explorer, *Tel. 56.12.86/78.70.72; www.mooreatransport.com.* Moorea Transport has a big fleet of Explorer yellow buses, vans and 4WD vehicles, all decorated with fish. You'll see them everywhere on the island. They'll take you on a half-day full Circle Island Tour (Belvedere) by a/c bus, or you can sign up for the Aito Safari off-road half-day tour by 4WD. They also offer private safari and sunset safari tours, as well as a special shopping tour at Le Petit Village.

Torea Nui Transport & Safari, *Tel. 56.12.48/77.01.52, enttoreanui@mail.pf.* They offer a half-day Safari Tour by 4WD and they also operate a transfer service for only 600 CFP per person, providing transportation from the airport or ferry dock to your hotel, or from your hotel to other locations on the island. You must reserve in advance. See additional information under *Tour & Transport Companies* in this chapter.

Special Activities & Sightseeing Stops Around the Island

Agricultural Lycée of Opunohu has a **Fare Boutique**, *Tel. 56.11.34, www.etablissement-opunohu.com.* On the right as you drive up the mountain to visit Le Belvedere. In addition to tasting the delicious fresh fruit juices, you can buy their vanilla and coffee beans, dried bananas, crystallized fruits, homemade jams and hand-painted *pareos*. You can also visit the high school farm and see the vanilla plantations, greenhouse, tropical orchards and vegetable gardens. The Fare Boutique has maps of three discovery walkways that will take you along marked paths for hikes of 1-2 hrs. for each choice. Open Mon.-Thurs. 8am-4:30pm, on Fri. 8am-3:30pm, and on Sat. 8am-2:30pm. If you want to hike a trail be sure to arrive at least 2 hours before closing time.

Moorea Fruit Juice Factory and Manutea Tahiti, *Tel. 55.20.00*, on the mountainside at PK 12 in Cook's Bay. Boutique open Mon.-Fri. 8:30am-4:30pm and Sat. 9am-4pm. Visit distillery Mon.-Thurs. You can taste the various liqueurs, including the prize-winning ginger brandy, and you can take home Rotui fruit juices, Paina Colada (*paina* means «drunk» in Tahitian), chocolate and coconut liqueur, Tahiti Drink rum punch, bottles of Tahitian rum and a whole range of Tahiti-Manutea confections and candies made with local fruits.

Nature House of Mou'a Roa, *Tel. 56.58.62; www.lamaisondelanature.com*, is located in the Vaianae Valley between Haapiti and Atiha. You turn off the circle island road at PK 21 (there is a sign) and walk up the valley until you come to the big colonial house that was built in 1900. It is surrounded by lush green foliage and tropical flowers and twin rivers flow through the property. Be sure to sample the farm's homemade organic jams, honey and fruit pies. Phone ahead if you want to stay for lunch or spend the night. You may even want to participate in one of the sports activities organized by Bernard Genton. These include archery, rope rappelling down to the river, mountain skating, riding mountain bikes and hiking. A 4WD Photo Safari takes you into the heart of Vaianae valley for 5.000 CFP per person. Morning and afternoon departures daily.

Painapo Beach, *Tel. 55.07.90*, is on the seaside at PK 33 in Haapiti. Just look for the giant sized tattooed warrior beside the road. It is open daily except Tues. and Wed. and you can spend the day in this welcoming place. Bring your swimsuits, towels, protective shoes and snorkeling equipment, and rent a kayak to explore the lagoon or just take it easy on the beach, playing in the lagoon and sipping a cold beer under the shade of big almond trees on the big grassy lawn overlooking the beach and lagoon. There is no admission charge and there are toilets and showers. You can also order sandwiches, salads and other light meals, as well as drinks, at the thatched roof snack bar, or you can enjoy a fresh fish platter at a table under the shady trees. See more information under *Where to Eat* and *Tahitian Feasts* in this chapter.

Motu Moea, *Tel. 56.55.37/74.96.96*, also known as Motu Tiahura, is across the channel from Les Tipaniers and the ex-Club Med beach. You can spend a few hours snorkeling in the coral gardens, enjoying the private white sand beach or lounging in a hammock under the shady trees in this privileged setting. **Restaurant La Plage** serves lunch, specializing in French and Tahitian cuisines. Paid boat transfers are provided at 10am and 12pm, returning at 2pm and 4pm. Call them for information on boat transfers.

Maiau Beach, *Tel. 70.78.58*, is on Motu Moea (Motu Tiahura). A private section of the white sand beach has been transformed into a protected environment where individuals, organized groups, clubs or associations can spend the day on the beach, take a private snorkeling tour, sunset cruise or enjoy a feast of *ma'a Tahiti* cooked in an underground *ahima'a* oven. Bill Gates celebrated his 40th birthday here in Nov. 2005, along with Paul Allen and 22 other guests from Allen's super yacht. Maire and Jean-Pierre transfer their clients from the beach at Hotel Les Tipaniers to their private paradise, where you will find lounge chairs, an ice chest, refrigerator, barbecue grill, and picnic tables. This is not a snack or restaurant, but they do have bottled water and ingredients for a barbecue.

Tahiti Arome, *Tel. 56.14.51*, is at PK 26 in Haapiti, behind the Royal Tahiti Noni factory. Open Mon.-Thurs. 8:30am-3:30pm. The botanical gardens here contain the largest plantation of Tiare Tahiti in French Polynesia, as well as 50 species of plants used throughout the world in the manufacture of cosmetics and perfumes. Here you will see how the vanilla orchids are "married" and learn about the healing powers of tamanu oil.

Temae Beach is where the locals go to swim, play games on the beach and in the water and have picnics on the white sand. A good surfing spot is located nearby. This is also the starting or ending point for outrigger canoe races, international marathons and other big events. There are public toilets and showers, as well as trashcans, but unfortunately, the whole area gets littered during busy holidays or long weekends. Turn off the circle island road across from the old post office at PK 0, and follow the dirt road for about one km, bearing left where you see a fork, and you can park in the shade across from the public park. This beach connects with the private beach fronting the Sofitel Moorea Beach Resort, which is off-limits to the public.

NIGHTLIFE & ENTERTAINMENT

Tiki Theatre Village, *Tel. 55.02.50*, at PK 30 in Haapiti, is a cultural and folkloric center that you can visit by day or four evenings a week. Multilingual guides lead you through the village of thatched roof *fares* where you will see demonstrations of how to carve tikis from stone, how to sculpt wooden bowls, weave a hat, make a floral crown and tie-dye a pareo. You can get a traditional Tahitian or Marquesan tattoo and learn how the ancient Tahitians built their homes and meeting houses. You can swim in the lagoon, paddle an outrigger canoe, visit their black pearl farm in the lagoon or sunbathe on the beach. You can also browse around in the Tiki Village boutique, Virgin's black pearl shop and the Maison du Jouir art gallery, where Paul Gauguin prints are for sale. You can enjoy an *a la carte* lunch in Le Papayer restaurant and watch a mini-dance show at 1pm. Tiki Village is open Tues.-Sat. from 11am to 3pm. They are closed on Sun. and Mon. The entrance fee to the village during the daytime is 1.500 CFP, which includes a visit around the village and to the pearl farm, plus the mini-show. Transportation from the hotels, airport or boat docks is 1.150 CFP per person.

Each Tues., Wed., Fri. and Sat. evening the 60 dancers and musicians at the Tiki Theatre Village present a Polynesian extravaganza. The program begins at 6pm with a welcome fruit drink or rum punch. You will be immersed in the culture and tradition of Polynesia, with demonstrations of arts and crafts and dancing techniques. After the opening of the *ahima'a* underground oven a bountiful buffet is set out, featuring Tahitian specialties, Continental cuisine, barbecued fish, chicken and meats, along with a salad bar and dessert table. Be sure to sample the delicious fried coconut beignets.

While you are enjoying your meal you'll be treated to a very lively demonstration of how to wear the *pareo*. After dinner the big show gets underway at 9pm in the open-air theater with a white sand floor. This spectacular dance show includes several fire dancers, all muscular men with beautiful tattoos. Everyone here works very hard and puts all their energy and enthusiasm into entertaining you. I highly recommend this **Great Polynesian Revue**. The cost of the buffet dinner, all the punch you want, as much wine as you wish to drink during dinner, plus the extravaganza show, is 8.700 CFP. You can also come back to visit the Tiki Village during the daytime without paying an additional entry fee. Round-trip transportation is 1.150 CFP per person. The cost of seeing the show without dinner is 4.300 CFP, plus transfer.

Maria Tapas, *Tel. 55.01.70*, in Maharepa has live or recorded music for dancing on weekends and sometimes during the week.

La Plantation, *Tel. 56.45.10*, in Haapiti has live entertainment every other Thurs. evening, with music for dancing. No reggae or Tahitian style music is played.

PK 0, *Tel. 56.55.46/28.06.70*, is a restaurant/lounge in Haapiti that is transformed into a nocturnal hot spot on Thurs., Fri. and Sat. evenings. Musical groups from Tahiti and Moorea play jazz, blues, rock, and other kinds of music, and there's room for dancing.

Ron plays the auto harp and harmonica and sings songs from the 1960s and 1970s, plus a little country and Celtic folk songs. You can catch his act at **Alfredo's** every Thurs. and Sun. evening and at **Les Tipaniers** every other Sat. night.

Several of the larger hotels have barbecues, special theme evenings and Tahitian feasts, followed by Tahitian dance shows. The regular events are listed for each hotel in the *Where to Stay* section of this chapter. More entertainment is added during the high seasons of July-August and for the Christmas-New Year holidays.

Some of the smaller hotels as well as individual restaurants also offer live entertainment once or twice a week throughout the year. In addition to the places listed above, you can listen to live music at **Rudy's**, **Aito's**, **Vaimoana** and **Tumoana**. See more information under *Where to Eat* in this chapter.

Billy's Club in Haapiti has occasional all-night dancing, with live bands playing Tahitian and disco music, and the atmosphere is very local. Special all-night balls (*bals*) are held at the sports stadiums (Salles Omnisports) on occasion, usually on a Sat. night. These dances are usually sponsored by soccer teams, outrigger canoe teams and other sports groups, and provide the perfect occasion to meet some of the local young people and to learn how to dance Tahitian style.

SPORTS & RECREATION

All Terrain Vehicle/Quad

ATV Moorea Tour, *Tel. 56.16.60/70.73.45; www.atvmooreatours.com.* Located at PK 24.6 in Tiahura, across road from Intercontinental Moorea Resort. Free pick-up. A 2-person ATV 4WD can be rented with a guide for 2 1/2 hours for 14.000 CFP or 3 1/2 hours for 19.000 CFP.

Golf

Moorea Green Pearl Golf Course Polynesia, *Tel. 56.27.32; www.mooreagolf-resort.com.* Open daily 7:30am-5pm. This 18-hole, par 70 Jack Nicklaus Design golf course lies on both sides of the circle island road between Moorea's airport and the village of Temae. A tunnel under the road allows golf carts to circulate from the lagoon to the mountain side of the course, which is 6,002 m. (6,596 yds). There is a clubhouse, pro shop, driving range on the lake, a putting green and chipping green. Green fees start at 6.000 CFP for 9 holes and an 18-hole green fee with golf cart is 14.000 CFP. You can rent clubs, golf balls, shoes, caddies and golf carts, and professional golf lessons are also available.

The overall golf course project is spread out over nearly 165 hectares (408 acres) of land with a 650-m. (710-yd.) white sand beach. When the Moorea Golf Resort is completed it will also offer a spa and fitness center, a 150-room 5-star hotel managed by the Warwick chain, a 3-star 130-room hotel owned by a group of Polynesian and New Caledonian investors, and a complex of 115 residential villas located in the hills, next to the golf course, and next to the beach. Mountain villas will range from 2-4 bedrooms, built on plots varying in size from 2,000-2,500 sq. m. (21,528-26,910 sq. ft.). Villas next to the beach and the golf course will offer 2-3 bedrooms on plots ranging in size from 1,000-1,500 sq. m (10,764-16,146 sq. ft.). Construction on all these projects is supposed to get underway in early 2008.

Hiking

Opunohu Agricultural College has opened three circular trails that you can walk alone or with a guide, where you can see the work of the school students and explore one section of the Opunohu domain. A small brochure with the detailed notes on the plant life on the trails is available in four languages (French, English, German and Spanish). Ask for information on guided tours at the Fare Boutique on the right side of the road leading to Le Belvedere lookout.

Moorea Hiking-Tohie'a Excursions, *Tel. 56.16.48/79.41.54; hiking@magicmoorea.com; www.mooreahiking.com.* Hiro Damide and his guides operate 3-hour hikes through the agricultural trails in Opunohu Valley for families and older people. They start at the Marae Titiroa and hike up to the Belvedere lookout and return to the *marae*, explaining the geology, plants, birds, and Polynesian culture along the way. The hikers are served fresh pineapple, *pamplemousse* (grapefruit) and other fruits, and the cost is 5.000 CFP. They also lead 5-hour hikes into the Opunohu Valley, 18-23 km. (11-14 mi.) hikes across the island from

Vaiare to Haapiti, and mountain climbing expeditions up Rotui Mountain and Moua Puta, the mountain with the hole in the top. The all-day hikes are 10.600 CFP and include lunch.

Polynesian Adventure, *Tel./Fax 43.25.95, cell 77.24.37; polynesianadv@mail.pf.* Vincent Dubousquet is a specialized professional guide who will accompany you on a day's hike to walk across the mountains of Moorea from Vaiare to Pao Pao or to visit the Three Coconut Trees pass. These are easy to medium level walks for a minimum of four people and each hike costs 7.200 CFP per person. He will take you for a day's hike to Mou'a Puta or Rotui Mountain, or to cross Moorea from Haapiti to Vaiare, walking over two passes. You should be in good physical condition and fit for these hikes, which also require a minimum of four people. Each hike costs 9.300 CFP per person. The above rates do not include taxes, food and drinks and boat transfers from Tahiti. Bring a casse-croûte sandwich and water.

Tahiti Evasion, *Tel./Fax 689/56.48.77, cell 70.56.18; tahitievasion@mail.pf; www.tahitievasion.com.* Michel Veuillet is the guide who will take you into the green sanctuary of Moorea's valleys and mountains for half- or full-day treks. He will introduce you to the archaeological sites in the Opunohu Valley, the pineapple fields and the Three Coconut Trees pass. This is an easy 2.5- to 3-hour hike for 4.500 CFP. A medium level hike takes you to the *marae* temples and the *mape* (chestnut tree) forests of Opunohu Valley and then to the Three Coconut Trees pass. This 3- to 3.5-hour trek is 4.500 CFP.

An all-day hike takes you to the waterfalls in Afareaitu and on to Mou'a Puta, the mountain with a hole in the top. From this height you will have a magnificent 360-degree view of the island of Moorea and you can also see Tahiti from here. You must be in good physical condition and not subject to vertigo to attempt this climb. A minimum of 2 people is required and transfers are included for the cost of 8.000 CFP per person.

Horseback Riding

Opunohu Valley Ranch, *Tel. 56.28.55/78.42.47,* is located on the *route des ananas* (pineapple road) in Opunohu Valley, on the right side of the road past the turn-off for Le Belvedere, 2 km (1.2 mi.) from the circle island road at Opunohu Bay. Terai Maihi leads 2-hour guided excursions for a maximum of 8 riders through mountain trails and into the valley, passing the river, forests of Tahitian chestnut trees (*mape*) and pineapple plantations. The morning ride is from 8:30-10:30am and the afternoon ride is from 2:30 to 4:30pm. Closed on Sun. afternoon and all day Mon. Each 2-hour ride is 5.500 CFP per person when you book direct and up to 8.250 CFP if you book at the big hotels.

Helicopter Tours

Polynesia Hélicoptères, *Tel. 689/54.87.20/78.65.05; Fax 689/54.87.21; helico-tahiti@mail.pf; www.polynesia-helicopter.com.* A 5-seat "Squirrel" AS 350 BA helicopter is based at the Tahiti-Faa'a airport and is available for tourist flights, transfers to Moorea and specific charters on request. A 35-minute "Moorea Discovery" flight-seeing tour for a minimum of four passengers costs 26.300 CFP per person with a departure from the Faaa Airport in Tahiti. A 20-minute flight over Moorea costs 16.300 CFP per person (minimum of 4) when it leaves from the Temae Airport in Moorea. Private transfers from a hotel in Tahiti to a hotel in Moorea are 56.000 CFP, and a private charter is 173.100 CFP per hour.

Nautical Activities Centers

Intercontinental Moorea Resort, *Tel. 55.19.19.* You'll find a variety of interesting activities here, which are available to hotel guests and anyone else who wants to explore the lagoon. In addition to snorkeling, windsurfing, scuba diving, day sailing, parasailing, fishing, lagoon tours, and pedal boat rentals, you can also get a round-trip boat transfer to a *motu* for 1.060 CFP, or rent a 5-passenger Spyder boat with captain for 18.060 CFP for 1 hr. An Aquavision boat with a 4 HP engine is 7.350 CFP for 2 hrs., and 9.450 CFP for 4 hrs. You can rent a jet-ski or wave-runner with a guide for 8.920 CFP for 1/2 hr. or 13.970 CFP for 1 hr., water-ski for 2.700 CFP for a 10-minute tour, join a snorkeling and ray-feeding expedition in the lagoon for 4.220 CFP, take a sunset cruise for 4.000-6.500 CFP, view the coral gardens through the windows of a self-piloted glass bottom boat for 8.250 CFP, or through an Aquablue diving helmet as you Aqua-Walk on the bottom of the lagoon for 6.900 CFP. You can also rent a talking snorkel for a 40-min. excursion in the lagoon.

Moorea Pearl Resort, *Tel. 55.17.50.* Hotel guests can use the snorkeling equipment, kayaks and outrigger canoes free of charge. They rent jet skis for 9.500 CFP for 30 min. and 14.500 CFP for 1-hour guided tours. Small motorboats are 9.000 CFP for 4 hrs. and 11.000 CFP for 8 hrs. A 45-min. Aquablue helmet dive is 6.900 CFP, water-skiing is 5.000 CFP for beginners, a 4-hr. deep-sea fishing outing for 3 people is 18.000 CFP each, and a Mahana private boat tour is 56.000 CFP for 2 people. A shark and ray-feeding excursion that includes a picnic on the motu is 7.000 CFP and a half-day catamaran cruise is 9.000 CFP. There are also scuba diving, dolphin and whale watching excursions, and boat tours to a private island.

Sheraton Moorea Lagoon Resort, *Tel. 55.11.11.* Guests staying in the hotel have free use of the snorkeling equipment, kayaks and outrigger paddle canoes. A Jet Ski with guide is 8.900 CFP for 30 min. or 13.970 CFP for 1 hr. Water-skiing is 2.750 CFP for 10 min. and 3.950 CFP for 20 min. for beginners. A speedboat with pilot is 17.200 CFP per hour, a circle island boat tour with ray feeding is 6.660 CFP, a circle island tour with a picnic on the motu is 9.850 CFP, or you can go directly to the motu at 9:45am for the picnic and return to the hotel at 2:30pm for 7.360 CFP. A half-day deep-sea fishing charter for 1-5 people is 16.500 CFP each, and a private fishing charter is 66.000 CFP for a half-day outing. A romantic sailing sunset cruise with cocktail is 6.500 CFP, and a private sunset cruise with cocktail is 72.000 CFP. TOPdive has a scuba dive center on the premises.

Sofitel Moorea Beach Resort, *Tel. 55.12.12.* The Fare Nautique is open daily from 7:30am-5pm. They rent pedal boats, sea trailers, small boats with or without a license, Jet-skis, windsurf boards, Hobie cats, sea kayaks, and water skiing. Snorkeling gear is free. They can also arrange boat tours to a motu for a picnic, deep-sea fishing, scuba diving, and dolphin watch tours. A 2 1/2-hr. guided excursion to the Lagoonarium is 6.000 CFP and 10.500 CFP for an all-day excursion, including a lunch of grilled fish and a drink.

Tip'Nautic, *Tel. 78.76.73*, is a nautical base located at Hotel Les Tipaniers, open daily from 9am to 6pm. You can go water-skiing, rent snorkeling gear, kayaks and wakeboards, or you can catch a boat transfer to the motu. You can join an excursion to discover the sharks and rays, which can also be combined with a boat trip around the island.

Boat Rentals, Glass Bottom Boat, Kayaks, Cata-Jet, Jet-Ski and Wave Runners
Cata-Jet, *Tel. 56.43.37/77.88.49*, is located on the beach at Hotel Hibiscus, They rent catajets with an awning and 6 HP or 25 HP engines that you can drive yourself without a license if you are at least 16 years old. The 6 HP catajet costs 7.000 CFP for one hour and a two-hour guided excursion on the 25 HP catajet is 14.000 CFP for two people. You can also rent a catajet at all the big hotels for around 16.500 CFP.

Glass Bottom Boat, *Tel. 74.32.50; www.glass-bottom-boat.com.* Tuatini Activities Moorea is located behind the bicycle rental *fare* adjacent to Le Petit Village. Glass bottom boat excursions are 2.500 CFP for 1:15 hrs. and 4.500 CFP for 2 hrs. Transfers to the motu are 700 CFP per person and a sunset cruise with Maitai punch is 5.500 CFP. They can organize picnics or a Tahitian feast for groups on Maiau Beach, and private tours for snorkeling and ray feeding.

You can rent a glass bottom boat with no license at Intercontinental Moorea for 8.250 CFP for 2 hrs. and 10.450 CFP for 4 hrs.

Moorea Locaboat, *Tel. 78.13.39*, is located on the beach at Moe Moea (Fare Condominium). Open daily 8am-5pm. Isabelle and Vanessa have small boats with a 6 HP engine that you can rent without a license. Rates start at 5.000 CFP for one hour, gas included. Transfer service provided.

Deep Sea Fishing
Tea Nui Services, *Tel./Fax 56.35.95; teanuiservices@mail.pf.* Captain Chris Lilley has a 31-ft. Bertram Flybridge Sportfisher named *Tea Nui* that is professionally equipped with Penn International reels and all that you need to realize your dream of catching marlin, tuna, wahoo or mahi mahi offshore Moorea. Chris, who is an American resident of Moorea, has more than 20 years' experience in local waters. The *Tea Nui* is based at Intercontinental Moorea. Chris charges US$150 per person for a minimum of 4 on a half-day charter and US$600 for a maximum of 6 people on a private half-day fishing excursion, including tax.

Moorea Fishing Charters, *Tel. 73.93.48/77.02.19; halfon@mail.pf;*

www.halfon-vip-tours.com. Jean Pierre Halfon has a 29-ft. Riviera fishing boat with a flybridge, 200 HP diesel Volvo engine and luxury accommodations for 6 guests. There are two game fishing chairs, two outriggers and all the fishing equipment is provided. Rates start at 18.000 CFP for a minimum of 4 people for 4 hours of fishing, and go up to 65.000 CFP for 4 hours for a maximum of 4 people on a private charter. His **VIP Tours** offer deep sea fishing, lagoon tours, a full-day excursion with fish and ray feeding and a BBQ on a private motu. This boat is also available for sunset cruises, and looking for dolphins and whales (in season).

Moorea Sportfishing, *Tel. 76.76.36,* is a Kevlacat 2400 Offshore fishing boat owned by Fiston Amaru, a Tahitian man who speaks English. His *Wet Dream* is available for deep sea fishing charters.

Dolphin & Whale Watching Eco-Tours

Dolphin and Lagoonarium Tour, *Tel. 56.50.05/78.42.42; courset.loisirs@mail.pf; www.dolphinlagoonarium.com.* This very popular excursion is operated by Paul Courset and Harold Wright, who worked with Club Med on Moorea until it closed in 2001. Their fully covered catamaran *Rava IV* makes daily trips around the island to look for the spinner dolphins and they also sight humpback whales between July and late October. Harold makes a stop to let the passengers play with the stingrays— an activity that he created in 1996. Another highlight of this excursion is an hour's visit to Motu Ahi, where the tourists can snorkel among the fish, sharks, rays and turtles in the enclosed lagoonarium. Then they are served rum punch, juice, water, coconut and pineapple under the shade on the beach. A cameraman is on board to record this memorable occasion and you can buy a video or DVD film that may even show you caressing a nurse shark. This tour lasts for 4-5 hrs. and costs 7.000 CFP per person. Pick-ups from Les Tipaniers, Hotel Hibiscus, Vaimoana and Intercontinental Moorea start at 8am and the boat leaves the last dock at 8:30am.

Dolphin & Whale Watching Expeditions is owned by Doctor Michael Poole, *Tel/Fax 56.23.22; cell 77.50.07; **www.drmichaelpoole.com,*** whose fiberglass boat will seat up to 40 people. On Sun. and Thurs. mornings a 3-4 hr. Dolphin & Whale Watching Expedition (see sidebar) is guided by Doctor Michael Poole or his staff, which takes you through the lagoon and outside the reef to search for, observe and learn about the dolphins and whales that inhabit local waters. Free fruit and juice are provided, and time permitting, a snorkeling stop is offered inside the lagoon. This tour costs 7.400 CFP for adults, half price for children 3-12, and free for children under 3. Supplementary excursions are sometimes made on Tues., and special group charters can be arranged.

Manu Eco Tours Catamaran, *Tel./Fax 56.28.04; cell 79.03.28; www.mooreaecotour.com. Manu* is a 10.8 meter (36-ft.) motorized catamaran owned by Bernard Calvet, which operates out of the Nautical Center at the Intercontinental Moorea. A 4-hr. eco-tour around the island takes you to look for dolphins and whales (between July and early November), and also includes snorkeling with the rays and fish, for a minimum of 4 passengers at a cost of 8.500 CFP per person. A 3-hour

---

DOLPHIN & WHALE WATCHING EXPEDITIONS

Dr. Michael Poole, *Tel/Fax 56.23.22; cell 77.50.07; www.drmichaelpoole.com,* is an American marine biologist who lives in Moorea and has devoted his life's work to the study of dolphins and whales. He is a very good teacher who loves sharing his knowledge with other people. The enthusiasm he feels for the mammals he studies in their natural environment is very contagious. Michael and his staff lead 3-4 hour **Dolphin & Whale Watching Expeditions** on Thurs. and Sun. mornings and special tours for passengers on ships. A maximum of 40 people are picked up at their respective hotel docks between 8 and 9am, and Michael or one of his staff boards the boat at the Moorea Pearl Resort pier. The search begins, as you head through the lagoon or through a pass into the open ocean. The wild spinner dolphins (*Stenella longirostris*) are the easiest to find and the most fun to watch because of their acrobatic aerial leaps. Michael and his staff will tell you that 120 of these mammals live around Moorea all the time.

When the sea is calm and the mammals seem approachable, you can sometimes swim with the rough-toothed dolphins, pilot whales and humpback whales. The giant humpback whales can be seen and heard singing off Moorea between July and early November, when they come up from Antarctica to mate and give birth. These are the most exciting mammals to watch as they frolic close to the shore and splash in the vicinity of the surprised surfers, who ride the waves beside the passes.

---

snorkeling and ray-feeding cruise for a minimum of four people costs 7.000 CFP each, departing daily at 9:30am and 1:30pm and also includes a visit to Cook's Bay and Opunohu Bay. A half-day private charter for 6 passengers is 55.000 CFP. You can also join a sunset cruise. See information under *Sunset Cruises* in this chapter.

Moorea Boat Tours, *Tel. 56.28.44/78.68.86; www.mooreaboattours.com.* Heifara Dutertre has 2 boats for dolphin and whale watches and private tours.

Lagoon Excursions, Snorkeling, Ray Feeding & Picnics on the Motu

Hiro's Tours/What To Do On Moorea, *Tel. 78.70.10/56.57.66; wtdmoorea@mail.pf.* Hiro Kelley's **Motu Picnic Tour** is very popular with tourists and features photo stops, a visit to Cook's Bay and Opunohu Bay, an exciting Shark Show and Ray Feeding, plus a sumptuous barbecue picnic on a motu islet, with punch, beer and soft drinks included. This 5 1/2-hr. tour is 7.000 CFP and includes free pick-up service. Hiro's team of friendly Tahitian guides will also take you on a 1 1/2-hour **Snorkeling Excursion** for 1.000 CFP a person, departing Club Bali Hai at 1:30pm each Mon., Thurs. and Sat. Hiro Kelley is the son of the late Hugh Kelley, one of the famous "Bali Hai Boys", and his activity desk at Club Bali Hai can also book other island excursions.

Moana Lagoon Tour, *Tel. 55.21.10/55.21.11/78.46.60; www.albert-transport.net.* Albert Transport and Activities has earned a good reputation for their barbecue picnic on the *motu,* which takes place every Tues., Wed., Fri. and Sun. You'll view Cook's Bay and Opunohu Bay from the water and stop to feed the stingrays and go snorkeling. The all-inclusive cost for this 6-hr. excursion is 7.000 CFP, including pick-ups at hotels.

Moorea Mahana Tours, *Tel. 56.20.44.* They have excursions from the Intercontinental Moorea and Sheraton Moorea Lagoon that will take you in a covered outrigger speed canoe to visit the two bays, snorkel and feed the stingrays, including a picnic on the motu. A full-day Dolphin Watch boat tour around the island with a picnic on the *motu* is 9.840 CFP per person.

Moorea VIP Tours, *Tel. 73.93.48; www.halfon-vip-tours-com.* Lagoon tours for a maximum of 12 people are provided on board a local catamaran with a small pool, shower and music. A special full day package on Moorea includes a lagoon excursion, dolphin tour, and picnic on the motu. The regular price of 21.400 CFP for this combination has been discounted to 12.900 CFP per person. Private excursions can include dolphin watching, ray feeding, lunch on a private motu, sunset cruises, and romantic dinners. A private half-day tour is 29.000 CFP, a full day is 49.000 CFP, and a sunset cruise from 5-6:30pm is 19.000 CFP. Prices include drinks, water, diet Coke and Hinano beer. This company also has Jet skis, wave runners and a deep-sea fishing boat.

Day Sailing Excursions & Sunset Cruises

Tahiti Cruise & Moorea Sailing, *Tel. 72.23.45, www.tahiticruise.pf.* Half-day sailing and lagoon snorkeling are 9.000 CFP per person on board the *Margouillat,* a 43-ft. luxury catamaran. Romantic sailing sunset cruises are made every evening from 4-6pm, except Thurs., Sat. and Sun., for 6.500 CFP, including a cocktail. A private half-day sailing and snorkeling cruise is 84.000 CFP, and a 7-hr. private cruise is 119.000 CFP, including the skipper, hostess, food, cocktail, wine and private transfers. A private sunset cruise is 72.000 CFP.

Lagoon Games, *Tel. 55.12.12,* at the Sofitel Moorea Beach Resort Nautical Activities Center, sells sailing cruises aboard the 42-ft. deluxe Leopard catamaran *Kokiri.* A half-day picnic outing is 10.000 CFP and a 7-hr. excursion with on-board picnic is 16.000 CFP. Private sailing tours are 70.000 CFP for a half-day and 110.000 CFP for a full day. The skipper, barman and chef are included in rates.

Polynesian Spirit, *Tel. 77.97.19/56.11.74; www.kaveka.free.fr.* The *Kaveka* is a traditional Polynesian outrigger sailing canoe that makes half-day sailing and snorkeling tours for a maximum of 5 passengers, for 6.900 CFP per person. A sunset sailing cruise is 5.900 CFP.

Sunset cruises are also provided by the following boats:

Hiro's Tours/What to Do on Moorea, *Tel. 78.70.10/56.57.66.* A Cook's Bay Sunset Cruise can be arranged, departing from the Club Bali Hai dock at 4pm for a 2-hour sunset celebration on board Hiro Kelley's modern version of the famous

Bali Hai Liki Tiki ("Leaky Tiki") catamaran. A Tahitian band plays Polynesian songs. Rum punch, beer, wine and soft drinks are included. Minimum of 12 people required for 6.000 CFP each.

Manu Catamaran, *Tel./Fax 56.28.04; cell 72.62.22/79.03.28. Manu* is a 10.8 meter (36-ft.) motorized catamaran that operates out of the Nautical Center at the Intercontinental Moorea. The sunset cruise leaves the dock every afternoon at 4:30-5pm and returns 1 1/2 hrs. later for a minimum of 4 passengers. Drinks are included in the price of 4.000 CFP.

Tuatini Activities Moorea, *Tel. 74.32.50; www.glass-bottom-boat.com.* A 2-hr. sunset cruise aboard a glass bottom boat on the lagoon in Haapiti includes Maitai punch and costs 5.500 CFP per person.

Sailing – Charter Yachts

Archipels, *B.P. 1160, Papetoai, Moorea, 98729. Tel. 689/56.36.39, Fax 689/ 56.35.87; information@archipels-croisieres.pf; www.archipels.com; Skype: archipels.* The main office for Archipels Croisières is on the mountainside at PK 17 in Opunohu Bay.

The English speaking staff will help you plan your own sailing holiday to visit the Leeward Society Islands or the Tuamotu atolls aboard one of their four new Eleuthera 60' sailing catamarans with 5 passenger cabins or one of their two Marquises 57' catamarans with 4 passenger cabins. Archipels Croisières charters primarily to individuals or "by the cabin" in a shared-boat cruise, or you can charter the entire yacht. The private charter rates include fuel for the boat and dinghy, all meals and hotel services aboard, organized shore activities and airport/yacht transfers. The per-passenger rates also include meals and hotel services aboard, double occupancy cabins, taxes, airport/yacht transfers, and all the excursions and events specified in the program you choose.

The 2008 low season in the Society Islands and the Tuamotu atolls is Jan. 5-Mar. 28 and Oct. 18-Dec. 19. The high season is Mar. 29-Oct. 17 and Dec. 20-Jan. 2, 2009.

A 7-day/6-night Leeward Islands cruise in low/high season is €1,880/2,090. A 7 day/6 night Tuamotu cruise from Fakarava to Toau to Rangiroa is €1,880/ 2,090; a 4 day/3 night Tuamotu cruise inside the atoll of Rangiroa is €1,092/1,207, and €820/935 per person for a 3 day/2 night cruise inside the Rangiroa lagoon. Departures for these cruises are guaranteed for a minimum of 2 passengers.

Scuba Diving

A qualified English-speaking instructor heads each dive center in Moorea. All diving equipment is available, and dive packages with special lodging can be arranged. If you are not a certified diver bring a health certificate from your doctor with you. The protected lagoons, passes and outer coral reefs offer ideal conditions for scuba diving year-round in water temperatures that range from 77° to 86° F.

There are more than a dozen dive sites no deeper than 75-90 ft. that you can discover with the following diving professionals.

Ia Ora Diving, *Tel. 77.86.44 or 55.12.12, ext. 1311; www.iaoradiving.pf.* This PADI dive center is located at the Sofitel Moorea Beach Resort. Certified divers leave the hotel beach daily at 8am and 10am, and pay 6.800 CFP for one dive and 11.560 CFP for 2 dives the same morning. An introductory dive for beginners is 7.200 CFP, and a night dive is 9.800 CFP. Packages are available for 5 and 10 dives.

Moorea Blue Diving, *Tel. 55.17.04/74.59.99; www.mooreabluediving.com.* This small dive center is based at the Moorea Pearl Resort & Spa and is owned by Lino and Solange Facondini. Lino is a BEES 1/OWSI PADI/CMAS** instructor/ MF1 FFESSM, and a shark diving specialist. An exploration dive is 6.850 CFP, an introductory dive is 7.500 CFP, and a night dive is 8.500 CFP. A package of 5 Fun dives is 32.500 CFP and 10 Fun dives costs 59.500 CFP. The rates include all the equipment, which is new. PADI certification is 45.000 CFP, not including the open water diving book. Other diving certificates possible.

Moorea Fun Dive, *Tel. 56.40.38; www.moorea-fundive.com.* This dive shop is adjacent to Moorea Camping at P.K. 27 in Haapiti, and is operated by Gregory and Catherine Kister. He is a master scuba diver trainer, PADI instructor and a CMAS** international instructor. Their equipment includes a 24-ft. aluminum boat for 14 passengers, but they limit the diving to 10 people with one dive guide for a maximum of 5 divers. All the necessary equipment is provided. They charge 6.200 CFP for an exploration dive, 11.500 CFP for two dives and 31.500 CFP for a 6-dive package. Whale watching excursions during season (July-Oct.).

New Bathy's Diving, *Tel. 56.31.44; bathys@mail.pf; www.dive-moorea.com.* This PADI 5-star center is located at the Intercontinental Moorea Resort & Spa. Four experienced PADI instructors speak English, French and Spanish and the dive gear is quite new (Aqualung). Nitrox is available for the same price as air. Full service features 2 aluminum dive boats, air fill, professional video service, dive shop, certifications and courses for beginners or certified divers. A specialty of New Bathy's Diving is feeding the sharks in the open ocean (for certified divers only). A Fun Dive costs 7.000 CFP air or Nitrox and an introductory dive is 9.000 CFP. A 4-day PADI Open Water Dive package is 59.000 CFP, and a 3-day PADI Advanced Open Water Dive package is 45.000 CFP for 3 days. Rates are the same for divers with their own equipment.

Scubapiti Moorea, *Tel. 56.20.38/78.03.52; scubapitidaniel@mail.pf; www.scubapiti.com.* Daniel Cailleux runs this popular dive center, which is located on the property of Les Tipaniers in Haapiti. He is a French State supervisor BEES 1, 1st degree French federal monitor, CMAS instructor, and monitor for PADI and ANMP (Association National des Moniteurs de Plongée). Daniel and his highly qualified instructors are available to take you for an exploration or first dive for 6.100 CFP. A 2-tank dive is 11.600 CFP and a 4-dive package is 22.000 CFP. Lessons available. Most dives are drift dives and they do no shark feeding. A cameraman records your dives, which you can then see on an instant replay system.

MOOREA'S BEST DIVE SITES

Moorea's dive sites outside the reef offer special treats of feeding the large lemon sharks and a rendezvous with the friendly giant-sized Napoleon fish. Divers also see black and white-tip sharks, gray sharks and moray eels. The water is clear with insignificant currents, assuring easy dives that attract scuba divers from all over the world. One of the most popular sites is "Le Tiki", where you'll be able to see wild sharks, including lemon sharks more than 2.4 m (8 ft.) long. The Toatai Pass through the barrier reef offers drift diving among nurse sharks, leopard rays and schools of jackfish. A site known as "Napoleon Plateau" offers Napoleon fish that weigh up to 80 lbs., as well as sharks. Inside the lagoon is a site called "The Wreck", which is an artificial haven for fish, with the ship's hull spread over 82 ft., complete with anchors, chains and a gangway. Other sites include the "Ray Corridor," "The Canyon," "The Blue Island," the "Shark Dining Room," the "Bali Hai Wall," "Temae," "Atiha," the "Avamotu Pass" and the "Taotaha Pass," all offering a concentration of eels, barracudas, coral fish, rays or sharks. The depth for these dives is usually 60-70 ft., with an average visibility of 150 ft. and sometimes more than 250 ft. Many of the dive spots are less than 10 minutes by boat from the shore.

TOPdive Moorea, *Tel. 56.17.32; Moorea@topdive.com; www.topdive.com.* This PADI 5-star dive center is located beside the pier at the Cook's Bay Resort (the hotel is now closed), and they also have a branch at the Hotel Sheraton. Manager and dive master Nicolas Buray is assisted by four qualified instructors, offering beginner, certified and night dives, each for 7.000 CFP, including taxes and all equipment. A package of 10 dives is 63.000 CFP and can also be used at TOPdive centers in Bora Bora, Rangiroa, Fakarava and Tahiti. Topdive Moorea also has Nitrox, which costs the same as air.

More Water Fun

Aqua Blue, *Tel. 56.53.53, aquablue_pf@hotmail.com* is a novel way to say hello to the fish in the lagoon in Moorea. This activity is based at the Intercontinental Moorea Resort and is available 3 times daily except Sunday. You do not have to be a certified diver nor even a swimmer to discover this new sensation. A qualified diving instructor will help you to put on a funny looking yellow diving helmet that weighs 40 kg (88 lbs.). But you don't feel the weight when you are under the water, and you can actually walk around on the bottom of the lagoon just as you would walk on any land, wearing special water shoes. An air hose connected to a compressor on board the boat allows you to descend to a depth of 3.7 m (12 ft.). Your Aqua-Walk lasts 30 min. and costs 6.900 CFP. Free transfers.

Aquadisco, *Tel. 56.40.90/76.40.90; aquadisco@mail.pf; www.aquadisco.com.* This is 12-passenger boat with an a/c room that has submarine windows for viewing marine life in the lagoon without getting wet. A 3-hr. Eco Tour is 7.000 CFP per adult and 4.500 CFP for a child. A sunset cruise from 5-7pm is 6.000 CFP for adults and 3.500 CFP for children. Night excursions are also available.

Moorea Dolphin Center, *Tel. 55.19.48; www.mooreadolphincenter.com.* This organization is based at the Intercontinental Moorea Resort & Spa. You can participate in encounter programs with trained dolphins that live inside a lagoon park. A Kid's program for 5-11 year olds is a 1-hr. adventure on request for 12.000 CFP. A Guided Lagoon discovery is on request and lasts for 1 1/2 hrs. at 18.400 CFP. A 1-hr. Dolphin Experience is available at 9am, 1:30pm, and 2:45pm for anyone over 12 years old, and costs 19.800 CFP. This encounter combines elements of hands-on contact, education, fun and adventure. A 30-min. Apnea is 24.300 CFP. A 3-hr. Trainer for a Day program starts at 8:30am and costs 45.000 CFP. A 1-hr. Special Romance for couples starts at 11am and costs 48.000 CFP, and a 30-min. Family program is 56.000 CFP.

Lagoonarium of Moorea, *Tel. 78.31.15; Fax 43.89.30; lagoonarium@mail.pf; www.lagomoorea.com.* This activity is operated by Teiki Pambrun on Motu Ahi, at PK 8 in Afareaitu. Stop at the Curios *fare* on the seaside beside the road and a shuttle boat will take you to the motu. The fee is 2.500 CFP for each adult and 1.800 CFP per child, which allows you to spend the day on the motu, snorkeling in a lagoonarium filled with tropical fish of all colors. You can swim with the stingrays, small blacktip reef sharks, moray eels, and turtles in a protected marine zone inside the lagoon. Fins, facemasks, snorkels, plastic shoes, and safety jackets are provided. Beach volleyball and French bowls are available. You can also go scuba diving, starting at 4.000 CFP per person. You can bring a picnic or buy your lunch at the Beach Snackbar on the motu. The menu varies during the week and on Sundays they prepare a Tahitian underground oven or a spit roasted veal. Some of the organized lagoon excursions come here for their barbecue picnic on the motu. There is a Tahitian style outhouse and a few simple A-frame shelters for those who want to spend the night in this *sauvage* environment. Just remember that it is not a hotel or pension, but an opportunity to sleep on a motu and commune with Nature. Round-trip bus transfers from the hotels are 1.500 CFP per person and bus or boat transfers from the Vaiare quay are 700 CFP.

Lakana Fly Kite Surfing, *Tel. 70.96.71; bdflyfr@yahoo.fr.* David Bourroux is a young Frenchman who gives lessons in kite surfing and he speaks good English. He is based next door to Les Tipaniers on the site of the former Moorea Beach Club. His rates are 10.000 CFP for 2 hours, 18.000 CFP for 4 hours and 40.000 CFP for 10 hours of lessons, which are spread out over several days.

Polynesian Parasailing, *Tel. 56.20.44,* is a way to let you float over Moorea's lagoon without getting your feet wet. You have a 10-12 min. ride aloft, up to 180 m (600 ft.) above the lagoon, where all you can hear is the wind. This activity is available at the Intercontinental Moorea for 7.190 CFP per person or 10.710 CFP tandem for one adult and one child. The Sheraton Moorea Lagoon charges 6.850 per person for a minimum of 2 people; and the Moorea Pearl Resort charges 8.000 CFP per person.

SHOPPING

When you take a guided circle island tour of Moorea the bus or 4-wheel drive vehicle will most likely stop at a boutique and a pearl shop, which are probably owned by the guide's family or friends. If you rent a car or scooter or bike around the island you'll have a better chance of finding out which shops you prefer.

My favorites are the shops that sell locally made products, rather than clothes, pareos and souvenir items imported from Bali. **Boutique Polynesia** is in Centre Tumai on the mountainside at PK 2.7 in Tiaia, between the airport and Maharepa. Jean-Luc, the talented owner, creates jewelry from Tahiti cultured pearls, nacre, bone, tou, tutu, purau and other local wood. He also sells Marquesan wood sculptures, pareo outfits, shirts and lamps made by Tahiti Art, and he carries Te Mana shirts from Tahiti for men and women. His wife has **Boutique Océane** across the road, where half the merchandise is locally made and half is imported. **Green Lagoon Gallery**, on the mountainside around PK 3.8 in Tiaia, presents oil canvases by Nataly Jolibois and sculptures of driftwood, wood and metal and wood and stone by Hans Jörg Stübler.

There are a few curio shops and boutiques in and close to the Maharepa Center, where you'll also find the post office and banks. **La Maison Blanche** is one of the most popular tourist stops, even though most of their curios are imported. **Michou Creations** is a well-known dressmaker whose shop is next to Rudy's Restaurant at PK 6 in Maharepa. **Van der Heyde Art Gallery**, on the mountain side at PK 7, is owned by Aad van der Heyde, a Dutch artist whose oil paintings are displayed all around his enclosed garden. Inside his shop you'll find authentic primitive art from throughout the South Pacific and sculptures of coral and wood from the French Polynesian Islands. He also sells Tahitian cultured pearls and unset *keshis*.

Art Marquisien is in the Cook's Bay Center across from Hotel Kaveka. In addition to carvings of wood, bone, stone and mother-of-pearl, they also have Marquesan tapa and *tifaifai* bed covers or wall hangings. **Moorea Arts Creation**, on the mountainside in Pao Pao, features the paintings of local artist, Stanley Haumani, as well as hand painted *pareos*. The boutique at **Club Bali Hai** carries local and imported items.

Maeva Center, across the road from Club Bali Hai, is a small artisan's village of 7 shops and a **Living Museum** of stone artifacts found in the lagoon or valleys of Moorea, as well as carved wooden tikis and umete bowls. At **Robert Aka's** shop, you can find his slit wooden toere drums, Tahitian ukuleles, carved umete bowls and coconut bras, as well as seashells from his Marquesan Island of Ua Pou. At **Tahiti Stained Glass** you will meet Tom Newbrough, an American who makes stained glass windows, lamps, candle covers and fish mobiles. This shop is shared by Xavier, a Frenchman who makes lap steel guitars and Kamaka cutoff ukuleles. Some of the shops sell locally made clothes, *pareos* and grass dancing skirts, and there is also a deli and beauty shop here.

Honu Iti Boutique, PK 8.5 in Cook's Bay, has Tahitian clothing and souvenirs, as well as pareos and trinkets imported from Indonesia. They also have some pearl jewelry. **Boutique Ra**, on the mountainside at PK 12.8 in Pihaena, displays the bamboo artifacts made by American expatriate, Ruth Konvalinka, as well as paintings, stone and coral sculptures created by local artists and artisans. **Kaimana Boutique** at the Sheraton Moorea Lagoon Resort & Spa is well-stocked with gift items, silk painted pareos, tropical clothing, men's shirts and T-shirts, and some pretty wall hangings or bed covers called *tifaifai* in Tahitian. **Outre-Mers** is a nice boutique at PK 25 in Tiahura that has some really pretty dresses, *pareos* and unusual souvenir items.

In the hotel area of Haapiti you'll find a number of boutiques that carry *pareos*, T-shirts, swimsuits and gift items. **Le Petit Village** is a small shopping center with an ABC store, pearl shops, boutiques and a magazine stand. **Linareva Boutique** at PK 34.5 in Haapiti sells original necklaces made by Mama Fauura, a noted artisan who lives in Tahiti. You should also visit the **bazaars** at the boat docks in Cook's Bay and Papetoai village when a cruise ship is in port. Local artisans set up display stands under awnings to sell their *pareos*, tee-shirts, dresses and beachwear, costume jewelry made of shells and mother-of-pearl, woven hats and bags and numerous other souvenirs that are made in Moorea.

Tahitian Cultured Pearls

Ann Simon Boutique, *Tel. 56.44.55/72.42.41; www.annsimonblackpearl.com.* This little pearl shop is in the shopping center across the street from the Banque de Tahiti in Maharepa. Each time I go inside I am impressed by the friendliness of Ann Simon and her very helpful sales staff. They are all young attractive French women who speak good English. I also like the beautiful colors and quality of the pearls, the originality of the settings, and their reasonable prices. Everyone I have sent here agrees with me and usually buys some of Ann's fine pearls, which they will happily set on request. Free shuttle service is also available.

Eimeo Fine Jewelry, *Tel. 56.47.07*, is located on the same road as the Moorea Fruit Juice Factory at PK 12 in Cook's Bay. Open Mon.-Fri. 10am-4pm. This cute little cottage is the workshop and showroom of Elizabeth (Beth) Eyler-Wong, a very talented American jewelry designer, jeweler and goldsmith.

In 2007 Beth won first prize for a pair of pearl earrings she created for the 5th national edition of the Tahitian Pearl Trophy design competition, and took second prize for an 18kt gold ring containing a big keshi pearl, two Tahitian cultured pearls and a rose tourmaline. Beth's distinctive designs tend to have an Etruscan look, combining cultured pearls with chalcedony, moonstone, tourmaline and other semi-precious stones. She took the jewelry design course at the Gemological Institute of America (GIA) in 1977, and worked in the best jewelry stores in

Southern California before moving to Moorea in 1988. Now she has one of the best jewelry shops on this island, with designs for all tastes and prices for all budgets. **Eva Perles**, *Tel. 56.10.10*, is next to the Banque de Tahiti in Maharepa. Eva and Thierry Frachon are the very amiable hosts in this pleasant shop, and their selection of fine Tahitian cultured pearl jewelry will be sure to please you. Eva was trained as an art metalist in Wisconsin during her college years, and now uses this knowledge to design and fabricate a lot of the jewelry she sells. She has also completed the pearl course given at the Gemological Institute of America, as well as the Accredited Jewelry Professional training. Her first goal is to educate people so that they will be free to choose the best for themselves, no matter where they buy their pearls. She never pushes for a sale, choosing instead to share her passion with the visitor, opening them up to the uniqueness of this magical gem, to recognize the true beauty of each pearl, even though that beauty may not be perfect. Eva also displays some of her paintings in the gallery, as well as works by other resident artists.

Golden Nugget Perles, *Tel. 56.13.05*, is on Motu Temae close to the public beach and the Sofitel Moorea Beach Resort. You take the coral sand road opposite the post office at PK 0 in Temae and follow the signs pointing to Kerebel Jeweller. Kerebel is a goldsmith who creates most unusual jewelry, which often reflects his interest in the American Southwest. Some of his masculine rings are a golden or silver eagle set with a big Tahitian cultured pearl.

Heivai Black Pearls, *Tel. 55.00.80*, is across the road from Club Bali Hai in Pao Pao, and **Moorea Black Pearls**, *Tel. 55.01.40*, is across the road from Intercontinental Moorea Resort. Anyone who takes a circle island tour or 4WD Safari with Albert Transports and Activities will certainly stop at one or both of these pearl shops, as they are owned by Albert's son, William Haring. Like all the Haring family, William is a hard worker and dedicated salesman.

Island Fashion Black Pearls, *Tel. 56.11.06*, at PK 6.9 in Pao Pao, is open Mon.-Sat. from 9am-6pm. Owner Ron Hall is an American from California, who sailed to Tahiti with Peter Fonda aboard the yacht *Tatoosh* in the mid-1970s and settled in Moorea. Ron was one of the first successful Tahitian cultured pearl salesmen on the island, and some of his customers return time and again to add to their collection from his impressive selection of quality pearls and jewelry. He also carries bikinis, beach wear, *pareos* and Hawaiian style shirts. Transportation from your hotel is provided on request.

Tahia Collins, *Tel.55.05.00; www.tahiacollins.com*. Look for the sail-like canopies on the red building across the road from the former Club Med in Haapiti. Open daily from 9am to 6pm. Courtesy shuttle transfers available.

This business began as The Black Pearl Gem Company in 1993, and has now developed from one small sales room to a highly successful chain of 5 pearl shops with a team of 40 employees. In addition to the main showroom in Moorea, you will also find Tahia Collins Exquisite Tahitian Pearls across from the boat dock in Papeete, at the Hotel Bora Bora and Intercontinental Resort and Thalasso Spa Bora Bora, and on board the *M/S Paul Gauguin* cruise ship.

Tahia Collins is a young Polynesian-Swiss woman from Moorea, who is President and CEO of her own company as well as an award-winning jewelry designer. Her exclusive Tahitian pearl jewelry features only rare pearls in the most exotic colors from the top 1% of each pearl harvest. These stunning top-of-the line colors include varying nuances of blues, greens and purple, as well as the rare peacock. An on-site master jeweler is available to adjust the length of chains and pearl strands, resize rings or tailor each piece to your individual needs. Tahia Collins also has established service centers in Los Angeles, Germany and Tokyo to assist you with any after-purchase needs.

Every Tahia Collins sales representative has received specialized training and the staff includes consultants who were trained by the Gemological Institute of America (GIA). Everyone here speaks very good English, in addition to a few other languages, and the service is friendly and helpful, never pushy. The a/c showroom is designed to make shopping for your pearls an enjoyable and memorable experience. You are welcome to help yourself to a beer, soda or bottle of water kept on ice at the back of the shop. The Moorea boutique also has a private, luxuriously appointed VIP Lounge to accommodate those clients who, because of the high value of their selections, wish to complete their transaction in an atmosphere of privacy and seclusion.

Woody's Black Pearl Paradise, *Tel. 56.37.00/79.45.70,* is beside the lagoon at PK 23.9 in Papetoai, 400 m. from Intercontinental Moorea. Free shuttle service. Woody Howard is an American resident of Moorea who creates exquisite sculptures from the roots of trees and local wood. He has now added a Tahitian cultured pearl showroom to his gallery, selling pearls from his own farm in the Tuamotu atolls. His jewelry has won top prizes in the Tahitian Pearl Trophy design competitions.

MASSAGES & SPAS

Hélène'Spa, *Tel. 55.19.70; infos@helenspa.com; www.helenespa.com.* For more than 7 years this award-winning spa has been ranked among the most beautiful Spas in the world. Hidden in the exuberant foliage of private tropical gardens on the grounds of the Intercontinental Moorea Resort & Spa, there are 9 treatment areas in an indoor/outdoor Polynesian jungle setting of thatched roofs, bamboo walls, basaltic rock walkways, river baths, waterfalls and rain showers. Hélène Sillinger is a qualified professional, certified in naturopathy. Using holistic secrets transmitted from wise Polynesian healers, she has created a new range of Tahitian cares inspired by unique recipes. Her Polynesian Escapes packages of Well-Being Rituals suggest 6 combinations that last from 35-145 min. and cost from 5.000-38.400 CFP. The Herenui Love Ritual for couples starts with a traditional river bath, followed by a soft body scrub with fresh coconut pulp, a smooth body wrap with fresh coconut milk, a mask and vegetal lotion for the face, a natural massage of hands and feet, a relaxing rain shower and Polynesian massage, topped off by a bath filled with fresh exotic flowers. A snack of coconut, traditional beverage and tropical fruits is included in the cost of 22.000-89.000 CFP per couple, for 35-145 min. A la carte treatments include Polynesian massages for 9.400 CFP for 25 min. up to 30.200 CFP for 100 min. Or you can choose an aromatic spa with tropical essential oils, a fresh flower bath, traditional river bath, regenerating rain shower, scrubs and vegetal wraps. She also provides facial care, manicures, pedicures, makeup and waxing.

La Magie de l'Orient, *Tel. 56.20.20*, is a Beauty Shop and Spa located in the Cook's Bay Center in Maharepa, across the road from the former Cook's Bay Hotel. Open Mon. 9am-12pm, Tues.-Fri. 9am-5pm, and Sat. 9am-2pm. Hammam and Spa, body scrubs, wrapping, hair, facial and body care, massages, waxing, hair removal, manicures and pedicures. A one-hour massage starts at 7.900 CFP and a Balinese Voyage Hammam and Spa treatment for the body and face is 24.000 CFP.

LeSpa, *Tel. 55.12.12*, is on the beach at Sofitel Moorea Beach Resort, offering 7 tranquil treatment rooms and 2 Jacuzzis with panoramic views across the lagoon. Open daily 9am-7pm. Regular rates for massages range from 13.000 CFP for a one-hour massage to 24.000 CFP for two hours. Reduced Happy Hour rates from 11am to 4pm offer a 30-min. body exfoliation for 6.500 CFP and a one-hour massage for 9.950 CFP. Facials, manicures and pedicures are also available.

Mandara Spa, *Tel. 689/55.10.40; Fax 689/55.11.55; tahiti@mandaraspa.com; www.mandaraspa.com.* is located at the Sheraton Moorea Lagoon Resort & Spa. Open daily 8am-8pm. Reserve. You'll love this place from the moment you walk in the door. Mandara Spa originated in Bali and the unique spa treatments you'll receive here reflect the beauty, spirit and tradition of Asia. The staff of technicians includes massage therapists who are available to pamper you, and a menu of indulgences will tempt all your hedonistic tastes. You may choose a relaxing footbath, an aromatic floral Jacuzzi bath, a Mandara body scrub, Elemis hydrating facials for men and women, aromatherapy massage, sports massage, hot stone massage, reflexology massage, a manicure, pedicure, Kérastase hair and scalp care, haircut and blow-dry, waxing hair removal, steam bath, sauna, Vichy shower, or a combination of indulgences.

A 50-min. Heaven and Earth massage combines touches from around the globe and costs 11.500 CFP. A Shara Dhara is a 50-min. ritual when warm oil is poured steadily over the forehead, followed by a relaxation massage for 14.500 CFP. An exotic lime and ginger salt glow is an 80-min. exfoliation ritual for 18.000 CFP. A Time for Two massage for couples is a 50-min. double pleasure for 25.000 CFP. A Mandara Four-Hand Massage lasts 50-min. and costs 28.500 CFP, and a South Pacific Indulgence lasts 2 hours and 50 min. and costs 39.500 CFP. A 30-min. manicure is 6.000 CFP and an Ultimate Spa pedicure is 6.500 CFP.

Manea Spa, *Tel. 55.17.97*, is the spa at the Moorea Pearl Resort and Spa. There are 3 rooms for massages, facials, hair and body and care, and a room for tattoos by Albert. Facilities include a Hammam, Jacuzzi and rain shower, but no sauna. A new addition is an outdoor pool for Watsu massages performed in the water. Manea Spa carries its own line of 100% natural products made from local herbs, fruits, flowers and plants. These oils and cosmetic creams can be purchased at the Spa. The house special in Moorea is the Monoi Painapo, a complete massage of 30, 50, or 80 min. using monoi oil made from locally grown pineapple.

Treatments range from a 30-min. massage for 7.500 CFP to a 3 hour and 20 minute Manea Manea combination for 30.000 CFP for one person and 53.000 CFP for two. A 50-min. Hohoa Ofai, hot & cool stone facial is 15.000 CFP. Manicures, pedicures, waxing, and scalp exfoliation are also available.

Philippe Girodeau, *Tel./Fax 689/56.40.42, cell 77.54.79*, is my preferred massage therapist. He will bring his massage table to your room and make you feel like a new person after he works on your body, mind and soul. He opens your chakra energy centers and heals your aches and pains with magnetism and a pair of very strong hands. He charges 10.000 CFP, but the massage lasts more than an hour.

TATTOOS

Masters of the art can design tattoos for those of you who wish to wear a permanent souvenir of your trip to Moorea. All the tattooers are required to follow strict standards of hygiene. The cost of a Maohi tattoo depends on the design, and you'll pay around 10.000 CFP for a simple drawing.

Gilles Lovisa, *Tel. 77.58.23; www.lovisatattoo.com.* Gilles is a Frenchman who moved to French Polynesia in 1993 and learned to tattoo from the local tattoo masters. He formerly worked out of a tattoo *fare* on the beach at the Sofitel Moorea Resort, and now he works out of his house beside the lagoon at PK 5 in Maharepa, 150 m. (492 ft.) from Moorea Pearl Resort. Look for the blue *pareo* tied on a pole beside the road.

Moorea Tattoo, *Tel. 76.42.60/56.25.33; www.mooreatattoo.com.* James Samuela is a young Tahitian man who specializes in traditional tattoos, and also uses the tattoo machine on request. He studied at l'Ecole National des Beaux Arts in Paris and learned tattoo techniques from local tattoo masters who now come to admire James as he works. His tattoo shop is at his home on the mountainside of the road at PK 32 in the Varari section of Haapiti. James speaks English and is married to Laurel Samuela, an American woman who owns True Tahiti Vacation and Dive Tahiti Blue, as an online tour operator.

Taniera Tattoo, *Tel. 56.16.98, tanieratattoo@mail.pf,* is located on the mountainside at PK 27.3 in Haapiti, across road from Restaurant PK 0. He is noted for his personalized Tahitian tattoos.

You can also get tattooed at **Tiki Village**.

Note: Some of Moorea's most popular tattoo masters are no longer living on the island. Roonui and Tautu Ellis have moved to Canada and Purutu has gone to France for a while. Chimé will be in Europe for several months during 2008 before returning to Moorea.

PRACTICAL INFORMATION
Banks
All the banks are closed on weekends and holidays. They charge a commission for each transaction, which varies from bank to bank. They all have an ATM ready cash window.

Banque de Tahiti, *Tel. 55.00.55*, is on the lagoon side near the Maharepa Post Office. Open Mon.-Fri. 8am-12pm and 1:30-4:30pm. **Socredo Banque**, *Tel. 47.00.00*, is in the same shopping center as the Maharepa Post Office, Open Mon.-Fri. 8am-12pm and 1:30-4:30pm. Across the road in the Centre Noha is the **Banque de Polynésie**, *Tel. 55.05.80*. Open Mon.-Fri. 7:45am-12pm and 1:15-3:45pm. There is also a branch located in Le Petit Village in Haapiti, *Tel. 55.04.30*. Open 8am-12pm and 1:30-4:30pm.

Books, Newspapers & Magazines
•**Kina Maharepa**, *Tel. 56.22.44*, is in the same commercial center as the Post Office and Socredo Banque,
•**Supersonics**, *Tel. 55.05.30*, is in Le Petit Village in Haapiti,

Churches
If your hotel is in the Cook's Bay area, the Protestant church at PK 5 in Maharepa is a good choice. The Protestant church Ebenezer at PK 22 in Papetoai Village is octagonal and was built on the site that was once the royal Marae Taputapuatea, where heathen gods were worshipped. The first church in the South Seas was built here in 1827 and rebuilt in 1889. It has since been restored a few times. Another Protestant church is located at PK 35 in Haapiti, and the beautiful Catholic Church, Eglise de la Saint Famille Haapiti, is at PK 24 on the mountainside.

Saint Joseph's Chapel at PK 10 beside Cook's Bay contains a large mural depicting a Polynesian Nativity scene, painted in 1946 by Swedish artist Peter Heyman. The members of this little church wrote a letter to the Pope, asking permission to have a religious painting made, with Mary, Joseph and the Christ child portrayed as Polynesians. The Pope agreed to their proposal, stipulating that the painting should be a mural so that it would always remain in the church and not be transported elsewhere. When the building began to deteriorate, a new church was built next door, where services are still held. A wealthy Moorea resident had the chapel restored in 1999, and it is now used for weddings, baptisms and other special occasions.

Dentist
Dr. Fréderic Avet and Dr. Nicole Lebreton, *Tel. 56.32.44*, share offices in the Centre Noha, opposite the post office in Maharepa, They have modern equipment and good dental knowledge and techniques. Dr. Nicolas Marchadier, *Tel. 56.47.51*, is at PK 27.2 on the mountainside in Haapiti.

Doctor

In the Maharepa area Dr. Sonia Woerth, *Tel. 56.18.18*, has an office on the mountainside at PK 4.4, and Dr. Augustin Lejeune, *Tel. 56.30.31*, is at PK 6. Dr. Fréderic Foucher, *Tel. 56.32.32*, has an office in the Centre Noha, opposite the post office in Maharepa. Dr. Franck Gaudard and Dr. Jean-Marc Jouve, *Tel. 56.44.63*, are general practice doctors whose offices are above the pharmacy in Maharepa. Dr. Anabelle Montagne, *Tel. 56.56.82*, is at Le Petit Village, and Dr. Dominique Barraille, *Tel. 56.27.07*, and Dr. Pierre Birckel, *Tel. 56.15.55*, are also in the Haapiti area.

Drugstores

Pharmacie Tran is at PK 6.5 in Maharepa, *Tel. 55.20.75*. The hours are 7:30am-12pm and 2-6pm Mon.-Fri., 8am-12pm on Sat. and 8-11am on Sun. and holidays. Dr. Tran is Vietnamese and speaks good English. In case of emergency, knock on the door. The **Pharmacie of Haapiti** is located on the mountainside at PK 30.5, *Tel. 56.38.37/56.41.16*.

Glasses

Optique Moorea, *Tel. 56.55.44*, is in the small shopping center across from the Banque de Tahiti. They can make or repair glasses.

Hospital

The small government **Hospital of Afareaitu** is at PK 9 in Afareaitu Village, *Tel. 56.24.24/56.23.23. Tel. 17* or *56. 22.22* for ambulance service. Seriously ill or injured patients are evacuated by helicopter or airplane to Mamao Hospital in Tahiti.

Internet Service

There are several places on Moorea that provide Internet service, but the two best locations are:

Arts Polynésiens, *Tel. 70.66.38, www.arts-polynesiens.net*. The computers and printer are located in the back room of this boutique located in Le Petit Village in Haapiti. Open Mon.-Sat. 8:30am-6pm and on Sun. from 8am-12pm. They charge 15 CFP per min. for Internet connections in ADSL 512. They also have Wifi.

Top Phone Cyber Space, *Tel. 56.57.57*, is in the Cook's Bay Center of Maharepa, across from Hotel Kaveka. Open Mon.-Fri. 8am-5pm and Sat. 8am-12pm. They have 6 computers with ADSL Internet connection and a printer. They charge 200 CFP for 20 min.

You can also go to the following places to check your email:

Photo Magic, *Tel. 56.59.59/71.69.51*, is adjacent to La Plantation Restaurant in Haapiti. Open daily 8am-6:30pm. You can bring your own laptop and connect to ADSL with Wifi and Skype for one hour at 650 CFP and two hours at 1.100 CFP. Unlimited package rates are also available.

Iguane Rock Café, *Tel. 56.17.16*, is in Le Petit Village in Haapiti.

Maria Tapas, *Tel. 55.01.70*, is in the Kikipa Center at PK 6 in Maharepa.

Moorea Vision, *Tel. 55.01.75*, is at PK 9 in Pao Pao village, located across the road from the Ecole Maternelle de Pao Pao in Cook's Bay.

System Tek, *Tel. 55.20.70*, on the mountainside in the Centre Tumai at PK 2.7 in Tiaia, between the airport and Maharepa.

Internet service is also available at all the big hotels, and some of the family pensions, such as Residence Linareva and Pension Motu Iti.

Laundry

La Laverie Beatrice, *Tel. 56.17.19/70.64.65*, at PK 5.5 in the Orovau Center in Maharepa and near Chez Vina Restaurant and ICH Moorea. This pick-up and delivery laundry service is open Mon.-Sat. They charge 750 CFP to wash 5 kilos of clothes and 750 CFP to spin dry and fold 5 kilos. Ironing is also available for 200 CFP per piece.

Marina

The **Marina of Vaiare**, *Tel. 56.26.97; rporoi@mail.pf;* Rocky Poroi is in charge of this marina, which has 120 places for sailboats and deep-sea sportfishing boats up to 60 ft. on the pontoon and 60 places for boats on the embarkment. Showers, restrooms, telephone box and Wifi Internet access.

Police

The French *gendarmerie* is at PK 7 in Maharepa, *Tel. 17* or *Tel. 55.25.05*. Open daily 7am to 12pm and 2 to 6pm.

Post Office & Telecommunications Office

The **Maharepa Post Office**, *Tel. 56.10.12*, is located in the shopping center at PK 5.5. Hours are 7:30am-12pm and 1:30-4pm Mon. through Thurs., and on Fri. it closes at 3pm. It's also open on Sat. 7:30-9:30am. All telecommunications and postal services are available here. **Papetoai Post Office**, *Tel. 56.13.15*, is on the lagoon side in the center of Papetoai village. Open Mon. through Thurs. from 8am to 12pm, and from 1:30 to 4pm and until 3pm on Fri. Open on Sat. from 8 to 10am.

Tourist Information

Moorea Visitors Bureau, *Tel. 75.01.01; etm@mail.pf; www.gomoorea.com*. Their office is beside the road at Le Petit Village shopping center in Haapiti. The English-speaking hostess is on duty Mon.-Thurs. from 8am-12pm and 1-4pm, on Fri. from 8am-12pm and 1-3pm, and on holidays from 8am-12pm. Closed weekends.

Wedding Ceremonies

Tahitian Weddings are performed at the **Tiki Theatre Village** for lovers who get married back home and want to splurge for a fun-filled colorful wedding ceremony in the authentic tradition of old Polynesia. It's not just newlyweds who are getting married in the Tahitian style, but also loving couples who are celebrating their anniversaries or who want to renew their vows. The ceremony takes place on a *marae* stone altar with a Tahitian priest officiating. **Olivier Briac** and his Tiki Village artisans will transform you into a Tahitian prince and princess for your wedding ceremony for a marriage made in Paradise. There is even a floating *fare* in the lagoon where you can spend your honeymoon. Contact Olivier Briac at B.P. 1016, Haapiti, Moorea, *Tel. 689/55.02.50; Fax 689/56.10.86; tikivillage@mail.pf; www.tikivillage.pf.*

13. Huahine

Huahine (WHO-ah-HEE-nay) is a magical island. I discovered the special qualities of Huahine in 1977, when I was shipwrecked on the reef in Parea, on the south end of Huahine Iti, during a dark and stormy night, while sailing with American friends aboard their luxury yacht. The story has a happy ending, because the yacht was saved and we were adopted into a Tahitian family in Parea. I stayed there for six weeks just because the people were so nice.

On that first morning in Parea, from the cockpit of the yacht that was embedded on the coral reef, I watched the early dawn turning the whole world pink from the mountains to the village to the sea. There is a certain light and color of the air on this island that I haven't found anywhere else. The senses are heightened so that the colors of nature seem more vivid, the air more calm, yet at the same time charged with a feeling of anticipation. I realized that I was listening more intently for—perhaps the primeval call of the jungle.

I still have the same feeling for Huahine. The people are happy and relaxed and they have maintained their traditional lifestyle of fishing and farming. Family and friends are more important than television and Internet. The mountains of Huahine form the shape of a beautiful Tahitian woman when seen from the sea in the moonlight. And there's a definite aura of sexual energy in the air.

Huahine is 175 km. (110 mi.) northwest of Tahiti, the nearest of the Leeward Society Islands to the capital of Papeete. The two islands that comprise **Huahine-Nui** and **Huahine-Iti** (big and little Huahine) are connected by a bridge and have a combined surface area of 73 sq. km. (28 sq. mi.). Legend claims that the two islands were once united and the isthmus was formed when Hiro, a great warrior and god of thieves in Polynesian mythology, sliced his canoe through the island, dividing it and producing two beautiful bays on each side of the isthmus. Folklore tells us that Hiro used the Leeward Islands as his favorite hangout, and on Huahine you can see Hiro's paddle and parts of his anatomy in the stone formations of the cliffs overlooking the channel.

A common barrier reef surrounds the two islands, with several passes providing openings from the sea to the deep harbors. Offshore *motu* lie inside the reef, where watermelons and cantaloupe are grown in the white coral sand. These islets are surrounded by white sand beaches, ideal for a picnic outing with snorkeling in the living coral gardens.

A paved road winds 32 km. (20 mi.) around the two islands, passing through the little villages of Fare, Maeva, Faie and Fitii on Huahine Nui, and Haapu, Parea, Mahuti, Tefarerii and Maroe on Huahine Iti. The modest homes of the 6,070 inhabitants are built beside the lagoon in the small villages. Another paved road,

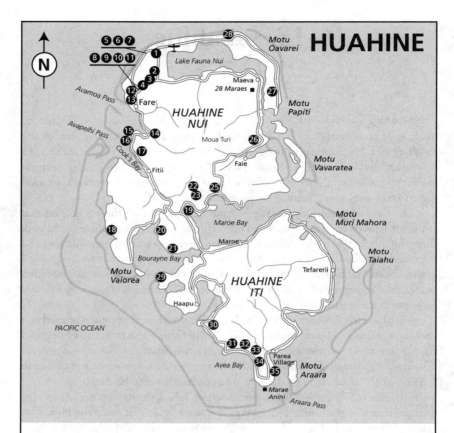

1. Chalet Tipanier
2. Motel Vanille
3. Chez Ella
4. La Petite Ferme
5. Fare Maeva
6. Pension Vaihonu
7. Pension Mama Roro
8. Rande's Shack
9. Fare Ie Fare
10. Pension Ariitere
11. Fare Punalea
12. Pension Enite
13. Chez Guynette

14. Pension Poetaina
15. Fare Ara L'ile Sauvage
16. Chez Henriette
17. Chez Meri
18. Te Tiare Beach Resort
19. Hotel Bellevue
20. Pension Tupuna
21. Fare Iita
22. Huahine Vacances
23. Villas Bougainville
24. Villas Standing
25. Residence Loisirs Maroe
26. Pension Te Nahe Toetoe

27. Vanaa Camping & Snack
28. Pension Fetia
29. Pension Hine Iti
30. Pension Te Nahe Toe Toe II
31. Pension Mauarii
32. Chez Tara
33. Hotel Relais Mahana
34. Fare Ie Parea
35. Huahine Camping
    (ex-Ariiura)

called *la route transversale*, crosses part of the island of Huahine Nui, and is best explored by Land Rover or Jeep or any 4WD vehicle, which are called 4x4 (*quatre-quatre* in French and pronounced like cat-cat). This road is close-hemmed by giant ferns and vines that look as though Tarzan might be seen swinging around these parts.

Skirting the shoreline and climbing a little higher into the fern-covered mountains, you will see spectacular views of natural bays and seascapes, with the white foam of the indigo ocean leaping into spray on the coral reef, giving birth to sapphire and emerald lagoons. One multihued bay near the village of Haapu is pointed out on tours as "Gauguin's palette." All around both islands are plantations of vanilla, coffee and taro, and groves of breadfruit, mango, banana and papaya. Trees of *purau* and kapok grow among tangled masses of untamed wilderness. Swiftly flowing streams make their way from their mountain origins, winding through the *mape* forests to form delightful pools for fresh water shrimp.

Mou'a Tapu is the sacred mountain overlooking the prehistoric village of Maeva, which is built beside Lake Fauna Nui. The mountain forms a pyramid, and the people of Maeva say there is a power spot on its summit, which is 429 m. (1,407 ft.) high. A tiki of white coral and a Tiare Taina (gardenia) bush are found here. You can reach this spot by going up the road where the television antenna is located on the southern side of the mountain.

According to ethnohistory, Maeva was the ancient capital of Huahine, and all its ruling families lived there and worshipped in their individual *marae* temples of stone. The great Marae Manunu on the coral islet on the opposite side of Maeva Village was the community temple for Huahine Nui, and Marae Anini at Point Tiva in Parea was the community *marae* for Huahine Iti.

European Discovery

Lieutenant James Cook (who was later promoted to Captain) was the first European to discover Huahine, when he anchored the *Endeavour* in the harbor of Farenui-Atea on July 15, 1769. You can see the islands of Raiatea, Taha'a and Bora Bora from Huahine, which Cook named a Society of Islands, 'because they lay contiguous to one another'.

Cook returned to Huahine in 1773 aboard the *Resolution*, along with the *Adventure*, under the command of Captain Tobias Furneaux. When the two ships set sail, a young man from Raiatea who lived in Huahine went with them. His name was Mai but the Englishmen call him Omai. He became the first Tahitian to discover England, where he was presented to King George III on July 17, 1774. Cook brought Omai back to Huahine in 1777 during his third and final voyage to the South Seas.

After Cook's departure there were few Europeans who visited Huahine, until 1808-09, when a party of Protestant missionaries from the London Missionary Society made it their headquarters for nearly a year. When Christianity was adopted in Tahiti in 1818 the missionaries returned to Huahine and opened a

HUAHINE'S ARCHAEOLOGICAL SITES

The royal village of **Maeva** was the traditional headquarters of Huahine, the capital of a complex and highly centralized system of government. This was the only place in the entire Polynesian triangle where the royal families lived side by side. The people of Maeva say that the sacred mountain of Mou'a Tapu protected them. Each of the eight district chiefs of Huahine held court at Maeva and ruled in his province through envoys. Each royal household had a marae stone temple in Maeva as well as in his provincial seat. When the children of each household approached maturity, they, too, each had a temple erected. Consequently, there are some 200 marae in Maeva.

Doctor Yosihiko H. Sinoto, Senior Anthropologist of the Bernice P. Bishop Museum in Honolulu, restored several of the marae temples in Maeva Village and on nearby Matairea Hill in 1967 and 1968. He also restored the stone fish weirs in Lake Fauna Nui, which were used by the ancient fishermen of Maeva. In 1972 Doctor Sinoto began excavation of two archaeological sites on the grounds of the former Hotel Bali Hai in Huahine. Over a period of years he and his assistants unearthed a village community that existed between 850 and 1200 AD, which had been destroyed by tidal waves. Doctor Sinoto has restored some 200 sites, including 35 marae temples, plus council platforms and housing sites on Matairea Hill in Maeva Village. Inside the Fare Pote'e, an oval-shaped traditional meetinghouse that is built over Lake Fauna Nui is a museum where you can pick up a map of Matairea Hill. Follow the cultural and scenic hiking trail to visit the restored sites and learn the story of the royal village.

station. The Reverend William Ellis in *Polynesian Researches* tells a first-hand account of this story.

Huahine's warrior-queen Teha'apapa defended her island against the aggressions made by the men of Bora Bora, and she won a great naval battle against the forces of Tahiti's Queen Pomare, who tried to gain control of Huahine. In 1846 Teha'apapa won a land battle against French troops at Maeva, and 24 Frenchmen are buried in Maeva Village, surrounded by seven broken cannon. Huahine defended its independence until 1888, when the regent Marama accepted the French protectorate. In 1898 Huahine became a French colony, but it was not until 1946 that the people of Huahine became French citizens, 58 years after the residents of Tahiti.

ARRIVALS & DEPARTURES
Arriving By Air
Air Tahiti has 4-6 flights daily between Tahiti and Huahine. The 40-minute

non-stop flight is 10.600 CFP one-way for adults, and 19.500 CFP round-trip, tax included. There is also a daily direct flight from Moorea, which costs 13.000 CFP one-way. You can fly from Raiatea to Huahine every day except Sun. for 5.600 CFP, and with 1-2 daily flights from Bora Bora, for 7.900 CFP. **Air Tahiti reservations:** Tahiti, *Tel. 86.42.42;* Moorea, *Tel. 55.06.00;* Huahine, *Tel. 68.77.02/ 60.62.60.*

If you have hotel reservations then you will be met at the airport and driven to your hotel. There are also taxis at the airport, as well as **Avis** and **Europcar** counters. Brochures of hotels, pensions and activities are available in a wall rack close to the arrival gate. A couple of small boutiques and the **Vakalele II** snack bar are located in the airport terminal.

You can also get to Huahine by chartering an airplane in Tahiti from **Air Archipels,** *Tel. 81.30.30;* or **Air Tahiti,** *Tel. 86.42.42.*

Arriving By Boat

All the inter-island transport boats dock at the quay in Fare village, the main town of Huahine, and it would be advisable to arrange with your hotel or pension to have someone meet you when you arrive in the middle of the night. The car rental agencies will also meet you at the Fare quay. A travel agency and visitors information center is across the street from the quay.

Hawaiki Nui, *Tel. 54.99.54/Fax 45.24.44, contact@stim.pf.* This 12-passenger ship leaves the Motu Uta dock in Papeete each Tues. at 4pm and arrives at Fare quay in Huahine on Wed. at 2am. The Thurs. trip leaves Papeete at 4pm, and arrives in Huahine on Fri. at 4:30pm, after visiting Raiatea, Bora Bora, Taha'a and Raiatea again. The cost of sleeping on deck is 1.800 CFP per person and a berth in one of the 4 double cabins costs 5.000 CFP from Papeete to all the Leeward Islands. Meals are available on board. Passengers must sleep in cabins on the Thurs. voyage as the ship also transports fuel then.

Vaeanu, *Tel. 41.25.35; Fax 41.24.34, torehiatetu@mail.pf.* This ship can transport a total of 90 passengers, with 32 berths in cabins and 58 places on the deck. It departs from the Fare-Ute quay in Papeete at 4pm on Mon., Wed. and Fri., arriving in Huahine at 12:30am the following morning. The ship continues on to Raiatea, Taha'a, Bora Bora and Raiatea again, then stops in Huahine on its way back to Tahiti each Tues. and Thurs. at 5:30pm and each Sun. at 4pm. One-way fares for deck passengers are: 2.120 CFP from Tahiti to Huahine; 1.690 from Bora Bora; 1.400 CFP from Taha'a and 1.060 CFP from Raiatea. A berth in a cabin costs 4.400 to 5.989 CFP per person depending on accommodations chosen, and the entire cabin can be rented for 9.858 to 13.197 CFP. Meals are served on board. Reservations for cabin space must be paid in full before 9am on the fixed date of departure from Papeete.

Departing By Air

You can fly from Huahine to Raiatea or Bora Bora or return to Moorea (1 flight daily) or Tahiti (3-6 daily flights) by **Air Tahiti**, *Tel. 68.77.02/60.62.60* in Huahine. Tickets can be purchased at the airport or at the Air Tahiti office in Fare village. If you already have reservations and a ticket and need to reconfirm your flight, most hotels will take care of this for you or you can do it yourself one day in advance. Check-in time at the airport is one hour before scheduled departure.

Departing By Boat
You can continue on to Raiatea, Taha'a and Bora Bora by boat from Huahine, or you can return to Papeete.
Hawaiki Nui, *Tel. 68.78.03* (Huahine); *Tel. 54.99.54* (Tahiti), leaves Huahine for Raiatea, Bora Bora, Taha'a and back to Raiatea each Wed. at 3am. On Fri. it leaves Huahine for Tahiti at 6:30pm, arriving in Papeete on Sat. at 5am.
Vaeanu, *Tel. 68.73.73* (Huahine); *Tel. 41.25.35* (Tahiti), leaves Huahine at 1:30am each Tues., Thurs. and Sat. for Raiatea, Taha'a and Bora Bora and back to Raiatea and Huahine (also stopping again in Taha'a on the Sun. voyage). The return trips from Huahine to Papeete leave Fare each Tues. and Thurs. at 6pm, arriving in Papeete at 3am the following day. On Sun. the ship leaves Huahine at 4:30pm for Papeete, arriving each Mon. at 2am.

ORIENTATION

To get from the airport in Huahine to the hotels you will turn right to reach the road that circles the island of Huahine-Nui. When you come to this road you will turn right to go to the main village of **Fare** (pronounced Fah-rey) and the land base for Te Tiare Beach Resort. Turn left if you want to go to **Maeva Village**. You can drive in either direction to reach Huahine-Iti, where Hotel Relais Mahana and a few pensions are located. If you arrive by boat you will disembark on the dock at Fare, right in the center of Huahine's "downtown" area. Fare looks like a sleepy little village, shaded by acacia and South Seas almond trees, but it certainly wakes up on boat days when the passenger or supply ships arrive. Then you have traffic jams in the center of the village. On the waterfront street opposite the quay are the Banque de Tahiti, a couple of snack bars and small restaurants, two pensions, car, scooter and bicycle rentals, service station, scuba diving center, a supermarket, general merchandise and clothing stores, boutiques, a photo shop and jewelry shop. The post office, *gendarmerie*, private doctors, pharmacy and a 15-bed dispensary are within easy walking distance.

GETTING AROUND HUAHINE
Car, Scooter & Bicycle Rentals
Europcar has a sales office facing the post office in Fare, *Tel. 68.82.59*; at the Port of Fare, *Tel. 68.88.03*; and a sales desk at the Relais Mahana, *Tel. 68.71.62*. A 3-door Punto rents for 6.500 CFP for 4 hrs., 8.000 CFP for 8 hrs. and 9.400 CFP for 24 hrs. A 5-door a/c Peugeot 206 rents for 9.100 CFP for 4 hrs., 11.800 CFP for 8 hrs. and 13.000 CFP for 24 hrs. A Bugxter is 5.500 CFP for 4 hrs. and 6.500

CFP for 8 hrs. Scooter rates are 4.800 CFP for 4 hrs., 5.800 CFP for 8 hrs. and 6.200 CFP for 24 hrs. These rates include unlimited mileage and third party insurance. Gas is extra.

Fare Nui Avis, *Tel. 68.73.34; Fax 68.73.35; avis.tahiti@mail.pf.* They have a sales counter at the airport and at the Mobil service station behind the Super Farenui store in Fare village. A 5-door a/c Hyundai Getz is 7.590 CFP for 24 hrs. Rates include taxes, unlimited mileage and insurance. Gas is extra.

Huahine Location/Hertz, *Tel. 68.76.85; huahinelocation@mail.pf; www.huahinelocation.com.* The sales office is located on the waterfront in Fare village and they have a counter at the airport and at Pension Mauarii on Huahine Iti. Free delivery. An a/c 5-door Hyundai Getz rents for 7.900 CFP for 24 hrs., including unlimited mileage and insurance. Gas is extra. Scooters rent for 4.800 CFP for 24 hrs.

Bicycles/Boats/Kayaks

Europcar, *Tel. 68.82.59,* rents bikes for 1.200 CFP for 4 hrs. and 1.600 CFP for 8 hrs. Longer rentals possible.

Huahine Lagoon, *Tel. 68.70.00,* on the quay of Fare adjacent to Pension Chez Guynette. You can rent beach bikes, kayaks, and small boats.

Taxis

Taxi service is provided by **Enite Excursions,** *Tel. 68.82.37/73.05.07,* and **Taxi Moe,** *Tel. 72.80.60/68.83.75.* **Hei Maohi Taxi,** *Tel. 68.73.60/73.65.10,* makes transfers to Huahine Iti.

Le Truck

The local transportation service, *le truck,* operates between the boat dock in Fare and the outlying villages around Huahine Nui and Huahine Iti, coordinating their runs with the arrivals and departures of the inter-island ferries and school hours. The name of the destination is painted on the wooden sides of each *le truck.* Although the fares are affordable for all budgets, hopping aboard a *le truck* is not recommended if you don't know your way around Huahine, and especially if you don't speak any French or Tahitian. But if you are adventurous, this is a fun way to discover the island and its inhabitants.

WHERE TO STAY
Huahine Nui – Deluxe

TE TIARE BEACH RESORT, *B.P. 36, Fare, Huahine 98731. Tel. 689/ 60.60.50; Fax 689/60.60.51; frontoffice@tetiarebeachresort.pf; res@spmhotels.pf; www.tetiarebeachresort.com. Located on the coast of Fitii, 20 min. by boat from the main village of Fare. 41 bungalows. 2008 EP Rates sgl./dbl.: Garden Bungalow 39.000 CFP; Beach Bungalow 58.000 CFP; Lagoon Bungalow 62.000 CFP; Deep Overwater Bungalow 78.000 CFP; add 5.000 CFP for 3rd person. Round-trip arrival/*

departure boat transfers 5.900 CFP per person. Add 7.700 CFP for MAP and 11.000 CFP for AP. Add taxes. All major credit cards.

This 4-star hotel is owned by American businessman Rudy Markmiller, and is managed by Tahiti-based South Pacific Management as a Pearl Resort. It opened in March 1999 and closed in Feb. 2007 for a big sprucing up program that included new roofs and varnish for the woodwork. The accommodations consist of 19 garden bungalows, 6 beach bungalows, 5 lagoon bungalows and 11 deep overwater bungalows, beside and over the lagoon in the district called Fitii. The hotel property can be reached only by boat, about a 12-min. ride from Fare village to the resort. All of the bungalows face west, so guests may enjoy the island's spectacular tropical sunsets as well as admire the nearby islands of Raiatea and Taha'a. Your first impression when you arrive here will be a sense of spaciousness and total tranquility. The reception, lobby, lounge, main bar, restaurant and boutique are built over the lagoon, suspended over the water on sturdy concrete pilings. The motif of this complex is tastefully Polynesian, with a huge thatched roof, ceiling fans, shell chandeliers, rattan tables and chairs, bamboo and woven pandanus decorations, and a Tahitian trio playing island tunes in the evening, while lovely *vahines* dressed in Polynesian colors and flowers take your order and serve you an excellent meal that combines French and local style cuisine.

On land the hotel site covers 28.17 acres (11.4 ha.) of tropical plants and flowers and flat ground. The deluxe bungalows are among the largest rooms you will find in Tahiti and Her Islands. You may not even want to leave your room because they are so comfortable. You don't even have to go out to eat if you want to order from room service, which is available from 7:30am to 9:30pm.

Each bungalow features a king-size bed comprised of 2 mattresses, and a living room with sofa, chairs and tables, a/c and ceiling fan, a wet bar, refrigerator, coffee and tea facilities, cable TV, IDD telephones, and a separate dressing room in which you will find a personal safe. The overwater bungalows have a large Jacuzzi bathtub and a separate shower with powerful water pressure. (The water at Te Tiare Resort comes from a fresh underground spring, which is filtered, offering you a very high quality of drinking water.) All the bathrooms have separate toilets and hair dryers. There is twice-daily maid service to bring you more towels, bath gels and lotions. All the doors and windows are screened and you even have blackout curtains for more privacy. The terraces for these units are L-shaped and partially covered, with deck chairs for sunbathing or reading and snoozing in the shade. A ladder leads down a few steps into the shallow lagoon.

Next to the lagoon are a free form swimming pool and new beach restaurant and bar, as well as the water sports facilities. Complimentary activities include scheduled boat transfers to and from the main town of Fare, snorkeling equipment, outrigger paddle canoes, kayaks, beach volleyball, ping-pong and board games. Optional activities include land tours by 4WD, horseback riding, sunset catamaran cruises, deep sea fishing, shark feeding, island tour by outrigger speed canoe, picnic on a motu, jet-skiing, scuba diving and sailboat excursions. Car, scooter and bicycle rentals, as well as Jeep safaris and other land excursions, are operated from the Te Tiare land base in Fare village. You can also enjoy a relaxing massage in the privacy of your bungalow for 12.000 CFP per hr., you can practice your asanas with a yoga teacher for 6.000 CFP per person, or you can get a tattoo. There are 3 computers in the overwater lounge and you can buy tickets at the reception for 450 CFP for 15 min. or 900 CFP for 30 min. Boutique Pearls by Corrion is located in the overwater restaurant/bar/reception complex.

Special evenings at the Ari'i Restaurant at Te Tiare Resort include an Exotic Buffet for 5.800 CFP, which is accompanied by a Polynesian dance group. During high seasons there is also a Seafood Buffet and dance show for 6.200 CFP. See more information under *Where to Eat* in this chapter.

Various cultural demonstrations are given each evening at the Hawaiki Nui Bar at 6pm, while Tahitian musicians play romantic island songs to complete your dream come true. Honeymooners and couples celebrating anniversaries or other special events can contact the hotel directly for a list of the Romantic Rendez-Vous programs that are designed especially for lovers. These even include a non-binding Polynesian wedding ceremony on the white sand beach, with the bride and groom arriving by outrigger paddle canoe.

Family Pensions, Guest Houses, B&B, Backpackers' Lodgings, & Campgrounds
Moderate

MOTEL VANILLE, *B.P. 381, Fare, Huahine 98731. Tel./Fax 689/68.71.77; yvesmotelvani@hotmail.com; www.motelvanille.com. Located beside the road 1 km. (0.62 mi.) from the airport, 1 km. from the beach, and 1 km. from Fare village. Free transfers and breakfast. 2008 Rates: EP bungalow 9.900 CFP sgl/dbl, plus taxes. MAP meals add 3.500 CFP per person. Minimum stay 2 nights. MC, V.*

This small family hotel is the first lodging you come to when leaving the airport, as it is built on the corner between the airport road and the circle island road. There are 5 bungalows with a choice of sleeping accommodations for 2-4 people, private bathroom with hot water, and a terrace. All the Tahitian style *fare* units are built of local woods, bamboo and thatched roofs, and the windows are screened. They are set in a tropical garden around a swimming pool, and you cannot see the ocean from here. Bicycles are free for guests and a restaurant-snack is located on the premises. See more information under *Where to Eat* in this chapter.

PENSION POETAINA, *B.P. 522, Fare, Huahine 98731. Tel. 60.60.06; 78.86.39; Fax 689/60.60.05; pensionpoetaina@mail.pf; www.poetaina.com. Located on the mountainside of the road in Fare village, 3 km. (1.8 mi.) from the airport and 1 km. (.62 mi.) from the ferry dock. Free transfers. 2008 EP Rates sgl./dbl.: Room with fan and shared bathroom 8.480 CFP; Room with a/c and private bath 11.130 CFP; Family room with private bathroom, kitchen and electric fan 12.720 CFP; 14.520 CFP triple. Breakfast included for all rooms. Add municipal tax. MC, V.*

Jean-Pierre Amo and his wife Damiana have built a big 3-story white concrete house in the South Seas neo-colonial style, with a huge sun deck on the top floor.

There are 4 rooms with a double and single bed, sharing 2 communal bathrooms and hot water; 3 family rooms with a/c, a double bed, single bed and private bathroom; and a family room with a king size bed, single bed, private bathroom and kitchenette. Downstairs is a living room with TV and activity area, a kitchen and dining room, which are all shared, as well as the big terrace and swimming pool. Jean-Pierre has a cute little *le truck* that he uses to transport his guests to and from the airport and village. He also operates Poetaina Cruises, providing a choice of lagoon excursions and picnics on the motu. Bicycles, horseback riding, scuba diving and all other activities can be arranged through the pension. Poetaina Restaurant is located in Fare village facing the fishermen's wharf. Guests staying in Pension Poetaina are driven to the restaurant and back for dinner on request. The MAP plan is 2.000 CFP per person, which includes the appetizer, main course and a dessert. Or you can order from the menu and pay a little extra. See *Where to Eat* and *Lagoon Excursions* in this chapter.

HOTEL BELLEVUE, *B.P. 21, Fare, Huahine 98731. Tel. 689/68.82.76; Fax 689/68.85.35. Located on the mountainside overlooking Maroe Bay, 6 km. (4 mi.) from the airport and 5 km. (3 mi.) from the ferry dock in Fare village. Round-trip transfers 1.600 CFP per person. 10 garden bungalows. 2008 EP Rates: bungalow without kitchen 6.000 CFP sgl, 7.000 CFP dbl, 8.000 CFP triple; bungalow with kitchen 7.000 CFP sgl, 8.000 CFP dbl, 9.000 CFP triple. Add taxes. MC, V.*

Most visitors to Huahine see the Hotel Bellevue when they are riding around the island in a tour bus. It is perched on the top of a knoll overlooking the panoramic scenery of Maroe Bay and the hills beyond. This is one of those places that is discovered by travelers who have the time to get to know an island, its people and its delightful secrets.

Each of the 10 colonial style bungalows contains a double bed with mosquito net, a private bathroom with hot water provided by solar heating, and individual terraces overlooking the fresh water swimming pool and the view of Maroe Bay. 4 of these units are equipped with their own kitchen, and guests staying in the other 6 bungalows without kitchens share the communal kitchen.

This small hotel is owned by Eliane and François Lefoc, a Chinese couple from Huahine who were once noted for the delicious seafood they served in their restaurant, before they turned the kitchen over to their guests. The Lefocs do not speak much English, but they say a lot with their eyes and gestures. Eliane will drive you to Fare village for supplies or you can also walk down to the road and catch *le truck.*

PENSION VAIHONU, *B.P. 302, Fare, Huahine 98731. Tel. 689/68.87.33/ 79.20.65/71.96.03; Fax 689/68.77.57; vaihonu@mail.pf; www.iaorana-huahine.com/fr/vaihonu.html. Located beside the sea at PK 1 in Fare, between the airport and the village. Free transfers. EP 2-story cottage 8.000 CFP sgl/dbl, extra adult 1.800 CFP; child 9-12 years 900 CFP; beach hut 3.500 CFP sgl, 5.000 CFP dbl; dormitory 1.800 CFP per person. Add taxes. 2-night minimum stay at rates quoted. Add 2.900 CFP per person for MAP and 4.800 for AP. MC, V.*

Owner-manager Etienne Faaeva has worked in tourism in Tahiti and Huahine for several years, and his English is excellent. His facilities are clean and attractive and the atmosphere is laid back and fun. If you are coming from Fare village look for the dirt road just past La Petite Ferme; turn left there and head toward the sea; turn left again at the last road before you get to the end at Fare Maeva; continue a short distance until you see the Vaihonu sign.

Available for guests are 2 concrete 2-level duplexes, 3 small wooden beach huts facing the sea, and a 7-bed dormitory. The duplex cottages are equipped with 2 double beds and a ceiling fan upstairs, and on the ground level there is a bright, cheerful kitchen with a dining area, plus a private bathroom. The windows are screened and the floors are tiled. Each beach hut has a double bed, and the kitchen and bathroom with cold-water showers are in another block, shared with guests staying in the dorm. Sheets are furnished and regularly changed for all guests, but you must bring your own towels when staying in beach huts or dorm.

The restaurant serves Chinese and local style dishes on request. See *Where to Eat* in this chapter. Etienne also owns Huahine Explorer and can organize your safari excursions and other activities. This is a family of excellent musicians, and if you are in residence during one of Etienne's frequent barbecue parties, you'll truly enjoy the beautiful island songs they sing while playing the guitar and ukulele.

FARE MAEVA, *B.P. 675, Fare, Huahine 98731. Tel. 689/68.75.53/72.89.60; Fax 689/68.70.68; faremaeva@mail.pf; www.fare-maeva.com. Located beside the sea on the outskirts of Fare, 3 km. (1.8 mi.) from the ferry dock and 1 km. (.62 mi.) from the airport. Free transfers and breakfast. EP Rates sgl. /dbl.: Room 7.000 CFP; Bungalow 12.100 CFP. Add municipal tax. MC, V.*

Ten yellow concrete bungalows with sheet metal roofs are built in a garden setting 20 m. (66 ft.) from the sea. Each small unit is a/c and furnished with cheerful colors and contains a double bed, a salon with 2 single beds, dining area and equipped kitchen, a private bathroom with cold water, and a terrace. 4 bungalows have easy access for handicapped guests. There are also 10 a/c rooms with a double bed and a private bathroom. Restaurant Tehina is part of the pension, where you can eat all your meals if you don't want to cook. See information under *Where to Eat* in this chapter. Guests have free use of the swimming pool. You can also rent bicycles here and the reception people will help you organize your tours and excursions.

FARE ARA L'ILE SAUVAGE, *B. P. 13,779 Carrefour, Punaauia, Tahiti 98717. Tel. 689/74.96.08; Fax 689/68.75.08; fare-ara@mail.pf; www.fare-ara.blog.fr. On the mountainside, 5 min. from the center of Fare. Free transfers. 2008 Rates: Room 7.000 CFP sgl. /dbl; 11.000 CFP 3-4 people. Extra person 1.500 CFP. See package rates below. No credit cards.*

There are 2 comfortable houses, each with 2 bedrooms, living room, equipped kitchen, bathroom with hot water, washing machine, TV, and house linens. Free activities include bikes, canoes, snorkeling gear, barbecue grill and visits to a vanilla farm. You can also rent a house with a car and boat. A 3-day minimum package for a house + car is 14.500 CFP for 2 and 18.500 CFP for 3 people. Add 1.500 CFP per person, for a maximum of 6. A 3-day package for a house + car + boat for 3 days is 19.000-23.000 CFP; and a 2-night package for the house, car for 24 hrs. and the boat for 1 day is 32.000-40.000 CFP.

Economy

CHEZ GUYNETTE CLUB-BED, *B. P. 87, Fare, Huahine 98731. Tel./Fax 689/68.83.75; chezguynette@mail.pf; www.iaorana-huahine.com/fr/guynette.html. In the center of Fare village, opposite the ferry dock and 3 km. (1.9 mi.) from the airport. 7 rooms and an 8-berth dormitory. One-way transfers 500 CFP per person. 2008 EP Rates: Room 4.900 CFP sgl, 5.900 CFP dbl, 6.900 CFP triple; for 1 night only add 300 CFP per person; bed in dormitory 1.750 CFP; for a 1-night stay the dormitory bed is 2.000 CFP per person. Rates include all taxes. MC, V.*

This is my favorite place to stay in Huahine when I want to meet all kinds of interesting people while sitting on the terrace facing the road and beach in the middle of Fare village. If you arrive in Huahine by inter-island ferryboat you can walk across the road from the boat dock and you'll be at Chez Guynette, which is operated by my friend Marty Pratt Temahahe, an American expatriate who bought the pension in April 1998. The hostel has 7 large rooms, each with a double bed and 1-2 bunk beds, and a private bathroom with hot water. There is also an 8-bed dormitory, sharing a communal bathroom with hot water, and a big, clean and homey kitchen where you can cook your own food. The windows are all screened and each room has a ceiling fan. Linens are furnished. Marty and her Tahitian husband, Moe, gave Chez Guynette a thorough face-lift in 2004 and continue to upgrade and improve the facilities year-round. In the reception area Marty has all the information posted on the activities available on Huahine. You'll enjoy eating the breakfasts and snacks prepared in the local style even if you're not sleeping in the pension. See information under *Where to Eat* in this chapter.

You'll be right in the center of village life on a small tropical island here, with the benefit of walking across the road to a white sand beach for a wonderful swim in the warm lagoon, or watching the inter-island freighters and luxury passenger ships coming and going.

PENSION ENITE, *B.P. 37, Fare, Huahine 98731. Tel./Fax 689/68.82.37. Located at the end of the waterfront street in Fare. Round-trip airport transfers 1.200 CFP per person. 2008 Rates: Room with MAP 9.000 CFP sgl; 6.900 CFP per person if there are 2 or more people; child 2-12 years 4.800 CFP. Room only with one dbl. bed 6.000 CFP sgl. /dbl.; Room only with a dbl. bed and sgl. bed 7.000 CFP for 1-3 people. Add taxes. No credit cards.*

This is one of the oldest pensions on the island, with 8 rooms located next to the lagoon. Guests share a living room and a bathroom with hot water. Owner Enite Temaiana has earned a worthy reputation for the cuisine she serves her guests in the open-air restaurant. She also operates a taxi service and will take you on excursions around the island.

PENSION FETIA, *B.P. 73, Fare, Huahine 98731. Tel. 689/72.09.50; Fax 689/68.83.71; pension-fetia@caramail.com; www.ifrance.com/polynesie-pension-fetia. On the beach at Motu Maeva, 2.5 km. from the airport and 5 km. from boat dock in Fare village. Free transfers and breakfasts. 2008 EP Rates: Bungalow 8.000 CFP dbl, 10.000 CFP for 3-4, and 15.000 CFP for 6-8 people. No credit cards.*

Réjane and Pierre Ah-Min have 5 bungalows in a coconut grove beside the ocean shore on Motu Maeva. Made of wood, bamboo and stone, they can sleep a couple or up to 8 guests. Each bungalow has mosquito nets over the beds, a private bathroom and a kitchen. Réjane's generous meals are served family style in a restaurant overlooking the ocean.

RANDE'S SHACK, *B.P. 112, Fare, Huahine 98731. Tel./Fax 689/68.86.27; randesshack@mail.pf. On the beach between the airport and boat dock, a short walk from Fare village. 2008 EP Rates: 1-bedroom house for 3 people, 10.000 CFP per night; 2-bedroom house for 4-5 people, 15.000 CFP per night. Min. of 3 nights required. Add municipal tax. No credit cards.*

American expatriate Rande Vetterli and his Moorean wife Emere have 2 fully equipped houses that are set in a garden full of fruit trees. The houses are very clean and completely screened, with full kitchens, private bathrooms, hot water, linens, washing machines and bicycles. You will need to provide your own toiletries and car transportation and there is no maid service available. A 15-min. walk along the white sand beach or on the road will bring you to Fare village, where you can find restaurants and supermarkets. You can also spend hours snorkeling in the marvelous lagoon in front of the property or walk down the beach to the site where the Hotel Bali Hai used to stand, and swim in this lost paradise. Rande's Shack is highly recommended by discerning Canadian friends who visit Huahine frequently. They think this is the best buy in French Polynesia and stay here each year for 2-3 months.

PENSION MEHERIO, *Tel. 689/60.61.35; Fax 689/60.61.36; meherio.huahine@mail.pf. Located 10 min. by car from the airport and 2 min. from Fare village. 2008 EP Rates sgl. /dbl.: 10.000 CFP, breakfast included. MC. V.*

This is a new lodging in the midst of a lovely flower garden of Tiare Tahiti, gardenias and hibiscus, 200 m. (656 ft.) from the public beach of Fare. There are 3 buildings covered with woven bamboo, with the reception in the middle building and the 7 rooms divided in 2 side buildings. Each room is decorated in a colorful Polynesian style with woven bamboo wall coverings, pareo curtains and bedding, and paintings by local artists. There is a double bed, mosquito net, electric fan and a private bathroom and covered terrace. Two rooms are equipped for people with reduced mobility. The rooms are cleaned every 2 days.

Breakfast and dinner are served in the restaurant, which is closed at noon. The good meals feature local products, and the Sunday morning breakfast also contains coconut bread and *firi firi*, the famous Tahitian doughnut. There is a TV and DVD player in the lounge, as well as a small library and board games. A safety deposit box is available at the reception and laundry service is optional. Guests have free use of the kayaks, snorkeling equipment and bicycles, as well as the lounge chairs and parasols. All the island's activities and excursions can be arranged on request.

FARE IITA, *B.P. 629, Fare, Huahine 98731. Tel. 689/68.70.21; www.fare-iita.net. On mountainside in Bourayne Bay. 2008 Rates: Room only 6.000 CFP sgl., 7.500 CFP dbl., extra person 2.000 CFP; add 3.000 CFP per person for MAP and 5.000 CFP for AP. Breakfast and day transfers included; night transfers 1.000 CFP. Entire house with 12-ft. motor boat 25.000 CFP for maximum 8 people, with breakfast and transfers included.*

The Papaya House (Fare Iita) is in Bourayne Bay, between Huahine Nui and Huahine Iti. You can cook your own meals or let Christine, your French landlady and neighbor, do it for you. This 4-bedroom wooden house is from Chile, and includes a bathroom with bathtub, a bathroom with shower, plus an outdoor shower. There is an American style kitchen and a big covered terrace, plus solar hot water, fans and mosquito nets. This is a good choice for families as there are 2 kids next door. Daniel, the landlord, will transfer you to the beach for 2.000 CFP each, and you can paddle a kayak, or rent a boat without license for 5.000 CFP for a half-day and 8.000 CFP for all day.

Huahine Iti – Moderate

RELAIS MAHANA, *B.P. 30, Fare, Huahine 98731. Tel. 689/60.60.40; Fax 689/68.85.08; relaismahana@mail.pf; www.relaismahana.com. Located at Avea Bay on Huahine's best white sand beach, (25 km.) 15.5 mi. from the airport, on the southwest side of Huahine Iti, just outside Parea Village. Round-trip transfers from airport 4.136 CFP. 2008 EP Rates sgl./dbl.: Garden Room 21.500 CFP; Deluxe Garden Bungalow 22.500 CFP, Superior Garden Bungalow 26.500 CFP; Deluxe Beach Bungalow 25.000 CFP; Superior Beach Bungalow 28.500 CFP; extra person 2.474 CFP. Add municipal tax. All major credit cards.*

This 3-star hotel opened in 1985 with 12 bungalows, and added more units over the years. Then the hotel closed in Nov. 2006 for rebuilding, adding new bungalows and remodeling some of the old ones. It reopened in March 2007 with 32 units, including deluxe and superior bungalows in the garden and on the white sand beach, plus 10 garden rooms with connecting doors. The superior bungalows, on the right side of the reception area, were only redecorated as they were still fairly new. These are the larger units usually occupied by families. The new rooms and deluxe bungalows on the left side of reception are built of balau wood from Bali. They have thatched roofs, tiled floors, woven wall mats, and a covered terrace with wicker table and chairs. The deluxe bungalows have a king size bed and a twin bed and the superior units have a king and 2 twin beds. The bedding is all white with accent cushions. All the rooms have ceiling fans, a long vanity desk with telephone, flat screen TV with satellite cable; coffee/tea making machines, and mini-bar. The bathrooms in the deluxe units have a separate toilet, a shower with rainshower and wand nozzles, a hair dryer and an iron in the closet. In all 12 of the deluxe bungalows you can step down from the shower into a walled garden with a locked gate that opens with your room key. Glass doors between the bathroom and bedroom may give a feeling of space, but they allow no privacy in either room, and there is no fresh air circulation in the bedroom when the sliding glass doors to the terrace are closed. There is maid service twice a day. Owner Franck Guillot said he plans to add free ADSL Internet service in the rooms in 2008.

There is a restaurant and bar in the main building, where breakfast and dinner are served. Lunch is normally served on the terrace, where there is a barbecue grill. See more information under *Where to Eat* in this chapter.

The white sand beach in front of the hotel curves along the aqua and deep turquoise waters of Avea Bay, which offers some of the island's best coral gardens for snorkeling. This bay is also a haven for cruising yachts and the swimming here is especially delightful. During the renovations of 2006-2007, the hotel's long pier was also rebuilt. The hotel grounds at the edge of the beach are partially shaded by enormous trees. These include tamanu, almond, miro (rosewood), tahinu, tiare kahaia and purau (wild hibiscus) trees. A bench has been built into the convoluted root system of an ancient almond tree that has grown together with a tamanu tree, a coconut palm and some bushes. This is a wonderful place to relax and watch the sunset. I sat here while it rained one afternoon and never even got wet because the overhead branches are so thick.

Free activities include beach towels, snorkeling gear and kayaks. The hotel works with the local suppliers for rental cars, scooters, bikes, beach buggies, Quads, horseback riding, and 4WD tours. Relais Mahana has its own 12-place outrigger speed canoe that is used to take the in-house guests on a lagoon excursion and picnic on Motu Ara Ara facing Parea village. This outing leaves the hotel at 8:30am and returns at 4pm and costs 8.500 CFP per person. Following a morning discovery of the lagoon, the pearl farm, snorkeling in the coral gardens and feeding the sacred eels of Faie, you arrive on the white sand beach of Motu Ara Ara for a picnic of grilled fish and meats, fresh fruits and drinks (punch, beer, fruit juice, mineral water or coffee). The picnic tables are placed in the shallow lagoon water to keep you cool while you dine. A traditional *fare potée* with a roof of coconut fronds provides shade, and lounge chairs allow you to relax. There are 2 toilets and a changing cabin on the motu. After lunch you will board the outrigger canoe again and visit the friendly rays that live in the lagoon.

PENSION MAUARII, *B.P. 17, Parea, Huahine 98731. Tel. 689/68.86.49/ 73.90.26; Fax 689/60.60.96; vetea@mail.pf; www.mauarii.com. Beside a white sand beach in Parea, 17 km. (10.6 mi.) from the ferry dock and 19 km. (11.8 mi.) from the airport. Round-trip transfers to/from airport 3.000 CFP per person. 2008 EP Rates sgl. /dbl.: Room 5.000-11.500 CFP; Mezzanine 9.000 CFP; Garden bungalow 12.500-15.000 CFP; Beach bungalow 18.500 CFP; Bungalow with kitchen 20.000 CFP; Add 4.500 CFP per person for MAP and 8.500 CFP for AP, plus taxes. AE, M, V.*

This Polynesian style pension is close to Parea village on Huahine Iti, beside the island's most beautiful lagoon and white sand beach. There are 5 rooms for 2-

4 people, 5 bungalows for 3-6 people, a mezzanine for 4 maximum, and a large *fare* can accommodate 10 people. All the units are clean and attractively decorated, with ceiling fans and mosquito nets over the beds, and they all have private bathrooms with hot water showers, either indoors or outside.

Guests have free use of kayaks, snorkeling gear, pedal boats and lounge chairs. Manager Vetea Breysse also owns Huahine Locations, and you can rent an A/C car, a scooter or bicycle at the reception desk. You can also book an island tour by 4WD vehicle. Moana Turquoise is the on-site nautical center, where you can rent a no-license boat, sign up for a jet ski tour, boat excursions, or a ride on a wakeboard. See more information under *Boat Rentals* and *Lagoon Excursions* in this chapter.

Chez Mauarii Restaurant has a very good reputation for its food, and the menu includes fish and seafood specialties, as well as tasty Chinese dishes. See more information under *Where to Eat* in this chapter.

FARE IE PAREA, *B.P. 746, Fare, Huahine 98731. Tel./Fax 689/68.86.51; www.tahitisafari.com. Located on a white sand beach in Parea 20 km. (12.4 mi.) from the airport, 30 min. by car from Fare. 2008 EP Rates sgl. /dbl.: Garden Cottage 16.500 CFP, Beach Cottage 27.000 CFP; extra person 2.500 CFP. Transfers and breakfast included. Add taxes. No credit cards.*

These cottages are actually 4 canvas tents like you would stay in on an African safari, and 2 more will be installed in 2008. They are built on a wooden platform with a deck and the beach units contain a private bathroom, while the garden cottages share a communal exterior bathroom. The beach bungalows also have a private kitchen in a *fare potée* adjacent to the tents, and guests staying in the garden tents share a communal kitchen. Each tent contains 1-2 big beds for a maximum of 4 people, and they have teak furniture, lamps, and electric floor fans. All the windows and doors are screened and the tents feel cool inside even on a hot day.

Marguerite and Nato are the very friendly and energetic Polynesian caretakers of this location, and they live on the premises. I stayed with Nato's family for 6 weeks when I was shipwrecked in Parea in 1977. Their English is rather skimpy, but they have generous smiles.

The bikes and kayaks are free for guest use, and you can rent a scooter or car at the reception. They will also help you arrange your excursions or order take-out meals from the nearby snacks, which can be delivered to your cottage. They will also show you Marae Ta'iharuru on the white sand beach in front of the Fare Ie property, and the very powerful Marae Anini at the end of Point Tiva.

Fare Ie Fare, *Tel. 60.63.77,* has 2 tent cottages beside the lagoon just 2 km. (1.2 mi.) from the airport and a 15-20 min. walk to Fare village. These beach cottages are 60 sq. m. (646 sq. ft.) and can sleep up to 4 people. Each unit has a private bathroom, but the kitchen is communal. Breakfast ingredients are supplied and Nadia, your hostess, delivers fresh bread and pastries to you each morning. Bicycles, snorkeling and fishing gear are available, as well as kayaks and beach chairs. Each cottage is priced at 16.500 CFP dbl. per day, plus 1.900 CFP for an additional person.

Villa Rentals With Cars & Boats

In the Maroe Bay area there are furnished villas to rent, and a car and boat are usually included. All villas have access to the water, and there are 2 tennis courts, a swimming pool and a marina in this complex of rental villas.

HUAHINE VACANCES, *B.P. 10, Fare, Huahine 98731. Tel./Fax 689/ 68.73.63; cell 689/23.03.26; www.huahinevacances.com. At PK 10 on the north shore of Maroe Bay. Free transfers. 2008 Rates including room, car and boat: 17.500 CFP sgl, 20.500 CFP for 2-3, up to 27.500 CFP for 6-7. Reduced rates for longer stays. Taxes included. MC, V.*

These 3 modern white plantation-type houses beside Maroe Bay have 2-3 bedrooms and 1-2 bathrooms. They include a fully equipped kitchen, hot water, screened windows, mosquito nets, baby bed, washing machine, TV, barbecue grill, house linens, and a covered porch facing the bay. There is direct access to the water. Baby-sitting is available, but no housekeeping. A car and boat are included in the package.

VILLAS BOUGAINVILLE, *B.P. 258, Fare Huahine 98731. Tel. 689/ 60.60.30/79.70.59; Fax 689/60.60.31; bougainville@mail.pf; www.villas-bougainville.com. At PK 10, Maroe on the north shore of the bay. Free transfers. 2008 EP Rates: 1-room villa 20.500 CFP dbl, 23.500 CFP with a/c; 2-room villa 26.500 CFP for 4-5 people; 31.500 CFP with a/c; 3-room villa 28.500 CFP for 5-6 people; 32.500 CFP with a/c. Minimum 3 days, reduced rates for longer stays. Taxes included. MC, V.*

Raphael Matopho has 4 modern houses built on 2 acres (1 ha.) of land near the water in Maroe Bay. Each villa is at least 1,000 sq. ft. (90 sq. m.) and contains a living room with ceiling fan and satellite TV, DVD player, bedrooms with a ceiling fan or optional a/c. There is a fully equipped kitchen, dining area, private bathrooms with hot water, covered terrace, washing machine, household linens, outdoor barbecue and fishing rods. A long dock has a palapa type shelter at the end, white a table and chairs. The house is cleaned once a week and a groundskeeper rakes leaves daily. Baby sitting services and cribs are available. Included with each villa is a new 5-door car with a/c, and a motorboat with 9.9 HP or 15HP motor. Reports on this place are very positive.

Other villas in the Maroe Bay complex include: **Residence Loisirs Maroe,** *Tel. 689/42.96.09/68.88.64,* with a 4-bedroom villa; **Villas Standing,** *Tel. 689/82.49.65/ 78.09.36; Fax 689/85.47.69; villas-standing@iaroana-huahine.com.* with 4 villas and a bungalow. Rental prices on request.

Other Family Pensions, Guest Houses, Bed & Breakfast, Backpackers' Lodgings & Campgrounds on Huahine Nui and Huahine Iti

Chalet Tipanier, *Tel. 689/68.78.91/78.05.69; chalet.tipanier@mail.pf; www.chalet-tipanier.fenuatravel.com.* 2 new chalets each with 2 rooms in Fare, 5 min. from airport. Free bicycles and option to rent a car. **Chez Ella,** *Tel. 689/ 68.73.07/77.92.78; chezellahuahine@yahoo.fr.* She has 2 houses and a cottage, all with kitchens, next door to Motel Vanille near the airport. **Chez Henriette,** *Tel. 689/68.83.71,* has 6 bungalows with kitchenettes in Haamene Bay. **Fare Punalea,** *Tel. 689/73.44.71,* is a local style *fare* for 4 people in Fare, with direct access to the beach at the site of the old Hotel Bali Hai. **La Petite Ferme,** *Tel./Fax 689/68.82.98; www.la-petiteferme.com,* is beside the road between the airport and Fare, with a bungalow, room and 6-bed dormitory. **Pension Ariitere,** *Tel. 689/74.40.30; Fax 689/68.82.26; leejuanito@mail.pf; www.iaorana-huahine.com/fr/ariitere.html.* There are 4 simple and practical bungalows with cooking facilities or meals on request, plus a pool, free bikes and kayaks in this pension in Fare, 10 min. from the village and 3 min. from the beach. Boat rentals possible. **Pension Hine Iti,** *Tel./Fax 689/68.74.58,* has a 3-story house for 6 people in Haapu. **Pension Mama Roro,** *Tel./Fax 689/68.84.82,* has two bungalows with kitchens close to the sea and airport, across the road from Pension Vaihonu. **Pension Meri,** *Tel. 689/68.82.44, cell 79.56.11; mataireameri@yahoo.fr,* has 5 fares with kitchens on the mountainside in Fare village.

Pension Te Nahe Toetoe, *Tel./Fax 689/68.71.43/78.13.53; www.pension-armelle.com* is in Faie and has simple rooms as well as a dormitory, plus meals, free bicycles and paddle canoes. They also own **Pension Te Nahe** in Parea on Huahine Iti. **Pension Tupuna,** *Tel./Fax 689/68.70.36; cell 79.07.94; lorettafranck@mail.pf; www.pensiontupuna.com* is in a coconut plantation near Bourayne Bay, with 3 very small local style bungalows. **Chez Tara,** *Tel. 689/68.78.45/72.98.76,* has 2 garden bungalows and 1 tree house beside the lagoon at Avea Bay in Parea on Huahine Iti. A local style restaurant on the premises serves good meals, with *ma'a Tahiti* on Sunday.

Backpackers and campers will find inexpensive accommodations at **Vanaa Camping and Snack,** *Tel. 689/68.89.51,* on Motu Maeva, which has 13 small *fares* and a campground. **Huahine Camping (ex-Ariiura),** *Tel./Fax 689/68.85.20,* has cabins, tents and a campground on a white sand beach in Parea village on Huahine Iti. Rooms are 6.000 CFP and camping is 1.200 CFP per night.

WHERE TO EAT
Deluxe
TE TIARE BEACH RESORT, *Tel. 60.60.50. Open daily for B, L,D. All major credit cards.*

Arii Restaurant, the main restaurant, is built over the water, where you can see numerous fish swimming in the clear water. During dinner guests frequently see manta rays performing their ballet just below the restaurant terrace.

A Continental breakfast is 1.800 CFP and an American breakfast is 2.400 CFP. At lunch you have a choice of a hot dog for 650 CFP, casse-croute sandwiches or paninis for 800 CFP, burgers for 1.350 CFP, salads and cold appetizers for 850-1.750 CFP, or a hot dish of shrimp, grilled salmon, calamari, lamb chop, or steak for 2.250 CFP. A vegetarian menu includes 6 choices for 1.500-1.650 CFP, and there is also a Junior menu for 1.550 CFP. Desserts are 850-1.250 CFP. The dinner menu lists French onion soup for 1.350 CFP, appetizers and salads for 1.300-1.800 CFP, pasta for 1.500-1.900 CFP, fish dishes for 1.850-2.400 CFP, fresh crab from Huahine with curry and coconut milk (when available) for 3.600 CFP, and grilled reef lobster (when available) for 3.600 CFP. The chef's specialty is a Polynesian platter for 2, which has to be ordered a day in advance and costs 12.000 CFP. Meat and poultry dishes are 1.950-2.850 CFP, and a Chateaubriand sauce béarnaise for 2 is 6.500 CFP. Homemade sorbets and ice cream are 850 CFP, and a tempting dessert menu is 1.050-1.200 CFP. A cheese platter is 1.500 CFP. You can order wine by the glass or a bottle of wine from France, Italy, Spain, Chile, California, New Zealand and Australia.

Special evenings at the Ari'i Restaurant include an Exotic Buffet for 5.800 CFP, which is accompanied by a Polynesian dance group. During the high season there is a Seafood Buffet for 6.200 CFP with a dance group.

Hawaiki Nui Bar is built over the water adjacent to the reception. They serve all your favorite libations plus some exotic cocktails of their own.

Beach Restaurant and Bar is built between the swimming pool and the white sand beach. This covered shelter can seat 40 people and is used for wedding receptions and other private parties. Drinks and snacks are served during the day, and the luncheon menu is the same as in the Arii Restaurant. No dinner is served here.

Moderate

RELAIS MAHANA, *Tel. 60.60.40. Te Nahe Restaurant is open daily for B, L D. All major credit cards.*

Breakfast and dinner are served in the 2 seaside dining rooms and you eat lunch outside on the terrace. Some of the tables are partially covered by the roof of the restaurant, while others are open to the elements, or covered by a big umbrella. Containers of carnelian and purple bougainvillea border the dining terrace. A breakfast buffet is 1.828 CFP. Lunch choices include burgers and fries for 1.350 CFP, pizzas for 1.350-1.600 CFP, *poisson cru* for 1.400 CFP, salads for 1.700 CFP, fish and seafood for 1.800-1.950 CFP, or grilled meats for 1.650-1.900 CFP. The dinner menu has starter courses for 1.650-2.650 CFP, fish and seafood for 2.100-3.950 CFP, meat and poultry for 2.350-3.150 CFP and desserts for 900-1.300 CFP. I enjoyed the chef's specialties, which included oven baked lamb with taro crust for 2.950 CFP and the crisp lobster ravioli for 3.400 CFP. A 3-course tourist menu is 3.885 CFP. Wine is sold by the carafe or bottle, and you can also order a cold pression of Hinano beer. A Buffet dinner with a Polynesian dance show is held on occasion, and costs 4.931 CFP.

CHEZ MAUARII, *Tel. 68.86.49, beside lagoon at PK 17 in Parea. Open daily 7:30am-9pm with non-stop service. AE, MC, V.*

This beachside restaurant is noted for its fresh seafood specials and local dishes. For breakfast you can order fruit, eggs and bacon or pancakes for 1.500 CFP. For lunch and dinner lagoon and ocean fish are served with a variety of sauces, priced from 1.600-3.200 CFP. Poultry dishes are 1.900-2.350 CFP and meats are 1.800-2.350 CFP. Shellfish choices are 2.300-4.500 CFP and include crab and lobster in season, and *varo*, a sea centipede that is a rare and tasty delicacy from the lagoon. Desserts are 500-750 CFP. You can buy wine by the glass, carafe or bottle. Their temperature-controlled wine cellar contains 60 bottles of red Bordeaux Grand Crus, as well as French champagne and Chilean wines. A snack menu is served from 12-5pm, offering sandwiches or grilled fish. Tahitian food is available any day of the week, including the staple diet of the Polynesians—*punu puatoro* (canned corned beef) and *mitihue* (fermented coconut milk), for 1.500 CFP, or a Polynesian plate for 2.650 CFP.

RESTAURANT BAR NEW TEMARARA, *Tel. 68.70.81, is at the edge of the lagoon at the beginning of Fare Village when you come from the airport. Open Mon.-Sat. Open Sun. only on boat days. Bar open 8am-10pm. Food served 11am-2pm and 6:30-9pm. MC, V.*

Marc Garnier, who also owns Huahine Nautique, is the energetic owner of this popular restaurant/bar. Burgers and fries are 800-900 CFP. The menu features fresh fish such as mahi mahi and tuna for 1.600-2.100 CFP, poisson cru and other appetizers for 1.200-1.800 CFP, crab and lobster (at dinner only when in season) for 3.200 CFP, and you can also get a filet mignon steak for 2.000 CFP. Wines are 1.800-4.800 CFP.

RESTAURANT VANILLE, *Tel. 68.71.77, is located at Motel Vanille close to the airport. Open Tues.-Sun. for L, D. Closed Mon. MC, V.*

Starter courses include raw vegetables, *poisson cru*, sashimi or tuna tartare. The main courses may be fish steak with lemon sauce, mahi mahi or wahoo with Roquefort, curry, black butter or green pepper sauce, shrimp dishes, chicken with cashew nuts and honey, or rib-eye steak and vegetables. The wine list is good and reasonably priced.

RESTAURANT POETAINA, *Tel. 68.80.50/60.60.06/78.86.39, is on the Fare waterfront facing the fishing dock. Open Tues.-Sun. for L, D. Closed Mon. MC, V. Free transfers.*

Poerava Amo, whose parents own Pension Poetaina, manages this small restaurant that specializes in seafood and Chinese dishes that you can eat here or take away.

Economy

CHEZ GUYNETTE, *Tel. 68.83.75, facing the waterfront of Fare village. Open daily 7am-7pm. MC, V.*

This is a great place to eat breakfast or just to stop in for a coffee, smoothie or beer and meet people while you watch what's happening on the waterfront. My very close friend, Marty Temahahe, and her Tahitian husband, Moe, own the pension and snack bar. Marty is an American who has lived for more than 30 years in the islands. They serve breakfasts, light lunches, hamburgers, poisson cru and other fish dishes when in season. The snack is busy most of the day, and especially in the mornings and late afternoon. Local residents and some of the visitors to Huahine are usually having so much fun that they don't want to go home when it's closing time.

RESTAURANT TEHINA, *Tel. 68.75.53/72.89.60, beside the sea at the Fare Maeva pension at PK 3, near Huahine airport. Open daily for B, L, D. except Sun. noon. MC, V.*

The dining tables of this restaurant are placed on a covered terrace beside the small swimming pool, overlooking the ocean. There is a *fare potée* (gazebo shelter) where groups can eat. They specialize in barbecue and fresh local fish dishes, such as tuna sashimi, poisson cru, tuna tartare or carpaccio of tuna, and the main courses often include tuna with mustard sauce, shrimp curry or steak with pepper sauce. Happy Hour at the bar is held from 5:30-6:30pm.

RESTAURANT VAIHONU, *Tel. 68.87.33, is beside the sea, between the airport and Fare village. Open daily for B, L, D. MC, V.*

Even if you are not staying at Pension Vaihonu, you are welcome to join Etienne Faaeva and his group for a good meal in a relaxed setting beside the sea. Breakfast is 850 CFP, lunch is 2.000 CFP and dinner is 2.300 CFP. You may order your meals 2 hrs. in advance, which cost 1.000-2.200 CFP. He has a tempting menu of Chinese dishes and there is a house specialty every Wed. and Fri.

VIVI ET VONVON, *Tel. 60.63.70, is upstairs above the Huahine Shop on the waterfront street in Fare. Open for B, L, D. This small restaurant-tearoom also carries art supplies, paintings and books on French Polynesia.*

HAAMENE PIZZA, *Tel. 68.71.70, is on the mountainside of the road in Fare village on the way to Fitii, between the French gendarmerie and Pension Poetaina. Open Tues.-Sat. from 12-2pm and every night from 6:30-9pm. Closed Sun. noon and Mon. noon. No credit cards.*

American residents of Huahine, as well as visitors, say that the pizzas made by this Polynesian family are the best they have tasted in Tahiti and Her Islands. You can order from a menu of 14 pizzas that are priced 900-1.500 CFP for a medium pizza for 2, and 1.200-1.800 CFP for a large pizza that is plenty for 3-4 people.

VAKALELE II, *at the Huahine Airport.*

This snackbar is open for all Air Tahiti arrivals and departures. A Continental breakfast is 800 CFP, or a local style breakfast with poisson cru is 1.000 CFP. You can get cookies, pies and ice cream for 200-600 CFP, a slice of pizza, quiche, a casse-croute or panini for 350-450 CFP, or a Caesar salad or chicken salad for 700 CFP.

Other restaurants and snacks include **Les Dauphins,** *Tel. 74.56.69,* which is on the mountainside of the circle island road, adjacent to the post office in Fare. Titiane, the Tahitian owner, serves local style meals, specializing in fresh fish, lobster and crab dishes. She's open sometimes and closed sometimes, as the mood strikes her. **Chez Tara** is close to the Relais Mahana in Parea, where you can eat right next to a beach of powdery white sand while sitting at a table under the shade of a tonina tree. There is also a big covered dining area. Tino, the Chinese-Tahitian chef from Parea village, serves delicious local style meals as well as French dishes, and a ma'a Tahiti feast of traditional Tahitian food is presented on Sundays.

You'll also find a few *roulottes* (mobile diners) and small snack bars on the quay of Fare, which are open during the day and evening, and some of them are still there when the inter-island boats arrive from Papeete or Bora Bora during the wee hours of the morning.

SEEING THE SIGHTS

Eden Parc, *Tel. 68.86.58; Fax 68.84.04; info@edenparc.org; www.edenparc.org. The park is open Mon.-Sat., 7am-5pm. Restaurant and bar open 9am-4pm. No credit cards.*

This tropical garden is located in Vaiorea Bay at Port Bourayne close to Fitii Village. Look for the sign at the junction just past Hotel Bellevue. Gilles Tehau Parzy and his wife Anne have created an ethno-botanical Garden of Eden in 7 acres (3 ha) of fruit trees, flowers and exotic plants. A visit package costs 500 CFP per person and includes three tours. Be sure to protect yourself with mosquito repellent. You can follow the guidebook they give you to visit the **Botanical Orchards**, where you will see exotic vegetables and fruits from many parts of the world. A show on **Eco-Energy Systems** starts at 1pm, and you can also join the **Great Panoramas** tour to admire and photograph the 3 magnificent bays beyond Eden Parc. You can taste some of the healthy foods grown in the gardens here by ordering an à la carte lunch or a fixed menu. Fresh fruit juices include pineapple, mango, guava, carambola, guanabana, cashew apple, starfruit, papaya, pamplemousse (grapefruit) and banana. In the gift shop you can also purchase vanilla-flavored coffee, tropical herbal teas, sun-dried bananas, jams, herbs and spices, pickled bilimbi peppers, and monoi insect repellent.

Fare Pote'e is a museum and handcrafts center built over the water at Lake Fauna Nui in Maeva Village. It is a replica of a traditional meetinghouse of classic Polynesian oval shape, with a high curved roof of pandanus thatch, bamboo walls, and a bamboo covered floor. The exhibits include a variety of useful tools that were used by the Polynesians before the arrival of the Europeans. Kites, canoes, tops and other traditional games are also displayed, as well as musical instruments and a copy of the wooden headrest used by Omai, the first Tahitian to discover England. Arts and crafts made by the residents of Huahine are for sale, and you can get a map of the hiking trails on nearby Matairea Hill, where you can see the restored *marae* temples of stone, the house and council platforms and other work in progress. Dorothy Levy, one of Polynesia's most interesting characters, is the curator extraordinaire who takes care of the Fare Pote'e. She will happily answer your questions about the history and culture of Huahine and the Maohi people.

Huahine Nui Pearl Farm & Pottery, *Tel. 78.30.20; www.huahinepearlfarm.com* is owned by American expat Peter Owen and his Tahitian wife, Ghislaine. This is Huahine's only black pearl farm. They are open daily from 10am-4pm, and offer a free tour by boat to visit the pearl farm, leaving the Marina of Faie every 15 min.

In 2006 they harvested 10,000 cultured pearls, and you can see some of them set in jewelry in their overwater boutique. Also on display are some of their creative pottery. You are welcome to snorkel in the mini-farm and see how the oysters are suspended under water. This area is not as deep as the pearl farm but it has lots of tropical fish to goggle back at you.

Land Tours

Island Eco-Tours, *Tel./Fax 68.79.67; pauljatallah@mail.pf; www.www.island-eco-tours.com*. Paul Atallah is an American archaeologist who offers half-day tours by 4WD Ford Ranger that will give you an in-depth briefing on Huahine's unique charm, history, culture and tropical flora as you discover the authentic island, mountains, valleys, rivers, beaches, islets and people. This is also an interesting botanical experience for lovers of nature and green open spaces. But the main advantage that sets Paul's tours apart is his extensive knowledge of the ancient *marae* temples and other archaeological sites. He worked with Professor Yosihiko H. Sinoto to help restore the stone *marae* in Huahine and in other islands and the knowledge he gained through his scientific research helps to make his tours even more interesting. Paul charges 5.000 CFP per person for his tour if you book directly through him.

Huahine Explorer, *Tel. 68.87.33; Fax 68.77.57; h-explorer@mail.pf; www.association@iaorana-huahine.com*. Etienne Faaeva has three 8-passenger Land Rovers to take you to discover the magical wonders of the two islands. Etienne and his brother Daniel are very good tour guides. They speak excellent English and know all about the legends and history of their native island. The Explorer Tour is 4.250 CFP per person and takes you around Huahine Nui and Huahine Iti. You will see the watermelon, cantaloupe and noni plantations, visit the *maraes*, fresh water eels, and enjoy the panoramic views. The 2-hr. Cultural Tour is 3.000 CFP and takes you to discover Huahine Nui, to visit the *maraes*, Belvedere lookout, the fresh water eels and the plantations. A Combined Tour is 10.500 CFP, and after you have visited the island by 4x4, you will board a comfortable canoe to visit a black pearl farm, snorkel and swim, and have lunch and a coconut show on a *motu* islet. The tours operate daily and water and fruit juices are served on board during each excursion.

Huahine Land, *Tel. 68.89.21/78.58.31, Fax 68.86.84; www.huahineland.com*. This company is owned by Joel House, an American who has lived in French Polynesia for more than 3 decades. He has 3 8-seater Mitsubishi 4x4 vehicles and English-speaking guides who lead the half-day excursions. The tour begins at 8am or 1pm and takes you off the track into the hidden valleys and sites of the two islands.

Huahine Local Tours, *Tel./Fax 68.89.14*; *atea.taipuna@mail.pf.* Pascal Taipuna has a/c buses and he will take you to visit the vanilla plantations, Tahitian chestnut forest of *mape* trees, ancient fish traps and the archaeological sites.

Enite Tours, *Tel. 68.82.37,* has big buses and mini-vans that are used for Circle Island Tours and Archaeological Tours.

SPORTS & RECREATION
Hiking
Huahine Camping, at PK 18 in Parea, *Tel. 68.85.20,* leads hiking expeditions into the flatlands, valleys, plateaus and mountains of Huahine. These Camping Ecology outings leave from the Huahine campground at 9am, and return at 1pm. Your qualified guides will teach you all about the traditional medicinal plants that you will see growing along the pathways.

Horseback Riding
La Petite Ferme, *Tel./Fax 68.82.98.* The little farm is located on the ocean side of the road between Fare Village and the airport. Brigitte and Vincent Pouzet will take you riding on trained Marquesan horses along the beach and on the shores of Lake Maeva for 5.500 CFP for 2 hrs. A 2-hr. ride with magical sea bathing in Lake Maeva is 7.000 CFP per person. Reserve at least a day in advance. Boarding facilities are also available.

Boat Rental
Huahine Lagoon, *Tel. 68.70.00.* Jean-Luc Eychenne rents 13-ft. aluminum boats with a 15-h.p. motor that you need a license to pilot. All safety equipment is included for a maximum of 4 people. Masks, fins and snorkel are included, as well as icebox and map of the lagoon. Gas is extra. Rental kayaks and bicycles are also available.

Moana Turquoise, *Tel. 77.59.58,* is the nautical activities center at Pension Mauarii in Avea Bay on Huahine Iti. A taxi boat service is available on request and transfers between Pension Mauarii and Hotel Te Tiare are 3.500 CFP per person. No-license boats are also available for rent.

Deep Sea Fishing
Huahine Sport Fishing, *Tel. 68.84.02; Fax 68.80.30; huah.mar.trans@mail.pf.* Ruau II is a 36-ft. Hatteras owned by American expatriate, Richard Shamel. He uses tackle approved by the International Game Fishing Association (IGFA) and the tag and release system is used on request. If you contact Rich directly he charges 90.000 CFP for a half-day fishing excursion and 120.000 CFP for a full day outing. Soft drinks, beer and water are included. Bring your own food.

Lagoon Excursions, Picnics on the Motu, Jet-Ski & Shark Feeding Excursions
Huahine Nautique, *Tel. 689/68.83.15; Fax 689/60.67.75; reservation@huahine-nautique.com; www.huahine-nautique.com.* Marc Garnier has a 12-passenger 36-ft. long glass bottom boat, 2 speed boats, 4 covered outrigger speed canoes and 12 Wave Runner Jetskis, as well as an 8-passenger mini-bus that he uses to transfer his clients

from their hotel, pension or cruise ship to the marina or boat dock. Marc's tours are highly praised by former customers, and some of the participants on Internet forums say that he offers the best excursions in the Leeward Islands. His tours are well described on his website, along with special Internet discounts.

On the **Island Picnic** tour you will take a boat ride around part of Huahine Nui and all of Huahine Iti by outrigger speed canoe, with stops to visit the stingrays and eagle rays, snorkeling in a big coral garden, and a picnic on a small motu islet. On the way back to Fare you will stop and watch your guide feeding the black tip lagoon sharks. This full-day excursion is 8.500 CFP per person.

A **Private Picnic** Luxury Lagoon cruise can be made by Jetski or on board Marc's comfortable catamaran, which is complete with a toilet and shower on board, as well as a sunbathing deck and awning for shade. After visiting the cultured pearl farm in Faie Bay and snorkeling in the coral gardens of Tefarerii, Marc's guide will take you to a motu islet where he will set up a table and chairs in the shallow lagoon and shade them with a gazebo type tent. You will be served a Royal lunch that includes grilled lobster and champagne. Then you continue on around Huahine Iti and return to the dock around 3pm. This unforgettable treat is priced at 80.000 CFP per couple.

Shark Feeding excursions take on another dimension with Huahine Nautique, due to the unique submerged platform that lets you descend from the boat into the lagoon without the risk of getting coral cuts. You can also observe the sharks being fed while standing on a structure especially built for this purpose, 4 m. (13 ft.) above the water's surface. This excursion costs 4.200 CFP per passenger.

A guided 2.5-hr. **Safari Jet** excursion aboard a Wave Runner Jetski costs 23.000 CFP per Jetski, and includes a stop on a *motu*, snorkeling in a coral garden, meeting the gray stingrays and spotted eagle rays, and a cocktail in a hotel.

Marc also has special programs for passengers who arrive in Huahine aboard the **Tahitian Princess** or other cruise ships. You can join an outrigger excursion for a barbecue picnic on a motu and boat cruise around Huahine Iti, which costs $100 per person, including the excursion, food and drinks. You can also combine the picnic tour with a circle island tour by 4x4 vehicle, which is $125 per person, including the food and drinks.

Poetaina Cruises, *Tel. 60.60.06/78.86.39; Fax 60.60.05; www.poetaina.com.* This company is headed by Jean Pierre Amo, who also owns the Poetaina Pension and Restaurant Poetaina. He has a 43-ft. outrigger speed canoe for 6-38 passengers and a 43-ft. double-decker catamaran named *Te Aito* that can accommodate up to 70 passengers. The excursion begins at the Fare quay daily at 9:30am and returns at 4pm, taking you around Huahine Nui and Huahine Iti inside the lagoon, with a stop at Vaiorea motu for snorkeling and a visit to a pearl farm. Lunch is served in the clear shallow water of the lagoon and you sit with your feet in the water as you dine. This all-day picnic excursion is 8.000 CFP per adult, 4.000 CFP for kids 6-12 years old and is free for those under 5 years. A half-day picnic excursion is 6.000 CFP per adult. You can also join the picnic cruise in the morning and at

1:30pm you will board a 4x4 Land Rover for a Huahine Explorer Safari Tour around the island. The combined tours are 12.000 CFP per adult and half-price for children. Taxes are included in all rates.

Vahine Api Cruises, *Tel. 68.84.02; Fax 68.80.30; huah.mar.trans@mail.pf.* Richard Shamel has a 22-ft. fiberglass hull boat for 2 to 8 passengers that can be used for personalized or individual transfers on the lagoon. He also has a body board and banana-ski boat. On request he will take you for a sunset cruise.

Vaipua Tour, *Tel. 68.86.42/72.10.51; here@mail.pf,* is managed by Marie-Colette Teaurai. She has two 30-ft. outrigger speed canoes and a 36-ft. double catamaran available for half- or full-day cruises for 6-60 passengers. You can board the boat at the quay in Fare at 9:30am for an all day excursion inside the lagoon to visit the bays, swim with the rays, snorkel and hunt for shells in the best spots and visit a black pearl farm. Your barbecue lunch of chicken or fresh fish with local vegetables and fruits will be prepared on the white sand beach of Motu Topatii in Tefarerii. Your Polynesian guide will teach you how to weave protective sun hats and other items from the coconut fronds. The tour ends at the Fare boat dock at 4pm. If you are on a cruise ship anchored in Maroe Bay, the catamaran will meet you at the dock there. This tour is 6.000 CFP for adults and half-price for children 5-12 years, which they advertise as the "best in the west."

Moana Turquoise, *Tel. 77.59.58,* is the nautical activities center at Pension Mauarii in Avea Bay on Huahine Iti. Manager Jérémie Czermak leads 4-hr. boat tours that include snorkeling in Huahine's most beautiful coral gardens, wakeboard riding and a visit to a pearl farm, for 8.000 CFP. A 7-hr. Mauarii Boat Tour includes fishing on the reef, snorkeling, wakeboard, encounters with dolphins and whales (in season), and a gastronomic meal with drinks included, for 12.000 CFP. A 7-hr. V.I.P. Tour includes lobster and champagne for 2 and costs 70.000 CFP. A Sunset Tour starts at 4pm and includes a cocktail at Hotel Te Tiare, for 5.000 CFP for min. of 2.

Sailing Yachts

Sailing Huahine Voile, *B.P. 661-98731 Fare, Huahine, Tel./Fax 689/68.72.49; cell 689/23.23.79; eden@sailing-huahine.com; www.sailing-huahine.com.*

Claude and Martine Bordier's 50-ft. sailboat *Eden Martin* is based in Huahine, offering half- and full-day sailing cruises, sunset cruises and private charters. The half-day cruise departs daily at 9am from the quay in Fare and sails down the lagoon to Motu Vaiorea, where passengers snorkel in the coral garden and swim beside the white sand beach of Hana Iti, arriving back at the Fare quay at 1pm. The cost is 7.200 CFP per person. The full-day cruise is 12.500 CFP and lasts from 9am-5pm, following the same course as the half-day cruise during the morning. From Hana Iti the cruise continues on to Avea Bay, where lunch is served on board. You can then relax or visit the reef by dinghy before sailing back. Snorkeling gear is available on board. A sunset cruise for a minimum of 4 leaves the Fare quay at 4:30pm and returns at dusk. The cost of 6.500 CFP per person includes cocktails, and champagne can be ordered at extra cost.

The *Eden Martin* can also be chartered for 2-5 passengers to cruise the Society Islands or the Tuamotu Archipelago. A 7-day/6-night cruise in the Leeward Islands is 69.000 CFP per day or 483.000 CFP for 7 days, and includes the boat rental, skipper and fuel for the main engine. A good cruise for scuba divers is the 7-day/6-night cruise in the northern Tuamotu Islands, which begins in Rangiroa and ends in Tikehau, or the 12-day/11-night cruise to the central Tuamotu Islands, sailing from Makemo to Tahanea, then to Fakarava. Preferential conditions for Internet reservations.

You can also rent a sailboat from one of the yacht charter companies based in Tahiti, Moorea or Raiatea and sail to Huahine, or you can arrange for a yacht to be delivered to Huahine in time for your arrival. See chapter on *Planning Your Trip*.

Scuba Diving

Mahana Dive, *Tel. 73.07.17; Fax 68.76.63; kbi@mail.pf; www.mahanadive.com.* The dive center is based in Fare village and is managed by Annie Brunet. She and another qualified instructor lead exploratory dives for 5.900 CFP. Baptism dives and 4-dive packages are also available.

Pacific Blue Adventure, *Tel. 68.87.21/71.96.55; Fax 68.80.71; pba@divehuahine.com; www.divehuahine.com.* This dive shop is located on the dock in the main village of Fare. Theophile Samourcachian is an international PADI and CMAS diving instructor who leads lagoon and ocean dives for beginners and certified divers. He has an outing at 9am, 11am and 2pm daily, taking a maximum of 10 divers to the best sites inside the lagoon or in the open ocean, adapting to the diving level of the participants. The cost is 5.900 CFP for one dive and 21.600 CFP for 4 dives, including equipment, transfers and taxes.

Surfing

American surfers discovered the passes of Huahine in the early 1970s, and a couple of them are still here, now sharing their favorite surf spots with their children. The local surfers jealously guard the passes with the best breaks, and a few foreign surfers have been given black eyes when they intrude. The big attraction in Huahine is the consistency and perfect shape of the waves rather than their size. Three of the best breaks are in the Fare area, and another good site is at the Ara Ara pass in Parea on the southern tip of Huahine Iti. Try to find a local surfer to accompany you to the passes, which may eliminate any problems from the other surfers.

Water Skiing

Vahine Api Cruises, *Tel. 68.84.02.* Richard Shamel, at the land base for Hotel Te Tiare, has a banana-ski boat and a kneeboard, plus all the equipment for water-skiing. He charges 10.000 CFP per hr.

SHOPPING

In addition to the boutiques and pearl shops in the resort hotels, you can also find original creations and some imported items in the boutiques in Fare and around the island. **Mihinda** on Fare's main street has Tahitian cultured pearls and other jewelry and perfumes. **Exotica Boutique** is also located in Fare village.

The **Rima'i Te Nui Taue** has the most original clothing and souvenir items, including pottery made by Peter Owen, an American resident of Huahine, who owns **Huahine Pearl and Pottery** at his pearl farm in Faie.

Vana Creations, *Tel. 68.72.49/23.23.79; martine@tahiti-arts.com; www.artisanat-tahiti.com.* Martine Bordier (sailboat *Eden Martin*) makes and sells original handmade necklaces from the green or purple pencil sea urchins found on the coral reefs. You can shop online.

Galerie 'Umatatea, *Tel. 68.70.79/27.27.17; melanie.artiste@free.fr; www.polynesiapaintings.com.* The studio and showroom of Melanie Dupré includes her paintings of Huahine in oils and watercolors. Located on Motu Maeva across the road from Vanaa Camping.

SPECIAL SERVICES, MASSAGE, NATURAL THERAPY, RELAXATION

Patricia Matthews Nanua, *Tel. 68.72.32/77.94.65*, is an Australia expatriate and long-time resident of Huahine who does intuitive healing massages, working with the body's energy. She also gives private yoga lessons. Her base is Te Tiare Resort, and she will also come to your house, room or yacht to work her wonderful magic on your body.

TATTOO ARTISTS

Tihoti (Georges), *Tel./Fax 68.77.27; tihotitatau@yahoo.com,* has a very good reputation for his creative Polynesian style tattoos.

PRACTICAL INFORMATION

Banks

Huahine has two banks, which are located in the main village of Fare. Both have ATM windows. **Banque de Tahiti**, *Tel. 68.82.46*, is open Mon.-Fri. 7:45-11:45am and 1:30-4:30pm. **Banque Socredo**, *Tel.47.00.00,* is located on the mountainside of the circle island road in Fare village.

Doctor

There are three private doctors in Fare who speak English, and the 15-bed government infirmary is on the mountainside in Fare, *Tel. 68.82.48.*

Drugstore

The **Pharmacy of Huahine**, *Tel. 60.60.41/60.62.41,* is on the circle island road of Fare, on the way to the post office, one block inland from the waterfront.

Open Mon.-Sat. 7:30-11:30am and 2:30-5:30pm. The pharmacist speaks English.

Internet

AO API–New World, *68.70.99; aoapi2000@yahoo.com* is a cyber center located upstairs above the pharmacy and the Tahiti Tourisme Bureau on the waterfront in Fare Village; They also have Xerox facilities and can print out digital photos and color photocopying.

Video Shop Huahine, *Tel. 60.67.40; videoshop@mail.pf.*

Te Tiare Beach Resort, *Tel. 60.60.50,* has 3 Cyberpoint computers in their overwater lobby, and you can hook up your laptop to the data port on the telephone in your bungalow.

Police

The French gendarmerie, *Tel. 60.62.05,* is beside the lagoon in Fare.

Post Office and Telecommunications Office

The Post Office, *Tel. 68.82.70,* is in Fare on the circle island road. All telecommunications and postal services are available here. Hours are 7am-3pm, Mon.-Thurs., and 7am-2pm. on Fri.

Tourist Bureau

Tahiti Tourisme, *Tel. 68.78.81,* is a tourist information office located on the waterfront street in Fare, Open Mon.-Sat. 7:30-11:30am. Georgette Itchner is the pretty Tahitian hostess who will give you brochures on all the lodgings and activities and answer your questions with a smile.

14. Raiatea

A panorama of green carpeted mountains, azure shoals and indigo bays greets your eyes as your Air Tahiti flight descends at **Raiatea** (Rye-ah-TEY-ah). The Temehani plateau rises to heights of 792 m (2,598 ft.) in the north, and Mount Tefatoaiati touches the clouds at 1,017 m (3,336 ft.) in the south. Small coral islets seem to float at the edge of the bays, rising from the submarine foundation that surrounds Raiatea and the smaller island of Taha'a. Eight passes provide entry into the vast lagoon.

Raiatea does not have the glamour of its neighboring island of Bora Bora. There are no white sand beaches except around the *motu* islets, and the tourist facilities do not include world-famous luxury resorts. Neither does it have the dramatic skyline of Moorea or the majesty of the mountains of Tahiti. Raiatea's big attractions include the ideal conditions the island and its surrounding lagoon and ocean offer for year-round sailing, scuba diving and fishing. There are 4 major yacht charter bases on the island, 2 scuba diving centers and several game-fishing boats.

Raiatea is 220 km. (136 mi.) to the west-north-west of Tahiti. It is the largest of the Leeward Society Islands, which also include the high islands of Taha'a, Huahine, Bora Bora and Maupiti, plus the coral atolls of Tupai, Mopelia, Scilly and Bellinghausen. It has a surface area of 170 sq. km (105 sq. mi.) and is shaped rather like a triangle. When I look at a map of Taha'a and Raiatea together and see the barrier reef that protects the two islands, I think that it looks like a *penu*, the phallic-shaped stone pestle used by the Polynesians to prepare their traditional medicines of plants and herbs. Taha'a is the head of the *penu* and Raiatea is the base.

Havai'i, The Sacred Island

Raiatea means "clear sky" and is still referred to as the **Sacred Island of Havai'i**, the ancestral home of the **Maohi** people. The Polynesian Creation Chant tells how Havai'i was created by the god Ta'aroa, as the birthplace of land, the birthplace of gods, the birthplace of kings and the birthplace of man. And it was to Havai'i, deep within the sacred Temehani mountain, that the souls of the dead must return.According to Polynesian mythology, fragments of the sacred island broke off to create other lands, swimming like a fish to become the Windward Islands of Tahiti, Moorea, Maiao, Mehetia and Tetiaroa. Havai'i was also the cradle of royalty and religion in Eastern Polynesia, as well as the center of the Maohi culture, history and heraldry.

Ta'aroa, the creator god, was considered too aloof for the dynamic religion that soon developed among the ancient Polynesians. He was eventually retired to

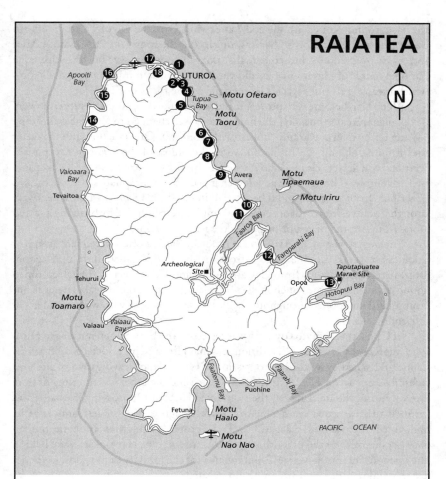

RAIATEA

Apooiti Bay

UTUROA

Tupua Bay

Motu Ofetaro

Motu Taoru

Avera

Motu Tipaemaua

Motu Iriru

Vaioaara Bay

Tevaitoa

Faaroa Bay

Fareparahi Bay

Archeological Site

Tehurui

Opoa

Taputapuatea Marae Site

Hotopuu Bay

Motu Toamaro

Vaiaau

Vaiaau Bay

Faatenu Bay

Faarahi Bay

Puohine

Fetuna

Motu Haaio

Motu Nao Nao

PACIFIC OCEAN

1. Uturoa Boat Dock
2. Public Marché
3. Hotel Bajoga-Hinano
4. Hawaiki Nui Hotel
5. Pension Tepua
6. Pension Manava
7. Kaohi Nui Ranch
8. Peter's Place
9. Pension Yolande
10. Vini Beach Lodge
11. La Croix Du Sud
12. Pension Te Maeva
13. Pension Atiapiti
14. Raiatea Lodge Hotel
15. Sunset Beach Motel
16. Marina Apooiti
17. Pension Tiare Nui
18. B&B Raiatea Bellevue

the background, along with the god **Tane**, while **Oro**, the son of Ta'aroa, came to be revered as the god of war, harvest, music and the founder of the famous Arioi society of troubadours and comedians. Long before Oro was born at Opoa the national *marae* of Havai'i or Havaiki was called Tinirauhinimatatepapa o Feoro, which means "Fruitful myriads who engraved the rocks of Feoro."

When Oro became very powerful and was acknowledged as the supreme every day god of the earth and sky, the name Feoro was changed to Vaiotaha, meaning "Water of the man o' war bird," because this bird was Oro's shadow and the water meant human blood. To his *marae* were taken most of the heads of decapitated warriors, which were cleaned and stacked in shining white rows on the black stones of the temple. The name was later changed to **Taputapuatea**, which means, "Sacrifices from abroad," and it became an international *marae*, where chiefs were brought for investiture. All other *marae* temples were founded by bringing a sacred stone from Taputapuatea or one of its descendant *maraes*.

The sacred pass of **Te Ava Moa** at Opoa in Raiatea offered frequent scenes of grandeur as great double canoes from many islands sailed into the lagoon, streaming long pennants from Hawaii, Tonga and New Zealand. The deep-toned sound of drums and the conch shell trumpets announced the arrival of delegations from island kingdoms throughout the Polynesian triangle, who were members of a friendly alliance.

At Opoa, the **Tamatoa** dynasty was reputed to go back 30 generations to **Hiro**, who was Raiatea's first king. Tradition says that Hiro and his associates built a great canoe and sailed away to Rarotonga and New Zealand, leaving two of his sons behind. One succeeded him as King of Raiatea and the other was the King of Bora Bora. During the meetings of the friendly alliance at Opoa, King Tamatoa was entitled to wear a red feather belt or *maro*, a sign of the highest honor, as he welcomed the visiting delegations. Each group of pilgrims brought human sacrifices to offer to the bloodthirsty Oro, and awesome ceremonies were held in the open-air temple of Marae Taputapuatea for the festivity of the gods, to render respect and sacrifices to Oro on his home soil.

These pagan rites ended with the arrival of the missionaries. Oro and the lesser gods were banished and Marae Taputapuatea is now silent, except for an occasional reenactment ceremony, which does not involve human sacrifices!

European Discovery

Captain James Cook was the first European to discover Raiatea, when he anchored the *Endeavour* in the lagoon at Opoa in July 1769. On board the ship was a man named **Tupia**, a native of Uliatea, as the island was then called. Tupia was the rejected lover of **Queen Purea** in Tahiti, and he and his servant boy Tayeto sailed with Cook when the *Endeavour* left Uliatea 11 days later. Both of the Polynesians died in Batavia in October 1770, of scurvy or malaria or both.

Cook returned to Raiatea in September 1773, and took a young man from Raiatea to England with him. This was a 22-year old fellow named Mai (**Omai**) who was then living in Huahine. Cook brought Omai back to Huahine in 1777 and once again visited Raiatea on a prolonged visit before sailing to Hawaii, where he was killed.

A number of other explorers touched at Raiatea following Cook's visits, but very few of them wrote about their experiences. After them came the traders and whalers, whose primary objective was to recover from scurvy, get provisions and find a woman.

John Williams from the London Missionary Society arrived in Raiatea in 1818, when he was just 21 years old. A few years later he founded the town of Uturoa. The island remained under the influence of the English Protestant missionaries long after Tahiti had come under French control. The people of Raiatea are still predominantly Evangelical. Following a *coup de force* in Tahiti by French **Admiral Du Petit-Thouars** in 1842, there followed a long period of instability. The French did not attempt a real takeover until 1888. In 1897, more than 50 years after the conquest of Tahiti, two war ships filled with French marines mounted a full-scale attack, with massive fire-power, driving the Raiateans back, until the surrogate chief Teraupoo was captured and exiled to New Caledonia. The French flag first flew over Raiatea in 1898.

Raiatea Today

The Raiatea airport is at the northern tip of the island and the town of Uturoa is southeast of the airport. A mostly paved road encircles the island for about 150 km (93 mi.), following the contours of the deeply indented coastline, with occasional forays into the exuberant vegetation of the valleys. You can drive for several miles without seeing any houses or people. Raiatea's 12,545 inhabitants live beside the road in Uturoa and in the villages and hamlets of Avera, Faaroa, Opoa, Puohine, Fetuna, Vaiaau, Tevaitoa and Apooiti.

Driving in a southeasterly direction from Uturoa you will see the **Hotel Hawaiki Nui** on your left, and you will pass impressive new homes and lovely flower gardens on both sides of the road. By the time you reach Avera you are in the country and at PK 6 you will round a curve to the right that takes you down the deeply indented road that winds quietly around the edge of the **Faaroa Bay**. Your senses are heightened as you breathe in the perfumes of fresh mountain ferns, wild mangoes, kava, kapok and ripening breadfruit.

This bay merges with the **Apoomau River**, which is navigable by small ships and boats for a distance of 4 km (2.5 mi.) into the interior. At the mouth of the river is a spring containing effervescent water. A woman from Raiatea told me that people come from Hawaii and New Zealand to drink this water, which is guarded by the spirit of the spring. She said that photos taken here always show an extra person, or part of a face, which is supposedly that of the spirit. But this image fades in time.

A road from Faaroa Bay takes you into the interior of the island for 8 km (5 mi.), connecting with Fetuna at the southern tip of the island. Winding through the fertile valleys and wide flatland, you will pass plantations of pineapple, tapioca, papaya and vanilla, and farms with horses, cows, pigs and chickens. Far below the lacy fronds of acacia trees bordering the road you can see the wild, untamed southern coast of Raiatea. If you continue along the coastal route instead of cutting across the valley, you will come to **Marae Taputapuatea** at PK 32, 19.2 miles from Uturoa center, just beyond the village of Opoa. This is Raiatea's most famous landmark. The huge slabs of coral flagstone and basaltic rock slumber under the shade of coconut palms, a shrine to Polynesia's rich and varied Maohi culture.

Between Puohine and Fetuna a road has been built along an embankment, with small *motu* islets, some with just one coconut tree, within wading distance from the shore. The pre-fabricated box-like houses on stilts that you will see are supposedly built to withstand cyclones like those that destroyed the former homes on these sites. The Tahitian government sells these houses to qualified property owners at very low cost.

Along the west coast you will see mountain streams meandering to the sea and gaily-colored cocks following their harem of clucking hens. The fishermen still use stones to enclose their fishponds, instead of wire netting. You can see them mending their nets on the beach, while their children play in the shallows of the lagoon. There are no stores in these remote settlements, except for the mobile *magasins* operated by the Chinese vendors, who make their daily rounds with fresh *baguettes*, frozen chickens and Piggy Snax.

The lagoon narrows between Vaihuti and Vaiaau Bays, with palm-shaded *motu* islets on the reef edge of the lagoon. Sharp peaks delineate the central mountain chain and in Vaiaau valley are remnants of fortifications that were built by the warriors of Faterehau, the great chiefess of Raiatea, who opposed the takeover by the French in 1897.

TIARE APETAHI-RAIATEA'S ENDANGERED FLOWER

In the heights of the sacred Temehani Mountain grows the **Tiare Apetahi**, refreshed by the cool, dense clouds and mountain showers. When touched by the first rays of the rising sun, this rare white flower bursts open with a slight exploding sound.

The five-petal Tiare Apetahi is the symbol of Raiatea, and it is believed that this particular variety of the Campanaulacées family grows nowhere else in the world. Legend says that the delicate petals represent the five fingers of a lovely Tahitian girl who fell in love with the son of a king and died of a broken heart because she could not hope to marry him.

In order to protect the rapidly disappearing Tiare Apetahi, which the flower vendors in Raiatea were selling at the airport, the local government has declared it an endangered species. Offenders may be fined up to one million French Pacific francs if caught. Repeat offenders can be given a stiff fine and imprisoned.

Behind Tevaitoa village the magnificent **Temehani Plateau** rises in formidable walls of basalt. The historic peaks shimmer in shades of blue and gray, and countless waterfalls cascade in misty plumes to splash far below into crisp pools fringed with tropical fern trees and shrubbery. **Marae Tainuu** is on the shoreline in the middle of the village. The Protestant church here is the oldest on the island, and partially covers the flagstones of the *marae*. Petroglyphs engraved in the basaltic stones include a Polynesian sundial and 10 turtles, depicting a sort of Polynesian treasure hunt that the Maohi warriors had to perform to achieve valor and esteem.

Copra drying in the sun, pigs grunting in the mud and pearl farms in the lagoon just beside the road are left behind as you arrive at Apooiti Bay and see the sleek charter yachts moored at **Apooiti Marina**. Soon you round the north end of the island, pass in front of the airport and end your tour back in Uturoa.

Although there is an increase in the flow of traffic in the town center, the lifestyle here is still unhurried and the calm, friendly feeling of a small island lingers still. It is this wonderful magic of Polynesia that tempts you to return again to Raiatea.

ARRIVALS & DEPARTURES
Arriving By Air

Air Tahiti has 6-9 flights daily between Tahiti and Raiatea, including several direct flights for the 40-min. connection. The fare is 12.100 CFP one-way for adults, and 22.200 CFP round-trip, tax included. You can also fly direct to Raiatea from Moorea each Mon., Tues., Wed., Fri. and Sun., with a stop in Huahine on Fri. and for one Sun. flight. You can fly direct from Bora Bora to Raiatea daily except Tues. and there are direct flights from Maupiti to Raiatea each Tues., Fri. and Sun. The one-way Moorea-Raiatea fare for adults is 13.000 CFP, between Huahine-Raiatea it is 5.600 CFP, Bora Bora-Raiatea is 6.300 CFP, and from Maupiti to Raiatea the one-way fare is 6.900 CFP. **Air Tahiti reservations**: Tahiti, *Tel. 86.42.42*; Moorea, *Tel. 55.06.00*; Huahine, *Tel. 68.77.02*; Raiatea, *Tel. 60.04.44*; Bora Bora, *Tel. 60.53.53*; Maupiti, *Tel. 60.15.05*.

If you have reservations with a hotel, pension or yacht charter company, then you will be met at the airport and driven to your hotel. Avis and Europcar have sales counters at the airport and there are also taxis that meet the arrival of each flight.

You can also get to Raiatea by chartering an airplane in Tahiti from **Air Archipels**, *Tel. 81.30.30*; or **Air Tahiti**, *Tel. 86.42.42*.

Arriving By Boat

All the inter-island transport boats dock at the quay in Uturoa, the main town of Raiatea, and it would be advisable to arrange with your hotel or pension to have someone meet you when you arrive in the middle of the night. The car rental agencies will also meet you at the Uturoa quay. The Raiatea Tourism office is adjacent to the quay.

Hawaiki Nui, *Tel. 54.99.54; Fax 45.24.44; contact@stim.pf.* This 12-passenger cargo ship has 4 double cabins and deck space. Passengers must sleep in cabins on the Thurs. voyage as the ship also transports fuel then. It leaves the Motu Uta dock in Papeete each Tues. at 4pm and arrives at the Uturoa quay in Raiatea on Wed. at 5:30am, after stopping in Huahine. The Thurs. trip leaves Papeete at 4pm, and arrives in Raiatea on Fri. at 3:30am. The ship continues on to Bora Bora and Taha'a and returns to Raiatea on Fri. at 4pm on its way back to Huahine and Tahiti. The cost of sleeping on deck is 1.800 CFP per person and a berth in one of the cabins costs 5.000 CFP from Papeete to all the Leeward Islands. Meals are available on board the ship.

Vaeanu, *Tel. 41.25.35; Fax 41.24.34; torehiatetu@mail.pf.* This ship can transport a total of 90 passengers, with 32 berths in cabins and 58 places on the deck. It departs from the Fare-Ute quay in Papeete at 4pm on Mon., Wed. and Fri., stopping in Huahine and arriving in Raiatea the following morning at 3:30am. One-way fare for deck passengers is 2.120 CFP; a berth in a cabin costs 4.400 to 5.989 CFP per person depending on accommodations chosen. Meals are served on board. Reservations for cabin space must be paid in full before 9am on the fixed date of departure from Papeete.

Maupiti Express II, *Tel. 66.37.81/78.27.22/72.30.48; www.maupitiexpress.com.* . This 140-passenger boat transports passengers between Raiatea and Bora Bora and from Bora Bora to Maupiti. In Raiatea it docks at the Uturoa quay where all the Taha'a boats tie up. It arrives in Uturoa direct from Bora Bora and Taha'a at 8:35am each Mon., Wed. and Fri., and at 5:35pm each Fri. and Sun. The one-way fare from Bora Bora to Raiatea is 3.000 CFP and round-trip is 4.000 CFP. The fares from Maupiti to Raiatea are 4.000 CFP and 6.000 CFP. Passengers under 12 years pay half-fare.

Enota Transport Maritime, *Tel./Fax 65.61.33.* Enota Tetuanui has 3 covered launches that can transport passengers each between Taha'a and Raiatea. *Te Haere Maru V* leaves from the east coast of Taha'a twice a day, starting from Faaaha, stopping in Haamene (at 6:30am and 12pm) and Vaitoare for the trip to Uturoa. *Te Haere Maru IV* leaves from the west coast of Taha'a twice a day, with stops at Tapuamu (5:30am on Mon. and 5:45am Tues.-Sat. and again at 11:45am), Tiva, Poutoru and Marina Iti, and then makes the 15-minute crossing to Uturoa. *Te Haere Maru VI* goes to around the island of Taha'a as needed. One-way fare starts at 500 CFP.

Tamarii Taha'a I, *Tel. 65.65.29* or 20.93.11, can transport a maximum of 66 passengers in a 46-ft. aluminum boat that operates a shuttle service between Taha'a and Raiatea. The boat leaves the Patio boat dock at 5:20am and 11:25am Mon.-Fri., and at 5:30am on Sat. Stops are made at Murifenua, Tapuamu, Tiva, Hatupa, Patii, and Poutoru, then continue on to Uturoa, arriving at 6:30am, 12:30pm and 6:40pm. The fare is 700 CFP from Patio and the other stops cost 500 CFP per person.

Tamarii Taha'a II, *Tel. 25.80.58.* This sturdy 47.5-ft. boat was formerly the *Maupiti Express I*. It leaves Ra'ai dock in Taha'a at 5:20am Mon.-Sat., arriving in

Uturoa at 6:40am. A second service starts in Haamene at 11am, arriving in Uturoa at 11:40am. The fare starts at 500 CFP for the closest docks.

Departing By Air
You can fly from Raiatea to Bora Bora, Maupiti and Huahine, or return to Tahiti by **Air Tahiti**, *Tel. 60.44.44/60.04.40* in Raiatea. There is no direct return flight service between Raiatea and Moorea. Tickets can be purchased at the airport. Check-in time at the airport is one hour before scheduled departure.

Departing By Boat
You can continue on to Taha'a, Bora Bora and Maupiti by boat from Raiatea, or you can return to Papeete with a stop in Huahine.
Hawaiki Nui, *Tel. 54.99.54* (Papeete), *Tel. 66.42.10* (Raiatea); *Fax 45.24.44*, leaves Raiatea for Bora Bora and Taha'a each Wed. at 7am, returning to Raiatea at 4:30pm, and then departs for Tahiti at 5:15pm, arriving in Papeete on Thurs. at 5am. It leaves Raiatea each Fri. at 4:30am for Bora Bora and Taha'a and returns to Raiatea at 4pm, then leaves at 4:30pm on Fri. for Huahine and Tahiti, arriving in Papeete at 5am Sat. morning.
Vaeanu, *Tel. 41.25.35* (Papeete), *Tel. 66.22.22* (Raiatea); *Fax 41.24.34*, leaves Raiatea at 5am each Tues. for Taha'a and Bora Bora, and on its return voyage it leaves Raiatea at 3:30pm each Tues. for Huahine and Tahiti, arriving in Papeete at 3am on Wed. On Thurs. the ship leaves Raiatea at 5am for Taha'a and Bora Bora, then returns to Raiatea at 2:30pm and departs at 3:30pm for Huahine and Tahiti, arriving in Papeete at 3am Fri. On Sat. the Vaeanu leaves Raiatea at 5am for Taha'a and Bora Bora, and returns to Raiatea at 1pm on Sun., then departs at 2pm for Huahine and Tahiti, arriving in Papeete each Mon. at 2am. The deck fare from Raiatea to Taha'a is 800 CFP, to Bora Bora it's 1.400 CFP, from Raiatea to Huahine is 1.060 CFP and from Raiatea to Tahiti it costs 2.120 CFP. A berth in a cabin is 4.400 to 5.989 CFP.
Maupiti Express II, *Tel. 66.37.81/78.27.22/72.30.48/www.maupitiexpress.com*. The boat departs from the Uturoa quay each Mon. and Wed. at 4pm for Taha'a and Bora Bora, arriving in Vaitape at 5:35pm. On Sun. it leaves Raiatea at 6pm, arriving in Bora Bora at 7:35pm. During the school period the *Maupiti Express II* leaves Raiatea at 2pm and 6pm each Fri. During school vacations there is a 4pm departure each Fri. for Bora Bora. The one-way fare to Bora Bora is 4.000 CFP. Passengers under 12 years pay half fare. The captain is not allowed to transport passengers from Raiatea to Taha'a only.
Enota Transport Maritime, *Tel. 65.61.33*. Te Haere Maru V leaves from the boat dock in Uturoa at 10:30am and 4:30pm for the east coast of Taha'a, stopping in Vaitoare, Haamene and Faaaha. *Te Haere Maru IV* leaves from the boat dock in Uturoa at 10:30am and 4:30pm for the west coast of Taha'a, stopping at Poutoru, Tiva and Tapuamu. The crossing takes 20 to 45 minutes, depending on your destination. Te *Haere Maru VI* is used as needed. One-way fare starts at 500 CFP.

Tamarii Taha'a I, *Tel. 65.65.29/76.37.20*. This 46-ft. aluminum catamaran leaves the Uturoa boat dock Mon.-Fri. at 10:20am and 4:20pm, and on Sat. at 10:20am. Stops are made in Poutoru, Patii, Hatupa, Tiva, Tapuamu, and Murifenua, arriving in Patio at 11:15am and 5:15pm Mon.-Fri., and on Sat. at 11:15am. One-way fare starts at 500 CFP for the closest stops.

Tamarii Taha'a II, *Tel. 25.80.58*. This sturdy 47.5-ft. boat was formerly the *Maupiti Express I*. It leaves Uturoa dock Mon., Tues. and Thurs. at 10.20am, 3:30pm and 4:20pm. On Wed. and Fri. it leaves Uturoa at 10am and 4pm. Stops are made at Vaitoare, Amaru Quay, Haamene and Ra'ai.

ORIENTATION

The town center of **Uturoa** (oo-too-RO-ah), which means, "long jaw," is 2 km (1.2 mi.) south of the airport. This is the second largest town in French Polynesia. Here you will find the administrative seat for the Leeward Islands. Buildings reminiscent of former colonial days stand adjacent to modern government buildings, post office, banks, boutiques, general stores, supermarkets and small restaurants. There is a hospital, *gendarmerie*, courthouse, a Catholic school, a lycée, technical schools and boarding facilities for students from throughout the Leeward Islands. A community nautical center and marina are on the edge of town, and the public market, port facilities and shipping warehouses in the center of Uturoa provide the focal point of a relaxed pace of business life.

Mount Tapioi rises 294 m (964 ft.) behind Uturoa, with a TV relay at the summit. You can hike up or drive 3.5 km (2.2 mi.) to the top in a 4WD, where you'll enjoy the panoramic view of Taha'a and Huahine, Bora Bora and Maupiti.

Big government projects have modernized Uturoa's public facilities. A wharf provides 430 m (1,410 ft.) of docking space for the passenger ships that are based in Tahiti or the Leeward Islands year-round, as well as the inter-island cargo/passenger ships from Tahiti. On or adjacent to the quay are the port captain's office, warehouses, cold storage for fish, public restrooms, arts and crafts center and public gardens. A Gare Maritime shopping mall also embellishes the waterfront, with fancy 2-story buildings painted pink. Granite from Portugal was imported to pave rue Tiare Apetahi in front of the mall. In addition to the restaurants, pearl shops, boutiques, gift shops and florist shop downstairs, the Tahiti Tourism Bureau occupies an enormous space on the ground level, and the post office has a branch upstairs.

Uturoa's downtown area has been improved with a new public market and a by-pass road on the hill behind the main street, to ease the flow of traffic on the main street. There are also traffic round-abouts at each end of town. This modernization program will mean losing the old Fare Vanira, a little wooden shack on the main street to which you are drawn by the enticing aroma of fragrant vanilla wafting on the breeze. This is the oldest building downtown, built in 1938, and it is the domain of "Madame Vanilla," Jeanne Chane, a lively Chinese woman who sells dried vanilla beans, powdered vanilla and extract. She is the third generation of vanilla experts in her family. If the Magasin Vanira is still standing when you visit

Uturoa, be sure to ask Madame Chane to show you her six diplomas and the silver cups she's won as a vanilla professional. Just follow your nose to her store and you'll find her counting her beans— vanilla, that is.

GETTING AROUND RAIATEA
Car, Scooter & Bicycle Rentals
Europcar, *Tel. 66.34.0678.33.53/75.53.74; Fax 66.16.06; raiatea@europcar.pf.* Sales offices are located at the airport, at the main office between the airport and Uturoa, and at the Hawaiki Nui Hotel, *Tel. 66.05.00.* A 3-door Twingo/Punto rents for 6.500 CFP for 4 hrs., 8.000 CFP for 8 hrs., and 9.400 CFP for 24 hrs. A 5-door Panda with a/c costs 7.500 CFP for 4 hrs., 9.300 CFP for 8 hrs., and 11.500 CFP for 24 hrs. Scooter rates start at 4.800 CFP for 4 hrs. These rates include unlimited mileage and third-party insurance. Gas is extra.

Raiatea Location, *Tel. 66.19.20/66.16.06,* which represents Europcar, offers special Tiare Nui packages starting at 10.930 CFP a day for two. This includes a Twingo or Punto and a bungalow, or 17.530 CFP for a Twingo/Punto, a bungalow for two people and a boat. The simple bungalows are located adjacent to Europcar's main office near the airport. All rates include taxes.

Hertz, *Tel. 66.44.88/77.66.69; Fax 66.44.89,* is located in the office of Raiatea Motors, on the mountainside across the street from the Mairie (town hall) of Uturoa. They also have a counter at the airport, *Tel. 66.44.90.* An a/c 5-door Skoda manual drive car rents for 6.500 CFP for 4 hrs., 8.000 CFP for 8 hrs., and 9.500 CFP for 24 hrs. A 5-door a/c Toyota Yaris with automatic drive rents for 8.900 CFP for 4 hrs., 11.900 CFP for 8 hrs., and 12.900 CFP for 24 hrs. Rates include VAT and unlimited mileage, plus collision insurance.

Bicycles
Europcar, *Tel. 66.34.06,* rents bicycles for 1.800 CFP for 4 hrs., 2.400 CFP for 8 hrs., and 3.500 CFP for 24 hrs. Longer rentals possible. Many of the pensions also rent bikes.

Taxis
There are at least 10 taxis in Uturoa and you can usually find one at the Uturoa airport for each flight arrival. A taxi stand is located at the boat and ferry dock in the center of Uturoa, *Tel. 66.20.60/66.36.74 /72.30.54.* The Raiatea taxi drivers pride themselves on their good reputation, although there is a variance in the fares they charge. Taxi fare from the airport to Uturoa center is 1.000 CFP and from the airport to the Hawaiki Nui hotel is 1.500 CFP, plus 100 CFP for baggage. The rate from the port in Uturoa to Hawaiki Nui is 700 CFP. The hourly rate is 4.000 CFP, and 1.800 CFP for waiting time. A circle island tour by private taxi is 20.000 CFP.

Le Truck
A *le truck* service operates between the public market in Uturoa and each

village, coordinating their schedules with the arrivals of the ferries and school hours. They charge a minimal fee to transport passengers to their destination in Raiatea.

Taxi Boats

La Compagnie des Taxis-Boat (Corto), *Tel.65.66.44/79.62.01, VHF 16; www.taxi-boat.com.* William Donzelot has 2 locally built polyester and aluminum boats that will accommodate 2-6 passengers. He provides taxi boat service on request, daily from 6am-6pm. He will pick you up at the airport, the quay in Uturoa or from any boat dock specified. Night transfers cost 100 percent more. You can also charter a taxi boat for 17.000 CFP an hour.

Limousine Boat, *Tel. 60.81.21/79.63.81; tahaa-marine@mail.pf.* Patrick Braindot has a 28-ft. teak and mahogany boat that can take up to 6 passengers on private excursions or transfers. Shower, towels, refrigerator, 2 salons, and snorkeling equipment. Hostess, champagne, picnic or snack basket available on request.

WHERE TO STAY

Superior

RAIATEA HAWAIKI NUI HOTEL, *B.P. 43, Uturoa, Raiatea 98735. Tel. 689/60.05.00; Fax 689/66.20.20; res@spmhotels.pf; www.pearlresorts.com. Beside the lagoon, 2 km (1.2 mi.) south of town. Round-trip transfers from the airport or ferry dock: 1.500 CFP per person. 2008 Low/High Season EP Rates sgl/dbl: Garden Room 26.000/28.000 CFP; Garden Bungalow 26.000/28.000 CFP; Lagoon Bungalow 29.000/31.000 CFP; Overwater Bungalow 33.000-35.000 CFP; Premium Overwater Bungalow 36.000/38.000 CFP. Add 5.000 CFP for 3rd person. American breakfast 2.300 CFP; Canoe breakfast 8.500 CFP. Add 7.600 CFP for MAP and 10.900 CFP for AP, per person per day. Add taxes. All major credit cards.*

Situated on the fringe of the lagoon in Tepua Bay, this 3-star hotel has 28 rooms and bungalows built in the Polynesian style with thatched roofs and bamboo furniture. Recently renovated, all the units are screened and equipped with a king-size bed or 2 twin beds, a single bed, ceiling fan, mini refrigerator, TV, telephone, coffee and tea making facilities, safety box and hairdryer. An iron and board are available on request. The garden bungalows have an interior lounge area and the overwater units provide a spacious terrace with direct access to the lagoon. A glass floor in the overwater bungalows lets you watch the fish at night as they feed in the coral gardens below. The garden rooms and bungalows all have a/c.

Adjacent to the Nordby Restaurant is an indoor-outdoor bar and a fresh water swimming pool that overlooks the lagoon. There is no beach here, but there is a pier for sunbathing. Snorkeling equipment is provided free of charge as well as outrigger canoes and kayaks. Hemisphere Sub Diving Center will take qualified divers to visit the *Nordby* wreck at the bottom of the giant aquarium close to the hotel pontoon. Pronounced "Nordbou", this 3-masted barque was built of iron in 1873 in Dundee, Scotland, under the name *Glencarn* for a British ship owner. It was sold in 1893 to the Winther Shipbuilders in Denmark. It sank in August 1900 in front of Teavarua pass in 25 m. of water.

The Raiatea Hawaiki Nui Hotel is truly an integral part of the community. The Rotary Club and Chess Club meet here in the a/c conference room. Manager Pierre (Pierrot) Dinard began a Happy Hour and resumed the Sun. brunch, which attracts the island's well established residents, including the mayor and his family and older families who arrive on Sun. dressed in Polynesian shirts, lovely *mama ruau* gowns and crowns of flowers. They dance the Tahitian two-step, fox trot and waltz to the tunes of old Polynesia that are played by a 3-piece band. A Polynesian dance show is presented on Fri. nights, and sometimes on Tues. evenings.

Guest services include a computer with Internet access in the lobby, room service, laundry service, and a snack service in the afternoon. You can rent cars, scooters and bicycles, and there is a boutique adjacent to the lobby. There is an on-site dive center and an excursion desk. You can participate in the fish feeding at the end of the pontoon each morning, and you can also join others for a snorkeling excursion in the shallow water beside Motu Ofetaro, opposite the hotel. Or you can be dropped off at the *motu* and they will pick you up later. See *Where to Eat* in this chapter for information on the restaurant and bar.

RAIATEA LODGE HOTEL, *B.P. 680, Uturoa, Raiatea 98735. Tel. 689/ 66.20.00; Fax 689/66.20.02; raiateahotel@mail.pf; www.raiateahotel.com. On the mountainside at PK 9.8 in Tumaraa, 4 km (2.5 mi.) from the airport and 7 km (4.3 mi.) from the ferry dock. Round-trip transfers 1.000 CFP for maximum 5 passengers. 2008 EP rates sgl/dbl: Room 12.000 CFP; add 3.000 CFP for 3rd person; Suite 22.000 CFP. Continental breakfast 1.200 CFP, American breakfast 1.500 CFP. Add 4.000 CFP per person for MAP and 6.000 CFP for AP. Add taxes. MC, V.*

This 2-story colonial style hotel opened as the Hotel Tenape in 1999, with 15 a/c rooms and a 2-bedroom a/c suite with a living room. The present owners are two French women who claim it is an international 3-star hotel. The hotel is situated on 4.9 acres (2 ha) of land on the northwest coast of Raiatea, with 120 m. (394 ft.) of lagoon frontage across the road. Each room contains a king-size bed or twin beds, ceiling fan, refrigerator, TV, telephone, individual safe, and a separate bathroom with a hot water shower. The suite has two bedrooms, living room, bathroom and all the other amenities as the rooms. A covered terrace overlooks the lagoon, the islands of Bora Bora and Maupiti, and the spectacular sunsets. This may be a convenient place to stay if you have a car and want to be close to the marina and yacht club, but keep in mind that only the Tahitian cook speaks English.

Public facilities include a restaurant and bar, swimming pool and pool bar, front desk, lounge, activities desk and boutique. There is a helicopter-landing pad on the premises, and they work with Europcar, who will come to the hotel to pick you up when you want to rent a car. Other tours and excursions are also available, such as scuba diving, deep-sea fishing, 4WD safari tours, lagoon outings and picnics on the *motu*. The owners planned to build a pier for easier access into the lagoon. Guests have free use of snorkeling equipment, fishing gear, kayaks and bicycles. They also have free Internet service with WiFi. See *Where to Eat* in this chapter for more information.

Moderate

PENSION TEPUA, *B.P. 1298, Uturoa, Raiatea 98735. Tel. 689/66.33.00; Fax 689/66.32.00: pension-tepua@mail.pf; www.raiatea.com/tepua. Beside the lagoon in Tepua Bay, 2.5 km (1.5 mi.) south of Uturoa center. Round-trip transfers from Uturoa port or airport 1.000 CFP per adult. 2008 EP rates: Room 5.000-13.000 sgl; dormitory 2.500 CFP. Breakfast 1.250 CFP. Meal plan available. AE, MC, V.*

Manager Joe Ungaro-Alves speaks Portuguese, Spanish, Italian, French and English, and his wife Guylaine is the cook. Since this couple took over in 2001 they have renovated, repainted and redecorated whatever needed attention on the premises. They installed a "Cyberpoint" service with Internet connections for guests, and will soon offer the WiFi international system and IP phone.

The pension has a seaside bungalow, a bungalow facing the pool, and a garden bungalow; all with a queen size bed and two single beds, ceiling fan, kitchenette and private bathroom. There are 3 rooms with a double bed, 1 room with a single bed, and a 12-bunk dormitory. The rooms and dorm have ceiling fans and guests share the bathroom facilities and kitchen. All the bathrooms have hot water showers. There are refrigerators in all the bungalows.

The restaurant serves breakfast and dinner to the in-house guests and there is also a bar, swimming pool and a pier over the lagoon. There's a lot squeezed into one small space here, and all land and sea activities that are available in Raiatea can be arranged at the pension.

HOTEL ATIAPITI, *B.P. 884, Uturoa, Raiatea 98735. Tel./Fax 689/66.16.65; atiapiti@mail.pf; www.raiatea.com/atiapiti. Beside the lagoon at PK 31 in Opoa, near Marae Taputapuatea, 30 km (18.6 mi.) from the ferry dock and 32 km (19.8 mi.) from the airport. Round-trip transfers 3.900 CFP per person. 2008 EP Rates sgl./dbl.; Garden suite or Beach bungalow 13.900 CFP; add 4.800 CFP per person for MAP. Breakfast only 1.500 CFP. Add visitor tax. MC, V.*

This is the only accommodation available anywhere near the famous Marae Taputapuatea. 7 concrete bungalows with wood shake roofs are well spaced in 2.5 acres (1 ha) of land beside a narrow strip of white sand beach. The grounds are planted with fruit trees, rainbow shower trees and lots of flowers. Each of the 5 beach bungalows has a bedroom with a king-size bed, living room with tamanu wood furniture, a kitchenette, mini-bar, bathroom with hot water, and a terrace overlooking the sea and the distant island of Huahine. The 2 garden bungalow suites contain a lounge with a double bed and 2 single beds, a small room with a single bed, a kitchen, terrace, and a bathroom with hot water. All bungalows have an electric fan and TV and can accommodate up to 5 people.

Marie-Claude Rajaud, the friendly and energetic French woman who owns this small family hotel, speaks English and Spanish, and she is a very good cook. See more information under *Where to Eat* in this chapter. Free activities include snorkeling from the long pier or pontoon, fishing, outrigger paddle canoes, feeding the eels, petanque (French bowls), ping-pong, society games and a lending library. Rental bicycles are available for 1.500 CFP per day, and a single kayak or outrigger paddle canoe costs 1.000 CFP for a half-day and 1.500 CFP per day for a double canoe or kayak. You will have an interesting choice of optional activities, including a guided visit to the Marae of Taputapuatea for 1.000 CFP per person. Guided walking tours take you into the valleys on the wild southern end of Raiatea. A 4WD excursion around the island is 6.000 CFP per person. You can also go horseback riding, scuba diving and deep-sea fishing, or take a boat trip to a nearby *motu* or to Taha'a.

VINI BEACH LODGE, *B.P. 1384, Uturoa, Raiatea 98735. Tel. 689/60.22.45/ 78.48.34; Fax 689/60.22.46; vinibeach@mail.pf; www.raiatea.com/vinibeach. On seaside in Faaroa Bay at PK 12 in Avera, 7.4 mi. southeast of Uturoa center and 15 km from the airport. Round-trip airport transfers 1.220 CFP per person. 2008 EP rates sgl/ dbl: Garden bungalow 12.920 CFP; Lagoon bungalow 15.850 CFP. Continental breakfast 1.500 CFP, lunch or dinner 2.850 CFP, including taxes. No credit cards.*

Five hillside bungalows and two units beside the water overlook the Faaroa River. The first of these attractively decorated bungalows were built in 2003 and each unit can sleep 4 people. The windows and doors are screened, and there is a ceiling fan, kitchenette, bathroom with hot water shower and a terrace and balcony. Guests can use the swimming pool, bicycles and kayaks. Excursions and rental cars arranged.

SUNSET BEACH MOTEL, *B.P. 397, Uturoa, Raiatea 98735. Tel. 689/ 66.33.47; Fax 689/66.33.08; sunsetbeach@mail.pf; www.raiatea.com/sunsetbeach. Beside the lagoon in Apooiti, 5 km (3 mi.) from the ferry dock and 2 km (1.2 mi.) from the airport. Free round-trip transfers. 2008 EP Rates: Bungalow 10.000 CFP sgl/ 11.000 CFP dbl. Camping 1.100 CFP per person per day. MC, V.*

This small family hotel offers one of the best values and most pleasant experiences in the islands. The 20 American style wooden cottage type houses or bungalows are placed far apart on a 24.7-acre (10 ha) property that is still a working coconut plantation. The bungalows are all on the waterfront with a fabulous view of Taha'a and Bora Bora. Each bungalow has screened windows and sliding glass doors, and contains a bedroom with a double bed, a living room with three single beds and television, ceiling fan, picnic table, kitchen, bathroom with solar hot water, covered terrace and carport. A narrow strip of white sand beach fronts the property, and you can sunbathe on the long private pier or feed the fish at the end of the dock. Snorkeling equipment, outrigger paddle canoes and volleyball are provided. You can rent a bicycle, scooter, car, or a motorboat. Free car transfers are provided for shopping expeditions in town.

Separated from the bungalows by a large garden is a campground for up to 25 tents, with a large kitchen and big covered dining terrace. Campers share the communal cold-water bath facilities, with access to a pay phone, luggage room and library on the premises.

Sunset Beach is owned and managed by Moana Boubee, whose enthusiasm and friendliness are welcome assets, and he speaks good English. There is no restaurant, but a breakfast including fresh fruit grown on Moana's farm will be delivered to your bungalow on request for 1.200 CFP. You can also order bread or croissants the night before and pick them up at the reception in the morning.

BED & BREAKFAST RAIATEA BELLEVUE, *B.P. 98, Uturoa, Raiatea 98735. Tel./Fax 689/66.15.15; raiateabellevue@mail.pf; www.raiateabellevue-tahiti.com. On the mountainside behind the Lycée of Uturoa, 2 km. (1.2 mi.) from the airport and 2 km. from the Uturoa ferry dock. One-way transfers 1.000 CFP per person. 2008 EP Rates including breakfast: Room 7.250 CFP sgl, 8.500 CFP dbl. Add visitor tax. No credit cards.*

This Bed and Breakfast guesthouse is located on top of a very steep hill reached by a road north of Uturoa center. Take the first paved road on the left after PK 1 and follow it past the school, upward for 800 m. (2,624 ft.). Owner Max Bucher has transformed what were formerly 4 very small rooms into 3 larger rooms, which are much more comfortable for his guests. Each room has a double bed, mosquito net, ceiling fan, electric fan, TV, and private bathroom with hot water, and they all have a private terrace. There are also 2 studios with a kitchenette for long stays. The rooms are all romantically decorated with Tahitian *tifaifai* bedspreads. Guests share a refrigerator and a small bar has been added. There is a small swimming pool with a parasol table. You'll have a lovely view of the *motu* islets and island of Taha'a from this mountainside location. Three restaurants provide pick-up service for dinner.

HOTEL BAJOGA-HINANO, *B.P. 1689, Uturoa, Raiatea 98735. Tel. 689/66.13.13/70.82.40; Fax 689/66.14.14; bajoga-hinano@mail.pf; www.hotel-hinano-tahiti.com. On the main street in the center of Uturoa, a 2-min. walk from the ferry dock. Transfers from the airport 800 CFP per person. 2008 Rates EP: Standard room with fan 6.350 CFP sgl/7.700 CFP dbl; standard room with a/c 7.350 CFP sgl/8.700 CFP dbl; extra person 1.350 CFP. Breakfast 600 CFP per person. Add visitor tax. MC, V.*

This old hotel is upstairs in the center of town and is the only lodging in the downtown area of Uturoa. The 10 motel-type rooms have a/c or ceiling fans and can sleep 3 people. They also have cable TV and private bathrooms with hot water shower. Although the reception closes at 8:30-9pm, the door to the street downstairs is locked at night. Chez Michele restaurant is on the ground floor facing the boat dock and several good restaurants and snack bars are just a few steps away.

LA CROIX DU SUD, *B.P. 769, Uturoa, Raiatea 98735. Tel./Fax 689/66.27.55. On the mountainside at PK 12, overlooking Faaroa Bay. EP room and breakfast 7.300 CFP sgl/7.700 CFP dbl; room and MAP 8.900 CFP sgl/13.500 CFP dbl. No credit cards.*

This pension has a lovely panoramic view from a large covered terrace and is surrounded by a flower garden, with a swimming pool in the front yard. Hostess Annette Germa is Marquesan and worked in the charter boat business for many years with her late husband, Eric Germa. The three bedrooms are clean and attractively furnished, each with a double bed, mosquito net, fan and private bathroom with hot water.

PENSION TE MAEVA, *B.P. 701, Uturoa, Raiatea 98735. Tel./Fax 689/ 66.37.28; temaeva@mail.pf; www.temaeva.com. On the mountainside at PK 23 in Opoa, 25 km (15.5 mi.) from the airport and 23 km (14.3 mi.) from the boat dock. Free round-trip transfers for 3-night stay. EP bungalow with breakfast 7.200 CFP sgl/ 7.800 CFP dbl. Lunch or dinner 2.500 CFP. No credit cards.*

You'll have a panoramic view of the *motu* islets of Avera from this mountainside retreat, which is 7 km (4.3 mi.) north of Marae Taputapuatea. It's far from the sea, far from the main village and tourist attractions, far from noise, far from everything. The two modern style bungalows have a double bed and single bed, fan, refrigerator, terrace and private bathroom with hot water. Guests can use the swimming pool and bicycles. Owner Claudine Leclerc-Hunter has been awarded a 2-Tiare rating by the Tahiti Tourist office for the quality of her pension.

PENSION MANAVA, *B.P. 559, Uturoa, Raiatea 98735. Tel. 689/66.28.26; Fax 689/66.16.66; manava@free.fr; www.manavapension.com. On mountainside in Avera, 6 km (3.7 mi.) southeast of town. No charge for round-trip transfers. 2008 EP Rates sgl/dbl: Room with shared kitchen and bathroom 4.700 CFP; Bungalow with private bathroom and shared kitchen 7.000 CFP; Bungalow with totally private bathroom and kitchen 8.000 CFP person. Add 1.000 CFP for one night stay only and 1.000 CFP for 3rd person. Breakfast on request 800 CFP. No credit cards.*

Roselyn and Andrew Brotherson have 4 clean and attractive bungalows and a large house, located in a pretty setting of trees, grass and flowers, across the road from the lagoon. Two bungalows have individual kitchens and toilets with solar hot water; 2 have individual toilets with hot water and share a kitchen. In the large house are 2 bedrooms with shared kitchen and a communal bathroom with hot water. Each bungalow has screened windows and a covered terrace. All the rooms have an electric fan and bed linens are furnished. If you want to eat dinner in a local restaurant someone from the pension will drive you to the good dining places, and the restaurant will drive you back after dinner or the Brothersons will come get you. Manava Excursions is across the road, where Andrew Brotherson will take you on an outrigger canoe ride to Taha'a for the day, complete with a picnic on a *motu*, for 7.500 CFP per adult and half-fare for a child less than 12 years old. Or you can join a half-day boat tour to visit the Faaroa River and Marae Taputapuatea, for 4.500 CFP per adult and half-price for each child. You can be dropped off on a *motu* and picked up later, for 1.500 CFP per person. There are no excursions on Sat.

KAOHI NUI RANCH, *B.P. 568, Uturoa, Raiatea 98735. Tel./Fax 689/ 66.25.46; Cell 689/74.37.13; kaoha.nui@mail.pf; www.tahitidecouvrir.com. On mountainside in Avera, 6 km (3.7 mi.) southeast of town. Round-trip transfers are free. 2008 EP Rates sgl./dbl.; Bungalow 7.800 CFP; add 1.200 CFP for 3rd person; Room with 2 beds and shared bathroom 3.800 CFP. Reduced rates for 2nd night. Breakfast is 800 CFP and dinner is 2.700 CFP. Taxes included. MC, V.*

The grounds resemble a Western movie setting, with a corral, bank (reception area) and saloon, which is the mini-bar. Lodging is in 2 bungalows with a double bed and 1-2 single beds, a fan, private bathroom with hot water, and a terrace. A 4-bedroom house has 2 single beds in each room, with a fan and shared bathroom facilities with hot water. Be aware that the walls do not go all the way up to the ceiling in these rooms. House linens and anti-mosquito products are furnished. Guests have use of the kitchen and share the dining room.

The Kaohi Nui Ranch includes a stable of horses, and a 2-hour ride is 5.000 CFP, and a half-day ride is 6.500 CFP. You can also rent bicycles, or join an outrigger excursion to visit the Faaroa River, Marae Taputapuatea, coral reef and a *motu* islet, for 5.500 CFP. A 7.5-hour boat excursion to Taha'a is 8.500 CFP, and a boat transfer to a nearby *motu* is 1.700 CFP.

Economy

Other family lodgings include: **Pension Yolande**, *Tel. 689/66.35.28*, has 4 studios with kitchen in a large bungalow beside the lagoon at PK 10 in Avera, starting at 6.000 CFP sgl. MAP available. **Pension Tiare Nui**, *Tel. 689/66.34.06; Fax 689/66.16.06; europcar-loc@mail.pf; www.raiatea.com/tiarenui*. Adjacent to Europcar Agency, who has special packages for bungalow and car or bungalow, car and boat rental. EP rates start at 5.300 CFP sgl for bungalow only. **Peter's Place**, *Tel. 689/66.20.01*, has 8 very basic backpackers' rooms and a campground for 6 tents on the mountainside at PK 6.2 in Avera. Share kitchen and bathroom facilities.

WHERE TO EAT

Moderate

ATIAPITI RESTAURANT, *Tel. 66.16.65, is located at Hotel Atiapiti, PK 31, beside the lagoon in Opoa, near Marae Taputapuatea. Open daily for BL. Closed for D. Guests not staying in their hotel-pension are welcome at lunch only. MC, V.*

This is a good luncheon stop when you are driving around the island or visiting Marae Taputapuatea. Marie-Claude Rajaud likes to serve fresh fish, crab and lobster from the lagoon, which she says is still not polluted. The river shrimp she prepares can be served with saffron or curry. She also cooks chicken with Coca-Cola, grilled New Zealand beef, and she makes a sumptuous coconut cake. Fresh fruits from the garden are also served. Meals are served à la carte and there is a well-stocked bar and a good wine list.

BRASSERIE MARAAMU, *Tel. 66.46.64, is in the Gare Maritime building. Open for BLD, Mon.-Sat. noon. Closed Sat. afternoon and all day Sun. AE, MC, V.*

This Chinese restaurant is popular with local residents, who sometimes reserve the entire restaurant for private parties. You can have a breakfast of coffee, bread and butter for 300 CFP, poisson cru for 700-1.100 CFP, eggs or an omelet for 700 CFP, or fried fish for 800 CFP. The lunch and dinner choices are *ma'a tinito* (Chinese stew with pork, red beans, vegetables and macaroni) for 1.000 CFP, and other Chinese dishes of beef, chicken or shrimp start at 1.000 CFP.

CHEZ MICHELE, *Tel. 66.14.66, occupies the ground floor of the Hotel Bajoga-Hinano, facing the boat dock. Open for BLD. Closed Sat. night and Sun. No credit cards.*

You can get Polynesian food at all times in this small in-door, out-door restaurant that has been in business for many years. In addition to poisson cru for 900 CFP, you can order *fafa* (Tahitian spinach), *uru* (breadfruit), taro, bananas and other Tahitian specials on request. The quality of the food is usually good, and includes Chinese dishes for 1.200-1.400 CFP, and European dishes such as steak, chicken and fish, prepared in the local style for 1.500-2.200 CFP. There are three choices of daily specials, which cost 1.500 CFP each.

JADE GARDEN, *Tel. 66.34.40, is on the mountainside of Uturoa's main street in the downtown shopping area. Open Wed.-Sat. from 11am-1pm and 6-9:30pm. Closed Sun., Mon. and Tues. AE, MC and V.*

There are 60 choices of Cantonese cuisine and local style food on the menu, plus the specials, such as Tapen Lou, the Chinese seafood fondue that requires a day's advance notice to prepare. I have always enjoyed my meals here, which have included the steamed chicken with black mushrooms and ginger for 1.650 CFP, the shrimp stuffed with taro for 2.300 CFP, and taro steamed fried duckling for 1.750 CFP. The a/c dining room is upstairs and has an elaborate ceiling decorated with gold dragons. The tables are covered with red or pink cloths and a vase of plastic flowers. You pay the owner, Soufa Chung, at the bottom of the stairway when you've finished eating.

L'ESPADON, *Tel. 66.43.19, (formerly Le Quai des Pecheurs-Fisherman's Wharf) is in the Gare Maritime building facing the quay for small boats. Open daily for L, D, except Sat. noon and Sun noon. Open holidays and boat days. MC, V.*

This French and seafood restaurant is located in the big, pink Gare Maritime building beside the ship dock. Agnès and Guy, who also own Restaurant Patoti in Bora Bora, took over this restaurant in May 2007, and Raiatea residents say that it is one of the best restaurants on the island. You can eat on the terrace overlooking the dock area or inside the restaurant, where the tables are covered with tablecloths. The menu lists starter courses for 1.200-1.550 CFP, fish dishes for 1.800-2.400 CFP, and meat selections for 1.950-2.950 CFP. Desserts are 700-850 CFP, and the luncheon special is 1.600 CFP. Guy's specialties include homemade fish soup for 1.500 CFP, frog legs for 2.400 CFP, beef tartar for 1.950 CFP, calamari steak for 1.950 CFP, roast beef for 2.950 CFP, and lobster fricassee for 3.900 CFP.

LE CLUB HOUSE RESTAURANT, *Tel. 66.11.66, is located at the Apooiti Yacht Harbor. Open LD Tues.-Sun. Closed Mon. MC, V. Dinner transfers from Raiatea Lodge and Hawaiki Nui Hotel.*

This open sided restaurant and bar faces the marina and charter yachts, and appears to be more of a bar than a restaurant, although the manager said they can serve up to 60 people. Burgers and fries are served at lunch for 1.200-1.500 CFP, a chef's salad is 1.300 CFP, and a steak with fries is 1.600 CFP. The dinner menu lists appetizers for 1.600-2.300 CFP, fish dishes for 2.400-2.900 CFP, and meats for 1.950-3.200 CFP. Desserts are 650-1.200 CFP. A 3-course tourist menu is 4.900 CFP and a child's menu is 1.300 CFP.

LE NAPOLI, *Tel. 66.10.77, is on the lagoon side of the road between Uturoa village and the airport. Open Tues.-Fri. for lunch and dinner, and on Sat. and Sun. evenings. Closed Sat. noon, Sun. noon and all day Mon. MC, V.*

This little restaurant is right beside the road near the airport, with shoji screens and bamboo walls. They serve Italian cuisine and pizzas cooked in a wood oven.

MOEMOEA, *Tel. 66.39.84, is between the Uturoa quay and the main street in the center of town. Open Mon.-Sat. from 6am-5pm. Closed Sun. No credit cards.*

This indoor-outdoor snack café is very local style with no pretensions of any sort, and it's usually packed with a noisy, happy crowd. It's a good place to people watch, as the residents of Taha'a and Raiatea come to town to shop, do their banking and take care of business, but also to visit, gossip and giggle. The menu offers 5 choices of poisson cru, from 800-1.600 CFP, Chinese dishes, such as chow mein, chop soy or Kai fan, are 1.450-1.700 CFP, fried or grilled Mahi Mahi is 1.850 CFP, grilled lobster is 3.100 CFP and burgers are 750-800 CFP.

RAIATEA HAWAIKI NUI HOTEL, Tel. 60.05.00. Open daily for BLD. Sun. brunch 10:30am-2:30pm. All major credit cards.

The **Nordby Restaurant** serves an American breakfast buffet for 2.300 CFP. Lunchtime fare includes burgers, sandwiches and pizza for 1.400 CFP and pasta is 1.250 CFP. The lunch or dinner menu offers a good selection of hot or cold appetizers for 1.300-1.750, fish and shellfish for 1.980-2.600 CFP, roasted lobster for 3.850 CFP, meat and poultry for 2.100-2.700 CFP. The dessert menu lists choices for 850-1.000 CFP, including a cheese platter for 900 CFP. A set luncheon menu is 3.200 CFP, the Sun. brunch is 4.500 CFP, and a set dinner menu is 5.600 CFP.

The bar serves a variety of exotic cocktails, and Happy Hour is held each Wed. and Fri. from 6-7pm, with 2 drinks for the price of 1. Snacks are available at the bar from 2-6pm.

RAIATEA LODGE HOTEL, Tel. 60.01.00, Open daily for BLD. MC, V.

The hotel's restaurant is an attractive open sided dining area overlooking the gardens and swimming pool and the lagoon across the road. A hamburger is 1.500 CFP and poisson cru is 1.800 CFP. The dinner menu changes every week and a 3-course set dinner menu is 3.500 CFP. Shrimp is 1.500 CFP, steak is 2.200 CFP, desserts are 600 CFP and wines are 2.050-9.000 CFP. They also have cocktails for 1.300 CFP.

SEA HORSE, *Tel. 66.16.34; leogite@mail.pf, is in the Gare Maritime building on the quay, next to Le Quai des Pecheurs. Open Mon.-Sat. from 10am-9:30pm. Closed Sun. AE, MC, V.*

This is a very popular Chinese restaurant. It is open on three sides, giving you a good view of the quay and activities taking place in the harbor. You can buy Chinese food to go, such as chow mein or chop soy, for 1.200-1.650 CFP, or you can dine here. A selection of Chinese soups is priced from 1.000-1.300 CFP; spring rolls are served with a sweet and sour sauce for 1.000 CFP, and fried wonton is 1.000 CFP. Spicy salted shrimp is 2.100 CFP; fish and seafood dishes are 1.500-3.800 CFP; beef with satay sauce is 1.500 CFP, lemon chicken is 1.200 CFP, and tofu dishes are 1.500 CFP. The list goes on and on, and even includes the Sea Horse Tapen Lou for a minimum of 2 people, which is a Chinese seafood fondue for 3.500 CFP per person. On Fri. and Sat. you can order roast suckling pig with coconut milk for 1.800 CFP. Wines are priced from 2.200 to 13.000 CFP a bottle.

Economy

There are small snack stands all around the island where you can buy casse-croute sandwiches on baguette bread, *poisson cru*, *maa tinito* and other local dishes while driving around Raiatea. Several rolling food trucks called **Roulottes** park on the Uturoa waterfront at night, serving steak and fries, chicken legs and *salade russe* (red potato salad), *poisson cru*, brochettes of beef hearts, and other grilled fish, along with soft drinks and juices in cartons. The prices are usually about 1.200 CFP per food order. You can also get casse-croûtes and other prepared foods in the well-stocked supermarkets in Uturoa.

SEEING THE SIGHTS

Almost Paradise Tours, *Tel. 66.23.64*, is owned by American Bill Kolans, who will take you in his 8-passenger minibus on a 3-hour tour to visit Marae Taputapuatea and five other *marae* temples. Bill's tours are highly praised by English-speaking visitors, who learn about the migration, anthropology and navigation of the ancient Polynesians. He gives detailed explanations of the rocks, gods, religious ceremonies and human sacrifices performed at this international *marae*. Cost is 4.500 CFP per person.

Hinerani Tours, *Tel. 66.25.75*, is owned by Lysis and Heiariki Terooatea, who have an 8-passenger Land Rover. They will take you into the interior of the island in the Faaroa valley, stopping at a botanical garden, splashing through rivers, and visiting Marae Taputapuatea. This 4-hr. tour costs 5.000 CFP per person for a minimum of 4 people. A combination excursion takes you on a 4WD tour, then by boat to the Faaroa River, for a swim and picnic at Motu Iriru. This all-day excursion is 8.500 CFP per person for a minimum of 8 people.

Jeep Safari Raiatea, *Tel. 66.15.73/79.62.21*, is operated by Mirella and Petero Mou Kam Tse, who have 4 4WD vehicles and a motorized outrigger canoe for 32 passengers that they use for combined land and lagoon tours. They have daily departures in the morning and afternoon for 4-hour tours through the mountain valleys, with stops at vanilla plantations, Marae Taputapuatea and a pearl farm. You will learn about the botanical treasures of the hidden valleys and tropical plantations and all about the cultivation of the pearl oyster. This tour is 5.000 CFP per person. Boat tours will take you to the *motu* for a picnic.

Raiatea Discovery, *Tel. 66.24.16 / 78.33.26; raidiscovery@mail.pf* is operated daily at 8:30am and 1pm by Maria Cowan and Gérard Duvos. Their 4x4 safari tours by open air Land Rover are 4.770 CFP per person for a minimum of 6 passengers.

Raiatea Tourism, *Tel. 66.20.86/78.33.13; raiateatourisme@mail.pf.* Christophe Bardou has a 45-seat a/c bus that is used to transfer groups between the airport and hotel or pensions or for tours around the island. He also provides 4WD excursions.

Special Places to Visit

Marae Taputapuatea, at PK 32 in Opoa, faces Te-Ava-Moa pass on the east coast of the island. This is Raiatea's most famous landmark and the most significant archaeological site in the whole South Pacific area. This international *marae* has been in existence since 1600 A.D. and was the most important *marae* in eastern Polynesia during the pre-Christian era. Raiatea was then known as Havai'i, the Sacred Island. This marae was not always international and did not always carry the name of Taputapuatea. At a very remote time before the birth of the god Oro it was only the national marae of Havai'i (Raiatea) and its full name was Tini-rau-hui-mata-te-papa-o-Feoro (Fruitful myriads who engraved the rocks of Feoro), and its abbreviated name was Feoro. It contained 8 memorial stones representing the 8 kings who had reigned over the land. These stones later became 8 symbols of the royal insignia of the kings and queens in long succession afterwards. They were named: Te'iva, Feufeu, Nuna'a-e-hau, Te-ata-o-tu, Manava-taia, Paie-o-te-fau-rua and Te-ra'i-pua-tata. On the seashore is **Marae Hauviri** with an investiture stone that served as a royal throne and as a measuring stone for warriors who served as representatives to the outside world. See introduction to *Raiatea chapter* for more information.

Marae Tainuu is located beside the sea at PK 15 in the little fishing village of Tevaitoa on the northwest coast of Raiatea. This marae has one of the most imposing *ahu* altars in the Leeward Islands. Petroglyphs engraved in the basaltic stones include a Polynesian sundial and 10 turtles, depicting a sort of Polynesian treasure hunt that the Maohi warriors had to perform to achieve valor and esteem. The chief's platform, called Taumatini, is at the edge of the road. Upstream from these ruins, on the hill there are several structures. First of all is the Marae Tetuira, which belonged to the chief and was considered to be very sacred. Above that a succession of small terraces takes you to the platform of the war chiefs, the *paepae* Taputuari'i.

Chez Lovine Botanical Garden, *Tel. 66.14.45*, is at PK 14,5 in Faaroa Bay. For an admission fee of 200 CFP you can visit a lush garden filled with a wide variety of local plants and flowers, and also learn all about how the vanilla vines are grown.

Mama Kapu's Garden is on the mountainside at PK 31 in Vaihuti in the district of Vaiaau on the west coast of Raiatea. Her garden has 25 species of hibiscus, 18 kinds of bougainvilleas, 17 different *aute* plants, bird of paradise, opuhi ginger flowers, torch ginger and roses in all colors. She also has 30 species of fruit trees, several acres of flowers that she sells to the hotels in Bora Bora, plus a garden of 121 medicinal herbs. A small stream on her property provides irrigation and provides a home for some 40 fresh water eels.

La Vanillère is located at PK 33.5 Opoa in Hotopuu Bay, *Tel. 66.15.61/ 79.16.56; info@tahiti-vanille.com; www.tahiti-vanille.com.* While driving around the island be sure to stop at this vanilla farm with 18,000 vanilla plants and learn how the vanilla orchids are "married" by hand to cross-pollinate the flower that produces the vanilla bean. You can also buy dried vanilla beans, powder, extract and vanilla soap in their farm shop. Guided tour at 2pm Mon-Sat. Closed Sun. Admission 300 CFP. Hidden in the bushes nearby is a pretty waterfall where you can splash around in the basin, which is called "The Queen's Bathtub."

Magasin Vanira, *Tel. 66.30.06*, on the mountainside in Uturoa center, sells dried vanilla beans, powdered vanilla and vanilla extract. This is the oldest building on the street and may even be destroyed by the time you arrive. If so, ask around to find out where Madame Jeanne Chane has relocated her vanilla business. She is the third generation of the Chane family to buy and sell vanilla, and she has earned two silver cups, six diplomas and other honors for her knowledge. A package of plump, fragrant vanilla beans costs 1.000 CFP.

Pearl Farms you can visit include: **Anapa Pearl Farm**, *Tel. 66.34.52/70.76.07*; www.anapapearls.com is owned by Philippe Blanc, who says that "the best little pearl farm in the South Pacific", is located in Tevaitoa, in front of the Protestant church and Marae Tainuu. He invites the public to call for a free visit. Don't forget your snorkeling gear and they accept all major credit cards. **Tahi Perles**, *Tel. 60.20.20, tahiperles@mail.pf* at PK 4 in Avera, is owned by Roma and Moana Constant. **Vairua Perles**, Tel. *66.12.12/66.42.57/78.25.62; vairuaperles@mail.pf* is located at PK 8.7 in Avera. The owner is Hundrew Brodien.

NIGHTLIFE & ENTERTAINMENT

Club Zenith Discothèque, *Tel. 66.27.49*, is upstairs in the Léogite Building in Uturoa center. The disco opens at 10pm each Fri. and Sat. Entry is free before 11pm and after that the cover charge is 1.500 CFP, including a drink.

SPORTS & RECREATION
Horseback Riding

Kaohi Nui Equestrian Tourism Center is on the mountainside at PK 6 in Avera, *Tel. 66.25.46/74.37.13*. Patrick Marinthe leads 2-hour rides for 5.000 CFP and half-day rides for 6.500 CFP, using saddled Marquesan horses of Chilean stock. Lodging is also available.

Hiking

Eric Rando, *Tel. 66.49.54/73.61.23; ktiki@mail.pf.* Eric Pelle is a licensed guide who belongs to an association of hiking guides. He leads hikes to the Faaroa Valley, the 3 cascades or waterfalls, Marae Taputapuatea, and to the Faaroa River by canoe. Rates are 3.600 CFP, 4.500 CFP, 6.000 CFP and 6.953 CFP, respectively. He also leads a hike to the Temehani mountain for 7.600 CFP, which includes a sandwich and drink. Transfers are made by 4WD vehicle.

Other hiking guides are: Thierry of Raiatea Randonee, *Tel. 77.91.23*; Paul of Hava'i Rando, *Tel. 66.13.77*; and Sandrine, *Tel. 76.38.00.*

Boat Rentals, Kayaks and Day Sailing
    Europcar, *Tel. 66.34.06*, rents boats with a 6-HP engine that requires no permit or a 15-HP engine that does require a license. The cost of either boat is 7.000 CFP for 4 hrs., 9.300 CFP for 8 hrs. and 10.400 CFP for 24 hrs.

    Lagon Aventure, *Tel. 79.26.27; h.clot@mail.pf; www.lagonaventure.com.* Hubert Clot operates this new activity at Marina Apooiti and provides free transfers from the hotels and pensions. He rents 1-place sea kayaks for 2.500 CFP for 4 hrs. and 5.000 CFP per day. A 2-place kayak is 3.500 CFP for 4 hrs. and 7.000 CFP for the day. A guided tour of the lagoon by kayak is 4.000 CFP for 4 hrs. and 7.000 CFP for all day. A 4-berth Tilapia sailboat is 20.000 CFP per day for a maximum of 6 people. A 4-hr. sail with a skipper is 15.000 CFP and for all day you pay 26.000 CFP for a maximum of 4 people. You can also rent the "Kalim", an 11 m. (36-ft.) trimaran with skipper for a minimum of 5 passengers, which costs 6.500 CFP per person for the day.

Deep Sea Fishing
    Game fishing is especially rewarding in the Leeward Society Islands, where prize catches of marlin, yellow fin tuna, mahi mahi and wahoo are frequent events. The Raiatea Haura Club holds local competitions several times a year, and the private charters report good fishing year-round.

    Te Manu Ata Charter, *Tel. 66/21.09/66.32.14; temanuatapf@yahoo.fr* is a 28-ft. Bertram owned by Jean-Luc Liaut, who also provides half-day fishing expeditions and full-day outings. A 4-hr. fishing trip costs 60.000 CFP and an 8-hr. outing is 100.000 CFP. Bring your own sandwiches.

    Moanavaihi II Charter, *Tel./Fax 66.10.22; cell 72.10.57/72.03.38; jpconstant@mail.pf.* This Viking 40-ft. fishing boat is owned by Jean Pierre Constant, who is one of the top captains in the Leeward Islands. The boat is equipped with Shimano heavy tackle. Half-day fishing for a maximum of 6 people is 80.000 CFP, with soft drinks, and full-day outings are 120.000 CFP with soft drinks and snacks.

Lagoon & Motu Excursions
    Faaroa River is a cool, green haven bordered by wild hibiscus *purau* trees and modern homes. One of the most popular excursions is to explore this historic river by outrigger speed canoe. Around the year 1350 hundreds of brave Maohi families left Raiatea from this river, navigating their voyaging sailing canoes by the wind, stars and ocean currents to settle in Hawaii, the Cook Islands, the Samoas and

finally in New Zealand. Their Polynesian descendants are called Maori in New Zealand and Tahitians in French Polynesia.

A Day Tour to Taha'a Island takes you on a 30-min. boat ride across the protected lagoon that is shared by Raiatea and Taha'a. On the main island you will visit a picturesque little village and a vanilla farm. Then you will explore the lagoon by boat, visiting a pearl farm and stop on a *motu* islet to swim and snorkel in the clear lagoon waters. Most full-day excursions to Taha'a also include a picnic on the *motu*.

Trips to the Motu provide an ideal destination by canoe or speedboat, where you will find white sand beaches, privacy, and time for daydreaming and swimming in the lagoon. Taxi boats are available to drop you off and pick you up later, or you can arrange transfers with your hotel or pension. Should you wish to make a day of it, your hotel will pack a picnic lunch for you or you can buy food already prepared in the supermarkets in Uturoa or order a take-out dish from any of the restaurants and snack stands. Several of the *motu* islets around Raiatea and Taha'a are off limits to the public, as they are privately owned. Others are partially private while the rest of the *motu* is open to visitors seeking sun, sand and sea. On these sometimes fiercely protected properties you will see Tabu signs warning you to keep out. Some of the people who operate the boat excursions have access to private *motu* islets where they take their passengers.

Motu Iriru, located at the entrance to the Iriru pass on the east coast of Raiatea, is open to the public. The government has built a *fare pote'e* shelter here, along with a small changing room, shower, water faucets, toilets with handicap access, picnic tables and barbecue grills. You have to take your garbage away with you. To camp on Motu Iriru you need a permit from the commune of Taputapuatea. There are no mosquitoes, no nonos and no grouchy owners here. **Motu Oatara**, on the southeast side of Raiatea in front of Hotel Atiapiti, is also known as Bird Island. There is good snorkeling here. **Motu Nao Nao**, on the south end of Raiatea, is used by some of the boat service providers who take visitors to enjoy the pretty white sand beach. A 3,000-foot landing strip was built on this 65-acre flat islet by the US Navy Seabees during World War II. **Motu Ceran** (Motu Mahaea on a map of Taha'a) has fences to close off some of the private properties, but you can visit one part of the islet for a nominal fee and use the beach. **Motu Atger** (also known as Motu Toahotu) is also privately owned. Boat excursions take their passengers to visit a lagoonarium and marine park beside this *motu*, which is called "Titi ere ere" (black breasts). There are toilets on the islet, as well as a few small bungalows to rent.

Here is just a partial list of the people who provide boat tours in Raiatea and Taha'a. You may also want to look at the lagoon excursions listed in the Taha'a chapter, as many of those excursions begin in Raiatea.

Faaroa Tours, *Tel. 66.32.70*, is owned by Noma Wong, who managed the Hotel Bali Hai in Raiatea for several years. (This hotel is now the Raiatea Hawaiki Nui). Noma has an outrigger speed canoe to take up to 30 passengers to visit the Faaroa valley and Apoomau River, with a stop at Marae Taputapuatea, and a swim at a *motu* islet with a white sand beach. This 4-hr. excursion starts at 8:30am or 1:15pm. She also offers half-day boat tours to Taha'a, or a full-day tour with a barbecue picnic on a *motu*.

Hinerani Tours, *Tel. 66.25.75; lysis@mail.pf.* Lysis and Heiariki Terooatea can take 6-12 passengers on lagoon excursions in their 27-ft. long covered boat. A combination land and lagoon excursion takes you on a 4WD tour, then by boat to the Faaroa River and for a swim and picnic at *Motu* Iriru. This all-day excursion is 8.500 CFP per person for a minimum of 8 people.

Jeep Safari Raiatea, *Tel. 66.15.73/79.62.21,* is operated by Mirella and Petero Mou Kam Tse, whose 32-place outrigger speed canoe provides excursions inside the lagoon and picnics on the *motu*.

L'Excursion Bleue (formerly Taha'a Pearl Tour), *Tel. 66.10.90/78.33.28; tpt@mail.pf; www.tahaa.net*, is owned by Bruno Fabre, who has outrigger speed canoes with awnings that he uses to transport 4 to 12 passengers for half- or full-day excursions. On the all-day tour, from 9am to 5pm, your guide (a former journalist on Taha'a) will take you to a vanilla plantation and a pearl farm on the main island of Taha'a. He will present the eco system and history in a pleasant ambiance. You will be served a local type meal on a *motu* islet with a lagoonarium, and then you can drift snorkel in the best spots. Bring plastic shoes, a towel and snorkeling gear. This excursion is 9.500 CFP, including beverage. An underwater photographer will capture the memories for you on digital camera. Bruno works with the *Tahitian Princess* during her visits to Raiatea. AE, Paypal.

Manava Excursions, *Tel. 66.28.26, manava@free.fr; www.manavapension.com.* This company is owned by Andrew Brotherson of Pension Manava. He provides excursions by a 27-foot longboat with a sun awning, offering half-day trips to the Faaroa Bay, Apoomau River and Marae Taputapuatea for 4.500 CFP. An all-day trip to Taha'a to visit a pearl farm, fish park, vanilla plantation and stop for a swim and picnic of grilled fish and fresh fruits at a *motu* costs 7.500 CFP. He will also take you to a nearby *motu* and return at your convenience, for 1.500 CFP per person. No excursions on Sat.

West Coast Charters, *Tel. 66.45.39/79.28.78.* Tony and Marie Tucker are a very friendly couple who speak good English. He's from South Africa and she is French. They offer a program of scenic lagoon excursions around Raiatea and Taha'a aboard their two boats with sun awnings. A full-day circle island tour of Raiatea includes a visit to Marae Taputapuatea and a snorkeling stop at a *motu*. A half-day Raiatea River Tour takes you along Faaroa River and to Motu Iriru for a swim or to snorkel at Motu Oatara. Or you can visit Marae Taputapuatea. A full-day boat trip to Taha'a takes you to visit a pearl farm and vanilla plantation, to feed the turtles, rays, tropical fish and sharks at a marine park, and snorkeling on a spectacular coral drop and in coral gardens.

Sailing Charter Yachts
   Archipels Croisières (Archipels Polynesian Cruises), *Tel. 689/56.36.39; Fax*

689/56.35.87; information@archipels-croisieres.pf; www.archipels.com; Skype: archipels. This yacht charter company has a nautical base at Opunohu Bay in Moorea with a fleet of 2 Marquises 57' catamarans and 4 new Eleuthera 60' catamarans. Three of these yachts are based permanently in Raiatea. Their 7 day/ 6 night Leeward Islands sailing program starts in Bora Bora and calls at Taha'a, Raiatea and Huahine, or they can begin in Huahine and end in Bora Bora, also visiting Raiatea and Taha'a. These cruises are guaranteed to operate with a minimum of 2 people, and the per passenger cost is 1,880-2,090, according to seasons. Private charters for 2-10 passengers are 11,280-16,920 in the low season and 12,540-18,810 in the high season.

The Moorings, *B.P. 165, Uturoa, Raiatea 98735. Tel. 689/66.35.93/78.35.93; Fax 689/66.20.94; moorings@moorings.pf; www.moorings.com; North American reservations: Tel. 800/669-6529; outside US and Canada 727/535-1446.* The nautical base is located at Apooiti Marina, 1 km (0.6 mi.) from the Raiatea airport and 4 km (2.5 mi.) from the boat dock in Uturoa.

The Moorings has been operating in Raiatea since 1985. In 2007 both The Moorings and Sunsail operations were taken over by First Choice Holidays, headed by Patricia Hubbard in Raiatea. The Moorings has an average fleet of 25 yachts, including 36-51 ft. long monohulls and 40-46 ft. long catamarans. You have a choice of 3, 4 or 5 cabins in a frequently renewed fleet. Yachts can be chartered bareboat, ready to sail away or with skipper and hostess/cook. Provisioning is available on request.

If you visit their Website you can select your level of luxury and plan your vacation, then get an estimate of what your cruise will cost. The Moorings is the charter company most frequently chosen by Americans who want a cruising vacation in the Leeward Society Islands.

Sunsail, *B.P. 331 Uturoa, Raiatea, 98735 Tel. 689/60.04.85; Fax 689/ 66.23.19; sunsail.tahiti@mail.pf; www.sunsail.com.*

This nautical base was formerly operated by Stardust Yacht Charters with a nautical base in Faaroa Bay. The Sunsail company, as well as The Moorings, was taken oven by First Choice Holidays and in September 2007 the Sunsail base was moved to Apooiti Marina, but it still maintains a separate office. Sunsail's fleet of 25 boats includes 11 monohulls 34-50-ft. and 14 catamarans 38-46 ft. Bareboat charters for a minimum of 3-days are available for sailing in the Leeward Islands. The yachts can also be chartered ready to sail away, complete with fuel, water, dinghy and outboard engine, bed linens and towels, barbecue grill and charcoal, snorkeling equipment and with complete provisions on request. Optional services include skippers and hostess-cooks, spinnaker and windsurf boards.

Tahiti Yacht Charter, *Tahiti office: Monette Aline, B.P. 364, Papeete, Tahiti 98713; Tel. 689/45.04.00; Fax 689/42.76.00; tyc@mail.pf; www.tahitiyachtcharter.com. Raiatea base: Tel. 689/66.28.86; Fax 689/66.28.85.*

Tahiti Yacht Charter is a 100% locally owned company. They have a fleet of 20 catamarans, most of them are less than 2 years old, all based at the Apooiti

Marina in Raiatea, with Papeete as a possible departure point. The catamarans are from 38-46 ft.: Athena 38, Lagoon 380, Lavezzi 40, Belize 43, Bahia 46, Lagoon 440, Lagoon 500 and more new models from Fountaine-Pajot and Lagoon are due to arrive in 2009.

Their sailing range is mainly the Leeward Islands, including Maupiti when weather conditions allow it. You can also sail to the Tuamotu and Marquesas Islands with a Tahiti Yacht Charter skipper on board. Charter rates vary according to seasons. A Lagoon 380, bareboat, with 4 cabins (8 passengers) starts at 408.000 CFP for an 8-day/7 night cruise during the low season (Jan.1-Mar. 31 and Sept. 29-Dec. 31), which is 7.300 CFP per night per person for 8 people.

The company is very service oriented and keeps creating new and original programs and cruises targeted to couples as well as families or group of friends. The staff and crew speak English. All the skippers have their own fishing rod. The "Tropiques" models have generator, water maker, a/c and 2 kayaks, and 2 floating hammocks on board. Boats are being equipped with Wifi (for email retrieval from your own laptop) and VOIP telephones (call your country at your local telephone rates).

Atara Royal, *Tel. 450.400; Fax 42.76.00; tyc@mail.pf; www.motoryachtchartertahiti.com.* From March 2008 Atara Royal is represented by Tahiti Yacht Charter at Marina Apooiti. This 46-ft. Grand Banks Europa motor yacht can be chartered for cruises in the Leeward Islands of French Polynesia. It was built in 1999 and has two Caterpillar 375 HP engines. Accommodations include 1 double cabin with ensuite bathroom, plus crew quarters, a/c, water maker, TV, video and DVD players, 2 stereos, dinghy with 40 HP engine, plus equipment for fishing. With the boat cruise is linked a day on the Atara Motu in the lagoon of Taha'a.

Two specific cruises are proposed: Atara Twosome, a 7-day/6-night honeymoon cruise starting in Raiatea and ending in Bora Bora, including one day on the private Atara Motu, from 1.500.000 CFP for 2, a dinner at Le Taha'a Private Island Resort & Spa, a complimentary Polynesian Monoï massage at the Deep Ocean Spa at Hotel Intercontinental Thalasso & Spa on Bora Bora, all other meals and drinks on board, taxes, transfers, fuel and gas (up to 3 hours. of daily navigation). A bottle of champagne is complimentary. A similar, shorter 4-day/3-night cruise, Atara Iti Iti (small in Tahitian), is also possible from Raiatea to Bora Bora, from 750.000 CFP for 2. Private diving sessions can be arranged with a CMAS-PADI Instructor for 50.000 CFP for 2 dives/day.

Catamaran Tane, *Tel. 73.96.90; charter.tane@mail.pf; www.chartertane.free.fr.* This 46-foot catamaran was specially designed for sailing in the tropics and has been based in Raiatea for many years. Hostess Martine and Christian the skipper provide professional, personalized cruises for 2-8 passengers. Cruises in the Leeward Islands include 5-days/4-nights and 7 days-6 nights, and longer cruises will take you to the Tuamotu and Austral Islands on request. Private cruises, day cruises and sunset cruises are also available. E-mail them for rates.

Scuba Diving

A short boat ride takes you to the **natural aquarium** at Teavapiti, and 50 different exciting dive spots are found in the four most beautiful passes of the Raiatea-Taha'a lagoon. These include exploring a sunken three-masted yacht, the hull of a Catalina seaplane, feeding gray sharks, barracuda, moray eels and the Napoleon fish that inhabit an underwater wall. The Octopus Grotto is a cave 120 m (394 ft.) long at a depth of 50 m (55 ft.); a dive for experienced divers only. There are rainbow-hued Jack trevally fish, caves of orange corals, black coral forests and dancing coral gardens of blues, violets and yellow.

Hémisphere Sub Plongée, Tel. 66.12.49/72.19.52; Fax 66.28.63; hemissubdiving@mail.pf; www.hemispheresub.com is based at the Marina Apooiti. A team of qualified instructors led by dive masters Sedira Farid and Durie Julien offers French CMAS-certification courses and PADI lessons. Daily diving excursions leave the marina at 8am, 10am, 2pm and 7pm to discover the lagoon, passes, caves, wreck and open ocean depths around Raiatea and Taha'a. Daily introductory dives; night dives on the wreck are available on request. A day tour with a picnic lunch on a *motu* and diving cruises can also be arranged. They also have dive centers at Hawaiki Nui Hotel and Sunset Beach Motel. Rates are 5.900 CFP per dive, 7.200 CFP for a night dive and 51.300 CFP for a 10-dive package.

Te Mara Nui Plongée, *Tel./Fax 66.11.88; cell 72.60.19, temaranui@mail.pf; www.temaranui.pf.* This dive center is located at the Marina in Uturoa and is open daily. Floriane Voisin, the manager, is an international CMAS ** instructor and BEES 1 State instructor. An introductory dive or exploration dive is 5.500 CFP, an initial dive is 5.900 CFP; a night dive is 6.500 CFP and a 10-dive package is 52.000 CFP. Boat transfers to the *motu* for snorkeling is 2.000 CFP per person round-trip.

SHOPPING

Coco-Vanille, *Tel. 66.17.63*, is next to the drugstore on Uturoa's main street. Isabelle is the friendly English-speaking sales person who also makes the darling hand-painted dresses and T-shirts, plus the original patchwork designs of the Tahitian bed covers. They also have quality pearls in pretty colors that come from the Bernard Champon pearl farm in Taha'a, and a selection of paintings by local artists. **La Palme d'Or**, *Tel. 60.07.85*, on Uturoa's main street, sells pearl jewelry. **Tico Pearls**, *Tel. 60.06.88*, has an impressive showroom in the Maritime building. They also sell wood and coral sculptures by the late Mara, Tahiti's most renown coral sculptor. **Rai-Teva**, *Tel. 60.04.20*, in the Maritime building, is a jewelry shop that carries a good selection of small pearl earrings. This size black pearl is not easy to find in most shops. They also carry a fashion collection of jeans, tops and other clothes. **Vairua Perles**, *Tel. 66.38.39*, is on the Uturoa waterfront, adjacent to Snack Moe Moea. In addition to 18-karat gold jewelry, they carry engraved mother-of-pearl shells and pottery.

Sephora Boutique, *Tel. 66.21.21*, is in the pink Gare Maritime building on the Uturoa wharf. They carry woven hats, tapa covered photo albums, paintings and other gift items, as well as pearls. **Te Fare Boutique**, *Tel. 66.17.17*, is behind the Gare Maritime across the street from the Arts and Crafts Village. They offer a colorful selection of Polynesian art deco linens, pottery, basketwork and jewelry. **Arii Creation**, *Tel. 66.35.54*, on Uturoa's main street, sells locally made fabrics, pareos and tee shirts, and **Habillez-Moi (Boutique Mariki)**, *Tel. 66.44.88*, on the mountainside facing the Mairie (town hall), sells clothes for children and women. **Wasa Nui Shop** in downtown Uturoa, *Tel. 66.18.00*, sells pareos, T-shirts and Indonesian clothes. **My Flower**, *Tel. 66.19.19*, is a florist and gift shop in the Maritime building. **Havai'i Sport**, Tel. 60.25.20, is upstairs at the Gare Maritime building. This is the only sporting goods store in the Leeward Islands.

Be sure to visit the **Arts and Crafts Village** or "**Fare Mama**" adjacent to the ship dock in Uturoa. There are 10 thatched roof *fares* decorated with *tifaifai* wall hangings, where the artisan mamas display their hand painted dresses and pareos, woven hats and bags, woodcarvings and shell jewelry. You can also find locally made souvenir items. The **Hawaiki Nui Association**, *Tel. 66.12.37*, at the airport, sells *pareos* and tee-shirts, wood sculptures, and traditional woven hats and bags, plus seashell jewelry.

Anuanua Art, *Tel. 66.12.66*, is on the mountainside of the main street in Uturoa center. A unique selection of paintings, sculptures, etchings, pottery, tapa, sandalwood and seashell jewelry is on display. Some of the local painters, sculptors and other artists represented are: Erhard Lux, Jean-François Favre, Christian Deloffre, André Marere, Joannis, Martiale, Philippe Dubois, Maryse Noguier, Roland Marti's sculpture and Peter Owen's pottery. Open Mon. to Fri. 8am to 12pm and 1:30 to 5:30pm, and on Sat. from 8am to 12pm.

SPECIAL SERVICES, MASSAGE, NATURAL THERAPY, RELAXATION

Lylou Beauté, *Tel. 66.15.16*, is upstairs in the Socredo building across the road from the Arts and Crafts Village and the Uturoa wharf. Their services include manicures, pedicures, facial care, waxing, makeup and relaxing massages. Beauty shops in Uturoa include **Style et Tendance Coiffure**, *Tel. 66.21.77*, and **Tehina Coiffure**, *Tel. 66.10.20*.

TATTOO ARTISTS

Isidore Haiti, *Tel. 66.15.97/72.86.63*, specializes in Marquesan tattoos.

PRACTICAL INFORMATION
Banks

Raiatea has 3 banks, which are all located in the center of Uturoa. All of them have ATM windows. **Banque de Polynésie**, *Tel.60.04.50*, is open Mon.-Thurs. from 7:45am-3:45pm, and on Fri. 7:45am-2:45pm. **Banque Socredo**, *Tel. 60.07.00*, is open Mon.-Fri. from 7:30-11:30am and from 1:30-4pm; **Banque de Tahiti**, *Tel. 60.02.80*, is open Mon.-Fri. from 7:45am-12pm, and from 1-3:45pm.

Bookstores

Librarie d'Uturoa, *Tel. 66.30.80*, is in the center of town, on the mountainside of the main street. They have calendars and books (mostly in French) about Tahiti and Her Islands.

Drugstore

The **Pharmacie de Raiatea** is on the mountainside of the main street in Uturoa center, across the street from the Catholic Church, *Tel. 66.15.56* (emergency), *Tel. 66.35.48*. It is open Mon.-Fri. from 7:30am-12pm and 2-5pm; on Sat. from 8am-12pm and on Sun. and holidays from 9-9:30am.

Hospital

There is a government hospital close to the boat dock in Uturoa, *Tel. 60.08.00* (all services) and *Tel. 60.08.01* (emergency), which serves all the Leeward Society Islands. Several private doctors and dentists have practices in Raiatea as well as physical therapists (kinésithérapeutes) and there is also an optician, **Te Mata Ora**, *Tel. 66.16.19*.

Internet

ITS Multimedia *Tel. 60.25.25*. Informatique Technologie Services has moved its Internet Cyber Café to the Gare Maritime building facing the Tahiti Tourist office. They have 6 computers with flat screens and ergonomically designed keyboards including a Qwerty board. You pay 500 CFP for a 45-min. prepaid card. Open Mon.-Fri. 7:30am-12pm and 1-5pm; on Sat. from 7:30am-12pm.

Vaitronic, *Tel. 60.00.01*, is also in the Gare Maritime. There are cyber point computers at the Raiatea Hawaiki Nui Hotel, at Raiatea Lodge, and at Pension Tepua.

Laundry

Laverie Jacqueline, *Tel. 66.28.36*, is in Apooiti and will also pick up and deliver your laundry. She's closed Sat. afternoon and all day Sun.

Police

The French *gendarmerie* is close to the post office in Uturoa center, *Tel. 60.03.05* or *17*. The number for the Municipal Police is *Tel. 66.38.97*.

Post Office & Telecommunications Office

The **Post Office** has a branch at the Gare Maritime building on the boat dock in Uturoa, which is open Mon.-Fri. from 8am-12pm and 1:30-4:30pm, and on Sat. from 8-11:30am. The main post office, *Tel. 66.35.50*, is in a modern building north of Uturoa on the main road, facing the hospital. It is open Mon.-Thurs. 7:30am-3pm, on Fri. from 7:30am-2pm and on Sat. from 8-10am. There is an

ATM window here. All telecommunications and postal services can be handled at either office.

Tourist Bureau
    Tahiti Tourism, *Tel. 60.07.77, Fax 60.07.76, raiateainfo@tahiti-tourisme.pf.* This information center is located in the Gare Maritime Building on the quay in Uturoa, and is open Mon.-Fri. from 8am-4pm. Marianne Amaru is the very helpful hostess and she also speaks good English.

Yacht Services, Marinas & Nautical Bases
    Apooiti Marina is at PK 3 in Apooiti, west of Uturoa center, *Tel. 66.12.20; Fax 66.42.20; VHF 68 or 12; noc_fr@yahoo.fr.* This is the home base of The Moorings, Sunsail and Tahiti Yacht Charter. There are 70 berths for boats up to 50 ft. with a maximum draft of 8 ft. Visiting yachts pay 160 CFP per linear meter plus tax for overnight stays. Water and electricity supplied. Contact the marina manager for extended stays. Sailboat rentals, sailing school, sail loft, scuba diving club, 2 restaurants and bars, laundry service.
    Uturoa Harbor Master's Office, *Tel./Fax 66.31.52; Cell 78.36.94 (Port Captain); VHF Channel 16 or 12.* This is a public marina in the harbor of Uturoa that has a quay for liners up to 210 m. (688.8 ft.) Large vessels are welcome. There is also a nautical base with 100 berths for boats from 26-55 ft. and a maximum draft of 3 m. (9.8 ft.). A diving club is on the premises and fuel service is available in the Uturoa port complex adjoining the wharf. Overnight stays for up to 10 sailboats are free for one night only at the loading dock.
    Uturaerae Marina is at PK 4.5 in Apooiti. This large marina is on the northwest side of Raiatea and is used by all vessels needing repairs or services, as well as by people on extended stays. It is privately owned by the **Chantier Naval des Iles** (Naval Shipyard of the Islands), *VHF Channel 72 or Tel. 66.10.10, Fax 66.28.41;* raiatea.marine@mail.pf; www.raiateamarine.com. This is the base of 4 companies that service the marine industry, providing construction and repair facilities for 30 vessels from 10-60 ft., including barges. Maximum draft 2.30 m. (7.5 ft.). Dry-docking, ships chandlery, take-away food, point phone.
    Raiatea Carenage Services, Tel. 60.05.45, Fax 60.05.46, VHF Channel 68; raiateacarenage@mail.pf; www.raiatea.com/carenage. This full service boatyard has everything you need to repair your boat and sails and also provides long-term moorage during your absence. It is located at Uturaerae Marina and is managed by Dominique Goché, who speaks English.

15. Taha'a

This small circular island that is known today as **Taha'a** (or Tahaa) was settled by Maohi pioneers several hundred years ago, estimated between 850 and 1200 AD. They called the island Uporu, a name that is also found in Samoa (Upolu). Polynesian folklore declares that this island was the natal home of Hiro, the famous god of thieves in Polynesian mythology, whose favorite hangout was in the area we now call the Leeward Society Islands. Huge black volcanic boulders on Taha'a's east coast are considered parts of Hiro's body or objects that belonged to him.

During the 17th century the kings of Raiatea and Taha'a fought for possession of Taha'a. Bora Bora's feared warriors were more powerful, and both Taha'a and Raiatea were subjugated to the rule of Bora Bora's King Tapoa, descendant of Puni the Conqueror. Although the Leeward Islands became a possession of France in 1888, the French flag was raised in Taha'a only in 1897, following years of rebellion.

For many years you didn't hear much about the quiet little island of Taha'a, which formerly lived in the shadow of its big sister island of Raiatea and within sight of the glamorous island of Bora Bora. Then, without making much hoopla about it, Taha'a began stretching in many directions. Its reputation as Polynesia's "**Vanilla Island**" has now expanded to include 3 dozen pearl farms in the clear lagoon waters near the white sand beaches of the *motu* islets.

Word began to spread among cognizant travelers when the 9-bungalow Hotel Vahine Island was built on a private *motu* in the mid-1990s. In July 2002 the 5-star Taha'a Pearl Beach Resort & Spa opened 60 bungalow suites on Motu Tautau, a lovely little islet just a 5-min. boat ride from the main island of Taha'a. One of its best selling points is a clear view of Bora Bora across the sea. This hotel was designed to be the most luxurious resort in the entire South Pacific region. In Jan. 2004 Le Taha'a Private Island & Spa, as it was then called, was accepted as a member of the elite Relais et Châteaux. This chain and The Leading Hotels of the World, Ltd., have created the Luxury Alliance group, representing the most prestigious hotels in the world. Although the official name of the hotel today is Le Taha'a Island Resort & Spa, to most people it is simply "Le Taha'a."

The Taha'a Golf Resort is an on-going project of TB Promotion, who also owns the Radisson Plaza Resort in Tahiti, and is building the deluxe Four Seasons Hotel in Bora Bora. The TB developers plan to build a 199-room hotel on a 247-acre (100-ha.) motu located off the north coast of Taha'a. The golf course will be surrounded by the hotel and its 60 overwater bungalows, 10 beach villas and 43 hotel villas, each with 3 bedrooms and kitchenette for long stays.

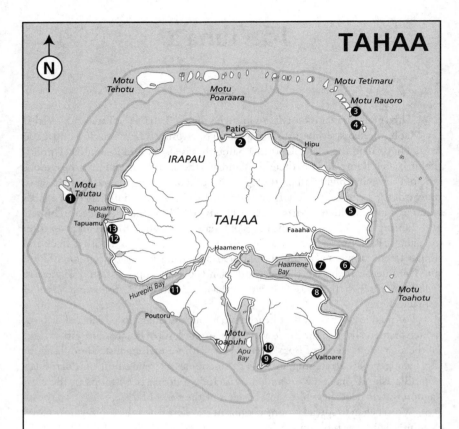

1. Le Taha'a Island Resort & Spa
2. Fare Poe Iti
3. Hotel Le Pirogue
4. Hotel Vahine Island
5. Residence Le Passage
6. Vai Poe (Chez Patricia & Daniel)
7. Pension Hibiscus
8. Tiare Breeze
9. Taravana Yacht Club
10. Pension Api
11. Pension Vaihi
12. Pension Au Phil Du Temps
13. Chez Pascal

While other hotel developers are looking for new properties on which to build their big resorts, there have been a few recent additions to the small hotel category that are quite impressive. La Pirogue is a 3-star hotel that opened 9 units on Taha'a's Motu Porou in June 2004. Fare Pea Iti opened 3 beach bungalows near Patio village in 2006 and has become a member of the Chateau & Hôtels de France selection, as well as receiving a 3-Tiare rating from the Tahiti Tourist Bureau. Another 3-Tiare lodging is the Tiare Breeze, a luxurious self-contained bungalow on the hillside in Haamene. Four small family pensions received a 2-Tiare rating and another one has earned a 1-Tiare status. See details in *Where to Stay* in this chapter.

The former Marina Iti hotel and yacht club on Taha'a was bought by a group of investors in 2005 and renamed the Taravana Yacht Club. According to investor Richard Postma, an expatriate American who also owns Taravana Island Sport Charters Bora Bora, the former bungalows of Marina Iti will be replaced by three 3-bedroom villas plus 10 small bungalows. See details under *Yacht Services* in this chapter.

Several Frenchmen with yachts have chosen the peaceful island of Taha'a as retirement retreats. There are good marina facilities and all yachts are welcomed.

Taha'a's inhabitants lead quiet, industrious lives, earning their living in agriculture, fishing and breeding livestock. Plantations of sumptuous fruits and vegetables add their lushness to the palette of vibrant colors you'll see all around the island. The produce from Taha'a is sold at the public market in Raiatea and the watermelons are shipped to the market in Papeete.

Taha'a is known as the Vanilla Island because of the numerous plantations of this aromatic "brown gold" that flourish in the fertile valleys. After the vanilla beans are harvested and laid out to dry, the whole village is filled with the rich perfume of vanilla. You can visit a vanilla plantation and some of the pearl farms that are built in the warm, clear lagoon near the *motu* islets.

Taha'a has no airport, but there are good port facilities, with service by inter-island ferry and cargo ships several times a week, and water-taxi or shuttle boat service from Uturoa. Taha'a has a *gendarmerie*, infirmary and dispensary, two post offices, banks and small general stores. Accommodations are available on a small but steadily growing scale, either in traditional Polynesian style hotels, elegant beach and overwater bungalows on a *motu*, a berth aboard a sailboat or a room in a village home. Wherever there is a room there is usually an excellent meal available. You can paddle a kayak or hire a boat and guide to visit the *motu*, where you can picnic on the white sand beaches. The protected lagoon is also ideal for sailing, windsurfing, snorkeling and fishing. You can hike into the valleys or rent a car or bike to explore the island.

Taha'a still remains virtually undiscovered by the general tourist market, although it is now awakening to the world of tourism. Peace, tranquility and natural beauty combine with the island's friendly, unhurried pace, offering you a relaxed and happy vacation with a taste of Polynesia of yesteryear. Wherever you go on this island you will find that the people smile and wave to you, nod their heads or raise their eyebrows in a traditional Polynesian greeting.

ARRIVALS & DEPARTURES

Arriving By Air

There is no airport on Taha'a. You can fly to Raiatea and take a boat to Taha'a. If you have made reservations at a hotel or pension on Taha'a, your host may send a boat to meet you at the airport. The dock is to the right of the terminal building as you face the street. There is no sign indicating this is where you should wait. You can sit at the snack bar and watch for the arrival of your boat. You can also go to the quay in Uturoa and get a regular shuttle boat to Taha'a or take a private taxi boat.

Arriving By Boat

Vaeanu, *Tel. 41.25.35; Fax 41.24.34, torehiatetu@mail.pf.* This ship can transport a total of 90 passengers, with 32 berths in cabins and 58 places on the deck. It departs from the Fare-Ute quay in Papeete at 4pm on Monday, Wed. and Fri., stopping in Huahine and Raiatea before arriving at Tapuamu quay in Taha'a the following morning at 6am. One-way fare for deck passengers is 2.120 CFP; a berth in a cabin costs 4.400 to 5.989 CFP per person depending on accommodations chosen. Meals are served on board. Reservations for cabin space must be paid in full before 9am on the fixed date of departure from Papeete.

Hawaiki Nui, *Tel. 54.99.54 (Tahiti); Tel. 65.61.59 (Taha'a); Fax 45.24.44, contact@stim.pf.* This 12-passenger cargo ship has 4 double cabins and deck space. It leaves the Motu Uta dock in Papeete each Tues. at 4pm and arrives at the Tapuamu quay in Taha'a on Wed. at 3pm, after stopping in Huahine, Raiatea and Bora Bora. The Thurs. trip leaves Papeete at 4pm, and arrives in Taha'a on Fri. at 2:30pm, after going to Bora Bora and before returning to Raiatea and Huahine on its return trip to Tahiti. The cost of sleeping on deck is 1.800 CFP per person and a berth in one of the cabins costs 5.000 CFP from Papeete to all the Leeward Islands. Meals are available on board the ship. Passengers must sleep in cabins on the Thurs. voyage as the ship also transports fuel then.

Maupiti Express II, *Tel. 66.37.81/78.27.22/72.30.48; www.maupitiexpress.com.* The *Maupiti Express II* leaves Bora Bora at 7am. on Mon., Wed., and Fri., arriving in Taha'a at 8:20am. The boat leaves Bora Bora at 4pm on Sun. and arrives in Taha'a at 5:20pm. The one-way fare from Bora Bora to Taha'a is 3.000 CFP and round-trip is 4.000 CFP. The fares from Maupiti to Taha'a are 4.000 CFP and 6.000 CFP. Passengers under 12 years pay half-fare.

Enota Transport Maritime, *Tel./Fax 65.61.33.* Enota Tetuanui has 3 covered speedboats that transport passengers between Raiatea and Taha'a. *Te Haere Maru V* leaves from the boat dock in Uturoa at 10:30am and 4:30pm for the east coast of Taha'a, stopping in Vaitoare, Haamene and Faaaha. *Te Haere Maru IV* leaves from the boat dock in Uturoa at 10:30am and 4:30pm for the west coast of Taha'a, stopping at the Marina Iti, Poutoru, Tiva and Tapuamu. The crossing takes 20 to

45 min., depending on your destination. *Te Haere Maru VI* makes stops all around the island. One-way fare starts at 500 CFP.

Tamarii Taha'a I, *Tel. 65.65.29/76.37.20*. This 46-ft. aluminum catamaran leaves the Uturoa boat dock Mon.-Fri. at 10:20am and 4:20pm, and on Sat. at 10:20am. Stops are made in Poutoru, Patii, Hatupa, Tiva, Tapuamu, and Murifenua, arriving in Patio at 11:15am and 5:15pm Mon.-Fri., and on Sat. at 11:15am. One-way fare starts at 500 CFP for the closest stops.

Tamarii Taha'a II, *Tel. 25.80.58*. This sturdy 47.5-ft. boat was formerly the *Maupiti Express I*. It leaves Uturoa dock Mon., Tues. and Thurs. at 10.20am, 3:30pm and 4:20pm. On Wed. and Fri. it leaves Uturoa at 10am and 4pm. Stops are made at Vaitoare, Amaru Quay, Haamene and Ra'ai.

Taxi Boats

La Compagnie des Taxis-Boat (Corto), *Tel.65.66.44/79.62.01, VHF 16; www.taxi-boat.com.* William Donzelot has 2 locally built polyester and aluminum boats that will accommodate 2-6 passengers. He provides taxi boat service between Raiatea and Taha'a or Taha'a and Raiatea on request, daily from 6am-6pm. He will pick you up at the airport, the quay in Uturoa or from any boat dock specified. The per person fare from Uturoa to Taha'a starts at 3.000 CFP for Zone 1, the villages closest to Uturoa, and escalates to 8.000 CFP per person for Zone 5, which includes Hipu, Patio and Iripau. Night transfers cost 100 percent more. You can also charter a taxi boat for 17.000 CFP an hour.

Limousine Boat, *Tel. 60.81.21/79.63.81; tahaa-marine@mail.pf.* Patrick Braindot has a 28-ft. teak and mahogany boat that can take up to 6 passengers on private excursions or transfers. Shower, towels, refrigerator, 2 salons, and snorkeling equipment. Hostess, champagne, picnic or snack basket available on request

Monique Taxi Boat, *Tel. 65.62.48*. Fares quoted on request.

Departing By Air

You can take a boat from Taha'a directly to the airport on Raiatea or go to Uturoa town by taxi boat and take a land taxi to the airport. Air Tahiti's number in Raiatea is *Tel. 60.04.44/60.04.40.*

Departing By Boat

Hawaiki Nui, *Tel. 54.99.54 (Papeete)*, *Tel. 65.61.59 (Taha'a); Fax 45.24.44*, leaves Taha'a each Wed. at 3:30pm for Raiatea and Tahiti, arriving in Papeete on Thurs. at 5am. It leaves Taha'a each Fri. at 3pm for Raiatea, Huahine and Tahiti, arriving in Papeete at 5am on Sat. morning. The one-way deck fare is 1.800 CFP and a berth is 5.000 CFP.

Vaeanu, *Tel. 41.25.35 (Papeete); Fax 41.24.34*, leaves Taha'a at 7am each Tues., Thurs. and Sat. for Bora Bora, arriving at 10am. Each Tues. and Thurs. the ship skips Taha'a on its voyage back from Bora Bora to Raiatea, Huahine and Tahiti. But on Sun., after spending the night in Bora Bora, the ship returns to

Taha'a, arriving at 11am on Sun. and then leaves at 12pm to continue its voyage back to Raiatea, then to Huahine and Tahiti, arriving in Papeete at 1am on Mon. The deck fare from Raiatea to Taha'a is 800 CFP, to Bora Bora it's 1.400 CFP, from Raiatea to Huahine is 1.060 CFP and from Raiatea to Tahiti it costs 2.120 CFP. A berth in a cabin is 4.400 to 5.989 CFP.

Maupiti Express II, *Tel. 66.37.81/78.27.22/*72.30.48. The boat stops in Taha'a each Mon., Wed., Fri. and Sun. between Raiatea and Bora Bora. See schedule in the Raiatea chapter.

Enota Transport Maritime, *Tel. 65.61.33*. *Te Haere Maru V* leaves from the east coast of Taha'a twice a day, starting from Faaaha, stopping in Haamene (at 6:30am and 12pm) and Vaitoare for the trip to Uturoa. *Te Haere Maru IV* leaves from the west coast of Taha'a twice a day, with stops at Tapuamu, Tiva and Poutoru, and then makes the 15-min. crossing to Uturoa. The boat begins its journey at 5:30am Mon.-Fri. during school days, and at 5:45am during vacation time. They also make another trip starting at 11:45am. *Te Haere Maru VI* also provides service from Taha'a to Raiatea. One-way fare is 500 CFP.

Tamarii Taha'a I, *Tel. 65.65.29/76.37.20*, leaves the Patio boat dock at 5:20am and 11:25am Mon.-Fri., and at 5:30am on Sat. Stops are made at Murifenua, Tapuamu, Tiva, Hatupa, Patii and Poutoru, then the boat continues on to Uturoa, arriving at 6:30am and 12:30pm Mon.-Fri., and at 6:40am. on Sat. The fare is 700 CFP from Patio and the other stops cost 500 CFP per person.

Tamarii Taha'a II, *Tel. 25.80.58*, leaves from the Ra'ai dock in Taha'a at 5:20am Mon.-Fri. It stops at Haamene, Amaru dock and Vaitoare, arriving in Uturoa at 6:40am. The 11am shuttle leaves Haamene and stops at Amaru and Vaitoare, arriving in Uturoa at 11:40am. On Sat. the boat leaves Ra'ai at 5:20am and arrives in Uturoa at 6:40am, with stops in Haamene, Amaru and Vaitoare.

ORIENTATION

Taha'a lies 3 km (2 mi.) northwest of Uturoa, sharing the same coral foundation and reef-protected lagoon that surrounds the island of Raiatea. The shape of the island, with its scalloped shoreline, resembles a hibiscus flower. A narrow isthmus separates the deeply indented bays of Apu, Haamene and Hurepiti on the south of the island. Some 60 *motu* islets lie inside the coral reef in the north and this protective barrier is unbroken except by the two navigable passes of Toahotu on the southeast side and Tiamahana on the southwest coast. Yachts and even ships can completely circumnavigate the island inside the lagoon, often accompanied by porpoises.

Taha'a has a land surface of 88 sq. km (34 sq. mi.), and **Mount Ohiri**, at 598 m (1,961 ft.), is the highest peak of the volcanic mountain range. The mountains are not high enough to attract enough rain to meet the needs of the 5,094 residents, who live in the small villages of Patio, Pahure, Hipu, Faaaha, Haamene, Motutiairi, Vaitoare, Poutoru, Patii, Tiva, Tapuamu and Murifenua. **Tiva** is considered the prettiest village, **Tapuamu** has the main port facilities, **Patio** is the administrative center, and **Haamene Bay** is 6 km (3.7 mi.) long, providing good anchorage and a haven for sailors.

A road winds 67 km (42 mi.) through the coastal villages and up mountain roads, where you have panoramic views of the bays, offshore islets and the ever-changing colors of the sea beyond the white foam on the barrier reef.

GETTING AROUND TAHA'A
Car Rentals
Europcar, *Tel. 65.67.00*. The main sales office is located at the service station on the ferry dock of Tapuamu. A Fiat Panda rents for 6.500 CFP for 4 hrs., 7.500 CFP for 8 hrs. and 8.600 CFP for 24 hrs. A 5-door a/c Panda costs 7.500 CFP for 4 hrs., 9.300 CFP for 8 hrs. and 11.500 CFP for 24 hrs. These rates include taxes, unlimited mileage and third-party insurance. Gas is extra.

Hibiscus Location, *Tel. 65.61.06/79.28.81*, is located at Hotel Hibiscus in Haamene. The rental rates are the same as those charged by Europcar.

Monique Location, *Tel. 65.62.48*, is located at the ferryboat dock in Haamene. She rents Ford Fiesta cars and gas is not included.

Bicycles
Taravana Yacht Club, *Tel. 65.61.01/28.08.08; VHF 68*. This is the only place on the island with rental bikes, which are 2.000 CFP a day.

WHERE TO STAY
Prestige
LE TAHA'A ISLAND RESORT & SPA, *B.P. 67, Patio, Taha'a 98733. Tel. 689/60.84.00; Fax 689/60.84.01; letahaa@relaischateaux.com; www.letahaa.com/ www.relaischateaux.com. Reservations: 689/50.84.45; Fax 689/43.17.86; res@spmhotels.pf. Located on Motu Tautau, 35 min. by boat from the airport in Raiatea and 5 min. by boat from the main island of Taha'a. One-way boat transfer from airport in Raiatea 4.500 CFP per person; private limousine boat transfer for 2 passengers min. with half a bottle of French champagne 12.500 CFP each. A 7-min. helicopter shuttle from the Bora Bora airport is 29.545 CFP per person. 60 bungalows. 2008 EP rates low/high season sgl/dbl: Taha'a Overwater Suite 95.000/99.000 CFP; Beach Villa 108.000/115.000 CFP; Sunset Overwater Suite 118.000/125.000 CFP; Bora Bora Overwater Suite 118.000/125.000 CFP; End of Pontoon Overwater Suite 138.000/145.000; Royal Beach Villa 250.000/290.000 CFP. American breakfast 3.000 CFP; Canoe breakfast for two 9.900 CFP; Add 10.500 CFP per person per day for MAP and 14.300 CFP for AP. Add taxes. All major credit cards.*

This 5-star 60-unit resort opened in July 2002 as the Taha'a Pearl Beach Resort & Spa, and the name was changed to Le Taha'a Private Island & Spa when it became associated with Relais et Château in Jan. 2004. Another rebranding took place in 2007, in an effort to more accurately reflect its secluded location, thus changing the name to Le Taha'a Island Resort & Spa. This resort sanctuary has garnered its share of industry honors and has appeared on many lists of the world's best places to stay.

Reached by boat from the airport on the neighboring island of Raiatea, 45 min. away, or better still from Bora Bora via an incredibly scenic 7-min. helicopter flight, Le Taha'a is located on Motu Tautau, an offshore islet facing the island of Taha'a. Designed in pure, authentic Polynesian style, Le Taha'a sits in a stunningly beautiful natural setting of 40 acres (16 ha.). Long white sand beaches and an unimaginably translucent lagoon offer horizon vistas of Bora Bora's mystical silhouette and the lusciously green mountains of Taha'a.

The best local craftsmen have combined their know how and talent to produce an architectural gem. The 48 overwater units are 90 sq. m (969 sq. ft.) large, and they are classified according to the views they offer. The 34 Taha'a Overwater Suites face Mount Ohiri on Taha'a's main island; the 6 Sunset Overwater Suites have a view of the lagoon and romantic sunsets; and the 8 Bora Bora Overwater Suites look out over the ocean and the island of Bora Bora. Each overwater unit has a wraparound deck outfitted with cushioned lounge chairs, thatched-roof dining areas and steps leading down to another solarium platform and a ladder that provides access to the lagoon. At the foot of the majestic bed in the center of the room, there is a see-through "lagoonarium" feature complete with nighttime lighting so that you can watch the tropical fish. Three of the overwater suites are equipped for disabled guests in a wheelchairs and do not have direct access to the lagoon.

Each of the 12 Beach Villas faces the lagoon and a terrace overlooking the beach. These spectacular villas have 180 sq. m (1,937 sq. ft.) of living space, including a private enclosed garden with a small self-cleaning plunge pool, shaded sitting area and an open sundeck. All of the above villas and suites have a/c and ceiling fans, a full shower and separate bathtub, a king size bed or 2 twin beds, plus a sofa bed. They have IDD phones and Internet outlet, flat screen TV's with satellite cable, DVD and CD players, mini-bar, Espresso coffee machine/tea making facilities, individual in-room safe, ironing board and iron, hair dryer and magnifying mirror. The bathrooms contain a generous supply of Manea Spa products. Housekeeping service is provided twice daily and room service is available from 7am to 9:30pm.

Two Royal Beach Villas were added in 2007, each offering 250 sq. m. (2,690 sq. ft.) of living space, including 2 bedrooms, and 2 full shower bathrooms plus a bathtub in a tropical garden. They also have a spacious lounge with desk, 3 flat-screen TV's with CD/DVD player, and a private enclosed garden and terrace with a private pool. These villas have all the amenities as the 1-bedroom units, plus a few extras such as a personalized VIP welcome, linen bathrobes and sea shoes, which are also available to guests staying in the Sunset, Bora Bora and End of Pontoon Suites.

Other additions completed in 2007 include a state-of-the-art fitness center, a new building for the Blue Nui Dive Center, an entertainment and relation room, an a/c computer room with game tables and a big screen TV, and another treatment room at the award-winning Manea Spa. The resort offers 3 dining venues, including a casual beach restaurant, an open-air dining room artfully conceived in a cathedral-like structure built into the trees, and an intimate, 18-place-setting gourmet restaurant. Two bars offer a variety of spirits, wines and tantalizing tropical cocktails. There is also a boutique and pearl shop, and 4 transit-day rooms. The fresh water infinity swimming pool has swim-up bar stools at the Manuia Bar. Besides the pool, other free activities include a lighted tennis court, volleyball, badminton, board games, magazines and books, snorkel gear, pedal boats, kayaks, outrigger paddle canoes and windsurfing.

You can take a free shuttle boat from Motu Tautau to the main island of Taha'a and go exploring on your own or join an organized tour. At the activities desk in the hotel lobby you can book a 4x4 safari tour of Taha'a for 7.273 CFP, rent a jet ski starting at 10.500 CFP for 30 min., take a catamaran day cruise for 36.363 CFP, or a champagne sunset cruise for 18.181 CFP, or a private sunset cruise for two for 55.000 CFP. A private picnic for two on a motu is 38.000 CFP. You can go sport fishing for 84.000 CFP for a half-day or 125.455 CFP for an all day outing. There are many other ways to spend your day, including snorkeling in the magnificent coral gardens adjacent to the hotel, or lying in a *chaise longue* on Motu Paari, an islet just a few steps from the beach, while you gaze at the mountains of Bora Bora in the distance. You can even take a scenic flight or an all day excursion to Bora Bora, departing from the helicopter pad on the hotel grounds. A 15-min. scenic flight over Taha'a is 23.182 CFP per person, and a 45-min. grand tour over Taha'a, Tupai and Bora Bora is 43.182 CFP each. The day excursion to Bora Bora ranges from 79.545-88.636 CFP for a minimum of two passengers.

If ever a hotel was created with honeymooners in mind, it is here at Le Taha'a Island Resort & Spa. Contact them directly for a brochure on their Special Romantic Rendez-Vous services. These include Romantic Welcomes, Romantic Interludes, Romantic Escapades and Polynesian Wedding Ceremonies. They can also recommend several private tours for two. Families are also welcome, and special beach toys are provided for the children. See further information under *Where to Eat*, *Massages & Spas*, *Seeing the Sights* and *Scuba Diving* in this chapter.

Deluxe

HOTEL VAHINE ISLAND, *B.P. 510, Uturoa, Raiatea 98735. Tel. 689/ 65.67.38; Fax 689/65.67.70; resa@vahine-island.com; www.vahine-island.com. Located on Motu Tuvahine (Island of the Woman), 15 km. (9.3 mi.) from the Raiatea airport and 12 km (7.4 mi.) from the ferry dock in Raiatea. One-way boat transfers from Raiatea are 3.460 CFP per person for a minimum of 2 people. 9 bungalows. 2008 EP Rates sgl./dbl.: Beach Bungalow 44.988 CFP; Deluxe Beach Suite 57.995 CFP; Overwater Bungalow 57.995 CFP. Add 7.040 CFP for child less than 12 years sharing bungalow with parents. Add 9.904 CFP per person per day for MAP. Minimum of 2 nights and MAP required. Add taxes. All major credit cards.*

This private hotel is located on a 10-acre *motu* facing the village of Hipu on the northeast side of Taha'a, with a beautiful view of Bora Bora. Clients are greeted at the Raiatea airport and taken to Vahine Island by speedboat over the lagoon in 30 min. On this motu you will find white sand beaches, snorkeling in the coral gardens of the lagoon, and a calm setting for relaxing. The reception-lounge and dining room are on the beach facing the 3 overwater bungalows, and you walk through a coconut grove to get to the beach bungalows and suites. All the accommodations were refurbished in March 2006, transforming 3 of the small beach bungalows into 3 deluxe beach suites. These new accommodations have a total floor size of 115 sq. m. (1,238 sq. ft.); the overwater bungalows have 70 sq. m. (753 sq. ft.), and the standard beach bungalows have 50 sq. m. (538 sq. ft.) The deluxe suites have a king size bed and the other categories have either king size or twin beds. All units include a bathroom with 2 sinks, a shower with hot and cold drinking water, separate toilets, telephone, Internet WiFi, fan, and a minibar with cups for tea and coffee. The beach bungalows and suites have a deck with a hammock, a beach shower, and an LCD screen with DVD player. The overwater bungalows have a sitting area with a sofa and aquarium table, and a covered terrace and hammock. The 3 deluxe beach suites also have a sitting area with a sofa and two armchairs, plus an extra fan.

The shallow water in the lagoon around Vahine Island is sometimes filled with spiny sea urchins and *bêche de mer*, the elongated black sea cucumber that lives on the white sand bottom. You have to step carefully through these obstacles to get to the deeper water where you can swim and snorkel.

Activities free of charge include Polynesian outrigger canoes, windsurf board, lagoon kayaks, snorkeling equipment, fishing equipment for the reef, beach games, board games, fish feeding, DVD selection and library. A beach boy is on hand to take you snorkeling, to visit the reef, and to learn all about the coconut. Optional activities organized by the hotel include boat transfers to Raiatea and the main island of Taha'a, snorkeling excursions by outrigger speed canoe, visit to a pearl farm, sailing on a 14-ft. Hobie Cat, and small motor boats for 2-4 passengers. The management will help you to book any of the other excursions listed in this chapter. There is also a helipad on the premises. The restaurant and bar are open to the public, but reservations must be made for meals if you are not staying in the hotel. See more information in *Where to Eat* in this chapter.

Superior
   HOTEL LA PIROGUE, *B.P 668, Uturoa, Raiatea 98735. Tel. 689/60.81.45; Fax 689/60.81.46; hotellapirogue@mail.pf; www.hotellapirogue.com. Located on Motu Porou on the northern barrier reef facing Bora Bora, a 30-min. boat ride from the port of Uturoa and 35 min. by boat from the airport in Raiatea. Boat transfer 6.500 CFP. 2008 EP rates sgl./dbl.: Garden Bungalow 26.000 CFP; Beach Bungalow 30.000 CFP; Beach Suite 42.000 CFP. Continental breakfast 1.850 CFP; American*

breakfast 2.250 CFP; add 7.000 CFP per person for MAP and 10.500 CFP for AP. Add taxes. AE, MC, V.

This 3-star hotel opened in June 2004 on Motu Porou, a private islet on the northern side of Taha'a, offering a superb view of the lagoon of Taha'a as well as the romantic sunsets over Bora Bora. Giuliano Tognetti and his wife Séverine and their two daughters welcome guests to their cozy little resort, which offers 1 beach suite, 4 beach bungalows and 4 garden bungalows. These are built in the local style of wooden walls and floors and thatched roofs of coconut fronds that were woven by the people of Hipu village. Each bungalow has a double bed, mosquito net, ceiling fan, television, teak and kohu furniture, DDD telephone and Internet connection for your laptop, a private bathroom with hot water shower, and a small terrace with lounge chairs. Fresh water is piped in from the main island under the lagoon and electricity is provided by solar energy and an electric generator. The restaurant proposes a local menu, with seafood specialties and Polynesian nights organized. Room service is available from 8am to 10pm. Canoes, snorkeling equipment and fishing gear are free to in-house guests. Optional activities include boat excursions to visit pearl farms, a 4WD trip around the island or a picnic outing on a motu. A private shuttle boat transfers hotel guests from the port of Uturoa or the airport in Raiatea to La Pirogue on Motu Porou. See more information under *Where to Eat* in this chapter.

FARE PEA ITI, *B.P. 128, Patio, Taha'a 98733. Tel. 689/60.81.11/76.98.55; Fax 689/60.81.12; farepeaiti@mail.pf; www.farepeaiti.pf; Beside the lagoon 1.2 km. (0.7 mi.) from Patio village and 45 min. by boat from Raiatea airport. Round-trip boat transfers 13.200 CFP sgl./16.800 CFP dbl. 2008 EP rates: Beach bungalow 30.000 CFP sgl., 36.000 dbl.; child 3-12 yrs. 3.000 CFP. Continental breakfast 1.800 CFP, Dinner 5.500 CFP per person. Add visitor tax. V.*

The name of this charming place means "A little luck" in Tahitian, and you will indeed feel lucky to stay here, as this small hotel is part of the prestigious Chateau & Hôtels de France selection. It has also been given a 3-Tiare rating by the Tahiti Tourist office. In a dream landscape facing a garland of motu islets, owner Brigitte Guerre has built 3 attractive bungalows in the Polynesian style and has decorated them with refinement and a high quality of comfort. Bungalow facilities include a king size bed with very nice bedding and a mosquito net, ceiling fan, cable TV and DVD player, a private bathroom with hot water shower, hair dryer, makeup mirror, linens, bathrobe, slippers, and Chateaux & Hôtels de France toiletries. The covered terrace includes a recessed kitchen area with hotplate, microwave, barbecue, fine china and silverware, and a stocked mini bar. There is daily housekeeping service and laundry service is optional.

A Continental breakfast of gourmet food is served on your dining terrace and dinner can be a private affair on your terrace or you can join other guests at the main table for this deliciously prepared table d'hôte meal. There is a magasin food store, a restaurant, snack and roulotte in nearby Patio village for lunch or dinner. Beside the white sand beach at Fare Pea Iti there is a salt-water swimming pool with deck chairs, and a fitness area with exercise bike and running mat. Guests have free use of the snorkeling gear, kayaks, canoes, bicycles, French bowls and ping-pong. In the main house there is a library with a relaxing area, board games and DVD films. Internet access is available for 500 CFP for 30 min. and Fax service is 200 CFP per page.

Activities can include a tour of the island by car for 4.500 CFP per person, a boat excursion with snorkeling for 6.400 CFP, a lagoon excursion with a picnic on the motu for 9.500 CFP, and a sunset cruise with cocktail for 7.800 CFP. You can also have a massage, Tahitian dance lesson or an arts and crafts demonstration, which are all extra.

TIARE BREEZE, *B.P. 178, Haamene, Tahaa 98734. Tel. 689/65.62.26/ 73.83.97; castagnoli@mail.pf; www.tiarebreeze.com. On hillside in Haamene, a 20-min. boat ride from airport in Uturoa. EP rates: 35.000 CFP per night, plus 10% during high seasons. Add taxes. V.*

This Polynesian style thatched roof luxury bungalow has earned a 3 Tiare rating from the Tahiti Tourist office. It contains a king size bed and a single bed, a full bath with hot water shower and a half bath, a fully equipped kitchen, barbecue grill, bar-dining area, entertainment center with CD player and stereo system, ceiling fan, and expansive decks overlooking the bay. All activities can be arranged. Fresh island fruits and French pastries are delivered to your doorstep each morning.

Moderate

LE PASSAGE, *B.P. 150, Haamene, Taha'a 98734. Tel./Fax 689/65.66.75; cell 72.07.71/79.17.17; residencelepassage@mail.pf; www.tahitilepassage.com. On the mountainside in Faaaha, a 20-min. boat ride from the airport in Raiatea. Round-trip transfers 5.000 CFP per person. A/C bungalow with MAP 18.000 CFP per person. Add visitor tax of 50 CFP per person per day. No credit cards.*

Bruno and Marie-Thérèse Meunier-Coeroli have built 3 bungalows on the side of a hill in Faaaha on the wild east coast of Taha'a, facing the rising sun and overlooking Motu Atara, Vahine Island and Motu Mute, as well as the boat passage near the village of Patio. It has been given a 1-star rating by the Tahiti Tourist office. The furnishings and decorations are all done in good taste, offering two smaller units with a double bed and a private bathroom, and a 2-bedroom family bungalow with double beds and 2 bathrooms. Mosquito nets and electric mosquito repellents are provided. Each a/c unit has a covered terrace overlooking the marvelous lagoon.

The biggest attraction at Le Passage is the gastronomic restaurant, where Marie-Thérèse practices her culinary arts. She specializes in fish and seafood, using local products and organically grown fruits and vegetables from her own garden. Amenities also include a bar with wine cellar, a barbecue pontoon, and a living room-library with satellite TV. Free activities include kayaks, bicycles, ping-pong, snorkeling equipment, swimming pool, private marina, 4WD Landrover excursions and free transfers to eat lunch elsewhere. Optional choices include renting a boogy board or car, deep-sea fishing, scuba diving and visiting Raiatea. A private boat tour around the island of Taha'a with a champagne picnic is 60.000 CFP for two people.

VAI POE (CHEZ PATRICIA & DANIEL), *B.P. 104, Haamene, Taha'a 98734. Tel. 689/65.60.83/79.26.01; v.p@mail.pf; www.vaipoe.com. On mountainside in Haamene, 15 min. by boat from the Apooiti marina in Raiatea and 13 km. (8 mi.) from the boat dock in Tapuamu. Round-trip boat transfer between Uturoa and Amaru quay in Haamene 4.000 CFP per person. Round-trip taxi transfer between Tapuamu and Haamene 4.000 CFP per passenger. 5 bungalows. 2008 EP rates: Bungalow 10.000 CFP sgl/dbl. Extra person 1.500 CFP, 750 CFP for child 4-12 years. Breakfast 1.000 CFP, dinner 2.500 CFP. Add taxes. AE, MC, V.*

This small family pension has a 2-Tiare rating from the Tahiti Tourist office. It is owned by Patricia and Daniel Amaru, who are some of the most organized people involved in tourism in French Polynesia. They have built 5 very clean and attractive thatched roof bungalows situated on a large lot of grassy land facing the lagoon and the family's pearl farm in Haamene Bay. Two bungalows each have a double bed, a kitchen with a mini-refrigerator stocked with drinks, and a private bathroom with hot water shower. The other bungalows are family size, with one double bed and two single beds and a small desk or dressing table, all with a Polynesian touch. Each unit has a ceiling fan, screened windows, mosquito net, TV, a kitchen, bathroom with hot water shower, and a terrace overlooking a flower garden.

Patricia cooks family style meals on request, and will bring your meals to your room. Guests have access to the laundry facilities, telephone, and computer with Internet connection. Vai Poe Boutique sells pearls from their own farm, and there are 5 boat moorings close to the Amaru dock. Guests staying in the pension pay reduced rates with Vai Poe Excursions. A 4x4 Safari Tour is 4.000 CFP and a boat tour of the lagoon with a picnic on the motu is 7.500 CFP. See more information under *Seeing the Sights* and *Sports & Recreation* in this chapter.

PENSION HIBISCUS, *B.P. 184, Haamene, Taha'a 98734. Tel. 689/65.61.06/ 79.28.81; Fax 689/65.65.65; hibiscus@tahaa-tahiti.com; www.tahaa-tahiti.com. At the end of Haamene Bay, 20 min. by boat from the Raiatea ferry dock. Round-trip boat transfers between airport and pension 2.250 CFP per person; transfers between Uturoa boat dock and pension 2.000 CFP. EP Rates: Bungalow with private bathroom 9.434 CFP sgl/dbl, 11.130 CFP tpl; plus choices up to 8-person bungalow for 26.500 CFP. MAP 4.392 CFP per person; AP 6.629 CFP per person. Rates include taxes. AE, MC, V.*

This is classified as a 2-Tiare small family hotel with 7 small bungalows built in a tight space. It is also a nautical base. The smallest bungalow contains 2 double beds and a single bed, a private bedroom with hot water and a small terrace. The largest bungalow can sleep up to 8 people, with beds downstairs and on the mezzanine, plus a bathroom with hot water. All the bungalows have screened windows, refrigerator and fan.

Across the road is the 200-seat restaurant and bar, which also serves as a yacht club. The ambiance at Leo and Lolita Morou's bar can become quite lively when a group of yachties tie up at the 10 moorings provided at the big pier and adjourn to the "watering hole." If you're looking for a rollicking good time, with lots of sea tales, this is your place. If you seek a tranquil, private environment, maybe the bungalows in back will give you enough distance from the noise to get a good night's sleep. You'll have to go further, however, to escape the sound of the *toere* drums when there is a dance group, so you may as well join them and learn to dance the hip-shaking *tamure*. Be prepared to chip in to pay for the entertainment when Leo passes the hat. He has a reputation for adding a lot of extra charges to the bill. See more information under *Where to Eat* and *Yacht Services* in this chapter.

PENSION AU PHIL DU TEMPS, *B.P. 50, Patio, Taha'a 98734. Tel. 689/ 65.64.19/74.71.08; Fax 689/65.64.19; E-mail: moutte.junior@mail.pf; www.pension-au-phil-du-temps.com. On mountainside on Taha'a's west coast, near the Tapuamu ferry dock. Round-trip boat transfers from the airport in Raiatea to the pension 12.000 CFP dbl. Free land transfers from Tapuamu dock to pension. EP room with breakfast 10.000 CFP sgl/dbl; EP bungalow with breakfast 12.000 CFP sgl/dbl. Add 5.000 CFP per person for MAP meals and 8.000 CFP for AP meals, including taxes. V.*

Two small thatched roof bungalows are built on stilts beside the main house inside a fenced yard across the road from the lagoon and boat dock. Each unit has 2 single beds and a double bed in the mezzanine, a mosquito net, fan, TV, mini-bar, terrace and private bathroom with hot water. Rooms are also available in main house. Meals are served in the communal dining room.

This small family pension has a 2-Tiare rating by the Tahiti Tourist office. It is owned by Philippe and Babeth Moutte, a French couple who will include a free excursion per day starting on the 3rd day of your stay if you choose the American Plan. Guests have free use of the bicycles and canoes. Philippe's 12-passenger boat has a sunroof, and he will take you fishing in the lagoon or outside the reef, and for tours around the island or to the motu islets. Kite surfing and scuba diving, as well as land tours by 4WD can also be arranged.

Other Family Pensions

Pension Api, *Tel./Fax 689/65.69.88.* 2 rooms beside lagoon in Vaitoare, with kayaks, bicycles and snorkeling equipment. EP 8.000 CFP sgl/dbl; MAP and AP available. No credit cards.

Pension Vaihi, *Tel. 689/65.62.02.* 3 fares beside Hurepiti Bay for 8.000 CFP sgl/dbl. Add 3.500 CFP for MAP and 5.000 CFP for AP.

Chez Pascal, *Tel./Fax 689/65.60.42.* A house and 4 simply furnished bungalows with communal bathrooms and kitchen on mountainside near Tapuamu ferry dock. EP room or bungalow with breakfast 3.000 CFP; MAP 4.500 CFP; AP 6.500 CFP.

WHERE TO EAT
Prestige

LE TAHA'A ISLAND RESORT & SPA, *Tel. 60.84.00. There are three restaurants and two bars. All major credit cards. Reserve.*

Restaurant Vanille is the main restaurant, situated in the heart of the resort on the upper level among the trees. A breakfast buffet is served from 7-10:30am and costs 3.000 CFP. Dinner is served nightly except Tues., from 6:30-9:30pm, featuring an international menu with an emphasis on fresh seafood and fish with French and Polynesian flavors. Starter courses are priced from 2.700-4.200 CFP, fish and seafood dishes are 3.600-3.800 CFP, and meat and poultry selections are 3.600-4.500 CFP. A 3-course set dinner menu is 7.800 CFP. A Manea Spa menu offers 4 selections of light, healthy choices for 2.500-3.600 CFP, and the Vegetarian Menu includes 6 dishes for 2.500-3.500 CFP. A seafood buffet and dance show for 8.000 CFP is served on Sat. evenings from May-Oct.

Restaurant Ohiri is an elegant room with a/c and seating for 18 that is open for dinner except on Sun. and Tues. You must reserve to savor a gourmet Chef's Menu dreamed up by the Executive Chef. You are served a starter course, fish, meat, cheese and dessert for 18.000 CFP per person, or 24.000 CFP including wine tasting. *A la carte* dining starts with appetizers from 3.100-6.500 CFP, and the main courses range from 3.900 CFP for the fisherman's lagoon catch to 7.600 CFP for local rock lobster. A set 3-course menu is 12.000 CFP, with an additional 8.200 CFP for wine pairing. A slice of Brie cheese stuffed with truffle and pistachio is 2.900 CFP and desserts are 2.300 CFP, accompanied by a glass of wine ranging from 850-2.600 CFP.

La Plage is the poolside restaurant that gifts you with a magnificent view of the lagoon and Taha'a island while you are enjoying your lunch, served daily from 11:30am-4:30pm. You can order burgers and light dishes and serve yourself from the salad bar. Prices start at 1.850 CFP for cottage cheese and cucumber and escalate up to 7.800 CFP for grilled beef rib. A hamburger or chicken hot dog is 1.900 CFP. La Plage is also the setting for Polynesian Evening each Tues., when a Polynesian barbecue buffet is served, accompanied by a Polynesian dance group and a fire dance performance. This theme dinner is 7.500 CFP per person.

Tehutu Bar is the hotel's main bar on the upper level, which is open daily except Tues. from 3-11pm. You can cool off in the swimming pool and swim up for a tropical cocktail at the **Manuia Bar**, which is open daily from 10am-6pm. Maurice, the bartender, is from Taha'a, and makes great cocktails, including a super Mojito.

Deluxe

HOTEL VAHINE ISLAND, *Tel. 689/65.67.38. In-house guests are required to pay the MAP rate of 9.904 CFP for breakfast and dinner. All major credit cards. Reservations are required for guests not staying in the hotel.*

The American breakfast includes fresh fruit salad, fruit juice, fresh croissants and bread, fresh homemade cakes and jams, and vanilla yogurts, omelet or any style eggs, a selection of cereals, tea and coffee. For lunch there is a large selection of fresh salads, grilled fish and meat sandwiches, or fresh pasta, marinated fish or fish tartar, and desserts. The gastronomic dinners offer a selection of 2 starters, 2 main courses and 2 desserts. A vegetarian menu can be offered on request.

Superior
   CHEZ LOUISE, *Tel. 65.68.88/71.23.06, beside the lagoon in Tiva village. Open daily with non-stop service from 8am-10pm. MC, V. Free transfers.*
   Louise has earned a good reputation for her crab and lobster and river shrimp specialties and other local style cuisine that is often flavored with vanilla. She serves a bamboo canoe filled with poisson cru, rock lobster (in season), grilled lagoon fish, shrimp, rice and bread for 4.900 CFP. A rare treat that you will find on her menu is *cigale de mer,* a very tasty slipper lobster that is priced at 3.350 CFP. Even more delicious and almost impossible to find on anyone's menu is *varo,* which Louise also serves for 5.650 CFP when it is in season. Special hooks and skills are required to capture these sea centipedes that live in pairs in a hole in the white sand bottom of the lagoon. Louise is considered "the" specialist in preparing *maa Tahiti* for groups. Prompted by some of the hotels and passenger ships to put the price up so that they can get a commission, she now charges 5.500 CFP per person, which includes a bottle of wine for 4 people. Yachting people can tie their dinghy to the boat dock in front of the restaurant.
   LA PIROGUE, *Tel. 60.81.45, on Motu Porou. BLD, lunch and dinner. Add 6% VAT. AE, MC, V. Reservations are required for guests not staying in the hotel.*
   Fresh fish and seafood, local favorites and international cuisine. A la carte lunch usually consists of poisson cru, sashimi or tuna carpaccio, and a 3-course dinner costs around 5.000 CFP per person.

Moderate
   RESTAURANT HIBISCUS, *Tel. 65.61.06. BLD, are served. AE, MC and V. Reservations are required for guests not staying in the hotel.*
   The emphasis is on local specialties and the fish catch of the day and the average meal costs around 4.000 CFP per person. The Hibiscus hosts a Tahitian *tamaara'a* feast each Saturday night. Guests are expected to chip in to pay the musicians and dancers who entertain.
   RESTAURANT TAHA'A MAITAI, *Tel. 65.70.85. On the waterfront in Haamene village. 3 moorings for boats. Open 10am-2:30pm and 6:45-8pm Tues.– Fri. Closed Sat. noon and open at night. Open Sun. noon and closed at night. Closed all day Mon. MC, V.*
   Frenchman Bruno François serves salads from 1.400-2.200 CFP, poisson cru for 1.380 CFP, fish and seafood for 1.600-2.100 CFP, and 1.150 CFP meat dishes for 1.600-2.400 CFP. Burgers and fries or salad are 1.250-1.400 CFP, and there are 14 choices of ice cream for 200-850 CFP. You can also buy a beer or bottled wine. He caters to the local clientele, as well as French residents and visitors from many countries.

TARAVANA YACHT CLUB, *Tel. 65.61.01/28.08.08; VHF 68. Open Fri.-Tues. 11:30am-1:30pm and 6:30-8:30pm. Reserve the night before for breakfast. Closed Wed.-Thurs. MC, V. Reserve.*

This restaurant has earned a good reputation for the quality and variety of food it serves as well as the ambience of good fun generated by manager Maui Postma and his crew. The menu is the same for lunch or dinner and does not include burgers or snack items. Starter courses of shrimp cocktail, snails in puff pastry, poisson cru or sashimi are 1.200-1.950 CFP, depending on the size you order. Salads are 1.150-2.600 CFP, seafood dishes are 2.150-2.950 CFP, frog legs are 2.550 CFP, meat choices are 2.950-3.350 CFP, and burgundy beef filet fondue for a minimum of 2 is 3.500 CFP. Reserve 30 min. ahead. Desserts are 900-1.250 CFP, and wines are 2.150-6.320 CFP. A kid's menu of main course plus drink and ice cream is 1.500 CFP. Maui makes great cocktails for 1.000-1.300 CFP.

Polynesian night is held every Tues. evening, with a buffet of local foods followed by a traditional dance show. Reserve before noon on Tues. See more information under *Yacht Services* in this chapter.

Economy
SNACK MAC CHINA 99, *Tel. 65.67.81.* In Haamene village across road from post office. Breakfast, pastry shop and Chinese food to go.

SEEING THE SIGHTS
Land Tours
Guided excursions by 4WD vehicles take you on safari tours into the mountains and across the island, passing through Taha'a's luxuriant vegetation from bay to bay. Stops are made at lookout points to let you admire the panoramic views of the bays and lagoons. You will visit a tropical fruit garden and vanilla plantation, where you will learn about this fragrant "brown gold" and how it is "married" by hand. Most of the tours also include a visit to a cultured pearl farm, and some tours even include the turtle park. Most half-day tours cost 4.500 CFP per person.

Land tours are provided by: **Dave's Tours,** *Tel. 65.62.42;* **Hanalei Tours,** *Tel. 65.67.60;* **Hibiscus Activities,** *Tel. 65.61.06/79.28.81;* **Poe-Rani Tours,** *Tel. 65.60.25/78.80.25;* and **Remuna Tours,** *Tel. 65.63.28/72.93.28;* **Taha'a Tours Excursion** (Edwin and Jacqueline Mama), *Tel.65.62.18/79.27.56;* **Vai Poe Excursions,** *Tel. 65.60.83/79.26.01;* and **Vanilla Tours,** *Tel. 65.62.46.*

Lagoon Excursions & Cultured Pearl Farms
Aquatic Explorer, *Tel. 75.71.20,* is a 24-ft. glass bottom boat operated by Catherine Briy in Apu Bay, taking 6-11 passengers to discover the natural aquarium with its fauna and flora.

Dave's Tours, *Tel. 65.62.42,* is operated by Dave Atiniu in Haamene. He has a 28-ft. locally built Fiberglas boat with a sun awning that he uses for excursions that begin in Uturoa or Taha'a. Full-day excursions include snorkeling in the coral gardens and a picnic on a motu. These tours can also be combined with 4WD land excursions.

Mata Tours, *Tel. 74.11.43/65.68.08; matatours@tahaa.org.* Stephane Toimata offers a half-day tour for 6.000 CFP that takes you by outrigger canoe to feed the sting rays and fish, snorkel in a natural aquarium and enjoy a fruit tasting while visiting a vanilla plantation. You can also opt for a half-day tour that includes shark feeding instead of the rays, as well as snorkeling, the vanilla plantation and fruit tasting for 6.000 CFP per person. A half-day private tour for 2-4 passengers is 45.000 CFP, and an all day-tour for 2-4 includes a BBQ on the motu for 78.000 CFP.

Poe-Rani Farm, *Tel. 65.60.25/78.80.25,* is owned by Teva and Rooverta Ebbs in Haamene Bay. Guided excursions take you to the pearl farm, where you will learn about how the oysters are grafted and the beautiful cultured pearls are produced. You can also buy Tahitian products here.

Taha'a Discovery/Motu Pearl Farm, *Tel. 65.66.67/79.28.92/72.33.01.* Matahiarii Laughlin takes you by 30-passenger motor launch or a 60-passenger covered catamaran on a half-day excursion to visit Motu Pearl Farm, the pearl farm of the Laughlin family in Faaaha Bay. Demonstrations are available from 9am to 5pm to explain how the pearl is cultivated inside the mother-of-pearl oyster. Their boutique is open from 9am to 10pm and you'll surely want to see their collection of pearls for sale. Optional visits can also be made by 4WD vehicles to visit a vanilla plantation and see the panoramic sights of Taha'a. Taha'a Discovery also specializes in organizing barbecue picnics and Tahitian buffets on the motu for groups up to 200 people. They can provide VIP tours on request.

Taha'a Terapu Tours, *Tel. 65.69.55,* is owned by Reynald Vaiho of Vaitoare. He has a 36-ft. locally built wooden motorboat for 6-12 passengers.

Taha'a Tours Excursion, *Tel. 65.62.18/79.27.56.* Edwin and Jacqueline Mama provide lagoon excursions on board their motorized outrigger canoes, which include a visit to a pearl farm and a picnic and swim at a motu. These tours usually originate in Raiatea and can be combined with a 4WD land excursion in Taha'a.

Vai Poe Excursions, *Tel. 65.60.83/79.26.01; vaipoe.excursions@mail.pf.* Patricia and Daniel Amaru operate have 2 boats for 6-24 passengers, providing an all day boat and safari excursion from Raiatea to Taha'a. This outing includes snorkeling in the coral gardens, a picnic on a motu and a visit to their **Vai Poe Pearl Farm** for 7.500 CFP per person. You can also combine this excursion with a 4WD tour of Taha'a for 9.000 CFP per person.

The Raiatea chapter also lists several tour operators under *Lagoon and Motu Excursions* who provide boat excursions to Taha'a and its motu islets. Some of these guides are: **l'Excursion Bleue**, *Tel. 66.10.90*; **Noma Tours**, *Tel. 66.32.70*; and **West Coast Charters**, *Tel. 66.45.39.*

HIBISCUS FOUNDATION SAVES THE SEA TURTLES

Leo and Lolita Morou, who own the Hotel-Restaurant Hibiscus in Taha'a, started the **Hibiscus Foundation** in 1992. Their goals are to fight against underwater spearfishing and turtle poachers, and to rescue the turtles that have been injured or accidentally trapped in fish parks inside the lagoon near the passes. When they find these turtles Leo and his volunteer helpers shelter them in a special enclosure for a few days, then tag them for future identification before releasing the turtles into the open ocean. By the end of 2006 the Hibiscus Foundation had saved 1,380 turtles, mostly the Chelonia Midas, the green sea turtle, which is the most common and the tastiest. Several hawksbill turtles, Eretmochelys imbricata, the large-headed turtle, have also been rescued by Leo and Lolita, and their network of yachting friends.

In the olden days when the arii, the Polynesian chiefs, ruled the people, the honu (turtles) were considered sacred and their meat was reserved only for the kings, priests and keepers of the marae, where the Maohi people worshipped their god Oro. The marae that were dedicated to Oro were distinguished by stones that were shaped in the form of turtle heads, and turtle petroglyphs were carved in the basaltic rocks. The turtles are just as tapu (taboo, sacred or forbidden) today as they were then, because they have been declared an endangered species by the local government.

SPORTS & RECREATION
Charter Yachts
Information on the yacht charter companies is given in *Tahiti, Moorea* and *Raiatea* chapters.

Day Sailing
Bisou Futé Charter, *Tel. 65.64.97/79.11.42; Fax 65.69.08; jeanyvon@mail.pf; www.bisoufute.com.* This 51-ft. Beneteau monohull is owned by Jean-Yvon Nechachby and is based in Apu Bay, Taha'a. This yacht is available for full-day sailing cruises inside the Raiatea-Taha'a lagoon. Lunch is served on board or on a motu islet. Private cruises can be organized on request to other Society Islands.

Fai Manu Cruises, *Tel. 65.62.52; Fax 65.69.08; www.faimanu.com.* This 50-ft. fast speed catamaran is owned by Louis Corneglio and is based in Apu Bay in Taha'a. A maximum of 16 passengers can sail around the island, with a picnic on request. Long distance cruises are available for 8 passengers.

See information on **Atara Royal** and **Catamaran Tane** under *Charter Yachts* in the Raiatea chapter. They also offer day sailing and sunset cruises.

Deep Sea Fishing
See the section on Deep Sea Fishing charters in the *Raiatea* chapter.

Scuba Diving
There are more than 25 recorded dive spots, including 8 passes, around Taha'a and Raiatea, all reachable by boat within 10-25 min. from Taha'a. You can see reef sharks and humphead wrasses year-round in water temperatures of 60-80° Fahrenheit. Of special interest to divers are underwater caves and a wrecked ship.

Taha'a Blue Nui Diving Center, *Tel./Fax 689/65.67.78; tahaabluenui@mail.pf; www.bluenui.com* is located at Le Taha'a Island Resort & Spa on Motu Tautau. The PADI/CMAS dive instructor can take certified divers for a Fun dive for 6.818 CFP, a 2-tank Fun dive for 13.182 CFP, an introductory dive or lesson for 7.727 CFP, or a private dive for two people for 45.455 CFP. A package of 5 Fun dives is sold for 31.818 CFP and a 10-dive package is 59.091 CFP. Both packages are available and usable in the four Blue Nui Diving Centers in Taha'a, Bora Bora, Manihi and Tikehau. A PADI Open Water training is 7.273 CFP, and after the initiation you must add a minimum of 4 lessons and purchase the diving logbook, which costs 1.818 CFP. Rates include basic equipment (instructor, boat ride, tank, jacket, regulator, weight belt, fins, mask, shorty wetsuit and underwater flashlight for night dives).

SHOPPING
Pearl Farms and Boutiques
Champon Pearl Farm, *Tel. 65.66.26; www.champonperles.com*. This cultured pearl farm is next door to Taravana Yacht Club at Point Toamaro in Apu Bay. Direct pearl sales are made in the boutique here. **Motu Pearl Boutique**, in Faaaha, *Tel. 65.69.18,* sells pearls, keishis, mabes and pearl jewelry. They also sell locally made clothing, *pareos,* curios, and traditional arts and crafts combining mother-of-pearl with local woods and woven coconut fibers. **Poerani Pearls**, *Tel. 65.60.25*, and **Vai Poe Pearls**, *Tel. 65.60.83,* both in Haamene Bay, sell pearls from their own farms, as well as locally made jewelry and arts and crafts. **Sophie Artisanant Boutique** in Hurepiti Bay, *Tel. 65.62.56,* sells hand painted *pareos.* **Strands of Pearls**, *Tel. 65.62.26/73.83.97; www.tiarebreeze.com.* Tama Castagnoli's pearl farm is open to the public in Haamene, with free demonstrations and a good selection of their own pearls for sale.

MASSAGES & SPAS
Manea Spa, *Tel. 60.84.00,* is built of natural materials in Polynesian style at the edge of a salt-water lake on Motu Tautau, providing body and facial care for men and women, most of whom are guests at Le Taha'a Island Resort & Spa. Among its many awards, this Spa was named the Top Island Spa in the World by *AsiaSpa*, May/June 2006, and Top Spa Destination in the South Pacific Islands, Luxury by *SpaFinder*, Sept. 2005.

The Manea Spa features twin massage rooms beside the lake, a double massage room with Jacuzzi viewing the lake, as well as a double open-air Vichy-shower. Treatments include traditional Polynesian massage, reflexology, exfoliation, body masks and wraps, facial care and hydration. All services are available for 1-2 people. A 30-min. massage starts at 8.500 CFP, a 50-min. massage starts at 13.000 CFP and an 80-min. massage is 18.500-21.500 CFP. You can even get treated with a Mahana Manea (16.000 CFP for 50 min. to prepare you for sun tanning, and if you stay in the sun too long, for 13.000 CFP you can have the Vea Manea, a 30-min. calming treatment with tamanu and sandalwood products. Facial care for ladies includes the 50-min. Hohoa Matai treatment for 13.000 CFP and the Hohoa Patitifa, a 50-min. natural treatment using hibiscus, coconut, honey and fruit, for 14.000 CFP. The Tino Tane for 13.000 CFP and Tane Vanira for 16.000 CFP are 50-min. hydrating, cleansing and exfoliating treatments for men. The ultimate choice is the Poe Manea (Manea pearl) that is a complete treatment that lasts 2 hours and 50 min. and costs 35.000 CFP for one person and 60.000 CFP per couple.

TATTOOS

Tavita Manea is a well-known tattoo artist who lives in Patio. He worked for many years at Tiki Village in Moorea. He does tattoos on request at Le Taha'a Island Resort & Spa and at most of the other hotels and pensions. Ask at the hotel's activity desk.

PRACTICAL INFORMATION
Banks

Banque Socredo, *Tel.60.80.10*, is located in Patio, and **Banque de Tahiti**, *Tel. 65.63.14*, is in the Teva Uri building in Haamene.

Doctors

There is a government operated medical and dental center in Patio, *Tel. 65.63.31*, and a medical center in Haamene, *Tel. 65.67.51*. Doctor Régis Rouveyrol has a private practice in Haamene, *Tel. 65.60.60*, and Doctor Patrice Reynaud, *Tel. 65.65.67*, has a private practice in Patio. Cathy Anais and Jérôme Gence are physical therapists in Taha'a, *Tel. 65.61.11*.

Drugstore

Pharmacie Taha'a, *Tel. 60.86.08*, is in the Commercial building in Haamene.
Police

A brigade of the French *gendarmerie* is posted in Patio and Haamene, *Tel. 60.81.05*.

Post Office and Telecommunications Office

There is a **Post Office** in Haamene, *Tel. 65.60.11*, and another in Patio, *Tel. 65.64.70*. All telecommunications and postal services are available.

Yacht Services

Hibiscus Yacht Club, *B.P. 184, Haamene, Taha'a 98734; Tel. 689/65.61.06/ 79.28.81; Fax 689/65.65.65; VHF 68-Hibiscus; hibiscus@tahaa-tahiti.com; www.tahaa-tahiti.com.*

The Hotel-Restaurant Hibiscus is at the entrance to Haamene Bay. There are 10 free yacht moorings and services include fresh water, showers, garbage disposal, message service and, on request, fresh bread can be delivered to your yacht daily except Sun. You can rent a car, join a 4x4 tour, or sign up for a variety of activities.

Taravana Yacht Club Tahaa, *B. P. 1026, Uturoa, Raiatea 98735; Tel. 689/ 65.61.01/28.08.08; Fax 689/60.81.40; VHF 68; taravanayc@mail.pf; www.taravanayachtclub.com.*

There are moorings for 12 boats close to the Taravana Yacht Club dock at Toamaru Pointe in Apu Bay. This was formerly the Marina Iti and is now owned by American expatriate Richard Postma, who operates Taravana Island Sport Charters Bora Bora. His son Maui lives on the premises to manage the restaurant and yacht club. Mooring fees are 2.000 CFP per night, and the fee is waived with dinner in the restaurant. Yacht services include filling your boat at the dock with clean Taha'a ground water for 1.000 CFP, hot showers for 300 CFP each, a 10-lb. bag of ice cubes for 550 CFP, use of washing machine for 1.500 CFP per load; fresh bread 50 CFP per baguette, and time cards for Internet WiFi access, 700 CFP for 1 hr. Be sure to order your bread in advance and make advance reservations for meals in the restaurant. Marlboro cigarettes are 1.200 CFP.

Activities for visiting yachties includes free use of snorkeling gear and kayaks. Maui Postma rents bicycles for 2.000 CFP per day, and he can arrange for a rental car, 4x4 tour around the island, a picnic on a motu or deep-sea fishing. You can also visit the Champon Pearl Farm next door to the Taravana Restaurant.

The bungalows were closed to the public in 2007 and were to be torn down to make way for a new building project. The project is to build three 3-bedroom villas and 10 small bungalows on the 3.3 acre property. These will be sold as a time-share prepaid vacation and rented out as hotel rooms when not in use by club members.

16. Bora Bora

When you tell your friends: "I'm going to **Bora Bora**," you can be sure that this simple phrase will bring envy and longing to their romantic hearts and stir a feeling of wanderlust in their vagabonding souls.

Bora Bora has become the center of tourism in Tahiti and Her Islands. Some of the world's famous stars of stage, cinema and television vacation here, flying their private jets to the international airport in Tahiti and on to Bora Bora, without a thought of seeing the other islands of French Polynesia. European royalty, sheiks, emirs, maharajas and international jet-setters find the serenity and privacy they seek on this magnificent little island. Cinematographers discover the ideal tropical setting for movies, often starring the islanders themselves.

Bora Bora, perhaps more than any other island in the South Seas, teases the imagination of travel writers, who search for adequate phrases of 'purple prose' to describe the spectacular beauty of its craggy, sculpted mountains, the palm-crowned islets that seem to float just inside the coral reef, surrounded by a confection of white sandy beaches that dip down into a lagoon of opalescent blues and greens.

Bora Bora lies 260 km. (161 mi.) northwest of Tahiti in the Leeward Society Islands. Your first glimpse of Bora Bora may be from the window of an Air Tahiti plane, at the end of a direct flight from Tahiti or Moorea. Bora Bora from aloft appears as a precious emerald in a setting of turquoise, encircled by a protective

---

PAUL-EMILE VICTOR - THE COLORS OF BORA BORA

Paul-Emile Victor, a French polar explorer, artist and writer, retired to Bora Bora with his wife **Colette**, and lived on Motu Tane in Bora Bora until his death in 1995. His impression of seeing Bora Bora from the cockpit of an airplane in 1958, after a 25-year absence from the island, was published in the 1970s in *Distance*, the in-flight magazine of the former UTA-French airline: "...Never before had I seen waters the colour of the rainbow or like fireworks, springing right out of some maddened imagination, or from Gauguin's own palette. Waters the colour of bronze, of copper, gold, silver, mother-of-pearl, pearl, jade, emeralds, moonlight or the aurora borealis. The stars themselves seemed to have fallen into the sea, scintillating brilliantly on the lagoon's surface, in bright sunlight...Who could find the words, what poet the images, what painter even the colours, to describe this scene? I give up."

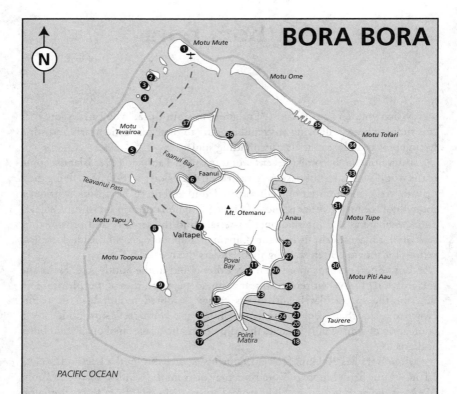

1. Bora Bora Airport
2. Pension Le Paradis
3. Blue Heaven Island
4. Mai Moana Island
5. Bora Bora Pearl Beach
Resort & Spa
6. Farepiti Wharf
7. Vaitape Boat Dock
8. Bora Bora Lagoon Resort &
Spa
9. Bora Bora Nui Resort & Spa
10. Pension Moon
11. Rohotu Fare Lodge
12. Chez Rosina
13. Hotel Bora Bora

14. Temanuata Iti
15. Hotel Matira
16. Pension Chez Nono
17. Pension Robert et Tina
18. ICH Bora Bora Le Moana
Resort
19. Chez Maeva Masson
20. Temanuata Beach
21. Le Maitai Polynesia
22. Novotel Bora Bora Beach
Resort
23. Sofitel Bora Bora Beach
Resort
24. Hotel Sofitel Motu
25. Club Med Bora Bora

26. Pension Anau-Chez Teipo
27. Pension Bora Lagoonarium
28. Camping Chez Aldo
29. Chez Henriette
30. Eden Beach Hotel
31. ICH Bora Bora Resort &
Thalasso Spa
32. Le Meridien Bora Bora
33. Lagoonarium
34. St. Regis Resort & Spa
35. Four Seasons Resort Bora
36. Pension Bora Vaiete
37. Bora Bora Condos

LEGEND OF HIRO

One of the most famous characters in Polynesian oral history was **Hiro**, god of thieves. Hiro hid out on **Toopua Island**, across Povai Bay from the main island. Using the dragonfly to distract attention, Hiro and his band of thieves robbed their victims at night, between sunset and the first cockcrow. Hiro's constant companion was a white cock, the moa uo. This rooster became excited when Hiro was trying to steal Toopua Island and began to crow, breaking the magic power and so enraging Hiro that he hurled the bird against the face of Pahia mountain, where the imprint still remains. Although Hiro abandoned his plan to steal the island, he detached a large chunk of it that is called Toopua-Iti, the islet that is separated by only a few feet from Toopua.

The view of Bora Bora's famous mountains of **Otemanu** (sea of birds) and the twin peaks of **Pahia** and **Hue** are best photographed through this opening, where just underneath the clear surface of the lagoon lie rocks known as **Hiro's Canoe**. Ashore on Toopua Island are giant stones said to have been left by Hiro and his son Marama, tossed about in a game played by the 2 giants. Deep inside the coconut forest is a gigantic rock, **Hiro's Bell** that used to reverberate when struck. This basaltic boulder was damaged during the construction of a hotel on Toopua Island, however, and now sits as a silent witness to Polynesia's past.

necklace of sparkling pearls. You will have a great view of Bora Bora as the ATR-72 banks for landing on Motu Mute. On most flights you will usually have the best views of Bora Bora if you are sitting on the left side of the plane, but this all depends on the landing pattern used for that particular flight.

If you arrive in Bora Bora by cruise ship, inter-island ferryboat or by sailboat, you will also be impressed by the kaleidoscope of shimmering iridescence that greets your eye at every turn. Aquamarine. Lapis lazuli. Turquoise. Cobalt. Periwinkle. Sapphire. Emerald. Jade. Ultramarine. Indigo. You'll love counting the shades of color in the sparkling waters of Bora Bora's world-famous lagoon.

Mythology

Polynesian mythology claims that Ofai Honu, a volcanic boulder carved with petroglyphs of turtles, was possessed with godly power and mated with the Pahia Mountain, then called Hohorai. From their union a son was born, whose name was Firiamata O Vavau. This first great chief gave his name to the island and for many years this fabled paradise was known as **Vavau**, which means first-born. Legend says that Vavau was the first island that sprang up after the mythical creation of the sacred island of Havai'i (Raiatea). The beautiful little islet beside the pass of Vavau was named Motu Tapu, the sacred islet.

BORA BORA – TODAY & TOMORROW

Today Bora Bora is an island devoted to tourism, with more luxurious hotels than on any other island of French Polynesia. In addition to the 7 major hotels (not counting **Bora Bora Dive Resort-Topdive**, which has closed its hotel and restaurant), at publication time in Feb. 2008 there were 8 international class hotels in operation on the offshore motu islets, and the **Four Seasons Resort Bora Bora** will open in June 2008. This gives you a fabulous choice of 16 beautiful big hotels in Bora Bora, as well as the dozen or so family pensions on the main island and motu islets. And let's not forget the condos, millionaire's villas and other luxurious accommodations on the main island, as well as the privately owned motu islets.

A new hotel project for Bora Bora (yes, another one) was announced in Feb. 2007 to build a 40-unit hotel on a 17-acre (7 ha.) property in the Commune of Faanui on the main island. The French-Canadian investor plans to open this hotel in 2010. His ecological, cultural and recreational project also involves building a vacation village for 25-40 people on Nukutepipi, a remote atoll in the Tuamotu Archipelago. Thus he can offer guests the pleasures of vacationing on a high island as well as a low atoll.

Everyone complains about the heavy traffic on Bora Bora's circle island road. Repeat visitors will be happy to learn that some parts of the road were widened in 2007 and the dangerously huge holes have not only been filled, but the road has been repaved as well. The public dump has been closed, therefore putting an end to the acrid smoke that burned the noses of guests staying in prestigious and deluxe class overwater bungalows across the lagoon from Anau.

Although a ride around the island still reveals too many errant dogs, too many overturned garbage containers, too much discarded trash and too many unsightly construction sites for hotel land bases or lodging for hotel employees, Bora Bora's lagoon is still a prize-winner. Each year since 2000 the island of Bora Bora has been awarded the Blue Flag (the European Pavillon Bleu) for their successful efforts in environmental management. These awards are for the quality of the water in the lagoon and the frequency of samples the health department takes from the water at hotels and public beaches.

In 2007 the mayor of Bora Bora, Gaston Tong Sang, also received the Marianne d'Or award, an environmental recognition for the island's 3 water treatment systems and desalinization plants. Bora Bora began its environmental improvement program in 1989 by providing its inhabitants and visitors with potable water. However, the water you get from your faucet in Bora Bora tastes and smells like chlorine. Therefore, the hotels recommend bottled water to their guests.

Geology

Bora Bora was formed by volcanic eruptions some three to four million years ago. It is one of the oldest in the chain of the Leeward Islands. Through eons and centuries it has been eroding and sinking. 1-2 miles inside the fringing reef rise the sharp cliffs of basaltic rock that form the central mountain chain running through the principal island of Bora Bora. Mount Otemanu, at 727 m. (2,384 ft.), Mount Pahia, at 661 m. (2,168 ft.), and Mount Hue at 619 m. (2,030 ft.), are the most spectacular chimney peaks of the crater that once spewed molten lava. The center of this sunken volcano lies far beneath the electric blue of Povai Bay, and the smaller islands of Toopua and Toopua-Iti are the opposite walls of the crater, formed when the earth erupted beneath the ocean. The Teavanui Pass is the only navigable break in the coral wall that has formed on top of the caldeira of the sunken volcano.

If you want to see what an atoll is like without heading out to the Tuamotu archipelago, then you should visit a *motu* in Bora Bora. These islets have the same flora and fauna of the atolls, with the advantage of having a high island just a 5-min. boat-ride away. Walk along the ocean side of a motu and you will find *miki miki* bushes, sea grape, pandanus, the South Seas rosewood tree called *miro*, the huge *tou* trees with their orange flowers and precious wood so desired by sculptors, *tamanu* trees whose fruit gives us a healing oil for the treatment of deep burns and cuts, the Australian pine, which is called *aito* in these islands, and the *tiare kahaia*, whose decorative branches are used in the construction of the typical Polynesian bungalows built by most hotel owners. Go for a walk along the seashore early in the morning and you will see the herons fishing, and during a picnic on the *motu* perhaps you will catch a glimpse of the lovely white fairy tern with its black button eyes.

ARRIVALS & DEPARTURES

Arriving By Air

Air Tahiti has 7-10 direct flights daily for the 50-min. hop between Tahiti and Bora Bora, as well as flights that stop in Huahine and/or Raiatea. More flights are added during high seasons. The fare is 14.500 CFP one-way for adults, and 26.700 CFP round-trip, taxes and airport shuttle boat in Bora Bora included. There are 3 flights daily from Moorea, either direct or stopping in Huahine or Raiatea. The one-way fare from Moorea to Bora Bora is 18.400 CFP, from Huahine to Bora Bora it is 7.900 CFP, and from Raiatea to Bora Bora the fare is 6.300 CFP. On Sun. there is a Maupiti-Bora Bora flight for 6.500 CFP. You can also fly to Bora Bora from Rangiroa each Mon. and Fri. for 23.400 CFP, from Fakarava on Tues. and Fri., for 26.400 CFP, from Manihi on Mon. and Fri. for 26.400 CFP, and from Tikehau on Mon. and Fri., for 23.400 CFP. Some of the Tuamotu flights stop in Rangiroa.

Air Tahiti reservations: Tahiti, *Tel. 86.42.42;* Moorea, *Tel. 55.06.00*; Huahine, *Tel. 68.77.02/60.62.60*; Raiatea *Tel. 60.04.44/60.04.40*; Bora Bora, *Tel. 60.53.53/ 60.53.00*; Maupiti *Tel. 60.15.05/67.81.24*; Rangiroa, *Tel. 93.11.00/93.11.01*;

Tikehau *Tel. 96.22.66*; Manihi, *Tel. 93.30.70/93.30.75*; Fakarava, Tel. *93.40.25/ 93.40.20*.

The **Bora Bora airport** is located *on Motu Mute*, a 15-min. boat ride to the main village of Vaitape or 10-15 min. by luxury launch direct to your deluxe hotel, depending on its distance from the airport. If your hotel doesn't have a private launch to the airport, then you will be met at the boat dock in Vaitape village and driven to your hotel. Land transportation from the Vaitape quay to the small hotels, pensions and campgrounds is also provided by *le truck* or mini-vans. The Air Tahiti office is located on the quay of Vaitape, and there are public phone booths just outside.

You can also get to Bora Bora by chartering an airplane in Tahiti from **Air Archipels**, *Tel. 81.30.30*; or **Air Tahiti**, *Tel. 86.42.42*.

Arriving By Boat

All the inter-island transport boats dock at the Fare Piti quay in Faanui, 3 km (1.9 mi.) from Vaitape village. It would be advisable to arrange with your hotel or pension to have someone meet you when you arrive. A *le truck* also provides service from the boat dock to the hotels in Matira.

Hawaiki Nui, *Tel. 54.99.54, Fax 45.24.44, contact@stim.pf* leaves the Motu Uta dock in Papeete each Tues. and Thurs. at 4pm. On the first voyage it arrives at the Fare Piti quay in Bora Bora at 10am on Wed., after stopping in Huahine and Raiatea. For the Thurs. departure the ship arrives in Bora Bora on Fri. at 8:30am after stopping in Raiatea. Passengers are limited to 12, who sleep on the deck for 1.800 CFP or in one of four cabins containing 2 berths and a toilet. A berth costs 5.000 CFP from Papeete to all the Leeward Islands. Meals are available on board the ship. Passengers must sleep in cabins on the Thurs. voyage as the ship also transports fuel then.

Vaeanu, *Tel. 41.25.35, Fax 41.24.34, torehiatetu@mail.pf* departs from the Motu Uta dock in Papeete at 4pm on Mon.,Wed. and Fri., stopping in Huahine, Raiatea, and Taha'a, arriving in Bora Bora at 10am the following morning. It spends overnight in Bora Bora. This cargo ship carries 90 passengers and has sleeping space for 32 people in cabins with 2-3 berths, private or shared toilets. The one-way deck fare from Tahiti to Bora Bora is 2.120 CFP, from Huahine to Bora Bora deck fare is 1.690 CFP; and from Raiatea or Taha'a to Bora Bora it costs 1.400 CFP. The one-way fare for a berth ranges from 4.400 CFP to 4.929 CFP and the cabins are 9.858 CFP, 11.978 CFP and 13.197 CFP, depending on the number of berths and toilet facilities. There is a snack-restaurant on board and meals are extra. Reservations for cabin space must be paid in full before 9am on the fixed date of departure from Papeete.

Maupiti Express II, *Tel./Fax 689/66.37.81* (Raiatea), *Tel. 67.66.69, Fax 60.37.16* (Bora Bora); *Cell 78.27.22/72.30.48*; *www.maupitiexpress.com*. The 140-passenger *Maupiti Express II* leaves Raiatea at 4pm each Mon. and Wed. and arrives at the Vaitape quay in Bora Bora at 5:45pm. On Fri. it leaves Raiatea at 2pm and arrives in Bora Bora at 3:45pm, and on Fri. and Sun. it leaves Raiatea at 6pm, arriving in Bora Bora at 7:45pm. On Tues., Thurs. and Sat. the Maupiti-Bora Bora shuttle leaves Maupiti at 4pm and arrives in Vaitape at 5:45pm. The one-way fare is 3.000 CFP and round-trip is 4.000 CFP. Passengers under 12 years pay half price.

Departing By Air
The main office of **Air Tahiti**, *Tel. 60.53.53/60.53.00*, is at the boat dock in Vaitape village. Most of the hotels take care of reconfirming your departure flight, or you can do it yourself by telephone. The Bora Bora Navette, Air Tahiti's shuttle boat, leaves the Vaitape village dock 1:15 hrs. before each scheduled departure and check-in time at the Air Tahiti office on Motu Mute is 1 hr. before your flight departs. Air Tahiti has 9-12 flights flies from Bora Bora to Tahiti times a day. Most of the flights are direct and the other flights stop in Huahine or Raiatea. There is a daily flight from Bora Bora to Moorea with a stop in Huahine, daily non-stop flights from Bora Bora to Huahine and 1-2 daily direct flights from Bora Bora to Raiatea except Tues. You can fly direct from Bora Bora to Maupiti on Sun. and via Raiatea on Fri. There are daily flights from Bora Bora to Rangiroa, to Fakarava each Tues. and Fri., to Manihi on Mon., Wed., Fri. and Sun., and to Tikehau daily except Tues. Some flights require a change of planes in Rangiroa.

Departing By Boat
Hawaiki Nui, *Tel. 67.72.39* (Bora Bora), leaves the Fare Piti dock in Bora Bora at 1pm each Wed. for Taha'a and Raiatea, then heads directly back to Papeete, arriving at 5am Thurs. On Fri. the ship leaves Bora Bora at 12pm, stopping in Taha'a, Raiatea and Huahine, and arrives in Papeete at 5am on Sat.
  Vaeanu, *Tel. 67.68.68* (Bora Bora), leaves Bora Bora at 11:30am each Tues. and Thurs., stops in Raiatea and Huahine, and arrives in Papeete at 3am on Wed. and Fri. After spending Saturday night in Bora Bora, the ship leaves at 8:30am on Sun., stops in Taha'a, Raiatea and Huahine, and arrives in Papeete at 2am on Monday. Buy your ticket at the counter on the dock or on board the ship.
  Maupiti Express II, *Tel. 67.66.69, cell 78.27.22/72.30.48*, leaves Bora Bora for Taha'a and Raiatea at 7am each Mon., Wed. and Fri., at 4pm on Mon., Wed., and Fri. and at 3pm on Sun. It leaves for Maupiti at 8:30am each Tues., Thurs. and Sat. The trip to Maupiti is 1 hour and 45 minutes and gives you plenty of time to enjoy a day tour on one of the lovely motu islets. See chapter on *Maupiti* for further information. The one-way fare from Bora Bora to Taha'a and Raiatea is 3.000 CFP and round-trip is 4.000 CFP. The same rates apply for the Bora Bora-Maupiti voyage. Passengers under 12 years pay half-fare.

ORIENTATION
In the vicinity of the boat dock in **Vaitape village** you will find the *mairie* (town hall), *gendarmerie*, post office, banks, schools, churches, dispensary, pharmacy, Air

Tahiti office, tourist information, arts and crafts center, food stores, small restaurants and snack stands, shops, boutiques and rental agencies for helicopters, cars, scooters and bicycles, plus service stations and public telephones.

Bora Bora's main island is only 10 km (5.2 mi.) long and 4 km (2.5 mi.) wide. A partially paved road circles the coastline, winding 29 km (18 mi.) through the villages of Vaitape, Faanui and Anau. You'll see little settlements of modest *fares*, the homes of Bora Bora's 8,992 inhabitants, which are often surrounded by flower gardens.

GETTING AROUND BORA BORA
Car & Bicycle Rentals

Rates for all rental cars include unlimited mileage and third-party insurance. Gas and flat tires are extra. Rental rates are considerably higher at the hotels.

Bora Bora Tours (Fredo & Fils Rent A Car) operates out of the Hotel Bora Bora and from an office in Vaitape, *Tel. 67.70.31; Fax 67.62.07; boraboratours@mail.pf.* They rent 3-door Hyundai cars for 4.800 CFP for 2 hrs., 6.600 CFP for 4 hrs., 7.800 CFP for 8 hrs., and 9.240 CFP for 24 hrs. They rent bicycles for 1.730 CFP for 4 hrs. and 2.310 CFP for 8 hrs. The Hotel Bora Bora rents the same cars, with rates at 7.800 CFP for 2 hrs., 9.800 CFP for 4 hrs., 11.000 CFP for 8 hrs., and 14.000 CFP for 24 hrs. The bikes are 1.500 CFP for 2 hrs. and 2.000 CFP for 8 hrs.

Europcar has its main sales office in Vaitape facing the quay, *Tel. 67.70.15/ 67.70.03,* with sales desks at all the hotels. A 2-seat Mini Cabriolet or Bugxter starts at 6.900 CFP for 2 hrs. A 3-door Fiat Panda rents for 6.600 CFP for 2 hrs. up to 9.000 CFP for 24 hrs. A 5-door a/c automatic drive Kia Picanto is 7.500 CFP for 2 hrs. and 13.000 CFP for 24 hrs. Their bicycles are 1.300 CFP for 2 hrs. and 1.900 CFP for 24 hrs.

Fare Piti Rent A Car is in Vaitape, *Tel. 67.77.17,* and at Le Maitai Polynesia, *Tel. 67.69.69.* The lowest car rental price for a Peugeot 106 is 6.000 CFP for 2 hrs. and 9.000 CFP for 8 hrs. Bicycles rent for 1.300 CFP for 2 hrs. and 2.000 CFP for 24 hrs.

Taxis

There are taxis in Bora Bora that can be flagged down or called by phone. Most of them wait for customers at the boat dock in Vaitape. Each hotel and pension has its own *le truck* or mini-van service between the hotel and the boat dock in Vaitape or Faanui, coordinating their runs with the arrivals and departures of Air Tahiti and the inter-island ferries. There is no official public transportation service on Bora Bora. See information under *Circle Island Tours* in this chapter.

WHERE TO STAY
On the Main IslandPrestigious

HOTEL BORA BORA, *B.P. 1, Bora Bora 98730. Tel. 689/60.44.60; Fax*

689/60.44.66; hotelborabora@amanresorts.com; North America Reservations: Tel.
800/421-1490, Los Angeles Tel. 818/587-9650; Fax 818/710-0050;
mbogusz@amanresorts.com; www.amanresorts.com. Beside the lagoon at Raititi Point,
14 km (8.7 mi.) from the airport and 5.8 km (3.6 mi.) from the village of Vaitape.
Round-trip transfers provided from airport to hotel by private launch. 54 bungalows.
EP Rates sgl/dbl through Mar. 31, 2009: Bungalow 60.000 CFP; Garden Pool Fare
83.500 CFP; Overwater Bungalow 95.500 CFP; Beach Fare 101.500 CFP; extra bed
10.200 CFP. Add taxes. All major credit cards.

The Hotel Bora Bora is my favorite hotel anywhere in the world. I stayed here for 2 weeks when I first came to the island as a tourist in 1968 and again in 1970. After moving to Tahiti in 1971 I have had many more opportunities to visit, and I usually choose to celebrate my special birthdays in this wonderful old hotel. It feels like home to me. Although I can see the signs of weathering, I still feel that the Hotel Bora Bora is as solid as the Otemanu Mountain that rises from the heart of the island behind the hotel. This establishment has stately, royal class and the comfort of a privileged country club.

The Hotel Bora Bora opened in June 1961 and since June 1989 it has been a member of the prestigious Amanresorts. Some of the world's most discriminating travelers choose to stay here, returning again and again, where they can still find the magical charm that entranced them during their first visit. Often these repeat visitors celebrate their special wedding anniversaries in the same bungalow where they spent their first honeymoon. Some of them have given the name of the bungalow to their babies, who were conceived while the parents were honeymooning at the Hotel Bora Bora. And several of these children come to this hotel years later for their own honeymoons.

You will be greeted with a glass of champagne as soon as you arrive at the Hotel Bora Bora boat dock on board their private launch, and you will be treated as a very special guest throughout your stay. This is the smallest 5-star resort on Bora Bora, and because the management and staff know the meaning of truly personalized service, this is what you will receive.

The Hotel Bora Bora was the first international hotel built on the island, and naturally it has the most exclusive setting. The main building is located on a bluff overlooking Point Raititi, a private peninsula that faces the southwest, with sunset views of the neighboring island of Maupiti. The famous Matira Beach is just an extension of one of the hotel's 3 private white-sand beaches. The vast sparkling lagoon of Bora Bora is a tableau of at least 7 shades of blue and green.

Guest accommodations include 54 individual units, featuring Bora Bora's first overwater bungalows. These 15 bungalows are built on stilts over the fringing reef section of the lagoon. Each unit has a spacious bedroom with a king-size four-poster bed, a bathroom with a bathtub and separate shower, and a sundeck terrace with a shower at the water level next to the steps set into the lagoon. The lush established coral gardens are one of the hotel's best attributes, offering some of the island's best snorkeling. There are hundreds of tropical fish of every hue, as well as spotted eagle rays, stingrays and turtles. Guests often see the graceful manta rays perform their nightly ballet next to the boat dock and below the steps of the deep overwater bungalows.

The premium beach *fares*, superior beach bungalows and garden pool *fares* are situated in 17 acres of luxuriant tropical gardens of trees, flowers and exotic foliage, All *fares* are 1,200 sq. ft. (117 sq. m.) with a living room, bedroom with a king-size four-poster bed, en suite sitting room, bathroom and large sundeck. The beach bungalows offer a spacious bedroom, bathroom and sitting area leading to a small patio facing the lagoon bordered by a lovely beach of fine white sand. Each bungalow has a hammock nearby, where you can enjoy the beach and sea breeze. The pool *fares* are surrounded by a rock garden wall for added privacy, enclosing a small plunge pool and outdoor sun pavilion.

All the spacious bungalows are built in the Polynesian style with hand-tied thatched pandanus roofs, ceiling fans and natural woods. The decor is neutral with plenty of natural light, drawing the vivid colors of the lagoon and gardens into every room. Each bungalow has a/c in the bedroom, ceiling fans, a freestanding bathtub and separate shower, hairdryer, private bar, coffee and tea facilities, telephone with Internet connection, radio, CD player and personal safe. The bathroom amenities carry the Hotel Bora Bora label and include a light monoi oil, which is difficult to find anywhere else. And the king size mattresses make you feel like you are indeed floating on air.

The management of the Hotel Bora Bora takes pride in not placing TV sets in the guest rooms as they find this is a good selling point; however, there is a satellite-cable TV in the Fare Raititi lounge. The staff can add a TV or DVD player to your room on request.

From the Matira Terrace Restaurant you can watch the hotel's outrigger sailing canoe skimming across the lagoon while you enjoy a bountiful breakfast buffet. The French *chef de cuisine* ensures that the menu upholds the reputation of the hotel, and each dinner is a gourmet's treat. Complimentary Tea is served in the Matira Terrace Bar at 4pm, followed by cocktails for sunset gazing. The Pofai Beach Bar is ideal for light lunches and special theme buffets are held on the beach several nights a week. See information under *Where to Eat* in this chapter.

The reception area, guest relations and boutique are located in the main building. In the Fare Raititi lounge you will find an activities desk staffed by very helpful personnel. There is also a library of paperback books and international newspapers, a TV with international broadcasts, and a pool table and board games. Complimentary Internet access is provided on a computer in the lounge, plus there is Wifi connection here and in the lobby area.

Next door to Raititi lounge is the Fare Taurumi, whose massage therapists are well trained. See more information Under *Massages & Spas* in this chapter. Tahia Collins Pearls presents her collection of fine jewelry and loose pearls of rainbow hue in a separate bungalow on the hotel's premises. This is definitely worth a visit.

The hotel's 2 complimentary tennis courts, basketball court and volleyball court are located across the road, and the Beach Boy Fare is located near the Pofai Beach Bar, providing snorkeling equipment, towels and canoe rides in an outrigger sailing canoe. Other complimentary activities include transfers between the hotel and airport, a daily bus shuttle to Vaitape village, a Sunday shuttle to local church services, pareos displayed on the bed on arrival, daily turndown service, a weekly management cocktail, canapés served during the Mama Show on Friday evening, and bottled water and a fruit bowl provided daily in the room.

The favorite optional activities of guests staying at Hotel Bora Bora include a full day of sailing and fishing aboard the "Taravana", the Blue Lagoon Cruise, a Shark and Ray Safari, Scuba Diving, and a menu of Massages. All the other excursions available on Bora Bora can also be organized by the activities staff. See more information under *Activities* in this chapter.

Honeymooners are welcomed at the Hotel Bora Bora as very special guests. Contact the hotel directly for information on their Island Romance packages, which include a 3-night *Honeymoon Escape*, a *Polynesian Ceremony* on the beach at sunset, or a *Marriage of Hearts Ceremony* with a private 2-hour sunset sail aboard a catamaran. A non-binding sentimental ceremony is performed during the cruise in Tahitian and English by the captain, fragrant flower leis are offered, and champagne and canapés are served. When you return to the Hotel Bora Bora with your children, be assured that baby-sitting service is available.

Deluxe

INTERCONTINENTAL BORA BORA LE MOANA RESORT, *B.P. 156, Bora Bora 98730. Tel. 689/60.49.00; Fax 689/60.49.99; lemoana@interconti.pf; www.lemoana.interconti.com; Reservation Tel. 689/86.51.78; reservationspf@interconti.com. Beside the lagoon on Point Matira. 2008 Low/High Season EP Rates sgl./dbl.: Beach Junior Suite Bungalow 64.580/71.750 CFP; Overwater Lagoon Junior Suite Bungalow 70.220/ 78.020 CFP; Overwater Horizon Junior Suite Bungalow 76.480/84.970 CFP; additional person 10.000 CFP; MAP 9.690 CFP, AP 13.000 CFP; Canoe breakfast 6.990 CFP per person. Mandatory round-trip transfer airport/hotel/airport; one-way boat transfer 2.750 CFP; one-way bus transfer to/from other hotels, heliport, nautical bases 800 CFP. Add taxes. All major credit cards.*

This hotel offers 62 junior suite bungalows or 60 junior suite bungalows and 1 suite, with a choice of units built over the water or on the white sand beach. The modern Polynesian style bungalows have pointed pandanus thatch roofs and are beautifully furnished with contemporary wood and wicker furniture, live plants, natural fabrics, and paintings by resident artists. All the units have a/c and ceiling fans, a bathroom with separate shower and bath, and a private sun terrace with exterior shower. A king-size bed can be converted into twin beds, and in the living room is a sofa that can sleep a third person. There is a writing desk, fully stocked mini-bar, coffee and tea facilities, complimentary toiletries, personal safety box, 2 TV's, with cable, CD and DVD players, 2 international direct dial telephones with voice mail and dataports for Internet. 2 beach bungalows are wheelchair accessible.

The overwater bungalows are the perfect haven for lovers. Room service is available 24/24 and you can even treat yourself to an American breakfast delivered by outrigger canoe to your private terrace. Lounge chairs on the terrace are ideal for hand-in-hand stargazing. Step down from your sun deck into the warm embrace of the clear lagoon for the feel of paradise. Or look through your glass table in the living room and watch the fish swimming around in the crystalline lagoon.

Meals are served in the Noa Noa Restaurant and Terrace overlooking the white sandy beach. See more information under *Where to Eat* in this chapter. The Vini Vini Bar is beside the 2-level swimming pool, which is enhanced with a waterfall and tropical foliage. Four fully equipped transit bungalow units are available for day visitors or guests arriving before the 2pm check-in or departing after the 11am check-out. Public facilities and services include a reception desk that is open 24/24, a concierge and guest relations/activities center, with a car rental desk, business center and computers for guest use with Internet connection. There is also a Robert Wan Tahiti Pearls shop and the Te Anuanua boutique.

The Beach Boys at the Fare Plage will give you pointers on how to use the complimentary snorkeling gear, outrigger paddle canoes for 2, windsurf boards and kayaks. A snooker lounge and board games are also available for your enjoyment. Entertainment includes a *pareo* show, demonstrations of Tahitian cooking, or a slide show presenting the hotel's activities and excursions. The Activities Director will explain the full range of land and water sports available, and help you book your optional excursions.

Le Moana Resort has long been a favorite destination for honeymooners. Contact them directly for information on romantic dinners and Polynesian wedding ceremonies that are performed on the beach.

The room rates at this hotel dropped with the 2006 opening of their sister property, the Intercontinental Bora Bora Resort & Thalasso Spa that is located on Motu Tiarepuomu, just a short boat ride away. When booking your room, ask for a bungalow that faces Mt. Otemanu and try to get as far away as possible from the noisy end of the resort closest to Point Matira, where there are several houses, children, dogs and roosters.

Superior
SOFITEL BORA BORA BEACH RESORT (ex Sofitel Marara), *B.P. 6, Bora Bora 98730. Tel. 689/60.55.00; Fax 689/67.74.03; H0564@accor.com; www.accorhotels.pf. Reservations: 689/86.66.66; Fax 689/41.05.05; reservation.tahiti@accor.com. Beside the lagoon at the end of Taahana Bay, north of Point Matira on the east side. 2008 Low/High Season EP Rates sgl./dbl.: Deluxe Garden Bungalow 38.496/45.133 CFP; Beach Bungalow 46.903/54.867 CFP; Lagoon Bungalow 46.903/54.867 CFP; Overwater Bungalow 66.372/76.549 CFP. Round-trip airport boat transfers 5.000 CFP per person. American breakfast 2.901 CFP, set lunch 3.148 CFP, set dinner 5.803 CFP. Add taxes. All major credit cards.*
The hotel Marara, (flying fish in Tahitian) was built by Dino de Laurentiis in

1977 to house the crew of his film, "Hurricane". When the Accor Group bought the hotel a few years later, it became the Sofitel Marara. The name was changed to Sofitel Bora Bora Beach Resort in mid-2006 following a major renovation project that upgraded it to a 5-star resort and spa. There are now 64 individual bungalows and 1 villa, crafted from wood and pandanus, all with a private terrace. These include 13 new bungalows built over the deep water, with spacious decks that have bamboo screening for privacy and in-floor viewing platforms that are illuminated at night for fish-watching. The beach and lagoon front bungalows have hammocks in the garden. All the bungalows offer guests the patented Sofitel MyBed with canopy, as well as a plush daybed, decorated in a retro Hollywood style of red wine and gold satin covers and cushions. All units have a/c, a ceiling fan, plasma TV with cable/satellite, radio, IDD telephone with voicemail, Wifi Internet access, in-room safety deposit box, minibar, coffee/tea facilities and bathrobes. The mosaic tiled bathrooms have a rainshower, a separate toilet with telephone, a hair dryer and magnified mirror.

The public areas of the resort also have a new look and new additions. French and international dishes are served in Latitude 16°, the main restaurant, and the Wakaba restaurant serves teppanyaki, sushi and other traditional Japanese dishes. Exotic cocktails are available in the Hurricane Bar, at Le Snack or on the deck beside the infinity swimming pool, which has been extended. See more information under *Where to Eat* in this chapter.

The ambiance at the Sofitel Bora Bora Beach Resort is lively, with a list of daily activities that are posted in the reception area. Guests have free use of snorkeling equipment, kayaks, outrigger paddle canoes, and board games. The activities desk can book any land tour or lagoon excursion you want, plus rent you a car or bicycle. A shuttle bus to Vaitape village is 700 CFP round-trip. The Nemo World dive center is located on the premises, and Le Spa at Sofitel provides body care, massages and flower perfumed Jacuzzi baths. There is something going on every evening, with nightly entertainment at the bar, including Polynesian dance shows twice on Wed. and Fri. Non-binding Polynesian wedding ceremonies are performed in the traditional wedding *fare* beside the beach or on a hillside of a motu opposite the hotel, where the Sofitel Motu is located. Contact the hotel directly for details and rates.

Moderate to Superior

LE MAITAI POLYNESIA, *B.P. 505, Bora Bora 98730. Tel. 689/60.30.00; Fax 689/67.66.03; info@bora.hotelmaitai.com; www.hotelmaitai.com. At Taahana Beach in the Matira area, 15 km (9 mi.) from the ferry dock and 12 km (6 mi.) from Vaitape. Round-trip airport transfers to/from Vaitape and hotel 1.750 CFP per person. 74 units. 2008 Low/High Season EP Rates sgl./dbl.: Garden Room 24.225/26.650CFP; Ocean View Room 32.300/35.500 CFP; Beach Bungalow 38.950/42.850 CFP; Overwater Bungalow 48.450/53.300 CFP; 3rd person 5.800 CFP. MAP with Continental breakfast 7.000 CFP; MAP with American breakfast 7.400 CFP. Add taxes. All major credit cards.*

This hotel opened in June 1998 and added more rooms in 2000, offering 4 types of lodging, all with a/c. The garden view rooms are located in 2-level concrete buildings behind the reception, Haere Mai Restaurant and Manuia Bar. Ocean view rooms are located in adjacent buildings across the road from the lagoon. The mountainside rooms have 312 sq. ft. (29 sq. m) of living space and provide either twin or king size beds. The ocean view rooms also have a day bed that can sleep a third person. The mountainside rooms are not recommended for anyone who has difficulty walking, as there are stone steps leading up to these units. The beach bungalows and overwater bungalows are all 323 sq. ft. (30 sq. m) in size and are built in the traditional Polynesian style, with thatched roofs and woven pandanus walls. These units all have king-size beds plus a daybed. All the hotel's rooms and bungalows are furnished with a writing desk, blackout curtains, TV and in-house video, mini-bar fridge, direct dial telephone with data jack, personal safe, shower with massage nozzle, hair dryer, bath and beauty amenities, extension mirror and full length mirror in bathroom, and a sliding glass door onto a private terrace or balcony. The overwater bungalows have a glass-viewing table that enables you to see the fish swimming in the clear water below, steps providing direct access into the lagoon and a shower on the landing below the terrace.

Maitai means 'all is well,' and you'll certainly have a good feeling about this place from the moment you enter the reception area and are welcomed by a smiling Tahitian hostess, who offers you a refreshing fruit punch. The reception desk, Haere Mai Restaurant and Manuia Bar are all under one huge woven pandanus roof. Vivid shades of bougainvillea, hibiscus, colored leaves, tree ferns and hanging baskets of exotic ferns fill the gardens of the hotel and the South Seas setting is completed with a decor of tapa, bamboo and huge chandeliers of seashells. Breakfast and dinner are served in the Haere Mai Restaurant, and the weekly buffets are popular events, accompanied by a Polynesian dance show. The Manuia Bar is a gathering place during Happy Hour, when the musicians play island tunes and demonstrations are given on how to make *poisson cru* or tie the *pareo*. The Tama'a Maitai Restaurant is located on the beach side of the property, providing non-stop service from 11:30am to 8:30pm. See information under *Where to Eat* in this chapter.

Room service is available from 7am to 9:30pm. The hotel also provides next day laundry service, luggage room, fax and photocopy facilities. Guests can buy an Internet card at reception to use on the computer in the lounge. Keana boutique and jewelry shop are also located on the premises. You can rent a car or bicycle from the Fare Piti Agency in front of the main building, and there is an activity desk in the lobby, where you can book your tours and excursions. Guests have free use of the hotel's snorkeling equipment, kayaks and outrigger paddle canoes.

Moderate
NOVOTEL BORA BORA BEACH RESORT, *B.P. 174, Bora Bora, 98730. Tel. 689/60.59/60; Fax 689/60.59.51. novotelbora@mail.pf; www.accorhotels.pf;*

Reservations: Tel. 689/86.66.66; Fax 689/41.05.05; reservation.tahiti@accor-com; Located north of Matira Point adjacent to Sofitel Bora Bora Beach Resort. 2008 Low/ High Season EP Rates sgl./dbl.: Garden Room 15.487/21.681 CFP. American breakfast 1.875 CFP, set lunch 2.500 CFP; set dinner 4.236 CFP. Round-trip airport transfers 1.700 CFP by bus and 5.000 CFP by boat per person. Add taxes. All major credit cards.

This hotel opened in May 2003 as the Bora Bora Beach Resort, replacing the former Bora Bora Beach Club that was supposed to have been taken over by the French company, Les Nouvelles Frontières, to be rebuilt as a Paladian hotel. In August 2004 it was taken over by the Accor Group as a Novotel outlet and put under the management of Sofitel, which also has the Sofitel Bora Bora Beach Resort just next door to this hotel, and the Sofitel Motu, a 5-minute boat ride from the Novotel.

There are 80 a/c rooms in 10 two-story concrete motel-like buildings on the mountain side of the road, and the reception, restaurant, bar and activities center are on the lagoon side. There are 3 connecting rooms and 4 reduced mobility rooms, and all rooms are simply furnished with a double bed or 2 twin beds and a sofa bed, writing desk with lamp, cable TV, direct dial telephone with Internet access, fan, safe, coffee/tea facilities. There is a tiled bathroom with a lavabo, shower, separate toilet and hair dryer, and each unit has a small balcony or terrace overlooking the gardens.

The reception area is large and there is an activity center, a beachfront and outdoor restaurant for 180 diners, a beachfront bar and a swimming pool. Nautical activities depart from the overwater pier. Round-trip transfers 4.000 CFP per person and the Nemo World Diving center is located on the white sand beachfront. Free activities include snorkeling equipment, outrigger paddle canoes, transfers to the motu, and entertainment several nights a week, especially on weekends, where there is music for dancing. Guests can also go next door to watch the Polynesian dance shows at the Sofitel Bora Bora Beach Resort. See more information under *Where to Eat* in this chapter.

HOTEL MATIRA, *B. P. 31, Bora Bora 98730. Tel. 689/67.70.51/60.58.40; Fax 689/67.77.02; hotel.matira@mail.pf; www.hotel-matira.com. On Matira Beach at the turnoff to Point Matira. Round-trip transfers on arrival and departure 2.332 CFP. EP Rates sgl./dbl: Standard Bungalow 21.090 CFP; Garden View Bungalow 26.640 CFP; Lagoon View Bungalow 31.080 CFP; Beach Bungalow 35.520 CFP; 3rd person 8.325 CFP. Add taxes. AE, MC, V.*

This small hotel is on the beach side of the road right at the turn onto Point Matira. 14 modern Polynesian style bungalows are built in the garden and facing the white sands of Matira Beach. There are 2 beach bungalows, 4 with a lagoon view, 5 with a garden view and 3 standard units near the parking lot. Each of the bungalows has 2 double beds in the bedroom, a sofa bed in the living room, ceiling fan, small refrigerator, coffee and tea facilities, bathroom with hot water shower, and a terrace. There is no a/c and no TV or telephone. An iron and hair dryer are available at reception.

The hotel has no restaurant, but there are several good restaurants and snacks very close by and some of them provide pick-up service for dinner. There is also a food store within easy walking distance and an excellent roulotte sets up shop practically across the street every evening. All activities and excursions, such as lagoon trips and mountain safaris are available.

CLUB MED BORA BORA, *B.P. 34, Bora Bora 98730. Tel. 689/60.46.04; Fax 60.46.11; clubmed@mail.pf; www.clubmed.com. Reservations: 689/42.39.41; Fax 689/42.16.83. Beside the lagoon on Faaopore Bay, between the villages of Anau and Faanui, on the east coast. 150 twin-share units. AP Rates: garden room 24.000 CFP sgl., 20.000 CFP per person dbl.; beach bungalow 30.000 CFP sgl., 26.000 CFP per person dbl. Add taxes. All major credit cards.*

An annual membership fee of 3.281 CFP is also applicable. People of all ages and from many countries choose the Club Med Bora Bora because it offers a great vacation package in an attractive, amiable environment. Only in the bar and disco will you find any noise, and you can join in or do your own thing without any pressure. The garden rooms and beach rooms are in motel-style concrete buildings and stand-alone bungalows, all painted in pastel shades of yellow, chartreuse and mauve, intended to resemble a coral garden. The units are well spaced throughout the village, each with a view of the lagoon. Each room has a/c, a ceiling fan, twin beds that can be transformed into a king size bed, Polynesian *tifaifai* bed covers, reading lights overhead and on the bedside tables, a writing desk, small refrigerator, telephone with Internet connection, and a cable TV with an inhouse video channel that introduces each G.O (*gentil organisateur*) by name and job. Ample closet space and shelves are provided in the dressing area and there also is a safety box in the closet. The bathroom contains a hair dryer and personal amenities. The shower has an overhead nozzle plus a hand held nozzle, and a full length mirror covers the door to the separate toilet. A blackout shade provides privacy when it is pulled down to cover the sliding glass door that leads to the balcony or terrace. Laundry service is available and drinks can be ordered from room service. The village is fumigated every evening at dusk, and there is also an anti-mosquito electric plug in each room.

An enormous thatched-roof beachside pavilion is the central gathering place, with the reception, boutiques, dining room, bar and nightclub located here. A full range of Club Med activities is presented, free of charge, including snorkeling equipment, boat shuttles to the motu, Hobie Cat sailing, windsurfing, kayaking, paddling an outrigger canoe and fitness classes. There are optional sailboat excursions with a picnic on the motu, shark feeding, water skiing, jet skiing, scuba diving, fishing in the lagoon, lagoon excursion, safari tours, helicopter flights and shuttle service twice a day to Vaitape village. You can even get massages and beauty treatments at Club Med Bora Bora. In the evening you can party in the disco bar following the Club Med show presented by the G.O.'s nightly except Thurs. and Sun., when you can watch a Polynesian dance group perform on stage. For more information see *Where to Eat* in this chapter.

Small Family Hotels, Family Pensions, Guest Houses, Guest Rooms, Dormitories, Camping on the Main Island

ROHUTU FARE LODGE, *B.P. 400, Bora Bora 98730. Tel. 689/70.77.99; info@rohutufarelodge.com; www.rohutufarelodge.com. On mountainside overlooking Povai Bay, 4 km. (2.5 mi) north of Vaitape village. Free round-trip transfers. 2008 EP Rates 18.900 CFP sgl./dbl., extra person 3.500 CFP, including taxes. Children under 10 years free. MC, V.*

For many years Israeli expatriate Nir Shalev was the friendly manager of the popular backbacker's hangout, Village Pauline. In 2005 he moved 50 m. (150 ft.) up the mountain slope and built 3 exotic wooden bungalows on stilts in the midst of a botanical garden. This unique lodging has been awarded a 3-Tiare rating by the Tahiti Tourist office—the only pension in Bora Bora in this category. There are two lagoon view bungalows and a double-size mountain view bungalow for families, which has a separate bar-salon and an extra bed. Each bungalow has its own design, with teak floors and thatched roofs, a four-poster queen size bed with mosquito net, ceiling fan, safe, a bathroom with a marble floor, outdoor shower in a private garden, kitchenette with refrigerator, microwave oven, and coffee maker, plus a wide veranda. The bungalows and gardens are decorated with original works of art, including some erotic paintings and statues. Even the showers are suggestive!

You can relax in a rope hammock in a special hut facing the lagoon, browse through the library's collection of books, ride a free bike to the main village, or take advantage of the free transfers Nir offers his guests to the beach, stores, shopping or wherever they want to go. He has all the information you need to book your activities to discover Bora Bora by land or lagoon. He also rents sturdy USA made sea kayaks, complete with snorkeling and fishing gear.

VILLAGE TEMANUATA, *B.P. 544, Bora Bora 98730. Tel. 689/67.75.61; Fax 689/67.62.48; village.temanuata@mail.pf; www.temanuata.com.*

Temanuata Beach: On the beach side at Matira, just past the turnoff to Point Matira. Round-trip transfers 1.200 CFP per person. 2008 EP Rates sgl./dbl.: Garden Bungalow, 15.000 CFP; Lagoon View Bungalow 17.000 CFP; Beach Bungalow 18.000 CFP; Family Bungalow with kitchen 18.000 CFP. Add taxes. V.

This is a good location on Matira Beach, very close to restaurants, snacks, food stores and activities. The 11 Polynesian style thatched roof bungalows sit in a spacious grassy area between the white sand beach and the road, adjacent to Restaurant Fare Manuia. They all have a terrace, private bathroom with hot water, double or single beds, a closet, refrigerator, electric kettle and ceiling fan. They are attractively decorated with pareo curtains and bedspreads and are cleaned daily. You can rent a bicycle at reception and Martine, the manager, will happily help you arrange your tours and excursions.

Temanuata Iti: *On the mountain side between Hotel Bora Bora and Point Matira. Round-trip transfers 1.200 CFP per person. 2008 EP Rates: 21.000 CFP sgl./ dbl., add 4.000 CFP per night for 3rd person. Add taxes. V.*

Four large thatched roof bungalows are located in a private garden setting across the road from Matira Beach and the lagoon. These well furnished family units are equipped with a king size bed, ceiling fan, coffee and tea making facilities, TV, private bathroom with hot water, kitchen and a terrace. Bungalows are cleaned daily. Two complimentary bicycles are provided for each bungalow.

PENSION MOON, *B.P. 307, Bora Bora 98730. Tel. 689/67.74.36; moonbungalow@netcourrier.com; munanui-teriitehau@hotmail.com. Beside lagoon in Pofai Bay, between Vaitape village and Hotel Bora Bora. Free round-trip transfers. EP Rates: room 7.000 CFP sgl./dbl. Min. stay 2 nights. Add taxes. No credit cards.*

Muna Teriitehau's 4 modern and clean bungalows are adjacent to Galerie Alain and Linda. Each unit has a private bathroom and kitchen.

PENSION ANAU-CHEZ TEIPO, *B.P. 270, Bora Bora 98730. Tel. 689/67.78.17/70.38.15; Fax 689/67.65.21; teipobora@mail.pf. At PK 12 beside the lagoon in Anau, 200 m (656 ft.) from Club Med. Free round-trip transfers. EP bungalow with cold water shower 7.000 CFP sgl, 10.500 CFP dbl; family bungalow with hot water shower 13.000 CFP 1-4 people, including taxes. MC, V.*

Six small thatched roof bungalows with a double bed, private bathroom, kitchen and coffee facilities. This guesthouse is clean and has a good reputation, even though it is far from the activity center of Matira and there is no beach here. Free fresh bread each morning and coffee, tea, butter and confiture are furnished in the bungalows. Bicycles and kayaks are available for guest use. Line fishing and reef fishing.

PENSION ROBERT ET TINA, *Vaitape, Bora Bora 98730. Tel. 689/67.63.55/79.22.73/73.53.89; Fax 689/67.72.92. Beside the lagoon at Point Matira. Round-trip transfers 1.000 CFP per person. 2008 EP Rates sgl/dbl: Lagoon Room with shared kitchen and cold water bathroom 8.000 CFP; Garden Room with shared kitchen and cold water bathroom 7.700 CFP; Room with shared kitchen and private cold water bathroom 7.700 CFP. Add taxes. MC, V.*

This Polynesian family has 3 individual houses with 4 or 5 bedrooms at the tip end of Point Matira. Two houses have private cold-water bathrooms and they all have kitchens and electric fans. You can rent a room and share the bathroom and kitchen or rent the entire house. A full-day circle island boat tour includes shark feeding, visit to stingrays and manta rays, snorkeling in coral garden and picnic on a motu. This costs 8.000 CFP. A half-day excursion is 6.000 CFP.

PENSION BORA LAGOONARIUM, *B.P. 56, Bora Bora 98730. Tel. 689/67.71.34, Fax 689/67.60.29, cell 79.73.67/79.22.90/79.15.82; lagonarium@mail.pf; www.boraboraisland.com. Beside lagoon in Anau village 900 m (2,952 ft.) after Club Med. Transfers by Le Truck 500 CFP one-way. EP rates sgl./dbl.: room 6.000 CFP; bungalow 8.000 CFP; extra bed 2.000 CFP; dormitory 2.700 CFP per person per day. Add taxes. No credit cards.*

Three garden bungalows are furnished with a double bed, mini-fridge and private bathroom with cold-water shower. Four rooms have a double bed and single bed and share bathrooms with guests staying in the 20-bed dormitory. All guests can use the kitchen. The pension and dorm are owned by the same people who operate a water park called the Lagoonarium, which is located on a motu near Le Méridien hotel. Claudine Teheiura, one of the owners, said it's not usually necessary to make reservations to stay in the pension. Just show up.

CHEZ NONO, *B.P. 282, Bora Bora, 98730. Tel. 689/67.71.38; Fax 689/ 67.74.27; nono.leverd@mail.pf. On the white sand beach of Point Matira, facing the Hotel Bora Bora and the distant island of Maupiti, 13 km (8 mi.) from the ferry dock and 6.8 km (4.2 mi.) from Vaitape village. Round-trip transfers Vaitape/Chez Nono 1.000 CFP per person. 6 rooms and 4 bungalows. EP Rates: room in big house 5.800 CFP sgl., 6.800 CFP dbl.; small twin bungalow with private bathroom 9.100 CFP sgl/ dbl; big round bungalow with private bathroom 12.100 CFP sgl., 13.100 CFP dbl. dbl; 3 adults and 2 children 16.100 CFP. Add taxes. MC, V.*

This guest house is one of the best choices for a budget accommodation on Bora Bora, because of its excellent location right on the white sand beach of Matira, facing Maupiti and the sunset sea. A grocery store and several restaurants and snack bars are within a 10-min. walk. Most of the guests stay in the big house, which has bedrooms on two levels. The communal kitchen and bathroom have solar hot water. There are also 2 twin bungalows, each with a queen-size bed and private bathroom with solar hot water; and 2 round bungalows with a king-size and single bed and private bathroom with solar hot water. Every room and bungalow has a fan. The family bungalows are especially recommended because they are a Polynesian style *fare*, with a big thatched roof and half-walls of woven bamboo, overlooking the incredibly beautiful lagoon. The biggest drawback here is lack of privacy, as Matira Beach is Bora Bora's only public beach. Nono operates Teremoana Tours and has a motorized outrigger canoe that he uses to take his guests around the island with a picnic on a motu. His very popular excursions depart from the beach in front of his pension at 9:30am and return at 4:30pm. A lunch of *poisson cru*, grilled fish, coconut bread, cake, fresh fruit and *po'e* is served on the *motu*. The cost is 8.500 CFP per person. Nono also operates a 4-wheel drive safari tour.

CHEZ MAEVA MASSON, *B.P. 33, Bora Bora 98730. Tel./Fax 689/67.72.04; www.tahitiguide.com. Beside the beach at Point Matira, 13 km (8 mi.) from the ferry dock and 6.8 km (4.2 mi.) from Vaitape village. 2008 EP Rates: room 6.800 CFP sgl./ dbl.; bed in dormitory 3.400 CFP. For one night only room is 8.000 CFP and dorm is 4.000 CFP. Add taxes. MC, V.*

This is a very good location on Matira Beach with a grocery store across the road and several restaurants, snacks and activities within easy walking distance. It was the former home of Polynesian artist Rosine Temauri-Masson and her late husband, the French painter Jean Masson, and it still has the decor and warmth of a home. The 2-story wooden house has 2 bedrooms on the ground floor, each containing a double bed, and the 4 rooms upstairs each have a double bed, plus there is a 3-bed dormitory and a sofa bed in the living room. The bathroom with hot water shower and the kitchen are communal. Use of the washing machine costs

1.000 CFP and the iron is also 1.000 CFP. Transfers are available from the airport boat dock in Vaitape village. Several of my friends have enjoyed staying here and getting to know Rosine, who still lives in the house.

Other Accommodations on Bora Bora's Main Island
Bora Bora Condominiums, *Tel./Fax 689/67.61.21, marcolundi@mail.pf, faces Bora Bora's airport.* They rent condos by week, month or year. **Chez Rosina,** *Tel./Fax 689/67.70.91, at PK 4.5, on mountain side in Paparoa section of Pofai Bay,* has 7 rooms. No credit cards. **Chez Henriette,** *Tel./Fax 689/67.71.32, beside the lagoon in Anau,* has 5 basic rooms, a 12-bed dormitory and a campground. **Bora Vaite,** *Tel./Fax 689/67.55.69, boravaiete@mail.pf, is on mountainside in Hitiaa Bay.* This new family pension rents 3 rooms in a big house overlooking lagoon, with meals and activities included. **Camping Chez Aldo,** *Tel. 689/67.71.34/78.58.97; Fax 689/67.60.29,* on mountainside in Anau village, has camping space, washing machine and rental bikes.

Hotels & Pensions on the MotuPrestige
ST. REGIS RESORT & SPA, *B.P. 506, Bora Bora, 98730. Tel. 689/ 60.78.88; Fax 689/60.78.60; www.stregis.com/borabora; www.starwoodhotels.com/ stregis. On Motu Ome'e, facing Anau village. Round-trip airport transfers by private launch 6.500 CFP per person. 2008 Low/High Season EP Rates: Pool Beach Villa 140.000/170.000 CFP sgl./dbl.; Overwater Villa 98.000/115.000 CFP sgl./dbl.; Deluxe Overwater Villa 136.000/160.000 CFP sgl./dbl.; Premier Beach Pool Villa 220.000 CFP sgl./dbl.; Royal Overwater Pool Villa 420.000 CFP 1-4 guests; Royal Beach Pool Villa 450.000 CFP 1-4 guests; Royal Estate 1.500.000 CFP 1-6 guests; Extra person add 15.000 CFP per day. Buffet breakfast 3.584 CFP per person; Canoe breakfast 8.000 CFP per person; MAP 11.320 CFP per person; AP 15.095 CFP per person. Add taxes. All major credit cards.*

Just a few days after the St. Regis Resort opened on June 20, 2006, actress Nicole Kidman and her new husband, Keith Urban, were honeymooning in the resort's Royal Estate. This ultra luxurious 3-bedroom retreat has 13,000-sq. ft. (1,207 sq. m) and costs $15,000 a night. At the same time, "Desperate House-wives" star Eva Longoria and her boyfriend (now husband), NBS star Tony Parker, also checked into the St. Regis Resort for their own romantic holiday. These power celebrity couples thus launched the St. Regis Resort, putting it on the world map as the latest "in" spot for high profile guests and anyone else in search of a spare-no-expense high-end luxury experience. By Jan. 2007 the St. Regis was being named the "Best Resort in the World" by travel magazines.

The St. Regis Resort features 91 overwater and beach villas, built on a 44-acre (17.8-hectare) property on a long motu islet across the lagoon from the village of Anau. The lush landscaping is edged by the largest expanse of beach access in French Polynesia. Le Méridien Resort and Intercontinental Resort Bora Bora are to the left of St. Regis and the Four Seasons Resort is on its right. All four resorts face Bora Bora's famous Otemanu Mountain and have the Pacific Ocean beyond the barrier reef at their back door.

St. Regis Resort Bora Bora boasts a number of firsts for French Polynesia, including 5 Royal Overwater Pool Villas with 3,455 sq. ft. and private swimming pools suspended over the lagoon. The 2 Royal Beach Pool Villas each provide 2,852 sq. ft. and 2 bedrooms, plus an infinity pool. They also have access to a private helicopter pad. The Royal Estate is located on a secluded cove with 3 separate pavilions, with magnificent tropical gardens bordering its own private white sand beach. In addition to the 3 bedrooms, the Royal Estate also boasts 2 luxurious living rooms, a chef's kitchen, and a dining room with sunset terrace. It has a private pool and a private spa area with treatment room, sauna, steam bath and Jacuzzi.

The 32 Overwater Villas and 32 Deluxe Overwater Villas each offer 1,550 sq. ft., and the 4 Pool Beach Villas have 1,636 sq. ft. and a plunge pool. The 8 Premier Overwater Villas have 1,905 sq. ft. and a Jacuzzi, and the 7 Premier Beach Pool Villas have 2,700 sq. ft. and a pool. Some of the villas face Bora Bora's main island and the Otemanu mountain, while others have a view of the inner lagoon. The units built over the water all have a glass floor under the coffee table for fish watching. All the accommodation designs are contemporary and showcase exotic woods and regional art. Each villa is a/c and has ceiling fans, light dimmers, mini bar, in-room safe, coffee and tea maker, Espresso machine, iron/ironing board, snorkel gear, hair dryer and magnified makeup mirror. The bathrooms also contain a deep bathtub and a separate shower with an oversize rain nozzle and a hand-held nozzle. Guests are truly pampered with big containers of Acqua di Parma bath products and Pratesi linens for the heavenly king size beds. (Watch out for the protruding black base under the mattress to avoid shin bruises). There are 3 telephones with voicemail, and wireless high-speed Internet. Free Internet access is also available in the library/lounge in the main building. Each villa also has two 42-in. plasma TV's, and Bose DVD/CD players, and the resort has a library of CD's and DVD's.

In addition to the twice-daily maid service, room service, guest relations and 24-hr. concierge staff, the St. Regis also offers the "legendary St. Regis Butler service". Your butler is supposed to ensure that everything is available at the touch of a button, from arranging a day of yachting and diving to dinner on a private island and even packing your suitcases on request. According to guests' comments, good service is a work in progress, as most of the staff are young French people who are still learning their jobs.

Guests have a choice of 3 restaurants, including Lagoon, the resort's signature overwater restaurant, as well as Sushi Take and Te Pahu, the Mediterranean Grill that offers all day dining. The Aparima Pool Bar & Grill serves snacks and drinks throughout the day, and the Lagoon Bar is a favorite destination for sunset cocktails. Room service is available 24 hours a day. See information in *Where to Eat* in this chapter.

The resort's main pool has a swim-up bar and the romantic Oasis pool has 6 private day-bed cabanas, each with its own private plunge pool that you must reserve. You can have lunch and drinks here too. Other water activities include snorkeling in the resort's man made lagoon, reef fishing, deep-sea fishing and the island's only catch and release fly-fishing at the resort's private lagoonarium.

The Miri Miri Spa is a 13,000 sq. ft. world-class spa located on a private island within the resort's lagoon. It features Tahitian and Pacific Rim treatments in 7 treatment rooms. See information under *Massages & Spas*. There is also a state-of-the art fitness center adjacent to the Spa, with Technogym equipment, open 24/24. Tennis players will enjoy the floodlit tennis court. Other complimentary activities include bicycles to ride around Motu Ome'e, outrigger paddle canoes, kayaks, Hobie Cats, windsurfing, and snorkeling gear. Optional excursions can be arranged to discover Bora Bora by land, lagoon or air, and a shuttle boat service operates 4 times daily (except Sun.) to take guests from the resort to the main village of Vaitape, returning 1-2 hrs. later. Night shuttles leave the resort at 6:30pm and 7:45pm for the land base and the last return is at 10:45pm.

St. Regis Resort, Bora Bora offers couples an array of wedding options—whether an intimate barefoot event on a private motu, a traditional Tahitian ceremony, or a reception in the resort's secluded beachfront 1,600 sq. ft. event villa. The resort offers an onsite St. Regis Travel Specialist who is available to assist with all individual and group travel planning needs. Families can take advantage of St. Regis' Creativity Club, which provides supervised activities for children. See information in chapter on *Taking the Kids*.

St. Regis Resort is Starwood's 4th managed property in French Polynesia in association with owner Louis Wane, a Chinese man from Tahiti who also owns Sheraton Hotel Tahiti, Sheraton Moorea Lagoon Resort & Spa, and Bora Bora Nui Resort & Spa.

BORA BORA NUI RESORT & SPA, *B.P. 502, Bora Bora 98730. Tel. 689/60.33.00; Fax 689/60.33.01. Reservations: in Tahiti, Tel. 689/47.88.00; Fax 689/47.88.01; reservations.tahiti@sheraton.pf; www.boraboranui.com; in US and Canada Tel. 800/325-3589; www.starwood.com/tahiti. On Motu Toopua, southeast of the main island of Bora Bora, 6 mi. from Motu Mute domestic airport. Round-trip airport transfers by private launch 6.500 CFP per person. 2008 Low/High Season EP Rates sgl./dbl.: Lagoon View 62.000/62.000 CFP; Beach Villa 74.000/83.000 CFP; Overwater Villa 89.000/99.000 CFP; Hillside Spa Villa (1 massage per person/day) 105.000/117.000 CFP; Horizon Overwater Villa 119.000/129.000 CFP; Royal Hillside Villa 215.000/215.000 CFP; Royal Horizon Overwater Villa 295.000/295.000 CFP. Extra person add 10.000 CFP per day. American breakfast 3.000 CFP; MAP 9.800 CFP; AP 13.300 CFP. Add taxes. All major credit cards.*

The Bora Bora Nui Resort & Spa is part of the Starwood Hotels Luxury Collection. This 5-star hotel has 120 villas and suites located on 16 acres of lush, terraced hillside and on the water of a private, protected cove. The white sand beach is 600 m (1,968 ft.) long, one of the longest hotel beaches on the island of Bora Bora. The spacious accommodations range from 90-100 sq. m. (900-1,000 sq. ft.)

offering a choice of beach, hillside and overwater units with views of Motu Toopua, Mt. Otemanu on the main island of Bora Bora, or the infinity of sky and sea on the horizon. These include non-smoking rooms, 4 rooms for handicapped guests and 16 connecting rooms. A Royal Hillside Villa of 135 sq. m (1,350 sq. ft.) is an oversize Spa Suite offering a unique panoramic view of the lagoon, and 2 Royal Horizon Overwater Villas also have 135 sq. m (1,453 sq. ft.) of living space. Two new overwater suites at the end of a pontoon each have 3 bedrooms, a living room and a swimming pool adjoining the sundeck. These are some of the finest overwater suites in French Polynesia.

The meticulously planned decor in all units features a stylish Polynesian motif with rich, exotic woods (Indonesian yellow balau walls, mahogany furniture, merbau decks, and teak outdoor furniture), plus Polynesian and Asian shell chandeliers. Paintings by resident painters adorn the walls in the living room and bedroom, and woodcraft objects were created by local artists. Tapa covered sconces are fixed in the corners of the living room, tapa covered sliding doors lead to the bathroom and there is a tapa covered lamp on the desk in the bedroom. There is a kingsize or 2 twin beds in the bedroom and a daybed-sofa in the living room, complete with very comfortable mattresses. In-room amenities include individual a/c, ceiling fan, CD player with tuner, DVD players, 2 color TV's with satellite channels including CNN, 3 direct dial telephones with data ports, voice mail and Internet access, and a mini-bar that is set up to bill your room the instant you remove an item from its place. Inside a wall of closets and shelves are two sets of snorkeling gear, a basket table for breakfast in bed, two plastic raincoats, shoe polish, electronic safe, iron and board. The pink marble bathroom is huge and very well lit. The floor and walls are tiled and there are dressing counters and lavabos on two opposite walls. On one side there is a magnified lighted makeup mirror, hair-dryer and a generous supply of Aveda personal toiletries. On the other counter are two pots for making coffee and tea, along with the supplies. Underneath the counter is a bathroom scale. There is an oversize bathtub and a separate shower with an overhead showerhead with a soft spray and a hand held shower nozzle with a jet spray. The toilet and bidet are in a separate room.

In the overwater villas and suites fish and coral viewing panels are provided in the living room, bathroom and on the deck, which is partially covered with a thatched roof. All the outdoor furniture is teak and includes two padded lounge chairs, a teacart and table and two dining chairs. A ladder leads to a lower platform, where there is a shower. From there you can dive into the deep water or descend slowly on another ladder to snorkel among the fish and coral gardens in the lagoon.

Should you decide to spend your entire day in your villa, be assured there is 24-hour room service. The regular room service menu has been expanded to include the Shabu Shabu experience, where you "swish swish" your fish, prawns, chicken, beef tenderloin and seasonal vegetables in a boiling broth in an electric pot. The cost of this Japanese type fondue is 14.000 CFP per person. A Tahitian barbecue is 12.000 CFP per person and the Zen experience is 15.000 CFP, which includes fish and seafood cooked on a hot stone. You can order a Continental, American, Fitness or Japanese breakfast to be served in your room and the romantic Canoe Breakfast can be delivered by outrigger canoe to the overwater villas. For special theme dinners see *Where to Eat* in this chapter.

The resort's public facilities are just as impressive as the bungalows. The overwater reception area is set in a natural aquarium. Among 600 coconut trees and hundreds of other palms, pandanus trees and tropical plants in the immense gardens and along the white sand beach there are 2 restaurants, 2 bars, a meeting room, library and computer room with free Internet access, a gift boutique, art gallery, Robert Wan Pearls boutique, a Mandara Spa built on the hillside, and a beauty salon for facials, manicures and pedicures. On top of the hill is a lovely little wedding chapel with a fabulous panoramic view. Secretarial and other business services are available, as well a tour and travel desk, same day laundry service, 2-day dry-cleaning, daily maid service and nightly turndown service, baby-sitting, private boat transfers between the airport and resort, electric shuttle carts and a heliport. Complimentary shuttle boat service between the resort and Vaitape village operates almost hourly starting at 8am, with the last boat leaving the village dock at 11:10pm.

One of the special touches offered is the food and beverage service that is brought to guests anywhere they may be in the pool and beach area. This includes complimentary sliced fruit, homemade cookies and sorbet that can even be delivered to you while you are enjoying the 10,000 sq. ft. infinity-edge swimming pool. Other complimentary activities include snorkeling equipment, canoes, kayaks and Hobie cats, as well as billiards and backgammon in the lounge, use of the fully equipped fitness center, sauna and steam bath. The activities desk staff can help you arrange your optional excursions, which include a barbecue picnic on Motu Tapu for 8.000 CFP per person. This exquisite little islet is the private domain of Bora Bora Nui Resort. Romantic dinners and ideas, wedding ceremonies and special honeymoon suggestions are available on request.

Deluxe

INTERCONTINENTAL BORA BORA RESORT & THALASSO SPA, *B.P. 156, Bora Bora 98730. Tel. 689/60.76.00; Fax 689/60.76.99; boraboraspa@interconti.pf; www.borabora.interconti.com. 83 units. 2008 Low/High Season EP rates sgl./dbl.: Emerald Overwater Villa 88.190/97.980 CFP; Sapphire Overwater Villa 102.050/113.380 CFP; Diamond Overwater Villa 110.990/123.320 CFP; Diamond Otemanu Overwater 133.190/147.980 CFP; Motu Family Suite 88.190/97.980 CFP; Extra person 10.000 CFP; "Heremoana" Beach Suite 152.820/169.800 CFP; "Poe Va'i" Overwater Suite 209.250/232.500 CFP. Mandatory round-trip transfers airport/hotel/airport. One-way boat transfers to/from airport 2.750 CFP; one-way bus transfers to/from other hotels, heliport or nautical bases 800 CFP. Add taxes. All major credit cards.*

This 5-star resort opened on May 1, 2006, between "the two hearts" of Motu

Piti Aau, a coral islet on Bora Bora's barrier reef, across the lagoon from the village of Anau on the main island. Some say that the 2 rows of overwater bungalows resemble the claws of a crab. This is the first resort in French Polynesia to feature only overwater villas. This eco-friendly resort is the first hotel in the world to use an air-conditioning system operating with deep sea water, which is 90% more energy efficient than electricity, and eliminates the use of potentially hazardous compounds that deplete the ozone layer and provoke climatic change. The Sea Water Air-Conditioning (SWAC) system pumps cold water (41°F, 5°C) from an ocean depth of 3,000 ft. (915 m.) to cool down the villas by thermic exchange. This is also the first luxury establishment to propose a deep sea water Thalasso center and Spa in the South Pacific.

Each of the 80 villas contains 65 sq. m. (700 sq. ft.) of space indoors and 100 sq. m. (1,076 sq. ft.) counting the terrace. All units are the same except for their view. The 21 Emerald Overwater Villas have a view of the beach and motu, the 24 Sapphire Overwater Villas face the lagoon and the main island of Bora Bora, and the 35 Diamond Overwater Villas have an extraordinary view of Mt. Otemanu and the lagoon. Each villa contains a living room with a glass-bottom coffee table for viewing the sea life in the lagoon, a separate bedroom with a walk-in dressing room, a large and bright bathroom with black slate floors and big tubs overlooking the lagoon. A large shaded terrace with sun beds and table, plus a spacious bathing deck with exterior fresh water shower. The bedrooms are furnished with a king size bed convertible into twin beds if required and in the living room is a sofa with a pull-out trundle bed. In addition to the seawater a/c, there are also 2 ceiling fans, 2 flat screened TV's with local and international channels, CD and DVD players, 2 IDD telephones, ADSL high speed Internet and Wifi connection, electronic safety box, a fully stocked mini bar, complimentary tea and espresso coffee facilities. The bathroom has a separate shower and bathtub and double sink, plus separate toilets. There is a hair dryer and a complimentary range of guest toiletries. Room service is available 24/24 and there is next day valet and laundry service. Butler service is also available on request. All the villas are decorated in a contemporary architecture with Polynesian accents that include traditional dance costumes on the walls.

Since the hotel opened, 3 Motu Family Suites have been added that can sleep 5 people. The "Heremoana" is a beach or overwater Junior Suite with beds in the bungalows and lounge. "Poe Vai" is an Overwater Suite comprised of 2 Junior Suites linked by a lounge with 2 single beds.

The hotel also offers 1,000 feet of private white sand beach, a freshwater infinity pool, 2 restaurants and bars, 12 transit bungalows, conference facilities, business center, concierge, guest relations/activities desk, car rental desk, boutique, a Tahia Collins pearl shop, a fitness and aerobic room, tennis court, and helicopter pad. Although the hotel's decor can be described as trendy—especially the all-white Bubbles Bar with Lucite ceiling fans that was inspired by Philippe Starck— their overwater wedding chapel can only be called romantic. The view from the picture window frames a perfect view of Bora Bora's famous Otemanu mountain, and a large glass floor lets you admire the tropical fish swimming below you. A "Blue Lagoon Chapel" wedding ceremony, including a beauty makeover in the honeymoon bungalow at the Spa, the ceremony, and a private gourmet dinner with champagne under the stars is 315.000 CFP per couple. Contact the hotel directly for a list of all their Romantic Ideas, Romantic Dinners, and Romantic Ceremonies.

A free boat shuttle service operates between the IC Thalasso and the IC Moana Resort Bora Bora. Other free activities include kayaks, outrigger paddle canoes, tennis, volley ball, snorkeling gear, pedal-boat, bocce-ball, star gazing sessions, pareo tying lessons and palm frond weaving. For a fee of 29.000 CFP you can even take gourmet cooking classes from the hotel's French chef. Special evenings at the IC Thalasso include a Polynesian dinner with dance show each Mon. evening, and an Island World Tour Dinner with show on Fri. night. Also see information under *Where to Eat* and *Massages & Spas* in this chapter.

BORA BORA LAGOON RESORT & SPA, *B.P. 175, Bora Bora 98730. Tel. 689/60.40.00; Fax 689/60.40.01; reservations@bblr.pf. www.boraboralagoon.com. US and Canada Reservations: 800/860-4095; www.orient-express.com. 76 units. 2008 EP Rates sgl/dbl: Motu Bungalow 56.086 CFP; Premium Motu Bungalow 71.002 CFP; Overwater Bungalow 82.935 CFP; Overwater End of Pontoon 99.641 CFP; Motu Suite with private pool 95.464 CFP; 2-Bedroom Villa with private pool 131.263 CFP; extra person 5.966 CFP. Buffet breakfast 3.103 CFP; Lunch 4.296 CFP; Dinner 7.876 CFP. Boat transfers from Bora Bora Airport to hotel 1.790 CFP one-way. Add taxes. All major credit cards.*

This exclusive Orient-Express property is located on the sunset point of Motu Toopua, a small, roadless coral island a mile across the bay from Bora Bora's main island. A quarter-mile stretch of white sand beach fronts the resort, which is set amid 12 acres of lush tropical gardens. Several improvement programs, along with a super friendly and helpful staff, have turned this into one of the most delightful tropical resorts in the South Pacific.

The 76 Polynesian style guest bungalows include a Presidential Villa with 2 bedrooms and 2 bathrooms. It faces the beach and has its own swimming pool in front and a rock wall and garden in the back. 3 Motu Suites each have a bedroom and a swimming pool. There are 5 End of Pontoon Overwater Bungalows and 44 Overwater Bungalows, 22 Motu Bungalows beside the white sand beaches, and 1 Premium Motu Bungalow with an outdoor soaking pool. All the units have a/c and ceiling fans. Features include yucca wood floors, floor-to-ceiling louvers and timber blinds. The furniture is made of bamboo and wicker, and the upholstery and draperies are neutral with accent cushions. Paintings by local resident artists decorate the walls. Each room contains a wonderfully comfortable king-size bed and a day bed, writing desk, bathroom with double basins, bathtub, separate shower and toilet, lighted makeup mirror and hair dryer. The amenities also include a mini-bar, private safe, tea and coffee facilities, international direct dial telephones, internet connection for laptops, satellite TV, in-house video channel and DVD player. The overwater bungalows have a glass-bottom coffee table, private sun deck and ladder leading into the lagoon, and a fresh water shower on the lower deck.

Guest services include ice delivery, laundry, daily maid service and nightly turndown, baby-sitting, and boat shuttle service between the hotel and Vaitape village. Room service is available 24-hrs. a day and a special treat for lovers staying in the overwater bungalows is to have a Continental breakfast of tropical fruits, pastries and juices delivered to their sundeck by a Tahitian style canoe. A Canoe Champagne Breakfast is 6.682 CFP per person.

Otemanu Restaurant, the 92-seat restaurant, is poised over the lagoon with breathtaking views on every side. An outdoor dining terrace was designed with lovers in mind who wish to take in the superlative sunsets. Café Fare offers informal indoor/outdoor dining for lunch and dinner beside the swimming pool. For special theme dinners see *Where to Eat* in this chapter.

The Pavilion library/lounge can also be used for private dining and meetings for small groups. This room contains a pool table, dartboard, card table, computer with Internet connections and a large screen TV and DVD player. The Putari Boutique carries gift items, film and clothing and there is a Nyco's Perles shop in the main building. The a/c Fare Fitness center has 17 Technogym machines and TV. The activities manager will help you with your exercise programs. The 160-ft. long swimming pool is supposedly the largest fresh water pool in Bora Bora. Guests also have free use of two floodlit tennis courts, beach volleyball, snorkeling equipment, Tahitian outrigger paddle canoes, kayaks, windsurf boards and Hobie cats. The friendly staff at the activities desk can book your excursions to discover Bora Bora by air, land or lagoon. One of the exclusive activities offered at this resort is a one-hour course in Qi-Gong or an initiation to Ney Yang Gong for 5.900 CFP.

The Special Events Pavilion is a Tahitian style meeting facility with open beams that is reached by a footbridge across a lily pond. Receptions for up to 100 people are held here, and this is also the computer room for guests who buy a card to use the Internet. A Fare Transit is available for guests who have an early arrival or late departure.

Marú Spa is a Polynesian inspired spa featuring 6 treatment rooms, 4 on the waterfront and the 2 massage rooms are built into the branches of 2 almost mythic Banyan trees, giving the property a true treehouse spa. See *Massages & Spas* in this chapter.

A Romantic Suggestions list of activities for two includes an exclusive Private Motu Lunch with your table set in the water. Tahitian Weddings may be performed on the hotel's main beach, followed by a special romantic dinner. The full-on ritual with Tahitian singers and dancers costs 159.305 CFP per couple and includes photos of the non-binding ceremony. You can also have a Tahitian Wedding performed on a private motu islet for 226.750 CFP, which includes a transfer with champagne and a romantic dinner served on the motu. A Honey-moon Dreaming Day is 277.000 CFP for two. These events are described in

Patrick's Activities under both *Mountain Safari 4x4 Excursions* and *Private Lagoon Excursions* later in this chapter.

FOUR SEASONS RESORT BORA BORA, *Motu Tehotu 98730, Bora Bora. Reservations: USA and Canada 1 800/819-5053; www.fourseasons.com. On a motu islet just north of St. Regis Resort, across the lagoon from Bora Bora's main island. EP Rates dbl: Mountain View Overwater Bungalow 97.500 CFP; Lagoon View Overwater Bungalow 112.500 CFP; Lagoon View Overwater Bungalow with Plunge Pool 121.000 CFP; Otemanu Overwater Bungalow with Plunge Pool 136.500 CFP; 2-Bedroom Beachfront Villa with Private Pool 304.000 CFP; 3-bedroom Otemanu Luxury Beachfront Villa with Private Pool 506.657 CFP. Supplementary charge for Dec. 24. Add taxes. All credit cards.*

Owner-promoter Thierry Barbion of Tahiti has announced that his new resort will open in mid-2008, and will accept reservations starting Oct. 1. The 121 spacious hideaways are located on 54 acres (22 ha.), with 100 units built over the lagoon. The overwater bungalows range in size from 1,080 sq. ft. (100 sq. m.) to 1,668 sq. ft. (155 sq. m.), offering views of the beach or lagoon and some with unobstructed views of Mount Otemanu. The 2-bedroom beachfront villas have a private pool and 3,228 sq. ft. (300 sq. m.) of living space, and the 3-bedroom beachfront villa has a private pool and 5,380 sq. ft. (500 sq. m.) of space. This one-of-a-kind Otemanu luxury villa has 2 king and 2 queen beds, 3 full marble bathrooms, plus powder room, and can sleep 5 adults or 2 adults and 4 children. The outdoor area of this presidential villa encompasses 1,000 sq. ft. (93 sq. m.) of expansive decks, a whirlpool, and shaded lanais, with spectacular views of the lagoon and Mount Otemanu. The overwater bungalows have sliding doors beside the deep bathtubs for panoramic, fresh air views of the lagoon and some of the units have private plunge pools. They also have separate showers and a double vanity in the marble bathrooms. Services and amenities in the a/c rooms include king or queen beds, satellite TV with plasma screens, CD player, DVD player, wired or wireless Internet access, multi-line telephones with voicemail, built in safe, refrigerated private bar, coffee/tea maker, thick terry bathrobes, hair dryer, hypo-allergenic pillows on request, iron and ironing board, and twice-daily housekeep-ing service. Inspired by local architecture, the guest quarters offer an airy restful ambience, complete with teak wood furnishings, Polynesian artwork, high ceil-ings, and thatched roofs made from pandanus leaves.

The resort's facilities include the Arii Moana, an open-air all-day restaurant, the Navé Navé French specialty restaurant, the Fare Hoa Beach Bar and the Sunset Bar. The Spa offers 7 a/c treatment rooms, steam rooms, an ice room, a mineral whirlpool, and an overwater cabana for treatments under the sun or stars. There will also be a full-service fitness center with overwater sunrise yoga platform. A wedding chapel and event pavilions will also be added. Barbion owns the Radisson Plaza hotel in Tahiti, as well as several commercial buildings. He wants to attract business clientele to the Four Seasons Resort, as well as families. The new resort will have a separate teen's island featuring a Young Adult Center with its own beach, and there will also be a "Kids for All Seasons" club for children 4-12 years old. In addition to the main pool with a swim-up bar, the resort will also have a children's pool in the supervised Kids Club area.

A project to build Four Seasons Private Residences Bora Bora is also underway on the Four Seasons property. This is another Thierry Barbion Development that will include 15 residences for homeowners, who will be able to enjoy the Resort's services and facilities. See *www.ownborabora.com* for more information.

HOTEL SOFITEL MOTU, *B.P. 516, Bora Bora 98730. Tel. 689/60.56.00; Fax (689) 60.56.66; h2755@accor.com; www.accorhotels.pf. Reservations: 689/ 86.66.66; Fax 689/41.05.05; reservation.tahiti@accor.com. On Motu Piti Uu'uta, across lagoon from Sofitel Bora Bora Beach Resort. 31 bungalows. 2008 Low/High Season EP Rates sgl./dbl.: Lagoon Bungalow 52.655/60.177 CFP; Hillside Bungalow 52.665/60.177 CFP; Overwater Bungalow 66.372/76.549 CFP; Overwater Horizon View Bungalow 74.779/88.053 CFP; Villa 76.991/89.381 CFP. Round-trip airport boat transfers 5.000 CFP per person. American breakfast 2.901 CFP, set lunch 3.148 CFP, set dinner 6.729 CFP. Add taxes. All major credit cards.*

This luxury resort opened in August 1999 on the private islet of Motu Piti Uu'uta, set in the middle of the Bora Bora lagoon, facing the Sofitel Bora Bora Beach Resort and the mesmerizing mountains of Otemanu and Pahia. The secluded *motu* features 3 beaches, one of which has sun all day long for sunbathing and snorkeling in the coral gardens surrounding the *motu*. People who have stayed here claim that the best snorkeling in Bora Bora is in the natural aquarium right beside this islet.

There are 30 bungalows built over the water, beside the lagoon or on high stilts on the hillside, which offer you choices of the sunrise, sandy beach or sunset views. A deluxe beach villa has been added, offering a spacious living area, private bar and dining room in addition to the bedroom and bath. The hotel is built of Indonesian kohu wood, which is similar to teak, and all the roofs are made of woven pandanus leaves. You have a choice of two twin beds or a king-size bed when they are pushed together, plus a day bed. Each bungalow has a/c and a ceiling fan, a private safety box, mini-bar, radio, DVD player, plasma TV with cable/satellite, plus coffee and tea facilities and 2-line phones with IDD and Internet access. The bathroom floor is covered with polished black volcanic stones and an enormous showerhead provides a relaxing massage in the very spacious shower. A long bathroom counter of kohu wood contains two lavabos and a selection of Sofitel amenities. There is also a lighted magnified makeup mirror, a hair dryer and a full-length wall mirror. The overwater bungalows each contain a round glass window on the floor for prime viewing of the natural marine life in the rich coral gardens below. Stairs from the covered terrace lead you directly into the inviting water and snorkeling gear and beach towels are provided in each room. There is an outdoor shower on the lower sundeck.

Because this particular *motu* is a natural reserve of the reef heron, *egretta sacra*, this graceful bird is used as the hotel's logo. It is called Manu Tuki in the Paumotu language of the Tuamotu atolls, which is also the name of the hotel's hilltop restaurant and bar. You will enjoy spectacular views of the multihued lagoon as well as the highly praised cuisine served here. For more information see *Where to Eat* in this chapter. Room service is also available.

Kayaks are available for guest use and you can also enjoy all the amenities, activities, and excursions that are available at the Sofitel Bora Bora Beach Resort. A complimentary on demand shuttle service takes you from the *motu* to the main island in less than 5 minutes. This hotel provides the perfect honeymoon hideaway, and you can even get married Polynesian style on the Sofitel Motu beach or in the gardens of the Sofitel Bora Bora Beach Resort. Contact the hotel for details and rates.

HOTEL LE MERIDIEN BORA BORA, *B.P. 190, Bora Bora 98730. Tel. 689/60.51.51; Fax 689/60.51.52. Reservations 689/47.07.29; Fax 689/47.07.28; rez@lemeridien-tahiti.pf; www.lemeridien-borabora.com. 99 units. 2008 Low/High season EP Rates sgl./dbl: Lagoon Bungalow 60.000/65.000 CFP; Beach Bungalow 70.000/85.000 CFP; Overwater Bungalow 80.000/92.000 CFP; Premium Overwater Bungalow 93.000/106.000 CFP. Third person 6.000 CFP. Round-trip airport transfers 4.600 CFP per person. American Breakfast Buffet 2.857 CFP; MAP 8.482 CFP; AP 12.634 CFP. Add taxes. All major credit cards.*

With more than 1 km (.6 mi.) of white sand beach, accessible only by a 20-min. boat ride from the airport or 5 min. by boat from the main island of Bora Bora, Le Méridien covers more than 23.5 acres (9.5 ha) on the southern end of Motu Piti Aau, an islet across the lagoon from the village of Anau. This 5-star hotel opened in June 1998 and was the first international class hotel to be built on this motu. Today, the Intercontinental Thalasso Resort & Spa is on its left, and neighbors on the right are the St. Regis and Four Seasons hotels. In late 2005 the Le Méridien group was acquired by Starwood Hotels & Resorts and a big renovation project has improved the bungalows and public buildings on the property.

Le Méridien Bora Bora is located between the sea and lagoon, with bungalows built over the lagoon and on the beach adjacent to a shallow interior lagoon. Each bungalow contains 60 sq. m (646 sq. ft.) of living space, which consists of a large bedroom with a sitting area, a walk-in closet and a spacious bathroom. There is also a partially covered outside deck, and for the bungalows over water, there are steps leading into the lagoon. Instead of the standard glass table that allows you to watch the fish in the lagoon underneath the overwater bungalows, Le Méridien has gone a step further and built a large glassed surface into the polished wood floor. A new category of accommodation is the lagoon bungalow, which has no glass bottom floor. These units are located over the channel of the interior lagoon. There is also a handicap accessible bungalow on the beach.

All the resort's bungalows are built with natural materials of pandanus-thatched roofs and precious kohu wood, which is dark and heavy, similar to teak. Each bungalow has a/c and a ceiling fan, and they are furnished with two twin beds that are pushed together to make a king-size bed. There is also a sofa bed, a big desk with a recessed make-up mirror, blackout curtains, satellite television and video, a mini-bar fridge, separate liquor or snack cabinet, international direct dial telephone with data port, personal safe, coffee and tea facilities. The bathroom contains a bathtub and separate shower, private toilet, a full-length mirror, magnified makeup mirror, hair dryer and a selection of Le Méridien toilet amenities. The premium overwater bungalows are the same size as the other overwater units, but they are located at the end of the deck with a direct view of Bora Bora's famous mountains. These units also have a DVD/CD player.

The boat-shaped central building houses the reception area, activities desk, the Miki Miki Bar, boutique, Nyco's pearl shop, lending library and a game room with billiards table. In the a/c lounge and TV room are 2 computers for guests to use at no charge, and they can also download pictures from digital cameras. Free Wifi is also available in the lobby and public areas.

Breakfast and dinner are served in the restaurant Le Tipanier, which can seat 180 people and looks out onto the private lagoon, complete with hungry fish looking for a handout. The chef caters to the taste preferences of the hotel guests, who are primarily French, Italian, American and Japanese, providing international and local cuisine. Lunch is served at Le Te Ava, a 120-seat beachside restaurant, where the atmosphere is informal and friendly. The Miki Miki bar and Tupa beach snack serve light meals and liquid refreshments. See information under *Where to Eat* in this chapter. Room service is available 24 hrs. a day, with a limited menu between 10pm and 6am, and you can even order picnic baskets to take with you while exploring the delights of the beautiful white sand beach and aquamarine waters of Bora Bora's incredible lagoon.

The choices of activities and excursions available at Le Méridien include the fresh water swimming pool, free snorkeling equipment, beach volley, ping-pong, pedal boats, windsurf boards, kayaks and Polynesian outrigger canoes. You can join the Kainalu Canoe Club and go sailing in a traditional dugout canoe built in Hawaii. Or you can rent a 14-ft. Hobie Cat for 2.000 CFP per hour.

As part of their ever-expanding family friendly program, the hotel management has added a fully equipped children's playground. They provide small snorkeling gear for kids from 2 years old, small cha-cha sailboats and a small windsurf board that an 8-year old can handle. An exclusive treat for guests of all ages at Le Méridien is to visit the turtle nursery on the hotel property and watch dozens of baby sea turtles being fed each morning. You can even swim with the turtles inside the clear waters of a *hoa* channel that flows from the ocean into the lagoon. The turtle eggs are hatched on the hotel's beach and the turtles are released from the nursery into the ocean a year later, then tracked by satellite as part of an environmental program. You can even become a godparent to one of the turtles and receive news of its progress.

One of the hotel's lagoon bungalows has been transformed into a massage and body care salon called Espace Bien-Etre, a place of well being. It is open daily and you can indulge your hedonistic nature with a rubdown with coconut fiber, crushed coffee beans or sand perfumed with oils, followed by an aromatic bath or floral bath, a seaweed wrap, facial and a choice of massages. See information under *Massages & Spas in* this chapter.

Honeymoon couples from Japan and other countries, who have already been legally married in their country, have their formal wedding ceremony in Bora Bora filmed in a romantic little chapel on the hotel grounds. Polynesian Wedding Ceremonies are performed on the beach at Le Méridien on request. For further details you should contact the hotel directly.

BORA BORA PEARL BEACH RESORT, *B.P. 169, Bora Bora 98730. Tel. 689/60.52.00; Fax 689/60.52.22; www.pearlresorts.com. Reservations: Tel. 689/ 50.84.45; Fax 689/43.17.86; res@spmhotels.pf. 80 bungalows. 2008 Low/High Season EP Rates sgl./dbl.: Garden Pool Suite 55.000/60.000 CFP; Premium Garden Pool Suite 60.000/65.000 CFP; Beach Suite with Jacuzzi 69.000/75.000 CFP; Overwater Bungalow 69.000/78.000 CFP; Premium Overwater Bungalow 79.000/ 88.000 CFP; third person 10.000 CFP. MAP 8.750 CFP; AP 12.000 CFP; Canoe Breakfast 9.900 CFP for 2. One-way boat transfer between the airport and hotel 2.750 CFP per person, private boat transfer 12.500 CFP, helicopter shuttle 26.364 CFP. Add taxes. All major credit cards.*

This 5-star resort is a member of The Leading Small Hotels of the World and has earned a well-deserved reputation as a honeymoon and family resort since it opened in June 1998. This well-maintained property is located on 47 acres (19 ha) of land between the ocean and lagoon on Motu Tevairoa, facing Faanui Bay and the famous Otemanu mountain of Bora Bora. It is a 10-min. boat ride from the airport and a 15-min. boat ride to the main village of Vaitape. The entire hotel is built in the traditional Polynesian style, with pandanus thatched roofs, local woods, woven pandanus wall coverings and a decor that includes tapa wall hangings and paintings and sculptures by Polynesian artists.

There are 50 overwater bungalows, 10 beach suites and 20 garden pool suites. All units have a/c as well as ceiling fans, a well-stocked refrigerated mini-bar, coffee and tea making facilities, hair dryer, safety box, iron and table, magnifying mirror, 20" LCD satellite television with DVD player, CD player, and IDD telephones in the bedroom and separate toilets. There are twin beds or a king size bed and a day bed in each unit, as well as writing desks and reading lights. Amenities include a wide range of Manea toiletries.

Honeymooners prefer the overwater bungalows that are classified as Premium, because they offer the best views of the mountain and lagoon. These attractively decorated units have 658 sq. ft. (61 sq. m) of living space, with a glass bottom table and glass windows in the bathroom to observe more than 70 species of fish that have settled and developed in the To'a Nui coral nursery beside these bungalows. This park also has a colony of 4,000 corals that are regenerating in perfect ecological conditions. All the overwater units have a bathtub and a separate shower, as well as Internet outlets. Guests staying in the overwater bungalows may also have the pleasure of their breakfast being delivered by outrigger canoe for 9.750 CFP per couple.

The very popular beach suites provide 786 sq. ft. (73 sq. m) of living space and have an indoor-outdoor bathroom with a full shower in a tropical garden, and a private enclosed sundeck with a Jacuzzi. The a/c bedroom can be completely closed off, and anyone sitting or sleeping in the living room, which has a day bed, will have the benefit of a ceiling fan but no a/c. The premium and garden pool suites provide 872 sq. ft. (81 sq. m) of living space, which is great for families. There is a gazebo type shelter with a table and benches, a sundeck with 2 lounge chairs, a private plunge pool and a small tropical garden. A privacy fence surrounds this area and another wall protects the covered shower in the garden adjoining the bathroom. The bedroom can be closed off from the bathroom to take full advantage of the a/c.

Three overwater bungalows are well equipped for wheelchairs and the hotel has wide cement paths and easily accessible public areas. There is an elevator in the main building, from the reception area to the restaurant and bar upstairs, a disabled access toilet in the main building and a changing room for disabled guests at the Manea Spa.

The hotel has 3 restaurants, 2 bars, a boutique and pearl shop, movie theater/conference center/computer room with paid Internet access, lending library, a fresh water swimming pool and Jacuzzi, a/c fitness center, day-use bungalows, heliport, floodlit tennis court, mini golf, table tennis, volley ball court and bacci ball court, billiards, and a wide variety of optional activities and excursions. Hotel guests have free use of the snorkeling equipment, outrigger paddle canoes, kayaks, Ping Pong, bacci ball, badminton and society games. On-site are the Blue Nui Dive Center and Manea Spa, both of which are top-rated in French Polynesia. See further information under *Where to Eat*, *Scuba Diving* and *Massages & Spas* in this chapter.

The Bora Bora Pearl Beach Resort & Spa is a favorite destination for honeymooners and other lovers who appreciate the romantic setting of this hotel. To make those moments together even more magical, you can have a non-binding wedding ceremony performed in the little wedding chapel or Polynesian style on the beach. Contact the hotel directly for a list of Romantic Welcomes, Romantic Interludes and Romantic Escapades.

Moderate

MAI MOANA ISLAND, *B.P. 164, Bora Bora 98730. Tel. 689/67.62.45/73.75.73; Fax 689/67.62.39; stan@mail.pf; www.mai-moana-island.com. On Motu Mute Iti, a private islet 5 minutes by boat from airport and 10 minutes from ferry dock. Boat transfers from airport 1.500 CFP per couple. One-way boat transfer to main island 3.000 CFP. 3 bungalows. Beach bungalow 24.000 CFP EP sgl/dbl; 34.000 CFP MAP dbl, 38.800 CFP AP dbl. Bungalow for a couple who wants to be alone, with no other guests on the island, 45.000 CFP EP, 55.000 CFP MAP. Add taxes. MC, V. No children allowed.*

This lodging is classified as a small family hotel. Owner Stan Wisnieswski speaks English, French, German, Russian and Polish, and he's a ham radio operator. His private paradise gets a lot of good comments from people who have stayed at Mai Moana Island, which is dotted with coconut palms and ironwood trees and surrounded by a white sand beach, with no dock. There are 3 Polynesian style deluxe thatched roof *fares*, each with a double bed, ceiling fan, mini-bar, TV, dressing room, private bathroom with solar hot water, and a covered terrace. Snorkeling equipment and four kayaks are available for guest use. French cuisine with a Polynesian touch is served in the panoramic restaurant-bar. Tahitian wedding ceremonies can also be performed.

LE PARADIS, *B.P. 243, Bora Bora 98730. Tel./Fax 689/67.75.53, cell 78.27.87; leparadis@mail.pf. On Motu Paahi, a private islet 5 min. by boat from the Motu Mute airport and 10 min. from the ferry dock. Free round-trip boat transfers between airport and motu. Paid boat transfers to Vaitape. 7 bungalows. 2008 EP Rates: fare 10.000 CFP sgl.; 15.000 CFP dbl; family fare 17.000 CFP dbl./tpl. MAP 3.500 CFP per person. Add taxes. No credit cards.*

Tehapai and Tipea Pahuiri, the Tahitian family who own this little pension, have a very good reputation for their local style cuisine, especially the *maa Tahiti* they prepare in the underground oven. The 7 thatched roof bungalows have bamboo walls and are located on a pretty white sand beach. The 5 small bungalows have beds for 2 people and 2 larger bungalows can sleep 3 people. They are all clean and have a mosquito net over each bed and house linens are supplied. Each unit has its own private bathroom with hot water, and all guests share the kitchen and dining room.

Other Lodgings on the Motu Islets

Bora Bora Eden Beach Hotel, *Tel. 689/60.57.60; Fax 689/67.69.76; borabora@mail.pf; www.boraborahotel.com.* A 16-bungalow eco-tourist hotel on Motu Piti Aau, a 15-minute boat ride across the lagoon from Anau village. This hotel has had several negative reviews because of owner.

Blue Heaven Island, *Tel. 689/72.72.61 (Bora Bora) or 310/989-5420 in Los Angeles monique@blueheavenisland.com; www.blueheavenisland.com.* A private motu near the airport in Bora Bora owned by Monique LaVoie, with 5 small Polynesian style bungalows and meals. Great snorkeling.

WHERE TO EAT

Hotel Restaurants on the Main Island

HOTEL BORA BORA, *Tel. 60.44.60. All major credit cards.*

Matira Terrace Restaurant. This is the main restaurant of the Hotel Bora Bora, located on the top level of the building that houses the reception, business office, and sundries boutique. Open daily for B.L. D. You can order room service from the same menu as the restaurant serves for breakfast, lunch and dinner, for an additional 20 percent cost.

The Continental breakfast is 3.500 CFP and American breakfast is 4.800 CFP. Your food is brought from the buffet to your table or you can order à la carte, which includes Eggs Benedict with smoked ham or salmon, French toast, waffles or pancakes, as well as miso soup and sashimi with rice and soy sauce.

Luncheon may be light or substantial fare, with appetizers, salads and sandwiches priced from 1.900-2.700 CFP, and the main courses are 2.500-2.900 CFP, plus grilled lobster for 5.500 CFP. Dinner at the Matira Terrace starts with soups from 2.100-2.300 CFP, pasta at 2.700-2.900 CFP, and cold or warm appetizers from 2.400-3.500 CFP. The fish and seafood dishes are 3.700-3.900 CFP, and spiny lobster risotto with Taha'a vanilla is 6.500 CFP. Side dishes include taro purée, sweet potato gratin, creamy polenta, wok vegetables and wild and basmati rice, which should please any vegetarian diner. Meat and poultry choices for 3.600-3.900 CFP include veal tenderloin with eggplant caviar, fried artichoke and thyme jus, and roasted loin of lamb with pomme dauphin, honey-glazed cherry tomatoes and mint sauce. Grilled beef rib for two is 6.800 CFP. The delightful desserts for 1.100-1.600 CFP may tempt you to try a crispy banana and coconut wrapper served with warm chocolate sauce and Ricotta ice cream.

Saturday night is Fisherman's Night at Restaurant Matira, when you can choose your red mullet, parrot fish, surgeonfish or other choices from the buffet and decide how you want it cooked. The price is 7.500 CFP per person, which includes a starter course and dessert.

The wine cellar has the right wine for every dish, with selections from California, Chile, Australia, New Zealand, South Africa, Spain, Italy and France. The Hotel Bora Bora also sells Cuban cigars—the only place on the island where you can still find this special treat.

Pofai Beach Bar. *Open daily for lunch and snacks. Special theme evenings.* This restaurant-bar is located on the white sand beach below the Hotel Bora Bora's main restaurant. Daily from 10am to 6pm you can order sandwiches, salads, *poisson cru*, fruit salads, milkshakes, cold beer or exotic cocktails, and enjoy your lunch while you take a break from sunbathing. Throughout the years, every time I go to Bora Bora, I make it a point to order their mahi mahi burger with fries and drink a draft beer while enjoying the scenery of the hotel grounds, beach and lagoon. Salads are priced from 2.000-2.600 CFP, pizza is 1.800-2.000 CFP, a cheeseburger is 1.900 CFP, and the mahi mahi burger with fries is now 2.100 CFP.

A Barbecue and Show takes place each Wed. evening on Pofai Beach, featuring a buffet of Tahitian specialties and fresh fish on the grill. The cost of 8.500 CFP includes a traditional Polynesian show and fire dancing. Starting at 5:30pm on Fri. evenings at Pofai Beach there is the very special Mamas of Bora Bora song and dance show, along with the spectacular Bora Bora sunset and complimentary canapés. Following this entertainment a dinner of typical Polynesian food is served on the beach, with a starter course, main course, dessert and glass of wine. A Romantic Dinner by candlelight can be served on the beach or in your room any evening except Wed.

INTERCONTINENTAL BORA BORA LE MOANA RESORT, *Tel. 60.49.00. All major credit cards.*

Noa Noa Restaurant and Terrace. *Open daily for breakfast, lunch and dinner.* A Continental breakfast is 2.510 CFP and a full American breakfast is 3.075 CFP. A Canoe breakfast delivered to your overwater bungalow is 6.990 CFP per person. A 3-course set luncheon menu is 4.700 CFP and a 3-course set dinner menu is 6.910 CFP. Light snacks are served on the Vini Vini Bar Terrace for lunch and the *a la carte* dinner menu in the Noa Noa Restaurant lists hot and cold appetizers from 1.920-3.400 CFP, fish and seafood dishes from 3.200-3.400 CFP, meat and poultry selections from 3.100-3.550 CFP, lobster for 6.760 CFP, surf and turf (lobster and beef filet) for 7.200 CFP, and desserts for 1.500-2.000 CFP. A lavish seafood buffet under the stars is served each Sat. evening, during the *Soirée Merveilleuse* (marvelous evening), followed by a Polynesian dance show on the beach. The cost is 8.530 CFP. Special theme evenings include a Tues. night Barbecue Buffet and Polynesian night on Thurs., with traditional foods and local entertainment.

The **Vini Vini Bar** has special cocktails and live music in the bar at sunset and during dinner in the Noa Noa Restaurant.

LE MAITAI POLYNESIA, *Tel. 60.30.00. All major credit cards.*

Haere Mai Restaurant, *in main building of Le Maitai Polynesia.* Open daily for breakfast and dinner.

An American breakfast buffet is served each morning for 2.200 CFP, and a Continental breakfast is 1.800 CFP. A Seafood & Polynesian Specialties Buffet with a Tahitian dance show is presented once a week, on Thurs. or Sat. night, according to number of in-house guests. The dinner menu on other nights features international cuisine with a French touch. Starter courses are 1.100-1.800 CFP, fish is 1.900-2.400 CFP, meats are 2.100-3.300 CFP, and desserts are 1.000 CFP. A 3-course tourist menu is 4.100 CFP.

Tama'a Maitai Restaurant, *on beach at Hotel Le Maitai Polynesia. Open daily with non-stop service from 11:30am to 9pm.*

This is a big open sided restaurant with a thatch roof, situated between the road and beach in the Matira area. The burger bar atmosphere is very casual, with indoor/outdoor seating. Burgers are served on sesame buns and are good, priced 1.400-1.650 CFP, including fries. Pizzas are 1.100-1.400 CFP, sashimi is 1.750, and a Maitai Polynesia salad with raw vegetables, fish and grilled chicken is 1.800 CFP. There are daily specials for around 1.950 CFP. You can also order fresh fruit juices, a glass of beer or house wine, or a bottle of wine.

NOVOTEL BORA BORA BEACH RESORT, *Tel. 60.59.60. All major credit cards. Open daily for B, L. D.*

Restaurant Tiare Anei is a 180-seat restaurant with tables on the terrace beside the beach. It has a good reputation for the food selections. An American breakfast is 1.875 CFP. A set lunch menu is 2.500 CFP, and there is also poisson cru, pizza or pasta for 1.430 CFP. The California plate gives you a choice of a hamburger, smoked turkey sandwich or teriyaki steak and toasted bread for 1.530 CFP. The dinner menu lists starter courses at 1.430-1.740 CFP, fish for 1.840-2.150 CFP, chicken and meats for 1.940-2.350 CFP and desserts for 1.130 CFP. A set dinner menu is 4.236 CFP. There are 3 dinner buffets a week, priced from 5.000-6.000 CFP, and on Mon. and Fri. there is a romantic dinner on the beach. The **V-6 Cocktail Bar** serves exotic cocktails for 1.390 CFP.

SOFITEL BORA BORA BEACH RESORT (ex Sofitel Marara), *Tel. 60.55.00. All major credit cards.*

Latitude 16° is the hotel's main restaurant, serving B., L.,D. in a pleasant decor that was inspired by tribal tattoos, with ironworks representing the local fishermen's nets. You can also dine on the terrace overlooking the lagoon. An American breakfast is 2.901 CFP and the set lunch menu is 3.148 CFP. For lunch you can also order burgers for 1.430-1.740 CFP, grilled mahi mahi for 2.350 CFP or filet of beef for 2.540 CFP. Starter courses on the dinner menu are 1.480-2.540 CFP, main course choices are 2.710-2.810 CFP, and surf & turf is 3.050 CFP. The set dinner menu is 5.803 CFP. A World and French buffet is served on Mon. evenings for 6.970 CFP; a Sea and Pacific buffet is held on Wed. for 7.680 CFP; and a Polynesian buffet is the big event for Fri. evening, for 6.970 CFP.

Wakaba Japanese Teppanyaki is open 6:30-9:30pm Thurs.-Mon. only. Gleaming stainless steel, natural wood and stone are combined in this ultra-stylish modern setting that features a menu of fresh sushi, teppanyaki and other Japanese specialties. Sushi selections are 1.400-2.700 CFP, beignets are 1.200-2.150 CFP and teppanyaki is 3.900-5.500 CFP. Desserts are 1.100-1.450 CFP. Should guests catch any fish during their excursions, the chefs can prepare their bounty as sushi or traditional Polynesian dishes.

Le Snack offers a menu of healthy salads, burgers or fresh sandwiches for a casual meal served to you beside the pool.

Hurricane Bar was named for the famous Dino De Laurentiis movie filmed in Bora Bora in the mid-1970s. The bar is inlaid with red and silver mosaic tiles and sparkling mirrored lights to complement the red-cushioned chairs. Live entertainment includes Polynesian shows on Wed., Fri., and Sat.

CLUB MEDITERANNEE, *Tel. 60.46.04. Open daily for B., L., D. All major credit cards.*

Even if you are not staying at Club Med you can go for a bountiful meal. The breakfast buffet costs 3.000 CFP; lunch is 5.000 CFP and dinner is 6.100 CFP, except for the Fri. night seafood buffet, which is 7.100 CFP. Beer and wine are included. A day pass for 5.000 CFP includes lunch and use of the Club's facilities from 11:30am-6:30 p.m. Each Thurs. and Sun. night is Polynesian night, featuring traditional Tahitian foods cooked in an underground oven and a Tahitian dance show. A nightly show is presented by the Club Med staff except when there is a Tahitian dance show. Starting at 9:30pm outsiders can attend the shows and spend an evening dancing without eating when you buy an entrance coupon for 1.500 CFP, which includes a free drink. After that you pay cash at the bar.

Hotel Restaurants on the Motu
  ST REGIS RESORT & SPA, *Tel. 60.78.88. All major credit cards.*
  Te Pahu is the Mediterranean Grill beside the beach with all-day dining for B., L., D. Closed Thurs. night. The young French wait staff provide very attentive service. You can choose a Continental breakfast for 3.000 CFP, a Healthy breakfast for 4.000 CFP or an American breakfast for 6.000 CFP, plus 4.000 CFP if you want to add a half-bottle of champagne. Or you can order à la carte. Luncheon choices of salads, antipasti, sandwiches, risotto and pasta are 2.500-3.300 CFP, grilled lagoon fish is 3.900 CFP and grilled meats are 3.900-6.600 CFP. The dinner menu has fish dishes for 4.000-4.300 CFP, and meats and chicken choices for 4.100-6.600 CFP. A 5-course tasting menu is 12.000 CFP per person. Tuesday is grilled fish night. Specialties here are the Citrus Shrimp Ceviche and Kobe Sirloin.

  Lagoon is the signature restaurant of the internationally acclaimed Chef Jean-Georges Vongerichten. This overwater restaurant features a limited but frequently changing menu of French- and Asian- influenced cuisine, using the freshest fish and ingredients indigenous to the islands. Try the bacon-wrapped shrimp with passion fruit mustard or the spiced chicken with coconut-caramel sauce and citrus salad. Appetizers and salads are 2.200-3.900 CFP and the main courses are 4.000-7.000 CFP, with desserts at 2.000 CFP. The wine cellar contains an awarded selection of fine wines spanning the old and new world. Open for dinner only.

  Sushi Take is the sushi and sake restaurant at St. Regis. Salads are 900-1.500 CFP, sashimi is 3.500-4.000 CFP and sushi is 2.500-4.000. A Sushi Take combo of seaweed salad, sashimi and sushi is 8.600 CFP.

  Aparima Pool Bar & Grill serves snacks and drinks throughout the day, and some guests take all their meals here. The **Lagoon Bar**, built over the water adjacent to Lagoon Restaurant, is a favorite destination for sunset cocktails. Try the Ginger Margarita or Pomelo-Mint Mojito and you'll surely want another one.

  BORA BORA NUI RESORT & SPA, *Tel. 60.33.00. All major credit cards.*
  Tamure Grill is a big open sided restaurant with a thatched roof and a floor of white sand, located next to the swimming pool and white sand beach. The luncheon menu includes burgers for 2.000 CFP, salads, pasta and sashimi for 1.500-2.300 CFP, and pizza from 1.900 CFP. Tamure Snacks are also available at the **Ta'ie'ie Beach Bar**, which is at one end of the Tamure Grill. The Tamure grill is also open nightly for dinner. The main courses are 2.900-5.850 CFP, and the chef's specialties include Thai style shrimp for 2.700 CFP. The Manager's Cocktail Party is held each Tues. and Fri. evening, followed by a Tahitian traditional feast and seafood buffet for 8.500 CFP on Tues. and a beach barbecue buffet for 5.500 CFP on Friday. Entertainment is provided by a Polynesian dance group.

  Iriatai is a panoramic restaurant on the upper level of the central building. Dinner is served here nightly except Tues. and Fri., when there are special theme evenings being held in the Tamure Grill. The Iriatai features a fusion menu with Polynesian, Pacific-Rim and Mediterranean influences. Starter courses are 1.400-

3.000, fish and seafood dishes are 2.500-4.800 CFP, and meats are 2.900-3.900 CFP. Desserts are 1.200 CFP each, and a dessert sampler for two is 2.500 CFP. You can order wines from Napa Valley, California, New Zealand, Australia, South Africa, Chile, Italy, and all the wine producing regions of France. In addition to an impressive list of Grands Crus from Bordeaux, there is also a good selection of French champagnes available.

A pianist plays popular tunes in the **Upa Upa Bar** adjacent to the Iriatai to enhance the romantic atmosphere.

INTERCONTINENTAL BORA BORA RESORT & THALASSO SPA, *Tel. 60.76.00. All major credit cards.*

Le Reef Restaurant & Terrace. Open daily for breakfast and dinner. You can dine in a/c comfort or sit outside on the patio that overlooks the white sand beach and lagoon. A Continental breakfast is 2.510 CFP and an American breakfast is 3.075 CFP. A 3-course set dinner menu is 6.910 CFP. The MAP rate is 9.690 CFP and AP is 13.000 CFP. The Polynesian dinner and show on Mon. night is 6.910 CFP, and the Island World Tour Dinner with show on Fri. is 8.530 CFP.

Sand's Bar & Restaurant is built beside the resort's private 1,000 ft. of white sand beach, providing the perfect rendezvous for light meals between 11am-9:30pm, as well as snacks and exotic cocktails. A 3-course luncheon menu is 4.700 CFP.

Bubble's Bar & Terrace is the ultra trendy bar designed all in white for the resort's Japanese tourists. There's music every night but very few people. Drinks, exotic cocktails and light snacks are served from 10am-11pm.

BORA BORA LAGOON RESORT & SPA, *Tel. 60.40.00. All major credit cards.*

Otemanu Restaurant. Open daily for breakfast and dinner. Proper attire is necessary. This 92-seat gourmet restaurant is on Motu Toopua, facing the main island of Bora Bora and its famous mountain peaks. You can also dine on the terrace. The breakfast buffet is 3.103 CFP and the set dinner menu is 7.876 CFP. Their Gastronomic Flavors of the World menu offers cold starters for 1.920-2.330 CFP (including fresh tofu and vegetables and herbs) and hot starters at 1.920-3.030, (with crab ravioli and spinach sprouts). Sea foods are 2.930-3.940 CFP and the meat dishes are 3.030-3.940 CFP. The Mediterranean Flavors menu has starters from 1.320-2.030 CFP, fish for 2.430 CFP and meats for 1.830-3.640 CFP. A Tahitian dinner buffet is presented on Thurs. evenings and costs 9.188 CFP per person. There is also a weekly Seafood Buffet.

Café Fare. Open daily for lunch and dinner. This restaurant offers informal indoor/outdoor dining with Mediterranean cuisine, serving from an open-air kitchen with service poolside. The luncheon menu suggests appetizers for 1.615-2.015 CFP, including red tuna tartar, poisson cru and shrimp cocktail served in an avocado. Salads are 1.615-2.515 CFP; pizzas and pasta dishes are 1.615-2.020; and the main courses are 1.615-2.220 CFP. These include a Club sandwich, burgers, panini, grilled fish and meats, or marinated pork ribs with barbecue sauce.

You can order your favorite libation from the **Rotopa Bar**, which is conveniently located between the pool and both beaches. The **Hiro Lounge** seats 50 and is open from 6-11pm. You can sit in a very high chair of wood and leather at the handcrafted wooden bar, relax in a big comfortable masculine chair, or enjoy the fresh breezes on the terrace while sipping your favorite libation. The Manager's Cocktail Reception takes place here each Monday evening, along with a fashion show of pearl jewelry.

HOTEL SOFITEL MOTU, *Tel. 60.56.00. All major credit cards.*

Manu Tiki Restaurant. Open daily for B., L., D. for guests staying at Hotel Sofitel Motu, and open for dinner only to outside guests who must reserve in advance. This restaurant is built on stilts on the hilltop of a *motu*, granting spectacular views of Bora Bora and its famous lagoon and mountains. An American breakfast is 2.901 CFP, the set luncheon menu is 3.148 CFP, and the set dinner menu is 6.729 CFP. The cuisine is French with a Polynesian accent and has earned a good reputation for quality. This cave has one of the most extensive wine lists in the region.

HOTEL LE MERIDIEN BORA BORA, *Tel. 60.51.51. All major credit cards.*

Le Tipanie Restaurant. Open daily for breakfast and dinner.

An American Breakfast Buffet is 2.857 CFP. You can feed the fish in the interior lagoon while dining in this 180-seat restaurant, where you can choose your favorite dishes from the buffet tables. A French buffet is served on Mon., a Pacific buffet is presented each Tues., followed by a Polynesian dance show, a Barbecue buffet is featured on Wed., an Asian buffet is the theme for Thurs., a Fisherman's buffet on Fri. night is followed by a Polynesian dance show, a Latino buffet is featured on Sat. evenings, and a Mediterranean buffet is served on Sun. Each buffet dinner is 6.716 CFP and there is live entertainment every night.

An à la carte menu is also available each evening in the Honu (turtle) section of Le Tipanie Restaurant, where you can watch the sea turtles and lagoon fish swimming in the lagoon just below your table. You must reserve in advance to dine here. Starter courses are priced from 2.200-3.600 CFP; fish and seafood dishes are 2.900-5.600 CFP; and meat and poultry choices are 2.900-4.500 CFP. The gourmet menu changes frequently and always includes some interesting vegetarian dishes for 2.500-3.000 CFP. Desserts for 1.300-1.500 CFP include the traditional crème brûlée served with a lime biscuit and strawberry sorbet; caramelized pineapple with a coconut biscuit and thyme sorbet, and a plate of Valrhona chocolate. Special menus include the 3-course Fenua Iti for 6.716 CFP, the 4-course Motu Tape for 8.000 CFP, and the 5-course Otemanu for 10.000 CFP. To accompany these delicacies you can order from an interesting list of wines from France, Chile, Australia and California.

Te Ava Restaurant, *open daily 11:30am-3pm.*

Le Méridien's 120-seat beachside restaurant Te Ava is adjacent to the fresh water swimming pool. In this relaxing atmosphere you can sit in a rocking chair and dig your toes into the white sand floor while enjoying your lunch. Salads, sandwiches, burgers, pasta, and pizzas (1.400-2.300 CFP) are supplemented by grilled meats and seafood (2.200-2.900 CFP). Desserts include a banana split or brownie for 1.200 CFP. Draft beer and wine by the glass or bottle are available.

The **Miki Miki Bar** at Le Méridien is shaped like the prow of a ship, pointing toward Mt. Otemanu. Open from 3-11pm, this is a good setting for sunset and cocktails. The **Fare Tupa** beach bar serves a "Tupa" breakfast from 10am-12pm and snacks from 10am-5pm.

BORA BORA PEARL BEACH RESORT, *Tel. 60.52.00. All major credit cards.*

Tevairoa Restaurant is the hotel's main dining room, which sits 20 ft. (6 m) above sea level and overlooks the myriad hues of the blues and greens of the Bora Bora lagoon. It is open for breakfast and dinner, serving a refined international menu. An American breakfast buffet is 3.000 CFP. International dining with a French flair is featured for dinner, with starter courses at 1.500-3.200 CFP, pasta for 2.100-2.700 CFP, fish choices for 3.200-3.800 CFP, and meats for 2.900-4.300. Grilled lobster is 6.900 CFP. A set dinner menu is 6.500 CFP. A Polynesian buffet and dance show is presented each Mon. evening for 6.900 CFP, and a seafood buffet and dance show is held on Fri. for 7.500 CFP.

Miki Miki Restaurant and Bar is located beside the swimming pool, and is open daily for lunch. This is a great place to hang out during a hot tropical day, sipping cold Hinano pression beer and munching on cheeseburgers, club sandwiches, poisson cru, fish and chips, or grilled sirloin steak. Most of the guests sitting at the friendly bar or at the tables on the terrace are American honeymooners or young French families with children. The atmosphere here is very casual. Salads and snacks are 950-2.300 CFP and a set luncheon menu is 3.700 CFP.

Fare Ambrosia, behind the Miki Miki Restaurant, features Italian specialties from 1.800-4.000 CFP and is open nightly except Mon. & Fri. Open for dinner only and reservations are required.

Taurearea Bar upstairs is open daily 3:30-11pm, providing the perfect setting to admire the sunset as you gaze at the peaks of Otemanu and Pahia mountains. Happy Hour is held from 5:30-6:30pm, featuring Polynesian cocktails at half-price. Live music in the evenings.

Private Restaurants on the Main Island – Deluxe
LA VILLA MAHANA, *Tel./Fax 67.50.63; damien@villamahana.com; www.villamahana.com. On the mountainside between Vaitape village and the Hotel Bora Bora. Open 7 days a week for dinner only. Free pick-up service. Reserve by email 2-3 months in advance. AE, MC, V.*

A young Corsican chef de cuisine named Damien Rinaldi Dovio opened this gastronomic restaurant in April 2004 and it became an immediate success. Residents and tourists alike must reserve months in advance during the high seasons, and when they leave the restaurant in a dreamy state of contentment, their comments in the guest book and by word of mouth are full of praise. This is indeed a unique experience that you do not want to miss when you visit Bora Bora, because people say that Damien, who studied at the prestigious Institut Paul Bocuse in Lyon, France, served them the best meal they have ever eaten.

There are six small tables on the courtyard patio or inside the restaurant during rainy weather. This area resembles a scene from the Mediterranean, with Bora Bora artist Garrick Yrondi's bright, colorful paintings and sculptures decorating the walls and garden. Another table for private dining is upstairs over the restaurant in the Tahitian room, which also has a couch. There's a small reflecting pool on the terrace. Damien will close the restaurant for private parties of up to 12 people.

Damien comes out of his kitchen to greet his guests, with a special smile for young honeymooners who dined here just a few nights ago. The barefoot Tahitian waitress serves their bottle of chilled champagne and Zampanetta, the black and white house cat, makes her rounds in search of handouts.

The gourmet menu features light cuisine influenced by Damien's origins, combined with Polynesian products and associated with the use of spices to magnify the flavors. He suggests several tempting menus starting at 39 Euros (4.654 CFP), but his piece de resistance is the Menu Royal, which is very popular with tourists, even though it costs 125 Euros (14.916 CFP) per person. You start with a light salad of shellfish and caviar on toast, followed by fried foie gras with sweet spices, served with green asparagus. The next course is king rock lobster with exotic flavors, followed by filet of beef tenderloin cooked in red wine and vanilla sauce, served with gnocchi. Dessert for this feast is chocolate souffle with a creamy chocolate sauce and petits fours.

Damien also proposes a wine tasting menu to accompany his special menus. His impressive wine list includes Cristal and Dom Perignon Rosé champagnes. Starting your evening with a glass of champagne seems a most fitting touch in this ambience of intimate hospitality.

Superior
LE MATIRA BEACH RESTAURANT, *Tel. 67.53.79. Beside the white sand beach between the Hotel Bora Bora and Point Matira. Open for lunch and dinner daily except Thurs. MC, V. Free pick-up for dinner.*

Lunch can be served on the beach, where your table is shaded by a big umbrella. Dinner is served in the dining room overlooking the sunset sea and sky. There's nothing fancy about the decor here, but the cuisine is billed as a fusion of gastronomic French, Polynesian and Chinese. Most of the hotel activities people push this restaurant, but I found it a bit disappointing. Appetizers begin at 1.800 CFP with a terrine of artichokes and smoked salad, and continue up to 2.950 CFP for pan fried foie gras, gingerbread and green apple vinaigrette. Meats and poultry are 2.900-3.300 CFP, and fish and shellfish dishes are 3.100-5.100 CFP. Desserts are 1.300 CFP, offering such delicacies as Tiare Crème Brûlée and a Cinnamon Biscuit sorbet.

SAINT JAMES RESTAURANT, *Tel. 67.64.62, www.stjamesborabora.com. On waterfront in Helen's Bay Center. Open for lunch and dinner Mon.-Sat. Closed Sun. AE, MC, V. Free pick-up for dinner. Reserve.*

This restaurant opened in Sept. 2007 in the building that was formerly La Pirate, and quickly became one of the most popular dining spots on the island. The French owners have remodeled and redecorated, placing tables and chairs beside the bay where guests can watch the magnificent Bora Bora sunsets as well as the manta rays that come to play in the evenings. Light lunches are served and the dinner menu lists appetizers from 1.100-2.000 CFP, plus homemade foie gras for 2.900 CFP. The main courses are 2.700-5.600 CFP, which consist of fresh local products prepared French style. Desserts are around 1.300 CFP and there is a good wine list. There are 2 moorings for boats in front of the restaurant.

BLOODY MARY'S, *Tel. 67.72.86. On the mountainside in Pofai Bay, 5 km (3 mi.) from Vaitape and 1 km (.62 mi.) from the Hotel Bora Bora. Open for lunch and dinner Mon.-Sat. and on boat days. Bar open 9:30am-11pm. Closed Sun. AE, MC and V. Free dinner transportation is provided from select locations.*

Most American visitors feel they haven't seen Bora Bora unless they have been to this world famous restaurant and bar. A long list of celebrities who have dined at Bloody Mary's is posted beside the road, adding to the legend that began when the restaurant opened in June 1980. This is the kind of funky and fun place where people get to know one another very easily. You can't be too reserved while you are sitting on a tree stump at the bar under a huge thatched roof or wiggling your toes in the white sand floor while eating your dinner. Be sure to check out the surprise in the men's room that keeps most of the young clients in giggles throughout the evening.

Appetizers start at 1.250 CFP, and include grilled shrimp, garlic crab, charred peppered sashimi, teriyaki fish kabob, and the house specialty, a very tender calamari steak that is breaded and sautéed in capers and white wine for 1.400 CFP. Choices of fresh lagoon or deep ocean fish are priced from 2.700-3.200 CFP. Fresh local lobster is 6.500 CFP. New Zealand beef may be rib eye steak, New York steak or babyback ribs, for 3.000 CFP. You can also order grilled chicken or a vegetarian plate. The main courses are accompanied by green salad, white rice, hot vegetables and fresh fruit. The dessert menu is also very tempting.

Lunch is served between 11am and 3pm, which includes salads, great burgers, chicken quesadillas, and deep fried shrimp and fish with chips. The house's special drink is the famous Bloody Mary for 600 CFP. They also serve cold draft Hinano, a good choice of wines, and an excellent frozen Margarita or Bloody Mary's Maitai.

RESTAURANT FARE MANUIA, *Tel. 67.68.08/72.52.84. On the lagoon side, just past the turnoff at Point Matira. Open daily for B,L,D. MC, V. Free pick-up for dinner.*

This attractive little Polynesian style restaurant serves gastronomic French cuisine and fresh island specialties. Their Continental breakfast is 1.600 CFP, snacks or burgers with fries are 1.400-1.900 CFP, and salads are 1.200-1.800 CFP.

Their starter courses are 1.200-3.200 CFP, the fish dishes start at 1.800 CFP, and meat choices are 1.900-3.900 CFP, including a grilled prime cut of beef with shallots for 2.600 CFP. A 3-course menu is 3.900 CFP. Try their famous Mouelleux, a warm chocolate cup cake. They have a good wine list and they also feature a daily cocktail for 1.000 CFP.

Moderate to Superior

SUNSET BOULEVARD, *Tel. 67.57.67/70.43.77; www.enjoybora.com. At Ellacott Marina in Tiipoto. AE, MC, V. Reserve for dinner and sunset cruises.*

Sandy Ellacott has a floating *fare* called *Lady Bora* that he uses to take 8-15 VIP guests from the hotels on sunset cruises. He has also opened a restaurant at his family's marina base, and he now combines sunset cruises with serving sushi, barbecue, Latino food, local dishes and other tasty meals. A complete meal at the marina will cost about 6.000 CFP per person, and a cruise and dinner is 12.000 CFP.

KAINA HUT, *Tel. 67.54.06, is on the mountainside in Pofai Bay. Open for dinner nightly except Tuesdays. Closed for lunch. All credit cards.*

A big thatch roof covers this open-sided Polynesian style restaurant that has a sandy floor, coconut wood furniture, pretty shell chandeliers and lots of plants and flowers. The signature dish here is crispy breadfruit gnocchis for 1.400 CFP. Starters and salads are 1.400-1.900 CFP, including homemade sushi. Meats include braised pork ribs and roasted loin of veal. Bouillabaisse is 3.200 CFP and a seafood platter is 3.900 CFP. Desserts are 1.000-1.400 CFP.

LE PANDA D'OR, *Tel. 67.62.70. On mountainside in Vaitape village. Open for lunch and dinner. Closed Sun. MC, V.*

The Golden Panda serves so-so Polynesian Cantonese food in its 200-seat a/c restaurant and also does a good take-out business. Their extensive menu includes breaded fried shrimp, cuttlefish, Coquille St. Jacques, and seasonal delicacies such as sweet and sour crab, and shrimp and lobster sautéed with broccoli.

Moderate

LA BOUNTY, *Tel. 67.70.43, on mountainside in Matira, close to Hotel Maitai Polynesia. Open for lunch and dinner. Closed Mon. MC and V.*

This restaurant has a good location and reputation. The menu includes pizzas for 1.150-1.650 CFP, and fish and meats cooked on "pierrade" stones. Their specialty is beef fondue starting at 3.000 CFP.

Economy

BEN'S, *Tel. 67.74.54. On mountainside in Matira, between Hotel Bora Bora and Point Matira. Open daily 8am-5pm. No credit cards.*

Ben Teraitepo, from Bora Bora, and his American wife, Robin, gave up their busy life in Southern California to settle in Bora Bora in 1987. They cook and serve home-style meals on their terrace across the road from the white sandy beach. Their menu includes American breakfasts for 1.195 CFP, pizzas from 1.000-1.700 CFP, spaghetti with different types of sauces for 1.300 CFP, and lasagna for 1.100 CFP, as well as Tex-Mex food, hot dogs, cheeseburgers and submarine sandwiches.

SNACK MATIRA, *Tel. 67.77.32, is beside the lagoon at Matira Beach, across the road from Ben's. Open 10am to 4pm. Closed Mon. No credit cards.* This simple 100-place beach snack serves sandwiches on baguette bread for 350-1.100 CFP, burgers for 600-850 CFP, *poisson cru* for 900-1.400 CFP, and pizza for 1.500 CFP. Beer and wine are served with food only.

ALOE CAFÉ, *Tel. 67.78.88. In Pahia Center in Vaitape village. Open 6am-9:30pm Mon.-Sat. Closed Sun. No credit cards.*

This cybercafé and pastry shop was formerly l'Appetisserie. They serve crêpes for 600-1.000 CFP, paninis, burgers, salads, lasagne, and lamb curry, and their daily special is 1.650 CFP. (See information under Cybercafé-Internet Service).

BORA BORA BURGER. *Adjacent to the post office in Vaitape. Open Mon.-Fri. 8am-5pm and on ship days. No credit cards.*

This sidewalk snack is conveniently located near the Vaitape boat dock. A hamburger is 670 CFP and fries are 400 CFP. A soft drink is 250 CFP and a Hinano beer is 400 CFP.

CAFÉ NOA NOA is a new fast food snack in Vaitape village, serving Mexican food and burgers. Owner Dino Dexter is a handsome young man from Bora Bora who was the first Mister Tahiti in 2001. He also won second runner-up in the Mister France 2002 competitions. He also owns Dino's Island Tours & Cab.

SNACKS AND ROULOTTES. Crêpes, burgers, pizzas, roast chicken and take-out Tahitian-Chinese dishes are available at small stands in Vaitape and the Matira Beach area. At least four *roulottes* (mobile diners) set up shop in Vaitape village at night, where you can enjoy a full meal for around 1.200 CFP. They all serve steak and fries, *brochettes* (kebabs), barbecued chicken legs, *poisson cru* and grilled fish. Roulotte Matira, across the road from the Intercontinental Le Moana Resort, is noted for its chicken Tandoori and other good food.

SEEING THE SIGHTS

To explore Bora Bora by car or bicycle, start at the Vaitape boat dock, if you head south around the island. All along the water's edge of Pofai (or Povai) Bay you will see spectacular views of the **Otemanu Mountain**. Beside the lagoon at the edge of the town center of Vaitape you will see a two-story white building that houses the Robert Wan Tahiti Perles boutique. Along the edge of Pofai Bay you will see Moon B&B just before coming to Alain and Linda's Art Gallery on the right. There are usually gaily-painted *pareos* hanging on a line in front of the boutique. Across the road from the nearby soccer field and gymnasium is a path that leads over the island to the village of Anau. The interior roads can only be traversed by mountain bike or on foot.

If you stay on the **circle island road** you'll see the Kaina Hut Restaurant, Tahiti Pearl Market, Mom's Boutique, Villa Mahana, Bloody Mary's Restaurant and The

Farm of Bora Pearl Company. Look to the right across the bay toward the point of Motu Toopua Iti and you will see some of the overwater bungalows at the Bora Bora Nui Resort & Spa. Continuing south on the main road, at Raititi Point, you will pass the entrance to the highly acclaimed Hotel Bora Bora.

Go past Bora Diving Center, Bora Bora Gallery and Alain Despert's gallery and you'll see the Matira Beach Restaurant beside the lagoon. When the American Armed Forces were stationed on Bora Bora during World War II they installed a battery of coastal defense guns on the hillside. You can reach them in just a 10-min. hike up a walking trail east of the restaurant. Ben's Place serves American food on the mountainside and Snack Matira serves local style dishes beside the lagoon. A sign indicates the turnoff at Point Matira, where you can visit the Bora Bora Intercontinental Le Moana Resort and the Hotel Matira and have a swim at Matira Beach. Chez Nono has a pension right on the white sand beach and Chez Robert & Tina have 3 rental houses right at the tip of Point Matira. Back on the main road, you'll see Chez Maeva Masson and the Fare Manuia Restaurant on the right, next to Village Temanuata. Matira Pearls is across the road.

Heading along the east coast of Matira, Le Maitai Polynesia hotel is on both sides of the road, with beach, mountain and overwater bungalows. Keana Art & Fashion, La Bounty Restaurant, Tiare Market, Nemo World dive shop, Novotel, Sofitel Bora Bora Beach Resort, and Snack Patoti (now closed) are all located on either side of this short stretch of road. Out on the motu in front of the Sofitel Bora Bora Beach Resort is the deluxe Sofitel Motu Bora Bora, a haven for honeymooners.

A steep hill leads you behind the Club Med Coral Garden Village at **Faaopore Bay**, just before Paoaoa Point. You can visit a lookout point on a ridge above the bay by taking Club Med's private tunnel under the road or by walking up the steps just beyond the Boutique Hibiscus. A trail to the right of the hill will take you down to Marae Aehautai, where you will have a good view of Otemanu Mountain and the islands of Taha'a and Raiatea beyond the reef. Other *marae* are also located in this vicinity, as well as coastal guns from World War II. Shortly after Club Med you will come to Chez Teipo and Pension Bora Lagoonarium, both on the lagoon side.

The road continues on to **Anau village**, which has some very modest homes sitting on rather marshy land with lots of land crab holes. Beside the lagoon are the land bases for the deluxe hotel resorts built on the motu islets facing the village. These are the Intercontinental Thalasso Resort & Spa, Le Méridien and the St. Regis Resort & Spa. The Lagoonarium is built on a motu between Le Méridien and St. Regis, and just past the St. Regis is the Four Seasons hotel that will open in June 2008. After passing a few houses on the road beyond Fitiiu Point, you'll come to Taimoo Bay. For the next few miles the only thing you will see are scattered houses, coconut plantations and *tupa* land crabs, until you come to the *Musée de la Mer*, the Marine Museum, which has replicas of famous ships that have visited Tahiti and Bora Bora.

Just before Point Taihi you'll see a steep track that leads up to a World War II radar station on top of Popoti Ridge. Across the lagoon you can see the Bora Bora airport on Motu Mute. Continuing on the circle island road you'll pass the Bora Bora Condos, which consist of 4 overwater bungalows and 11 mountainside apartments on stilts. Marlon Brando's estate owns 2 overwater bungalows and 1 on the mountainside. These condos are rented to visitors who wish to spend a week or more on the island.

At Tereia Point in **Faanui Bay** you'll see an old shipping wharf and a seaplane ramp that were built by the American Seabees during the war. Another US coastal gun is located on the hill above the concrete water tank, and right after the former submarine base is the Marae Fare-Opu, between the road and the bay. The stones of the temple are engraved with turtle petroglyphs. A road beside the Protestant church at the head of the bay runs inland, narrowing into an unmarked track that you can follow with a guide over the saddle of the ridge top to Bora Bora's east coast of Vairau Bay, south of Fitiiu Point.

On the western end of Faanui Bay is the main shipping wharf, where inter-island ferries and cargo vessels from Tahiti dock. This wharf was also built during the war. Just 100 m. west of the quay is the Marae Marotetini, a coastal *marae* that was restored by Dr. Yosihiko Sinoto in 1968. This was a royal temple and members of Bora Bora's chiefly families are buried nearby.

Around the bend from the Faanui boat dock is the Bora Bora Yacht Club, which was reopened in 2007, along with Le Manta restaurant. They are both closed now. On the hillside facing the island's only pass are 2 defense guns left over from the war. The Safari Tour excursions will take you to visit these guns. On 2 *motu* islets across the lagoon you will see the Bora Bora Pearl Beach Resort and the Bora Bora Lagoon Resort, as well as Motu Tapu, which is now the private domain of the Bora Bora Nui Resort & Spa. This little *motu* is famous for its white sand beach and is located just beside the Teavanui Pass, the only navigable entrance through the protective necklace of coral reef surrounding the island.

On the seaside just before you reach Vaitape village you will see the Topdive Center, all that remains of the Bora Bora Dive Resort and the gourmet Topdive or Kon Tiki restaurant. The hotel and restaurant are now closed.

You will also find a good little *patisserie* in the Centre Commercial Le Pahia, or you can shop at Magasin Chin Lee, which is truly an establishment of village life in Bora Bora. In addition to cold juices and drinks you can choose a *casse-croûte,* sandwich, Tahitian and Chinese pastries or a take-away container of good hot food—usually rice and fish, chicken or meat. Royal Helen's Bay is another small shopping center beside the lagoon in Vaitape.

To end your do-it-yourself tour around the island, spend a little time in Vaitape village and you will be able to observe the daily drama of life on a small island. You'll discover that Bora Bora is not just a tourist island, but the residents have their own private interests, as well as looking after visitors from all over the world. You may see the children bursting from the confines of their schoolrooms into the Bora Bora sunshine. Their parents or big brother or sister, auntie or grandmother may be waiting for the little ones in the car or on a scooter parked in the shade of a flamboyant tree.

Have a look at the fruits and vegetables the vendors have carefully placed on small tables beside the road. Take a picture of the brightly colored lagoon fish strung on a line that the fisherman and his family are selling. Watch the adolescent boys playing basketball on the court beside the road and enjoy the flirting that goes on between them and the young *vahines*. Walk down to the *mairie* (town hall) and you'll see the stately Polynesians coming and going, taking care of business that involves division of their land, or the marriages, births and deaths of family members. At the post office you'll see local residents standing in line to pay their telephone bills or mail a letter. Even if they're in a hurry to check their mailboxes, they always have time to greet a friend with kisses on both cheeks, and to share a bit of gossip, a joke and a laugh.

Then go to the arts and crafts center beside the wharf, which is adjacent to the Bora Bora Tourist Information Center. While you're looking at the hand painted *pareos* and dresses, the shell necklaces and woven hats, be sure to exchange smiles with the "mama" who spends all day here, waiting to make a sale. Just lifting your eyebrows is a form of greeting and you'll be happy with the response when you see her eyes light up with friendly warmth. This is Bora Bora at its best.

Circle Island Tours

To fully appreciate the history and beauty of Bora Bora, climb aboard an excursion bus or *le truck* and settle back to listen, learn and enjoy as the English-speaking guide tells all about this little island and its colorful past, exciting present and plans for tomorrow. While passing through the little villages on the 29-km. (18-mi.) circuit, you will see humble homes or modern concrete villas surrounded by pretty flower gardens, small snack stands and little boutiques selling *pareos* and shells.

The *marae* temples, where Polynesians used to worship in pre-Christian days, are pointed out, along with the Quonset huts, naval base and heavy artillery guns, left behind by the 5,000 American soldiers, sailors and Seabees who made a "friendly invasion" of Bora Bora during World War II, who also left many blue-eyed children. If you book through your hotel activity desk you will pay 3.000-6.000 CFP for a circle island tour by a/c van and more for private tours.

Circle island tours, as well as taxi and transfer service is provided by the following companies:

Bora Bora Tours, *Tel. 67.70.31; E-mail boraboratours@mail.pf; www.boraboratours.com.* Their 2-hr. excursions operate from several hotels. Transfers from hotel to hotel for site inspection start at 2.800 CFP per hour.

Otemanu Tours, *Tel. 67.70.49; otemanu.tours@mail.pf;* provides a circle island tour daily, using a/c vans or *le truck* to show you the island. If you are on a ship or yacht they will pick you up on the dock in front of your tender at 10am and 2pm.

Dino's Island Tours & Cab, *Tel. 79.29.65; Fax 689/67.57.40*; *dexterdino@yahoo.fr.* Dino Dexter charges 2.500 CFP for a regular tour around the island in his a/c van. A private tour is 6.000 CFP for the fist hour and 4.000 CFP for the second hour.

Simplet Taxi, *Tel. 79.19.31/73.85.72; kayhaut@yahoo.fr,* is operated by Matahi "Simplet" Tefana, who worked as guest relations manager for Sofitel Marara for years until he retired. You will enjoy his comical comments and anecdotes as he drives you around the island in his a/c van. A private tour is 6.000 CFP.

Charley Taxi, Tel. 67.64.37/78.27.71.

Jacques Isnard, Tel. 67.72.25.

Mountain Safari 4x4 Excursions

Viewing Bora Bora's majestic beauty takes on new dimensions when you bounce up and down the rutted mountain trails in a Land Rover or Jeep on a photographic safari excursion. Your guide will tell you the story of the American military base that was established in Bora Bora during World War II and you'll visit the gun emplacements and radar station on Popoti Ridge. At the end of the trail you walk uphill through the bush, where you are rewarded with a 360° panoramic vista of an ancient volcano crater, the lagoon and coral reefs around Bora Bora and the neighboring islands. These include Taha'a, Raiatea, Huahine, Maupiti and the atoll of Tupai, which are all clearly visible from this height. These tours also circle the island, where your guide points out the *marae* stone temples used by the ancient Polynesians, and the war relics used by the Americans. These are very interesting and scenic tours, but are not for the faint-hearted, pregnant or lazily inclined tourist. When you book through the hotel activity desks you will be charged 7.400-8.500 CFP for this tour.

Tupuna Mountain Expeditions, *Tel. 67.75.06; tupuna.bora@mail.pf; www.safaribora.com.* Owner Dany Leverd has several 4-wheel drive (4x4) vehicles and good guides. This half-day morning or afternoon tour costs 6.500 CFP and includes a visit to Bora Bora's only cultured pearl farm, owned by Dany and his wife.

Vavau 4x4 Adventures, *Tel. 72.01.21*, is operated by Heirama Fearon, whose American father, Steve, Fearon, owns Matira Pearls. Heirama and his English-speaking guides will take you on a historical and cultural tour by a/c Landrovers. Their off-road adventures include a visit to a fish farm, where you will learn about the effect these tropical fish have on Bora Bora's fragile ecosystem. Call direct for rates.

Patrick's Activities/Maohi Nui Private Excursions, *Tel. 67.69.94/79.19.11; patrick.bora@mail.pf; www.boraboraisland.com.* Patrick Tairua is your driver and guide during a private 4WD safari excursion by Land Rover Defender to let you discover the "back-country" of Bora Bora. Security belts are installed in the back for every passenger and a white cover protects you from the sun and rain. Raincoats are available if needed. Patrick speaks very good English and will give you details on the geological formation of Bora Bora, the history of the religious sites and information on the American presence on the island during World War II. He leads an easy 20-min. walk into the forest to reach a site where you can see an old turtle petroglyph carved in a basaltic boulder. Along the way you can learn about the tropical plants growing here. Mineral water is provided during the tour. Patrick's half-day safari tour is 37.000 CFP for 1-4 people and 45.000 CFP for 5-8 passengers. You can also combine a 4WD safari tour with a tour of the lagoon by outrigger canoe, starting at 92.000 CFP for 2-4 people. See information under *Private Lagoon Excursions and Picnics on the Motu* and *Wedding Ceremonies.*

Jungle Bike, ATV, Quad Mountain Tours

Most of the hotel activity desks can arrange guided excursions in the mountains with a Jungle Bike or quad all-terrain vehicle. A half-day tour will take you inland on a hidden trail where few people venture and you will experience the tropical wilderness of Bora Bora. No experience is required. A 2-hr. excursion for a minimum of 2 people is 18.500 CFP per quad. You can also rent a quad at Matira Jet Tours on Matira Beach, *Tel. 77.63.63.*

Helicopter & Airplane Tours

Polynesia Hélicoptères, *Tel. 67.62.59, helico-bora@mail.pf* is next door to the Air Tahiti office on the Vaitape quay. A 6-seat AS 350 BA Squirrel "Ecureuil" helicopter provides 15-min. flights over Bora Bora for 16.300 CFP per person. A 30-min. flight-seeing tour of Bora Bora and the nearby atoll of Tupai costs 27.100 CFP per person for a minimum of 4 people. These tours are available daily. You can also visit the neighboring islands by helicopter, which is rented by the hour. Helicopter transfers will also take you from Bora Bora to Le Taha'a Island Resort and Spa.

Skywalker Aviation, *Tel. 60.59.80/78.56.90; skywalker@mail.pf.* Steve Walker can take 1 passenger for a spin in his ULM ultralight aircraft. A 25-min. flight over Bora Bora is 13.420 CFP and a 40-min. flight over Bora Bora and Tupai costs 21.505 CFP. Steve also owns **Maraamu Lagoon Cruises** and can take several people for a sail on his 49-ft. yacht *Maraamu.*

Special Activities & Sightseeing Stops

Alain Gerbault's grave opposite the *gendarmerie* on Vaitape quay may be pointed out to you during your guided land tour. Gerbault was a Frenchman who had sailed the seven seas aboard his yacht *Firecrest* before dropping anchor in Bora Bora. He was most attracted to the young boys of Bora Bora, to whom he introduced the game of soccer. Due to the politics of war Gerbault left Bora Bora in 1941, and died on the island of Timor. His remains were brought back to his beloved Bora Bora in 1947, and a small tomb in the form of a *marae* was built in his honor.

Ancient temples of coral stone called *marae* are scattered around the island and on a few of the surrounding *motu* islets. The most easily accessible of these prehistoric sites of worship and human sacrifice are: **Marae Marotetini**, on a point by the lagoon between the Bora Bora Yacht Club and the Faanui boat dock; **Marae Taianapa**, on private property well off the mountain side of the road in Faanui, close to the Electra power plant; and **Marae Aehautai**, located on the beach at Fitiiu Point overlooking Anau Bay. **Fare Opu**, "House of the Stomach" is located between the lagoon and the road, close to the old navy docks in Faanui, immediately before the Faanui village. Petroglyphs of turtles are incised into 2 of the coral slabs. Turtles were sacred to the Maohi ancestors of today's Polynesians.

Matira Beach begins at the Hotel Bora Bora and continues past the Hotel Matira and Chez Nono at Point Matira, and on around the point past the Bora Bora Intercontinental Le Moana Resort. It joins Taahana Beach at Le Maitai Polynesia and the Sofitel Bora Bora Beach Resort, but most people still refer to the entire area as Matira Beach. This is where you will find a concentration of hotels, pensions, boutiques, black pearl shops and all kinds of nautical activities. The west side of Matira Beach, facing the Hotel Bora Bora, is Bora Bora's most popular beach. The soft, white powdery sand slopes gently into the aquamarine lagoon, where the water is very shallow until you see the deepening shades of blue. Point Matira was named in memory of a British ship named *Mathilda* that was wrecked

---

TUPAPAU

"Many vestiges of ancient times still linger on Bora Bora. The belief in **tupapau** (TWO-pow-pow), ghosts of the dead, is prevalent among the islanders. Walk alone on a dark Bora Bora night and you'll see why. It is still a common practice to keep a lamp lit at night to ward off these evil spirits. In 1973 my son Tom and I discovered a human arm and a portion of jawbone in front of the altar of Marae Marotetini. They had been pushed to the surface by land crabs digging their burrows. Despite warnings from the locals, we took the bones as souvenirs. Shortly after the discovery, my right arm became swollen to twice its normal size, followed by a swelling of the right side of my jaw. Upon taking the bones back to Los Angeles, Tom's leg was broken in several places during a freak motorcycle accident. This was followed by a period of family sickness and bad luck that didn't cease until we returned the bones to Marae Marotetini in 1976. In 1981, several giant human footprints were discovered at the water's edge near Marae Taianapa. The discovery was important enough to bring government officials and newsmen from Papeete to examine the huge prints and wonder at their origin. The elders of Bora Bora didn't wonder. They knew. The prints were an omen from the distant past." – from cinematographer Milas Hinshaw's booklet *Bora Bora E.*

on Moruroa Atoll in the Tuamotus in 1792. Three of the survivors remained in Tahiti, forming the first European colony. One of the crew, James O'Connor, married King Pomare's cousin, and their granddaughter was named Mathilda. She married a chief of the Leeward Islands and they settled in Bora Bora, where part of their property included the beautiful point and sand beach now called Matira, the Tahitian pronunciation of Mathilda.

Musée de la Marine is on the back side of the island, between the villages of Faanui and Anau, *Tel. 67.75.24.* French architect Bertrand Darasse displays his collection of ship models, which includes the *Mayflower,* dated 1615, the *H.M.S.Endeavour* that brought James Cook to Tahiti in 1769, the *Boudeuse* and *Etoile,* commanded by **Louis Antoine de Bougainville, Captain Bligh's** famous *Bounty,* and **Alain Gerbault's** *Firecrest,* which he sailed to Bora Bora. There are also models of outrigger sailing canoes, *bonitiers* and *poti marara* boats that are still used in these islands. Admission to the maritime museum is free.

Nightlife & Entertainment
Le Récif, *Tel. 67.73.87, north of Vaitape towards Faanui.*

This is Bora Bora's only public disco and it is open on Fri. and Sat. nights. The ambiance in this dark and crowded room is very Tahitian. If you are curious as to how the locals whoop it up, there's an entry fee of 1.500 CFP, which includes a drink. The drinking and dancing goes on until the wee hours of the morning.

All the big hotels have entertainment several nights a week and a nightly show is presented by the Club Med staff except on Thurs. and Sun., when there is a Tahitian dance show. Details are given under *Where to Eat* in this chapter.

Heiva in Bora Bora – Where the Fête Goes On & On
During the month of July, the island of Bora Bora pulsates to the rhythm of the **Heiva**, which means festival in Tahitian. Some people still call this event the Fête or Tiurai, the Tahitian word for July. Whatever name you choose to call it, this is the most colorful time to visit Bora Bora.

Most of the islands have their own Heiva celebrations, but the Fête in Bora Bora is the best, because the villagers put so much enthusiasm and effort into building their *baraques* (barracks). These are carnival type stalls or booths that are made of thatched roofs and walls woven of palm fronds. They are decorated with multicolored *tifaifai* wall hangings, ferns, bright blossoms and *ti* leaves. These *baraques* are transformed into restaurants, pool halls, shooting galleries and carnival booths with a roulette-type wheel called *taviri.* If you place a bet you may win a bar of soap, sack of rice or sugar, bolt of *pareo* cloth, or even a live suckling pig.

Each village presents a singing group and a troupe of dancers in the Heiva competitions. Some of these performers are just as talented as the professional entertainers in Tahiti, as Bora Bora has long been recognized for producing excellent dancers, choreography and costumes. The competitions are a big social event, when old friends get together to catch up on the latest happenings and to swap a choice bit of gossip. The bicycle races around the island are fun to watch on July 14, as the supporters stand beside the road and spray the riders with water. The fruit-carriers' race, javelin-throwing contest, soccer matches and outrigger sailing canoe races are just warm-up events for the outrigger paddle canoe races.

July 14 is a good combination of old style Polynesian celebrations and the French version of honoring Bastille Day in the tropics. This is the time to drink champagne at the mayor's office, aboard a visiting French ship and at the glamorous resort hotels. A huge fireworks display ends the day's festivities, and an all-night ball gets underway a little later. Although there are only 2-3 weeks of planned events during the Heiva in Bora Bora, the Fête still goes on and on, well into the month of August. After all, building the *baraques* did require a lot of work. What's more, they provide a great meeting place.

SPORTS & RECREATION
Hiking & Trekking

Amae Hiking Excursion (A.H.E.), *Tel. 24.03.96*, is operated by Erico and Alan, who will guide 2-10 people up Mata Pua mountain (235 m or 770 ft.) on Mon. and Sat. and up Mount Pahia (661 m 2,168 ft.) on Tues. and Thurs. Departure is at 9am and you'll return at 4:30pm. The Mata Pua hike starts from Tiipoto and the Mount Pahia climb departs from Vaitape. You must be fit, in good health, and not prone to vertigo. Children younger than 12 years are not allowed. Bring a sandwich and a bottle of water and wear mountain shoes or boots. The hotels sell the half-day hikes for 6.500 CFP; the all day hikes are 9.500 CFP; and a full day hike with a picnic is 10.500 CFP. A difficult level day trip to Mount Pahia is 14.000 CFP.

Taxi Boat & Boat Rental

Manu Taxi Boat, *Tel. 67.61.93/79.11.62*. Jean-François Ferrand has 3 motorboats and can accommodate up to 20 passengers for hourly, daily and half-day excursions, transfers and rental. Picnic on a private motu on request.

Taxi Motu, *Tel. 67.60.61/77.33.23; taximotu@hotmail.com*. Ronan and Chloé Delestre have a 15-ft. boat for transfers to the motu and a 28-ft. covered boat for a maximum of 12 passengers.

Matira Jet Tours, *Tel. 67.62.73/77.63.63*, has a 27-ft. covered boat for half- or full-day rentals to visit the hotels, circle the island or snorkel. Airport transfers on request.

Moana Adventure Tours, *Tel. 67.61.41*, provides boat transfers upon request from the airport and resort hotels or private lodgings. The cost of transporting up to 5 passengers from the Bora Bora Airport to your hotel is 20.000 CFP in a 21-ft. Bayliner. A 17-ft. Boston Whaler with sun top can be rented with a pilot, who will take you to places in the lagoon that visitors normally never get to see. Rates are 22.000 CFP for 2 hrs., 28.050 CFP for 3 hrs., and up to 50.600 CFP for 8 hrs. for a maximum of 6 passengers. Rental of a 6-passenger 21-ft. Bayline "Orama" with sun top starts at 33.000 CFP for 2 hrs. and goes up to 81.400 CFP for 8 hrs., pilot included.

Lagoon & Coastal Fishing
Moana Adventure Tours, *Tel. 67.61.41/67.75.97* uses a 17-ft. Boston Whaler for fishing close to the outside reef, where currents and high seas attract bonito, tuna, mahi mahi, jacks, barracudas and wahoo. A 4-hr. lagoon fishing excursion starts at 36.500 CFP and offshore or coastal fishing costs 40.000-42.500 CFP for 4 hrs., depending on which hotel books your trip.

Deep Sea Fishing
Sports fishing around Bora Bora is a very popular activity and the local fishing clubs hold tournaments throughout the year. There is even a Vahine Sport Fishing Club for the ladies, and any visiting female angler is welcome to join the competitions and fun. The fishing grounds are only a 20 min. boat ride outside the barrier reef, and the waters around Bora Bora are filled with marlin, yellowfin tuna, sailfish, wahoo, mahi mahi and bonito. The marlin are tagged and released at the anglers' request. Inter-island cruises are provided on request. The sea captains listed below all speak very good English.

Taravana is a 50-ft. prototype sportfishing/sailing catamaran owned by American expatriate, Richard Postma, which is based at the Hotel Bora Bora, *Tel. 67.77.79 (evening) or cell 689/72.30.99 (day); Fax 689/60.59.31; taravana@mail.pf; www.taravana.com.* Richard said that *Taravana* (which means 'crazy' in Tahitian) is the world's first sportfishing sailboat and has proven to be successful with an impressive record of tournament wins. The boat is equipped with the best gear, 20 custom rods from 8 lbs. to 130 lbs. test line, Penn international reels, custom gaffs, and 2 custom fighting chairs. She's tournament ready. If you book directly with Richard, a half-day's deep-sea fishing excursion costs 110.000 CFP and a full-day's outing is 154.000 CFP, including taxes, for a maximum of 8 people. The hotels charge 125.000 CFP for a half-day and 174.000 CFP for a full day. See more information under *Day Sailing Excursions and Sunset Cruises* in this chapter and in the chapter on *Planning Your Trip*.

Luna Sea is a Black Watch 34 that is also owned by Richard Postma of Bora Bora Sport Fishing, *Tel. 67.77.79 (evening) or 72.30.99 (day); 72.95.85 (Captain Tepoe); Fax 689/60.59.31; taravana@mail.pf; www.boraborasportfishing.com.* In spite of its name, this is a No Nonsense Big Game Fishing Boat built specifically for serious charter fishing in French Polynesian waters off the Leeward Society Islands. "Luna Sea" is based in Bora Bora but can easily fish the neighboring islands of Taha'a, Raiatea, Huahine, Tupai and Maupiti. The boat is dry, smooth, stable and very quick, and is equipped with Melton International Tackle custom-built rods from 8 lb. to 130 lb. test with Shimano Tiagra 2-speed reels and Shimano spinning reels. She has Top Shot gaffs and a Relax Marine fighting chair and outriggers. Captain Tepoe Pere has about 30 years of local and international experience and his goal is to give you the very best service possible. A half-day sportfishing excursion for up to 6 passengers is 99.000 CFP for the boat, and 135.000 CFP, including taxes, for a full-day charter. A full-day tour to Taha'a and Raiatea for up to 6 passengers is also 135.000 CFP, including taxes, for the boat. The hotels charge 110.000 CFP for a half-day outing, 148.000 CFP for a full day, and 158.000 CFP for a day tour to Taha'a and Raiatea.

Kaimana is a sport fishing boat based at the Bora Bora Nui, who charges 88.000 CFP for 4 hrs. and 132.000 CFP for 6 hrs., with drinks included. The St. Regis charges 99.000 CFP for a half-day and 150.000 CFP for a full day of deep sea fishing on board this boat.

Lagoon Excursions by Outrigger Canoe or Speedboat

Bora Bora's lovely lagoon offers many surprises, pleasures and photographic treasures. **A Boat Trip Around the Island** normally includes time for snorkeling, exploring a small motu islet, walking on the living coral reef, searching for the graceful manta rays, sharing a kiss with the sting rays, diving for the giant mussels buried in the white sand lagoon bottom (the mussels are not removed from their habitat) and donning mask and snorkel to view the fish and coral in the natural aquarium. **Feeding the Sharks and Stingrays** is included in most **Circle Island Tours**, and is Bora Bora's most popular and thrilling excursion. A **Picnic on a Motu** combined with your boat tour can mean you eat freshly grilled fish and fruit and drink coconut water, or you may be served a gourmet lunch, complete with cold drinks and wine. All lagoon activities depend on the whim of the weather and sea.

The hotel resorts and cruise ships have an agreement with their own qualified guides and charge from 9.000-12.500 CFP for a 3-hr. boat tour around the island. You may get a better rate if you contact them directly. Here are a few of the best known guides and excursions.

Shark Boy of Bora Bora, Tel./Fax 67.60.93, cell 78.27.42; sharkboy@mail.pf. Owner Evan Temarii of Evan Activities has several motorized outrigger canoes of various sizes, plus a catamaran for 60 passengers. On all the excursions you will be able to swim with the rays and watch the sharks being fed. Evan has starred in 2 movies filmed in Bora Bora: starting when he was 11 years old with *Heart*, made for the Wonderful World of Disney, followed by *Call It Courage* when he was 18. He traps the sharks with his bare hands and holds them over his head out of the water for the photographers. He was the first one to tame the stingrays, and even taught them how to kiss.

Raanui Tours, *Tel. 67.61.79/79.43.14*, is operated by Arieta Onee. He has 4 motorized outrigger canoes for half-day excursions that include shark and ray feeding and snorkeling.

Teremoana Tours, *Tel. 67.71.38*, is operated by Noel "Nono" Leverd, who also owns Chez Nono pension on Matira Beach. His very popular excursions aboard two 36-ft. outrigger speed canoes depart from the beach in front of his

BORA BORA'S SHARK FEEDING SHOW

Feeding the sharks is one of the most popular excursions on Bora Bora. Each morning the tourists board outrigger canoes to speed across the lagoon toward the barrier reef. When you make your own shark feeding tour, you will put on a mask and snorkel, and step into the clear waters of the warm lagoon, just inside the fringing reef. With just a few steps in water about 1.2 m (4 ft.) deep you will reach a rope that has been tied around 2 huge coral heads. You hold onto the rope for stability and watch through your mask as your guide performs the daily shark feeding show.

Thousands of tropical fish of all colors rush over to have a nibble at the huge head of tuna or mahi mahi that the guide holds out to them. You will see rainbow colored butterfly fish, black and white striped manini, the blue and yellow empress angel fish, the variegated and very territorial Picasso fish, plus many other families of more than 300 species of fish that inhabit the Bora Bora submarine gardens.

Gasps and squeals from the audience announce the arrival of the sharks as they appear for their breakfast. Sometimes you can see as many as a dozen sharks, about 1.5 m (5 ft.) long. These are the Carcharhinus Melanopterus, commonly known as the **blackfin** or **blacktip reef shark**.

The shark feeding show is so fascinating that you may forget your fear. As you are upcurrent of the sharks and the Tahitian guides keep their attention diverted with the proffered fish breakfast, the sharks normally pay little attention to their observers. If you are bold enough, you can even help to feed these hungry beasts. And if your nerve fails you, then the outrigger canoe is just a few steps away.

pension at 9:30am and return at 3:30pm. A lunch of poisson cru, grilled fish, coconut bread, cake, fresh fruit and *po'e* is served on the motu.

Bora Bora Lagoonarium, *Tel. 67.71.34; lagoonarium@mail.pf; www.boraboralagoonarium.com.* A half-day excursion operated by Teura and Claudine Teheiura takes you to their Lagoonarium on the northern point of Motu Piti A'au. Fenced-in sections of the lagoon contain fish, sea turtles, rays, and a huge moray eel. Most hotels charge 6.800 CFP for a half-day tour and St.Regis charges 8.000 CFP.

Private Lagoon Excursions & Picnics on the Motu

Private tours and excursions are very popular with Honeymooners in Bora Bora, and now there are several service providers who specialize in private boat tours around the island. They stop to let you swim in the coral gardens, feed the stingrays, observe the sharks and enjoy a romantic picnic on the motu.

Etienne, *Tel./Fax 67.63.14; cell 79.22.62*, was the first tour operator to provide a picnic in the water, and his private lagoon excursions and barbecues on the motu are highly praised by guests staying at the Bora Bora Lagoon Resort & Spa, his exclusive client. While you are swimming and snorkeling and enjoying the peace and quiet on the white sand beach of the motu, Etienne is preparing your lunch. He places a small table and 2 chairs in the shallow lagoon water, shades them with a big umbrella, dresses the table with a linen cloth and place settings, sets up his barbecue grill in the water and ices down the champagne in a bucket standing in the lagoon next to the table. The stylish lunch starts with mixed salad and poisson cru with coconut milk, and is followed by grilled lobster, mahi mahi and steak, accompanied by potatoes, and followed by a dessert of fresh fruit. There is beer, pineapple juice, Sprite and Coke in the cooler, and you can have wine if you prefer that to champagne. This excursion is available at the Bora Bora Lagoon Resort daily except Sat., and costs 75.000 CFP for 2 people.

Etienne told me that most of the so-called private picnic tours, except for Patrick's Activities, take place on a motu near the Lagoonarium, and you can see other couples or small groups while swimming and dining.

Patrick's Activities/Maohi Nui Private Excursions, *Tel. 689/67.69.94/ 79.19.11; patrick.bora@mail.pf; www.boraboraisland.com.* Patrick Tairua is well known and appreciated in Bora Bora for his Famous Nature Tours by 4x4 Jeep and outrigger canoe, his ma'a Tahiti feasts on a private motu, his Polynesian Wedding Ceremonies, and his spectacular fire-dancing when he performs with his Maohi Nui dancers at the hotels several nights a week. Patrick is indeed a busy man because he is really good at what he does and he's dependable; therefore, he is in demand by the hotels and individual clients.

Patrick speaks good English and he will tell you about the Polynesian culture and legends of Bora Bora as he takes you around the lagoon in his famous yellow outrigger speed canoe with a roof of coconut palm fronds. Patrick offers a half-day private tour around the island that costs 38.000 CFP for 2-4 people, and includes snorkeling gear to explore the coral gardens. You will also go ashore on the white sandy beach of a motu islet, where your guide will refresh you with mineral water, fruit juice, soft drinks and beer. Bring a beach towel, shoes or sandals, sunscreen and your cameras.

His 3/4 day tour from 9:30am-2:30pm, with a Polynesian lunch on a private island, is 70.000 CFP for 2-4 people. Patrick also has a full-day tour, from 9:30am-4:30pm, that includes a Polynesian lunch on a private island and costs 86.000 CFP for 2-4 people. On both these tours you can watch the opening of the underground earth oven, and you will be served a traditional Polynesian lunch on a shaded table set in the shallow lagoon water. The meal includes pork, chicken, tropical vegetables and local fruits and the food is cooked in banana leaves. Wine or champagne accompanies your lunch, according to your preference.

If you are going to be in Bora Bora only a short time, perhaps you would like to combine your Lagoon Tour and Polynesian lunch with a 4x4 Safari. This all-day private tour is 92.000 CFP for 2-4 people. See information under *Mountain Safaris and 4x4 Excursions* and *Wedding Ceremonies*.

Keishi Tours (Pierrot Picnic), *Tel. 67.67.31/79.26.56*, is owned by Pierrot Taati, who has 2 motorized outrigger canoes. He works with some of the hotels, taking their guests on boat excursions around the island with a private picnic on a motu, and the tourists are very happy with Pierrot's excursions.

Other private picnic tours are organized by **Ben Heriteau** of **Diveasy**, *Tel. 79.22.55;* **Moana Adventure Tours**, *Tel. 67.61.41*; and Thierry Mulatier of **Teiva Tours**, Tel. 67.64.26/73.75.74.

Sailing Charter Yachts

There is no big yacht charter company based in Bora Bora. You can rent a sailboat from one of the charter companies based in Tahiti, Moorea or Raiatea and sail to Bora Bora, or you can arrange for a yacht to be delivered to Bora Bora in time for your arrival. See Chapter 6, *Planning Your Trip*, section on Cruises.

Day Sailing Excursions & Sunset Cruises

Taaroa III, *Tel./Fax 67.64.30; boravoile@netcourrier.com*. This Formula 40 Fleury Michon racing catamaran accommodates 2-10 people for the morning excursions around the island and 16 passengers for a sunset sailing cruise. A sail around the island, from 8:45am-12:30pm, costs 6.600-7.500 CFP, depending on where you book it, and includes a swim in the lagoon. Sunset cruises for 2-16 passengers are from 4:30-5:15pm or 6:30-7pm daily except Sun., for a cost of 4.500-5.000 CFP per person. The boat can be chartered for 45.000-55.000 CFP for private sunset cruises.

Taravana, *Tel. 67.77.79 (evening) or cell 689/72.30.99 (day); Fax 689/60.59.31; taravana@mail.pf; www.taravana.com* is a 50-ft. prototype sportfishing/sailing catamaran based at the Hotel Bora Bora. Captain Richard Postma is an American who has lived in Bora Bora for about 30 years, and he works with several of the big hotels and passenger ships, offering half-day and full-day cruises. The sunset cruises for up to 20 people aboard the *Taravana* are ideal for lovers, departing each Tues., Thurs. and Sat. from the Hotel Bora Bora boat dock at 5pm for a 2-hr. sail on the lagoon waters inside the protected reef. When booking direct with Richard, this excursion costs 8.800 CFP, with taxes and complimentary beverage. The Hotel Bora Bora charges 9.800 CFP for the Taravana Sunset Cruise.

The boat can also be chartered for private sunset cruises, fishing charters, day sailing, sail and dive expeditions to the atoll of Tupai, the island closest to Bora Bora, or sailing excursions to Taha'a, where Richard owns the Taravana Yacht Club. Contact him for information and rates.

Hobie Bora is a 21-ft. Hobie Cat that offers sailing excursions around the lagoon, with snorkeling. Most hotels charge 25.000 CFP for a 2-hr. ride, 34.000 CFP for 3-hr. outings, and 25.000 CFP for a 1-hr. sunset cruise.

Motor Yacht Charters

ROA Yachting Company, *B.P. 511, Bora Bora 98730; Tel. 689/71.83.86; manager@roa-yachting.com; www.roa-yachting.com.* Motor Yacht Roa is a 23,55 m. Falcon 72-ft. Fiberglass French-owned a/c luxury yacht that is based in Bora Bora since Aug. 2007, providing charters or day trips for a maximum of 8 passengers. There are 4 cabins, crew quarters for 3, private bathrooms, a fully-equipped kitchen, living room, cockpit, flybridge, aft deck, sunbathing deck and swimming deck. Suggested itineraries include a 6-night/7-day cruise package for 6 or 8 passengers to visit Bora Bora, Taha'a, Raiatea and Huahine. The cost per person for 8 people is €4,000-5,000, and €5,000-6,000 on the basis of 6 people, depending on low or high season. You can also rent the boat and its crew for an "a la carte" cruise for €4,500-5,000 per day, which does not include food and drinks. A day trip from Bora Bora to Taha'a and back (9am-6pm) is €500-600 per person, including lunch on board.

Scuba Diving

Bora Bora's scuba diving clubs have qualified instructors who will introduce you to a large variety of diving spots inside the lagoon and beyond the barrier reef. Visibility is usually 20 to 30 m, with an abundance of marine life, including manta rays, sharks, barracuda, dolphins and turtles. The lagoon of Bora Bora is the only one in the world where a family of manta rays lives year-round. Initiation dives, fun dives and night dives are available, with up to 4 outings a day.

Bora Bora Blue Nui, *Tel. 67.79.07/60.52.00; Fax 67.79.07; boraborablue nui@mail.pf; www.bluenui.com.* This dive center is based at the Bora Bora Pearl Beach Resort, and is headed by Gilles Petre, who also supervises the Blue Nui Dive Centers in Taha'a, Manihi and Tikehau. He is an international CMAS ** monitor, State instructor BEES 1, PADI instructor and OWSI, and can give exams for CMAS, PADI and FFESM certificates. Rates are 7.000 CFP for one dive, 8.000 CFP for an initiation dive, and 8.000 CFP for a night dive, including all the equipment. Blue Nui offers packages that can be used in any or all of the 4 Blue Nui Dive Centers. These packages sell for 32.500 CFP for 5 dives and 62.500 CFP for 10 dives. They also offer a DVD video service on request.

Bora Diving Center, *Tel. 67.71.84; boradiving@mail.pf; www.boradiving.com* adjacent to the Hotel Bora Bora on Matira Beach. The friendly staff includes PADI instructors as well as BEES1 and BEES2 French State instructors who speak English. You can dive in the morning for 1 fun dive (7.500 CFP) or a 2-tank dive in the afternoon (14.000 CFP). Introductory dives and certification courses are held in the afternoon. Free pick-up by boat or car. Private boat or rebreather on request.

Diveasy, *Tel. 79.22.55; Fax 67.69.36; diveasy@mail.pf; www.boraboraisland.com/ diveasy/index.html.* Ben Heriteau offers private dives for 1-4 people, and this is reportedly a good dive center for beginners. He is a State Instructor BEES 1, Class II B. Examinations are given for ANMP and CMAS certification. He is equipped with an underwater communications system to allow comments during the dive and underwater camera rental is available. Several hotels use his services for private dives with personalized guidance.

Nemo World Bora Bora, *Tel. 67.77.85; mail@nemoworld.pf; www.nemodivebora.com.* This dive center is located on the beachfront adjacent to the Sofitel Bora Bora Beach Resort and Novotel Beach Resort. The multilingual staff includes certified PADI and BEES1 dive instructors who lead 2-tank dives in the mornings for 14.000 CFP and introductory dives in the afternoon for 7.500 CFP. A 6-dive package is 39.000 CFP. Video films can also be made of your dive.

TOPdive Bora Bora, *Tel. 60.50.50; Fax 60.50.51; info@topdive.com; www.topdive.com.* This is the biggest dive center in Bora Bora, and offers introductory dives and lessons inside the lagoon or in the swimming pool. Lessons in theory are given in the classroom next to the patio beside the pool. The equipment used is Scubapro, with 121 steel tanks and 8 tanks for children 8 years or older. There are 4 completely equipped dive boats to take you to special dive sites inside the lagoon or outside the coral reef. You can dive up to 4 times a day, and night dives in the lagoon are organized. Certification courses in CMAS and PADI are given, but it is best to check to find out when each course will begin. Public rates for scuba diving start at 7.500 CFP for an introductory dive, fun dive or night dive; and a package of 10 dives is charged at the rate of nine dives, which comes to 67.500 CFP. The diving rates include taxes and all equipment. This package can be used at TOPdive centers in Bora Bora, Moorea, Rangiroa, Fakarava and Tahiti. Nitrox scuba diving is also available and costs 7.500 CFP for an exploratory dive and 14.500 CFP for 2 tank dives. The resort and restaurant are now closed.

Other Ways to Discover Bora Bora's Marine World

Aqua Safari, *Tel. 67.74.83/72.03.56; aquasafari@mail.pf; www.aquasafaribora.com.* Anne and Michel Condesse offer you an unusual way in which to discover what's under Bora Bora's world-famous lagoon. You put a funny looking square yellow helmet over your head and you can walk on the lagoon bottom at a 3-m. (10-ft.) depth, without getting your head wet. And you don't even have to know how to swim or dive to discover this new sensation. The helmet is attached to air bottles just like the divers wear; only the bottles remain on the boat while you wander around under the water, breathing as you normally do. A bilingual guide accompanies 4-5 people while a dive master stays aboard the boat to check on the air supply. This 90-min. Undersea Walk takes you to a natural coral formation near Toopua Island, where nobody else goes. Here you can see a large variety of fish and maybe even some rays in the blue depths. The hotels charge 7.000-7.300 CFP for this Helmet Dive. A private helmet dive can be combined with snorkeling during a 3-hr. tour for 2, which costs 35.000-57.000 CFP for the boat. Half-price for children under 10 years old. Morning and afternoon departures daily except Sunday.

Bora Bora Submarine, *Tel. 67.55.55/74.99.99; www.spiritofpacific.com.* The *Spirit of Pacific* is a yellow submarine that will take 4-6 passengers down to 25 m.

(82 ft.) below the water's surface to observe the world of corals and their animal life. The cabin is a/c with a 360° viewing port. You are transferred by boat to the submarine, which remains inside the protected lagoon between Bora Bora's main island and Motu Toopua. There are 5 outings per day and the hotels charge 18.700 CFP for 30 min., and 24.900 CFP for 45 min., including transfers. Children under 12 years old pay half price. St. Regis charges 160.000 CFP for a private tour.

Snuba, *Tel.60.59.16, Fax 60.59.15, snubaborabora@mail.pf; www.marcus-diving.com.* Marc Biehler is a professional underwater instructor BEES 2 who will teach you all about Snuba, which is a cross between snorkeling and scuba diving. It is fun for the whole family and doesn't require any special training or diploma. You can dive down to 6 m. (18 ft.) inside the lagoon of Bora Bora, and instead of wearing the air tank on your back, it remains on a float above the water while you breathe through an attached tube. Marc leads private half-day Snuba trips for a maximum of 6 people. He will pick you up at your hotel in a 24-ft. long covered boat with a 150 HP engine, and the tour includes a stop for snorkeling and another stop at a private motu islet where you can practice the Snuba technique. The cost of this half-day excursion is 32.500-36.300 CFP for 2 people at most hotels. St. Regis charges 45.000 CFP for a half-day Snuba outing.

Funny Cat, *Tel. 67.60.61/77.33.25*; *funnycat@hotmail.com,* is a 2-person motorized catamaran that is easy and fun to ride. No experience required. You just follow your guide to discover the lagoon around the island and stop on a motu to go snorkeling. Free pick-up daily. Rates start at 17.500 CFP for a 2 1/2-hr. ride.

Glass Bottom Boat Excursions

Moana Adventure Tours, *Tel. 67.61.41* or *78.27.37*, has a covered glass bottom boat that operates tours from all the hotels on Mon., Wed. and Sat., between 9:45am and 12pm., for 3.850-4.000 CFP, and half-price for children under 12.

Jet-Ski or Wave-Runner Excursions

You can rent a jet ski for 1-2 hrs., with guides to take you around the island inside the lagoon. You'll stop on the *motu* islets, snorkel in beautiful coral gardens, feed the fish, visit the aquarium and even dive with the sharks and stingrays. The rental costs are 18.400 CFP for 1 hr. and 25.900-28.000 for 2 hrs. when you book through the hotels, and less if you contact the operators directly.

Matira Jet Tours, *Tel. 67.62.73/77.63.63*, is operated by Rainui Besineau on Point Matira. **Miki-Miki Jet Tours**, *Tel. 67.76.44/72.10.76/71.01.49*, is owned by Karl Chang, also on the beach at Point Matira.

Sea Kayaks

Bora Bora Kayak, *Tel. 70.77.99; www.boraborakayak.com.* Nir Shalev at Rohotu Fare Lodge rents single or double American made sea kayaks that include storage space, paddles, snorkeling gear, life vests. backrests, dry bags, fishing poles, and cooler.

Water-Skiing & Wakeboard

Bora Bora Laguna Ski, *Tel. 73.53.77, bobwaterski@mail.pf,* is operated by Karen Bonnevie, who works with several hotels, providing all levels of waterskiing: bi-ski, mono-ski, wakeboard, barefoot and buoy skiing. A 15-min. tour is 7.000-7.300 CFP, a 30-min. session is 12.000-12.500 CFP. Private water-skiing and snorkeling boat rides around the island available.

Parasailing

Bora Bora Parasail, *Tel. 67.70.34/70.56.62/78.27.10; parasail@mail.pf; www.dream-islands.com.* Their base is located adjacent to the Novotel Bora Bora Beach Resort in the south of the island. You can soar solo or duo from 330-990 ft. high above the Bora Bora lagoon for a fabulous view. The take-off and landing is gentle and you won't even get wet. No experience required. A 15-min. flight up to 100 m. (330 ft.) costs 18.000-19.000 CFP for 1 person and 23.000-26.000 CFP for 2. A 30-min. flight up to 300 m. (990 ft.) is 24.000 CFP solo and 32.000-34.000 CFP duo. There is no age limit to this thrilling flight, which was tested and approved by Walt Disney World. Half price for children under 12 years old. Free transportation.

SHOPPING
Art Galleries

Galerie D'Art Alain and Linda, *Tel./Fax 67.70.32, cell 79.15.89; alain-linda@mail.pf.* This interesting art gallery is on the beach side of Pofai Bay, between Vaitape village and the Hotel Bora Bora. Linda is a German painter and her French husband, Alain, paints the *pareos* and tee shirts that they sell. Their gallery has a collection of paintings, sculptures, pottery, etchings and lithographs by the finest artists from the Polynesian islands. They also carry art books and tapa bark paintings. Both of these friendly folks enjoy meeting people and Linda has a lot of stories to tell you about the legends and life of the island, where they have lived for 3 decades.

Garrick Yrondi, *Tel. 60.57.15,* displays his paintings, sculptures and bronzes in his mountainside gallery located between Vaitape and the Hotel Bora Bora. His former gallery houses the excellent restaurant, La Villa Mahana, which is also decorated with Yrondi art. Yrondi created the pink marble statue of *vahine ei'a,* the fish woman, which you should look for at the edge of the Motu Mute lagoon by the airport. This is the protector of Bora Bora.

Paarara Mountain Artist, *Tel. 67.65.31,* is located above Faanui Bay, overlooking the lagoon and the Bora Bora Pearl Beach Resort. **Emmanuel Masson** learned to paint from his father, Jean Masson, who was a very well known French artist who first discovered Tahiti in 1938. Years later he met Rosine Tamauri from

Bora Bora, who became his favorite model and student, and together they had four children. Emmanuel exhibits his paintings of Polynesian people and Bora Bora scenery in his art gallery, and all the Safari tours stop here. If you want to rent a car and drive there, you should turn off the main road beside the church in Faanui and follow the winding road up the mountain until you see his sign. You can even picnic in his garden and gaze at the lovely view.

Other galleries include: **Alain Despert Studio**, *Tel. 60.48.15*, on mountainside between Hotel Bora Bora and Point Matira; **Matira Beach Galerie**, *Tel. 67.66.75*, on mountainside between Hotel Bora Bora and Point Matira; **Bora Bora Art Naea Studio**, on mountainside in Faanui, *Tel. 67.71.17*; and **Atelier Patine**, *Tel. 67.74.09*, in Nunue.

Tahitian Cultured Pearls

Some of the pearl companies from Tahiti and Moorea also have outlets in Bora Bora. These include **Robert Wan's Tahiti Perles**, *Tel. 67.50.24*, **Nyco's**, *Tel. 60.58.20*, and **Tahiti Pearl Market**, *Tel. 60.38.60*. **Tahia Collins Pearls**, *Tel. 60.37.00*, is located at the Hotel Bora Bora, and Intercontinental Bora Bora Resort & Thalasso Spa, *Tel. 67.56.00*. They also have shops in Tahiti, Moorea and aboard the *Paul Gauguin* and other cruise ships. **Matira Pearls & Fashions**, *Tel. 67.79.14*, is a well-established shop on the mountainside at Point Matira. Owner Steve Fearon is an expat American who opened the first pearl shop on the island that was outside of the hotels. Steve's family used to own the Hotel Bora Bora and the Hotel Tahara'a in Tahiti.

I like the quality, colors and designs of the pearl jewelry at **Bora Pearl Company**, *Tel. 60.37.77/70.06.75*, next to Hotel Bora Bora. Owner Tea Suchard of Bora Bora gets her lovely pearls from a pearl farm in Taha'a and other sources, but she has also built a small pearl farm inside the lagoon, which is called **The Farm**. This is Bora Bora's only pearl farm, and visitors can learn all about how a cultured pearl is produced as they watch the process being demonstrated by trained technicians. A good sales gimmick here is to take a honeymoon couple in a boat to visit the grafted oysters suspended in wire baskets inside the lagoon and let the husband dive and choose an oyster. When the pearl is extracted, he then presents it to his bride. She can take it home unset or have the pearl drilled and set while they watch and drink champagne. Most of the pearl shops will provide complimentary shuttle service to visit their showrooms.

Clothing & Souvenirs

La Galerie Bora Bora, *Tel. 60.53.25*, is on the mountainside in the center of Vaitape village, across from the post office. This collection of Polynesian arts & crafts, jewelry, home interior accents, fashion accessories and Polynesian epicurean delights is owned by Nyco's Pearls.

Look for **Boutique Gauguin** and **Pakalola Boutique** in Vaitape; **Mom's Boutique**, next to Tahiti Market, is a good place to shop; and Royal Helen's Bay

Center and Pahia Center are two small shopping centers beside the lagoon in Vaitape village with pearl shops, a few clothing boutiques and miscellaneous gift shops. Be sure to check out the hotel boutiques on the motu islets as well as the main island. All around the island you will find little boutiques and thatched roof stands that sell hand-printed *pareos*, tee-shirts, swimwear and all kinds of creative souvenir items that were actually made on Bora Bora. Don't be fooled into buying an authentic made-in-Bali carving that has the name Bora Bora stamped on it. The **Arts and Crafts Center** at the Vaitape quay has grass skirts and coconut bras, shell jewelry and woven hats and bags that are handmade by the people who sell them, even though most of the seashells were imported.

Camera Rental

Jean-Luc Camera Shop, *Tel. 67.64.82/72.01.23, Fax 67.76.63*, is located on the Vaitape pier adjacent to the Air Tahiti office. He rents cameras for all occasions, sells film and provides express photo development. He can handle digital transfers and help you with your video and DVD requirements. Jean-Luc works with several of the top hotels, to photograph or film any occasion such as weddings, anniversaries, gatherings, reunions or whatever you want for your souvenir album. The photos can be delivered on paper, put on a CD-ROM or DVD-edited with sound effects.

MASSAGES & SPAS

Club Med, *Tel. 60.46.04*. Massages, hydrotherapy treatments and beauty treatments are available on the premises. You can get an anti-cellulite wrap, a sea mud application on your neck, shoulders and spine, various facials, foot and hand care, depilation treatments, waxing, or revitalizing massages.

Espace Bien-Etre, *Tel. 60.51.51*, is a massage and body care center located in a Lagoon bungalow at Lé Meridien, and is open daily from 9am-6pm. Treatments are available for the face, hands, feet and body, including scrubs, masks, body wraps, moisturizing massages and after sun care. Multisensory treatments include an 80-min. Paradise Wave back massage, facial and floral bath for 18.000 CFP, and a 3-hr. Polynesian Treasure body scrub, complete massage, bloom facial and bath for 32.000 CFP.

Ethy Kalombe, *Tel. 67.62.61/23.57.73*, is a certified masseuse and physiotherapist who gives relaxing Swedish massages, Chinese acupressure, reflexology of the feet, back and head, clears the lymphatic system, stretching massages, and a traditional massage with aromatic oils. You can also be a true hedonist and treat yourself to one of her special bath therapies. She will come to your hotel room on request.

Fare Taurumi at **Hotel Bora Bora**, *Tel. 60.44.04*, has 2 Indonesian therapists who were trained at the Amandari Spa in Bali, plus a local lady who specializes in the traditional Polynesian "Taurumi" massage given to children from birth to relax the whole body. The Indonesian lady gave me an Aman massage, which was the best massage I have ever had. An Aman full body massage or Taurumi massage is 12.000 CFP for 60 minutes and 18.000 CFP for 90 minutes. You can also get a facial, manicure, pedicure, after sun treatment, full body scrub, foot or head massage, or let a physical therapist and osteopath use his magic to help you create a balance in your body.

Le Spa at Sofitel, *Tel. 60.55.00*, is located in a bungalow at the edge of the lagoon at the Bora Bora Beach Resort & Spa. The menu of beauty treatments and massages includes a 1-hr. anti jet-lag body and face massage for 11.000 CFP, a 1-hr. Sacred Earth massage using warm stones, for 11.000 CFP, a 1:30 hr. aromatherapy based relaxation facial for 16.000 CFP; a 3-hr. Fruit & Exotic Flower ritual for 26.000 CFP, and a Double Decadence 3-hr. treatment that includes a bath for two, using essential oils, a signature massage and essential hydration facial for each person, for a total of 26.000 CFP.

Mandara Spa, *Tel. 60.33.00*, is built on the hillside at the Bora Bora Nui Resort & Spa. There are 3 private and luxurious treatment bungalows hidden within the lush vegetation. You have an unsurpassed view of the azure waters of Bora Bora's world famous lagoon and Otemanu mountain from one terrace and a panoramic sweeping view of the lagoon and Pacific Ocean from the other side of the spa. Each bungalow is equipped with its own Jacuzzi and all of the Mandara Spa treatments are available, such as Polynesian Aromatherapy full body massage, Hot Lava Stone Massage, Facials, Body Scrubs and much more.

Manea Spa, *Tel. 60.53.85, maneaspa@borapearlbeach.pf; www.maneaspa.com*. This spa at the Bora Bora Pearl Beach Resort has earned an excellent reputation. Spa managers Kamala and Anthony Nayelli are from Arizona, and the 10 massage therapists are well trained Polynesians. There are 8 treatment rooms spread over a 600 sq. m. (6,460 sq. ft.) area next to a lake in the heart of a tropical garden. The spa menu offers full body massage, body shaping, body wraps, hot stone healing, four hands massage, scalp massage and reflexology, after sun care, men's and women's facials, manicures and pedicures and waxing. There are also 2 saunas, 2 steam baths, a relaxation room, and the Manea line of 100% natural local products for complete body care. The Royale Pomare Suite, the Manea Spa's centerpiece, is a distinctive treatment room for honeymooners and couples, who can enjoy a private session that includes an exfoliating body polish, a coconut bath by candlelight, a relaxing couple's massage and a bottle of champagne. You can even get a tattoo in this spa. See information under *Tattoo Artists* in this chapter.

Marú Spa, *Tel. 60.40.00, spa@bblr.pf*, is a unique treehouse spa at the Bora Bora Lagoon Resort & Spa. It features 4 treatment rooms on the waterfront and 2 massage rooms built into the branches of banyan trees. Services include Tahitian based treatments using herbs and remedies that have been practiced in the South Pacific for hundreds of years. A 25-min. Tropical Rain Massage combines lomi-lomi with thalasso therapy for 10.979 CFP; I had a Sacred Tamanu treatment that began with a balm of Tamanu oil, followed by a hydrating face mask, a scalp massage with Monoi oil, a rain shower and a body massage with energizing noni and pamplemousse oil. This relaxing experience takes 1:50 hrs. and costs 28.043 CFP. The Honeymoon Bliss begins with a pineapple and brown sugar body exfoliation, followed by 80 min. of traditional Polynesian massage and a bath in coconut milk and flowers. This 2:30 hr. hedonistic delight costs 65.036 CFP per couple. Beauty treatments also include Thalgo facials for men and women, manicures, pedicures and waxing.

Miri Miri Spa, *Tel. 60.78.88*, is the world-class signature spa at the St. Regis Resort, Bora Bora. Occupying 13,000 sq. ft. of space on its own private island, the spa is accessible by a footbridge across its private lagoon. Tahitian and Pacific Rim treatments are available in 7 luxurious spa suites. These include Balinese, Table-Taï, Neuomuscular and Ayurvedic Abhyanga Massage.

Exclusive to Miri Miri Spa, Robert Wan, the world's largest cultivator and exporter of Tahiti pearls, has created two signature spa treatments utilizing his luxurious cosmetic product line "n@cre". These treatments integrate warmed black pearls, mother-of-pearl salve and mother-of-pearl powder. One of these treatments is the Heremoana Facial, a 50-min. facial that costs 17.000 CFP, and the 80-min. Poemana Body treatment for 20.000 CFP integrates a head-to-toe massage with monoi oil, a body scrub with pearl-powder and a mini-facial or foot massage, finishing with an application of the "n@cre" body milk.

The founding principles of the Miri Miri Spa are based on the Seven Pillars of Well-Being. A 3-day package was designed using the principles of harmony, beauty, vitality, aqua, life balance, nature and nutrition. This 3-day rejuvenation is 85.000 CFP per person.

Thalasso Deep Ocean Spa, *Tel. 60.77.00; www.boraboraspa.interconti.com.* This is the first thalasso spa in the world to harness the virtues of sea water from the ocean's depths. Built on a private motu at the Intercontinental Bora Bora Resort, the Deep Ocean Spa houses a complex of 13,200 sq. ft. (1,226 sq. m.), offering 14 treatment booths that are air-conditioned with water siphoned through a pipeline outside the coral that is 3,000 ft. (915 m. deep). This unique balneo-therapy and thalassotherapy center was conceived by Dr. Tregger, who designed Monaco's thermal baths. It is managed by the Algotherm company, whose reputation and expertise extend all over the world.

From the Deep Ocean Spa's glass-floored overwater treatment suites, individual guests or couples can admire maritime flora and fauna during sessions designed to help you relax and replenish your body's minerals and restore equilibrium. The facilities also include multisensorial outdoor spas, a phlebological course, a fitness room with cardio training area, steam baths and showers to awaken the senses, a traditional *fare* to relax while facing the ocean, a meditation garden, tea lounge and iced bath. There are changing rooms for men and women and an elevator for guests in wheel chairs.

At the entrance to the Deep Ocean Spa are 3 fountains where you can sample the desalinated, extraordinarily purified deep sea water. This cold water (41°F, 5°C), contains an excellent complement of nutritional mineral salts. It is bottled under the label "Vai Moana" (the ocean source) right at the Spa, and is sold in the **Boutique by Algotherm** that is located at the entrance to the Deep Ocean Spa. Algotherm and Hei Poa products, clothing, jewelry and wellness books are also sold here.

A 20-min. marine deep sea hydromassage bath with essential oils for 5.500 CFP is one of many à la carte choices for water treatments. An Algospa marine scrub and wrap lasts for 75 min. and costs 17.900 CFP. Facials include an eyelash tint for 5.300 CFP and a high performance facial for 18.400 CFP. The "Massage of the World" menu suggests a special 70-min. jet lag massage for 19.900 CFP or a 90-min. Bora Bora deep blue massage for 23.000 CFP. Body Care lists a Depressotherapy session with essential oils for 9.800 CFP and a bust firming care for 13.700 CFP. Discovery treatment packages offer a 2-hr. Detox for 32.900 CFP, a 2 1/2-hr. Honeymoon treatment for 2 in an overwater bungalow for 89.600 CFP, and a 4 hr. 40 min. "Chill Out in Bora Bora" for 2 people for 136.990 CFP. Treatment packages for 3 or 5 days are also available, under the themes of Vitality, Deep Serenity, Natural Beauty, Pure Slimming, Honeymoon (for 2), and The Ultimate by Algotherm. Waxings, hot stone foot massage, hand bliss and foot bliss are also available for men and women, as well as delightful add ons, such as a hot stone foot massage, collagen eyes or lips re-pulp care.

TATTOO ARTISTS

Herenui Teriitehau, *Tel. 60.53.85, maneaspa@borapearlbeach.pf; www.maneaspa.com*. Here has a massage studio at the Manea Spa located at Bora Bora Pearl Beach Resort and a desk in the hotel's reception area. He formerly tattooed at Tiki Village and Painapo Beach in Moorea and was Tahiti's first carnival king a few years ago. Exterior guests are also welcome.

Marama Traditional Tattoo, *Tel. 67.66.73/72.03.75*, is located on the lagoon side in Matira between Point Matira and Le Maitai Polynesia. Teriimarama Olson is a half-American half-Polynesian native of Bora Bora who designs the tattoo to suit the individual.

Tattoo Fati, *Tel. 71.54.84; fatitattoo@hotmail.com*. Look for Boutique Paiki in Matira, where Fati's Marquesan sculptures are on display. He does guaranteed hygienic tattoos by appointment.

PRACTICAL INFORMATION

Banks

Bora Bora has three banks, which are all located in Vaitape village. **Banque de Tahiti**, *Tel. 60.59.99*, **Banque Socredo**, *Tel. 60.50.10*, and **Banque de Polynésie**, *Tel. 60.57.57*. All the banks have ATM windows.

Books, Magazines, Newspapers, Cigars

Maison de la Presse, *Tel. 60.57.75*, is located on the mountainside in Vaitape village, adjacent to the Gendarmerie. They sell coffee table books, travel guides, local and international newspapers and magazines.

Cybercafé/Internet Service

You can check your E-mail while enjoying your morning coffee and croissant at Aloe Café in the Centre Commercial Le Pahia in Vaitape village, *Tel 67.78.88; Fax 60.56.80; aloecafe@mail.pf.* They are open 6am-9:30pm Mon.-Sat. and have four computers and printers. Rates start at 400 CFP for 10 minutes.

Most hotels also have computers and Internet service available for their clients, sometimes without extra charge. You can also plug in your laptop to the Internet connection in your hotel room, which costs much more, of course.

Doctors

There are private doctors and a dentist at the Medical Cabinet in Nunue and a government-operated dispensary is located in Vaitape, *Tel. 67.70.77.* Dentists are located in the Pahia Center, *Tel. 67.70.61.*

Drugstore

Pharmacie Bora Bora, *Tel. 67.70.30*, is located on the mountainside of the road in Vaitape village. It is open Mon.-Sat. 8am-6pm and on Sun. and holidays from 9-11am.

Police

The French *gendarmerie* is on the mountainside opposite the quay in Vaitape, *Tel. 60.59.05.*

Post Office & Telecommunications Office

The Post Office is in Vaitape village on the circle island road near the quay, *Tel. 67.70.74.* Hours are 8am-3pm on Mon., 7:30am-3pm Tues. through Fri., and 8-10am on Sat. All telecommunications and postal services are available here and there is an ATM window outside.

Tourist Information

Bora Bora Tourism Committee is on the quay in Vaitape, *Tel. 67.76.36; info-bora-bora@mail.pf.* Hours are 9am-4pm Mon.-Fri. They are closed on weekends and holidays unless there is a ship in port, when they remain open all day.

Wedding Ceremonies

Patrick's Activities/Maohi Nui Private Excursions. Tel. 67.69.94,79.19.11; patrick.bora@mail.pf; www.boraboraisland.com. I watched Patrick Tairua perform a Polynesian wedding ceremony on the beach at one of the resort hotels in Bora Bora, and I thought it was the most touching, romantic sensation a couple in love could experience. The bride and groom were dressed in white pareos and wore a crown of flowers on their heads. Patrick, the *tahua* priest, was dressed in a yellow costume with a necklace of mother-of-pearl and feathers. He conducted the ceremony in Tahitian and translated the words into English, with a gentle look at the couple he was marrying (unofficially). It was a magical moment for everyone who watched this performance. The Polynesians use the word *mana* to describe a sacred power, and Patrick is definitely filled with this presence, this *mana*.

Patrick has created his own Maohi Nui programs of ceremonies that are very popular with couples who want to be married in the traditional Polynesian style or anniversary twosomes who wish to renew their vows.

You can choose an **Intimate** Polynesian wedding on the beach of your hotel, which lasts for 12 min. and includes only the wedding couple and the priest. Patrick charges 30.000 CFP for this and you are given a wedding certificate made of tapa. The **Simple** ceremony lasts for 15 min., and includes the priest and one musician. This costs 42.000 CFP, and the couple receives 2 white pareos, 2 flower leis and crowns and a tapa wedding certificate.

The **Traditional Polynesian Wedding on the Hotel Beach** is a 30-min. ceremony that includes the Maohi Nui musicians and dancers. Two Polynesian "warriors" usually pick up the couple from their bungalow, by outrigger canoe if they are in an overwater unit. The bride and groom are dressed in white pareos and floral crowns and are carried to the beach in the arms of the warriors. Patrick charges 72.000 CFP for the Maohi Nui participation in this ceremony. The hotel charges the couple for the photographer, a romantic dinner with wine or champagne, plus a wedding cake. The Hotel Bora Bora charges 115.000 CFP for a traditional ceremony on the beach, IC Moana Resort charges 137.500 CFP, and Bora Bora Lagoon Resort charges 159.305 CFP.

A **Traditional Polynesian Wedding on a Motu** is normally scheduled from 3:30-5:30pm, including the outrigger canoe ride to and from the motu. The wedding couple dress in their white pareos and flowers once they are on the motu, and two Polynesian warriors take them in their arms to meet the priest for the ceremony. The Maohi Nui group sings and dances during the 30-min. ceremony. A bottle of champagne is opened and the happy couple sip their bubbly as they watch the sunset and listen to the tunes played on a ukulele during their outrigger canoe ride across the lagoon back to their hotel. Patrick charges 130.000 CFP for this wedding ceremony, which includes a bottle of *Moët et Chandon* champagne, 2 white pareos, 2 flower leis and crowns, and a certificate made of tapa. A **Simple** version of this ceremony is 90.000 CFP, which includes the champagne, pareos, flowers and wedding certificate, but no singers and dancers. The bride and groom are alone with the priest and one musician. The Hotel Bora Bora charges 190.000 CFP for the ceremony on a private motu, and the Bora Bora Lagoon Resort charges 226.750 CFP for this ceremony, as well as the photographer, and the romantic dinner that is served later at the hotel.

The **Honeymoon Day** program is especially made for the couple who wish to celebrate their love with a Polynesian wedding, as well as discovering Bora Bora's natural wonders. In the morning the couple are met at their hotel and transported in a flower-decorated canoe to a private motu islet in a very natural and beautiful setting. Once they are on the motu the couple can put on the white pareos, flower crowns and necklaces they are given. Tahitian warriors then come to carry the couple in their arms to meet the priest for the beginning of the ceremony. After repeating their vows, Patrick gives the newly united couple a Tahitian name, as well as a "wedding" certificate printed on tapa bark cloth. Songs, music and dances performed by the Maohi Nui dancers punctuate the entire ceremony, which lasts for 30 minutes.

The husband and wife are then taken to another motu on board the outrigger canoe, where a Polynesian lunch has been prepared in their honor. The couple listen to the explanation of the guide as they watch the opening of the traditional earth oven made with volcanic rocks and covered by banana leaves. An umbrella-shaded table is set in the lagoon, and the newlyweds are served a lunch of suckling pig, chicken with local spinach, manioc, plantain bananas, breadfruit, Tahitian fish salad (poisson cru) with coconut milk, and a traditional dessert made with bananas and vanilla, as well as fresh tropical fruits. The lunch comes with a good bottle of *Moët et Chandon* French champagne or red/white wine, depending on the guests' preference.

The couple can choose how they want to spend their afternoon. Maohi Nui usually suggests a lagoon tour around the island of Bora Bora, with one snorkeling stop at a coral garden, another stop for visiting the stingrays in shallow water, and finally, the observation of black tip reef sharks outside the lagoon. The guide is glad to give details on geology, ecology and the history of Bora Bora. Snorkeling equipment is provided.

The couple can also choose to stay at the motu and enjoy a walk to the coral reef, swim, relax, or take a basket weaving lesson, as well as traditional dance or pareo tying. The guide is pleased to satisfy the wishes of the guests.

This full day outing lasts from 10:30am-4pm and includes the Polynesian lunch, one bottle of champagne or wine, drinks for the entire day (water, soft drinks, juices, beer), 2 white pareos, 2 flower leis and crowns, and one wedding certificate made of tapa. Patrick charges 188.000 CFP for 2 people if you contact him directly. The Hotel Bora Bora sells this **Special Honeymooner's Day** for 260.000 CFP per couple, and the Bora Bora Lagoon Resort sells this **Honeymoon Dreaming Day** for 277.000 CFP per couple, including photographer services. The IC Moana Resort charges 327.800 CFP for a **Royal Ceremony on a Private Motu** with the traditional oven and private outrigger tour.

Wedding Chapels

Bora Bora Pearl Beach Resort, Bora Bora Nui Resort & Spa, Intercontinental Bora Bora Resort & Spa and Le Méridien, have wedding chapels for more classic type ceremonies. The Four Seasons Resort will also have a wedding chapel.

You can also get married on a catamaran or underwater in Bora Bora. But no matter how romantic or bizarre your ceremony is, it is still not legal unless you meet all the requirements outlined under *Getting Married* in Chapter 7 of this guide.

17. Maupiti

If you appreciate the beauty of Bora Bora but not the mass tourism, **Maupiti** offers similar scenery, peace and tranquility, as well as an authentic Polynesian experience, with genuinely friendly people who are not burned out by seeing too many tourists. If you want to find out what Bora Bora was like 40 years ago, then go to Maupiti. It offers so much more than sunshine, white sand beaches and a turquoise lagoon. The rhythm of life is slow and easy. There's gentleness to the place and the people that will answer a longing inside you to know the "real Polynesia." The villagers still smile and say "Ia Ora Na" when you meet. The longer you stay in Maupiti, the longer you will want to stay.

Lying just 40 km. (25 miles) west of bustling Bora Bora, Maupiti is considered the hidden jewel in the necklace of emerald islands and atolls that make up the Society Islands. Some people say it's one of the prettiest islands in the South Seas.

Like Bora Bora, Maupiti has a central island with a high mountain range of volcanic origins, and is surrounded by a shallow, sparkling lagoon with 5 long offshore *motu* islets bordered by beautiful white sand beaches. **Onoiau** is the name of a narrow pass leading into the lagoon. This formerly dangerous pass is more easily navigable since channel markers were added, but it can still be hazardous during high seas. The clear turquoise lagoon has pretty coral gardens, a plentiful supply of edible fish, lobsters, tridacna clams, *vana*, an edible sea urchin, and even *varo*, a sea centipede that is sought by gourmets. The *motus* provide coral gardens for watermelon and cantaloupe plantations, as well as secluded white sand beaches for sunbathing and excellent snorkeling grounds a few feet into the lagoon.

Mount Teurafaatiu rises 380 m. (1,246 ft.) above the central island, and is relatively easy to scale for panoramic views. **Point Tereia** on the main island is a lovely white sand beach in a natural environment, a favorite swimming site for the young people from the villages. Some of the older folks compare this beach to what Point Matira in Bora Bora was like 50 years ago. From here you can walk across the lagoon to the *motu*, in waist-deep water. Although you may encounter a few curious sharks, just hit the water hard with the palm of your hand and yell at them, and they will swim away. It works for the locals, and no tourists have been injured to date by the "friendly" sharks that grew up inside the lagoon.

Geologists say that Maupiti is the oldest of the high islands in the Society archipelago, and was formed some four million years ago.

Dr. Yosihiko H. Sinoto and Dr. Kenneth P. Emory of the Bernice P. Bishop Museum in Honolulu excavated a burial site in Maupiti in 1962 and 1963, unearthing 13 skeletons from the ninth century. Inside the tombs on Motu Paeao were adzes, fishhooks, lures and sperm whale tooth pendants that date back to circa

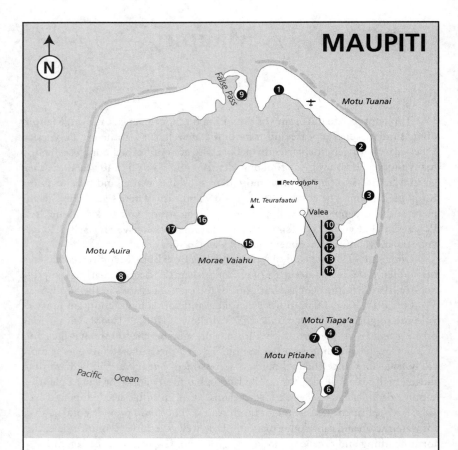

MAUPITI

N

False Pass

Motu Tuanai

Petroglyphs

Mt. Teurafaatui ▲

Valea

Motu Auira

Morae Vaiahu

Motu Tiapa'a

Motu Pitiahe

Pacific   Ocean

1. Pension Marau

2. Pension Poe Iti

3. Pension Terama

4. Pension Rose Des Iles

5. Maupiti Village

6. Kuriri Village

7. Pension Papahani

8. Pension Auira

9. Fare Pa'eao

10. Pension Eri

11. Chez Floriette

12. Chez Mareta Manu

13. Pension Taputea

14. Pension Tamati

15. Pension Tautiare Village

16. Visit Maupiti Pension

17. Tereia Beach

850 AD. This is one of the oldest archaeological sites in the Society Islands, and one of the most important. Doctor Sinoto said that the whale tooth pendants were the first material cultural link between the Society Islands and the New Zealand Maoris. Other archaeological sites include 2 more *marae* on the *motus* and 2 *marae* on the high island. In the valley of Heranae are petroglyphs representing turtles, a sacred animal for the ancient Maohi people.

At one time there were 9 districts and 9 royal Maohi chiefs on Maurua Ite Ra, as Maupiti was then called. Chiefs came from other islands to meet at the royal Marae Vaiahu for gatherings that included investiture ceremonies. A huge boulder at the stone temple has been engraved with the names of these chiefs, who came from Rimatara, Raivavae, Rapa, Atiu in the Cook Islands, and Hawaii. One of these kings was said to have come from Malaysia.

The Dutch explorer Roggeveen discovered Maupiti in 1722; 45 years before Samuel Wallis discovered Tahiti. It was united with Bora Bora during the reign of the last royal family. The 9 villages of ancient times have dwindled to the 3 contiguous villages of Vai'ea, Farauru and Pauma, where most of the 1,248 inhabitants live.

ARRIVALS & DEPARTURES
Arriving By Air
Air Tahiti, *Tel. 86.42.42* in Tahiti; *Tel. 60.15.05* in Maupiti, has a flight from Tahiti to Maupiti each Tues., 2 flights on Fri. and a Sun. flight, all with stops in Raiatea. During the high seasons there are non-stop flights from Tahiti to Maupiti on Mon. and Wed., and an additional flight on Fri. with a stop in Raiatea. There is a direct flight from Bora Bora on Sunday and a Fri. flight from Bora Bora that changes planes in Raiatea. The Maupiti airstrip is located on a *motu* islet across the lagoon from the main village. If you have reservations for a place to stay then you will be met at the airport and taken by boat to the pension. Otherwise, you can catch a ride with one of the taxi boats that goes to the airport for each flight arrival. The one-way airfare between Tahiti and Maupiti is 14.800 CFP and the round-trip fare is 27.200 CFP. The one-way fare between Raiatea and Maupiti is 6.900 CFP, and 6.500 CFP from Bora Bora.

You can also get to Maupiti by chartering an airplane in Tahiti from **Air Archipels**, *Tel. 81.30.30*; or **Air Tahiti**, *Tel. 86.42.42*.

Polynesia Hélicoptères, *Tel. 689/67.62.59; helico-bora@mail.pf*, provides helicopter transfers from Bora Bora to Maupiti on request.

Arriving By Boat
Maupiti Express II, *Tel. 689/67.66.69 (Bora Bora); cell phone 78.27.22/ 72.30.48; www.maupitiexpress.com.* This 140-passenger ship provides service between Raiatea, Taha'a, Bora Bora and Maupiti. The *Maupiti Express II* leaves Bora Bora on Tues., Thurs. and Sat. at 8:30am, arriving in Maupiti at 10:15am. The one-way fare from Bora Bora is 3.000 CFP and round-trip is 4.000 CFP.

Passengers under 12 years pay half-fare. If you want to take a day-trip from Bora Bora to Maupiti, you should contact Gérald Sachet at the above cell phone numbers. He is the owner/captain of *Maupiti Express II* and his wife runs the Pension Poe Iti, which serves as a land base for day-trippers. They have a small boat that is used for exploring the lagoon and motu islets. See information under *Where to Stay* and *Land and Lagoon Tours* in this chapter.

Departing By Air
Air Tahiti, *Tel. 60.15.05*; Tahiti Reservations *Tel. 86.42.42*. Air Tahiti has 4 flights from Maupiti to Papeete each week, stopping at Raiatea on Tues., twice on Fri. and once on Sun. During the high seasons there are direct flights to Tahiti each Mon. and Wed. There is a direct flight to Bora Bora on Sun.

Departing By Boat
Maupiti Express II, *Tel. 67.66.69/78.27.22/*72.30.48, leaves Maupiti at 4pm for Bora Bora each Tues., Thurs. and Sat. The trip takes 1:45 hrs. and the one-way fare is 3.000 CFP. Passengers under12 years pay half price.

ORIENTATION
The main village is **Vai'ea**, where the town hall, schools, Air Tahiti office, post office, church, school, airport boat dock, family pensions, snacks and a few small stores are located. This village suffered severe destruction in Nov. 1997 when Cyclone Osea destroyed 95 percent of the houses and buildings on the island. Most of the houses are now of the MTR variety, which is a box-like 'anti-cyclone' design, built on stilts. Each family has added their own touch of flowers and colored leaves planted around the houses to make them more attractive.

GETTING AROUND MAUPITI
By Bicycle
Arieta Firuu, *Tel. 67.80.63*, rents bikes for 1.000 CFP per day at the public boat dock in Vai'ea village. **Loana Manuarii**, *Tel. 67.81.46*, also rents bicycles on the boat dock for 1.000 CFP a day.

By Mini-Van
Visit Maupiti (ex Maupiti Loisirs), *Tel./Fax 67.80.95*. cell 21.88.21. Simone Chan speaks English and provides excursions around the island in her 9-seat a/c Mercedes-Benz minibus for 2.000 CFP. Day-trippers arriving on the *Maupiti Express* can spend the day with her and learn about life in Maupiti.

By Boat
Maupiti Poe Iti Tours and **Visit Maupiti** provide boat excursions around the island and picnics on the motu. See information under *Lagoon Tours* in this chapter.

WHERE TO STAY & EAT
On the Motus – Moderate
FARE PA'EAO, *B.P. 33, Vai'ea, Maupiti 98732. Tel./Fax 689/67.81.01; fare.pae.ao@mail.pf. On Motu Pa'eao, 10 min. by boat from the airport. Round-trip boat transfers between airport and pension 1.600 CFP per person; round-trip boat transfers to boat dock 1.500 CFP per person. MAP bungalow 14.470 CFP sgl/18.740 CFP double; taxes included. Family rates available. MC, V.*

This pension has 6 bungalows of the FEI type that have become the standard Polynesian bungalow partially financed by the local government. Tahiti Tourism has awarded them a 3-Tiare rating. These attractive units, which are wooden with a wood shake roof, consist of a double bed and a single bed, a ceiling fan, an electric anti-mosquito device, a mosquito net over the beds, a terrace and a private bathroom with cold water shower. Breakfast and dinner are served in the communal dining room. Owner Janine Tavearii is assisted by her son Nelson and his wife Linda, who also have a pension in Raivavae. Free kayaks are provided for guests, and an island tour by boat is 3.000 CFP per person. The snorkeling is very good here and the sunsets are sometimes incredible.

KURIRI VILLAGE, *B.P. 23, Vai'ea, Maupiti 98732. Tel./Fax 689/67.82.23; Cell 689/74.54.54; kuriri@mail.pf; www.maupiti-kuriri.com. Beside the ocean on Motu Tiapa'a, an islet 15 min. by boat from the airport. Free round-trip boat transfers between airport and pension. 2008 Rates: Bungalow with MAP 12.500 CFP per person; single supplement 2.120 CFP; light lunch 1.800 CFP, full lunch 2.800 CFP. VAT tax included. V.*

Since 2002 this lodging has been owned by Anne Marie Badolle and her husband, a French couple who sailed their boat around the world before settling down in Maupiti. There are 5 bungalows built of natural materials that face the beach or the garden. 3 of the *fares* contain a double bed or 2 twin beds, plus a private bathroom with cold water. The 2 family *fares* have a double bed, mattresses on the mezzanine, a living room and a private bathroom with cold water. All the beds are covered by a mosquito net. Lighting is by solar power, and guests have access to telephone, fax and email service in the reception area.

Rather than facing the inner lagoon, the view you'll have here is of the open ocean and Bora Bora in the distance, and if you get up early in the morning you can watch the sunrise behind Bora Bora. There is even a panoramic lookout deck built above the seaside dining area, for gazing at the sea and sky. The beach on the ocean side is always cooled by the trade winds and you can take a nice siesta under the thatched roof of the cushioned contemplation deck overlooking the sea. You can swing in a hammock or lie on a chaise longue. However, if you are visiting between Jul.-Oct. you may want to remain vigilant and be on the lookout for humpback whales. Snorkeling equipment and sea kayaks are free for guest use, as well as lagoon fishing and reef discovery walks. Paid activities include a boat tour around the island with a picnic on a motu, outrigger sailing canoe, and mountain hikes.

PENSION MARAU, *B.P. 11, Vai'ea, Maupiti 98732. Tel. 689/67.81.19/ 70.56.09/72.48.86; Fax 689/67.82.46; contact@pension-marau.com; www.pension-marau.com. On Motu Tuanai, 5 min, by 4WD from the airport and the village. Round-trip transfers 500 CFP per person. 2008 Rates: Bungalow sgl/dbl 8.000 CFP; add 1.000 CFP for extra mattress. Breakfast 1.000 CFP, lunch or dinner 2.500 CFP per person. Add taxes. No credit cards.*

This is a new pension with 7 modern bungalows on the same motu as the airport. Each bungalow has a double bed, a ceiling fan, a private bathroom with cold water, and a covered terrace. Mosquito repellents and house linens are provided, and the rooms are cleaned every 2 days. Polynesian type meals of lagoon fish, breadfruit, taro, sweet potatoes and plantains are served in a Fare Pote'e shelter. Paid activities include a 4WD tour around the main island, a boat tour around the island, deep sea fishing and a picnic on a motu.

PENSION POE ITI, *B.P. 39, Vai'ea, Maupiti 98732. Tel. 689/74.58.76; maupitiespress@mail.pf. On Motu Tuanai, 5 min. by boat or car from the airport and 5 min. by boat from the village. 2008 Rates: Bungalow 7.000 CFP sgl., 8.000 CFP dbl. Extra bed 1.000 CFP per night. Breakfast 700 CFP, lunch or dinner 2.500 CFP per person. Add taxes. No credit cards.*

This pension opened in October 2004, with 4 bungalows built in a garden setting on the same motu where the airport is located. Tahiti Tourism has awarded them the top rating of 3 Tiares, and this is also my preferred pension. The wooden bungalows with wood shake roofs are the government approved and subsidized FEI type units that are modern and attractive. Electricity is provided by wind generators. Each bungalow has a king size bed and a single bed, A/C, TV and DVD player, a private bathroom with hot water shower and a private covered terrace facing the white sand beach and lagoon. The kitchen and restaurant/bar are located in separate buildings, and the spacious dining area can accommodate day visitors who come over from Bora Bora on board the *Maupiti Express II*, whose captain, Gérald Sachet, is also owner of Pension Poe Iti and Maupiti Poe Iti Tours. His wife, Joséphine Ah-Yun, manages the pension and takes care of guests. The snorkeling equipment is complimentary, as well as the kayaks, bicycles, and society games. She provides free boat transfers to the village twice a day. Maupiti Poe Iti Tours will drop you at Motu Tiapa'a and return later to pick you up for 1.000 CFP per person, or you can join a boat tour around the island for 2.500 CFP, and have a picnic on an uninhabited motu for 3.500 CFP.

PENSION PAPAHANI, *B.P. 1, Vai'ea, Maupiti 98732. Tel. 689/60.15.35; Fax 689/60.15.36. On Motu Tiapa'a, 15 min. by boat from the airport. Round-trip boat transfers included. 2008 AP Rates per person: Small Garden Bungalow 10.000 CFP, Big Garden Bungalow 12.000 CFP, Beach bungalow 13.000 CFP. MAP also available. Add taxes. No credit cards.*

This pension is located on the lagoon side of the *motu* facing the pass and the village, and it has a beautiful beach of fine white sand on a point of land. Some of the old *fares* were destroyed by Cyclone Osea in 1997 and 2 are still standing. 3 new bungalows have also been built. The bungalows are very close together and are simply furnished with a double bed in the smaller units and a double bed in the family bungalows. Another bed can be added to the larger units on request. All the larger bungalows have ceiling fans, and the smaller units have electric fans. All units have mosquito nets, a bathroom with a hot water shower, and house linens. Vilna Tuheiava serves family style meals in the *fare pote'e* dining shelter beside the beach. Her husband Denis or their son Rudy can take you on a boat tour of the lagoon for 3.000 CFP or for a boat tour with picnic on a motu for 5.000 CFP. Snorkeling gear and kayaks are free for guests. You'll get a taste of the authentic Polynesian life when you stay here.

MAUPITI VILLAGE, *Vai'ea, Maupiti 98732. Tel./Fax 689/67.80.08; Cell 689/70.13.69/76.03.69; alain.colomes@mail.pf. On Motu Tiapa'a, 5 min. by boat from the airport and 3 min. by boat from the village. 2008 Rates: Bungalow and AP meals 12.000 CFP per person; Room and AP meals 7.000 CFP per person; beds in the lounge 6.000 CFP. Taxes included. No credit cards.*

There are 3 simple plywood bungalows beside a pretty beach, each containing 2 double beds with mosquito nets, and a bathroom with hot water. There is also a 3-bedroom house with a double bed and a single bed in each bedroom, plus a lounge with beds, and a communal bathroom with hot water. Another house has 2 bedrooms, a lounge-kitchen, refrigerator, 2 terraces and table tennis. There is plenty of fresh water and solar electricity day and night. Audine Colomes, the owner/manager, speaks a little English and serves fresh seafood, with Tahitian food served on Sun. Free activities include kayaks and outrigger paddle canoes, fishing gear, motu tour, a visit to the marae, and walking on the reef. Round-trip boat transfers are 1.500 CFP to the village and 2.000 CFP to the airport. A bicycle tour around the main island is 1.000 CFP, a boat tour of the lagoon is 4.000 CFP, and deep sea fishing is 5.000 CFP per person.

PENSION AUIRA, *B.P. 2, Vai'ea, Maupiti 98732. Tel./Fax 689/67.80.26. On Motu Auira, 20 min. by boat from the airport. Round-trip boat transfers 2.000 CFP per person. 2008 MAP Rates per person: Garden Fare 8.500 CFP; Beach Fare 9.500 CFP per person. Camping 2.000 CFP. Add taxes. No credit cards.*

The beach here is very beautiful when it is clean, with soft white powdery sand and clear shallow water in the lagoon that is deep enough for swimming if you walk out into the blue water several feet distant. All of the former *fares* were destroyed by the cyclone in 1997, and Edna Terai and her husband Gilbert, who are both Polynesian, have rebuilt 5 bungalows: 3 on the beach and 2 in the garden. All the units are furnished with a double bed, a private bathroom with cold water and mosquito screens. House linens are provided and there is a restaurant-bar on the premises. Campers can pitch their tent in the shaded garden or on the beach and they also have bathroom facilities with a cold water shower and can cook their meals in the kitchen, which has a refrigerator.

Edna can arrange for your boat excursions with a picnic or to watch the manta rays and feed the stingrays inside the lagoon. Her husband will take you by boat to the village on request, where you can bike around the island or hike in the mountains.

PENSION TERAMA, *Vai'ea, Maupiti 98732. Tel./Fax 689/67.81.96; cell 71.03.33; maupiti.terama@mail.pf. On Motu Tuanai, 5 min. by boat from the airport and the village. Free round-trip transfers. 2008 Rates: Room with MAP 7.000 CFP per person; half price for child up to 12 years. Add taxes. No credit cards.*

Melissa Firuu and her French husband, Marc Pinson, have built a 3-bedroom concrete house in the middle of a Tiare Tahiti plantation on the airport motu, but there are no neighbors and no noise in this remote area. There is a double bed in 2 of the guest rooms and 3 single beds in the other room. Both the interior and exterior bathrooms with cold water showers are shared. The kitchen is separate and a *fare pote'e* shelter serves as the dining room. Guests have use of the kayaks and can hop a ride to the village when Marc goes there to shop. Both Melissa and Marc speak some English and are very open and friendly.

On the Main Island

PENSION TAUTIARE VILLAGE, *B.P. 16, Vai'ea, Maupiti 98732. Tel./Fax 689/67.83.58; pension-tautiare@mail.pf. On seaside in Hurumanu, 2 km (1.2 miles) from the village. Round-trip boat transfers 1.500 CFP per person. 2008 Rates: Room and breakfast 5.000 CFP per person; Room with MAP 6.500 CFP; Room with AP 8.000 CFP per person per day. Add taxes. No credit cards.*

David and Dawn Domingo have a 4-bedroom guesthouse on the main island, located between the white sand beach of Tereia and the Vaiahu Marae. There is a hot water shower in the bathroom, plus a private terrace for each room. Snorkeling equipment and kayaks are available for guest use, and bikes can be rented. Tahiti Tourism has awarded a 2-Tiare rating to this pension.

Economy

PENSION ERI, *Vai'ea, Maupiti 98732. Tel. 689/67.81.29. Beside the lagoon in Vai'ea village, 700 m (763 yds.) from the ferry dock and 3 km from the airport. Round-trip boat transfers from airport 1.000 CFP per person; by car from boat dock 500 CFP. 2008 Rates: Room 3.000 CFP person; room with MAP 5.000 CFP per person; room with AP 6.500 CFP per person. Add taxes. No credit cards.*

This is a popular pension with young French people and other travelers who want to stay on the main island, but it is noisy here in the heart of the village. The 4-bedroom house is very clean, with a double bed in each room. Guests share the kitchen, living room and bathroom with cold water. House linens are furnished. Eri's daughter, Maeva Mohi, manages the pension, serving fresh fruits and vegetables from their farm, along with fresh fish. Snack Tarona is also close by. You can rent a bicycle or kayak, go by boat to the motu, fishing in the lagoon or on picnics to a white sand beach.

VISIT MAUPITI PENSION (ex **Maupiti Loisirs**), *B.P. 66, Vai'ea, Maupiti 98732. Tel./Fax 689/67.80.95; cell 21.88.21. The house is 4 km (2.5 miles) from the* *village on the main island. 2008 Rates: Room and MAP 5.000 CFP per person; Camping tent and MAP 4.000 CFP per person per day. No credit cards.*

This is the lodging closest to the white sand beach of Tereia, easily reached by bicycle or foot. Ui Teriihaunui and Simone Chan have a 2-bedroom house for guests, with ceiling fans and mosquito nets in each room. There are communal cold water showers indoors and outdoors. Meals are served family style. Bicycles and kayaks are free for guest use. Simone, who is Chinese-Tahitian, is a former schoolteacher and speaks English. She will take you around the island in her a/c mini-bus for 2.000 CFP per person.

Ui has an 18-ft. locally made fiberglass boat with a flat bottom that he uses to take people all the way around the island, a feat that cannot be accomplished by big boats unless it's at high tide. Ui's all-day excursion includes swimming in the sparkling lagoon, a visit to the petroglyphs carved in basaltic stone and a lunch stop at Snack Tarona, the island's only snack stand. In the afternoon he will take you to snorkel in the "false pass" and to visit the Vaiahu Marae ("sacred stone") if it is still low tide, as the marae is covered by water during high tide. Ui is a well-informed historian who loves to share his knowledge of Maupiti with others. I met him in 1977 when I first visited the island and he taught me a lot about the legends and culture of Maupiti. You will appreciate Ui's many stories much more if you speak French. Ui always greets their guests at the Maupiti airport with leis of Tiare Tahiti, and they also give visitors lots of fresh fruit from the garden.

Campers seeking a "sauvage" site to pitch their tent will enjoy the seclusion they'll find at Ui's property on Motu Auira. If you want to get "lost" for a while and just enjoy the beauty of nature on a small *motu* islet, this is a good place to do it, but no children are allowed. A huge bonus for this spot is that you can watch the sun drop behind the horizon every evening, and there's not anything to impede that view. It's all wide-open space—just the sky and the sea and the wonderful magic of an incredible tropical sunset.

Other Bed & Breakfast Lodgings
   CHEZ FLORIETTE, *Tel./Fax 689/67.80.85*. 1 bungalow with communal bathroom beside lagoon in middle of Vai'ea village, 7.000 CFP MAP and 8.000 CFP AP. **CHEZ MARETA MANU**, *Tel. 689/67.82.32*. Manuela Mohi has 3 guest rooms in the main village. EP Rates 3.000 CFP per person. MAP and AP meals available. **PENSION TAMATI**, *Tel. 689/67.80.10*, an old 2-story house with 9 rooms and private bathrooms for 4.500 CFP MAP. **PENSION TAPUTEA**, *Tel./Fax 689/67.82.78; pension.taputea@yahoo.fr*. A 3-room house in the main village, 6.500-7.000 CFP MAP. **PENSION ROSE DES ILES**, *689/70.50.70,* has 1 big beach bungalow on Motu Tiapa'a that can sleep 5 people. Camping for 2 tents also available.

SEEING THE SIGHTS
   You can walk around the main island of Maupiti in about 2-3 hours,

depending on your pace, and how many times you stop to take pictures, shake down a ripe mango from a roadside tree or stop for a swim in the inviting lagoon. A road circles the island for 9.6 km (5.9 miles). You can also bike around the island and visit the petroglyphs of turtles, the family and royal *marae* stone temples and other archaeological sites. The *maraes* are located on some of the *motu* islets, as well as the central island.

The hosts at each pension normally organize the activities for their guests, which include snorkeling and shelling, outrigger paddle canoes, fishing in the lagoon and pass for lobster and fish, and picnics on the *motu.*

Lagoon Tours

Maupiti Poe Iti Tours, *Tel.74.58.76*, is owned by Gérald Sachet, who owns *Maupiti Express* and Pension Poe Iti. He has a 20-ft. long flat bottom aluminum boat that is used for lagoon tours and transfers to Motu Tiapa'a. A circle island tour by boat includes fruit tasting and coconut water for 2.500 CFP, and you can also have a picnic on request for 3.500 CFP. The boat will drop you off on Motu Tiapa'a and pick you up later for 1.000 CFP per person. See information on *Where to Stay* in this chapter.

Visit Maupiti (ex-Maupiti Loisirs), *Tel. 67.80.95/21.88.21,* is operated by Ui Teriihaunui. He will take up to 4 passengers all the way around the island in his 18-ft. launch for 3.500 CFP, and will include a picnic on the motu for 5.000 CFP per person. Ui also has 2 kayaks and a 15-ft. polyester skiff boat for rent. See more information under *Where to Stay* in this chapter.

SPORTS & RECREATION
Mountain Climbing

Tefarerii Excursions, *Tel./Fax 67.81.83; nicolerichardo@mail.pf,* is operated by Auguste Taurua. He can take up to 10 people on hikes to the cliff of Hotu Parata, which is 165 m. (541 ft.) above the village of Vai'ea. Mango, wild hibiscus and Tahitian chestnut trees shade the fairly steep trail, but you have glimpses of the panorama of motu islets and the varying shades of the lagoon and coral gardens as you ascend. The path becomes harder and more dangerous to climb as you go higher and the crumbling rock sometimes causes landslides before you reach the end of the cliff. But once you get there and look out to the neighboring islands and infinity, you'll feel it was definitely worth the effort.

PRACTICAL INFORMATION
Bank

A representative from Banque Socredo calls at Maupiti once a month, which is also an occasion for arts and crafts vendors to set up shop in the Salle Polyvalente at the *mairie* (town hall).

Doctor

Dr. Patrick Henry provides medical assistance at Maupiti's Infirmary, *Tel. 67.80.18.*

Internet Service

Visitors can check their email messages on the computer at the *mairie* (town hall) in Vai'ea village, which will be connected in the wedding hall (*Salle des Mariages*) on request. Wifi service is also available. You can buy a Mana Spot card at most post offices in the islands that will allow access.

Tourist Information

Maupiti Tourism Committee, *Tel. 689/67.82.46/60.15.55/71.99.45; nicole.spitz@commune-maupiti.pf.* Nicole Spitz is the president. She also owns Tarona Snack.

18. Tuamotu Islands

The 77 atolls and one upraised island that form the **Tuamotu Archipelago** are mere specks of land out in the heart of the trade wind, lost in the vastness of the blue Pacific. Sprinkled across ten latitudes and covering a length of 1,500 km (930 mi.) and a width of 500 km (310 mi.), these are some of the most remote islands in the world.

This vast collection of coral islets conjures up castaway dreams on a tropical isle, the ultimate get-away for rejuvenation of the body and soul. Tiny green oases floating in the desert of the sea, with names as exotic as the trade winds and coconut trees. Wild windswept beaches, the sea and sunshine. And only the sound of the surf and the cries of the sea birds for company. Fragrant *miki miki* blends their perfume with aromas of salt spray and blossoms from the *tiare kahaia*, *geo geo* and *gapata* trees. The lagoons shimmer with a brilliance of light and color unsurpassed, and a submerged landscape of untouched magic and awesome beauty awaits beneath the sun-gilded waters tinged in turquoise.

Polynesian explorers, sailing from their homeland in the West, settled on the lonely shores of these atolls centuries ago. Pakamotu, they called their new home—a cloud of islands. Outcast chiefs from Tahiti and the Marquesas Islands named them Paumotu, the Submissive or Conquered Islands, the isles of Exiles. European ships from many nations rode the treacherous reef in this maritime maze, thus adding the names Low or Dangerous Archipelago and the Labyrinth. The **Paumotu people** now call their home the Tuamotu—many islands.

More than 400 varieties of fantastic, rainbow-hued fish glint like ornaments of gold in the iridescent waters of the sheltered lagoons, providing hours of enchantment for snorkelers and scuba divers. On many of the atolls you can visit pearl farms and fish parks inside the lagoons, take boat tours to visit the various *motu* islets and picnic under the black-eyed gaze of the white fairy tern.

You can go on fishing expeditions, hunt for tiny shells to string into pretty necklaces, learn to weave hats, mats and baskets from palm fronds, and eat delicious seafood direct from its shell while you stand at the edge of a Technicolor reef. In the evening you can sit under a starlit sky, watching the Southern Cross as you listen to musicians playing island tunes on guitars and ukuleles. Their songs tell of old gods and heroes, the spirits of sharks and fish, destructive hurricanes, people lost at sea, shipwrecks on the treacherous reef, *vahines* and *l'amour*.

More than two dozen of these atolls have airstrips and regular air service from Tahiti, and inter-island trading schooners transport supplies and passengers. The lack of potable water remains a problem on many of these remote islands, while solar energy provides electricity and hot water for villages and remote pearl farms.

"MANY LAGOONS" BY RALPH VARADY

You have to see an atoll to get its feeling. It leaves a vastly different impression than a high island does. There is something about the atolls that is magnetic. They are lost and, for the greater part, deserted, full of flies and copra bugs. They are remote, a death trap in a hurricane, a danger to navigation and often inaccessible except by small boat. They offer the minimum of human comfort, their maximum asset being their copra; and yet there is something wonderful about them, and truly they belong to the list of nature's wonders.

Many of the islands are uninhabited and seldom visited. Nevertheless, the traveler who wanders into this maritime maze will be rewarded by what he sees. These Dangerous Islands are not sizable or comfortable, but they are rich in the realm of color. The debauch of color found in the Tuamotu lagoons is incomparable to that of any other island group.

Personally, I hope that these islands never have "facilities" so that they will be kept as they are now: unspoiled, beautiful and natural. It is good to know that some of these islands will remain out of reach of a fast-moving civilization."

This archipelago is rapidly being developed, with modern telecommunications services now reaching even the most distant of the settled islands.

The atolls of Rangiroa, Manihi, Tikehau and Fakarava, which are described in this chapter, offer international class hotels, small hotels, pensions or guest houses with simple accommodations. These are the destinations most frequently visited by travelers, but the number of visitors in the Tuamotus is so minute that these islands still offer a natural environment and miles of empty beaches.

You will also find accommodations in family homes and pensions on the atolls of Ahe, Anaa, Apataki, Arutua, Kaukura, Mataiva, Takapoto and Takaroa. Unfortunately, we are not able to give the details of each atoll in this book, but you can obtain a list of lodging facilities from Tahiti Tourisme or the Haere Mai Association. The contact numbers are listed in the *Basic Information* chapter under *Where to Find More Information About Tahiti & French Polynesia*.

RANGIROA

Rangiroa, also called **Rairoa**, means 'long sky' in the Paumotu dialect, the language of the Polynesian inhabitants. The coral ring encircling the pear-shaped atoll of Rangiroa contains more than 240 *motu* islets, separated by at least 100 very shallow *hoa* channels and three passes. The Tiputa Pass and Avatoru Pass on the north of the atoll are deep and wide enough for ships to enter the lagoon, and the Tivaru Pass on the west is narrow and shallow. A vast inland sea measures

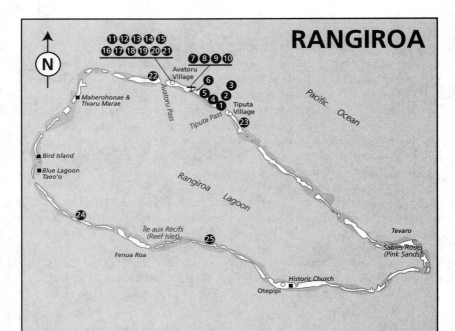

RANGIROA

1. Pension Glorine
2. Les Relais De Josephine
3. Chez Teina & Marie
4. Pension Bounty
5. Hotel Kia Ora Rangiroa
6. Novotel Rangiroa Beach Resort
7. Raira Lagon
8. Pension Tuanake
9. Ariitini Village
10. Pension Cecile
11. Turiroa Village
12. Pension Martine
13. Pension Henri
14. Pension Loyna
15. Pension Hinanui
16. Rangiroa Lodge
17. Chez Nanua
18. Miki Miki
19. Pension Herenui
20. Pension Henriette
21. Le Merou Bleu
22. Lagon Vert
23. Chez Lucien
24. Les Fare De Tiki Hoa
25. Hotel Kia Ora Sauvage

approximately 75 km (47 mi.) long by 25 km (16 mi.) wide, covering a distance of 1,020 sq. km (393 sq. mi.). This is the largest atoll in the Southern Hemisphere and one of the biggest atolls in the world.

The Dutch explorer Le Maire discovered Rangiroa in 1616, but the first European settlers did not arrive until 1851. The missionaries insisted that the population be grouped in Avatoru and Tiputa rather than dispersing in small villages around the atoll, where they could more likely continue their heathenistic practices. A cyclone in 1906 destroyed the village of Tivaru, and today the population of 3,384 inhabitants reside in the villages of Avatoru and Tiputa.

Rangiroa is the administrative center of the northern Tuamotu atolls. Children from the small atolls are sent to junior high school and technical schools in Rangiroa, where they are lodged throughout the school year, some of the students returning to their homes only during the two-month vacation in July and August.

Rangiroa's lagoon is world famous for unsurpassed scuba diving in the warmest and clearest water you can dream of. Favorite excursions include "shooting the pass," where hundreds of fish, moray eels and sharks swim beside and below you, swept along by the strong currents. You can view this exciting spectacle aboard a glass-bottom boat, or jump into the water with mask, snorkel, fins or even scuba diving bottles. Vacation memories are also made while paddling a kayak or outrigger canoe, sailing inside the lagoon, line or drag fishing, on boat excursions to the pink sand beach of Vahituri, while admiring the fossilized coral formations on Reef Island, and during a full day picnic trip to the Blue Lagoon or Green Lagoon.

Among this wealth of scenery is an attractive selection of international resort hotels, small hotels with thatched roof bungalows and simple family owned pensions with fresh lagoon fish on the menu. Across the lagoon from the villages are very basic sleeping facilities in camp-like settings that can be reached only by boat, where you can walk on beaches as remote as Robinson Crusoe's. On these beautiful little islets you can live a *sauvage* simplified life with freshly caught food from the reef and lagoon.

ARRIVALS & DEPARTURES
Arriving By Air
Air Tahiti has 1-3 direct ATR flights daily between Tahiti and Rangiroa. The 55-60 min. non-stop flight is 15.900 CFP one-way for adults, and 29.200 CFP round-trip, tax included. You can also fly from Bora Bora to Rangiroa with 70-min. direct flights on Mon., Tues., Wed., Fri. and Sun., and with a stop in Tikehau on Thurs., for 23.400 CFP one-way. Direct flight service is also provided to Rangiroa from Manihi each Tues., Wed., and Sun., for 10.400 CFP. There are direct flights from Tikehau to Rangiroa daily except Sun. for 5.600 CFP.

If you have reservations with a hotel, pension, cruise line or yacht charter company, then you will be met at the airport and driven to your accommodation. **Air Tahiti reservations**: Tahiti, *Tel. 86.42.42, www.airtahiti.aero.*

You can also get to Rangiroa by chartering an airplane in Tahiti from **Air Archipels**, *Tel. 81.30.30*; or **Air Tahiti**, *Tel. 86.42.42*.

Arriving By Boat
Mareva Nui, *Tel. 42.25.53, Fax 42.25.57*, is a 181-ft. steel ship that transports cargo between Tahiti and the Tuamotu atolls. It leaves Tahiti every 15 days, arriving in Rangiroa three days later. There are 12 berths for the maximum number of passengers allowed, but no cabins on board. The one-way fare to Rangiroa is 5.700 CFP. Add 2.200 CFP per person per day for three meals.
St. Xavier Maris Stella III, *Tel. 42.23.58*, can transport 12 passengers, sleeping in an a/c cabin or on the deck. The deck fare from Tahiti to Rangiroa is 7.070 CFP and a berth is 10.000 CFP per person, including meals. Bring your own sleeping mat, pillow and bed linen. Sometimes Rangiroa is the first stop after a 20-hr. crossing from Tahiti, and on other voyages it may be the 3rd island visited. The ship leaves Papeete every 15 days.

Departing By Air
Air Tahiti has 1-5 flights daily from Rangiroa to Tahiti, including up to 3 direct flights per day. You can fly direct from Rangiroa to Manihi daily except Thurs., direct from Rangiroa to Tikehau on Mon., Wed., Fri. and Sun., and direct from Rangiroa to Fakarava on Tues., Wed., and Fri., and with a stop in Manihi on Sat. There is a direct flight from Rangiroa to Nuku Hiva each Sat., continuing on to Hiva Oa. *Tel. 93.11.00* in Rangiroa. Tickets can be purchased at the Air Tahiti office in Avatoru. If you already have reservations and a ticket, reconfirmations should be made one day in advance, and most hotels will take care of this for you. Check-in time at the airport is one hour before scheduled departure.

Departing By Boat
The *Mareva Nui*, *Tel. 42.25.53, Fax 42.25.57*, calls at 11-12 other atolls after leaving Rangiroa each 15 days. *St. Xavier Maris Stella III*, *Tel. 42.23.58*, leaves Rangiroa every 15 days for Ahe, Manihi, and all the western Tuamotu atolls, before returning to Papeete. Fares are determined by length of voyage to Tahiti.

ORIENTATION
The villages of **Avatoru** and **Tiputa** are located on the northern coast of Rangiroa atoll, where most of the population lives beside the two deep passes, a 45-minute boat ride apart. A flat paved road 10 km (6.2 mi.) long extends from the Avatoru Pass to the Tiputa Pass, with the ocean on one side and the lagoon on the other side. Most of the hotels and pensions are on the lagoon side of this road and the airport is about halfway between the two passes. You will find churches, schools, post offices and small food stores in both villages and it is easy to walk around once you are there, but you will probably find that the people in Tiputa village are friendlier to visitors.

You can explore Avatoru village to the Tiputa Pass by car, scooter or bicycle. You have to take a boat across the Tiputa Pass to get to Tiputa village, which can be easily discovered in a short walk. Overlooking the Tiputa Pass is **Ohotu Point**, a favorite destination in late afternoon when dolphins can often be seen playing in the swift current that flows through the pass between the open ocean and the interior lagoon.

GETTING AROUND RANGIROA

The hosts at the hotels and pensions meet their guests at the airport and provide transportation to the lodgings. Taxi service is provided on the Avatoru side of the pass by Tauraa Taxi, *Tel. 77.28.02*, during the day only.

Maurice Snow, *Tel. 96.76.09/78.13.25*, provides taxi boat service between Tiputa and Avatoru, as well as other lagoon transfers. The fare from Ohotu Point to Tiputa village is 250 CFP one-way and 400 CFP round-trip. From the Hotel Kia Ora to Tiputa dock the taxi boat fare is 1.250 CFP.

Car, Scooter & Bicycle Rentals

Europcar Rangiroa (also called **Rangi Rent-A-Car**) has an office near Avatoru village, *Tel./Fax 96.03.28, cell 20.17.89*, and desks at the Hotel Kia Ora and the Novotel Rangiroa Beach Resort Hotel. The rate for a 2-passenger 4-wheel Fun Car starts at 5.500 CFP for 2 hours. A 2-passenger Mini Car rents for 6.900 CFP for 2 hours; a 5-passenger automatic drive car with a/c costs 8.000 CFP for 4 hours, and a 4WD a/c Suzuki is 9.000 CFP for 4 hours. Scooters rent for 4.200 CFP for 2 hours. Rates for cars and scooters include unlimited mileage, insurance and gas. Bicycles cost 900 CFP for 4 hours and bikes with a baby chair are 1.200 CFP for 4 hours.

Arenahio Locations is operated by Pomare Temaehu in Avatoru, *Tel./Fax 96.82.45, cell 23.37.20; carpom@mail.pf*. A 4-passenger a/c car rents for 6.200 CFP for 4 hours. Gas is not included. Scooters rent for 4.200 CFP for 4 hours, and bicycles cost 700 CFP for a half-day and 1.300 CFP for a full day.

Bicycles can also be rented from several of the hotels and pensions.

WHERE TO STAY
Deluxe

HOTEL KIA ORA RANGIROA, *B.P. 198, Avatoru, Rangiroa 98775. Tel. 689/93.11.11; Fax 689/96.04.93; Reservations: Tel. 689/93.11.17; Fax 689/96.02.20; resa@hotelkiaora.pf; www.hotelkiaora.com. 63 units beside the lagoon at Ohotu Bay, 2 km (1.2 mi.) east of the airport. 2008 EP Rates sgl/dbl: garden bungalow 32.000 CFP; garden suite 39.000 CFP; beach bungalow 46.000 CFP; beach suite 51.000 CFP; deluxe beach bungalow 63.000 CFP; overwater bungalow 68.000 CFP. Additional person 6.500 CFP. MAP 8.300 CFP, AP 11.500 CFP. Add taxes. Round-trip airport transfers provided. All major credit cards.*

The Hotel Kia Ora opened in 1973 as the Kia Ora Village, and for many years this was the only international class hotel on Rangiroa. The hotel's present capacity of 63 units includes 23 garden bungalows and 5 garden suites that are spread throughout 40 acres of gardens and coconut trees, and beside a white sand beach almost a mile long. The garden bungalows can sleep two in a king-size bed and the garden suites have accommodations for four adults, with a king-size bed in the bedroom and a sofa bed in the lounge.

The 19 beach bungalows have a bedroom with a king size bed and a living room with a single bed or day bed, with sliding doors to separate the two rooms. The 3 beach suites have a bedroom downstairs and another bedroom with two twin beds in the loft, plus a separate lounge, providing accommodations for four people. All these beach units have a Jacuzzi on the sundeck, facing a very white sand beach. Three new deluxe beach units have been added, which offer an outdoor bathtub as well as a jet stream infinity pool instead of a Jacuzzi.

The 10 overwater bungalows are so beautiful, comfortable and romantic you'll never want to leave. They stand on a wooden pontoon over the jade and blue water and are made of thatched roofs, local woods and woven bamboo walls. They are spacious junior suites with a separate lounge and a glass bottom coffee table for fish watching. The decor is a subtle Polynesian design in cool colors to complement the blues and greens of the lagoon. Each overwater unit has a shiny, modern bathroom, telephone and safe, plus a big terrace and a private solarium, with steps leading into the inviting lagoon, a huge liquid playground of a thousand delights.

All the bungalows are built in a traditional Polynesian style that blends noble and precious materials with international class comfort. All units include a/c and ceiling fans and they are equipped with telephones, dial-up Internet connections, safety boxes, refrigerator/mini bar, and tea and coffee making facilities. In the beach and overwater bungalows a door separates the bedroom from the large bathroom. All the bathrooms have a big tiled hot water shower and walls that are decorated with coral and mother-of-pearl shell. There is a hairdryer and the range of toiletries is replenished daily. Room service is provided on request.

In addition to an infinity swimming pool and adjacent Jacuzzi, the hotel provides free snorkeling equipment for its guests, outrigger paddle canoes, tennis, volleyball, basketball, *petanque* (French bowls), arts and crafts exhibits and frequent shows of Tahitian songs and dances. The Kahaia Lounge is equipped with a pool table, wide screen television with DVD and VCR players and films, computer with paid Internet access, library, and board games such as chess, backgammon, scrabble and dice. Another free service provided is round-trip transportation to attend services held each Sunday at the Catholic Church in Avatoru.

The activities desk in the hotel reception area can book your bicycle, scooter and car rentals, as well as excursions. These include glass bottom boat rides to snorkel and feed the sharks, lagoon tours to visit the dolphins and drift through the passes, picnic excursions to *motu* islets on the other side of the lagoon, deep-sea fishing, scuba diving, visits to a black pearl farm, boat rentals and excursions to visit the Kia Ora Sauvage. After a full day's activities, you can relax while enjoying a Thai or Oriental body massage or beauty treatment in the overwater spa.

While sipping your exotic cocktail in the overwater bar and lounge you can look through the big glass floor windows to watch the tropical fish in the coral gardens below. The menu selections in the open-air dining room were chosen to please discerning clientele from all parts of the world. Local fish and lobster are favorite choices, along with the fine French cuisine and the buffets that are served each Wed. and Sun. The wine cellar contains just the right vintage to enhance your meal, and the service provided by the friendly staff is also commendable. See more information under *Where to Eat* in this chapter.

HOTEL KIA ORA SAUVAGE RANGIROA, *(same contacts as for Hotel Kia Ora). 5 bungalows on a private motu islet, one hour by boat across the lagoon to Motu Avea Rahi, 30 km (20 mi.) from main village. Round-trip car transfers included between airport and Hotel Kia Ora. Round-trip boat transfers to Kia Ora Sauvage are 12.000 CFP per person. 2008 Rates: beach bungalow sgl/dbl 40.000 CFP (min. 2-night stay); additional person 6.500 CFP. AP meal plan compulsory for 9.000 CFP per person per day. Add taxes. All major credit cards.*

Motu Avae Rahi means "isle of the big moon". Here is your ultimate Robinson Crusoe Island—lost from the big world and all its problems. There are only five little thatched-roof bungalows on this 4-hectare (9.88-acre) islet. What you don't have here is of primary importance for your tranquility and totally relaxed getaway. No electricity, no telephones, no jet-skis, no excursion boats or helicopters buzzing around and overhead the lagoon, no cars, motorcycles and other traffic noises, and no roosters to crow all night. Your host and hostess and a staff of two assistants will take care of your meals, which are served family style in the restaurant-bar or on the beach. Your bungalow is an attractive *fare* built of local woods, and contains a king-size bed and a single bed with mosquito nets, a private bathroom with hot water shower and a terrace overlooking the white sand beach. Two kerosene lamps are placed on your front steps each evening. These units were renovated in 2007.

Activities include boat trips to nearby *motu* islets, fishing for dinner in the lagoon and trips to the reef for appetizers. You can also paddle an outrigger canoe, windsurf or feed the sharks. In this little haven of peace, you can breathe pure sweet air, listen to the thunder of the surf on the reef, and gaze at the Southern Cross while lying on the secluded beach. This little hotel is a favorite retreat for honeymooners and other travelers in the know.

Superior

NOVOTEL RANGIROA BEACH RESORT, *B.P. 17, Avatoru, Rangiroa 98775. Tel. 689/93.13.50, Fax 689/93.13.51; rbr@mail.pf; www.accorhotels.pf; reservations: Tel. 689/86.66.66, Fax 689/41.05.05; reservation.tahiti@accor.com. Beside the lagoon, 150 m (492 ft.) from the airport. Round-trip bus transfers 1.700 CFP. 2008 EP Rates: Garden Room 19.469 CFP; Garden Bungalow 24.336 CFP;*

Beach Bungalow 34.956 CFP. American breakfast 1.964 CFP, set lunch menu 2.592 CFP, set dinner menu 3.777 CFP. Add taxes. All major credit cards.

This hotel opened in April 2004 as a Polynesian Resort Hotel, and the French group Accor took over management in August 2004. The 38 units consist of 22 garden rooms with terrace, 10 garden bungalows and 6 lagoon bungalows with terrace. There are 4 adjoining rooms for a family or they can be used as a suite, and there are also 2 rooms for reduced mobility guests. The twin beds can also be transformed into one king size bed, and the sofa beds in the lagoon and garden bungalows can sleep a third person. All units include individual a/c and a fan, teak furniture, satellite/cable TV, IDD telephone, safe deposit boxes, mini refrigerator and coffee and tea making facilities. The bathrooms are tiled, have a separate toilet, hot water shower and lavabo, a hair dryer and a range of toiletries.

Public facilities include a reception area, where you will also find the activities desk and car rental center, as well as a small boutique and board games area. The indoor-outdoor restaurant offers lagoon-side dining and the beachfront bar is open daily from 11am to 10:30pm, serving Polynesian cocktails as well as standard drinks and fresh fruit juice. Local musicians and Tahitian dance shows are featured on special evenings.

Complimentary activities include a floating pontoon, *petanque* (French bowls), beach volleyball and use of snorkeling equipment. Optional activities include bicycle, scooter and car rentals, kayaks, outrigger canoes, glass bottom boat rides, day cruising on the lagoon with a skipper, picnics to the distant motu islets and scuba diving.

MOTU TETA, *Ilot Tetaraire, Tiputa, Rangiroa. Tel. 689/96.03.48; tetaraire@yourdreamisland.com; www.yourdreamisland.com. In US Tel. 559/447-2525; regina@yourdreamisland.com. On a private motu on the southeastern side of Rangiroa, an hour's boat ride from airport. Minimum stay 5 days. All inclusive price is US $2,250 per day plus $200 per adult per day and $100 per child under 15 years.*

Here is your own private hideaway with all the upscale comforts of an elegant Polynesian paradise. You will have this 9-acre (3.8 ha) Dream Island all to yourself during your stay. These well appointed accommodations are ideal for up to 6 adults or up to 10 including children.

The main house is 2,250 sq. ft. (250 sq. m), built in the typical breezy Tahitian style with open beams and no windows. It has 3 bedrooms, 2 bathrooms, dining and living area, and a kitchen complete with a private chef. A flat screen TV/DVD system with surround sound is complemented by a collection of music and DVD's. The guest bungalow, built in 2006, is 765 sq. ft. (85 sq. m) and has 2 bedrooms, a wet bar, walk-in shower and ample storage. Each house has a large veranda overlooking the lagoon.

All meals are prepared to order and drinks include champagne, a diverse wine list and a well-stocked bar. Guests have unlimited use of all sports equipment and watercraft, which includes snorkeling gear, 2 wind surfers, 3 outrigger canoes, a 14-passenger motor boat, 2 aluminum dinghies, kiting equipment, and a 2-person float to be pulled by a motor boat. Your own personal guide is on hand to help you explore the most interesting islets and sites, with lots of time for picnics on uninhabited motu, snorkeling in the lagoon and fishing or hunting for lobsters on the ocean side of the reef.

Moderate

LES RELAIS DE JOSEPHINE, *B.P. 140, Avatoru, Rangiroa 98775. Tel./Fax 689/96.02.00; relaisjosephine@mail.pf; http://relaisjosephine.free.fr. Beside the Tiputa pass close to the Ohotu boat dock, 5 km (3.1 mi.) from the airport. Bungalow MAP 18.840 CFP sgl; 14.600 CFP per person dbl; 10.300 CFP for 3rd adult, 7.300 CFP for child under 12 years. Add taxes. Lunch is available at extra cost. Free round-trip transfers. All major credit cards.*

Six attractive bungalows with thatched roofs are built in the garden and beside the beach in a sheltered cove along the lagoon opening of Tiputa pass. Each cozy unit is furnished in a colonial style with a canopied double bed and single bed, a private bathroom with hot water and separate toilet, a dressing room with individual safe, a ceiling fan, coffee and tea facilities and private terrace. The bar terrace overlooks the pass, where dolphins can often be seen dancing in the waves. Madame Denise Thirouard is noted for the refined atmosphere, gourmet cuisine and wines served in her restaurant, Le Dauphin Gourmand. Her clients are mostly French and Japanese. Activities can be arranged and there is a scuba diving center nearby.

RAIRA LAGON, *B.P. 87, Avatoru, Rangiroa 98775. Tel. 689/93.12.30; Fax 689/93.12.31; réservation@raira-lagon.pf; www.raira-lagon.pf. At PK 1.5, beside the lagoon in Avatoru commune, 6.5 km (4 mi.) from the Ohotu boat dock and 800 m (2,624 ft.)) west of the airport. Fare and MAP Rates (obligatory): 13.500 CFP sgl; 11.500 CFP per person dbl. Add taxes. Free round-trip transfers. AE, MC, V.*

There are 10 small *fares* for couples or families, with single or double beds and electric fans and electric anti-mosquito gadgets. Each bungalow has a private bathroom with hot water shower, and there is a sliding glass door leading onto a small terrace. Rooms are cleaned daily. Le Margouillat restaurant is on the beach, serving a Continental breakfast, salads and sandwiches for lunch, fresh local fish and gastronomic French cuisine for dinner. There is also a small bar in the restaurant. Beach chairs for guests are placed under the shade trees or on the coral beach and snorkeling equipment is provided. The new managers, Ghislaine and Raumati, will help you to plan your lagoon excursions and scuba diving.

LE MEROU BLEU, *B.P. 163, Avatoru, Rangiroa 98775. Tel./Fax 689/ 96.84.62, cell 79.16.82; lemeroubleu@mail.pf; www.merou-bleu.com. Beside the Avatoru pass, 5 minutes from the village. Free round-trip transfers from airport and Ohotu boat dock. Bungalow MAP 12.000-15.000 CFP plus taxes. No credit cards.*

The name of this pension means "Blue Spotted-Grouper" in English or "Roi" in Tahitian. Pierre and Sonya Friedrich are from Alsace and speak just a little English. Their three traditional style thatched roof bungalows are beside Avatoru pass, which is "the" surfing spot on Rangiroa. All the beds are protected by mosquito nets and electricity is provided by solar lighting and electric generator. Pierre is a decorator and has added his special touch to each bungalow with the use of local woods, bamboo, sea urchin shells, and mother-of-pearl and dolphin mobiles. Sonya serves her specialties of couscous, West Indian dishes and local foods. Bicycles are free for guests.

PENSION TUANAKE, *B. P. 21, Avatoru, Rangiroa 98775. Tel. 689/ 93.11.80; Fax 689/93.11.81; tuanake@mail.pf; www.sitetuanake.fr.st. Beside the lagoon in Avatoru, 2.5 km (1.6 mi.) from the airport and 7.5 km (4.7 mi.) from the boat dock at Ohotu. Free round-trip transfers between airport and pension. EP Fare 6.500 CFP sgl/9.700 CFP/11.800 CFP tpl. MAP Fare 10.500 CFP sgl/15.700 CFP dbl/20.800 CFP tpl. Add taxes. MC, V.*

This popular family pension has been awarded a temporary 2-Tiare rating by Tahiti Tourisme. There are six *fares* or bungalows on the white sand beach, with beds for 2, 5 or 6. Each *fare* is very clean and has a fan and private bathroom with cold water or a separate cold water shower outside. All guests share the big open-air living space with tables and TV. There is a pay phone for guests and an Internet point at the office.

Owner Vetea Terorotua takes good care of his guests, and his pension has a good reputation. A friendly, comfortable atmosphere reigns here, with beach chairs to read in the shade or sunbathe on the coral sand beach. A hoa channel runs from the ocean to the lagoon on one side of the property and Gauguin's Pearl farm is on the other side.

LES FARE DE TIKI HOA, *B.P. 235, Avatoru, Rangiroa 98775. Tel. 689/ 73.80.13/73.63.10; tikihoa@mail.pf; www.fare-tikihoa.pf. on Motu Tairua Manahune, 19 km (11.8 mi.) across the lagoon from the airport and 15 km (9.3 mi.) from the boat dock. Round-trip boat transfers 2.000 CFP per person. EP bungalow 6.000 CFP per person; AP bungalow 12.500 CFP per person per day. Taxes included. MC, V.*

This small family hotel has been awarded a temporary 3-Tiare rating by Tahiti Tourisme. The 10 high standard bungalows are located on Motu Tairua Manahune on the northwest side of the lagoon, a 30-min. boat ride from Avatoru village. Each unit is 29 sq. m (312 sq. ft.) with a terrace, constructed of wood on concrete pilings, with a roof of thatched coconut fronds. Each airy unit is beside the lagoon, facing the wind, and contains a double bed, mosquito net and private bathroom with cold water shower. Electricity is provided by solar panels and a generator. There is also a reception area, kitchen, dining terrace and bar, as well as a small boutique. The hotel grounds and a small salt water lake on the property are sprayed on a regular basis against mosquitoes. Boat excursions take you to other uninhabited motu, including the popular Blue Lagoon, which is much closer to this hotel than to the villages. Scuba divers can be transported by boat to the dive centers on the Avatoru side of the lagoon. Owners Michel Tavernier and Jacques Mouillie emphasize that the whole idea of staying on a remote motu is to be close to nature.

CHEZ LUCIEN, *B.P. 69, Tiputa, Rangiroa 98776. Tel./Fax 689/96.73.55. Near the pass in Tiputa village, 10 minutes by boat from the airport. Round-trip boat transfers 1.000 CFP per person. 2008 Rates: Bungalow with breakfast 9.000 CFP per person; Bungalow with MAP 13.000 CFP per person, including taxes. No credit cards.*
This well maintained pension is facing the lagoon at the edge of the Tiputa Pass. Lucien Pea has built 2 small bungalows and a 2-bedroom family bungalow, all with covered porches that overlook the pass. Each of the smaller bungalows has 2 double beds, a mezzanine with a double bed, a fan, refrigerator and a bathroom with hot water. The family bungalow has a double bed in each bedroom, 3 double beds on the mezzanine, a living room, fan, refrigerator and a communal bathroom with hot water. House linens are furnished. The meals are generous and pleasant, served in a covered dining room beside the lagoon. Bikes, lagoon fishing and a visit of the village are free.

PENSION BOUNTY, *BP 296, Avatoru, Rangiroa 98775. Tel./Fax 689/96.05.22; contact@pension-bounty.com; www.pension-bounty.com. Between the road and lagoon just past Hotel Kia Ora and 1/2 mi. from Tiputa Pass. Free round-trip transfers. Rates 7.000 CFP per person with breakfast; studio and MAP 10.000 CFP per person; add 4.000 CFP for sgl. Taxes included. AE, MC, V.*
This 4-bungalow boarding house has been awarded a temporary 2-Tiare rating by Tahiti Tourism. Newly constructed of Kohu wood and red cedar, each of the double studios has a double bed, kitchenette, bathroom with hot water, mosquito screens on doors and windows, ceiling fan, personal safe, and a large deck.
A private road leads directly to the nearby beach on Ohotu Bay. Owners Muriel and Alain Ruiz de Galaretta offer free use of bicycles to their guests and help them to organize their nautical activities. Alain is a level three diver and will direct you to the nearby dive centers.

PENSION MARTINE, *B.P. 68, Avatoru, Rangiroa 98775. Tel. 689/93.12.25; Fax 689/96.02.51; cell 71.30.12; pension.martine@mail.pf. On the lagoon side near the airport and 5 km (3.1 mi.) from the village of Avatoru. Free round-trip transfers. 2008 Rates: Bungalow with MAP 6.500 CFP per person; Bungalow with AP 7.500 CFP per person; including VAT. MC, V.*
This pension has a good reputation in Rangiroa and with former guests. There are three attractive and clean little bungalows, including a unit for singles, built beside the beach and lagoon. Each bungalow has a ceiling fan, private bathroom with hot water shower, and terrace. All guests share the living room and eat their meals in the dining room. Your hosts will take you to visit their family pearl farm if you wish.

PENSION CECILE, *B. P. 98, Avatoru, Rangiroa 98775. Tel. 689/93.12.65, Fax 689/93.12.66; cell 71.95.76. In Avatoru, 7.5 km (4.7 mi.) from the Ohotu boat dock and 2.5 km (1.6 mi.) from the airport. Free round-trip transfers. 2008 MAP Rates: Standard Bungalow 8.000 CFP person; Family Bungalow 8.500 CFP per person; VAT included. MC, V.*
There are 9 bungalows beside the beach and in the garden, including 4 new

units of the standard government approved model. Tahiti Tourism has awarded this pension a temporary 2-Tiare rating. There is a family bungalow with one double and one single bed, plus mattresses on the mezzanine, and a private bathroom with cold water. 8 bungalows contain a double and single bed, a private bathroom and cold water. Meals are served in an open-air dining room. Ruahatu Tetua, the manager, can help you arrange activities that can include a visit to a pearl farm, fishing in the lagoon and lagoon excursions.

TURIROA VILLAGE, *B.P. 26, Avatoru, Rangiroa 98775. Tel. 689/96.02.46, Fax 689/96.04.27, cell 78.90.19; pension.turiroa@mail.pf. Beside the lagoon in Avatoru, 6 km (3.7 mi.) from the airport and 5 km (3.1 mi.) from Avatoru village. Free round-trip transfers. EP Rates: fare without kitchenette 6.000 CFP sgl/dbl; bungalow with kitchenette 8.000 CFP for 1-4 people; add 2.750 CFP per person for MAP. Add taxes. No credit cards.*

There are two garden and two beach bungalows, each containing a double bed and a mezzanine with single beds. These units have a kitchenette, private bathroom with cold water, and a terrace. There is also a small *fare* with a private bathroom and hot water shower outside. Your hostess, Mrs. Olga Niva, will take you to visit her family pearl farm and she also offers free transfers daily to the village.

ARIITINI VILLAGE, *B.P. 18, Avatoru, Rangiroa 98775. Tel. 689/96.04.41, Fax 689/96.04.40. Located beside the lagoon at PK 4 in Avatoru, 5.6 km (3.5 mi.) from the Ohotu boat dock and 500 m (1,640 ft.) from the airport. Free round-trip transfers. 2008 MAP Rates: 8.000 CFP per person per day, VAT included. No credit cards.*

Felix and Judith Tetua have 9 bungalows in a garden setting beside the beach and lagoon. 8 units have one bedroom with a double bed and a single bed, a private bathroom with cold water shower and a small terrace. There is also a 2-bedroom unit.

Economy

RANGIROA LODGE, *Avatoru, Rangiroa 98775. Tel. 689/96.82.13. Beside the lagoon in Avatoru village, 8 km (5 mi.) from the Ohotu boat dock and 6 km (3.7 mi.) from the airport. Free round-trip transfers. EP Rates: Room with communal bathroom 5.000 CFP dbl; room with private bath 6.200 CFP 1-2 people per day; dormitory 2.200 CFP per person per day. Add taxes. No credit cards.*

Because of its location and facilities, this pension is appealing to low-budget travelers who want to stay in Avatoru and be able to cook their own meals. There are six simple rooms and two 3-bed dormitories built between the lagoon and the road—very close to the road. There is an equipped kitchen and a dining room on the coral beach, and Chez Filou is a popular snack located on the premises.

PENSION LOYNA, *B.P. 82, Avatoru, Rangiroa 98775. Tel./Fax 689/96.82.09; pensionloyna@mail.pf; www.pensionloyna.fr.st. 4 km (2.5 mi.) from airport and 2 km (0.8 mi.) from Avatoru village. Free transfers. Room and MAP 6.675 CFP; big bungalow 7.500 CFP MAP, taxes included. MC, V.*

Loyna Fareea can sleep up to 30 people in a 3-bedroom house, a 2-bedroom *fare* and 3 big new bungalows located 100 m. (328 ft.) from lagoon. Group rates provided starting with 6 people. Choices of hot or cold water showers. Living room and dining room facilities are shared.

LAGON VERT, *B.P. 54, Avatoru, Rangiroa 98775. Tel. 689/79.24.66/ 77.28.85. On a motu at Lagon Vert (Green Lagoon), a 10-minute boat ride from Avatoru village. Free ground transfers from airport to boat dock and 1.000 CFP per person for round-trip boat transfers to the motu. Fare and MAP 5.500 CFP per person; fare and AP 6.500 CFP per person. Campers pay 1.050 CFP EP or 4.500 CFP MAP per person. Taxes included. No credit cards.*

Punua and Moana Tamaehu have built three simple Paumotu style *fares* of coconut fronds and kahaia wood on a motu islet called Lagon Vert (Green Lagoon). There is also camping space here. Each fare has a private bathroom with cold water shower. Electricity is provided by electric generator.

Other Pensions

The pensions listed above are the most popular of the family lodgings that were available in Rangiroa at publication time. The other pensions near Avatoru village are: **PENSION GLORINE**, *Tel. 96.04.05; Fax 96.03.58; pensionglorine@mail.pf;* 4 bungalows beside Tiputa Pass; **PENSION HENRI**, *Tel./Fax 96.82.67; pensionhenri@mail.pf;* 5 bungalows on ocean side; **PENSION HENRIETTE**, *Tel. 96.84.68;* 1 bungalow; **PENSION HERENUI** *Tel./Fax 96.84.71;* 1 bungalow; **PENSION HINANUI**, *Tel./Fax 96.84.61;* 3 bungalows in Avatoru; **MIKI MIKI**, *Tel. 96.83.83; Fax 96.82.90;* 7 bungalows beside lagoon in Avatoru; **CHEZ NANUA**, *Tel./Fax 96.83.88;* 4 fares & campground in Avatoru; **CHEZ TEINA & MARIE**, *Tel. 96.03.94, Fax 96.84.44;* 7 bungalows at Tiputa Pass.

WHERE TO EAT
Deluxe

HOTEL KIA ORA, *Tel. 93.11.11. Open daily for B, L, D. All credit cards.*

This 120-seat restaurant caters to international palates, served in an open air setting beside the lagoon. An American breakfast buffet is 2.400 CFP.

The luncheon menu features burgers with fries, pizza, pasta, chow mein, lagoon fish and a fresh fruit plate. The dinner menu offers several different choices each evening, which usually include fresh fish from the lagoon or deep ocean, with a good selection of fine wines. Soups are 900-1.300 CFP, appetizers are 1.250-1.950 CFP, fish and seafood dishes are 2.650-3.000 CFP, meat and poultry selections range from 2.450-3.300 CFP and roast lobster is 4.300 CFP. The pastry chef creates an appealing dessert buffet. A barbecue buffet of grilled meat, chicken and fish is served on Wed. and Sun. night, and a Polynesian dance show is performed during the buffet. The cost for each event is 5.500 CFP per person. The overwater bar is open daily from 9am to 11pm, serving almost any drink you want to order, plus their own exotic creations.

Superior-Moderate

VAIMARIO, *Tel. 96.05.96, is located on the ocean side of the road between the Hotel Kia Ora and the airport. Open for L, D, except on Tues. when they are closed all day and at noon on Sat. MC, V. Free pick-up service provided.*

Dominique Soupot, who formerly worked at the Hotel Kia Ora, took over this restaurant and bar in 2003 and prepares excellent French cuisine and pizzas for his clientele, who always include a number of local residents. His wife Marcella manages the restaurant and takes orders for the *confits, magret de canard,* escargots and fresh fish dishes, as well as *poisson cru* and the daily specials. Pizzas are 1.100-1.300 CFP, appetizers are 950-1.750 CFP, fish and shrimp dishes are 1.950-2.650 CFP, meats are 1.950-2.950 CFP, desserts are 650-950 CFP, and wine is priced from 1.950-7.800 CFP a bottle. A 3-course tourist menu is 3.100 CFP.

NOVOTEL RANGIROA BEACH RESORT (Lagon Bleu), *Tel. 93.13.50. Open daily for B.L.D. All credit cards.*

You can dine in the thatched-roof restaurant or under an umbrella on the terrace beside the beach. A tropical breakfast buffet is 1.900 CFP, and at lunch you will pay 1.400 CFP for poisson cru, salads, burgers, pizzas or pasta, or 1.300-1.800 CFP for the main course. The dinner menu features international and Polynesian cuisine, with appetizers from 1.100-1.950 CFP, fish from 2.100-2.400 CFP and meat choices from 2.100-2.700 CFP. Desserts are 950-1.200 CFP.

LE KAI KAI, *on lagoon side next door to Pension Martine and across road from L'Atelier Corinne, Tel. 96.03.39. Open for lunch and dinner daily except Wed. night. Round-trip transfers provided. MC, V.*

This restaurant is managed by Gaëlle Coconnier, who serves her guests French home cooking on an outdoor terrace with a thatch roof and coral floor. The starter courses are priced from 800-1.500 CFP. Main course dishes are 2.300-2.400 CFP, with choices of grilled mahi mahi, shrimp curry or shrimp with ginger sauce. A dish of Paumotu style roast pork is excellent for 1.500 CFP and beef filet with Roquefort sauce is 2.000 CFP. An extensive dessert menu has tempting choices, including crêpes, from 450 to 600 CFP.

Economy

CHEZ AUGUSTE & ANTOINETTE (Chez Puhipuhi), *Tel. 96.85.01, is on your right opposite the marina at the entrance to Avatoru village when coming from the airport. Open Mon.-Sat. from 9am to 9pm. No credit cards.*

This is where the locals with big appetites go for very generous portions of mouth-watering dishes prepared local style. The menu includes fresh fish and Chinese dishes such as chow mein, lemon chicken and tamarind duck. Prices range from 950 to 1.200 CFP a plate.

SNACK DE LA MARINA, *Tel. 96.85.64, is at the Avatoru marina. Open daily except Mon. for L,D. No credit cards.*

You can buy chow mein, poisson cru, sashimi, shish kabob, grilled fish or meats for 900-1.200 CFP a plate.

SNACK MOETUA, *Tel. 28.06.96, is on the Ohotu quay, across the road from Pension Glorinne, overlooking the Tiputa Pass. Open Mon.-Sat. 8am-5pm, and on Sun. 5:30-7:30am. No credit cards.*

Fruit juices, beer, *casse-croûtes* (400-650 CFP) omelets, grilled chicken, steak, shish kebabs, fish and hamburgers (400-800 CFP) are served on the overwater terrace.

SPORTS & RECREATION
Glass Bottom Boat Excursions
Matahi Excursions, *Tel. 96.84.48/79.24.54*, based at Ohotu Point on the Avatoru side of the Tiputa pass, is operated by Matahi Tepa and his daughter. They have two glass bottom boats that provide 2-hr. excursions, with departures made according to the incoming current in the pass. You'll view the amazing wealth of sea life from the dry comfort of the boat as you drift through the pass and stop at the fishermen's *motu* islet inside the pass. The cost is 3.000 CFP per person.

Snorkeling & Dolphin Watch Excursions
Rangiroa Activities, *Tel. 96.73.59/77.65.86*. René Fels offers a 1 1/2-hr. snorkeling excursion to the natural aquarium of Motu Nohi Nohi for 3.500 CFP; a 2-hr. boat excursion to watch for dolphins and to drift snorkel through Tiputa Pass for 4.750 CFP; and a 2-hr. Dolphin-watch Ecotour for 4.750 CFP. You may see the big dolphins (Tursiops truncatus), a family of spinner dolphins (Stenella longirostris), or more rarely, the black and white dolphins (Peponocephala electra) that live around the coast of Rangiroa.

Marereva Excursions, *Tel. 96.84.51/76.71.82/26.95.01*. This dolphin watch and snorkeling excursion is guided by Fisher, who has worked in the tourist business for many years and speaks good English. He charges 4.500 CFP for the 2-hr. excursion.

Lagoon Excursions, Picnics on the Motu, Fishing, Motor Boat Rental
The most popular destination of the lagoon excursions is the **Blue Lagoon**, which is an hour's boat ride from the hotels and pensions in Rangiroa, on the western edge of the atoll. This lagoon within a lagoon is formed by a natural pool of aquamarine water on the edge of the reef, known locally as Taeo'o. Several *motu* islets are separated by very shallow *hoa* channels, and you can walk from one white sand beach to another. Be sure to take along your T-shirt, hat, sunscreen, mosquito repellent, protective shoes and snorkeling gear. Don't forget your camera.

Each hotel or pension has its own private *motu* used for barbecue picnics, and the cost varies from 7.500-10.400 CFP for an all-day picnic excursion to the Blue Lagoon.

Reef Islet, also called **île aux Récifs** and **Motu Ai Ai**, is on the south end of Rangiroa, an hour's boat ride across the lagoon. Here you can walk through razor sharp raised coral outcrops called *feo* that resemble miniature fairy castles formed during four million years of erosion. This excursion is sold for 7.500-10.400 CFP, which includes a picnic on the beach. The pink sand beaches of **Vahituri**, or **Les Sables Roses**, are 1.5-2 hours by boat from Avatoru to the southeastern edge of the lagoon. The pink reflections in the sand are caused by Foraminifera deposits and coral residues. You'll enjoy swimming and snorkeling in the lagoon in this lovely area. The cost of this excursion ranges from 9.500-12.400 CFP, including a picnic.

Here are some of the excursion operators who will take you to discover the wonders of the Rangiroa lagoon.

Atoll Excursions, *Tel. 96.04.49/26.73.27*. Hiria Arnoux has two motorboats used for snorkeling, lagoon excursions, picnics and fishing in the lagoon or deep sea. Hotel Kia Ora sells his half-day fishing charter for 54.000 CFP and 88.000 CFP for the full-day outing. Hiria's father, Serge Arnaux, was one of the original owners of the Kia Ora.

Hei Hei Te Vahine Te Pua Excursions, *Tel. 96.83.23/73.45.03* is operated by Raumati Sanford, who has two speedboats used for full-day excursions, which include a barbecue picnic on his private motu. He works with the Hotel Kia Ora as well as the family pensions and also provides fishing excursions in the lagoon or open ocean, as well as private tours to Reef Island or Sables Roses (Pink Sand Beach).

Maurice Taxi Boat, *Tel. 96.76.09/78.13.25*. Maurice Snow, who operates a non-stop taxi boat service between Ohotu boat dock, Tiputa village and the airport daily, also has a boat that is used for drift snorkeling in the pass and picnic excursions. The full-day outings include a visit to Otepipi, the site of an ancient village where the old Catholic church of Sainte-Anne is still standing.

Oviri Excursions, *Tel./Fax 96.05.87/26.07.05*. Ugo Angely speaks good English. His father, Robin Angeley, was one of the original owners of the Kia Ora and Ugo grew up at the hotel, then worked there for several years, managing the Kia Ora Sauvage. His wife and son still work at Hotel Kia Ora. Ugo has two powerful motorboats available for excursions.

Pa'ati Excursions, *Tel. 96.02.57/79.24.63*, is operated by Léon Revault. His full-day excursions for 4-9 people include a picnic on Motu Pa'ati and a stop at Pink Sand Beach.

Tane Excursions, *Tel. 96.84.68/72.31.51*, is operated by Marcel Tane Tamaehu, whose wife owns Pension Henriette, close to the Avatoru Marina. He has two locally built boats that he uses for lagoon fishing, deep-sea fishing, shooting the pass or for picnic excursions.

Te Reva Tane E Vahine, *Tel. 96.82.51/70.71.38*. Jean-Pierre Tavita has two 24-ft. boats for 4-7 people. He specializes in picnic excursions to Reef Island.

Pearl Farms

Gauguin's Pearl, *Tel. 93.11.30/78.79.78, Fax 96.04.09; phcab@mail.pf.* This working pearl farm is operated by Philippe Cabrall. Free transfers from your lodging to the farm, which is built over the lagoon close to the airport. Free guided visits are given Mon.-Fri. at 8:30am, 10:30am and 2pm. You can watch the black-lipped oysters being grafted, cultivated and harvested during the season. The pearl boutique is open Mon.-Sat. 9am- 5:30pm, and on Sun. from 10am-12pm and 2:30-5pm. Their reasonably-priced pearls have a very good luster and lovely colors, and they also have a pearl shop at the Hotel Kia Ora.

Visit a Vignard & Wine Storehouse

Rangiroa Loisirs, *Tel. 96.04.70/71.67.10.* You can visit a unique wine orchard on Motu Lagon Vert, where grapes are actually grown in the coral soil to produce red, rosé and white wine. A half-day excursion costs 6.000 CFP and a full-day outing with picnic is 9.600 CFP. When you return to the village you can taste the Rangiroa wines in the wine storehouse near Avatoru. Or you can simply do some wine tasting in the cave for 1.800 CFP without the boat trip.

Scuba Diving

The lagoon of Rangiroa is essentially a huge inland sea, with a maximum depth of about 27 m (90 ft.), which offers the finest and most abundant of nature's aquaculture. The two passes of **Tiputa** and **Avatoru** are submarine freeways for the passage of fish between the open ocean and the lagoon. The ocean normally has a moderate swell running and near the passes a five-knot current enters or exits rhythmically with the rise and fall of the tide. Static dives in or near the passes can only be done twice a day when the water is still and clear, which is normally at 12-hour intervals. Drift dives are possible on nearly any day, and these "shooting the pass" dives are exhilarating, as you are surrounded by hordes of fish, jacks, tuna, barracuda, manta rays, eagle rays, turtles, dolphins and sharks.

Between December and March huge hammerhead sharks gather to mate outside Tiputa Pass, and the graceful manta rays are most plentiful during their mating season between July and October. There are 15 popular dive sites inside the lagoon, in the passes and on the outer coral reef of Rangiroa. The following diving clubs have qualified instructors who speak English and schedule their dives between 8am and 2pm, depending on the tides, currents, swell and wind conditions. The cost of an exploratory dive varies between 6.400-7.700 CFP, an introductory dive is 7.000-9.900 CFP, and a night dive is 7.800-9.900 CFP. They all accept credit cards and dive packages are available. Equipment is included, but you may feel more secure if you bring your own buoyancy compensator, regulator and depth gauge. You'll also need to bring you certification papers and a medical certificate if you are not certified. Transportation is usually provided from your hotel or pension to the dive center.

Blue Dolphins Diving Center, *Tel./Fax 96.03.01, bluedolphins@mail.pf; www.bluedolphinsdiving.com.* This busy dive shop is located at the Hotel Kia Ora. They offer Nitrox dives and the equipment is 100 percent Scubapro that is renewed every two years. **Raie Manta Club**, *Tel. 96.84.80/72.31.45; raiemantaclub@mail.pf; http://raiemantaclub.free.fr.* The main office is beside the lagoon near Avatoru village, between Pension Herenui and Rangiroa Lodge. This is Rangiroa's oldest dive center, opened since 1985. Owner Yves Lefevre also has dive centers in Tikehau and Rurutu, all using Scubapro equipment. **Rangiroa Paradive**, *Tel. 96.05.55; paradive@mail.pf; www.chez.com/paradive.* This PADI dive center owned by Bernard Blanc is next door to Pension Glorinne near the Tiputa Pass. **The Six Passengers**, *Tel/Fax 96.02.60; the6passengers@mail.pf; www.the6passengers.com.* This dive center is located between the Hotel Kia Ora and Ohotu Point beside the Tiputa Pass. Owners Ugo Mazzavillani and Tanguy Bonduel have a limit of 6 passengers for dives and diving picnics. **TOPdive**, *Tel. 96.05.60/72.39.55; rangiroa@topdive.com; www.topdive.com.* This dive shop is located beside the lagoon just a minute's walk to the right of Hotel Kia Ora. It is a PADI center with modern equipment including NITROX. A 10-dive package can be used in any of the four Topdive centers on Tahiti, Moorea, Bora Bora and Fakarava.

Cruising, Sailing & Fishing Charters

Archipels Cruises (Archipels Croisières), *Tel. 689/56.36.39, Fax 689/56.35.87; information@archipels-croisieres.pf; www.archipels.com; Skype: archipels.* This Moorea-based company also has a Marquises 57' or Eleuthera 60' catamaran based permanently in Rangiroa. A Tues.-Fri. 4-day/3-night Robinson Crusoe cruise inside the atoll of Rangiroa costs €1,092-1,207 according to season. A Sat.-Mon. 3-day/2-night cruise in the eastern part of the atoll is €820-935 per person according to season. One-week cruises are also available from Fakarava to Toau and Rangiroa, boarding in Fakarava on Sat. morning and disembarking in Rangiroa at noon on Fri. The cruise dates are scheduled in conjunction with the full moon and guaranteed departure for a minimum of 2 passengers. The per person cost of this cruise is €1,880-2,090, including taxes, meals and hotel services on board in double cabin occupancy, airport/yacht transfers at boarding and landing sites, as well as all excursions and events specified in program. Private charters for 2-10 passengers are also available.

Haumana, *Tel. 689/50.06.74; Fax 689/50.06.72; contact@tahiti-haumana-cruises.com; www.tahiti-haumana-cruises.com.*

The *Haumana* (Spirit of Peace) offers all-inclusive cruises inside the Rangiroa lagoon for 3, 4, and 7 nights. The 147-ton luxury yacht is 33 m. (110 ft.) long, with a beam of 13.8 m. (45 ft.), and a draft of 1.8 m. (6 ft.). Each of the 12 passenger cabins is 160 sq. ft., with a large picture window, individual a/c, a queen-size bed, TV with DVD, CD and VHS, a safe deposit box and mini bar, plus a private bathroom with hot water shower, hair dryer and toiletries. Two cabins also have a child's bed. The public areas include a restaurant, lounge-bar, main lounge with panoramic views, a Jacuzzi, sun deck, and a marina platform with kayaks and 2 wave runners. Three tender boats are dedicated to activities, excursions and transfers and the 16 crew members from French Polynesia and Europe attend to the needs of their 24 guests.

Due to the relatively small size of the *Haumana* and her shallow draft, you will be taken into the heart of the lagoons and almost to the edge of the motu islets and their beaches of white or pink sand. A 3-night Blue Lagoon cruise operates Wed.-Sat. and takes you to the beautiful sites of the Green Lagoon, the Blue Lagoon, Faama and Motu Ai Ai. The 2008 rates are €1,790 per person in a double cabin, €2,319 for a single cabin, and €895 for a child under 12 years sharing a cabin with a parent. The 4-night Pink Sand cruise is from Sat.-Wed. and costs €2,126 per person double, €2,756 single, and €1,063 per child. You will discover Tiputa village, meet a local family on Shell Islet, participate in a shark feeding adventure at the Pink Sand Motu, visit a natural bird sanctuary at Teruatupua, discover the old village of Otepipi, hunt for shells at Anatia and explore the rock and coral formations at Mauahatea. The 7-night Rainbow cruise is from Wed.-Wed. or Sat.-Sat., and combines the 3- and 4-night itineraries, selling for €3,529 per person double, €4,588 single, and €1,765 for children. Rates quoted include transfers to/from Rangiroa's airport, all meals with complimentary wines for lunch and dinner, all non-alcoholic beverages, tea time and snacks, all Haumana activities and excursions, fishing and all tackle, free use of kayaks and snorkeling equipment, free access to the onboard DVD library, all port charges and taxes. The *Haumana* is also available for private groups such as including fly-fishing, diving and surfing charters.

SHOPPING

There is a well-stocked boutique at **Hotel Kia Ora** and an outlet of **Gauguin's Pearls**, which has another sales room at the pearl farm. **Black Pearl Island**, *96.05.75*, is close to Novotel and the airport, with displays of black pearl jewelry. **Ikimasho**, *Tel. 96.84.46*, close to the Shell Station, sells black pearl jewelry. **Au Petit Coin de Paradis** is a boutique in Avatoru village selling clothes and gift items. **Ocean Passion**, between the airport and Novotel Rangiroa Beach Resort, *Tel./Fax 96.02.72,* sells beautiful original T-shirts, *pareos* and wall hangings of dolphins, rays, fish and the coral gardens of Rangiroa's lagoon.

Une Fille A La Vanille Boutique is adjacent to the Six Passengers Dive Center between Hotel Kia Ora and Ohotu Point. **Vai Boutique** is in Avatoru village, selling homemade dresses and shirts, tee shirts and hand painted *pareos*. **Raie Manta Club Boutique** is adjacent to the scuba diving center in Avatoru, between Pension Herenui and Rangiroa Lodge. Here you will find a good selection of wildlife postcards, underwater video films, tee shirts and posters.

MASSAGES & BEAUTY TREATMENTS

The **Fare Massage** at Hotel Kia Ora offers a choice of traditional Thai body massages, starting with a 50-min. massage for 5.000 CFP, up to a 2-hour complete massage with oils for 13.000 CFP. A 50-min. Oriental massage is 13.000 CFP and various treatments for face and body include Oriental ideas and European aesthetic techniques. I do not recommend the Japanese masseuse.

TATTOOS

Rangiroa's tattoo artists are: **Clement Tattoos**, *Tel. 27.83.05*, **René Vaiaanui**, *Tel. 27.25.55;* and **Thavy**, *Tel. 78.74.63.*

PRACTICAL INFORMATION
Banks

Banque de Tahiti has an office in Avatoru village close to the Catholic Church and the *mairie* (town hall), *Tel. 96.85.52.* It is open Mon., Wed. and Fri., from 8 to 11am and 2 to 4pm, and on Tues. and Thurs. from 8 to 11:30am. Closed on Tues. and Thurs. afternoon.

Banque Socredo is located beside the *mairie* of Avatoru, *Tel. 96.85.63,* and is open on Mon., Wed. and Fri. from 8am to 12pm, and on Mon. through Thurs. from 1:30 to 4:30pm. Banque Socredo, *Tel. 93.12.50,* also has an office at the *mairie* in Tiputa, which is open Mon. and Thurs., 8am to 12pm.

Hospitals

A government operated medical center is located in Avatoru village, *Tel. 96.03.75,* between 7:30am and 3:30pm and on Fri. from 7:30am to 2:30pm. Outside these hours you can reach emergency service at *Tel. 78.60.18.* The hospital has an ambulance. There is an infirmary in Tiputa village, *Tel. 96.03.96,* and there are also private doctors and dentists in Rangiroa.

Internet

Photo Rairoa, *Tel. 93.12.85/22.00.25*, is open Mon.-Sat. 8am-12pm and 1:30-6pm. For 550 CFP you have 30 min. on line plus an espresso coffee or tea. CD albums and post cards also available. **Restaurant Kai Kai**, *Tel. 96.03.39*, also has Internet service. In Dec. 2007 the Post Office in Avatoru added a computer and Internet service.

Magasins (Food Stores)

Magasin Daniel is the best-stocked store in Avatoru village and sells wine, beer and a few fresh vegetables. **Magasin Heiura** is a food store located in the airport area close to the Novotel Rangiroa Beach Resort. **Magasin Kahaia** is a small store located on the lagoon side of the road between Hotel Kia Ora and Point Ohotu.

Pharmacy

The **Pharmacie de Rangiroa**, *Tel. 93.12.35*, is a new building in Avatoru village, across the road from the Catholic Church. It is open Mon.-Fri. from 7am to 12:30pm and from 2:30 to 6:30pm; on Sat. from 7am to 12:30pm and 4:30 to 6:30 pm; and on Sun. from 10 to 11:30am.

Police

The French *gendarmerie* is beside the lagoon between Hotel Kia Ora and the airport, *Tel. 93.11.55*. Municipal Police of Avatoru, *Tel. 96.84.74*.

Post Office & Telecommunications Office

A Post Office is located in Avatoru village, *Tel. 96.83.81* and another is in Tiputa village, *Tel. 96.73.80*. The Avatoru office also has a computer with Internet service.

MANIHI

Manihi is 520 km (322 mi.) northeast of Tahiti and a world removed from time and care. A tiny green oasis floating in the desert of the sea, with a name as exotic as the trade winds and a lagoon as pretty as a mother-of-pearl shell. Seen from the air, Manihi presents a picturesque palette of glimmering greens and blues, with white and pink beaches in a framing of feathery green coconut palms. A close range view of this crystal clear lagoon is even better, as you can see the vividly painted tropical fish feeding in the coral gardens on the white sand bottom, several feet below the water's surface.

Some visitors find that Manihi is still one of the friendliest villages in the Tuamotu Islands, although life for the 1,575 inhabitants has changed with the development of the cultured pearl industry. The first privately owned black pearl farm was started in Manihi in 1966. When it became known that the black-lipped oysters in this lagoon produced a high quality rainbow-hued pearl, Manihi became synonymous with the *po'e rava*. This is the local name for the rare and beautiful Tahitian cultured pearl.

Several dozen pearl farms were eventually built on stilts on almost every coral head inside the lagoon, which is about 8 km (4.9 mi.) wide by 27 km (16.7 mi.) long. Most of the people who live in Manihi were involved in the pearl business, even though they may have had other jobs as well. All but 10 or so of these pearl farms are now abandoned since the market for pearls took a dive, and the local government began demanding high taxes. All around the lagoon you can now see the buoys that once floated on the surface, marking the presence of pearl oysters suspended below the water in wire baskets. Some of these buoys and other flotsam from collapsed pearl farms have drifted onto the shores of the motu islets, creating a new form of pollution.

Turipaoa, which is also known as Paeua, is a sun-baked little village with colorful houses of limestone and clapboard lining the three main roads, one of which extends to the end of the motu. The houses are shaded by breadfruit trees and bordered with frangipani, hibiscus and bougainvillea. This village is home to most of Manihi's 800 residents. The favorite hangout in the village is to sit on the benches under the shade of a giant *tou* tree with orange flowers beside the Turipaoa pass. Here the inhabitants can talk politics and gossip as they watch the comings and goings of the supply ships from Tahiti and the boats from the pearl farms.

ARRIVALS & DEPARTURES
Arriving by Air

Air Tahiti flies from Tahiti to Manihi 7 days a week with a stop in Rangiroa and sometimes in Tikehau. There is a direct Rangiroa-Manihi flight daily except Thurs. You can fly from Bora Bora to Manihi every Mon., Wed., Fri. and Sun., with a stop in Rangiroa. There is a flight from Tikehau to Manihi each Mon. and Wed., with a stop in Rangiroa. You can fly direct from Ahe to Manihi during the high season each Fri. and Sun. The one-way fare from Tahiti to Manihi is 19.100 CFP and 26.400 CFP from Bora Bora to Manihi. The one-way fare from Rangiroa or Tikehau to Manihi is 10.400 CFP. **Air Tahiti reservations:** Tahiti, *Tel. 86.42.42*; in Manihi *Tel. 93.30.70*.

The airport is on a *motu islet* at the southwest end of Manihi, and the recently rebuilt airstrip has been extended to accommodate ATR-72 aircraft. Transfers from the airport to the Manihi Pearl Beach Resort are made by boat or golf carts, just a 5-minute ride either way. Air Tahiti does not provide any boat transportation from the airport to the village, a 15-min. boat ride from the airport.

You can also get to Manihi by chartering an airplane in Tahiti from **Air Archipels**, *Tel. 81.30.30*; or **Air Tahiti**, *Tel. 86.42.42*.

Arriving By Boat

Mareva Nui, *Tel. 42.25.53, Fax 42.25.57*, is a 181-ft. steel ship that transports cargo between Tahiti and the Tuamotu atolls. It leaves Tahiti every 15 days for the 8-day round-trip voyage, and calls at Manihi after stopping at several atolls, which may include Makatea, Mataiva, Tikehau, Rangiroa and Ahe. There are 12 berths but no cabins and the one-way fare from Tahiti to Manihi is 8.200 CFP, plus 2.200 CFP per day for 3 meals.

St. Xavier Maris Stella III, *Tel. 42.23.58, Fax 43.03.73*, can transport 12 passengers who sleep on the bridge for 8.484 CFP between Tahiti and Manihi, including three meals a day. A berth in an a/c cabin is 15.000 CFP, meals included. Bring your own bedding. The ship leaves Papeete every 15 days and the itinerary varies, taking from 7-10 days for the round-trip voyage.

All the ships stop at the Turipaoa quay beside the pass in Manihi. See more information in Chapter 6, *Planning Your Trip.*

Departing By Air

Air Tahiti has daily flights from Manihi to Papeete, either direct or with a stop in Rangiroa or Fakarava. There are daily direct flights from Manihi to Rangiroa and to Fakarava on Thurs. and Sat. **Air Tahiti** reservations in Manihi: *Tel. 93.30.70*, and the airport number is *Tel. 93.30.75*.

Departing By Boat

St. Xavier Maris Stella III, Tel. 42.23.58, leaves Manihi every 15 days, stopping at several of the western Tuamotu atolls before returning to Papeete. Meals are

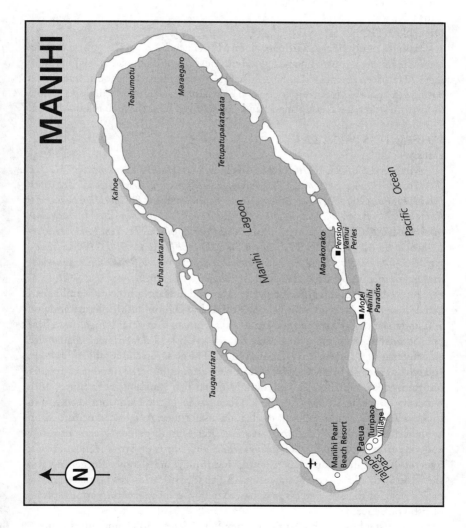

served on board. *Mareva Nui, Tel. 42.25.53, Fax 42.25.57*, calls at 9-10 other atolls after leaving Manihi each 15 days. A berth costs up to 8.200 CFP, depending on how long the journey takes, and three daily meals are 2.200 CFP extra. See more information under *Inter-Island Cruise Ships, Passenger Boats and Freighters* in Chapter 6, *Planning Your Trip*.

ORIENTATION

Manihi's only village, **Turipaoa**, is on Motu Paeua, 2.8 km (1.7 mi.) across the lagoon from the airport. The village is built next to the Tairapa Pass, which is 60 m. (197 ft.) deep and provides the only navigable entry into the lagoon. A sheltered basin with lights has moorings for several boats. In the village you will find a couple of *magasin* stores, a bakery, a snack, and a post office. There is no bank in Manihi.

WHERE TO STAY & EAT

Deluxe

MANIHI PEARL BEACH RESORT, *B.P. 1, Manihi Tuamotu 98771. Tel. 689/96.42.73; Fax 689/96.42.72; www.pearlresorts.com. Reservations: Tel. 689/ 50.84.45; Fax 689/43.17.86; res@smphotels.pf. 40 units. 2008 Low/High Season EP Rates sgl/dbl: Beach bungalow 30.000/35.000 CFP, Premium Beach bungalow 40.000/45.000 CFP; Overwater bungalow 52.000/57.000 CFP; Premium Overwater bungalow 60.000-65.000 CFP; 3rd person 8.000 CFP. Add 7.900 CFP per person for MAP and 10.900 CFP for AP. Canoe breakfast for two 9.900 CFP. One-way airport transfer 1.000 CFP. Add taxes. All major credit cards.*

All 5 editions of this guide book have featured the same photo of Manihi Pearl Beach Resort on the front cover. Look at the clear lagoon in this picture and you will understand why I recommend that you stay in an overwater bungalow. These coral heads are home to a vast array of tropical fish, Tridacna reef clams with colorful mantles, and even live Trochus shells. The glass top coffee table that allows you to view the fish below your bungalow has become almost *de rigeur* in overwater bungalows, but this hotel gives you additional fish watching possibilities with windows on 2 sides of a writing desk. Glass panels in the bathroom keep you in touch with what's happening in the lagoon at all times. A light can be turned on at night to attract the fish and you can even watch a family of blue, green, turquoise and red parrotfish nibbling their dinner while you're brushing your teeth after your own meal! Of course, you'll have a better view from your balcony or by getting into the water with all that fascinating fauna. A fish identification card is placed in the desk drawer of the overwater bungalows to help you recognize the various species of fish you're seeing.

This 4-star hotel with 40 units is a member of Select Hotels and offers a choice of 4 standard beach bungalows or 17 premium beach bungalows, 14 overwater bungalows and 5 premium overwater bungalows. They are built in traditional Polynesian style, with a roof of thatched pandanus fronds and wooden walls. Each unit has a king size bed or 2 twin beds, plus a day bed, covered with neutral beige covers with accent cushions the color of the turquoise and emerald lagoon. They are equipped with a ceiling fan, mini-bar refrigerator, coffee/tea facilities, hair dryer, international direct dial telephone with Internet connection, satellite TV, individual safe and sundeck. All units have a hot water shower and the superior beach bungalows have 2 entrances and an indoor garden with a coral floor. All bungalows have electric mosquito repellent plugs and laundry service is available.

The premium overwater bungalows are the same size as the overwater bungalows (51 sq. m. or 549 sq. ft.) but they are further apart, providing just a little more privacy. They also have a/c, CD player and bathrobes. There are 2 overwater bungalows designed for physically challenged guests in wheelchairs, and the hotel's public areas and pool are wheelchair accessible. The hotel staff will assist handicapped guests when being transferred by boat between the hotel and village or other boat excursions.

The Poe Rava restaurant serves deliciously prepared fish and French cuisine. An American breakfast buffet is 2.600 CFP, a set luncheon menu is 3.200 CFP, and a set dinner menu is 5.600 CFP. In addition to burgers, sandwiches, pizza and pasta (1.250-1.850 CFP), the luncheon menu suggests a salad topped with fresh fried parrotfish that is breaded in coconut for 1.800 CFP, or a Cob salad for 2.200 CFP. The dinner menu offers fish and seafood dishes for 2.500-2.900 CFP, including a whole parrotfish, and the meat choices are 2.500-3.600 CFP. Grilled lobster is 5.000 CFP. Papaya pie and other desserts start at 1.000 CFP and a cheese platter is 2.000 CFP. A local band plays island style music in the restaurant during dinner on Tues. and Fri., and a Tahitian dance show is presented at 8pm each Wed. and Sat.

The reception, bar, boutique, pearl shop, library-lounge and Manea Spa are all located in separate buildings. Beside the coral beach and the lagoon is a large fresh water swimming pool, and the Manihi Blue Nui scuba diving center is adjacent to the pier. Another place to feed and admire the fish is at the snorkeling pier, which has a shower and steps leading into the lagoon. You can also walk across a shallow part of the lagoon to a small islet, where you can relax in a lounge chair or hammock and read your favorite beach book. Hopefully, the hotel management will get rid of the sea cucumbers that are much too numerous in the lagoon facing the beach bungalows.

Free activities for hotel guests include use of bicycles, kayaks, snorkeling gear, volleyball, billiards and mini-golf. A coconut show, pareo tying demonstration, traditional weaving lessons and tamure dance lessons are scheduled regularly at the Miki Miki bar. Tahitian dance shows are presented in the restaurant twice a week during dinner. An interesting activity takes place at 7pm each Wednesday evening when guests accompany Celine, the Marquesan bartender, out to the airstrip to gaze at the huge bowl of stars and planets. There are no lights anywhere nearby, and you can clearly see the Milky Way, Southern Cross, Orion's Belt and all the other constellations visible in the Southern Hemisphere.

Paid excursions and activities include a visit to a pearl farm for 2.273 CFP, a picnic on an uninhabited motu islet for 7.927 CFP, hand line fishing for 1.727

CFP, drift snorkeling in the ocean for 1.727 CFP, and a sunset cruise for 1.818 CFP. You can go online at the computer in the lounge when you buy a code number from reception.

Manihi Pearl Beach Resort is one of French Polynesia's most popular destinations for honeymooners and other loving couples. The hotel offers a number of suggestions for Romantic Interludes, such as the canoe breakfast that is delivered by outrigger paddle canoe and served on your terrace, just as you see in the cover photo. Contact them for details and prices and be sure to have a look at their website as they have installed a webcam to entice you.

Because the Manihi Pearl Beach Resort is a small hotel, it is easy to get to know the employees and other guests. The feeling here is that of a small village, yet you still have all the privacy you desire.

Moderate

MOTEL NANIHI PARADISE, *Turipaoa, Manihi 98771. Tel. 689/93.30.40/ Fax 689/93.30.41; nanihiparadise@mail.pf; www.nanihiparadise.com. On Motu Kamoka, a private islet on the southeast side of the atoll, 10 km. (6.2 mi.) from airport. Round-trip boat transfers 2.100 CFP per person or free for 3 nights stays. EP Rates: 13.400 CFP for 1 room and 20.100 CFP for 2 rooms; AP 13.500 CFP per person per day, including taxes. MC, V.*

Vaiana Dantin owns this holiday family pension, which has been given a temporary 1-Tiare rating awarded by Tahiti Tourisme. There are two small bungalows, with each unit containing 2-bedrooms, kitchenette with refrigerator, bathroom and terrace. Activities include boat transfers to the village, boat tours around the lagoon, snorkeling, shelling, fishing in lagoon, visits to pearl farms, picnics on an uninhabited motu, and transfers to the Manihi Blue Nui Dive center at Manihi Pearl Beach Resort.

Economy

PENSION VAINUI PERLES, *B.P. 51, Turipaoa, Manihi 98771. Tel. 689/ 96.42.89; Fax 689/96.43.30; pension-vainui@mail.pf; www.pensionvainui.com. On Motu Marakorako, 12 km (7.5 mi.) from the airport and main village. Round-trip boat transfers 1.000 CFP per person. AP Rates: 10.000 CFP per person. Add taxes. MC, V.*

This is a large motu owned by Frenchman Edmond Buniet in a remote location 30 min. by boat from the airport. Very basic accommodations are available in 3 recently renovated bungalows facing the lagoon. Each bungalow has 2 rooms and all guests share the bathroom with cold-water shower. Meals are served on a shaded terrace next to the beach of white and pink sand. Rena and Manuel are the two Polynesians who take care of guests. Activities include fishing in the lagoon, picnics on a motu and a visit to Rena's private pearl farm.

SPORTS & RECREATION
Scuba Diving
Manihi Blue Nui Dive Center is located at the Manihi Pearl Beach Resort, *Tel./Fax 96.42.17; manihi.blue.nui@mail.pf; www.bluenui.com.* This well equipped dive shop has showers, lockers, hangers for wet suits and a covered aluminum boat for 16 divers. All diving gear and equipment is provided. Founder Gilles Petre, who is based in Bora Bora, supervises all the Blue Nui Dive Centers. His staff in Manihi are highly qualified instructors for PADI, BEES and CMAS. The rates are 6.818 CFP for 1 dive, initiation dives are 7.727 CFP, and night dives are 8.182 CFP. The Blue Nui Dive Centers in Manihi, Tikihau, Taha'a and Bora Bora all offer dive packages that can be used in any or all of the centers. These packages sell for 31.818 CFP for 5 dives and 59.061 CFP for 10 dives.

Dive Sites
Manihi offers excellent diving conditions in shallow, warm, clear water, with mild currents in the pass. The dive sites are only five minutes away from the dive center, reached by a comfortable speedboat that is custom designed for diving. The pass is south to north with the main wind from the east, and for beginners, a site outside the reef is used that is protected from the main wind by the village of Turipaoa.

Tairapa Pass is one of the most popular dive sites, offering drift dives with the incoming or outgoing currents. You'll feel as though you are soaring through space with the tuna, sharks, schools of barracuda, jack fish, rays and turtles. **The Drop Off** is a wall dive on the ocean side of Manihi, which descends from 3 to 1,350 m (10 to 4,500 ft.) deep. This site abounds with gray sharks, Napoleon fish, giant jack fish, schools of snapper and sea pike barracuda, plus the deep-sea fish like tuna and marlin. Each July thousands of groupers gather here to breed, offering one of the most fascinating underwater events in the world.

The Circus is the name given to a location between the pass and the lagoon, which is a favorite hangout for eagle and manta rays. Underwater photographers can get close to the graceful manta rays as they glide up and down in an average underwater depth of 9 m (30 ft.). These curious and friendly creatures sometimes have a wingspan up to four m (13 ft.) wide, and remain here all year long.

A scenic dive on the **West Point** of the ocean side reveals fire coral, antler coral and flower petal coral, among others, which are visible for up to 60 m (200 ft.) in the incredibly clear water. Shark feeding is best at **The Break**, a large cut in the outer reef, where a coral amphitheater provides the scenery for a multitude of reef sharks, including black tip, white tip, gray sharks and an occasional hammer head, who show up for the free handouts of tuna heads.

SHOPPING
The Manihi Pearl Beach Resort has the **Vahine Purotu Boutique** and **Pearls by Corrion** sells pearls and pearl jewelry on the premises. Just a 5-minute walk or

an even quicker bike ride from the hotel is **La Boutique Mareva,** *Tel./Fax 689/ 96.41.38/93.30.25; marevacoquille@hotmail.com.* This is the home of Mareva and Guy Coquille, who formerly owned and managed the Kaina Village before it became Manihi Pearl Beach Resort. Mareva has a nice selection of Tahitian cultured pearl jewelry.

Poetai Perles, *Tel. 96.42.36/75.12.97,* is across the road from the airport, adjacent to **Rebeta Snack & Boutique.** There is a very limited choice of pearls, but you can buy a sandwich and juice or soft drink.

You can also buy pearls in Turipaoa village, where you may encounter some of the pearl farmers who have set jewelry as well as loose pearls. It is best to learn something about pearls first, so that you will be able to determine if the pearl is not a reject or a pearl that has been harvested early for control purposes. The best quality pearls stay inside the oyster for 18 months, and have a lovely orient or luster. See more information under Shopping in the *Basic Information* chapter.

Visits to a Pearl Farm

Pearls by Corrion, also known as **CJC Perles Manihi,** is the only pearl farm in Manihi that allows regular visits, which are conducted each Mon., Wed. and Fri. morning. The boat leaves the Manihi Pearl Beach Resort at 8am, with a minimum of two people, and the excursion lasts about 2 hours. During this time you will learn practically all there is to know about the *Pinctada Margaritifera* black lipped oyster that gives us this precious gift from the rainbow-hued lagoon of Manihi. The guide is well informed, as she also works in the Pearls by Corrion boutique located at the hotel, where you can buy pearls from the farm. Please do not expect to fly into Manihi at noon and be taken to a pearl farm that afternoon. It just doesn't work that way because the farm is on the other side of the lagoon and the boat and pilot may be otherwise occupied. The guided boat tour to the pearl farm costs 2.273 CFP per person.

MASSAGES & SPA TREATMENTS

Manea Spa, *Tel. 96.42.73; maneaspa@manihipearlbeach.pf,* offers a selection of massages for men, women and couples. Prices start at 8.500 CFP for a 30-min. Monoi Maitai massage for one or 13.500 CFP for two. You can also get a 50- or 80-min. massage. The specialty here is the Monoi Poe, named for the cultured pearls that come from Manihi's famous lagoon. This exotic stimulating massage is applied with a rope of black pearls that arouses all your senses as the masseuse slithers the pearls over your body. You've got to try it! This 50-min. treat is 14.300 CFP. Ask for Mere.

If you are interested in a Reiki treatment, see **Cathy** in the CJC Perles Manihi shop at the hotel. She also does private meditation sessions under the stars at the airstrip.

PRACTICAL INFORMATION
Banks
There are no banks in Manihi.

Hospital
A government-operated infirmary is located in Turipaoa village, *Tel. 96.43.67*. The nurse is on duty from 7-11am and from 4-6pm.

Post Office
A **Post Office and Telecommunications Office** is located in Turipaoa village facing the marina, *Tel. 96.42.22*. You'll find telephone booths in this building, as well as a couple more in the village and at the airport, and a public phone is located at the Manihi Pearl Beach Resort. They all accept phone cards.

TIKEHAU
Tikehau is a South Sea island dream come true, an escapist's haven of seclusion that is less than an hour's flight from Tahiti and just 20 minutes by plane from Rangiroa. Tikehau is one of the most popular atolls in the Tuamotu Archipelago, because of its natural beauty and the friendliness of the 400 inhabitants.

In the Paumotu language Tikehau means "peaceful landing" and when the Russian navigator Kotzbue discovered the atoll in 1815, he named it Krusenstern Island. The old village was destroyed by a cyclone in 1906 and the residents moved to higher ground and built their homes in Tuherahera on the southwest side of the atoll. Here you'll find the *mairie* (town hall), post office and telecommunications center, school, infirmary, three *magasin* stores, bakery, Protestant temple, Catholic church, Seventh-Day Adventist church, Sanito temple, a snack, and most of the pensions and guest houses. There is no bank in Tikehau. Three coral sand roads connect Tuherahera with the airport and the road follows the coast line around the *motu*, where you will see new settlements of the anti-cyclone type houses, as well as new concrete houses, which are built by the new generation who have moved back to the old village.

Most of the guesthouses or pensions are located between the airport and a pretty white sand beach. Tall, stately ironwood trees, *Casuarina equisetifolia*, also known as Australian pine or *aito*, border the beaches, and you can hear the wind whistling through the branches while you watch the white fairy terns soaring overhead.

The barrier reef surrounding Tikehau is almost continuous and the 150-m (492-ft.) wide Tuhieava Pass, on the west coast, is the only entrance into the lagoon. Immediately to the left of the pass is Motu Teonai, which contains a small village of fishing families. Copra is produced in the old village of Maiai, on the northeast side of the atoll, and this is where you will find a religious community called Eden, where cruise boats are usually welcomed. Many members of this sect are Chinese from Tahiti who gather here during holidays and long weekends.

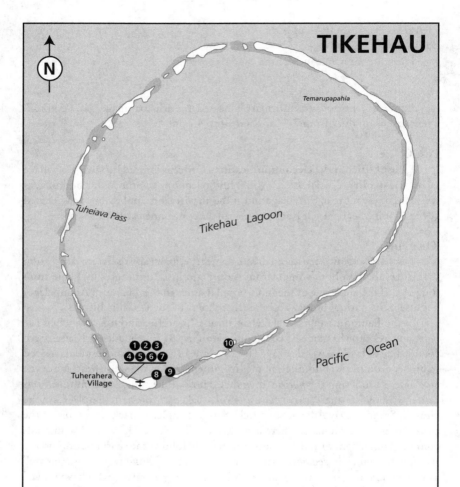

1. Tevaihi Village
2. Aito Motel Colette
3. Tikehau Village
4. Pension Tematie
5. Panau Lagon
6. Chez Justine
7. Pension Hotu
8. Royal Tikehau
9. Kahaia Beach
10. Tikehau Pearl Beach Resort

When **Jacques Cousteau's** research group made a study of the Polynesian atolls in 1987, they declared the lagoon of Tikehau to contain the most fish of any of the lagoons in French Polynesia. There has been no evidence of ciguatera fish poisoning in Tikehau, and all the lagoon fish are considered edible. The choice fish include parrotfish, grouper, long-nose emperorfish, soldierfish and jackfish. A few attempts were made to harvest the *Pinctada Margaritifera* oyster that produces pearls, but due to a lack of plankton in the lagoon, most of these pearl farms are now closed. Surfers seek the swells of the sea as it crashes on the reef beside Tuheiava Pass.

ARRIVALS & DEPARTURES
Arriving by Air
Air Tahiti flies direct from Tahiti to Tikehau daily with 55-min. flights and an additional flight on Fri. that stops in Rangiroa. There is a direct flight from Rangiroa to Tikehau on Mon., Wed., Fri., and 2 on Sun. You can fly direct from Bora Bora to Tikehau each Thurs., and with a stop in Rangiroa on Mon., Wed., Fri., and Sun. You'll have to change aircraft in Rangiroa on Fri. **Air Tahiti reservations**: Tahiti, *Tel. 86.42.42*, in Tikehau *Tel. 96.22.66.*

The one-way airfare from Tahiti to Tikehau is 15.900 CFP; the one-way fare from Rangiroa to Tikehau is 5.600 CFP; and the one-way fare from Bora Bora to Tikehau is 23.400 CFP.

You can also get to Tikehau by chartering an airplane in Tahiti from **Air Archipels**, *Tel. 81.30.30*; or **Air Tahiti**, *Tel. 86.42.42.*

Arriving by Boat
Mareva Nui, *Tel. 42.25.53, Fax 42.25.57*, is a 181-ft. steel ship that transports cargo between Tahiti and the Tuamotu atolls. It leaves Tahiti every 15 days, stopping in Makatea and Mataiva before arriving in Tikehau. There are 12 berths on board but no cabin. The one-way fare from Tahiti to Tikehau is 3.850 CFP and three meals a day cost 2.200 CFP per person.

St. Xavier Maris Stella III, *Tel. 42.23.58*, can transport 12 passengers, sleeping in an a/c cabin or on the deck. Bring your own bedding. The fare from Tahiti to Tikehau is 7.070 CFP on deck and 10.000 CFP for a berth in a/c cabin, including 3 meals a day. The ship leaves Papeete every 15 days for 7-10 day voyages.

See more information in Chapter 6, *Planning Your Trip.*

Departing by Air
Air Tahiti has daily flights from Tikehau to Tahiti, either direct or with a stop in Rangiroa plus a Mon. stop in Manihi. Direct flights from Tikehau to Rangiroa are daily except Sun. There is also a Wed. flight to Manihi via Rangiroa. **Air Tahiti reservations** in Tikehau, *Tel. 96.22.66.*

Departing by Boat

Mareva Nui, Tel. 42.25.53, calls at 12 other atolls after leaving Tikehau each 15 days, and the trip back to Tahiti takes 7 days. *St. Xavier Maris Stella III, Tel. 42.23.58*, leaves Tikehau every 15 days for Manihi, Fakarava and several other western Tuamotu atolls before returning to Papeete. Fares are determined by length of voyage to Tahiti. See more information under *Inter-Island Cruise Ships, Passenger Boats and Freighters* in Chapter 6, *Planning Your Trip*.

ORIENTATION

Most of the residents of Tikehau live in **Tuherahera village** on the southern end of the atoll, where small boats can enter the lagoon through a pass in the coral reef. The almost circular interior lagoon is 26 km (16 mi.) wide, bordered by white and pink sand beaches. A 10-km. (6.2-mi.) dirt road circles the *motu* of Tuherahera, which you can explore on a bicycle.

WHERE TO STAY

Deluxe

TIKEHAU PEARL BEACH RESORT, *B.P. 20, Tuherahera, Tikehau 98778. Tel. 689/96.23.00; Fax 689/96.23.01; www.pearlresorts.com. Reservations: Tel. 689/50.84.54; Fax 689/43.17.86; res@spmhotels.pf. 37 units. 2008 Low/High Season EP Rates sgl/dbl: Beach bungalow 40.000/45.000 CFP; Premium Beach bungalow with a/c 46.000/51.000 CFP; Overwater bungalow 49.000/54.000 CFP; Premium Overwater bungalow 63.000/69.000 CFP; Overwater suite with a/c 70.000/77.000 CFP; 3rd person 8.000 CFP. Add 7.900 CFP per person for MAP and 10.900 CFP for AP. One-way boat transfer between airport and hotel 2.500 CFP. Private boat transfer with champagne 12.500 CFP. Add taxes. All major credit cards.*

This 4-star hotel is located on Motu Tianoa, 3 km (1.9 mi.) east of Tuherahera village in a group of islets called Ohotu. The hotel opened in 2001 with 8 beach bungalows, 6 deluxe beach bungalows with a/c, 8 overwater bungalows and 8 premium overwater bungalows. A 2004 project added 8 premium overwater suites with a/c, and I have to tell you that these suites get my vote as the best overwater accommodation in all the islands.

All the bungalows have thatched roofs, walls of woven palm fronds, woven pandanus matting on the ceiling and split bamboo on the inside walls. The furniture is made of rich-toned local woods and consists of a king-size bed or 2 twin beds, a single daybed, writing desk, small table and chairs. There is a ceiling fan, telephone, satellite TV, mini-bar, coffee-tea making facilities, safe, umbrella and snorkeling gear in each room. The bathrooms in the beach bungalows open onto a garden and a high coral wall, and there are doors between the bedroom and bathroom. Each bathroom has a hair dryer and Manea amenities that are replenished daily when the rooms are cleaned. One of the nicest features of the beach bungalows is the partially covered terrace overlooking a beautiful white sand beach. You can recline in the lounge chairs on the sundeck and watch the sunrise or sunset, depending on which unit you have, and rarely do you see another person on the beach, nor even a passing boat. The very inviting lagoon is just a few steps away. This is the gentle side of the motu, so typical of the South Seas scenery that makes you dream of trade winds singing through the coconut palms, white sandy beaches that turn pink with the setting sun and a crystalline lagoon the color of green silk, turquoise and jade

The original overwater bungalows are 55sq. m. (595 sq. ft.), and are built over a *hoa* channel where the current flows from the ocean into the lagoon. Because the water can be as deep as 2 m (6.6 ft.) underneath some of the bungalows, the hotel management advises guests against swimming here when the current is very strong. You can stand on your balcony and see the waves crashing onto the coral reef and watch a family of reef herons fishing on a sandbar. The overwater bungalows have a glass window in the floor for fish watching. These units have all the same amenities as the beach units, with the addition of CD players in the premium overwater bungalows. 2 of the overwater units are equipped for guests in wheelchairs.

The fabulous premium overwater suites are 93 sq. m. (1001 sq. ft.) and are built over the lagoon just beyond the beach bungalows. These a/c units are furnished like all the other bungalows, but they also have CD players, bathrobes and bathtubs, as well as a big terrace partially covered with a thatched roof. There is a table next to a sofa and chairs under this *fare pote'e*, and there are 2 lounge chairs on the open sundeck. You have direct access into the lagoon by ladder from the swimming platform, plus a shower for rinsing off when you come back up. The fish are plentiful and greedy for free handouts of bread and croissants. There is also a glass table in the bedroom-sitting area designed for fish-watching.

In addition to the Poreho Restaurant and Tianoa Bar, the hotel has an activities desk at the reception area, plus an all-purpose room that can be used for meetings or a game room with a wide screen TV and DVD. There is also a sundries gift shop and boutique. Tikehau Blue Nui Dive Center is located on the hotel grounds, as well as Fare Manea Spa. Room service is offered during regular meal hours, and there is a 48-hr. laundry service and a secretarial service. The hotel grounds are fumigated daily to keep the mosquito and bug population to a minimum, and each room is furnished with an electrical repellent device, as well as bug spray.

The hotel's complimentary activities include an infinity swimming pool, kayaks, snorkeling gear, volleyball, bacci ball, ping-pong, billiards and library. For optional excursions and activities you can take a boat trip to visit Bird Island on Motu Puarua and snorkel in the lagoon for 5.909 CFP, or join a barbecue picnic on a pink-sand motu for 7.727 CFP. A local fisherman will also take 1-4 people for line fishing in the lagoon for 14.091 CFP, or trawling in the open ocean for 27.273 CFP for 2 passengers. A sunset cruise is 3.182 CFP. You can be dropped off on an uninhabited motu for 3.182 CFP, with a walkie-talkie and picnic and drinks if you so desire. A jetski excursion costs 17.727 CFP for 1 hr. and 45 min. or 11.818 CFP for a 1-hr. sunset ride.

The hotel operates a daily boat service between the village and the hotel, providing 5 round-trip shuttles. You can take this free shuttle to the village and pick up a rental bike at the boat dock for 900 CFP for half a day. A bike ride around the village motu takes about 45 min. and it is a lovely trip. The people of Tikehau are very friendly to one another and to visitors.

The Tikehau Pearl Beach Resort is a member of Select Hotels & Resorts and a favorite destination for honeymooners. Contact the hotel for details on their Romantic Rendez-vous Package, which includes a Canoe Breakfast for 2 for 9.900 CFP, a Blue Lagoon breakfast, a picnic for 2 on a secluded motu, or a gourmet picnic on the motu that includes champagne served at an elegantly dressed table.

Moderate

ROYAL TIKEHAU, *B.P. 15 Tuherahera, Tikehau 98778. Tel./Fax 689/ 96.23.37, cell 72.17.18/72.17.19. On a private islet across channel from the end of the airport runway and 5 min. by boat from Tuherahera quay. Round-trip car and boat transfers 1.160 CFP per person. 2008 MAP Rates: Room 15.750 CFP sgl, 20.570 CFP dbl; MAP hoa bungalow 23.250 CFP sgl; 30.250 CFP dbl; MAP beach bungalow 27.220 CFP sgl, 35.330 CFP dbl; Premium Beach Bungalow 31.460 CFP sgl, 42.350 dbl, including VAT. Lunch on request for 3.000 CFP. No credit cards.*

Tikehau's newest lodging opened in mid-2007 with 4 rooms in a concrete building and 5 wooden bungalows built over a *hoa* channel and beside the beach on a private motu. Each room can sleep 2 and has mosquito nets and a private bathroom with cold-water shower. The bungalows can also sleep 2 people and each has a fan and a private bathroom with hot water shower. There is also a Premium Beach Bungalow with a tester bed, TV and a bottle of wine for its guests. There is solar electricity plus an electric generator as back-up. Meals featuring Tahitian food with a seafood base are served in the overwater restaurant, and there is also a lounge with a pool table and rainy day games. Snorkeling equipment and kayaks are provided and lagoon excursions can be arranged for guests. Owners Jean-Claude and Monique Varney are well-known residents of Tahiti and their pension has already become a success due to the quality of cuisine served here.

Economy

PENSION TEMATIE, *Tuherahera, Tikehau 98778. Tel./Fax 689/96.22.65. Beside the beach in Tematie village, 400 m (436 yds.) from the airport and 2 km (1.2 mi.) from the main village of Tuherahera. 2008 Rates: EP bungalow 6.000 CFP sgl; 7.500 CFP dbl; MAP add 2.800 CFP per person per day. Lunch on request for 2.500 CFP. Add taxes. Free transfers. No credit cards.*

This original style pension is between Tikehau Village and Panau Lagoon, right on the pretty white sand beach that is shaded by *aito* trees (Australian pines) that whisper in the refreshing sea breezes. Owner Nora Hoiore is originally from Tikehau and her French husband, Yves-Marie Dubois, is an engineering consultant for airport landing strips. After living in Africa, St. Kitts, Indonesia and other countries for several years, they returned to Tikehau and built 3 bungalows for guests. Two of these units are octagon shaped and the walls are made of broken coral they collected from the reef. The smaller bungalows have a double bed and a single bed, and the family bungalow also has a mezzanine that will sleep two people. All the bathrooms are tiled and private, with cold water showers. The windows are screened and there is a portable fan. The bungalows are attractively decorated with Polynesian bed covers and woodcarvings.

Meals are served in the communal dining room. They both speak some English and can arrange activities for guests.

TIKEHAU VILLAGE, *Tuherahera, Tikehau 98778. Tel./Fax 689/96.22.86; cell 689/74.86.46. Beside the beach in Tematie village, 600 m (654 yds.) from the main village of Tuherahera and 400 m (436 yds.) from the airport. Free transfers. 2008 Rates: MAP bungalow 9.100 CFP per person. VAT included. MC, V.*

This small family hotel is also called Chez Pae'a and Caroline, and is located between Aito Motel Colette and Chez Tematie on a pretty white sand beach next to the airport. There are 9 recently renovated thatched roof bungalows facing the beach. All rooms have tiled floors, ceiling fans and private bathrooms with cold-water showers, and terraces. You have a choice of double or twin beds and mosquito nets are available on request.

The beach side restaurant and bar are open to the public. When business is good they have buffet dinners twice a week and a Tahitian feast is also prepared once a month or so, complete with Paumotu music.

Guests enjoy feeding the sharks and rays that come to the edge of the lagoon beside the white sand beach in search of handouts. Boat trips can be arranged with Naga Excursion to take you to visit other motu islets inside the lagoon, complete with a picnic. The Raie Manta Club diving center is located on the hotel premises.

TEVAIHI VILLAGE, *B.P. 42, Tuherahera, Tikehau 98778. Tel./Fax 689/96.23.04, cell 74.85.29; tevaihivillage@mail.pf; www.yozz-online.com/tevaihivillage. Beside lagoon in Tuherahera village, 5 minutes from the airport and 400 m (1,312 ft.) from the quay. Free transfers. 2008 Rates: EP bungalow 5.000 CFP; Bungalow and MAP 8.500 CFP; Bungalow and AP 10.500 CFP per person per day. Add taxes. No credit cards.*

Noella Poetai operates the only pension to the left of the boat dock. There are four wooden bungalows of the government-approved model, built on stilts facing a pretty beach of white sand. Each unit has a double bed and a single bed and a bathroom with cold water shower. You can sit on the covered terrace and watch flocks of sea birds as they fish in the lagoon and you can also watch the sunrise from here.

Meals are served in a restaurant on the beach that is also open to the public. The lagoon is shallow here, but you can swim if you walk further from shore. Noella rents bikes for 1.000 CFP a day and she will also arrange your boat excursions on request.

AITO MOTEL COLETTE, *Tuherahera, Tikehau 98778. Tel./Fax 689/96.23.07; Cell 74.85.77/74.85.88. Beside lagoon between Tuherahera village and the* *airport. Free transfers. 2008 Rates: Bungalow with MAP 17.500 CFP dbl; Bungalow with AP 22.800 CFP dbl, including taxes. No credit cards.*

Colette has 5 thatched-roof A-frame bungalows built on stilts on the beach within easy walking distance from the village. Tall Australian pine trees (called Aito in Tahitian) line the beach, providing shade and the melody of their whispering sounds as their feathery fronds sway in the ocean breeze. Two bungalows contain 2 double beds, 2 bungalows have a double bed, and 1 bungalow has a double bed and a sofa. Each unit has a private bathroom with a cold water shower. There is a restaurant and bar on the beach where you can enjoy Colette's home cooking. Colette doesn't speak much English, although she works at the airport for each Air Tahiti flight arrival and departure, so she can manage to communicate with non-French speaking guests.

Other Pensions

The pensions listed above are the ones I consider the best choices on Tikehau. You can also find accommodations and meals in the following lodgings, which are all located on a white sand beach. **PANAU LAGON**, Tel./Fax 96.22.99. 6 *fares*; **CHEZ JUSTINE**, Tel./Fax 96.22.87; cell 72.02.44. 5 *fares* and campground; **PENSION HOTU**, Tel. 96.22.89. 3 *fares*; **KAHAIA BEACH**, Tel. 96.22.77; Fax 96.23.75, 5 *fares* on motu.

WHERE TO EAT

Restaurant Poreho at Tikehau Pearl Beach Resort, *Tel. 96.23.00*. Open daily for BLD. All major credit cards. An American breakfast buffet is 2.600 CFP, a set luncheon menu is 3.200 CFP, and a set dinner menu is 5.600 CFP. You can get snacks at the Tianoa Bar from 2:30-4 pm.

Tevaihi Village, *Tel. 96.23.04*. The restaurant at this family pension is open to the public. No credit cards.

Tikehau Village, *Tel. 96.22.86*. A beachside restaurant/bar at this family pension welcomes the public. Regular buffet dinners and occasional Tahitian feasts served. MC, V.

Cathy's Snack in Tuherahera is also a good place to stop for lunch while you are biking around the village.

SEEING THE SIGHTS

You can view the beauty of the fish and submarine gardens through a snorkeling mask or while scuba diving with qualified instructors. Take a boat to **Motu Ohihi**, which is surrounded by shallow *hoa* channels and has a pink sand beach. Go to **Motu Puarua** and **Oe Oe**, the Bird Island where snowy white fairy terns and noddy birds nest. Snorkeling is especially good in Tikehau's crystal clear lagoon.

Boat excursions will take you to visit the fish parks and past one or more of the former pearl farms, and you have a choice of *motu* islets for a memorable picnic.

You can fish by line or spear, and Tuheiava Pass is a good surfing spot in December and January. On the main island bike through the coconut groves to the rose-colored reef, and take a guided land tour to the old village and surrounding area. Hina's Bell is a big rock beside the beach that resounds like a chime when struck. This is a lovely place to watch the sunset. And under the light of the tropical stars it becomes a romantic spot for lovers to meet.

SPORTS & RECREATION
Nautical Activities
Naga Excursions, *Tel. 689/74.84.85*. Roland Teriiatetoofa will take you in his boat with a sunroof to visit Bird Island, where hundreds of sea birds come to lay their eggs in the sand or on the bare limb of a tree. You can fish, snorkel and swim in the warm lagoon and then enjoy a Paumotu style picnic of grilled lagoon fish on an uninhabited motu. This all-day excursion also includes visiting a fish park and stopping on Eden Island, where there is a religious community. The cost is 7.500 CFP per person.

Scuba Diving
The dive sites are concentrated around the Tuheiava Pass at the southern or southwestern end of the atoll. The clarity of the water, moderate currents in the pass and impressive seascapes provide an exciting experience, especially when you are surrounded by white tip reef sharks, leopard rays, eagle rays, tunas, barracudas, jackfish, black surgeon fish, big groupers, napoleons and other brilliantly colored schools of tropical fish. You may even see the graceful manta rays gliding by.

Raie Manta Club Tikehau is located at Tikehau Village, *Tel./Fax 96.22.53; raiemantaclub@mail.pf; http://raiemantaclub.free.fr*. This dive center is owned by Yves LeFevre, who is also based in Rangiroa and Rurutu. The qualified English-speaking diving instructor takes a maximum of 5 divers for each outing, just a 20-min. boat ride from the village.

Tikehau Blue Nui, *Tel. 96.22.40; Fax 96.23.01; tikehaubluenui@mail.pf; www.bluenui.com* has their dive center at the Tikehau Pearl Beach Resort. The rates are 6.818 CFP for a fun dive, 7.727 CFP for a first dive and 8.182 CFP for a night dive. Dive packages can be used at any of the Blue Nui centers in Tikehau, Manihi, Bora Bora and Taha'a. A 5-dive package is 31.818 CFP and a 10-dive package is 59.091 CFP. A half-day private dive for two is 45.454 CFP. CMAS 1-star or PADI Open Water certification available.

MASSAGES & SPA TREATMENTS
Manea Spa, *Tel. 96.23.00; maneaspa@tikehaupearlbeach.pf*, is located in a beach bungalow at the quieter end of the hotel property. You can choose from a range of massages for 1-2 people that last for 30, 50, or 80 min., and start at 8.000 CFP for a 30-min. Monoi One. The specialty here is the Monoi Pape Miti, an unforgettable massage that is performed on a massage table placed in the lagoon.

The cost for this 50-min. treat is 15.000 CFP for one and 26.000 CFP for two. The Monoi Ofai hot stone healing is 16.500 CFP for a 50 min. massage.

PRACTICAL INFORMATION

There are no banks and no *gendarmes* in Tikehau. The *mairie* (town hall) is located in Tuherahera village, adjacent to the post office and school. Construction of a new marina began in 2007.

Food Stores

There are 2 stores in Tuherahera village that provide frozen products, canned foods, a few fresh vegetables, wine and beer. You can buy fresh baguettes of French bread each morning. Yachts can find a limited quantity of fuel in the stores. A municipal cistern at the foot of the wharf can supply yachts with water.

Medical Services

There is an infirmary in Tikehau, *Tel. 98.22.97*, with a nurse but no doctor.

Post Office

The **Post Office and Telecommunications Office** is in Tuherahera village, *Tel. 96.22.22*. There is an automatic telephone cabin here.

FAKARAVA

Fakarava is the second largest atoll in the Tuamotu Archipelago, after Rangiroa, and its rectangular-shaped lagoon is 60 km. (37 mi.) long by 25 km. (15 mi.) wide. The atoll is 488 km. (303 mi.) east-northeast of Tahiti and southeast of Rangiroa in the central Tuamotus.

A direct flight from Tahiti to Fakarava is just 70 min., which is helping to turn this atoll into a popular destination for those who seek vacation experiences off-the-beaten path. The lagoon of Fakarava is a magnificent marine realm of sharks, graceful manta rays, giant sized fish and a whole parade of beautiful tropical fish.

The Commune of Fakarava includes 7 atolls that received an official seal of approval as a Biosphere Reserve in Dec. 2007. Aratika, Fakarava, Kauehi, Niau, Raraka, Taioro and Toau are now protected as part of the UNESCO Man and the Biosphere (MAB) global network.

Fakarava's special features are columns of water in the lagoon and ocean and the importance and diversity of its fauna and flora, including the kingfisher, the Tuamotu palm tree and the lagoon crustaceans, such as *varo* (squill or sea centipede) and *tiane'e* (slipper lobster).

The **Garuae Pass** on the northwest coast is one km (.62 mi.) wide. It is the largest pass in French Polynesia and gives access to anchorages for yachts and even the big passenger liners that anchor in front of the village of **Rotoava** on the northeast coast facing the pass. The *Aranui III* calls here on the second day of its 14-day round-trip voyages between Tahiti and the Marquesas Islands. Rotoava village is home to most

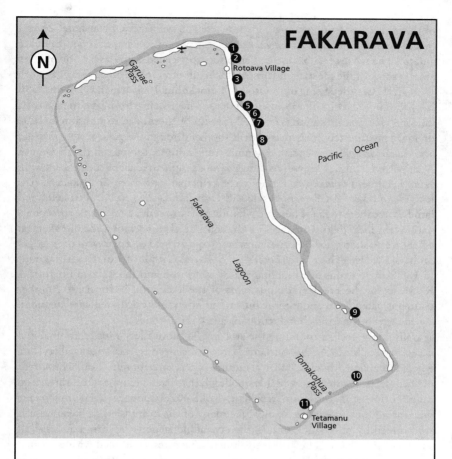

1. Relais Marama
2. Vahitu Dream
3. Havaiki Fakarava Guest
   House
4. Vekeveke Village

5. Pension Paparara
6. Hotel Maitai Dream
   Fakarava
7. Tokerau Village
8. Vaiama Village

9. Raimiti
10. Motu Aito Paradise
11. Tetamanu Village &
    Tetamanu Sauvage

of the atoll's 1,674 population. This is where you will find a 4-star hotel, several family pensions, a couple of *magasin* stores, the post office, grade school, churches and town hall. Three scuba dive centers offer experienced divers a selection of dives among some of the most abundant fish life in all of French Polynesia.

On the southeast side of the atoll is **Tumakohua Pass**, which is 200 m. (656 ft.) wide and 12 to 15 m. (39 to 49 ft.) deep. The distance from pass to pass is 58 km. or 35 nautical miles and takes 1 1/2 -2 hours by speedboat. In addition to scuba diving, a favorite activity here is to drift snorkel through the pass. Several decades ago Fakarava was the social, religious and cultural capital of the Tuamotu Archipelago, and was known to the *Paumotu* people in ancient times as Havaiki Nui. **Tetamanu** village was formerly the principal settlement on Fakarava. It is located on a very small *motu* beside the Tumakohua Pass, and only a couple of families live there today. There are 3 family pensions plus some simple accommodations for local folks who also seek the solitude of this remote side of Fakarava. There are no shops, no boutiques, nowhere to go on land except to visit the vestiges of the old village. There is the coral shell of an old Catholic Church that was built in 1862, the remains of a building that was a prison and the walls of the former Residence of the French Administrator of the Tuamotu Archipelago. Another church is dated 1874 and is more intact, but no mass is celebrated here anymore. A cemetery behind the church contains a few tombstones.

Inside the reef surrounding the atoll are 94 motu islets, mostly uninhabited except for sea birds. At the southern extremity is a very special motu called Irifa, where the lagoon provides a magical luminescence, a mirror reflection of hundreds of coconut palms that grow beside the beach that stretches on and on for several miles. Bring your mosquito repellent. Koka Koka motu is a favorite picnic destination for those in the know. Like many of the motu islets in Fakarava it is surrounded by pink sands, and in the crystalline lagoon you'll find a wealth of succulent fish that can be grilled for lunch. The forests are filled with trees that provide precious wood for building and carving: *kahaia, puatea, miro, tou, gnao gnao* and *autera'a*. Chances are you will also see a white fairy tern with black button eyes perched on the branch of a *tou* tree, along with her newly hatched chick. She provides no nest, but lays a solitary egg in the crook of a tree limb. Drinking coconuts are within easy reach without shinnying up the trunk. This is the domain of the *kaveu*, the giant coconut crab, which makes a very tasty dinner.

Whatever you do and wherever you stay in Fakarava, do not miss seeing the southern end of the atoll. Bring your camera and lots of film, and you may also want to bring your own booze and munchie snacks if you are staying on this side of the atoll.

ARRIVALS & DEPARTURES
Arriving by Air
Air Tahiti flies direct from Tahiti to Fakarava each Mon., Tues., Thurs., Sat. and Sun., with 70-min. flights. Each Tues., Wed. and Fri. the ATR flight from

Tahiti to Fakarava stops in Rangiroa, with a change of aircraft on Tues. You can fly from Bora Bora to Fakarava on Tues. and Fri. with a stop in Rangiroa each day and a change of aircraft on Fri. **Air Tahiti reservations:** Tahiti, *Tel. 86.42.42* in Fakarava, *Tel. 93.40.25/93.40.20.*

The one-way airfare from Tahiti to Fakarava is 17.100 CFP, the one-way fare from Rangiroa to Fakarava is 5.600 CFP, and the one-way fare from Bora Bora is 26.400 CFP. The airport is 4 km. (2.5 mi.) from Rotoava village, connected by a paved road.

You can also get to Fakarava by chartering an airplane in Tahiti from **Air Archipels**, *Tel. 81.30.30*; or **Air Tahiti**, *Tel. 86.42.42.*

Arriving by Boat
Mareva Nui, *Tel. 42.25.53, Fax 42.25.57*, is a 181-ft. steel ship that transports cargo between Tahiti and the Tuamotu atolls. It leaves Tahiti every 15 days, arriving in Fakarava after stopping at 8 atolls in the Western Tuamotu Archipelago. There are 12 berths on board but no cabin. The one-way fare from Tahiti to Fakarava is 5.700 CFP and three meals a day cost 2.200 CFP per person.

St. Xavier Maris Stella III, *Tel. 42.23.58*, can transport 12 passengers who sleep on deck or in the a/c cabin. Bring your own bedding. The deck fare from Tahiti to Fakarava is 11.830 CFP per person, including 3 meals a day, and 30.000 CFP in a berth, meals included. The ship leaves Papeete every 15 days for 7-10 day voyages.

See more information in Chapter 6, *Planning Your Trip*.

Departing by Air
Air Tahiti flies direct from Fakarava to Tahiti each Tues., Wed., Thurs., Fri., Sat. and Sun. The Mon. flight and a Sat. flight from Fakarava stop in Rangiroa enroute to Tahiti. **Air Tahiti reservations** in Fakarava, *Tel. 93.40.25/93.40.20.*

Departing by Boat
Mareva Nui, *Tel. 42.25.53*, calls at five or more atolls after leaving Fakarava each 15 days, and the trip back to Tahiti takes 4 days or more. The cost is determined by the number of days required and 3 meals a day are 2.200 CFP per person. *St. Xavier Maris Stella III*, *Tel. 42.23.58*, leaves Fakarava every 15 days for Papeete following an itinerary determined by freight to deliver or pick up. See more information under *Inter-Island Cruise Ships, Passenger Boats and Freighters* in Chapter 6, *Planning Your Trip*.

GETTING AROUND
Fakalocation, *Tel. 78.03.37*, rents scooters and bicycles.

WHERE TO STAY

Superior

HOTEL MAITAI DREAM FAKARAVA, *B.P. 19, Rotoava, Fakarava 98763. Tel. 689/93.41.50; Fax 689/93.41.51; info@fakarava.hotelmaitaifa.com; www.hotelmaitai.com. Beside lagoon 10.5 km (6.5 mi.) from airport. 30 bungalows. 2008 Low/High Season EP Rates sgl./dbl.: Tiare Bungalow 25.000/26.500 CFP; Beach Bungalow 29.900/31.500 CFP; Beach Premium Bungalow 35.700/37.500. 3rd person 6.500 CFP. American breakfast 2.300 CFP; MAP with Continental breakfast 7.750 CFP; AP with American breakfast 10.250 CFP. Add taxes. Round-trip airport transfers 2.500 CFP per person. All major credit cards.*

Fakarava's first and only hotel opened in September 2002, offering international class lodging and services just a 15-minute ride on the paved road from the airport and a 15-minute boat ride from the Garuae Pass, which offers nirvana for scuba divers in the kilometer-wide opening through the coral reef.

The sturdily built bungalows sit on raised islands in groups of three above the quarter-mile white sand beach that stretches the length of the property. There are 9 bungalows facing the magnificent lagoon, 6 beach bungalows in the second row and behind them are 15 bungalows, set in a garden of Tiare Tahiti bushes. All the bungalows have 45 sq. m (484 sq. ft.) of living space, plus a covered terrace. The only difference in price is where they are placed. The walls and roofs are constructed with rich teakwood from Bali. Each unit is furnished with a king size bed that converts into twin beds. There is also a sofa bed, office desk and chair, ceiling fan, international direct dial telephone, satellite TV, refrigerator with mini-bar on request, coffee and tea making facilities, and individual safe. The furniture is made of coconut wood from Bali and Polynesian artwork adorns the walls. The indoor/outdoor bathroom is decorated with coral and has a powerful hot water shower and hair dryer. Bring your own makeup mirror if you are near sighted. There are also facilities for physically challenged guests.

The Kura Ora restaurant and Kiri Kiri bar overlook the lagoon. Buffet or à la carte meals are served in the 48-seat dining room, on the open terrace, or on the adjacent white sand beach where the tables are shaded by big umbrellas. The Paumotu waitresses are sometimes barefoot and shy, but always friendly if you smile at them. There is no room service. The bar is open from 10 am-10pm, serving your favorite cocktails. Musical entertainment adds a Polynesian touch during special evenings. Internet service is available in the hotel's big reception area. You can buy a phonecard at the front desk.

A long pier is built over the lagoon in front of the hotel, which is the departure point for boat trips to visit pearl farms, fish parks, remote motu islets, picnics on deserted beaches, deep-sea fishing and other lagoon excursions. A half-day excursion starts at 6.000 CFP and a full-day boat trip to Tetamanu village with a picnic is 12.000 CFP. Guests have free use of snorkel gear, kayaks and outrigger paddle canoes. You can rent a bike or arrange for a village tour or lagoon excursion at the front desk. Topdive is a scuba diving center on the premises that offers a range of exciting dives to explore the wealth of big sea life in the passes and lagoon.

Moderate/Economy

I have listed the Pensions on the North side of Fakarava atoll in order of their proximity to the airport.

RELAIS MARAMA, *B.P. 16, Rotoava, Fakarava 98763. Tel./Fax 689/98.42.51, cell 72.09.42/70.81.98; teavanui@divingfakarava.com. On seaside in Rotoava village, 3.5 km (2.2 mi.) from airport. EP Rates: room 4.500 CFP sgl, 7.000 CFP dbl; ocean side bungalow 5.000 CFP sgl, 8.000 CFP dbl; camping 2.000 CFP per person per day, including taxes, breakfast and transfers. No credit cards.*

This is a popular bed and breakfast lodging with backpackers, campers and other budget travelers who prefer to spend a minimum amount on their sleeping facilities and save their money for scuba diving in one of the world's most spectacular lagoons. Owners Jacques Sauvage, a Frenchman, and Marama Teanuanua, a Paumotu man from Fakarava, speak English, French and Tahitian. They have built 6 bungalows and a 3-bedroom house, with two twin beds in each room. Camping space for 12 tents is available in a clearing overlooking the ocean and tents are available at no extra cost. There are 4 communal bathrooms and 2 showers with cold water and guests can also use the washing machine. A *fare pote'e* shelter contains a kitchen/dining area that has two gas burners and two refrigerators, plus a sink and tables. There is also a barbecue grill. Guests can cook their own food here as the bungalows are rented without meals included, but you can order dinner or barbecue for 2.000 CFP per person. Be sure to reserve before 2pm. Rainwater is used for drinking. There is a public telephone at the post office nearby, and there are 3 snacks and two small stores in the village. A bicycle costs 2.000 CFP for your entire stay. Lagoon excursions and scuba diving are available.

HAVAIKI FAKARAVA GUEST HOUSE, *Rotoava, Fakarava 98763. Tel. 689/93.40.15/74.16.16; Fax 689/93.40.16; havaiki@mail.pf; www.havaiki.com. Beside lagoon 5 km (3.1 mi.) from airport and 600 m (1,968 ft.) past Rotoava village. 2008 Rates MAP: panoramic garden room 11.500 CFP sgl, 17.900 CFP dbl; beach bungalow 13.950 CFP sgl., 21.900 CFP dbl., including taxes. Round-trip airport transfers 1.500 CFP. Minimum stay 3 nights. AE, MC, V.*

This is the most popular family pension in Fakarava and definitely my favorite place to stay on the north side of the atoll. Owners Clotilde (Havaiki) and Joachim Dariel have 5 plywood bungalows facing a pretty white sand beach, overlooking one of the most beautiful views of the lagoon and sky that Nature has created in these islands. There are also 2 duplex garden rooms on the second level of the main building across the road. Each bungalow and room contains a double bed and a single bed, a private bathroom with cold-water shower, and a ceiling fan.

Clotilde has a passion for flowers and she has placed big planters of hot pink bougainvillea, yellow and purple alamanda and other colorful flowers on both sides of the road to mark the limits of her land. Baskets of bright blossoms also hang under the eaves of each bungalow.

Meals are served at a table for 16 guests in the dining room across the road from the beach. Breakfast is European style and dinner includes local and imported products prepared for European tastes. They also sell wine and beer.

There is also a small pearl boutique in the dining/lounge/reception room. Here you can admire and buy the creations of Nicolas Dariel, Joachim's father, who is a goldsmith. Their family began Fakarava's first pearl farm in 1989, and you can see the grafting *fare* that is built overwater at the end of a very long pier in front of the pension. You can visit the pearl farm on request and even fish for your own mother-of-pearl oyster for 3.000 CFP. If there is no pearl inside, then you just keep fishing until you find one.

Bicycles and kayaks are provided and excursions are organized on request. These include snorkeling and fishing in the lagoon, visits to pearl farms, picnics on uninhabited motu islets, and scuba diving. Excursion rates range from 6.000-12.000 CFP. Or you can simply swing in a hammock or sit on the covered terrace of your bungalow and watch the setting sun slip behind the horizon at Garuae pass.

VEKEVEKE VILLAGE, *Rotoava, Fakarava 98763. Tel./Fax 689/98.42.80; cell 79.13.77; vekevekevillage@mail.pf; www.pension-fakarava.com. Beside lagoon 9 km (6 mi.) from airport. MAP 10.000 CFP sgl, 18.000 CFP dbl, plus visitor's tax. Round-trip airport transfers 1.000 CFP per bungalow. AE, MC, V.*

Owners Lenick and Thierry Amo have built 4 plywood bungalows beside a pretty cove with a narrow beach. Two beach bungalows have a double bed, one bunk bed, a ceiling fan and private bathroom with cold water shower. Two semi over-water bungalows each have a double bed, 2 single mattresses in upper level mezzanine and private bathroom with cold-water shower.

Chef Christian takes care of the guests, serving fine French cuisine in a dining *fare* at the water's edge. Bicycles and kayaks are provided free of charge to guests, and all optional excursions and picnics can be arranged.

PENSION PAPARARA, *B.P. 88, Rotoava, Fakarava 98763. Tel./Fax 689/ 98.42.66; cell 74.69.10; pensionpaparara@mail.pf; fakaravaexplorer@mail.pf; www.pensionpaparara.com; www.fakaravaexplorer.com. Beside lagoon past Rotoava village, 10 km (6.2 mi.) from the airport. MAP 9.000-11.500 CFP sgl; 16.000-19.000 CFP dbl, including taxes and transfers. MC, V.*

This Polynesian owned pension is one of the oldest guest houses on Fakarava. It is located beside the lagoon just before the Hotel Matai Dream Fakarava. There are 2 beach bungalows with ceiling fans, private tiled bathrooms and cold-water showers, and 3 traditional style bungalows with a communal bathroom and cold-water shower. One of the bungalows has a coral floor and a terrace hanging over the lagoon, where you can watch the parrotfish nibbling on the coral heads in the shallow water. All units have mosquito nets over the beds.

Corina Lenoir and her husband Ato Lissant serve European and local style meals in a spacious dining room/bar in the garden or at a picnic table beside the lagoon. Bicycles, kayaks and outrigger canoes are free of charge for guests. Ato, who speaks English, also operates Fakarava Explorer, providing boat excursions for snorkeling, dolphin watching, to visit distant motu islets, for picnics and deep-sea fishing. Fakarava Diving is also located on the premises, offering scuba diving packages.

TOKERAU VILLAGE, *B.P. 53, Rotoava, Fakarava 98763. Tel./Fax 689/ 98.41.09/88.06.82, cell 70.82.19/71.30.46; tokerauvillage@mail.pf; Beside lagoon 11 km (6.8 mi.) from airport. 2008 Rates: MAP bungalow 12.000 CFP sgl, 22.000 CFP dbl per day, plus taxes. A minimum of 2 nights required. Round-trip airport transfers 1.000 CFP per person. AE, MC, V.*

This attractive pension opened in February 2003 and has been awarded a 2-Tiare rating by Tahiti Tourism. It is located beside the lagoon just after the Hotel Maitai Dream Fakarava, and is owned by Flora and Patrick Bordes, who are assisted by their daughter, Gahina, who speaks English. The 4 bungalows built on stilts are the government backed models that consist of shingle shake roofs and wooden walls, a modern Polynesian style with *pueu* mats covering the walls, and room for a double bed and a single bed, desk and clothes closet in the bedroom/sitting room. The rooms are colorfully decorated with *tifaifai* bed covers and photographs of old Tahiti hang on the walls. The private bathrooms have a cold-water shower. A covered terrace overlooks the French style garden with sculpted bushes and there are flowers everywhere.

Polynesian style meals featuring fresh fish are served in a dining room near the beach, which is also open to the public. Bicycles and kayaks are provided free of charge for guests and car and boat excursions can be arranged on request. The scuba dive centers will come here to pick up clients who wish to dive.

Pensions on the South side of Fakarava atoll, close to Tumakohua Pass

MOTU AITO PARADISE, *B.P. 12, Rotoava, Fakarava 98763. Tel. 689/ 74.26.13; motu-aito@mail.pf; www.fakarava.org. On Motu Aito near the Tumakohua Pass and Tetamanu village, 55 km (34 mi.) by boat from the airport and Rotoava village. AP 14.880 CFP per person per day, including bungalow and 3 meals, round-trip boat transfers between airport and lodge, activities and taxes. Minimum stay 3 nights. No credit cards.*

When Manihi and Tila Salmon and their 3 children settled on Motu Aito more than 20 years ago, the islet was only sand and coral. Today it is an oasis bordered by *aito* trees (also known as Casaurina, ironwood or Australian pine. There are also *tamanu* and *tou* trees for shade, flowering Tiare Tahiti bushes, frangipani and lovely green bird's nest ferns. The main abode is a big concrete house with an enormous family lounge filled with sofas or beds to accommodate the Salmon children and grandchildren when they come to visit, or to provide extra sleeping space for friends and an overflow of guests.

Manihi has built six Polynesian style bungalows for clients, which are very well constructed and thoughtfully decorated with driftwood, coral, seashells and fresh flowers. Each *fare* contains a double bed and a single bed and a mattress can be added if needed. Each unit is different and very originally designed, with walls and ceiling of woven palm frond and terraces trimmed with the very useful *kahaia* wood found in the atolls. Manihi also built the furniture, using local woods. There is an individual bathroom for each bungalow, with a private outdoor shower in a little garden of ferns and other green plants. Two enormous concrete tanks catch the rain and provide a plentiful supply of water for showers. Solar panels generate the electricity.

Manihi has expanded the size of the bungalows and Tila makes new curtains and bedspreads each year. Recent improvements also include a new fast boat that can get you from the main village to their motu in 90 minutes. The boat dock has been extended and a new bridge built to join the next motu. He has added lights for better fishing here at night, and has rebuilt his fish trap.

Activities include walking around the islets, swimming, boat trips to visit the pink sand beaches and bird island, the old village of Tetamanu with its Catholic church that was built in 1874, and snorkeling in the Tumakohua Pass (bring your own snorkeling gear). You can accompany Manihi on a tuna fishing expedition in the open ocean, or you can help him choose dinner from the abundant selection of fish in his fish trap. Everyone eats together at a big table on the dining terrace and fresh fish is the base of their meals. They do not sell any wine or beer, so bring your own and they will chill it for you.

It is also easy to get away on your own. You can walk across a shallow *hoa* channel to visit adjacent motu islets. Yours will be the only footsteps in the sand, as these are truly desert isles. Should you desire, Tila will pack you a picnic lunch and Manihi will drop you off on a pink sand beach and pick you up whenever you wish.

Tila and Manihi are both Polynesians and they warmly welcome their guests. They lived in New Zealand for 10 years and speak very good English. Their three children are now grown and the two boys are professional tattoo artists in Tahiti. See information on Aroma Tattoo Art and Manu Tattoo Art under *Tattoos* in the *Tahiti* chapter.

RAIMITI, *Rotoava, Fakarava; raimiti@mail.pf; www.raimiti.com. On a big motu in the Tetamanu district, 60 km (37.2 mi.) from the main village of Rotoava and 15 km (9.3 mi.) from the nearest neighbor. 2008 AP Rates for 2 nights: Lagoon side Fare Robinson 47.000 CFP sgl., 84.000 CFP dbl.; Ocean side Fare Crusoe 54.000 CFP sgl., 97.000 CFP dbl; extra adult add 15.500 CFP per night. AE, MC, V.*

Guests who have stayed at Raimiti since it opened in Sept. 2005 have a tendency to wax poetic in their verbose praises of the charms of this remote paradise when they sign the guest book or make their trip reports on Tahiti forums online. Raimiti means "between the sky and sea," and the beauty of this very special place really does make you want to describe it in superlatives.

Raimiti's 3 owners jokingly say that the pension is located at the 5028th coconut tree from the church in Rotoava, the main village on Fakarava. Eric Lussiez and Florian Pilloud, who own Pension Linareva in Moorea, joined forces with Raimaru (Junior), a Polynesian who worked for them in their former restaurant, Le Bateau at Linareva, to make a dream come true in Fakarava. They leased 14.8 acres (6 ha.) of land on a very large motu that is bordered on the east by the Pacific Ocean, on the west by the lagoon, on the north by an immense coconut forest and untouched natural environment and on the south by Irifa, one of the most beautiful beaches in Fakarava. The only way to get to this isolated area is by boat, which takes about an hour. You'll know you're there when you hear the sound of a *pu* shell (triton) heralding your arrival at the small boat dock, where 3 excited dogs wait to welcome you ashore.

Accommodations include 4 identical "Fare Robinson" bungalows beside the lagoon or a "Fare Crusoe" spacious bungalow located on the reef side of the motu, with a panoramic view of the ocean. The lagoon-side units are built on stilts of coconut logs and the walls, roofs and windows are made of woven palm leaves, kahaia and other tropical woods. There are no doors and no keys—simply a curtain of pareo cloth over the entrance. A mosquito net hangs over the queen size bed and the private bathroom with cold-water shower is detached. There will eventually be 4 of the larger bungalows facing the ocean. These are made of gnao gnao and kahaia wood, as well as Brazilian mahogany. Each of these units has a king size bed and 2 single beds, plus a shower with hot water. Solar energy and oil lamps provide lights in the bungalows, and a powerful flashlight helps you to find your way to the "fare iti" (bathroom) in the middle of the night.

Raimiti's dining room/bar/lounge/boutique/reception *fare* has a thatched palm roof, low walls of coconut stumps, a coral floor and stools made of coconut logs. It is imaginatively decorated with shells, coral, woven hats, wood carvings, pottery from Huahine and Moorea, and candles in sand-filled coconut shells.

Meals are announced by the sound of the pu shell. And what a gourmet feast they are! Your natural reaction will be to take a picture of the generous portions of creatively arranged food on your plate before you eat. A Continental breakfast is served buffet style. Lunch may include various kinds of salads and raw vegetables, as well as smoked salmon or whole boiled shrimp, followed by fruit and cheeses. Dinner is another true work of art and a delight for gourmands, with temptingly prepared vegetables to accompany the main courses of fish, seafood, poultry or meat. French style desserts include crème caramel and Poire Belle Helêne. There is a limited supply of wines, beer and soft drinks, as well as sparkling water or you can drink rain water.

The cost of your stay includes your lodging and all meals, boat transfers between the airport and Raimiti, and free use of snorkeling gear, kayaks and board games. It also includes your "Discovery" activities, which may be visits to the old village of Tetamanu, drift snorkeling in the Tumakohua Pass, visits to the pink sand beach of Irifa and to the fish parks inside the lagoon, picnics on a neighboring motu, or being dropped off at a secluded beach with a sandwich and water to make your own private discoveries.

Two teams alternate between Raimiti and Linareva, so you will have either Eric and his daughter Maluha or Junior and his wife Elvina to take care of you when you visit. Both teams are assisted by a few friendly Paumotu workers, as well as all the Raimiti pets. These include the dogs, pigs, rabbits, red-footed booby birds and herons that gather in the kitchen or guest dining room at breakfast time.

Other Pensions

The pensions listed above are just a few of the family lodgings that were available in Fakarava at publication time. The other pensions are:

VAIAMA VILLAGE, *Tel. 98.41.13/70.56.41.* 4 basic palm-fond huts beside lagoon past Rotoava village. **VAHITU DREAM,** *Tel. 98.42.63,* 6-room house in Rotoava village. **TETAMANU VILLAGE** and **TETAMANU SAUVAGE,** *Tel. 77.10.06/78.03.67; Fax 42.77.70, tetamanuvillage@mail.pf; www.tetamanuvillage.pf.* Beside the pass in Tetamanu village on south end of atoll. 6 + 6 simple bungalows. Although I like the location, I am listing this pension rather than giving details due to negative reports of the owners' conjugal problems that affect guests.

WHERE TO EAT

Restaurant Kura Ora at Hotel Maitai Dream, *Tel. 93.41.50,* serves B, L, D. An American breakfast is 2.300 CFP. The lunch menu suggests salads and appetizers for 1.000-1.200 CFP, sandwiches and burgers with fries for 1.350-1.600 CFP, and main courses for 1.300-1.750 CFP. The dinner specials may be pheasant for 2.450 CFP or breaded parrotfish for 2.650 CFP. Desserts are 990 CFP and you can order wine by the glass or bottle. Bar Kiri Kiri is open 10am-10pm. All major credit cards.

Restaurant Teanuanua, *Tel. 98.41.58/70.98.50; cecile.enoha@mail.pf.* Open for L, D. This lagoon-side restaurant-boutique is just a 5-min. walk from Havaiki Guest House. Menu elections include hamburgers, poisson cru, fried filet of parrotfish and steak. Cecile, the French owner, also makes hand-painted pareos, caftans and tee shirts. V.

Snack Elda, *Tel. 98.41.33,* is on the lagoon side of the road between Hotel Maitai Dream and Havaiki Guest House. Elda is a Marquesan who serves hamburgers for 450 CFP, poisson cru or steak and fries for 1.200 CFP, and grilled fish with fries for 1.300 CFP. She also sells Marquesan wood carvings, tapa bark paintings and shell jewelry. No credit cards.

Faka Pizza, *Tel. 98.43.39,* is in the middle of Rotoava village. A pizza and soft drink is 1.500 CFP. No credit cards.

Tereka, *Tel. 98.42.13,* is a snack open only on weekends at the port. No credit cards.

You can also arrange in advance to eat at some of the family pensions, such as Havaiki Guest House and Pension Paparara.

SPORTS & RECREATION
Cruise & Dive Charters

Aqua Tiki. *Contact Patrice Poiry at Aqua Polynésie, Tel. 00 33 1 64 90 50 10; aquatiki@aquapolynesie.com; www.aquatiki.com.* This 46-ft. Bahia deep-sea catamaran can sleep 6 passengers/divers in 3 double guest cabins, each with its own bathroom. There is a TV and VCR player on board, as well as full scuba diving equipment. You can rent a cabin or charter the whole boat for cruises that begin in Fakarava, take you to Kauehi and Toau and back to Fakarava. The 8-day/7-night cruise for divers during the low season starts at €1,920 and for non-divers at €1,620 per person in double occupancy, including taxes. There are also 9-, 10-, 11-, 12- and 13-day cruises in the Tuamotu Islands, as well the Leeward Islands. Please see information under the chapter on *Planning Your Trip* for 2008 and 2009 programs.

Archipels Cruises (Archipels Croisières), *Tel. 689/56.36.39, Fax 689/56.35.87; information@archipels-croisieres.pf; www.archipels.com; Skype: archipels.* One-week cruises on board a 4-cabin Marquises 57' or a 5-cabin Eleuthera 60' catamaran are available from Fakarava to Toau and Rangiroa, boarding in Fakarava on Sat. morning and disembarking in Rangiroa at noon on Fri. The cruise dates are scheduled in conjunction with the full moon and guaranteed departure for a minimum of two passengers. The per person cost of this cruise is €1,880-2090, including taxes, meals and hotel services on board in double cabin occupancy, airport/yacht transfers at boarding and landing sites, as well as all excursions and events specified in program. A 7 day/6 night private charter from Fakarava-Toau-Rangiroa costs €11,280-12,540 for 2-4 passengers and €16,920-18,810 for 10 passengers, according to seasons.

Scuba Diving

TOPdive Fakarava, *Tel./Fax 98.43.76; cell 29.22.32; fakarava@topdive.com; www.topdive.com,* is based at the Hotel Maitai Dream Fakarava. Mathias is a master scuba diving trainer, assisted by another qualified instructor and a local boat captain. They provide morning dives for 12-14 open water divers and afternoon dives for 15 people for world class diving in the north passage of Garuae. Public rates for scuba diving start at 7.000 CFP for an introductory dive, fun dive or night dive; an open water certification course is 65.000 CFP, and a package of 10 dives is 63.000 CFP. The diving rates include taxes and all equipment. This package can also be used at TOPdive centers in Bora Bora, Moorea, Rangiroa and Tahiti. A special day trip to Tetamanu on the south side to dive the Tumakohua Pass is 19.000 CFP per person, including 2 dives and a picnic on the pink sand beach.

Fakarava Diving Center, *Tel./Fax 93.40.75, cell 73.38.22; fdc@mail.pf; www.fakarava-diving-center.com* is located on the premises of Pension Paparara. Serge Howald is a BEES 1 diving instructor and his wife Carine pilots the spacious and comfortable dive boat, which is used for 5-6 divers only. Dives for all levels are made, either inside the lagoon, in the two passes of Fakarava, on the outer reef, deep sea and on the neighboring atoll of Toau, a 45-minute boat ride across the open ocean. All necessary diving gear is provided, including Aqualung wetsuits. A first dive is 7.000 CFP, an exploratory dive is 6.000 CFP, and a day-trip to dive in the pass at Tetamanu is 20.000 CFP, which includes 2 dives and a picnic on a motu. Dive packages are available and discounts are given for guests staying at Pension Paparara.

Te Ava Nui Plongée, *Tel./Fax 98.42.50, cell 79.69.50; teavanui@divingfakarava.com; www.divingfakarava.com*. This dive center opened in 1999 in Rotoava village and is operated by Jean-Christophe Lapeyre, who is an international CMAS 3-star monitor and BEES 1 professional dive master. He is assisted by two qualified instructors and a local boat pilot and has 3 fast unsinkable boats available to take small groups of divers to explore some of the best dive sites in the wide and deep passes, inside the lagoon and outside the Garuae pass to the neighboring atoll of Toau. The diving center provides modern and state of the art Aqualung equipment and this is a Nitrox station. They also have a base at Motu Aito Paradise in Tetamanu and another at Pension Matarive in Toau. A first dive is 7.000 CFP, an exploratory dive is 6.200 CFP, a day-trip to Tetamanu or Toau is 15.000 CFP, including 2 dives, and an inter-island dive card valid at 21 dive centers starts at 30.000 CFP for 5 dives.

SHOPPING
Buying Pearls & Visiting Pearl Farms

In Fakarava you need only mention the word "pearls" and you will be escorted to someone's house to look at the pearls that came from their family's pearl farm. Very often they are pearls of poor quality. You can learn the difference by reading about Tahitian Cultured Pearls in the *Basic Information* chapter in this book. You should also be aware that jeweler's glue is not always used to set the pearls in these remote atolls, and you risk losing your pearl just hours after you buy it. If you cannot resist a piece of jewelry, then have a jeweler reglue it once you get home. A few of the unset pearls selling at bargain prices may even be magnificent, but most of the really good pearls are shipped to Tahiti and sold at auctions.

Pearls of Havaiki, *Tel. 93.40.15/74.16.16; havaiki@mail.pf; www.havaiki.com* is the pearl farm and boutique at Havaiki Guest House. Joachim Dariel, who owns the pension, also started Fakarava's first pearl farm in 1989 with his father, Nicolas Dariel, who is a goldsmith, painter and sculptor. The grafting *fare* is open for visits on request and you pay 3.000 CFP to fish for a pearl inside a mother-of-pearl oyster. A collection of Nicolas Dariel pearl jewelry creations is on display in the boutique at Havaiki. I would definitely trust the quality of the pearls here as well as the settings.

Hinano Pearls, *Tel. 98.41.51/71.68.41; hinanohellberg@mail.pf* is a pearl farm 10 km. from Rotoava village. Transfers are provided and there is no charge to visit the pearl farm, which is open on request.

PRACTICAL INFORMATION

There are no banks and no *gendarmes* in Fakarava. The *mairie* (town hall) is located in the center of Rotoava village, *Tel. 98.42.81.*

Food Stores

There are 2 well-stocked stores in Rotoava village that provide frozen products, canned foods, a few fresh vegetables, wine and beer. You can buy fresh baguettes of French bread each morning. One of the magasins sells fuel (diesel by the 200-liter drum only). They will deliver it to the quay for visiting yachts. Open 7am-12pm and 3-6:30pm.

Hospital

An infirmary is located in Rotoava village, *Tel. 98.42.24.*

Post Office

The **Post Office and Telecommunications Office** is in Rotoava village, *Tel. 98.42.22.* Open 7-11:30am. There are telephone cabins here that take phonecards.

19. Marquesas Islands

The South Seas Island images of tranquil lagoons protected by coral reefs are not part of the scenery in the **Marquesas Islands**. Rising like a mirage from the swells of the cobalt blue Pacific, the rugged volcanic cliffs soar like rock fortresses thousands of feet above the thundering sea. The wild ocean beats endlessly against the craggy, sculpted coasts, unbroken by any barriers for almost 6,400 km. (4,000 mi.).

Beyond the tumbling breakers lie the fjord-like bays, the narrow shores and curving beaches of golden black sand. Sheltered coves reveal a turquoise tide with pink and white sand beaches. Behind the seaside cliffs the electric green grasslands wander gently upward. Brooding and black with frequent rains, the jagged peaks and spires become a fairy castle in the clouds of the setting sun.

Lying north-northwest by south-southeast along a 350-km. (217-mi.) submarine chain, the Marquesas Islands are all of volcanic origin. Scientists believe that these islands rose from the oceanic depths and their foundations are submerged 4,000 m. (13,120 ft.) below sea level. The island of Fatu Hiva is the youngest of the chain, with an age of only 1.35 million years, while the most ancient island in the Marquesas group is the uninhabited island of Ei'ao, which was formed 5.2 to 7.5 million years ago. This is the youngest group of islands in French Polynesia and the farthest removed from any continent.

The Marquesas Islands are 7.50 to 10.35 degrees south of the Equator, and 138.25 to 140.50 degrees west longitude. They form two geographical groups about 111 km. (69 mi.) apart, with a combined land area of 1,279 sq. km. (492 sq. mi.) for the 20 or so islands.

The southern group consists of the 3 inhabited islands of **Hiva Oa**, **Tahuata** and **Fatu Hiva**, plus a few smaller islets. The northern group comprises the 3 principal islands of **Ua Pou**, **Nuku Hiva** and **Ua Huka**, and several uninhabited islands, including **Eiao** and **Hatutu**, which lie about 80 km. (50 mi.) northwest of the other islands in the northern group.

Nuku Hiva, the administrative center of the northern Marquesas, is about 1,500 km. (932 mi.) northeast of Tahiti. Hiva Oa, the main island in the southern group, lies approximately 1,400 km. (868 mi.) northeast of Tahiti, a 3 1/2-hr. flight by Air Tahiti's 48-passenger ATR 42 airplanes. Marquesan time is 1/2 hr. ahead of the rest of the islands in French Polynesia. When it is 6am in Tahiti, it is 6:30am in the Marquesas.

The average temperature of the Marquesas is about 27 degrees Celsius (80 degrees Fahrenheit), with the hottest weather in March and the coolest temperatures in August. Although there is usually more than 80% humidity, the climate

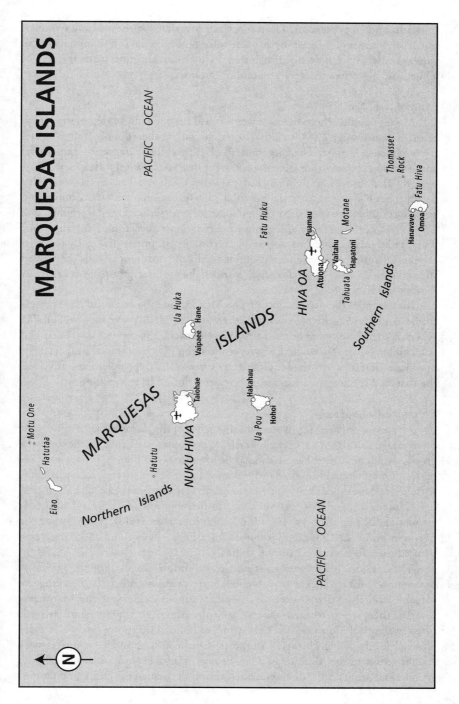

is healthy and fairly pleasant. The trade winds prevail between April and October, but at other times of the year there can be some hot, calm days. The annual rainfall varies greatly and is unevenly distributed. Fatu Hiva is the most verdant island of all because it receives the greatest amount of rain.

Land of the Men

Maohi people, whom the Europeans called Polynesians, settled in the valleys of these islands some 2,000 to 2,500 years ago, sailing their double-hulled canoes from Samoa or Tonga. Their legends tell of the god **Tiki**, ancestor of man, who conjured up a dozen islands from the ocean depths. These proud and fierce warriors were divided into clans, living in isolated valleys, separated by steep, knife-edge ridges. They had seasons of abundant food, but also seasons of draught, famine and tribal wars. They tattooed their bodies in intricate patterns learned from their god Tiki. As they evolved they made exquisite carvings in wood, stone, ivory and bone. They built their homes on *paepae* platforms, worshipped their gods in *me'ae* temples of stone, and were feared cannibals. In the northern islands they called their adopted home *Te Henua Te Enata*, and in the southern group it was *Te Henua Te Enana*, "Land of the Men."

In later years the descendants of The Men learned the origins of their islands from their legends, and had a story for the way their islands were named. Folklore tells that the islands were born of a marriage between the sea and sky. Their god Atua built a house: Nuku Hiva was its pointed roof; Ua Pou was its support posts or pillars; Ua Huka was the binding; Hiva Oa was the ridge pole; Fatu Hiva was the thatched roof; and Tahuata was the celebration of its completion.

European Conquerors

The history of the Marquesas with the arrival of the Europeans was varied and often tragic. In 1595 Spanish explorer Alvaro de Mendaña discovered the southern group, which he named Las Marquesas de Mendoza—in honor of the wife of his patron, Don Garcia Hurtado de Mendoza, Marquis de Canete, Viceroy of Peru. When Mendaña sailed away, some 200 islanders lay dead on the beach of Tahuata.

Captain James Cook claimed the southern group for England in 1774, estimating the population at 100,000. Joseph Ingraham of Boston discovered the northern group in 1791, and explorers from France, Germany and Russia also planted their flags on these distant shores.

These islands became a regular port-of-call for the men sailing the Pacific—crews hungry for a touch of land, women and recreation. Australians seeking the valuable sandalwood that grew in abundance in the valleys of the Marquesas brought their sailors to these shores. Later the American whaling ships arrived, often leaving behind those deserters who had jumped ship. Over the years there were all kinds of blackbirders, profiteers, beachcombers and adventurers who sought refuge in the Marquesas. They brought guns, alcohol, opium, smallpox, syphilis and other deadly diseases, which almost decimated the entire population.

In 1842 the whole archipelago was annexed to France under the name *Iles Marquises.* Catholic missionaries were installed and a new rule began. Yet the decline of the population continued. When the French took control in 1842 there were 20,000 people living in the Marquesas Islands, and 30 years later that number dropped to 6,200. The all-time low of 2,225 people was recorded in 1926, and 131 of this number were non-natives. The latest census of Sept. 2007 was 9,281, who are mostly Catholic.

Modern Marquesas

The Marquesas Islands today are quite modern, with electricity, international communications services, a radio and television station and efficient boat docks in the larger villages for the supply ships that provide regular service from Tahiti. The islands of Nuku Hiva, Hiva Oa, Ua Pou and Ua Huka have airports, and projects to build airports on Tahuata and Fatu Hiva still remain in the planning stage.

Farming and fishing are carried out on a family scale. The villagers live mostly from the land and sea, earning money for purchased supplies by copra production. For a few years the economy was boosted by the wild pickings of the *noni*, the *Morinda Citrifolia,* a potato-like fruit that grows on a tall bush. The juice from this fruit is sold worldwide by an American company as a tonic to cure anything from sore throats to syphilis, or as a panacea to heal a wide range of ailments from colds to cancers. The pulp is used in skin and hair care products, as well as a diet food supplement. While encouraging the exploitation of this business, the local government tried to discourage the islanders from abandoning their subsidized copra plantations in favor of planting *noni.* Their concerns proved accurate when the biggest noni company began buying the fruit for their Tahitian Noni Juice from Fiji and other countries at 20 CFP per kilo instead of paying 60 CFP per kilo to the Marquesans. Most of the Marquesans are now chopping copra again.

The *Aranui* cruises to the Marquesas Islands 17 times a year during its 14-day round-trip voyages from Tahiti. The ship calls at every principal valley and many smaller ones on each inhabited island. This is the most practical and enjoyable way to make a brief visit to the Marquesas, as the costs of land and sea transportation are very expensive for individual travelers. See information on the *Aranui* under *Inter-Island Cruises, Passenger Boats and Freighters* in the chapter on *Planning Your Trip.*

Accommodations are available in family pensions on each island, and Pearl Resorts has an international class hotel on Nuku Hiva and another on Hiva Oa.

Activities in the Marquesas Islands include 4WD excursions, helicopter flights, horseback riding, hiking over mountain trails and to inland cascades, picnics on the beach or in the mountains. You can go deep-sea fishing, on motorboat rides, scuba diving, visit the restored archaeological sites and stone tikis, and go to the workshops of crafts people to buy woodcarvings and tapa hangings.

A fragrant bouquet of flowers and herbs is worn in the hair or around the necks of the Marquesan women. This is called *kumu hei* in the northern group and *umu hei* in the southern islands. Their *monoi* is a delightful blend of coconut oil, sandalwood, spearmint, jasmine, gingerroot, pineapple, sweet basil, gardenia, pandanus fruit, ylang-ylang and other mysterious herbs. This is used as perfume, for massages, to seduce a boyfriend or to ward off mosquitoes.

For further information on the hotels, pensions, restaurants, rental cars, boats, horses, and boat or land excursions; *tourisme@marquises.pf; www.marquises.pf.* You can also find information on the family pensions and guesthouses at: *haere-mai@mail.pf, www.haere-mai.pf.* Nuku Hiva will host the 8th edition of the Marquesas Festival of Arts in 2011.

NUKU HIVA

In Marquesan mythology, **Nuku Hiva** was the first island to be raised from the ocean depths by the god Tiki, who created a wife from a pile of sand. Even today this beautiful emerald isle, located about 1,500 km. (932 mi.) northeast of Tahiti, is the leader of the Marquesas archipelago.

Captain Joseph Ingraham from Boston discovered Nuku Hiva in 1791, followed the same year by Etienne Marchand of France. When Russian Admiral Krusenstern landed in Taiohae Bay in 1804 they found an Englishman and a Frenchman who had deserted their ships to settle in Nuku Hiva. Cabry, the Frenchman, was tattooed from head to foot, just like his hosts in Taiohae.

With a surface area of 330 sq. km. (127 sq. mi.), Nuku Hiva is the largest island of the Marquesas group. The beauty of Nuku Hiva is truly breathtaking, whether viewed from the sea or the mountain heights. On the crenellated north coast is Taiohae Bay, a spectacular giant amphitheater dominated by emerald peaks and waterfalls. This is a welcome haven for cruising yachts from all over the world that drop anchor here after a month or more at sea. Taiohae is a pleasant village bordering the sea and serves as the administrative, economic, educational and health center of the Marquesas Islands. Here are the French and Territorial administrators, government buildings, *gendarmerie*, post office, general hospital, town hall, Air Tahiti office, banks and schools.

The 2,798 inhabitants live in the villages of Taiohae, Taipivai, Hatiheu, Aakapa, Pua, Ho'oumi, Anaho and Hakaui, which are separated by serrated mountain ranges, and connected by rutted roads best suited for 4WD vehicles and horses. These residents work for the government, the community, Catholic church or school system, or for themselves—chopping copra high in the mountains, fishing, raising cattle and other livestock, or sculpting bowls, platters, Marquesan ceremonial clubs, tikis and ukuleles.

The Notre-Dame Cathedral of the Marquesas Islands contains magnificently carved sculptures by craftsmen from each of the Marquesas Islands. You can visit the sculptors' workshops and arts and crafts centers in the villages of Taiohae, Hatiheu and Taipivai. You can rent a horse, a 4WD or pickup truck with chauffeur or a speedboat with pilot. A scuba diving center is located in Taiohae and the waters surrounding the island are rich with big fish, manta rays and an exciting variety of

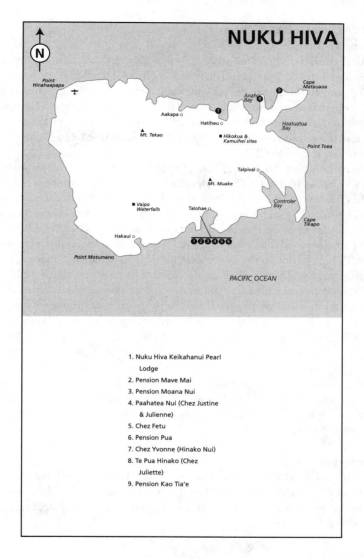

1. Nuku Hiva Keikahanui Pearl Lodge
2. Pension Mave Mai
3. Pension Moana Nui
4. Paahatea Nui (Chez Justine & Julienne)
5. Chez Fetu
6. Pension Pua
7. Chez Yvonne (Hinako Nui)
8. Te Pua Hinako (Chez Juliette)
9. Pension Kao Tia'e

sharks. You can take a helicopter flight to Hakaui Valley, with its steep gorges and Ahuii waterfall, one of the world's highest cascades, at an altitude of 350 m. (1,148 ft.). Near Hatiheu and Taipivai are ceremonial platforms, stone tikis and petroglyphs hidden deep in the valleys.

Taiohae has a few restaurants and snack bars, as well as general stores stocked with canned and frozen food, clothing and household items. Fresh vegetables are available some of the time. In Hatiheu you will find one of the best restaurants in the Marquesas Islands, as well as one of the most important ceremonial sites.

ARRIVALS & DEPARTURES

Arriving By Air

Air Tahiti, *Tel. 86.42.42*, in Nuku Hiva *Tel. 91.02.25*, flies ATR turbo jet planes from Tahiti to Nuku Hiva daily in 3 1/2 hrs. All the flights are direct except for Mon. and one of the Fri. flights, which stop first in Hiva Oa, and the Sat. flight, which stops in Rangiroa enroute to Nuku Hiva. Reminder: Marquesas Islands time is 30 min. ahead of Tahiti. The one-way airfare from Tahiti to Nuku Hiva is 27.800 CFP, and the round-trip fare is 50.800 CFP. From Rangiroa to Nuku Hiva the one-way fare is 27.600 CFP.

You can fly from Atuona to Nuku Hiva by ATR or Twin Otter plane daily for a one-way fare of 10.400 CFP. You can also fly to Nuku Hiva from Ua Pou aboard a Twin Otter every day except Mon. There is a direct Twin Otter flight from Ua Huka to Nuku Hiva each Tues., Wed., Fri. and Sun. The one-way fare for the 25-30 min. flights from Ua Pou or Ua Huka to Nuku Hiva is 6.400 CFP.

A partially paved road from the Nuku Ataha airport to Taiohae village winds 48 km. (30 mi.) through the Toovii plateau, 800 m. (2,624 ft.) above the valleys of ferns, giant mango trees and coconut palms. The trip takes about 1 1/2 hrs. by 4WD vehicle and the still unfinished sections of the road are often very muddy and uncomfortable. Some people prefer to take the helicopter shuttle service.

You can also get to Nuku Hiva by chartering an airplane in Tahiti from **Archipels**, *Tel. 81.30.30*; or **Air Tahiti**, *Tel. 86.42.42*.

Arriving By Boat

The *Aranui* stops at the main port of Taiohae during its 14-day round-trip cruise program from Tahiti to Fakarava and on to the Marquesas. See details in section on *Inter-Island Cruise Ships and Cargo/Passenger Boats* in Chapter 6, *Planning Your Trip*.

Departing By Air

There is a direct ATR flight between Nuku Hiva and Tahiti daily. There are also direct or 1-stop flights by ATR or Twin Otter from Nuku Hiva to Atuona, daily except Mon. **Air Tahiti reservations** in Taiohae, *Tel. 91.02.25*; Nuku Ataha airport, *Tel. 92.01.45*.

Departing By Boat

The *Aranui* arrives in Taiohae Bay on the 5th day of its 14-day voyage from Tahiti to the Marquesas Islands. An alternative to taking the entire trip is to fly to Nuku Hiva and join the ship there, which will give you the opportunity of visiting all the inhabited islands in the Marquesas, with a stop in Rangiroa on the return trip to Tahiti. Or you can make the round of the Marquesas on board the ship and fly back to Tahiti. If you're just looking for a one-way passage from the Marquesas to Tahiti, the *Aranui* calls again at Nuku Hiva on the 11th day of its schedule, and from there goes to Ua Pou, Rangiroa and Tahiti, which will give you only 3 nights aboard the ship. See details in section on *Inter-Island Cruise Ships and Cargo/ Passenger Boats* in Chapter 6, *Planning Your Trip.*

ORIENTATION
The main village of **Taiohae** follows the semicircular curve of **Taiohae Bay** for about 3.5 km. (2 mi.), from the ship dock on the east to the **Nuku Hiva Keikahanui Pearl Lodge** on the west. During the summer months of Dec.-Mar. flowering flamboyant trees shade the road that passes through the village.

GETTING AROUND NUKU HIVA
Helicopter Flights
Marquises Hélicoptères, *Tel. 92.02.17, Fax 92.08.40.* A 5-passenger "Squirrel" helicopter provides regular 20-min. shuttle service between the Nuku Ataha Airport and the Nuku Hiva villages of Taiohae, Hatiheu and Aakapa. The one-way transfer is 8.000 CFP per passenger. Reservations are required and the baggage limit is 10 kgs. (22 lbs.) per person and 20 kgs. (44 lbs.) if you are in possession of an international airline ticket. A 20-min. helicopter ride will take you on a flight-seeing tour of the island of Nuku Hiva for 20.000 CFP per person if there are 4 passengers and 16.000 CFP per person for 5 passengers. You can also charter the helicopter for inter-island connections.

Taxi & Transport Service
The one-way taxi fare between the Terre Deserte Airport to Taiohae village is 4.000 CFP per person. If you wish to go by way of Aakapa, Hatiheu and Taipivai to Taiohae, the cost is 5.000 CFP per passenger. Your hotel or pension can arrange for your transfers when you reserve your accommodation.
Marie Jeanne Bruneau, *Tel. 92.01.84/70.05.89,* and **Rose-Marie Transports,** *Tel. 92.05.96/74.36.76; r-transport@voila.fr,* provide taxi service. See more information under *Land Tours* in this chapter.

Rental Cars
You can rent a self-drive 5-passenger 4WD vehicle from **Nuku Rent-A-Car,** *Tel./Fax 92.08.87/73.51.67; atachristian@mail.pf.* The office is located at the public boat dock and the 24-hr. rate is 14.000 CFP. Rentals are also available at **Huki Location,** *Tel. 92.04.89/72.86.70/72.02.65;* **Moana Nui Location,** *Tel. 92.03.30/ 72.86.65;* and **Kohuhunui Locations,** Tel. 92.00.16/74.47.60. A list of all the rentals can be obtained at the Nuku Hiva Tourism Committee in Taiohae village.

WHERE TO STAY
Superior
NUKU HIVA KEIKAHANUI PEARL LODGE, *B.P. 53, Taiohae, Nuku Hiva 98742, Marquesas Islands. Tel. 689/92.07.10; Fax 689/92.07.11; keikahanui@mail.pf; www.pearlresorts.com. Reservations: Tel. 689/50.84.45; Fax*

689/43.17.86; res@spmhotels.pf. 20 bungalows overlooking Taiohae Bay, 2 km. (1.2 mi.) from the Taiohae pier and 48 km. (30 mi.) from the airport. 2008 EP Rates sgl./ dbl.: Bay view bungalow 25.000 CFP; Premium bay view bungalow 35.000 CFP; add 5.000 CFP for 3rd person. Add 7.600 CFP for MAP and 10.900 CFP for AP. One-way airport transfer by bus or 4WD 4.500 CFP per person. A private transfer is 15.000 CFP. Add taxes. All major credit cards.

This 4-star hotel opened in 1999 with 20 local style bungalows built on stilts on the hillside overlooking Taiohae Bay. The grounds cover 15 acres (6 ha.) of tropical gardens of fruit trees and flowers. Each bungalow is 39 sq. m. (420 sq. ft.), and has a king size bed or 2 twin beds and an extra bed, plus a separate bathroom with hot water shower, and a terrace facing the bay. The bamboo walls and shingle roof of the bungalows are complemented by an interior of pandanus and tapa, which are beautifully blended to create a very pleasant decor. Each bungalow has a/c, a mini-bar refrigerator, local TV, in-house movie channel, tea and coffee facilities, IDD telephone, safe and hair dryer. Two rooms are well equipped for disabled guests using a wheelchair. Room service, laundry service and baby-sitting services are available.

The public facilities include Le Pua Enana gourmet restaurant and Le Tiki bar, the reception, boutique and tour desk, plus the fresh water swimming pool, from where you can gaze out at the lovely scenery of Taiohae Bay. The hotel's tour desk can help you arrange excursions and outings to visit the island by land, sea or air. See information in the sections on *Where to Eat, Land Tours, Horseback Riding, Motor Boat Rental*, and *Scuba Diving* in this chapter.

As in all the Pearl Resorts, the Nuku Hiva Keikahanui Pearl Lodge has a special program for honeymooners and other romantic couples. A Starlight dinner served on the terrace of your bungalow is 28.000 CFP for two, and you can have your bed covered in flowers for 12.700 CFP. For other romantic touches please contact the hotel directly.

Moderate

MAVE MAI, *B.P. 378, Taiohae, Nuku Hiva 98742, Marquesas Islands. Tel./ Fax 689/92.08.10; Cell 689/73.76.01; pension-mavemai@mail.pf. On mountainside overlooking Taiohae Bay, 100 m. (328 ft.) from the boat dock and 48 km. (30 mi.) from the airport. Airport transfer by 4WD 8.000 CFP round-trip. Free transfers from heliport in Taiohae to pension. EP room 7.000 CFP sgl/8.000 CFP dbl. Add 1.000 CFP per person for breakfast, 3.000 CFP for breakfast and dinner, and 6.000 CFP for all meals. Rates include taxes. D, JCB, MC, V.*

This is a 2-story white house on a hill behind the tourist office, located close to the shops and restaurants in Taiohae village. There are 8 clean and cheerfully decorated bedrooms on the ground floor or the second level, with a terrace or balcony overlooking the bay. All the rooms have a/c, a ceiling fan, a private bathroom with hot water shower, and a double and single bed. Guests can use the washing machine and swimming pool.

Owners Jean-Claude and Régina Tata also operate the Kovivi restaurant, and guests are driven there for meals. An early breakfast is served at the pension on request. They will arrange day excursions for you or you can rent a 4WD vehicle from them for 12.000 CFP per day. Please see details under *Land Tours* in this chapter.

PENSION MOANA NUI, *B.P. 33, Taiohae, Nuku Hiva 98742, Marquesas Islands. Tel. 689/92.03.30/72.86.65; Fax 689/92.00.02; pensionmoananui@mail.pf; www.ifrance.com/pensionmoananui. On mountain side 600 m. (654 yds.) from the boat dock and 48 km. (30 mi.) from the airport. Round-trip transfers: 8.000 CFP per person by 4WD. EP room 6.360 CFP sgl/6.890 CFP dbl; MAP 9.010 CFP sgl/12.190 CFP dbl; AP 11.660 CFP sgl/15.370 CFP dbl, including taxes. D, MC, V.*

This 2-story renovated building has 7 rooms upstairs, with single or double beds and private bathrooms with hot water showers. Each room has a ceiling fan, and 5 rooms have A/C. There's nothing fancy about this hotel, but it's conveniently located if you want to be in Taiohae village, and the restaurant and bar downstairs serves good food for reasonable prices. The manager, Charles Mombaerts, also has a one-bedroom A/C bungalow for rent, with a double bed and a single bed, private bathroom with hot water shower, a living room and dining room. The owner also rents self-drive 4WD vehicles.

Economy

PAAHATEA NUI (CHEZ JUSTIN & JULIENNE), *B.P. 201, Taiohae, Nuku Hiva 98742, Marquesas Islands. Tel. /Fax 689/92.00.97; paahateanui@mail.pf. Overlooking the bay at the west end of Taiohae village, 3 km. (1.9 mi.) from the quay and 45 km. (28 mi.) from the airport. Round-trip transfers: 8.000 CFP per person by 4WD; 16.000 CFP per person by helicopter. Room and breakfast 4.000 CFP sgl./8.000 dbl.; bungalow and breakfast 5.500 CFP sgl./8.800 CFP dbl., including taxes. No lunch or dinner served. No credit cards.*

This bed and breakfast pension has an excellent reputation. Julienne and Justin have 3 rooms and 6 bungalows in a garden setting across the road from the black sand beach. One of the bedrooms and all bungalows are equipped with a private hot water shower and toilet, and the other 2 rooms share the bathroom facilities. One of the family bungalows has a kitchen and other guests share a kitchen. The bungalows also have a terrace, ceiling fan, TV and mosquito nets. All units are cleaned daily and guests can use the washing machine.

Other family lodgings in Taiohae:

Chez Fetu, *Tel. 689/92.03.66*, has a bungalow for 3 with kitchen and cold-water shower in Taiohae, for 2.000 CFP per person per day.

Pension Pua, *Tel. 689/92.06.87/21.47.53; Fax 689/92.01.35*, has 5 bungalows in the Nuku Hiva Village complex (now closed). 2 units have kitchens. Bungalow rates are 4.000 CFP sgl. /5.500 CFP dbl.; bungalow with kitchen 5.500 CFP sgl./7.500 CFP dbl.

Lodging Outside Main Village

CHEZ YVONNE (HINAKO NUI,) *B.P. 199, Taiohae, Nuku Hiva 98742, Marquesas Islands. Tel. 689/92.02.97; Fax 689/92.01.28; hinakonui@mail.pf. On mountain side in Hatiheu village, 500 m. (545 yards) from the Hatiheu boat landing, 75 km. (47 mi.) from the airport and 28 km. (17 mi.) from Taiohae Bay. Round-trip transfers: 8.000 CFP per person by 4WD; 16.000 CFP per person by helicopter. Bungalow and MAP 8.000 CFP sgl/12.000 CFP dbl, including taxes. No credit cards.*

These 5 simple bungalows facing the sea and the restaurant next door are owned by Yvonne Katupa, who is also the mayor of Hatiheu. She is reputed for serving the best food in all the Marquesas Islands. Four units have a double bed and the family bungalow can sleep three people. Each bungalow has a private bathroom with a cold-water shower. You can walk to the church, archaeological sites, to a small museum and to the artisan center. A black sand beach is across the dirt road in front of the bungalows. Be sure to protect yourself against the nonos. Guided excursions to Anaho village can be made by boat or 4WD.

TE PUA HINAKO (CHEZ JULIETTE), *B.P. 202, Taiohae, Nuku Hiva 98742, Marquesas Islands. Tel. 689/92.04.14. Beside the beach in Anaho Bay, 2 km. (1.2 mi.) from Hatiheu village, 30 km. (19 mi.) from Taiohae Bay and 77 km. (48 mi.) from the airport. Round-trip transfers by boat between Hatiheu Bay and Anaho Bay 12.000 CFP for 1-6 passengers. Room 2.500 CFP per person; breakfast 600 CFP, lunch, lunch or dinner 1.500 CFP, including taxes. No credit cards.*

It is worth staying here just to swim in the beautiful Anaho Bay, bordered by a beach of soft pink sand. Juliette Vaianui has a 2-bedroom house with both single and double beds, and a communal bathroom with cold-water shower. Free activities include line fishing, swimming and shelling. You can hike the trail along the beach to Atuatua Bay and to the peaks overlooking the bay. You can also find a horse to ride along the beach if you just ask Juliette. Her son Raymond owns the Kao Tia'e pension next door.

KAO TIA'E, *B.P. 290, Taiohae, Nuku Hiva 98742, Marquesas Islands. Tel. 689/92.00.08. EP bungalow 2.500 CFP per person; MAP 5.000 CFP, AP 6.500 CFP, including taxes. No credit cards.*

See information on Te Pua Hinako, as Juliette is the mother of Raymond Vaianui, the man who owns this 5-bungalow pension next door to her house in Anaho Bay. Kao tia'e is Marquesan for the Tiare Tahiti bud. Each unit has a double bed and a private bathroom with hot water. Both pensions combine meals and activities for their respective guests. Tel. *92.01.01* or *92.00.15* for round-trip boat transfers between Hatiheu Bay and Anaho Bay. The cost is 12.000 CFP for 1-6 passengers.

WHERE TO EAT

NUKU HIVA KEIKAHANUI PEARL LODGE, *Tel. 92.07.10. On hillside in Taiohae. All major credit cards.*

Le Pua Enana Restaurant is open daily for BLD. An American breakfast is

2.300 CFP; the set luncheon menu is 3.200 CFP and the set dinner menu is 5.600 CFP. **Le Tiki Bar** has a bartender who is trained to make your favorite cocktail. **MOANA NUI**, *Tel. 92.03.30. On the waterfront street of Taiohae village. Open daily except Sun. for BLD. D, MC, V.*

This is the most popular gathering place in the village, serving French and local cuisine. Main courses range from 1.500-2.300 CFP. Pizzas available at night only.

LE KOVIVI, *Tel. 92.03.85. On the waterfront street of Taiohae village. Open daily for BLD. D, JCB, MC, V.*

This restaurant is operated by the owners of Pension Mave Mai. The menu includes Chinese and local cuisine, and you can get take-away meals.

CHEZ YVONNE (HINAKO NUI), *Tel. 92.02.97 in Hatiheu village. BLD. Reserve. No credit cards.*

Although this popular restaurant is now called Hinako Nui, most people still refer to it as Chez Yvonne Katupa, because that's the name that earned it the reputation of serving the best food in the Marquesas Islands. The specialty here is the fresh water shrimp that are caught in the river nearby, which are battered and fried. They also serve very tasty barbecued chicken legs, tuna fritters, roast pig and goat. Main courses are priced from 1.750-2.800 CFP. This is where the *Aranui* passengers eat when they come to Hatiheu.

SEEING THE SIGHTS

The **Notre-Dame Cathedral of the Marquesas Islands** is located in the Catholic mission on the west side of Taiohae village. The cathedral was built in 1977, using stones from all the inhabited islands in the archipelago. The magnificent carvings were made by several of the local sculptors.

The **Herman Melville memorial** is a wooden sculpture made by Kahee Taupotini in 1992, which is on the bayside between the cemetery and the nautical club at the west end of the village. Melville wrote two books, *Typee* and *Omoo*, based on his short visit to Nuku Hiva in 1842, when he jumped ship from an American whaler and lived among the Taipi cannibals in Taipivai Valley for three weeks.

The **Koueva** and **Temehea** sites in Taiohae were used for ceremonies during the 5th Marquesas Festival of Arts in December 1999. The *tohua* Koueva was the ancient site for public festivities in ancient times, and during the 1800s the Temehea was the residence of one of the great chiefs of Taiohae Bay. You can see the carved stones at each site, as well as the millennium tree that was planted at Temehea.

Behind Taiohae village you can have a panoramic view of Taiohae Bay and the island of Ua Pou from the summit of **Muake Mountain**, which rises 864 m. (2,834 ft.). You can get there on foot, by horse or by 4WD.

Hakaui Valley is on the southern coast, about a 20-min. boat ride from Taiohae. You'll have to hike inland over stones for about 2 hrs. to reach the **Ahuii waterfall**. This is one of the world's highest cascades, with a single jet of water tumbling from the basaltic rock at an altitude of 350 m. (1,148 ft.). You can also reach Hakaui from Taiohae on horseback, riding 12 km. (8 mi.) along a bridleway that ranges from 400-500 m. (1,312 to 1,640 ft.) in altitude. You'll appreciate the refreshing pool of water when you get to the waterfall. It's best to go with a guide, and take mosquito repellent, plastic shoes and your swimsuit with you. This valley was featured in the "Survivor" television series that was filmed in Nuku Hiva in 2001 and telecast in 2002.

Hatiheu, on the northern coast, is 28 km. (17 mi.) from Taiohae and 12 km. (7.5 mi.) from Taipivai. The road between the two villages has been improved and now offers a smoother and easier trip by 4x4. Hatiheu was the favorite village of the Scottish writer, **Robert Louis Stevenson**, when he visited the Marquesas Islands in 1888 aboard his yacht *Casco*. This is also my first choice on Nuku Hiva, for the beauty and layout of the village, for the food at Chez Yvonne Katupa's restaurant (also called Restaurant Hinako Nui) and for the **Hikokua** *tohua* in the valley, beside the road to Taipivai. This archaeological site is about 1 km. (.62 mi.) from Chez Yvonne, and it was restored for the Marquesas Festival of Arts that was held in Nuku Hiva in 1999. It is a large flat surface 120 m. (394 ft.) long, used for dances and other public ceremonies. The *me'ae* are decorated with ancient stone tikis and modern sculptures also decorate the *paepaes*.

At the entrance to the site is a phallic-shaped fertility tiki. It is said that infertile women who touch the tiki will soon become pregnant. A 20-min. walk further up the road from Hikokua brings you to **Kamuihei**, a sacred place shaded by numerous trees, including an impressive old banyan tree that is 14 m. (46 ft.) wide and said to be more than 600 years old. **Dr. Robert Suggs** found skulls in the branches of this tree when he was doing archaeological research in Nuku Hiva in the 1950s. The **Te i'ipoka** *me'ae* of boulders and stone platforms is located near the banyan tree in a mysterious dark jungle setting of *purau*, mango, breadfruit and *mape* chestnut trees, with giant ferns and *ape* leaves. There are also big pits that were used for storing "ma", a paste made from fermented breadfruit. In a riverbed behind the banyan tree are boulders carved with petroglyphs of fish, turtles and humans. After crossing a log bridge on the main path below the banyan tree you will come to Kamueihei *me'ae*, where you can hear the *upe'e* pigeons hooting in the banyan forest and smell the fragrance of the slim yellow flowers of the ylang ylang trees bordering 2 *tohua* complexes.

In Hatiheu village a small **museum** inside the *mairie* (town hall) has a collection of traditional artifacts found in the valley. A French priest brought a white statue of the Virgin Mary to Hatiheu in 3 pieces in 1872, and it was placed on one of the cathedral-shaped peaks overlooking the village, some 300 m. (984 ft.) above the sea. Once a year people from Hatiheu climb the peaks to clean the Virgin Mary statue. The Catholic Church in this village was rebuilt in 2003 and is ideally situated, facing the sea with a backdrop of rolling hills carpeted in shades of green.

Anaho is just a 10-min. easy boat ride from Hatiheu, and you can also get there by 4WD, horse or hiking the difficult 2-km. (1.2-mile) trail, which takes about 90 min. round trip. Anaho Bay is one of the loveliest spots in the Marquesas Islands, with good swimming in tranquil turquoise water and a crescent-shaped beach with golden-pink sand. Only a few families live in this valley, and the simple little chapel here is perhaps the smallest church in French Polynesia. The manta rays and leopard rays live in the depths of this bay, and the dreaded *nono* hangs out in the beach area. Bring your repellent.

Ha'atuatua Valley can be reached by hiking from Anaho beach, and the best way to visit it is with Dr. Robert Suggs, who is a guest lecturer aboard the *Aranui* 2-3 times a year. Dr. Suggs will lead you to the archaeological site he excavated on the Ha'atuatua beach in 1956 and 1957-58. In addition to the human bones, basalt adzes, fishhooks, mother of pearl ornaments and basalt flake tools he uncovered, he also found potsherds of a type of pottery that is known as "Polynesian Plain Ware." This undecorated household ware belongs to the Lapita pottery category of ceramics that was used by the Lapita peoples in Eastern Indonesia and Western Melanesia as far back as 2000-1900 BC. The pieces of potsherds that Dr. Suggs found at the Ha'atuatua site were believed to be brought by the first Polynesian settlers, which radiocarbon dating of the pottery indicates was around 125 BC. For more information on this subject you should read Dr. Suggs' books, which are listed in the chapters on *Basic Information*.

A road connects the Nuku Ataha airport in the **Terre Déserte** with **Aakapa** village. The wind-battered bushes, dried grasses and red earth in this desert land make you think you've been transported to an African savanna, and the only living beings you normally see are herds of wild goats. The panoramic scenery is incredible, with vistas of Motu Ehe and its bay edged with a beach of fine white sand. You pass through the sacred valley of Pua, where the last queen is buried, and the road leads up to a hill where you can look out over the bays of Akahea and Hapapani with a pink sand beach and turquoise waters. Then you see the sentinel peaks of Aakapa and follow the road into the little village.

The **Paeke archaeological site** in Taipivai has 2 *me'ae* temples and 11 tikis of reddish colored stone. The trailhead, about 4 km. (2.5 mi.) from where the valley begins, is not marked, so it is best to go with a guide. In 1957 American archaeologist Dr. Robert Suggs excavated **Te Ivi o Hou**, a *tohua* ceremonial site that is 274 m. (300 yds. long). You'll need a guide to reach this hidden site, way back in the valley. **Pukiki**, a guide who lives in Taipivai, is familiar with both sites. Protect yourself against *nonos* in the valleys as well as on the beaches.

Taipivai Valley is 16 km. (10 mi.) northeast of Taiohae, which you can reach in 30 min. by boat from Taiohae, or by 4WD over a now improved road that crosses the **Toovii Plateau**, which has an average altitude of 800 m. (2,624 ft.). A navigable river connects Contrôleur Bay with the village boat dock and follows the road through the village into the valley. American writer Herman Melville made this village famous with his published account of the Taipi tribe who welcomed him into their village in 1842. A '**Cite Melville**' sign marks the place where Melville was supposed to have stayed during his 3-week visit. It is on the left side of the Hatiheu road about 4.5 km. (2.8 mi.) from the bridge in Taipivai village.

Land Tours

Nuku Hiva Keikahanui Pearl Lodge uses 2 of the best guides on the island: **Richard Deane**, *Tel. 28.08.36/24.66.43*, and **Jean-Pierre Piriotua**. The hotel's activity desk can arrange half-day excursions by 4WD vehicle for you to visit Taiohae village for 3.600 CFP per person. A half-day tour of the village plus the archaeological site of Koueva is 4.091 CFP, and a half-day excursion to Taipivai valley is 7.500 CFP. Full-day excursions by 4WD include a visit to Hatiheu for 10.000 CFP without lunch and 12.800 CFP with lunch. See *Boat Excursions* for further details.

Jocelyne Henua Enana Tours, *Tel. 92.00.52/74.42.23; Fax 92.08.32; jocelyne@mail.pf; www.marquises.com.pf.* Jocelyne Mamatui provides full-day safari excursions by 4WD vehicle to Taipivai, Hatiheu and the Aakapa lookout, for 16.000 CFP per car for 1-2 passengers, 6.500 CFP each for 3 and 5.500 CFP each for 4-5 passengers. Maximum 8 passengers. An optional lunch at Chez Yvonne is 2.500-3.000 CFP per person. Half-day tours will take you from Taipivai to Ho'oumi for 12.500 CFP per car for 1-2 people, with digressive rates for a maximum of 6 passengers. You can go to Muake Mountain and the Toovii Plateau during a half-day excursion, which includes a short hike. Rates are 12.500 CFP for 2 passengers and 3.500 CFP per person for 6. Visit Taiohae village, the artisans and the Koueva site, for 3.250 CFP per person for 1-3 passengers and 2.750 CFP per person for 4-6 passengers. Jocelyne also has all-inclusive package programs available to visit the other islands in the Marquesas group. Contact her directly for details.

Mave Mai Tours, *Tel. 92.08.10/92.00.01/73.76.01; Fax 92.08.10; pension-mavemai@mail.pf. D, MC, JCB, V.* Jean-Claude and Régina Tata, who own the Pension Mave Mai, also provide excursions by 4WD, which are sometimes combined with boat trips and hiking. You can take an archaeological tour by 4WD to visit the sites of Taipivai and Hatiheu and stop at the Aakapa Col for a panoramic view. At noon you will be taken by boat from Hatiheu to Anaho Bay where you will have a picnic of casse-croûte sandwiches and drinks, as well as time for swimming and enjoying the lovely white sand beach. This tour is 15.000 CFP for 1-2 people and 6.500 CFP each for 3 or more people.

Nuku Hiva Excursions, *Tel. 92.06.80/77.32.81, Fax 92.06.44*, is owned by Marcel Huveke in Taiohae. He also provides 4WD tours to visit the archaeological sites and panoramic lookouts.

SPORTS & RECREATION
Hiking

Marquises Rando, *Tel. 92.07.13/21.08.74; www.marquisesrando.com.* Frédéric Benne and William Teikitohe are both professional hiking guides who lead treks and walks in the mountains and hills. They can take you hiking on the ridges and Caldeira of Taiohae and the viewpoints of Nuku Hiva's South coast. This 5-1/2 hr. hike costs 6.600 CFP per person. A hike to the cliff edges of Aakapa and Hatiheu on the Northeast side of the island and to the observation sites of endemic birds from the Marquesas Islands takes 6 hrs. and costs 8.400 CFP. A 6-hr. hike to the Big Z Ridge and to Temokomoko Point offers views of Toovi, the Terre Deserte, Hakaui and the Hidden Valley, and costs 10.000 CFP per person. Included in all the hikes are transfers, sandwiches, cookies, hot and cold beverages, and the guide's services. Other hikes available on request.

Horseback Riding

Sabine and **Louis Teikiteetini** in Taiohae village, *Tel. 92.01.56/25.35.13,* have Marquesan horses for rent. A 1-hr. ride is 2.500 CFP, a half-day ride is 6.500 CFP, and a full-day ride is 8.000 CFP. They will organize excursions for you to explore the valleys by horseback.

Alphonse Teikiteetini, *Tel. 92.02.37,* also has horses for rent by the hour, half- or full day.

The Ranch is operated by Patrice Tamarii, *Tel. 92.06.35; danigo@mail.pf,* who has horses for rent. He can arrange 2-day excursions to Hakahui Cascade and to Hakatea, where you spend the night on the white sand beach. His 3-day outings will take you to the Terre Déserte.

Motor Boat Rental, Fishing & Excursions

The activities desk at the **Nuku Hiva Keikahanui Pearl Lodge** can arrange boat excursions for a minimum of 2 people. A 2-hr. boat trip around Taiohae Bay is 5.800 CFP per person. A half-day dolphin trip with snorkeling is 9.500 CFP. A full-day boat excursion to Anaho Bay for a maximum of 3 passengers is 12.000 CFP per person. Mixed land and sea excursions include a half-day boat excursion to Hakapaa bay, which includes a 1-hr. walk to 2 beautiful waterfalls, for 9.500 CFP. A full-day boat trip to Hakaui valley with a picnic is 10.000 CFP. This excursion includes a 4-hr. walk to visit the waterfall.

Jocelyne Henua Enana Tours, *Tel. 92.00.52/74.42.23; Fax 92.08.32; jocelyne@mail.pf; www.marquises.com.pf.*

Jocelyne Mamatui's boat, *Nils 1,* is a 26-ft. polyester hull motorboat that will take you to the Hakatea Valley and the Cascade of Hakaui, a 7-hr. excursion that costs 15.000 CFP for 1-2 people, 6.000 CFP per person for 3, and 4.500 CFP per person for 6-7 passengers. Bring your own sandwich and drinks. A 2 1/2 to 3-hr. outing will take you to the neighboring bays (Hakapaa, Taipivai, Hooumi, Hakahui, Hakatea, Colette), where you can snorkel and have a chance to see dolphins or manta rays. Rates are 13.000 CFP for 1-2 passengers, descending to 4.000 CFP per person for 6-7 passengers.

Marquises Plaisance, *Tel./Fax 92.08.75/73.23.48; e.bastard@mail.pf; www.marquises.pf.* Eric Bastard operates half- or full-day excursions in his 25-ft. boat, *Hitiaa.* He can take up to 5 people to visit Anaho Bay for a swim and picnic on the beach (picnic not included). He also combines a boat tour with hiking when he takes you to the Ahuii waterfall in Hakaui Valley. On the return boat trip you'll stop for a swim in Hakatea Bay. A half-day outing to the Southwest coast of Nuku Hiva also includes a swim at Hakatea Bay, and a half-day excursion to the Southeast coast of the island will take you from Taiohae to the site of the dolphins. He charges 25.000 CFP for trolling in the open sea for 3 hrs. and 45.000 CFP for 7 hrs. A boat trip around the island is 45.000 CFP. An all-day boat trip to Ua Pou is 35.000 CFP and to Ua Huka it's 45.000 CFP.

Pua Excursions Nuku Hiva is operated by Georges Pua Taupotini, *Tel. 92.06.87/21.47.53; info@puaexcursions.pf; www.puaexcursions.pf.* A day's outing with Pua will take you by 4WD to Hatiheu, where you will then continue on to Anaho Bay by speedboat, a ride of 20 min. Lunch will be served on the beach in Anaho, featuring lobster if the season is right. Then you have time for swimming in the coral gardens. Be sure to bring a snorkel. The cost of 12.000 CFP per person does not include drinks. Another excursion choice takes you by speedboat from Taiohae Bay to Hakaui Valley, where you will hike to the Ahuii waterfall. Here you will have a picnic lunch before hiking back to the boat for the return trip to Taiohae. The price of 12.000 CFP per person includes the boat and guide, but not the picnic.

Scuba Diving

Centre de Plongee Marquises (CPM) is based at the Taiohae Quay, *Tel./Fax 92.00.88; marquisesdives@mail.pf; www.marquises.pf.* Xavier Curvat is a French Federal Instructor who has lived in the Marquesas Islands for 18 years. He is a PADI OWSI, BEES 1 and CMAS two-star instructor, and he can give exams for diving certificates. His dive boat is the 33-ft. *Makuita,* with complete equipment for 15 divers, plus a compressor and additional bottles. He can take you to more than 20 dive sites in the immediate proximity of Taiohae, or on day trips to Ua Pou, Ua Huka and the other islands in the northern Marquesas group. The water temperature in the Marquesas Islands is 28º C (82º F) all year.

You can see an abundance of marine life near the rocky points, where the water is oxygenated continuously by the surf. Among the profusion of color, species and movement, you may see red snappers, groupers, perch and other rock fish seeking shelter in the hollows of rock slides and caves sculpted in volcanic stones, hiding from their predators—tuna, surgeon fish, lionfish and four kinds of jacks or trevally. Curious manta rays, with their graceful ballet movements, will approach you for a closer look. And everywhere you will see sting, eagle and marble rays, lobsters, sponges and rare seashells. A little deeper you can observe barracudas and sharks. These may include reef sharks, silvertip sharks, Galapagos and silky sharks, hammerhead sharks and melon-head whales. You may even see one or more orcas, as they have been regular visitors in this area for the past five years.

The rates for scuba diving are 5.500 CFP for an exploration dive, 6.000 CFP for an introductory dive, 10.000 CFP for a double-tank dive, 25.000 CFP for five dives and 50.000 CFP for 10 dives. All equipment is included.

SHOPPING

Musée Enana Boutique, *Tel. 92.03.82*, is operated by Rose Corser in a building just below the Nuku Hiva Keikahanui Pearl Lodge. Rose is an American who has lived in Nuku Hiva since the 1970s and she buys carvings from the best sculptors in the Marquesas Islands. The boutique features a large variety of art objects as well as tapa and original paintings by local artists. She also has a small library and museum of Marquesan artifacts and handcrafts, and she loves to share her wealth of information about life in the Marquesas Islands. Rose and her late husband, Frank Corser, built the original Keikahanui Inn, which had 6 bungalows. See information under *Yacht Services* in this chapter.

La Galerie d'Art des Marquises, *Tel. 92.08.62*, in Taiohae, is operated by Renaud Coquille and his wife, who present the works of the best contemporary artists in the Marquesas Islands. They sell Tahitian cultured pearl jewelry, pareos, T-shirts, and other items under the *chapiteau*, a big circus tent adjacent to the tourist bureau beside the main road in Taiohae village. Several artisans display their wares under this tent whenever a passenger ship is in port.

Beside the beach in Taiohae village is the arts and crafts workshop, where you can buy all kinds of Marquesan jewelry, stone, bone and wood carvings, scented monoi oils, Marquesan pareos and T-shirts, and anything else made in the Marquesas.

You can visit the sculptors' workshops to buy carved bowls, platters, saddles, tikis, ceremonial clubs and intricately carved tables. You can also visit the arts and crafts centers to buy woodcarvings. **Damien Haturau**, *Tel. 92.05.56*, is the best known of the Marquesan sculptors. His works include the statues in the cathedral in Taiohae and the Virgin with Child at the Vaitahu church in Tahuata.

Other noted wood carvers and stone sculptors include: **Edgard Tamarii**, *Tel. 92.01.67*; **Tahiahui Haiti, Damas Taupotini**, *Tel. 92.02.42*; **Pierrot Keuvahana**, *Tel. 92.05.58*; and **Philippe Utia**, *Tel. 92.00.51*. **Raphael Ah-Scha**, *Tel. 92.03.33*, is a wood carver and tattoo artist. If you're a serious collector, you can get a list of sculptors and arts and crafts centers from the Nuku Hiva Tourism Bureau.

TATTOOS

Mata Tiki Tattoo, *Tel. 23.02.51, 92.05.20, 92.06.40*, Jean Yves Tamarii. There are numerous other tattoo artists in Nuku Hiva.

PRACTICAL INFORMATION
Banks

Banque Socredo, *Tel. 92.03.63*, has a branch office in Taiohae. You can exchange currency and make credit card withdrawals here. The ATM machines are outside the bank.

Hospitals

There is a government-operated hospital in Taiohae, *Tel. 92.03.75*, and a dental center. The villages of Hatiheu and Taipivai each have an infirmary.

Police

The French gendarmerie has an office in Taiohae, *Tel. 92.03.61 or 17.*

Post Office & Telecommunications Office

All telecommunications and postal services are available at the post office, which is close to the boat dock in Taiohae, *Tel. 92.03.50.* It is open Mon.-Thurs. from 8am-3:30pm and on Fri. from 7:30am-2:30pm. Outside ATM available.

Tourist Bureau

Nuku Hiva Visitors Bureau is located on the mountainside between the marina and *mairie* (town hall) in Taiohae village and is open Mon.-Fri. in the mornings only. Jocelyne Piriotua is the president, *Tel. 92.03.73; Fax 92.08.25; tourisme@marquises.pf; www.marquises.pf.* She speaks English.

Yacht Services & Internet Connections

Rose Corser Yacht Club, *B.P. 21 Taiohae, Nuku Hiva, (ZIP 98742), Marquesas Islands; Tel. 689/92.03.82, Fax 689/91.02.35; rose.corser@mail.pf.*

Rose Corser is an American woman who sailed to Tahiti in 1972 with her husband Frank aboard their yacht *Corser*. After a couple more trips, they finally settled in Nuku Hiva in 1979, where they bought land and built a 6-bungalow hotel called the Keikahanui Inn. Rose and Frank ran the hotel together for the first 15 years, and Rose continued to run the hotel after her husband's death. She formed a partnership to build the 20-bungalow Nuku Hiva Keikahanui Pearl Lodge, which opened in Taiohae in September 1999. Now that she is free of all connections with that hotel, Rose is in the process of building another small first-class hotel all her own, which will consist of 8 a/c guest rooms, a restaurant and pool located on her beachside property below the Keikahanui Pearl Lodge. **Rose Corser's He'e Tai Inn and Restaurant** will also feature yacht club activities. In addition to providing a service for mail and packages, she also has facilities and equipment for faxes, e-mail and Internet connections for cruising yachts, Rose's yachting services are already a reality, and her new projects should all be finished in 2008. Be sure to visit Rose's Musée Enana Boutique, in a building just below the Nuku Hiva Keikahanui Pearl Lodge.

Nuku Hiva Yacht Services, *B.P. 461 Taiohae, Nuku Hiva 98742, Marquesas Islands. Tel./Fax 689/91.01.50; www.yachtservicesnukuhiva@yahoo.com.*

This service is operated by Anne Ragu and Moetai at the quay in Taiohae, who welcomes the people who arrive aboard cruising yachts. In addition to faxing facilities, they also have 3 computers (2 with Qwerty keyboards), and provide Wifi Internet connections even from your yacht. They can help visiting yachts with entry formalities, visa extensions, provide general information on the weather, the Marquesas Islands and French Polynesia. They do laundry, mechanical repairs for boats, repair sails, and advise on where to buy duty free fuel, shop for provisions, rent a car, boat, horse or helicopter. They can organize hikes, guided excursions, visits to the wood sculptors' workshops and other arts and crafts vendors, and can even send you to a good tattoo artist.

UA POU

When the Polynesians first settled on the island of **Ua Pou** they named it for the pillars of rock that resemble great cathedral spires. The mountain called Oave Needle, the tallest of the fantastic monoliths, thrusts 1,232 m. (4,040 ft.) into the clouds, and Ua Pou's dramatic silhouette is visible from Nuku Hiva, 35 km. (22 mi.) across the sea, and even from Ua Huka, some 56 km. (35 mi.) distant.

From the time of the old Polynesian chiefs Ua Pou has always been different from the rest of the Marquesas Islands. Although they formed tribes in the isolated valleys they recognized the authority of a single chief. The people seemed to be more peaceful, more unified and friendly, and the girls of Ua Pou are still considered the prettiest in all of Polynesia.

Ua Pou is the third largest island in the Marquesas archipelago, with 114 sq. km. (44 sq. mi.) of surface area. The 2,246 inhabitants live in the villages of Hakahau, Hakahetau, Haakuti, Hakamaii, Hakamoui, Hakatao, Hohoi and Anahoa.

The first stone church built in the Marquesas was constructed in Hakahau in 1859, and in Haakuti and Hakahetau villages there are small Catholic churches built on top of old *paepae* platforms. The main village of **Hakahau** has a dispensary, *gendarmerie*, bank, post office, food stores, boutiques, Air Tahiti office, port facilities, schools, small family pensions, plus a few simple restaurants and bars.

Ua Pou has experienced a cultural revival within the past several years. **Paepae Teavatuu** is a restored meeting platform in Hakahau, where traditional reenactments are held. The Marquesas Festival of Arts was held in Ua Pou in Dec. 2007. **Rataro** is a talented young singer from Ua Pou, who has become very popular throughout the Polynesian triangle and beyond. Videotapes and musical cassettes featuring his all-male performers are fast selling items throughout the islands. The **Kanahau Trio** is another popular singing group from Ua Pou.

The sculptors sell their wood or stone carvings from their homes and in the handcraft centers in the villages. Horseback or 4x4 vehicle excursions can be arranged to visit the **Valley of the Kings** at Hakamoui, archaeological sites in the interior valleys, to picnic on the white sand beach of Anahoa or to discover the flower stones (*phonolitis*) of Hoho'i, with their multi-colored drawings. Boats with pilot can be chartered for offshore fishing or to visit **Motu Ua**, a bird sanctuary on the south coast.

ARRIVALS & DEPARTURES

Arriving By Air

Air Tahiti, *Tel. 86.42.42* in Tahiti and *Tel. 91.52.25* in Ua Pou, has daily ATR flights from Tahiti to the Marquesas Islands of Nuku Hiva and Hiva Oa. A 19-passenger Twin Otter provides air connections from Nuku Hiva to Ua Pou daily except Mon., and there are flights from Hiva Oa to Ua Pou daily except Mon. From Ua Huka to Ua Pou there are 1-stop flights on Tues., Wed, Fri. and Sun. One-way airfare from Tahiti to Ua Pou is 31.000 CFP; the one-way fare from Hiva Oa to Ua Pou is 7.900 CFP; the one-way fare from Nuku Hiva to Ua Pou is 6.400 CFP; and from Ua Huka to Ua Pou the cost is also 6.400 CFP.

If you have reservations with a pension then you will be met at the Ua Pou's Aneou airport and driven to your lodging. Otherwise, you can get a taxi or hitch a ride. It's a 45-minute trip between the airport and Hakahau.

Polynesia Hélicoptères, *Tel. 92.02.17, Fax 92.08.40 Taiohae office; Tel. 92.04.40 Nuku Ataha airport; helico-nuku@mail.pf.* An AS 355 helicopter can transfer you between the Nuku Ataha Airport and Ua Pou for a flat fee of 120.000 CFP. These flights are normally made in connection with the ATR flights from Tahiti each Mon., Wed., Thurs. and Sun.

Arriving By Boat

The *Aranui* includes stops at Hakahetau and Hakahau during its 14-day round-trip cruise program from Tahiti to the Marquesas. See details in section on *Inter-Island Cruise Ships and Cargo/Passenger Boats* in Chapter 6, *Planning Your Trip.*

Motorboats can be rented in Nuku Hiva for trips to Ua Pou. See details in *Nuku Hiva* section.

Departing By Air

The **Air Tahiti** office in Ua Pou is next door to the post office in Hakahau, *Tel. 91.52.25/92.51.08.* The Twin Otter departure flight leaves from the Aneou airfield daily except Mon. and flies direct to Nuku Hiva to connect with the departure schedule of the ATR flights to Tahiti. Every day except Mon. you can fly the Twin Otter from Ua Pou to Atuona, Hiva Oa, which may have 1-2 two stops before reaching Atuona. There are direct flights from Ua Pou to Ua Huka on Tues.; on Wed. and Fri. a stop is made in Nuku Hiva and on Sun. the plane stops in Atuona on the way to Ua Huka.

Heli-Inter Marquises, *Tel. 92.02.17,* flies from Ua Pou to Nuku Hiva to connect with the ATR 42 flight schedule. The cost is 120.000 CFP.

Departing By Boat

See information on the *Aranui* and in Chapter 6, *Planning Your Trip* (section on Inter-Island Cruise Ships and Passenger Boats). It is also possible to make arrangements with the numerous speedboats and *bonitiers* that frequently make the crossing from Ua Pou to Nuku Hiva.

ORIENTATION

The **Aneou airport** is located between Hakahetau and Hakahau, 30 min. from the main village. **Hakahau** is spread along the Bay of Hakahau and continues inland for several blocks. Sailboats drop anchor in the bay, adjacent to a concrete dock for inter-island ships. The "pillars" rise above the seaside cliffs, and are often covered by clouds. A paved road leads from the boat dock throughout the village, and it is also an easy walk from the dock to the village center, where you'll find *magasins*, a few snack bars, a museum and the Catholic Church in the south end of the village.

A 22-km. (14-mi.) road from Hakahau to the airport and **Hakahetau** continues on to the tiny valley of **Haakuti** on the southwest side of the island, with a track from there to the village of **Hakamaii**, which is more accessible by boat. The road from Hakahau to the south leads to the villages of **Hakamoui**, **Haakau** and **Hoho'i**. A track leads from this road to **Pa'aumea**, but all the villages along this southeast coast are better reached by boat. The white sand beach of **Anahoa** is a 25-min. walk east of Hakahau. This is also a nice ride on horseback, where you have panoramic views of the volcanic mountains and Hakahau Bay. Look for the Restaurant Pukue'e sign, which also gives directions to Anahoa Beach.

GETTING AROUND UA POU

Taxi & Transport Service

Gilbert Kautai, *Tel. 92.51.80*, and **Jules Hituputoka**, *Tel. 92.53.33*, provide taxi service in Hakahau village, and **Bertrand Ah-Lo**, *Tel. 92.51.97*, has a taxi in Hakahetau.

WHERE TO STAY

Hakahau – Moderate

PENSION PUKUE'E, *B.P. 31, Hakahau, Ua Pou 98745, Marquesas Islands. Tel./Fax. 689/92.50.83; pukuee@mail.pf; http://chez.mana.pf/-pukuee. Overlooking Hakahau Bay, 12 km. (7.5 mi.) from the airport and 300 m. (984 ft.) from the boat dock. Round-trip transfers between airport and pension 4.000 CFP per person. 2008 Rates: Room and MAP 6.000 CFP per person. Add taxes. No credit cards.*

This is also known as Chez Hélène et Doudou. A big 5-room house sits on a hill overlooking the boat harbor, with a good view of the sugar-loaf mountains of Ua Pou. Rooms have 1-2 single beds or a double bed. Guests share the 2 bathrooms with hot water. A very spacious terrace is also used as a dining area for the restaurant. Hélène Kautai is from Ua Pou and spent several years in France with her French husband, before coming home to open her own pension. She serves French cuisine and local products with a French flavor and takes very good care of her guests, who are often government officials from Tahiti who are visiting the Marquesas as part of their duties as *fonctionnaires*. You can sign up for a guided excursion by 4WD for 15.000 CFP per car.

CHEZ DORA, *Hakahau, Ua Pou 98745, Marquesas Islands. Tel. 689/ 92.53.69; Fax 689/92.53.99. 500 m. (1,640 ft.) from the quay of Hakahau and 10 km. (6.2 mi.) from the airport. Round-trip transfers 4.000 CFP per passenger. 2008 Rates: Room or bungalow and MAP 7.000 CFP, AP 9.000 CFP. Add taxes. No credit cards.*

Tahiti Tourisme has awarded Chez Dora a 2-Tiare rating. This is the home of Dora Teikiehupoko, who has a 2-story white house in the heights of Hakahau at the end of the village. One of the 3 rooms she rents to guests is large and comfortable and has a private bathroom with a hot water shower. The other two rooms are also large and the bath facilities are shared. A big covered terrace overlooks the bay. There are also 2 bungalows on the premises, each with a private bathroom and cold water shower. Dora has a reputation for preparing some of the best local style meals in town, which are served in the communal dining room. Excursions by 4WD are 15.000 CFP per car.

PENSION VEHINE, *B.P. 54, Hakahau, Ua Pou 98745, Marquesas Islands. Tel. 689/92.50.63; Fax 689/92.53.21. Overlooking Hakahau Bay, 800 m. (2,624 ft.) from the quay of Hakahau and 13 km. (8 mi.) from the airport. Round-trip transfers 4.000 CFP per person. 2008 Rates: Room with breakfast 4.500 CFP per person; room and MAP 6.500 CFP per person; Bungalow with breakfast 5.000 CFP; bungalow with MAP 7.000 CFP per person. Add taxes. No credit cards.*

Tahiti Tourisme has awarded Pension Vehine a 2-Tiare rating. This pension in the center of Hakahau village is also called Chez Claire, and is owned by Marie-Claire and Georges "Toti" Teikiehuupoko, who are both involved in the cultural activities in Ua Pou. She rents out 2 rooms in a big 2-story house and in 2 separate bungalows. The rooms contain a double bed and a single bed and guests share the living room, dining room, terrace and bathroom with hot water. The bungalows are equipped with twin beds and a private bathroom with hot water. Meals are served on the big covered terrace upstairs or you can eat in Snack Vehine on the ground floor, which Claire also manages. A magasin food store is across the street. Excursions by 4WD can be organized for 15.000 CFP per car.

PENSION LEYDJ KENATA, *B.P. 105, Hakahau, Ua Pou 98745, Marquesas Islands. Tel. 689/92.53.19. On the hillside in Hakahetau village, overlooking the Bay of Hakahetau, 17 km. (10.6 mi.) from the airport. Round-trip transfers 4.000 CFP per person. 2008 Rates: Room with breakfast 3.500 CFP sgl, 5.000 CFP dbl; Room and MAP 5.500 CFP per person; Room and AP 7.000 CFP per person. Add taxes. No credit cards.*

You have a choice of 2 average size bedrooms or 2 big rooms, all with a double bed. Guests share a bathroom with hot water, plus the kitchen, dining room, living room and terrace. Tony Tereino, the owner, has a restaurant-bar on the premises, and meals are served family style on the covered terrace of his big white house. He also operates Ua Pou Evasion, organizing hikes, 4x4 excursions and horseback riding.

WHERE TO EAT

SNACK VAITIARE, *Tel. 92.50.95.* No credit cards. This snack serves good food.

SNACK VEHINE, *Tel. 92.53.21.* This is part of Pension Vehine and is in the center of Hakahau village. No credit cards. The cuisine is Marquesan, Chinese and French.

SEEING THE SIGHTS

Saint Etienne Catholic Church in Hakahau village is on the site where the first church in the Marquesas Islands was built in 1859. The carvings inside this stone and wood church include a pulpit of *tou* wood that represents the prow of a boat with a fishnet filled with fish. Adam and Eve and the serpent in the Garden of Eden and other Biblical designs are also presented. The statue of Christ rests his feet on the head of a tiki and the Virgin Mary and Christ child have Polynesian faces. Alfred Hatuuku, who lives in Hakahau, created these exquisite carvings.

Excursions by horseback or 4WD vehicle will take you to visit the white sand beach of **Anahoa** and the flower stones of **Hohoi**. These amber colored stones are pieces of volcanic *phonolite* that make a pinging noise when struck. They were formerly used to make carving tools and as weapons. Recent studies show that these *phonolites* are 2.9 million years old and the light colored basalt, which is very rich in black minerals, is different from that found in other places. In the vicinity of Hakahetau and Hakamaii a very unusual basaltic stone was dated as 4 million years old. Archaeological sites in the **Valley of the Kings** in Hakamoui and Hakaohoka valley include *paepae* platforms, *tohua* ceremonial plazas, *me'ae* temples and tikis.

Above the village of **Haakuti** a small Catholic Church is built on a high *paepae* stone terrace. **Hakahetau** also has an interesting Catholic Church with a red tower. Hakanai Bay, 11 km. (7 mi.) from Hakahau, below the track leading to Hakahetau, is a good picnic spot. This cove is also called Shark Beach.

Te Menaha Taka'oa is the site of what was once a holy temple, dedicated to Te Atua Heato, one of the Polynesian gods worshipped by the ancient Marquesans. The German ethnologist Karl von den Steinen visited this sacred site in the 1800s, when it was still *tapu* (forbidden). Georges Toti Teikiehuupoko, *Tel. 92.53.21*, can guide you there.

SPORTS & RECREATION

Horseback Riding

Tony Tereino in Hakahetau, *Tel. 92.53.19,* can arrange horseback rides on request. A half-day ride costs 3.500 CFP and an all-day ride is 7.000 CFP, with a picnic on request.

Cultural, Hiking & Eco Tours

Georges "Toti" Teikiehuupoko, *Tel. 92.50.63/92.53.21*, speaks good English and enjoys sharing his knowledge of Marquesan culture and history. He is a schoolteacher and president of Motu Haka, the Society for the Preservation of Marquesan Culture, and he is also director of l'Académie Marquisienne. Toti is an excellent contact for information on local sites, history and archaeology. His wife, Claire, who runs Pension Vehine and Snack Vehine, is also leader of a Marquesan dance group in Hakahau.

Oatea was created by Pascal Erhel Hatuuku, *Tel./Fax 92.51.28; oatea@mail.pf or pascal@mail.pf.* Pascal was born in Ua Pou and educated in France, then returned to Ua Pou in 1997 to discover his own island and culture and learn the Marquesan language. Oatea is an Eco-Tourism agency he started in 2001 that specializes in cultural hikes and "green" excursions with a team of Marquesan guides whom Pascal has helped train, complete with English lessons. His guides will lead you on walking trails that he has created from Hakahau to the Vaiea waterfall, or from Hakahetau to Hakahau, over the mountains and through the woods, along the seashore and beach of Hakanai, following a cleared path that takes you to the Pokoio pass and through the Keaoa valley, where you will be tempted to climb the Poumaka peak for a breathtaking panoramic view of the island and sea. This 4-hr. walk is relatively easy for most people, but you can also go by 4WD if you prefer. He also works as a guide for the *Aranui 3* as well as German tour operators and yachting groups. He can arrange lodging, transfers and excursions for private or professional groups or solo-travelers, reporters, scientists, tour operators and travel agents.

Ua Pou Evasion, *Tel. 92.53.19,* is operated by Tony Tereino, who will guide you on half- or full-day walks to discover the flora and fauna, archaeology and history of the island. A half-day walk is 2.000 CFP per person and a full-day's outing is 3.000 CFP. Tony doesn't speak much English.

Motor Boat Rental & Fishing Excursions

The following locally built speedboats are available for inter-island transfers between Ua Pou and Taiohae or the Nuku Ataha airport on Nuku Hiva, for excursions around the island, and for fishing trips.

Oceane is a 24-ft. Fiberglas boat owned by Antoine Tata, *Tel. 92.54.87* that he uses for fishing expeditions and other charters.

Kukupa is a 24-ft. 8-passenger Fiberglas boat owned by Rudla Klima, *Tel. 92.53.86; Fax 92.53.37,* that is available for deep-sea fishing and boating excursions or transfers.

Tahia O Te Tai is a 24-ft. 8-passenger Fiberglas boat owned by François Keuvahana, *Tel./Fax 92.53.31* that can be chartered for fishing and guided excursions.

SHOPPING

Tehina Boutique in Hakahau sells curios, local clothing and perfumes. There is an arts and crafts center near the boat dock in Hakahau. Some 2 dozen wood or stone sculptors live on the island of Ua Pou, and you can visit their workshops beside their homes. One of the finest sculptors is Alfred Hatuuku, *Tel. 92.52.39*, who carved the pulpit in the Catholic Church. He lives between the seafront and Snack Vehine.

In Hakahau village **William Aka**, *Tel. 92.53.90*, makes and sells jewelry, small tikis, lizards and miniature saddles of semi-precious woods. Artisans in Hakahetau village include **Marcel Kautai**, *Tel. 92.52.37*, **Beo Makario**, *Tel. 92.52.54*; **Tony Tereino**, *Tel. 92.53.19*; **Jacques Kaiha**, *Tel. 92.50.31*; in Hakamaii village **Eloi Hikutini**, *Tel. 92.52.53*, carves wood sculptures and **Kina Vaiauri**, *Tel. 92.50.32*, does tattoos.

PRACTICAL INFORMATION
Bank
Banque Socredo, *Tel. 92.53.63*, is located in the same building as the Hakahau Mairie. The bank is open Mon.-Thurs. from 7am-3pm, and on Fri. from 7am-2pm. There is an ATM window outside the bank.

Hospital
A government operated dispensary with a medical team and dentist is located in Hakahau, *Tel. 92.53.75*, and every village has an infirmary.

Information Centers
The **Ua Pou Tourism Committee** is presided by Tina Klima, *Tel. 92.53.86*; *Fax 92.53.41*.

Police
There is a French *gendarmerie* in Hakahau, *Tel. 91.53.05*.

Post Office & Telecommunications Office
The post office is in Hakahau. All telecommunications and postal services are available here. Phonecard telephone booths are located beside the post office, on the quay and opposite the Air Tahiti office.

UA HUKA
Welcome to **Ua Huka**, Marquesan cowboy country by the sea. On the southern coast untamed horses gallop freely in the wind on the tablelands. Herds of cows and goats graze in the ferns, wild cotton and scrub brush that grow in the desert-like topography on a vast plateau. Above this incredible and beautiful scene rises Mount Hitikau, the highest mountain at 855 m. (2,804 ft.). Breathtaking panoramas of the rugged coast and the sparkling sea greet the eye at every turn on the narrow winding mountain road that connects Vaipae'e, Hane and Hokatu, the 3 valleys where the 592 inhabitants live.

Ua Huka lies 35 km. (22 mi.) east of Nuku Hiva, and 56 km. (35 mi.) northeast of Ua Pou. It is the smallest of the inhabited islands in the northern

Marquesas group, with just 81 sq. km. (31 sq. mi.) of land. This crescent-shaped island is 8 km. (5 mi.) long and 14 km. (8.7 mi.) wide.

Ua Huka is one of the most interesting of all the Polynesian islands. The fern-covered valleys conceal *tohua* ceremonial plazas, *me'ae* stone temples and *tokai* burial platforms for women who died while pregnant or giving birth. Among the ruins from the 7 tribes who formerly inhabited the island are petroglyphs that can be seen at the archeological site of Vaikiki valley. From Auberge Hitikau (Chez Fournier) in Hane you can hike uphill for 30 min. or so to **Me'ae Meiaiaute**, a restored temple terrace where you will see 3 *tiki* that are sculpted from slabs of red tuff. A 4th *tiki* is a smaller version of the Maki'i Tau'a Pepe statue found in Puamau Valley on Hiva Oa, only this one in Ua Huka has been beheaded. (Read *Manuiota'a*, a book that was written by **Dr. Robert C. Suggs** and **Burgle Lichtenstein**, for more information on this subject).

In 1964 and 1965, **Dr. Yosihiko H. Sinoto**, Senior Anthropologist at the Bishop Museum in Honolulu, excavated a coastal village in Hane that was buried under sand dunes 2 m. (6.6 ft.) high. Among his findings were 2 fragments of pottery, dating from around 380 AD, which Dr. Sinoto said is the oldest site yet discovered by anyone in Eastern Polynesia, and an important link between Western and Eastern Polynesia. Other renowned archaeologists believe that the Marquesas were settled between 500-200 BC. When Dr. Suggs excavated the Ha'atuatua site in Nuku Hiva between 1956-58, he discovered the first pieces of pottery ever found in Eastern Polynesia. The radiocarbon technique dated these shards at 125 BC.

An archaeological site named Manihina is located on a sandy beach not far from the arboretum in Ua Huka. Dr. Sinoto first noticed this site in 1964 when he was excavating the sand dune in Hane. In 1991 the mayor of Ua Huka wanted to take sand from the beach to use in construction. Before doing so he notified the department of archaeology at the Centre Polynésien des Sciences Humaines (CPSH) in Tahiti. Their research in 3 stages uncovered a burial site at Manihina that contained 39 human skeletons of both sexes, along with skeletons of 2 dogs and 11 pigs. Studies date this site between 1000 and 1400 AD. Although these were robust people in general, some of the human skeletons revealed that the old folks suffered from rheumatism and one of them had leprosy.

Captain Joseph Ingraham, of the American trading ship *Hope*, sailed by Ua Huka in 1791. The northern Marquesas islands were then visited in quick succession by Captain Marchand of the French ship *La Solide*; Lieutenant Hergest aboard the *Doedalu*s, who surveyed the islands, and by Captain Josiah Roberts of the American ship *Jefferson* in 1793. Ua Huka was spared most of the carnage wreaked on the other Marquesas Islands by European discoverers, whalers and sandalwood seekers. During this period of discovery Ua Huka was named Ile Solide, Washington Island, Massachusetts, Ouahouka, Riou, Roahouga and Rooahooga.

Accommodations for tourists are available in the villages of Vaipae'e, Hane and Hokatu. These lodgings are located in separate houses and small bungalows, or in family homes or pensions.

ARRIVALS & DEPARTURES
Arriving By Air
Air Tahiti, *Tel. 86.42.42,* has daily ATR 42 flights from Tahiti to the Marquesas Islands of Nuku Hiva and Atuona. From Nuku Hiva you can connect directly to Ua Huka each Wed., Fri. and Sun., and a Tues. flight stops in Atuona. From Hiva Oa there are flights to Ua Huka on Tues. Wed., Fri. and Sun., either direct or with 1-2 stops. There are direct flights between Ua Pou and Ua Huka on Tues., and 1-stop flights on Wed., Fri. and Sun. One-way airfare from Tahiti to Ua Huka is 31.000 CFP; the one-way fare from Nuku Hiva to Ua Huka is 6.400 CFP; the one-way fare from Atuona to Ua Huka is 7.900 CFP, and from Ua Pou to Ua Huka the cost is 6.400 CFP. If you have reservations with a pension then you will be met at the Ua Huka airport and driven to your lodging.

Helicopter Service is provided by **Polynesia Hélicoptères** in Taiohae, Nuku Hiva, *Tel. 92.02.17,* on request.

Arriving By Boat
The *Aranui* includes stops at Vaipae'e and Hane in its 14-day round-trip cruise program from Tahiti to the Marquesas. See details in the section on Inter-Island Cruise Ships and Cargo/Passenger Boats in Chapter 6, *Planning Your Trip.* Motorboats can be rented in Nuku Hiva for trips to Ua Huka. See details in Nuku Hiva section.

Departing By Air
Air Tahiti reservations in Ua Huka is *Tel. 92.60.44.* The Twin Otter flight leaves Ua Huka each Tues., Wed., Fri. and Sun., connecting in Nuku Hiva for a direct flight to Tahiti on board the ATR plane. There are direct flights from Ua Huka to Atuona each Tues. and Sun., and flights with 1-2 stops on Wed. and Fri. One-stop flights from Ua Huka to Ua Pou operate on Tues., Wed., Fri., and Sun.

Departing By Boat
See information on the *Aranui* in Chapter 6, *Planning Your Trip,* section on Inter-Island Cruise Ships and Passenger Boats. Motorboats can be rented in Ua Huka to visit Nuku Hiva. Please see information in this chapter under Motor Boat Rentals.

ORIENTATION
Ua Huka's 3 villages of **Vaipae'e**, **Hane** and **Hokatu** are connected by a concrete road that winds along the edge of the cliffs for 14 km. (8.7 mi.). 4WD vehicles and horses are the means of transportation. The surf crashes against the steeply rising rocks of the coastline, creating a continuous spray that splashes high

into the sky, reflecting the sun in multiple shades of blue. After a rain the hills and plains glimmer in varying shades of green, but the plateaus become brown and desolate during the arid seasons.

If you arrive by ship you will probably disembark in **Vaipae'e Bay**, also called Invisible Bay, because a wall of basaltic rock protects the bay from the open sea. Landings are made by small boat onto a concrete pier. Vaipae'e is the largest village on Ua Huka, with the *Mairie*, post office and the Vaipae'e Archaeological Museum of Marquesan artifacts all in the same complex. The Catholic Church in Vaipae'e is worth a stop to see the artwork in the windows. The 6 panels of stained glass include illustrations of the Immaculate Conception that feature a Marquesan Mary against a background of the Invisible Bay. She is complete with tattoos and a ukulele, while the panels are bordered by figures from the petroglyphs found in the valleys.

The Nukumoo airport is located between Vaipae'e and Hane villages and the arboretum is close to the small airstrip. **Hane Bay** is distinguished by Motu Hane that sits just offshore facing the pretty little village. This is a dark violet and red rock 152 m. (508 ft.) high, shaped like a sugar loaf. A structure of stones on top of this huge rock looks like a giant tiki has been carved there. In Hane there is a post office, an infirmary, schools and churches. Small *magasins* offer limited food supplies in Vaipae'e, Hane and Hokatu. Handcrafts centers and wood carvers' shops are found in each village.

The coast off Haavei is rich in sea life, filled with sharks, dolphins, manta ray, big turtles, lobster and a variety of fish. Boats with captains can be rented for deep-sea fishing and excursions to Anaa Atua grotto and the islets of Teuaua and Tiotio. On these bird islands thousands of white and sooty terns (*kaveka*), red-footed booby birds, blue noddy birds, frigates, tropic birds, petrels and shearwaters lay their eggs. They screech and squawk as they feed on the abundance of fish in this area, while their fluffy white fledglings sit on the hard ground of the upraised *motu* islets, waiting for dinner to be served.

WHERE TO STAY
Moderate
MANA TUPUNA VILLAGE, *Vaipae'e, Ua Huka 98744, Marquesas Islands. Tel. 689/92.60.08, Tel./Fax 689/92.61.01; manatupuna@mail.pf. In Vaipae'e valley, 5.5 km. (3.4 mi.) from the airport and 2 km. (1.2 mi.) from the Vaipae'e boat landing. Round-trip transfers 2.000 CFP. Rates: Bungalow only 5.000 CFP sgl; 9.000 CFP dbl; Bungalow with MAP 7.000 CFP sgl, 11.000 CFP dbl; Bungalow with AP 9.500 CFP sgl, 16.000 CFP dbl per day. Add taxes. No credit cards.*

Three small wooden A-frame bungalows on stilts overlook Vaipae'e valley, where you can see goats and horses roaming freely and feeding on wild grass. Each of these *ha'e* contains a double bed and a single bed, a private bathroom with hot water, and a covered terrace. The furniture is made of bamboo and the posts on the terrace are sculpted coconut trunks from Ua Huka. Local style meals served. Karen

Taiaapu-Fournier is your hostess at Mana Tupuna Village, and she speaks good English and Spanish.

LE REVE MARQUISIEN, *Vaipae'e, Ua Huka 98744, Marquesas Islands. Tel./Fax 689/92.61.84; Cell 689/79.10.52/71.52.95; revemarquisien@mail.pf. In Pahataua valley, 800 m. (2,624 ft.) from Vaipae'e village, 5 km. (3.1 mi.) from the airport and 1.5 km. (0.93 mi.) from the boat dock. Free transfers. 2008 EP Rates: Room only 9.500 CFP sgl, 11.500 CFP dbl. Breakfast 1.000 CFP, lunch or dinner 3.000 CFP. No credit cards.*

Marie-France and Charles Aunoa have 4 bungalows in the middle of a bird sanctuary. Each unit has a double bed, electric fan, mosquito net, terrace, and private bathroom with hot water. A sofa bed can be added for a third person and house linens are furnished. Guests can watch television or DVD films in a communal room and enjoy their gourmet meals of Marquesan, Tahitian, Chinese and French cuisine served in the restaurant. The hosts will organize sports activities, deep-sea fishing and walking excursions. They rent a 4x4 car with driver for 6.000 CFP per day.

AUBERGE HITIKAU, *Hane, Ua Huka 98744, Marquesas Islands. Tel./Fax 689/92.61.74. In Hane village, 7 km. (4.3 mi.) from the airport and 11 km. (7 mi.) from the Vaipae'e boat landing. Round trip transfers 2.000 CFP. EP Room: 2.000 CFP sgl, 3.000 CFP dbl. Breakfast 700 CFP, lunch or dinner 2.500 CFP. No credit cards.*

This is a concrete house with 3 bedrooms, each containing a double bed, closet and desk. Shared bath facilities include 6 toilets, 1 lavabo and 1 shower with cold water. House linens are furnished. A big terrace in front is also shared by guests who come to eat local style cuisine in the Hitikau restaurant and bar, also operated by Céline Fournier and her family.

Economy

CHEZ ALEXIS, *Vaipae'e, Ua Huka 98744, Marquesas Islands. Tel./Fax 689/ 92.60.19; scallamera.florentine@mail.pf. In Vaipae'e valley, 5.5 km. (3.4 mi.) from the airport and 2 km. (1.2 mi.) from the Vaipae'e boat landing. Round-trip transfers 2.000 CFP per person. 2008 EP Rates: Room 2.000 CFP per person; a/c room 4.000 CFP; breakfast 1.200 ÇFP, lunch or dinner 2.700 CFP. Add taxes. No credit cards.*

This is a concrete house with 4 rooms for rent beside the main road in Vaipae'e village. Look for the sign on the right. Each room contains a double bed. The living room with TV, the large kitchen, terrace and 2 bathrooms with hot water are shared. House linens are furnished. You can rent a 4x4 vehicle with a driver for 7.000 CFP per day. Your host Alexis Scallamera will organize hikes for you on request. He is president of the Ua Huka tourism committee.

CHEZ MAURICE & DELPHINE, *Hokatu, Ua Huka 98744, Marquesas Islands. Tel./Fax. 689/92.60.55. In Hokatu valley, 7 km. (4.4 mi.) from the airport, 13 km. (8 mi.) from the boat landing of Vaipae'e and 2 km. (1.2 mi.) from Hane village. At the entry to Hokatu it is the first house on the left. Round-trip transfers* *between airport and pension 2.000 CFP per person. 2008 EP Rates: Room only 3.000 CFP per person. Breakfast 700 CFP, dinner 2.000 CFP. No credit cards.*

Five hillside bungalows overlooking the sea and Mount Hane are furnished with a double and single bed, private bathroom with hot water, and a terrace. House linens provided. Meals are served in the Rootuehine home in the village. A 4WD vehicle is available for rent with driver for 6.000 CFP a day, and a small self-drive car rents for 10.000 CFP a day if you are not staying in this pension. Delphine speaks English and Maurice handles the land excursions and boat trips, which include a picnic.

CHEZ CHRISTELLE, *Vaipae'e, Ua Huka 98744, Marquesas Islands. Tel. 689/92.60.04, Fax 689/92.60.85. In Vaipae'e valley, 7 km. (4.4 mi.) from the airport and 2 km. (1.2 mi.) from the boat landing. It's the 7th house on the left from the bridge, 5 m. (16 ft.) after Chez Alexis. Round-trip transfers 2.000 CFP per person. Rates: Room 2.000 CFP sgl, 4.000 CFP dbl. Breakfast is 700 CFP, lunch or dinner is 2.000 CFP each. House can also be rented by the month. Add taxes. No credit cards.*

This is a 4-bedroom concrete house, with a double bed in each room. Guests share the living room, equipped kitchen, dining room, 2 bathrooms with cold-water shower, and terrace. House linens are furnished. There is also a large garden here. You can rent a 4WD vehicle with or without driver for 6.000 CFP per day.

WHERE TO EAT

Whenever a ship arrives in Vaipae'e, the vendors sell fried fish, chicken legs, meats, banana fritters and sandwiches at the boat landing. Anne-Marie's snack at the Arboretum sells short-order food and soft drinks, and prepared food is also available from the *roulottes*, which may be a pick-up truck.

AUBERGE HITIKAU, *Hane village, Tel. 92.61.74. Advance reservations are needed for all meals. No credit cards.*

Breakfast is 700 CFP, and lunch and dinner are each 2.500 CFP. Feasts are prepared for groups, such as the *Aranui* passengers. These buffets may include kaveka (sooty tern) omelets, hard boiled kaveka eggs, goat cooked in coconut milk, *poisson cru*, sashimi, roast pig, goat and fish cooked in an underground oven, plus rice, *fei*, *uru*, banana *po'e*, cake and fresh fruit.

All the family pensions serve meals to their guests as well as to anyone else who reserves in advance.

SEEING THE SIGHTS

Papuakeikaha Arboretum, between Vaipae'e and Hane, *Tel./Fax 92.61.51*, is a botanical and plant nursery with more than 400 species of flora, including 144 varieties of citrus plants. Leon Lichtle, who is now the mayor of Ua Huka, started this nursery in the early 1970s. The gardens comprise 57 acres (23 ha.) and contain every kind of plant and flower you can think of that grows in this climate. There are huge trees of *miro* (rosewood), *tou*, bamboo, banyan, *uru*, teak, *puatea*, *pakai*, *cerrettes*, *tutui*, allspice, acacia, mangoes, mountain apples, custard apples, star apples, carambola and guava. You'll find several species of bananas and plantains, pomegranates, coffee, cacao, vanilla, hot peppers, hibiscus, auti and jasmine. Plus there are many bushes of Tiare Tahiti and Tiare Moorea. This is a refreshing stop in the shade of the lovely trees, as well as a very interesting and informative botanical lesson. The arboretum is open to the public from 8am-3pm Mon.-Fri. There is no admission charge.

Vaipae'e Archaeological Museum is adjacent to the Mairie or town hall of Vaipae'e on the left of the main road from the boat landing, *Tel. 92.60.74, Fax 92.60.39.* At the entryway is a small sandalwood tree, one of only a few that you will see in the Marquesas Islands. The small museum is filled with old photographs and ancient Marquesan artifacts, including replicas of a chief's burial grotto and a Marquesan stove. A collection of reproductions of ancient sailing canoes and outrigger canoes represents all the Polynesian archipelagoes. A contest is held each year at the end of June, when the sculptors carve reproductions of old Marquesan artifacts. The winner of this competition has the pleasure of seeing his creation sent off to Tahiti to be displayed in the Museum of Tahiti and Her Islands. Master sculptor Joseph Vaatete takes care of the museum in Vaipae'e, which is open Mon.-Fri. from 8am-3pm.

Hane Maritime Museum, *Tel. 92.60.74; Fax 92.60.39,* is managed by Joseph Vaatete, and is located beside the sea in Hane village. This small museum contains an old anchor, fishnets, ancient fishhooks, reproductions of outrigger canoes, and drawings of the Polynesian triangle, retracing the route of the first Polynesian sailors who settled the South Pacific islands. An arts and crafts center shares the building with the Musée de la Mer.

Hokatu Geological Museum, *Tel./Fax 92.60.55,* is managed by Maurice Rootuehine, and is open Mon.-Fri., 8am-3pm.

Museum of Wood "Jardin", *Tel. 92.60.13,* is another project realized by Léon Lichtle, the mayor of Ua Huka, who planted the first seeds in the botanical nursery in the 1970s. This museum is in the magnificent setting of the Arboretum and pays homage to trees. Contact Joseph Vaatete if you want to visit, as it is open on request.

Hokatu Stone Museum, *Tel. 92.60.13,* is also managed by Joseph Vaatete and open on request. Here you will see a display of petroglyphs carved into basaltic stone.

Land Excursions

Land tours will take you to visit the 3 villages, the archaeological sites, arboretum, museums and the arts and crafts shops. To arrange for an excursion by 4x4 vehicle you can ask at the pension where you're staying, or you can hire the following people: **Alexis Scallamera,** *Tel. 92.60.19,* **Denis Fournier,** *Tel. 92.60.62;* **Marie-Louise Fournier,** *Tel. 92.61.08;* **Maurice Rootuehine,** *Tel. 92.60.55;* **Benoît Teatiu,** *Tel. 92. 61.22;* and **Firmin Teikiteepupuni,** *Tel. 92.61.07.* In Hokatu valley arrangements can be made at *magasin* Maurice, *Tel. 92.60.55,* for land tours, horseback riding and boat rentals. Some of the cars and 4-wheel drive vehicles can be rented without a driver. The rates are 6.000 to 10.000 CFP per day, depending on where you are staying when you rent the vehicle.

SPORTS & RECREATION
Horseback Riding
Seeing Ua Huka on horseback is the way to go. The small Marquesan horses you see wandering around the desert-like plains are descendants from Chilean stock imported in 1856. You can ride bareback or astride wooden saddles softened by piling on copra sacks. The cost of horseback riding in Ua Huka is 5.000 CFP per day, plus 2.000-3.000 CFP for a guide. The following men rent horses and will accompany you on your outing.

Alexis Fournier in Vaipae'e, *Tel. 92.60.05*, rents riding horses for half- and full-day excursions. There are others who have horses but not the permit to rent them.

Motor Boat Rental
Offshore excursions can be made by speedboat to visit Ua Huka's unusual sites. Half-day excursions and all-day outings with picnics are also possible. Boats with captains can be rented for deep-sea fishing and excursions to **Anaa Atua** grotto and the bird islands of **Teuaua** and **Tiotio**.

Bird Island or **Teuaua Motu** is a steep rock 6 m. (20 ft.) high, 150 m. (492 ft.) long and 100 m. (328 ft.) wide, lying offshore Haavei valley. Attracted by the numerous fish in this area, millions of sooty terns lay their eggs on the open ground on top of this small island. You have to climb to the top by rope, which is very tricky and dangerous. The small eggs are white with black spots and the yolk is very orange. People gather these eggs by the bucket to boil or use in omelets.

The imprint of human footsteps can be seen in the sand at low tide in the **Anaa Atua** grotto and they disappear during high tide. Petroglyphs can be visited at the pretty beach of **Hatuana**. The **Pahonu beach** near the airport is a good place to swim and can be reached by boat.

Alexis Fournier, in Vaipae'e, *Tel. 92.60.05/92.60.72*, has a locally built 20-ft. fishing boat for 6 passengers. Excursions around Ua Huka include half-day outings to Bird Island and Anaa Atua grotto. Full-day excursions around the island of Ua Huka also include a picnic. In Vaipae'e you can also rent a boat from **Joseph Teatiu**, *Tel. 92.61.28*, and **Roland Teatiu**. **Maurice Rootuehine**, in Hokatu, *Tel. 92.60.55*, has a locally built 25-ft. fishing boat for 7 passengers, which is available for inter-island round-trips between Ua Huka and Nuku Hiva, and excursions around Ua Huka.

SHOPPING
Arts and crafts centers are located in the villages of **Vaipae'e**, **Hane** and **Hokatu**. The prices here are less expensive than in the other islands. You can also visit the sculptors' workshops at their homes. There are a dozen wood sculptors

living in Hane Village, 14 wood sculptors living in Hokatu, and up to a dozen wood sculptors living in Vaipae'e village.

You will also find artisans who carve stone and bones. **Joseph Vaatete**, *Tel. 92.60.74,* is one of the most noted sculptors in wood and stone, who makes pieces for the museums in Ua Huka. He lives in Hane village, a couple of blocks from the sea, on the left side of the road that goes up the valley. You can recognize his house by the tree trunks and pieces of wood and stone in his yard. Two of Joseph's statues are located at the International Airport of Tahiti-Faaa, and another carving is located at the *Mairie* of Papeete. Joseph also takes care of the Vaipae'e Archaeological Museum adjacent to the *Mairie* of Vaipae'e, the Hane Maritime Museum, the Museum of Wood and the Hokatu Stone Museum. **Daniel Naudin**, *Tel. 92.61.03/ 92.61.35,* the best-known sculptor in Ua Huka who carves bones, lives in Vaipae'e. He creates designs combining wood and bone, and he is also a tattoo artist.

Magasin stores are located in each village and are also open on Sundays.

PRACTICAL INFORMATION
Infirmary
A government-operated infirmary is located in the village of Hane, *Tel. 92.60.58.*

Post Office & Telecommunications Office
A Post Office is located in the main village of Vaipae'e, *Tel. 92.60.26,* and in Hane village, *Tel. 92.60.46.* All telecommunications and postal services are available here.

Visitors Bureau
You can get information from the Ua Huka Tourism Committee–Tupehe Nui. *Tel./Fax 92.60.19; Cell 79.09.48; scallamera.florentine@mail.pf.* Alexis Scallamera is the president. He also owns the pension Chez Alexis.

HIVA OA
According to some Marquesan legends, **Hiva Oa** was the first island in this archipelago settled by the Polynesians before they reached Nuku Hiva. Archaeological findings support this theory, based on a charcoal sample taken from a fireplace in a rock shelter at Anapua. This site was excavated in 1981 by Pierre Ottino of the ORSTOM research center in Tahiti, and the charcoal dates 150+-95 years BC. This is one of the oldest dates thus uncovered reflecting the presence of human occupancy in Eastern Polynesia.

Hiva Oa is located 1,400 km. (868 mi.) northeast of Tahiti. It is one of the youngest islands in the Marquesas chain, and has been described as a seahorse whose head faces the setting sun. The island measures 40 km. (25 mi.) long east to west and averages 10 km. (6.2 mi.) north to south. Atuona sits in the center of 3 adjoining craters, and Temetiu, whose peak reaches into the clouds 1,190 m.

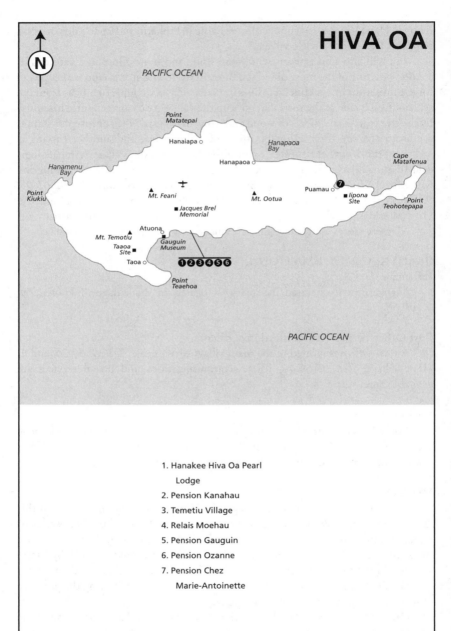

1. Hanakee Hiva Oa Pearl
   Lodge
2. Pension Kanahau
3. Temetiu Village
4. Relais Moehau
5. Pension Gauguin
6. Pension Ozanne
7. Pension Chez
   Marie-Antoinette

(3,900 ft.), crowns the ridge of mountains above the picturesque bays. The steep slopes of high altitude interior plateaus dominate this large fertile island of 330 sq. km. (127 sq. mi.). The 2,310 inhabitants live in the villages of Atuona, Puamau, Hanaiapa, Hanapaaoa, Nahoe, Tahauku and Taaoa, which are separated into isolated valleys by the dorsal spine and ridges.

The French painter **Paul Gauguin** came to Hiva Oa in 1901 in search of a primitive culture and savage wildness, and here he died in 1903. He is buried in Calvary Cemetery on a hill behind Atuona village. Fragrant petals from a gnarled old frangipani tree shower down on the simple grave, and a statue of Oviri, "the savage" stands at the head of the tombstone.

In the village of Atuona you can visit the **Paul Gauguin Center,** a complex of 3 large buildings on the original site where Gauguin lived. This center was inaugurated on May 8, 2003, during the commemorative services to honor the 100th anniversary of Gauguin's death in Atuona. The Gauguin Museum has some 100 reproductions of the French artist's paintings made in Tahiti and Hiva Oa, as well as sculptures, drawings, photographs, letters and other souvenirs of Gauguin. The entry charge is 600 CFP for adults and 300 CFP for 12-18 year olds. A replica of Gauguin's house, which he named **La Maison du Jouir** (House of Pleasure), is built beside the well into which Gauguin used to keep his liquor bottles, and there is a bamboo pole hanging out the window upstairs, which represents the pole Gauguin used to fetch his bottles of liquor from the well. This dried pit was uncovered during construction of the complex, and was filled with broken bottles, old paintbrushes, teeth and other cast off items. An open-sided shelter was erected near the sea for visiting artists, a replica of Gauguin's *Atelier des Tropiques,* where the ocean breezes fanned him as he painted. These Gauguin copyists are lodged in 4 bungalows on the premises. Across the street from the Gauguin Center is the Magasin Gauguin, where he used to buy his supplies.

A few graves distant from Gauguin's tombstone in Calvary Cemetery is the final resting place of the famous Belgian singer **Jacques Brel**, who lived in Atuona from 1975 until his death in 1978. Many of Brel's European fans make a pilgrimage to his grave, which is always decorated with flowers. When Brel was buried his mistress, Maddly Bamy, placed a plaque on his tombstone that contained an engraving of the two devoted lovers. The **Jacques Brel Memorial** is a black marble stele set in a stone overlooking the Hanakee Pearl Lodge and Atuona Bay east of Atuona. Brel wanted to build his house on this hillside, but was unable to do so because of his illness. There are 2 tracks leading to the site, and it is best to get clear directions before setting off on foot.

Jacques Brel's Beechcraft airplane, Jo Jo, has been restored and is on display in the **Jacques Brel Space** adjacent to the Gauguin Center. The **Traditional Arts Museum** (entrance is 400 CFP for adults and 200 CFP for 12-18 year olds) and an arts and crafts center are found in the area facing the **Pepeu** *tohua* meeting ground, where the ceremonies and dances were held during the Marquesas Festival of Arts in December 2003.

Atuona is the administrative center for the southern Marquesas. Framed in a theater of mountains with the Tahauku Bay providing safe anchorage, Atuona is a favorite port of call for yachts and copra/cargo ships. Atuona village has a *gendarmerie*, infirmary, new post office, bank, weather station, Air Tahiti office, restaurants and snack bars, stores and shops. There is a Catholic mission with a boarding school and a Protestant church.

You can rent a car with or without a driver or you can join an excursion by 4WD and visit the bays of Nahoe and Hanamenu, the black sand beach of Taaoa and the lovely white sand beach of Hanatekua. Near the little village of Hanaiapa is a cascade that splashes down a 249-m. (800-ft.) high cliff into the surging sea, wetting the black rocks so they sparkle like vaults of mica. Petroglyphs carved on stone have been found in the valleys of Eiaone and Punaei, and many other archaeological sites exist all over the island of Hiva Oa.

Gauguin's descendants still live in the Puamau valley, 48 km. (30 mi.) from Atuona. The restored archaeological site of I'ipona is also located in this valley. In this religious sanctuary is a *me'ae* on 2 large terraces, with 5 huge stone tikis. The most famous stone tiki represents the god Takai'i. Carved from porous red rock, this statue is 2.35 m. (7.7 ft.) tall, and is the largest stone tiki in French Polynesia.

You can also go deep-sea fishing, explore woodcarvers' shops, ride along a black sand beach on a Marquesan horse or charter a boat for a trip to visit nearby islands, including **Motane**, the sheep island. Accommodations on Hiva Oa are found in a 4-star hotel overlooking the cobalt blue Pacific and in small family pensions near the villages.

ARRIVALS & DEPARTURES
Arriving By Air
Air Tahiti, *Tel. 86.42.42* in Tahiti, *Tel. 91.70.90* in Atuona, flies ATR turbo jet planes from Tahiti direct to Hiva Oa each Mon., Fri. and Sun. Flights from Tahiti stop in Nuku Hiva on Tues and Thurs., with a change of aircraft on Thurs., then continue to Atuona. The one-way fare from Tahiti to Atuona is 31.000 CFP and the round-trip fare is 56.700 CFP. You can fly from Rangiroa to Atuona each Sat., with a stop in Nuku Hiva, for a one-way fare of 27.600 CFP. The fare from Ua Pou to Atuona is 7.900 CFP, flying by Twin Otter direct or with 1-2 stops daily except Mon. You can also fly direct from Ua Huka to Atuona on Tues. and Sun., and have 1-2 stops on Wed. and Fri. The one-way fare is 7.900 CFP.

You can also get to Nuku Hiva by chartering an airplane in Tahiti from **Air Archipels**, *Tel. 81.30.30*; or **Air Tahiti**, *Tel. 86.42.42*.

Arriving By Boat
The *Aranui* includes stops at Atuona, Puamau, and Hanaiapa in Hiva Oa during its 14-day round-trip cruise program from Tahiti to the Marquesas. See details in section on *Inter-Island Cruise Ships and Cargo/Passenger Boats* in Chapter 6, *Planning Your Trip*. The communal boats from Tahuata and Fatu Hiva connect

their islands with Atuona once or twice a week. See further information for these two islands in this chapter.

Departing By Air

Air Tahiti reservations in Atuona, *Tel. 91.70.90*. You can take an ATR plane from Atuona direct to Tahiti each Sun. There are flights on each day of the week, with 1-2 stops and sometimes a change of aircraft before you reach Tahiti.

Departing By Boat

The *Aranui III* leaves Tahuata on a Sunday and goes to Ua Huka, then to Nuku Hiva and back to Tahiti.

Auona II, *Tel. 92.80.23; Fax 92.80.39*, is the 51-ft. communal catamaran of Fatu Hiva. It can transport 30 passengers and when it is not broken down the boat leaves Atuona each Wed. around 12pm for Fatu Hiva. The one-way fare is 4.000 CFP.

Tahuata Nui is a 48.6-ft. long aluminum hull boat that can transport 60 passengers between Atuona and Tahuata. The boat leaves the quay of Atuona at 12pm each Mon. for Vaitahu, and each Fri. the boat leaves Atuona at 4pm for Vaitahu and Hapatoni. The one-way fare is 1.000 CFP. Reserve at the Mairie of Tahuata, *Tel. 689/92.92.19; Fax 689/92.92.10*.

Te Hinaonaiki, *Tel. 92.76.97*, is the 8-passenger boat of Médéric Kaimuko of Atuona. He provides inter-island transfers to Tahuata and Fatu Hiva.

Vaipuna O Hanamenu, *Tel. 92.76.57/70.71.97/78.82.98*, is a bonito boat that can transport up to 8 passengers to Tahuata or Fatu Hiva.

See information under *Boat Excursions & Deep Sea Fishing* in this chapter and *Departing by Boat* in chapter on *Tahuata*.

ORIENTATION

A road 17 km. long (10.5 ft.) is built on the **Tepuna Plateau**, 440 m. (1,443 ft.) above the sea, connecting the airport with **Atuona village**. The town is at the north end of Taaoa Bay, 3 km. (1.9 mi.) from **Tahauku Bay**, also known as Traitors' Bay, which provides a safe harbor for yachts and the inter-island cargo vessels that dock at the concrete pier.

Three paved roads pass through Atuona and it is easy to walk around the town center, where most of the businesses and administrative offices are concentrated, as well as the medical facilities, churches and Catholic schools.

GETTING AROUND HIVA OA

When you make reservations with a hotel or pension your hosts will meet you at the airport or boat dock on your arrival. You can also organize your excursions at the place where you're staying. The cost of transfers and land tours varies according to the lodgings, which are listed under *Where to Stay*.

Taxi Service
Ida Clark, *Tel. 92.71.33/72.34.73.* She charges 1.500 CFP per person for one-way transfers between the airport and Atuona village, and 1.000 CFP per car for a transfer from the ship dock to the village. A visit around Atuona village is 4.000 CFP and she can also drive you to visit the valleys and sites around the island. She charges 8.000 CFP to visit the Taaoa valley and 20.000 CFP for a trip to Puamau.

Car Rentals
With advance reservations a car can be delivered to the airport for your arrival. The gas station is located at the cargo ship dock at Tahauku Bay. Make sure there is a stockage of fuel on hand before signing your contract.

Atuona Rent-A-Car, *Tel. 92.76.07, cell 72.17.17,* operated by Abel Rauzy, has self-drive 4WD vehicles. A Suzuki Jimmy is 7.000 CFP for a half-day and 13.000 CFP for all day. A double cabin Toyota is 9.000 CFP for a half-day and 16.500 CFP for a full day.

David Locations, *Tel. 92.72.87; kmk@mail.pf,* is owned by David Kaimuko, facing Magasin Naiki in Atuona. He rents a 4WD self-drive vehicle for 15.000 CFP per day. Reserve 2 days in advance.

Hiva Oa Location, *Tel. 92.70.43/24.65.05.* Liliane Heitaa or Sandra Tamarii will rent you a Suzuki 4x4 for 6.500 CFP for a half-day and 13.000 CFP for all day.

WHERE TO STAY
Superior
HANAKEE HIVA OA PEARL LODGE, *B.P. 80, Atuona, Hiva Oa 98741, Marquesas Islands. Tel. 689/92.75.87, Fax 689/92.75.95; www.pearlresorts.com. Reservations: Tel. 689/50.84.45; Fax 689/43.17.86; res@spmhotels.pf. On hillside overlooking Tahauku Bay, 7 km. (4.4 mi.) from airport and 2 km. (1.2 mi.) from boat dock. 14 bungalows. 2008 EP Rates sgl. /dbl.: Mountain view bungalow 20.000 CFP; Ocean view bungalow 25.000 CFP; Premium ocean view bungalow 35.000 CFP; add 5.000 CFP for 3rd person. Add 7.600 CFP per person for MAP and 10.900 CFP for AP. One-way transfer from airport by 4WD 2.400 CFP per person. Add taxes. All major credit cards.*

This 4-star hotel is built on the hillside overlooking Tahauku Bay, above the port for the inter-island ships. All 14 bungalows are 39 sq. m. (420 sq. ft.) large, and each unit has a king size bed or twin beds, plus an extra bed. They all have a/c, ceiling fan, TV, a mini-bar, tea and coffee facilities, IDD telephone, safe, shower with hot water, hair dryer and a sundeck. Laundry service is available and you can get a babysitter on request. Two of the ocean view bungalows are equipped for handicapped guests in wheelchairs.

The main building houses the reception, boutique and a desk for excursions and car rentals. There is a gourmet restaurant and bar, and a swimming pool overlooks Traitors Bay, the Bordelais canal and the small island of Hanakee. Bicycles are provided free for guests.

The activities desk can arrange for your 4-wheel drive excursions to visit the Tehueto Petroglyphs for a half-day tour that costs 2.091 CFP, or the smiling tiki and paepae for the same price. A half-day tour to Atuona village is 3.000 CFP, including the museum entry fee; a half-day excursion to the Makamea sites is 2.636 CFP, and a half-day tour to the Taaoa valley is 3.500 CFP. You can also visit the Hanaiapa valley by 4WD, which includes an outrigger canoe trip, for 7.000 CFP. Full-day excursions by 4x4 take you to the Vaipikopiko waterfall for 5.909 CFP, or to Puamau valley and the Oipona sites for 10.500 CFP, which includes lunch. You can visit the island of Tahuata by boat for 8.636 CFP each, for a minimum of 4 passengers. Horseback rides are 6.364 CFP for a half-day outing, and your choices include Punaei Creek, Tehueto petroglyphs and the Belvedere lookout of Jacques Brel's stele. A full-day ride is 12.728 CFP, and you can have a bivouac on horseback by request.

You can also rent a 4WD car to drive yourself to see the historical and archaeological sites, the famous stone tiki in Puamau, and the picturesque scenes of Marquesan horses swimming in the lovely bays or galloping down a black sand beach. See information under scuba diving for underwater discoveries.

Romantic Rendez-vous at the Hiva Oa Hanakee Pearl Lodge include a Starlight Romantic Dinner for 25.000 CFP, and a private tour by boat to the island of Tahuata for 49.867 CFP. Prices quoted are per couple. The hotel can also arrange Polynesian Weddings, decorate your bed with flowers, bake a cake for 2 or 4, and bring it to your bungalow along with a bottle of chilled French champagne. Contact the hotel directly for details on the Romantic programs.

Moderate

PENSION KANAHAU, *B.P 101, Atuona, Hiva Oa 98741, Marquesas Islands. Tel. 689/91.71.31/70.16.26; Fax 689/91.71.32; pensionkanahau@mail.pf; www.ifrance.com/pensionkanahau. Rates: Bungalow with breakfast 10.400 CFP sgl., 13.300 CFP dbl., 16.700 CFO tpl, for less than 4 nights. Add 3.000 CFP per person for dinner. Round-trip transfers between airport and pension 3.000 CFP per person. Add taxes. No credit cards.*

Tahiti Tourisme has awarded this pension its highest rating of 3 Tiares. This 4-bungalow family pension managed by Stèphania Dubreuil opened in 2003 on the hillside of Atuona, overlooking Tahuku Bay, 9 km. (5.6 mi.) from the airport and 1 km. (0.62 mi.) from the boat dock. 2 of the wooden bungalows on stilts have a double bed and the other 2 units have twin beds. Each unit also has a ceiling fan, a convertible sofa, a private bathroom with hot water, local TV, electrical mosquito repellent, and a terrace. Meals are served on a big terrace with a marvelous view of the bay. Free laundry service is available for guests and free transfers are provided to the village, including excursions to visit the points of interest in Atuona village, and the artisan workshops. They will also introduce you to the local cuisine, weaving, tapa making and Marquesas dancing.

TEMETIU VILLAGE, *B.P. 52, Atuona, Hiva Oa 98741, Marquesas Islands. Tel. 689/91.70.60.70.72.07; Fax 689/91.70.61; heitaagabyfeli@mail.pf. EP Rates: Room only 6.550 CFP sgl, 8.735 CFP dbl; add 2.185 CFP for 3rd person or child more than 12 years old. Breakfast is 1.060 CFP and lunch or dinner costs 2.970 CFP per person for each meal. Round-trip airport transfers 3.180 CFP per person. Add taxes. AE, MC, V.*

Six neat and clean bungalows sit on the hillside in Atuona village, with a beautiful view of Tahauku Bay. Each bungalow has a double bed or 2 single beds, and some units also have a folding bed. All units have a private bathroom with hot water, a terrace, electric fan, TV, and electric anti-mosquito diffuser. The rooms are cleaned every 2 days and the towels are changed every day. There is a restaurant/bar and meals are served on the covered dining terrace overlooking the small swimming pool and the bay. There is also a communal living room with a TV, video and books, plus Internet access, and a small boutique of Marquesan arts and crafts. You can rent a self-drive 4WD vehicle for 13.000 CFP a day.

This is a favorite lodging because of its location, but mainly because of the owners, who are warm and welcoming. "Gaby" is the former president of the Tourism Committee in Hiva Oa. His wife speaks English and will guide you on a complimentary tour of Atuona village and the other main points of interest. Gaby also has an Excursion business. See information under *Land Tours & Safari 4x4 Excursions* in this chapter.

RELAIS MOEHAU, *B.P. 50, Atuona, Hiva Oa 98741, Marquesas Islands. Tel. 689/92.72.69/70.16.34; Fax 689/92.77.62; moehaurelais@mail.pf; www.relaismoehau.pf. On mountainside in Atuona, 9 km. (5.6 mi.) from the airport and 3 km. (1.9 mi.) from Atuona quay. Round-trip transfers between airport and pension 3.000 CFP per person. 2008 MAP Rates: Room with breakfast 8.005 CFP sgl; 12.110 CFP dbl.; 16.585 CFP tpl; room with MAP 11.005 CFP sgl., 18.110 CFP dbl.; 25.585 CFP tpl, including taxes. MC, V.*

This pension has been given a 2-Tiare rating by Tahiti Tourisme. Gisèle and Georges Gramont have 8 spacious guest rooms in their 2-story white house, with a choice of a double bed or two single beds. Each room has a ceiling fan, TV, in-house video channel, and bathroom with hot water shower. A big terrace spans the length of the house, offering a lovely view of Traitors Bay and Hanakee Rock. Wifi Internet service is available for guests with their own computers.

Meals are served in the restaurant on the premises, which is equipped with a wood-burning pizza oven. It is also open to the public. An *a la carte* menu features Marquesan, Polynesian and French cuisine. Excursions and guided tours can be organized on request to visit Hiva Oa and the sister island of Tahuata.

PENSION GAUGUIN, *B.P. 34, Atuona, Hiva Oa 98741, Marquesas Islands. Tel./Fax 689/92.73.51; cell 75.68.51; pens.gauguin@mail.pf. Rates: Room only 3.500 CFP per person; Room with MAP 6.500 CFP sgl, 12.000 CFP dbl. Round-trip airport transfers 3.000 CFP per person. Add taxes. MC, V.*

This popular small hotel overlooks the road that leads to Tahauku port at the eastern end of Atuona Bay, 7 km. (4.4 mi.) from the airport and 2.5 km. (1.6 mi.) from the boat dock. The 2-story building has 6 rooms, each with a double bed and a single bed, and a private bathroom with hot water. All guests share the living room, dining room and a big covered terrace with a panoramic view of the bay. The atmosphere is very homey and clean and the meals are good. The Make Make Snack is also close by, should you want a change. André Teissier, your host, will organize interesting excursions for you to visit the sites in Hiva Oa and to spend the day on Tahuata.

Economy

PENSION OZANNE, *B.P. 43, Atuona, Hiva Oa 98741, Marquesas Islands. Tel/Fax 689/92.73.43; Cell 70.16.34. Rates: Room only 3.500 CFP sgl., 4.500 CFP dbl; Room and MAP 5.500 CFP sgl., 10.000 CFP dbl. Bungalow only 4.000 CFP sgl., 5.000 CFP dbl. Bungalow and MAP 6.000 CFP sgl., 9.000 CFP dbl. Round-trip airport transfers 3.000 CFP per person. Add taxes. No credit cards.*

This pension is on the hillside on the eastern edge of Atuona, providing accommodations in a 3-bedroom house and 2 bungalows. In the house there is a double bed in each room, and guests share the living room, terrace and a communal bathroom with cold water. The bungalows each have a double bed and a single bed, a kitchen, and private bathroom with cold water. The Marquesan style meals are eaten with the family under a *fare pote'e* shelter overlooking the black sand beach and ocean. Owner John Ozanne Rohi speaks English and is very friendly. His wife takes care of the pension and he and his sons take care of their boats. They can take you fishing or on excursions to visit other islands.

PENSION CHEZ MARIE-ANTOINETTE, *Puamau, Hiva Oa 98741, Marquesas Islands. Tel./Fax 689/92.72.27; cell 70.92.24. Rates: Room with MAP 5.830 CFP per person; room with AP 7.000 CFP per person per day; half price for child under 10 years. Add taxes. No credit cards.*

This pension is in the valley of Puamau, on the northeast coast of Hiva Oa, 40 km. (25 mi.) from the airport and 3.5 km. (2.2 mi.) from the quay in Puamau. It is on the right hand side of the road that leads to the I'ipona or Oipona archaeological site with the 5 big tikis. There are 2 simply furnished rooms in the home of the former mayor, Bernard "Vohi" Heitaa, with a double and a single bed in each room. The bathroom with hot water is shared, as well as the living room and dining room. Marie-Antoinette cooks the local style meals. She also has a big yard with lots of noni trees and other kinds of fruit trees and flowers. She serves lunch for 2.000 CFP per person to those who stop here during day excursions to Puamau valley. Reserve in advance.

According to Marie-Antoinette, the tomb of Vehine Tetoiani, the last queen of Puamau valley, is also located on her property in the **Tohua Pehe Kua.** Although the queen was given a Christian burial when she died in 1926, two *ti'i* statues were placed beside her tomb. Those tikis are now beside the road.

Other accommodations include: **Bungalows Fa'e Isa,** *Tel./Fax 689/92.73.33,* owned by Aline Saucourt. She has 2 bungalows for rent by the day, week or month, which contain a double bed, equipped kitchen and bathroom with hot water, with a view of the mountain and Atuona village. Rates are 4.000 CFP sgl/, 5.000 CFP dbl; Weekly rates are 30.000 dbl. and monthly rates are 80.000 CFP for 1-2 people. No credit cards.

Communal Bungalows of Atuona, *Tel. 689/92.73.32; Fax 689/92.74.95; commune@commune-hivaoa.pf.* Claire and René Terme take care of the town hall's bungalows that are located in Atuona village, 200 m. from the beach. These units have beds, kitchenette and bathroom and are rented by the day for 3.000 CFP sgl, 2.500 CFP per person dbl., and 1.000 CFP for each additional person. Monthly rates are 50.000 CFP for 2 occupants and 70.000 CFP for 4 people, including electricity but no hotel services. No credit cards.

WHERE TO EAT

HANAKEE HIVA OA PEARL LODGE, *Tel. 92.75.87. Open daily for BLD. All major credit cards.*

An American breakfast is 2.300 CFP; the set luncheon menu is 3.200 CFP and the set dinner menu is 5.600 CFP. The chef's specialties include fresh fish and locally caught seafood. You can sit on the terrace overlooking the bay and listen to Jacques Brel music during Happy Hour, which is held at the bar every Fri. evening. There is a Marquesan dance show on special evenings.

HOA NUI, *in Atuona village, Tel. 92.73.63. No credit cards. Reserve.*

This is where the *Aranui* passengers eat when they visit Atuona. They get to enjoy Marquesan feasts of roast pork, curried goat, fresh river shrimp, smoked red chicken, *fafa poulet*, macaroni fritters, fried breadfruit, banana *po'e* and other delicious treats. Lunch or dinner costs around 2.300 CFP.

TEMETIU VILLAGE, *Tel. 92.73.02. BLD. Reservations are necessary. AE, MC, V.*

Meals are served on their terrace overlooking Tahauku and Taaoa bays. Breakfast is 1.060 CFP and lunch or dinner costs 2.970 CFP. Lobster and shrimp specialties are featured, along with goat in coconut milk and other Marquesan foods.

SNACK KAUPE, *Tel. 92.70.62, adjacent to Magasin Gauguin in the center of Atuona village. Open during the day Tues.-Sun. and for dinner on Fri.-Sat. No credit cards.*

Besides pizzas, Chinese dishes and fish, you can order spicy specialties from Réunion Island to eat there or to take away. Prices vary from 1.100-1.650 CFP per dish. Interested yachties should ask the manager, who speaks some English, about the laundry service they provide for cruising yachts.

SNACK MAKE MAKE, Tel. 92.74.26, on the mountainside in the center of Atuona village. Open Mon.-Fri. 8am-2pm and 6-8pm. Open Sat 8am-2pm. Closed Sat. night and all day Sun. No credit cards.

The Chinese owners still serve hamburgers for 600 CFP, but they specialize in Chinese dishes priced from 1.200-2.000 CFP.

SEEING THE SIGHTS

In the center of Atuona you can visit the Paul Gauguin Museum and Maison du Jouir in the Gauguin Center, Jacques Brel Cultural Center, Traditional Arts House, arts and crafts center and the sacred site of Tohua Pepeu, which was restored for the 1991 Marquesas Festival of Arts and used again as a stage during the 2003 Marquesas Festival of Arts. In Calvary Cemetery behind Atuona village you can visit the graves of French artist Paul Gauguin and Belgian singer Jacques Brel. The tourist office erected a stele or memorial to Brel in 1993 on a piece of open ground a few km. east of Atuona, overlooking the Hanakee Hiva Oa Pearl Lodge. This can be visited by 4WD, horseback, or on foot.

Sightseeing highlights away from Atuona include a visit to **Puamau Valley** to see the giant tikis at the **I'ipona** (or Oipona) archaeological site; the tiki and *paepae* platforms of **Taaoa Valley**; the petroglyphs on the **Tehueto** site in the **Faakua Valley**; the **Moe One tiki** in **Hanapaaoa Valley**; and the *paepae* and pretty little village of **Hanaiapa Valley,** where you can visit wood carvers' workshops and watch the surfers riding the waves in this recently discovered surf spot.

Land Tours & 4x4 Safari Excursions

Gabriel Heitaa of Temetiu Village, *Tel. 91.70.60/70.01.71/70.72.07; heitaagabyfeli@mail.pf.* Gaby leads guided 4x4 excursions to Puamau. The 2 1/2-hour ride to Puamau is a one-way distance of 48 km. (30 mi.). You will be taken to visit the famous tikis, the queen's grave, and return by way of Jacques Brel's stele. This is an all-day trip and you can include lunch for 2.000 CFP per person. You'll pay an entry fee of 200 CFP at the archaeological site of Oipona. Another excursion takes you to the restored archaeological site of Taaoa. This is a distance of 7 km. (4.4 mi.) and a 15-20 min. ride from Atuona. You can also visit the village of Hanaiapa, where you can buy tapa bark paintings and woodcarvings.

André Teissier at Pension Gauguin, *Tel. 92.73.51*, leads excursions to the historical sites in Hiva Oa.

Marie Thérèse Tehaamoana Deligny, *Tel. 92.71.59/72.80.70*, can take up to 4 passengers in an a/c 4x4 vehicle to visit the archaeological sites.

Frida Peterano, *Tel. 92.79.66/70.72.02*, is an English-speaking guide who will show you the highlights of Hiva Oa by 4WD.

SPORTS & RECREATION

Hiking

Moana O Te Manu Excursions, *Tel./Fax 92.74.44 (Atuona), Tel. 92.75.68 (Hanaiapa), cell 24.64.58/23.68.90.* Henry Bonno is a professional Marquesan guide who can take you around the island by foot or 4WD to Taaoa, Puamau, and Hanaiapa. He also organizes camping trips on request.

Hiva Oa Trek, *Tel. 20.40.90.* Alain Tricas is a professional guide who can suggest a choice of hiking trails, especially to explore the Taaoa valley, which is rich in archaeological sites. To hike Taaoa, Tehueto and the old cemetery, he charges 1.000 CFP per hr.

Horseback Riding

Hamau Ranch, *Tel./Fax 92.70.57, cell 28.68.21.* Lucien "Pako" Pautehea, leads "green tourism" expeditions by horseback to explore any of the dozen trails he knows, starting from Atuona. He is a nature lover and enjoys sharing his knowledge of the Marquesan fauna and flora with small groups of 3-4 riders. He uses 15 different trails for his rides, according to the riding level of his clients. You can ride by the hour, half day or all day, and hunting rides can also be organized. Free transfers provided from your hotel or pension.

Etienne Heitaa, *Tel. 92.75.28,* has Marquesan horses for rent in Puamau, with a guide if requested.

Boat Excursions & Deep Sea Fishing

Te Hinaonaiki is a 36-ft. bonito boat owned by Médéric Kaimuko, *Tel. 92.76.97.* Picnic excursions to Hapatoni or Vaitahu on Tahuata are 30.000 CFP for 8 passengers, and a trip to Fatu Hiva is 65.000 CFP for 8 passengers.

Vaipuna O Hanamenu, *Tel. 92.76.57/70.71.97/78.82.98,* is a 12-m. (39-ft.) bonito fishing boat owned by Leo Rohi of Atuona that can accommodate 8 passengers. He charges 20.000 CFP for a round-trip from Atuona to Vaitahu on Tahuata and return, and 25.000 CFP for an outing that also includes Hapatoni. A round-trip to Fatu Hiva is 50.000 CFP plus 10.000 CFP to spend the night. Deep-sea fishing and picnics on request.

Scuba Diving

SubAtuona Plongée, *Tel./Fax 92.70.88, cell 27.05.24; eric.lelyonnais@wanadoo.fr.* Hiva Oa's scuba diving center is headed by Frenchman Eric Le Lyonnais, a BEES1 monitor. He charges 6.000 CFP for one dive and 11.000 CFP for a 2-tank dive. He can take 4-8 people on all-day outings in his 9.5 m. (31-ft.) bonito boat **Te Pua O Te Tai,** for a picnic on the white sand beaches of Tahuata, with a dive included on request. The excursion and picnic are 9.500 CFP per person, and 13.000 CFP including a dive. The outing without meal or dive is 7.500 CFP.

SHOPPING

One of several arts and crafts centers in Atuona is adjacent to the Gauguin Museum and a very good handcraft shop and boutique is across the road. You can buy tee shirts with Marquesan designs, hand-painted pareos, *monoi* oil made with sandalwood and a thousand flowers, and *mille fleurs* honey. Artisan shops are also located in Puamau and Taaoa.

Marquesas Creation, *Tel. 92.70.77,* is operated by Stéphanie Citeau and Jean-Baptiste Gueldry and is adjacent to Tohua Pepeu in the center of the village. They sell Marquesan shirts, pareos, T-shirts, tapa, sculpted wood and stone, and Marquesan seed necklaces. The **Atuona Artisans Association** is headed by Aline Saucourt, *Tel. 92.73.33*, and is located on the western side of Tohua Pepeu. **Jean and Nadine Oberlin**, *Tel. 92.76.34*, have the small boutique at the airport and they also exhibit their oil paintings, tapas, engraved gourds and other arts and crafts in Atuona village whenever a passenger ship is in port. **Curios Vaiaka**, *Tel. 92.74.03/ 26.68.02*, is owned by Simone Teriivahine, who sells jewelry and specializes in hand painted sheets.

If you want to buy woodcarvings you can visit the sculptors at their home workshops. The Atuona artisans include: **Jean-Marie Otomimi**, *Tel. 92.76.55*, who carves wood sculptures; **Gilbert "Tuarai" Peterano**, *Tel. 92.70.64*, who carves on wood, stone and bone; **Fernand Tetuaveroa**, *Tel. 92.74.07*, who carves stone "penu" pestles; and **Maurice "Mori" Poevai**, who lives close to the *me'ae* Poevau in Puamau, and carves wood sculptures.

TATTOOS
Tuarae Peterano, *Tel. 92.70.64*; **Santos Nazario**, *Tel. 92.70.11*;

PRACTICAL INFORMATION
Banks
Banque Socredo, *Tel. 92.73.54*, has a branch on the main street in Atuona, next to the Air Tahiti office. Business hours are Mon., Tues., Thurs. and Fri. 7:30-11:30am, and 1:30-4pm, Wed. 7:30-11:30am.

Hospitals
There's a government-operated infirmary in Atuona, *Tel. 92.73.75*, a dental center, *Tel. 92.78.17*, an infirmary in Puamau, *Tel. 92.74.96*, and first aid stations in Nahoe and Hanapaaoa.

Information
Hiva Oa Tourism Committee, *Tel. 92.78.93; comtourismhiva@yahoo.fr* is located in a small building in front of the Paul Gauguin Center in the village of Atuona. There is also an annex office at the boat dock when ships arrive. Georges Gramot of Relais Moehau is the president.

Ernest Teapuaoteani works for the Mairie (town hall) of Atuona, *Tel. 92.73.32*, and he is a good source of information on Marquesan culture, dance and history. He speaks English.

Internet
Cyber Services, *Tel./Fax 92.79.85, cell 23.22.47, VHF 11; cyber-services@mail.pf* is one of the activities headed by Sandra Wullaert in Atuona. She has Wifi Internet access. She is also the local agent of Polynesia Yacht Services.

Laundry

Sandra Wullaert, *Tel./Fax 92.79.85, cell 23.22.47, VHF 11; cyberservices@mail.pf.* She charges 250 CFP per kilogram to wash your clothes, and for 400 CFP a kilo she will wash, dry and fold your laundry.

Police

The French *gendarmerie* has a brigade in the center of Atuona, *Tel. 92.73.61.*

Post Office & Telecommunications Office

The post office is located adjacent to the town hall (*mairie*) in the center of Atuona village, *Tel. 92.73.50.* It is open Mon.-Thurs. from 7:30-11:30am and from 1:30-4:30pm, and on Fri. until 3:30pm; on Sat. it is open from 7:30-8:30am.

TAHUATA

Tahuata has the only coral gardens in the Marquesas and the prettiest white sand beaches. There is no airport, although plans are underway to construct a runway. Nor is there any helicopter service, but you can easily reach Tahuata by boat from Hiva Oa, which is just an hour's ride across the Bordelais Channel. This is a popular port-of-call for cruising yachts that drop anchor in coves with beautiful secluded beaches accessible only by boat. The *Aranui* passengers enjoy visiting the friendly little village of Hapatoni and playing on the beach at Hanemoenoe whenever the ship stops there.

Tahuata is the smallest populated island in the Marquesas archipelago, with only 50 sq. km. (19 sq. mi.) of land. A central mountain range crowns the crescent shaped island, reaching 1,040 m. (3,465 ft.) into the ocean sky.

It was in Tahuata's Vaitahu Bay that Alvaro de Mendaña's expedition of 4 caravels anchored in 1595. He named the island group *Las Marquesas de Garcia de Mendoza de Canete*, in honor of the wife of Peru's viceroy. The Spanish explorer came ashore at Vaitahu Bay, which he named *Madre de Dios*, Mother of God. It was here that the first crosses were raised and mass was held. When the Spanish-Peruvian ships set sail, 200 inhabitants lay massacred on the beach.

Following Captain James Cook's visit in 1774, Vaitahu's harbor was named Resolution Bay. When the first Protestant missionaries came in 1797, the generous local chief left his wife with missionary John Harris, with instructions that he should treat her as his own wife. Harris fled when the wife and 5 of her women friends visited his room.

The French took possession of the Marquesas in Vaitahu, establishing a garrison at Fort Halley in 1842. Monuments, ruins and graves of the French soldiers killed during the skirmishes can be seen in Vaitahu, but no indication is given to the Marquesans who lost their lives. The Catholic missionaries chose Tahuata as the site of their first Marquesan church. The Catholic Church that stands today in Vaitahu was built in 1988 with funds from the Vatican. It has a stained-glass window depicting a Marquesan Madonna, plus carvings from the wood sculptors.

Although Tahuata's past has been violent and grim, the 706 inhabitants live a quiet life today, working peacefully in their verdant valleys, raising livestock and making copra. The rich waters surrounding the island attract an amazing variety of fish, sharks and even whales.

Boat day in Tahuata's small villages is a main event when a ship arrives with food and supplies. Getting ashore in Hapatoni has always been dangerous, and this process is now easier with the addition of a jetty that was built to protect the enlarged concrete quay so that the new communal boat can dock here. The 60 residents of Hapatoni are especially welcoming. The seafront road is made almost entirely of ancient paved stones and is shaded by the sacred *tamanu* trees.

ARRIVALS & DEPARTURES

Arriving By Boat

The *Aranui 3* includes stops at Vaitahu and Hapatoni during its 14-day round-trip cruise program from Tahiti to the Marquesas. See details in section on *Inter-Island Cruise Ships and Cargo/Passenger Boats* in Chapter 6, *Planning Your Trip*.

The 48.6-ft. long *Tahuata Nui* is an aluminum hull boat operated by the Commune of Tahuata that transports 60 passengers between Atuona and Tahuata. The boat leaves the quay of Atuona at 12pm each Mon. for Vaitahu, and each Fri. the boat leaves Atuona at 12pm for Vaitahu and Hapatoni. The one-way fare is 1.000 CFP. Reserve at the Mairie of Tahuata, *Tel. 689/92.92.19; Fax 689/92.92.10*.

Philippe Tetahiotupa, *Tel. 92.92.65*, has a 5-passenger boat *Tehaumate* that makes private transfers between Atuona and Vaitahu. The round-trip fare is 22.000 CFP for the boat. **Louis Timau**, *Tel. 92.93.19*, charges 15.000 CFP for a round-trip for up to 6 passengers between Atuona and Tahauta. **Hervé Barsinas**, *Tel. 20.35.43*, charges 15.000 CFP for 4-5 passengers for inter-island transfers. **Frédéric Timau**, *Tel. 92.92.28*, charges 18.000 CFP for his boat.

Departing By Boat

Tahuata Nui, *Tel. 92.92.19*, is Tahuata's communal boat that leaves Vaitahu each Mon. and Fri. at 6:30am for Atuona. The boat stops at Hapatoni village each Fri. enroute to Hiva Oa. The one-way fare is 1.000 CFP and reservations are a must. See information above under *Arriving by Boat* for private boat transfers.

ORIENTATION

You can walk from the boat landing to the small village of **Vaitahu**. **Hapatoni** is just a 10-min. boat ride from Vaitahu, or you can take the road between the 2 villages. The **Valley of Hanatehau** is a 30-min. horse ride from Hapatoni. A track joins Vaitahu and **Motopu** in the northeast, a distance of about 17 km., which is ideal for riders. **Hanatetena** was formerly approachable only by boat and getting ashore through the turbulent surf is a dangerous maneuver. A road is under construction to connect this small valley with Hapatoni, Motopu and Vaitahu.

WHERE TO STAY & EAT
PENSION AMATEA, *Vaitahu, Tahuata 98743, Marquesas Islands. Tel./Fax 689/92.92.84, cell 76.24.90/29.37.49. Located in the center of Vaitahu village, with access to the sea. Free transfers from quay. Rates: Room only 4.000 CFP; breakfast 1.000 CFP, lunch or dinner 2.500 CFP. Add taxes. No credit cards.*

There are 4 rooms in a big white concrete house owned by Marguerite Kokauani and her husband, François. Each room contains a double bed and guests share 2 bathrooms with cold water shower, as well as the living room, dining room and terrace. The beach is close by and you can easily walk around the village from here. Land and sea activities are also available on request. They provide round-trip transfers between Vaitahu and Hapatoni for 12.000 CFP, and to visit Motopu for 15.000 CFP

SEEING THE SIGHTS
Vaitahu is the main village, and the small museum **Haina Kakiu** is located in the *mairie* (town hall), which contains exhibits, photos and illustrations of an archaeological site excavated in Hanamiai. **Monuments** in Vaitahu commemorate the 400th anniversary of the Spanish discovery of the Marquesas Islands; the 150th anniversary of **Iotete**, the first Marquesan chief; French Admiral Dupetit-Thouars; and the French-Marquesan battle of 1842. There are also the remains of a French fort and the graves of French sailors.

The big **Meipe Eia** in Hapatoni was renovated by the youths from the village. **Petroglyphs** can be found in the Hanatu'una valley, which can be reached by boat or horseback from Hapatoni. There are also stone **petroglyphs** in Hanatehau and **archaeological sites** in Vaitahu valley.

In front of the **Notre Dame de l'Enfant Jesus Catholic Church** in Vaitahu is a wooden statue of the *Virgin with Child* that is nearly 4 m. (13 ft.) tall. This beautiful work of art was carved by **Damien Haturau** of Nuku Hiva, whose Christ child is holding an *uru* (breadfruit) as an offering.

SHOPPING
A specialty of Tahuata is the fragrant *monoi* oil made from coconuts, herbs and flowers, sandalwood, pineapple and other aromatic plants. You will also enjoy the smoke flavored dried bananas wrapped in leaves. Wood carvers have their workshops in the valleys of Vaitahu, Hapatoni, Hanatetena and Motopu.

One of the best bone carvers in the Marquesas is Teiki Barsinas, *Tel. 92.93.24*, who lives in Vaitahu. Other noted sculptors in Vaitahu are: Edwin Fii, *Tel. 92.93.04*; Felix Fii, *Tel. 92.92.14*, In Hapatoni contact Frédéric Timau, *Tel. 92.92.55*, Ernest Teikipupuni, *Tel. 92.92.51*, Paul Vaimaa, *Tel. 92.93.20*, Jules Timau, and Sébastien "Kehu" Barsinas, *Tel. 92.92.38*. Be sure to visit the handcrafts center in Hapatoni for woodcarvings.

Felix Barsinas in Vaitahu, *Tel. 92.93.23*, is one of the best tattoo artists in the Marquesas and passengers aboard the *Aranui 3* can arrange to get a tattoo during their time ashore, providing it doesn't take too long. Edwin and Felix Fii are also tattoo masters whose designs are very original.

FATU HIVA

The beautiful island of **Fatu Hiva** will show you the mysterious Marquesas you have dreamed of discovering. Deep within **Hanavave Bay** you may feel that you are inside a gigantic cathedral, a green mansion of moss and fern covered mountains, often encased in misty rain. White patches of goats and sheep look down from their green mansions above the quiet harbor. Nature's chiseled image of the Polynesian god Tiki is visible in the mountain formations, which may give inspiration to the talented sculptors of wood and stone. This is the famous Bay of Virgins, so named by Catholic missionaries, who said that the phallic shaped stone outcrops were formed as veiled virgins.

When the Spanish explorer Alvaro de Mendaña sighted the island of Fatu Hiva in 1595, he believed he had discovered Solomon's kingdom, complete with gold mines. He named the island La Magdalena and killed his first Polynesian on the shore of Omoa village.

The wild, spectacularly beautiful island of Fatu Hiva is the most remote, the furthest south and the wettest and greenest of the Marquesas Islands. Stretching 15 km. (9.3 mi.) long, a rugged mountain range is topped by Mt. Tauaouoho, at 960 m. (3,149 ft.), overlooking 80 sq. km. (31 sq. mi.) of land.

Fatu Hiva is about 70 km. (43 mi.) south of Hiva Oa, and can be reached by communal catamaran, private bonito boats or inter-island ships. Although government plans include building an airport here sometime in the future, the only approach is still by sea, and this view alone is worth a trip to the Marquesas Islands.

The jungle greenery begins at the edge of the sea, which is like blue glass after a rain. Narrow ravines, deep gorges and luxuriant valleys briefly open to view as your boat glides past, close to the sheer cliffs that plunge straight into the splashing surf.

Due to the abundant rain and rich, fertile soil, sweet and juicy citrus fruits fill the gardens. Large, tasty shrimp live in the rivers that rush through each valley and rock lobsters are plentiful in the submerged reefs offshore Omoa.

Fatu Hiva is a center of Marquesan crafts. In the villages you will see the women producing tapa cloth from the inner bark of mulberry, banyan or breadfruit trees. They hammer the bark on a log until the fibers adhere, and when it is dry they paint it with the old Marquesan designs like their ancestors wore as tattoos. Sculptors carve the semi-precious woods of rosewood, *tou* and sandalwood, as well as coconuts, basaltic stones and bones. They produce bowls, platters, small canoes, turtles, tiki statues and war clubs. You are welcome to visit their workshops at their homes.

A rare collection of ancient Marquesan woodcarvings can be viewed at a private museum in Omoa for a small entrance fee. You can rent a horse for a bareback ride into the valley, charter a motorized outrigger canoe to explore the coastline and line fish, swim in the rivers or open ocean, go shrimping or lobstering with the locals, and if you're really adventurous, you can join a Marquesan wild pig hunt.

Smoke flavored dried bananas are a specialty of the industrious people of **Omoa village**. Fatu Hiva's special bouquet is the *umu hei*—a delightful blend of sandalwood powder, spearmint, jasmine, ginger root, pineapple, vanilla, sweet basil, gardenia, pandanus fruit, ylang-ylang and other mysterious herbs. This seductive concoction is all tied together and worn around your neck or in your hair.

ARRIVALS & DEPARTURES
Arriving By Boat
The *Aranui* includes stops at Hanavave Bay and Omoa during its 14-day round-trip cruise program from Tahiti to the Marquesas. See details in Chapter 6, *Planning Your Trip*, section on Inter-Island Cruise Ships and Cargo/Passenger Boats.

Auona II is a locally built 51-ft. catamaran owned by the Commune of Omoa, *Tel. 92.80.23* that can transport 30 passengers. It used to be a big joke in Fatu Hiva that their boat spends more time on land than it does in the sea, due to so many repairs it has had to undergo. After a few years of doing without transportation to Hiva Oa, they are no longer laughing. The family pensions have closed because the tourists cannot get to the island. On the rare occasions when the *Auona II* is functioning normally, it leaves Atuona, Hiva Oa, each Wed. around 12pm for Fatu Hiva. The one-way fare is 4.000 CFP. You can also charter a boat in Atuona to visit Fatu Hiva. See information in *Hiva Oa* chapter.

Departing By Boat
The best advice is to leave on the boat that brought you here, unless you're staying a long time and have made other arrangements that you can count on. You can take the *Auona II* catamaran to Atuona from Omoa or Hanavave each Wed., which leaves Fatu Hiva around 4am. and costs 4.000 CFP per person. Reserve at the *mairie* in Omoa, *Tel. 92.80.23.*

Private boats can be rented in Omoa for transfers to Atuona. **Joel Coulon**, *Tel. 92.81.17*, can transport 4 passengers and the one-way fare is 40.000 CFP for the boat. **Xavier Gilmore**, *Tel. 92.81.38*, also charges 40.000 CFP for a one-way trip and 80.000 CFP for a round-trip to Atuona.

ORIENTATION
The 629 inhabitants of Fatu Hiva live in the villages of **Omoa** and **Hanavave**, which are separated by 5 km. (3 mi.) of sea. Omoa, in the south of the island, is a wide-open valley with a black sand beach lined with several outrigger canoes painted blue. Just behind the beach are a soccer field and a paved road that leads through the village past the little Catholic Church, which has a red roof and a lovely background of mountainous peaks and spires. Beautiful flower gardens, pamplemousse (grapefruit) trees, citrons and oranges, bananas and other tropical

fruit trees surround almost every house. This village is clean and the people are open and friendly. A spring-fed river runs through the village, bordered by ferns and flowers, and villagers say it is safe to swim in this water, as there are no pigpens beside the river.

Getting ashore in Omoa can be an adventure in itself, as the small boat landing is slippery. When the ocean is wild, as it often is, the whaleboat bobs up and down beside the pier and you have to time your jump with the crest of the waves.

A protective seawall has been built on the left bank of Hanavave Bay, which greatly facilitates the problem of getting ashore. The whaleboat discharges passengers at a concrete quay, where they are welcomed by the artisan group. The tourists are led to the arts and crafts center, where tables are covered with tapa cloth paintings, sculptures, monoi oil, dried bananas, seashells and other wares for sale.

A serpentine path winds over the mountains between Omoa and Hanavave, offering a 17-km. (10.5-mile) challenging hike and panoramic views through the curtains of rock. Majestic waterfalls are visible from the path deep inside **Vaie'enui Valley**. In Hanavave valley you should avoid swimming in the basin at the bottom of the waterfall, as it is polluted and you risk catching leptospirosis. Facilities include food stores, a post office, a town hall and primary schools in each village.

GETTING AROUND FATU HIVA
Car Rentals
Henri Tuieinui, *Tel. 92.80.23*, **Didier Gilmore**, *Tel. 92.80.86*, **Xavier Gilmore**, *Tel. 92.82.08*, **Roberto Maraetaata**, *Tel. 92.81.02*, and **Joseph Tetuanui**, *Tel. 92.80.09*, all have a 4WD vehicle they will use to drive you to Hanavave. Cars have to be rented with a chauffeur, as the roads are very rugged.

WHERE TO STAY
Economy
PENSION CHEZ LIONEL, *Omoa, Fatu Hiva 98740, Marquesas Islands. Tel./Fax 689/92.81.84. 2008 EP Rates: Room and breakfast 4.500 CFP sgl, 6.500 CFP dbl, 3rd person 1.500 CFP; Bungalow and breakfast 6.500 CFP sgl, 8.500 CFP dbl, 3rd person 2.000 CFP. Lunch or dinner 2.500 CFP. Free round-trip transfers from boat landing to pension. Add taxes. No credit cards.*

Tahiti Tourisme has given this pension a 1-Tiare rating. It is the last residence in the village, located beside a river 1.5 km. (.9 mile) from the quay. Lionel and Bernadette Cantois rent a room in the main house, which has a double bed and a single bed. As in many Polynesian homes, the walls do not go all the way to the ceiling. You share the bathroom with hot water and the living room with the family. A small bungalow next to the house has a double bed and a single bed, a fan, kitchenette and tiled bathroom with hot water. Two rooms can also be rented in their son's house on the premises, sharing the bathroom and kitchen. Meals are served on a big covered dining terrace in the main house. Lionel has a 4WD that he uses to take guests over the mountain road to Hanavave for 15.000 CFP. You can also include a picnic lunch on this excursion. He will also take you to visit Omoa valley where there are waterfalls, ancient paepae and petroglyphs. He also has a small boat and can take guests fishing. He can take you hunting by horseback if you stay 8 days. You can also take a refreshing bath in the spring-fed river that gurgles behind his house.

Note: All the other family pensions in Omoa are now closed because the communal boat is always broken down and there are no tourists to fill their rooms. The women are now working as artisans to make tapa and the men have become carvers.

WHERE TO EAT

Chez Lionel is also a public restaurant. There are two *magasin* stores in Omoa village that sell food supplies and cold beer, and there is also a *boulangerie* that bakes long *baguette* loaves of French bread. There are no snacks or restaurants.

SEEING THE SIGHTS

The most beautiful sight in Fatu Hiva is the **Bay of Virgins** in Hanavave, which is best seen from the sea. In Omoa a giant **petroglyph** featuring a huge fish and stick figures is engraved in a boulder at the edge of the village, and there are stone *paepae* house terraces in the valleys. A private collection of ancient Marquesan woodcarvings that belonged to former chief **Willie Grelet** are on display in a house owned by his grandchildren in Omoa. The **Catholic Church** in Omoa, with its red roof, white walls and rock fence, is one of the most picturesque scenes in any Marquesan village.

A 17-km. (10.5-mile) **hiking trail** will lead you across the rugged mountains between Omoa and Hanavave village. Walking alone in the mountains of Fatu Hiva is not recommended, even if you are an experienced hiker.

SPORTS & RECREATION

Horseback Riding

In Omoa village you can rent a Marquesan horse with a wooden saddle for daily excursions to Hanavave Bay or to ride around Omoa Valley. Contact Roberto Maraetaata, *Tel. 92.81.02*, or Isidore Mose, *Tel. 92.80.89*.

Boat Rental

You can rent an outrigger canoe with an engine and guide to get from Omoa to Hanavave Bay or vice-versa. Skimming across the incredibly blue water close to the untamed shore and gazing up at the rock formations and the wild cattle and goats staring down at you are moments to remember forever.

Lionel Cantois at Pension Lionel, *Tel. 92.81.84*, has a small boat he uses to take his guests fishing. Other rental boats: in Omoa contact Xavier Gilmore, *Tel. 92.81.38*, or his brother Napoléon. They have an aluminum speedboat. Joel Coulon, *Tel. 92.81.17*, has a locally made *poti marara* fishing boat, and Roberto

Maraetaata, *Tel. 92.81.02*, has a boat for hire. Jacques Tevenino, *Tel. 92.80.71*, Mathias Pavaouau, *Tel. 92.80.45*, also have boats. In Hanavave call Daniel Pavaouau, *Tel. 92.80.60*.

Deep Sea Fishing

The Marquesan men are experienced fishermen and you can arrange with your pension to accompany one of them. Most of the boats used for fishing are the outrigger speed canoes or *poti marara* wooden boats.

SHOPPING

Most of the women in Fatu Hiva make tapa bark paintings, which they sell in their arts and crafts center adjacent to the *mairie* (town hall). They also take or send their tapa creations to Papeete for arts and crafts exhibits. Appoline Tiaiho, *Tel. 92.80.66*, in Omoa village is one of the most noted tapa makers. When passengers from the *Aranui 3* or other ships visit the village, she demonstrates how the bark cloth is made. Marie-Noëlle Ehueinana, who also lives in Omoa, has won prizes for her tapa paintings.

Their *monoi* is a delightful blend of coconut oil, sandalwood, spearmint, jasmine, gingerroot, pineapple, sweet basil, gardenia, pandanus fruit, ylang-ylang and other mysterious herbs. This is used as perfume, for massages, to seduce a boyfriend or to ward off mosquitoes. Some of the men even consider drinking it. The women wear an *umu hei* bouquet of flowers and herbs in their hair or around their necks, which has an enticing aroma. Dried bananas are also a specialty here.

In the village of Hanavave the artisans have started displaying their tapa, carvings and other handcrafts on tables near the dock whenever a ship comes to call.

Fatu Hiva has several sculptors in both villages. They carve wood, stone, shell and even coconuts, creating lovely designs taken from the ancient Marquesan tattoos. There are at least a dozen sculptors in Omoa village and two or three in Hanavave. Some of the noted sculptors are: Stéphane Tuohe, *Tel. 92.81.87*, David Pavaouau, *Tel. 92.80.45*, and Marc Barsinas, *Tel. 92.80.44*.

PRACTICAL INFORMATION
Doctors

There is a government-operated **infirmary** in Omoa village, *Tel. 92.80.36*, and a **First Aid Station** (*Poste de Secours*) in Hanavave village, *Tel. 92.80.61*.

Post Office and Telecommunications Office

There is a **post office** in Omoa Village, *Tel. 92.83.74,* and in Hanavave, *Tel. 92.82.32*.

20. Austral Islands

In the Polynesian language the **Austral Islands** of French Polynesia are collectively known as *Tuhaa Pae*, referring to the 5 parts or islands that make up the archipelago. Folklore tells of Maui, the South Seas Superman, who fished up this chain of islands from the sea, using a magical fishhook that now forms the tail of Scorpio in the sky. This same hero is said to have cut away the great octopus that held the earth and the sky together, and he pushed up the sky so that people could walk upright. The arms of this octopus fell to the earth to form the Austral Islands, with Tubuai as its head.

Tane was a powerful god who used his many colored seashells to help separate the earth and sky, decorated the Austral heavens with twinkling stars, a golden sun and silvery moon, cool winds and billowing clouds. Ro'o, God of Agriculture and the Harvest, can be seen as a gilded rainbow and heard as the voice of thunder. Ruahatu-Tinirau, a Polynesian Neptune known as God of the Ocean and Lord of the Abyss, is said to have a man's body joined to a swordfish tail. Everyone knows that this powerful god lives in the reefs of Raivavae. And Tuivao, a fishing hero from Rurutu, sailed on the back of a whale to an enchanted island ruled by the goddess Tareparepa. Fleeing her spell Tuivao rode his whale to the island of Raivavae, where the mammal landed so hard on the beach that its imprint is still seen there today.

Past and present blend in harmony in the Austral Islands today. Islands of quiet beauty, peace and pride; these are Polynesia's Temperate Isles.

The Austral Islands include the high islands of **Rurutu**, **Tubuai**, **Rimatara**, **Raivavae** and **Rapa**, plus the low, uninhabited islands of **Maria** (or Hull) and the **Marotiri** (or Bass) **Rocks**. These islands lie on both sides of the Tropic of Capricorn, extending in a northwest-southeasterly direction across 1,280 km. (794 mi.) of ocean. They are part of a vast mountain range, an extension of the same submerged chain that comprises the Cook Islands 960 km (595 mi.) further to the northwest.

The 141 sq. km. (54 sq. mi.) of land surface in the Austral Islands is home to some 6,669 Polynesians, who live peaceful lives in their attractive villages, where their houses and churches are usually built of coral limestone or concrete. Due to the rich soil and the cooler climate of the Australs, good quality vegetables can be produced, including taro, manioc, potatoes, sweet potatoes, leeks, cabbage and coffee, as well as apples, peaches, figs and strawberries.

Archaeological diggings in these isolated islands have uncovered habitation sites, council platforms and *marae* temples in the village of Vitaria on Rurutu, showing man's presence around the year 900 A.D. Tubuai, Rimatara and Raivavae also have ruins of open-air *marae* stone temples, and giant sized stone *tikis* have

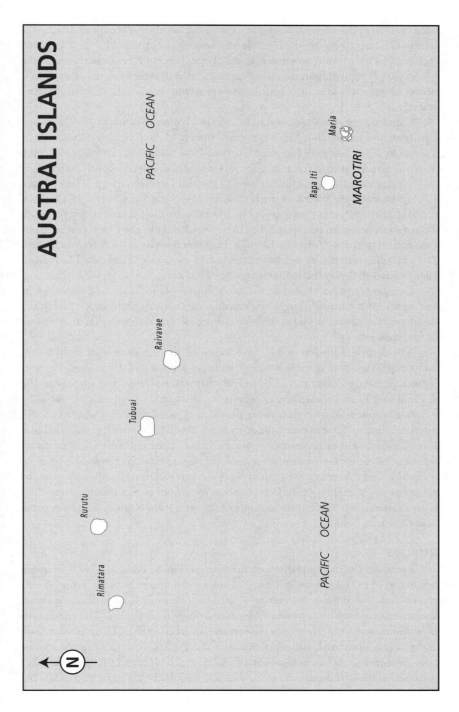

AUSTRAL ISLANDS

PACIFIC   OCEAN

Maria

Rapa Iti

MAROTIRI

Raivavae

Tubuai

Rurutu

Rimatara

PACIFIC   OCEAN

N

been found on Raivavae that resemble those in the Marquesas Islands and on Easter Island. On Rapa there are the remains of 7 famous *pa* fortresses on superimposed terraces that were found nowhere else in Polynesia except New Zealand where the Maori people settled. Exquisite woodcarvings, now in museums, tell of an artistic people highly evolved in their craft, who were also superb boat builders and daring seafarers.

Captain James Cook discovered Rurutu in 1769 and Tubuai in 1777. Fletcher Christian and his band of mutineers from the H. M. S. *Bounty* tried to settle in Tubuai in 1789, but were forced to flee the island because of skirmishes with the men of Tubuai. Spanish Captain Thomas Gayangos discovered lovely Raivavae in 1775 and remote Rapa was first sighted by English Captain George Vancouver in 1791. Rimatara, the lowest of the high islands, was not found until 1821, when Captain Samuel Pinder Henry of Tahiti arrived, returning the following year with 2 native teachers who converted the entire population to the Protestant religion. Evangelism still predominates, although there are now Mormon, Adventist, Sanito and Catholic churches, as well as Pentecost and Jehovah's Witnesses. The Austral Islands have all flown the French flag since 1901.

European and South American crews aboard whalers and sandalwood ships during the 19th century brought epidemic diseases to the islands, which practically decimated the strong, proud and highly cultured Polynesian race that once existed in the Australs.

The Austral Islanders today have many of the advantages of civilization, including electricity, potable water, telephone service and television. There is regular air service to Rurutu, Tubuai, Rimatara and Raivavae, and the *Tuhaa Pae II* cargo ship from Papeete brings supplies to all the islands on a regular basis.

Accommodations for visitors are provided in small pensions, where you will often eat, sleep and live in close proximity to the host family, which usually includes small children. Other guests may be people from Tahiti who are in the islands on business for the local government, school system or a church group. They may be technicians who have come to repair some broken machinery or bakery oven, or commercial representatives who take orders for school books and other supplies. Or it's just as likely you'll meet a couple of travelers from Norway who have come here to write a book.

RURUTU

Rurutu is the most northerly of the Austral Islands, lying at 22°27' Latitude South and 151°21' Longitude West, 572 km. (355 mi.) southwest of Tahiti. A very pretty island with a circumference of 30 km. (19 mi.), Rurutu is an upthrust limestone island with steep cliffs rising dramatically from the sea. The crannies in these bluffs were formerly used as shelters and burial chambers. There are also caves and grottoes decorated with stalactites and stalagmites. Rurutu's highest mountain, **Manureva**, reaches an elevation of 385 m. (1,263 ft.), and the coral reefs that surrounded the island eons ago are now raised *makatea* bluffs some 90 m. (300 ft.)

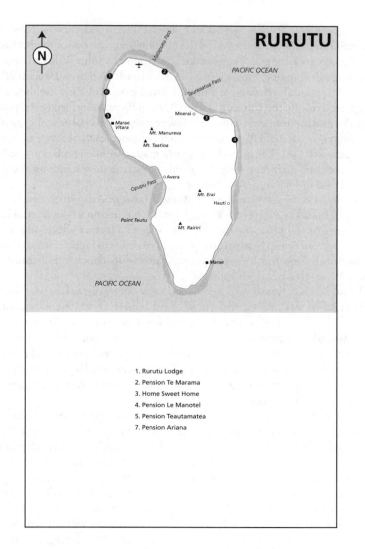

1. Rurutu Lodge
2. Pension Te Marama
3. Home Sweet Home
4. Pension Le Manotel
5. Pension Teautamatea
7. Pension Ariana

high above the sea. Rurutu does not have the wide lagoons found in the Society Islands or in Tubuai and Raivavae. Swimming and snorkeling are still possible in certain areas, however, and there are a few white sand beaches.

The original name of this island was *Eteroa*, which means a long measuring string. The current name of *Rurutu tu noa* is an old Polynesian saying that means a mast standing straight. *Manureva* (soaring bird) was formerly the name of one of Rurutu's famous sailing boats that carried produce between the islands. The men are still noted sailors, and several of them work aboard the inter-island cargo ships that serve as a lifeline between Tahiti and the remote islands of French Polynesia.

The people of Rurutu were also highly skilled wood carvers. Most of the ancient tiki statues were destroyed by the missionaries, and one of them, the statue of the Rurutu ancestor god A'a, was taken to London by John Williams, one of the pioneering missionaries. This original tiki, which is 45 in. tall and weighs 282 lbs., is in the Museum of Mankind in London, but 5 plaster of Paris molds of the A'a statue were made by the British Museum. One of them was willed to the people of Rurutu by an American man who died a few years ago. This statue is now on display in the Mairie in Moerai village. Christi's has evaluated each of the A'a tiki statues to be worth $50,000. A Rurutu dance group made a wooden replica of the A'a tiki for a Heiva performance in Tahiti and this big statue now stands as guardian in front of Pension Le Manotel in Moerai.

In the old village of **Vitaria** is the **Marae Taaroa** or Arii, which dates from the year 900. This is the oldest known site of man's habitation in the Austral Islands. Nearby is a council platform and 70 house sites of a former village and warriors' house. In ancient times the warriors of Rurutu were feared for their strength. Today they are admired for their industriousness, seamanship, dancing skills and physical beauty.

The 2,210 handsome, intelligent and industrious Polynesians who live in the 3 villages of Moerai, Avera and Hauti, have houses of white concrete or coral limestone, bordered by flower gardens and low fences of white limestone.

In the main village of **Moerai** there is a *gendarmerie*, a post office and infirmary, a bank, primary and junior high schools, a few small *magasin* stores, bakeries, snack bars and roulottes (mobile diners). Each village is dominated by a Maohi Protestant Church, with smaller buildings for the Catholic, Mormon, Adventist, Pentecostal and Jehovah's Witness faiths.

The men harvest their taro, potatoes, tapioca, sweet potatoes, cabbages, leeks and carrots. The women form artisan groups to weave specially grown fibers of *paeore* pandanus into attractive hats, bags and mats, which are sold both locally and in Tahiti. The people of Rurutu enjoy a pleasant communal spirit, working together, singing *himenes* in their churches, and pitching in to prepare a big feast.

A New Year's custom on Rurutu is to visit each house in the village, where you are sprinkled with talcum powder and eau de cologne before entering. Once inside the house, you can enjoy the refreshments and admire the women's nicest woven products and *tifaifai* bed covers and wall hangings. Also during the month of January the youth groups of the Protestant churches participate in a ritual called the *Tere*. A long caravan of flower-decorated pickup trucks, 4WD vehicles and motorcycles makes a tour of the island, stopping at each historical site, where one of the orators recites the legends of each significant stone or cave. One of the stops is on top of a mountain, where you have a lovely view of the village of Avera. Here is the Ofai Maramaiterai (intelligence that lightens the sky), which folklore claims is the center and origin of the island.

During the *Tere* circle island tour and also during the 2-week Heiva Festival in July the young men and women of each village prove themselves in a show of strength. Following a custom called *amoraa ofai*, unique to Rurutu, they attempt to lift huge volcanic stones to their shoulders. The village champions hoist one sacred stone that weighs 150 kgs. (330 lbs.). This accomplishment is followed by exuberant feasting and dancing.

Another big event in Rurutu, as well as in all the Austral Islands, takes place during the month of May, when the Protestant parishioners gather in their temples for a religious fête called Me. The "mamas" dress for this occasion in their white gowns and elaborate hats and blend their voices with those of the men to sing their *himenes* and to donate money to support the church's projects for the coming year.

Activities on Rurutu include horseback riding and hiking to waterfalls, where refreshing showers cascade into fern bordered pools. The limestone grottoes form a natural stage for cultural reenactment ceremonies and cinematographers from all parts of the world come here to film these natural formations. Circle island tours by 4WD wind over concrete or dirt roads into cool valleys where fields of wild miri (sweet basil) scent the breeze. Picnic lunches can be packed for these trips or to play in the sun on deserted white sand beaches. Humpback whales can be seen offshore Rurutu during the austral winter months of July-Oct., and observation platforms have been built across the bluffs overlooking the ocean at each end of Moerai village.

The aroma of pineapple mingles pleasantly with *ylang ylang*, Tiare Tahiti, wild *miri* basil and *avaro*, some of the fragrant flowers, fruits and spices that are used to make the welcoming leis you will smell as soon as you arrive on this island of fragrant perfumes.

ARRIVALS & DEPARTURES
Arriving By Air
Air Tahiti has a 1 1/2-hr. direct ATR flight from Tahiti to Rurutu each Mon., a Mon. flight that stops in Tubuai, a flight each Wed. with a stop in Rimatara, a Fri. flight with a stop in Rimatara, a Fri. flight that stops in Raivavae, and a Sun. flight with a stop in Tubuai. The one-way airfare from Tahiti to Rurutu is 19.100 CFP; from Tubuai to Rurutu the fare is 9.900 CFP; from Raivavae to Rurutu is 13.400 CFP, and from Rimatara it is 7.700 CFP. **Air Tahiti reservations:** Tahiti *Tel. 86.42.42; Rurutu Tel. 93.02.50;* Tubuai, *Tel. 93.22.75.*

You can also get to Rurutu by chartering an airplane in Tahiti from **Air Archipels**, *Tel. 81.30.30*; or **Air Tahiti**, *Tel. 86.42.42*.

Arriving By Boat
Tuhaa Pae II, *Tel. 41.36.06/41.36.16, Fax 42.06.09; snathp@mail.pf* makes 3 voyages a month from Tahiti to the Austral Islands, calling at Tubuai, Rimatara, Raivavae and Rurutu, then returning to Papeete. This itinerary changes according to the freight requirements of each voyage. The one-way fare to Rurutu is 3.817 CFP on the deck and 7.348 CFP for a berth in a cabin. Meals are extra. See further information in Chapter 6, *Planning Your Trip.*

Departing By Air
You can fly from Rurutu direct to Tahiti on Wed., Fri. and Sun. The Mon. flight stops in Rimatara and a Fri. flight stops in Tubuai. **Air Tahiti reservations** in Rurutu, *Tel. 93.02.50.*

Departing By Boat
The **Tuhaa Pae II** calls at Moerai village in Rurutu on its way back to Papeete or enroute to the other Austral Islands, according to the needs of the islanders. You can purchase your ticket on board the ship.

ORIENTATION
The oblong-shaped island of Rurutu is 10 km (6.2 mi.) long and 5.5 km (3.4 mi.) wide, or 36 sq. km (14 sq. mi.) in circumference. The main village of **Moerai** on the east coast is about four km (2.5 mi.) from the airport, connected by a paved road, which also extends to the village of **Hauti,** also on the east coast. Another concrete road links Moerai with **Avera**, a village 6 km (3.7 mi.) distant, located on the western coast. Avera has a small harbor for fishing boats, within the island's only real bay. The road around the island does not circle the coastline, but climbs up and down, from sea-level to almost 200 m (656 ft.), with panoramic views of white sand beaches and lagoons alternating with craggy cliffs and limestone caves and grottoes. The interior roads are bordered by fields of potatoes and taro and plantations of pandanus, bananas, coffee and noni. There are also several off-track dirt roads that can be explored by 4WD, horseback or on foot.

GETTING AROUND RURUTU
Car, Scooter & Bicycle Rentals
If you reserve a room at a family pension they will provide free round-trip transportation between the airport and their lodging. They charge for other transfers requested. **Rurutu Rent A Car,** *Tel. 93.02.80, Fax 93.02.81, pensiontemarama@mail.pf,* is located at Pension Temarama in Unaa, between the airport and Moerai village. Rentals start at 7.000 CFP for 8 hours for a small car, or you can pay more for a 4WD vehicle. Bicycles start at 1.100 CFP for 4 hours. Weekly and monthly rates are also possible.

WHERE TO STAY
RURUTU LODGE, *B.P. 87, Moerai, Rurutu 98753. Tel. 689/93.03.30/ 79.0901; Fax 94.02.15; www.rurutulodge.com. Beside lagoon in Unaa Vitaria, close to airport. 2008 High Season EP Rates: Standard Garden Room 5.000 CFP sgl, 4.000 CFP per person dbl/twin; Deluxe Garden Bungalow 9.750 CFP sgl, 8.435 CFP per person dbl; 8.285 CFP 2 twin beds; Deluxe Beach Bungalow 11.000 CFP sgl, 8.750 CFP per person dbl; 9.750 CFP 2 twin beds; extra bed 1.000 CFP. MAP and AP available. VAT included.*
This small 2-star hotel has 9 bungalows and is operated by Raie Manta Club,

the scuba diving center headquartered in Rangiroa. They have rebuilt the old Hotel Rurutu Village bungalows, providing 3 choices of accommodations. The simple standard rooms have a shower and the comfortable bungalows have a full-sized bath. The main building houses the reception, dining room and bar, library and dive shop. Among the tropical gardens is a fresh water swimming pool and there is a white sand beach in front of the property. Scuba diving is the main theme here, especially during the peak season of July-Oct., when the humpback whales come up from Antarctica to give birth and mate. Because there is no barrier reef, the whales come in close to shore, and it is easy to dive with them from a safe distance and have good visibility in the transparent water. Other activities include biking, hiking and horseback riding.

PENSION TE MARAMA, *B.P. 68, Moerai, Rurutu 98753. Tel. 689/ 93.02.80, Fax 689/93.02.81; cell 689/72.30.20; pensiontemarama@mail.pf. On mountainside in Unaa with access to the sea, 2 km (1.2 mi.) from the airport and 500 m (1,640 ft.) from the village of Moerai. Room 4.300/5.000 CFP sgl, 5.300/6.000 CFP dbl; MAP from 8.100 CFP sgl; 12.900 CFP dbl. Breakfast 800 CFP, Lunch 2.000 CFP, Dinner 3.000 CFP. Taxes not included. Free round-trip transfers between airport and pension. MC, V.*

This is a big two-story white house with 8 bedrooms located just outside the main village of Moerai. Each attractively decorated room has one or two double beds, a writing desk, ceiling fan, and a private bathroom with hot water shower. Daily maid service and clean towels. Each floor also has a living room with sofas, a television and bookshelves. A long, wide covered balcony outside the rooms overlooks the ocean, which is only about a block from the pension, and they have a swimming pool and Jacuzzi in their front yard. A bar and restaurant are on the ground floor, where well-prepared meals are served family style. Dinner is accompanied by a pitcher of red wine. Owners Tania and Landry Chong also operate Rurutu Rent A Car and they can arrange island tours, a special picnic, hiking excursions, horseback riding, fishing and diving expeditions.

PENSION LE MANOTEL, *B.P. 11, Moerai, Rurutu 98753. Tel./Fax 689/ 93.02.25, cell 689/71.74.77; manotel@mail.pf; www.lemanotel.com. On the mountainside, 6 km (3.7 mi.) from the airport and 2 km (1.2 mi.) from the boat dock in Moerai village. 2008 Rates: Bungalow with MAP 9.014 CFP sgl, 12.726 CFP dbl, bungalow with AP 11.136 CFP sgl, 16.968 CFP dbl, taxes included. Free round-trip transfers between airport and pension. MC, V.*

Hélène and Yves Gentilhomme have four wooden bungalows in a lovely garden of flowers and ferns, located in Peva, across the road from a long white sand beach that is shaded by tamanu trees. Each colorfully decorated unit has a double bed, a single bed, a fan and television, a private bathroom with hot water shower and a covered terrace with two lounge chairs. Meals are served in the restaurant and the water is potable.

Yves is president of the Rurutu Visitors Bureau and speaks a little English. He can provide land tours by 4WD and will take you to visit the grottoes, caves, beaches and blowhole, with or without lunch included. He can also put you in touch with a qualified hiking guide. Just across the road from Le Manotel you can easily see the humpback whales swimming close to shore during their visit each July through October.

PENSION TEAUTAMATEA, *B.P. 35, Moerai, Rurutu 98753. Tel. 689/ 93.02.93; Fax 689/93.02.92; pension.teautamatea@mail.pf; www.teautamatea.com. Across the road from the sea in Vitaria, 3 km (1.9 mi.) from the airport and 6 km (3.7 mi.) from Moerai quay. Room 4.600 CFP sgl, 6.200 CFP dbl; MAP 7.700 CFP sgl, 12.400 CFP dbl; AP 9.500 CFP sgl, 16.400 CFP dbl, including taxes. Breakfast 600 CFP, Lunch 2.000 CFP, Dinner 2.500 CFP. Free round-trip transfers between airport and pension. No credit cards.*

This modern house in Vitaria is situated in a magnificent coconut grove shading an archaeological site that includes a royal *marae*. There are five guest bedrooms with one or two double beds and wooden furniture built by the owner, Viriamu Teuraurii. The four private bathrooms and one communal bathroom all have hot water showers. A half-day excursion by 4WD vehicle is 4.000 CFP, and bicycles rent for 1.000 CFP a day. Viriamu also has rental horses. There is a pretty white sand beach here that faces the setting sun. Viriamu's sister, Darianne, takes care of the pension and cooks the meals. She speaks a little English.

Other Family Pensions:

PENSION ARIANA, *Tel. 689/94.06.69; Fax 689/94.07.14*, has 7 simple bungalows and a 4-bedroom house sloping down the hillside to the lagoon in Vitaria. She serves meals and has an arts and crafts counter. HOME SWEET HOME, *Tel. 689/77.76.87*, is a Bed and Breakfast that opened in Sept. 2007. The 3-bedroom house in Moerai overlooks the sea and is built like the bow of a ship. Owners Jean-Claude and Virginia are a young Polynesian couple who have even included a honeymoon suite that has a king size bed, bathtub, terrace and private entrance. Guests can cook their own meals or let Virginia cook for them.

WHERE TO EAT

Visitors usually take their meals in the pension where they are staying. If you wish to dine in another pension then you must reserve in advance.

The **Omiri Ferme** (Farm), *Tel. 94.02.39*, in Moerai, makes various kinds of goat cheese, yogurt and confitures, and on Fri. nights you can get pizzas and fresh homemade pasta to go. There are also a few snack bars and roulottes that are located near the schools and at the port in Moerai. Most of the Chinese food stores sell prepared dishes to go, and it's best to shop before noon. There are also 3 bakeries turning out fresh baguettes daily.

SEEING THE SIGHTS

Some of the interesting sites you will want to visit in Rurutu are the grottoes and *marae* temples of Vitaria, the Tetuanui Plateau and dam, the beautiful view of

Matotea between Vitaria and Avera, the Lookout Point at Taura'ma, where you can see the villages of Avera and Hauti, the Trou de Souffleur (spouting hole) and the beautiful white sand beaches of Naairoa, Narui and Peva, the Vairuauri Grotto at Paparai, and the Underwater Grotto of Te Ana Maro at Teava Nui.

You may also be interested in visiting the final resting-place of **Eric de Bisschop**, a French explorer who was noted for his ocean voyages in unseaworthy rafts. He died at Rakahanga in the Cook Islands in 1972, and is buried in the second cemetery of Moerai, off the main road, south of the village. All the pensions can provide a 4WD excursion to visit the highlights for about 4.500 CFP per person.

Hiking

Retii Mii, *Tel. 94.05.38*, is Rurutu's only trained hiking guide. He will take you on excursions that may include a visit to the Metuari'i domain on the north coast of the island. You can visit the Matonaa promontory overlooking Moerai village, and climb to the summits of Teape, Taatioe and Manureva mountains, which shouldn't present any major difficulty unless you are subject to vertigo. The Ana Aeo grotto in Vitaria resembles a baroque cathedral with its stalactites and stalagmites. President François Mitterand came here in 1990 when he was still president of France, and this grotto became a stage where the traditional songs and dances of Rurutu were performed. Following this visit the residents now calls this Mitterand Grotto. The Pito circuit covers the beautiful south end of the island, with its numerous beaches of white sand. You will climb plateaus and explore numerous grottoes, cross the cliffs and follow a road that takes you from Avera to Auti villages. The Peva circuit between the villages of Moerai and Auti is the shortest hike in distance, but the richest in various kinds of sites. This is where you will find the most beautiful grottoes on the island, complete with stalactites and stalagmites. The Varirepo grotto is comprised of two immense chambers with a ceiling that is 20 m high. One of the calcite formations is in the amazing shape of a giant sized *cocoro* (penis) that stands 2 m. high.

Horseback Riding

Viriamu Teuruarii at Pension Teautamatea in Vitaria, *Tel. 93.02.93*. You can ride a horse along the white sand beach for an hour for 2.500 CFP, and a half-day ride in the mountains is 5.000 CFP per person.

SPORTS & RECREATION

Boat Rentals, Sports Fishing and Whale-Watching Excursions

Rurutu Baleines Excursions, *Tel. 94.07.91/94.02.13, Cell 70.30.53/70.79.74; Fax 94.02.22; www.rurutubaleines.com. Princesse Inanui* is a 16-passenger Bertram fishing boat that is used for deep-sea fishing, excursions around the island, and for whale watching between the months of July and October. The captain and crew are all certified in first aid and life saving at sea.

Pierre Harua in Avera, *Tel. 94.06.36,* also has a boat for rent with a skipper.

Diving

Raie Manta Club Rurutu is based at the Rurutu Lodge, *Tel. 93,03.30/ 79.09.01.* and their main tourist season is from July-Oct., when the humpback whales (*Megaptera novaeangliae*) come up from the cold Antarctic waters. The calm waters and low predation in the warmer waters of the tropics allow the females to calve in peace after their 11-12 month gestation period. Two observation platforms have been built on either side of Moerai village to watch the humpback whales, which are easily sighted as the reef is close to the shore. The islanders say that when the orange flowers of the African tulip tree start to blossom this is a sure sign that the whales will arrive at any moment. Although the air temperature in Rurutu may drop to 15º C. (59º F.) in July-Aug., the ocean temperature doesn't get any cooler than 21-22º C. (70 to 72º F). Although more whales are sighted each year in Tahiti and Moorea, visitors from several countries make their reservations months in advance so that they can dive with the humpback whales in Rurutu because the water is so clear. Sept. is usually the best month.

SHOPPING

The "mamas" of Rurutu are noted for their finely made hats, baskets, tote bags, mats and other woven products. You can visit the arts and crafts shops in each village and you will also see the women sitting together on the grass or on their front terraces, creating an outlandish hat for them to wear to church or a beautiful traditional hat for you to buy. The Artisans Association has stands at the airport.

Taofe Tapiti, *Tel. 94.07.03*, is on the mountainside in Unaa, past the airport heading toward Vitaria. This is a small shop where you can learn how coffee is grown and ground and you can even taste the different coffees that are produced in the Austral Islands. Here you can buy coffee and confitures made in Rurutu. In some of the *magasins* you can also buy 500-gram (1 lb.) bags of Cafe Teautoa, which is 100% Arabica Cafe de Rurutu.

PRACTICAL INFORMATION
Banks

Banque Socredo, *Tel. 94.04.75*, has an agency in Moerai village, with an ATM distributor.

Doctors

There is a small medical center in Moerai, *Tel. 94.03.12*, and an infirmary in Avera village, *Tel. 94.03.21*.

Police

The French *gendarmerie* of Rurutu, *Tel. 93.02.05*, is located in Moerai.

Post Office

There is a Post Office and Telecommunications Center in Moerai, *Tel. 94.03.50*.

Tourist Bureau

Rurutu Visitors Bureau (Ano Mai Association) is at Le Manotel Pension in Moerai, *Tel. 93.02.25, Fax 93.02.26; rurututourisme@mail.pf; www.rurutu.info.* Yves Gentilhomme is president.

TUBUAI

Tubuai is 568 km (352 mi.) due south of Tahiti, located just above the Tropic of Capricorn in the center of the Austral Island group, offering a pleasant combination of the tropics and temperate zone.

This is the largest of the Austral Islands, with a land area of 45 sq. km. (17 sq. mi.) and a population of 2,216 inhabitants. An immense turquoise lagoon is bordered by brilliant white sand beaches and dotted by 7 palm shaded *motu* islets, surrounded by superb snorkeling grounds. From the village of Mahu the reef is 5 km. (3 mi.) from the shore. These shallow lagoon waters provide an ideal nursery for colorful and delicious tropical fish, clams, sea urchins and lobsters. There are 3 main passes and several smaller passes through the coral reef into the lagoon, and cargo ships can offload supplies at a concrete pier near Mataura village. This sheltered harbor is located close to the former site where Fort George was established by Fletcher Christian and his mutineers from the *H.M.S. Bounty* when they tried to settle on Tubuai in 1789. This was one of the most important events in the history of Tubuai, when the mutineers tried twice to live on the island, but were fought off by the unfriendly warriors of the island.

Captain James Cook discovered Tubuai in 1777 during his 3rd voyage to Tahiti, but he did not go ashore. The London Missionary Society sent native teachers to the island to convert souls to Christianity in 1822 and the Protestant faith is still predominant in Tubuai. The first Mormon missionary to settle in these islands arrived in Tubuai in 1844, and this religion is today an important part of the lifestyle.

Tubuai is the administrative center for the archipelago, and the main village of **Mataura** has the administrative offices, town hall, gendarmerie, small hospital, post office, schools and some of the churches. Chinese families operate the island's 5 grocery stores and 2 bakeries. Electricity and hot water are provided in the small bed and breakfast pensions, where you can also share lunch and dinner with the host family in their big dining room, or cook your own meals in a well-equipped kitchen. Activities can be arranged at your pension to visit the island by car or bicycle or to explore the motu islets and lagoon by boat. Hiking is popular here and can easily be accomplished without a guide.

Tubuai is a pretty island with gentle slopes and contours. It does not have the dramatic coastlines of Rurutu, Raivavae and Rapa, and the people here seem to lack the zestful spirit, the *joie de vivre* that you'll find on Rurutu. This is one of the few remaining islands in French Polynesia where the untreated tap water is still totally safe for consumption, even for babies.

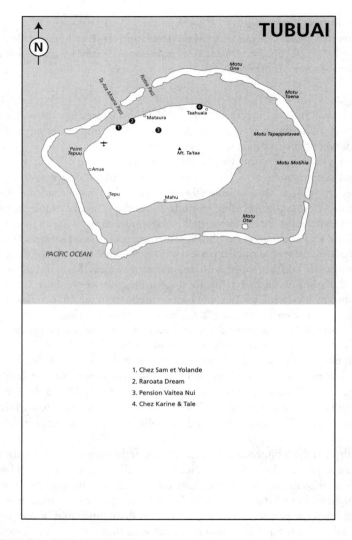

TUBUAI

N

Motu One

Motu Toena

Ta Ara Moena Pass

Roroa Pass

Mataura

Taahuaia

4

Motu Tapappatavae

Point Tepuu

Mt. Taitaa

Motu Motihia

Anua

Tepu

Mahu

Motu Otai

PACIFIC OCEAN

1. Chez Sam et Yolande
2. Raroata Dream
3. Pension Vaitea Nui
4. Chez Karine & Tale

ARRIVALS & DEPARTURES

Arriving By Air

Air Tahiti has a 1:40 hr. direct flight from Tahiti to Tubuai each Sun. and Mon. A Mon. and Wed. flight also stops in Raivavae, and the Fri. flight stops in Rurutu. The one-way airfare from Tahiti to Tubuai is 21.300 CFP; the fare from Rurutu to Tubuai is 9.900 CFP; and from Raivavae to Tubuai the one-way fare is 9.700 CFP. **Air Tahiti reservations:** Tahiti *Tel. 86.42.42;* Tubuai *Tel. 93.22.75.*

You can also get to Tubuai by chartering an airplane in Tahiti from **Air Archipels,** *Tel. 81.30.30*; or **Air Tahiti,** *Tel. 86.42.42.*

Arriving By Boat

    Tuhaa Pae II, *Tel.41.36.06, Fax 42.06.09; snathp@mail.pf* makes 3 voyages a month from Tahiti to the Austral Islands, calling at Tubuai, Rimatara, Raivavae and Rurutu, then returning to Papeete. This itinerary changes according to the freight requirements of each voyage. The one-way fare to Tubuai is 3.817 CFP on the deck and 7.348 CFP for a berth in a cabin. Meals are extra. See further information in Chapter 6, *Planning Your Trip.*

Departing By Air

    You can fly direct from Tubuai to Tahiti each Wed. and Fri. The Mon. departure from Tubuai makes a brief stop in Raivavae before returning to Tahiti and the Sun. flight stops in Rurutu on its way to Tahiti. More flights are added in July and August. **Air Tahiti reservations** in Tubuai, *Tel. 93.22.75.*

Departing By Boat

    The **Tuhaa Pae II** calls at Tubuai enroute to the other Austral Islands or on its way back to Papeete. You can purchase your ticket on board the ship.

ORIENTATION

    Tubuai is an oval shaped island with no indented bays. Two mountain ranges rise from the heart of the island, with **Mount Taitaa** the highest peak at 422 m (1,393 ft.) in altitude. A 24-km (15 mi.) paved road circles the island, connecting the quiet villages of **Mataura, Taahuaia** and **Mahu**. The airport is about 4 km (2.5 mi.) west of Mataura village and the ship wharf is on the east side of Mataura. Beside the pretty mint green Protestant church in the center of Mataura village a transversal road heads inland and crosses the island from Mataura to Mahu, passing through fertile plains and marshlands, where taro, potatoes, sweet potatoes and peaches grow alongside coffee, corn and oranges. The island is bordered by soft sandy beaches that range in color from white to rose and yellow to ochre, an artist's palette of at least 8 varying shades. Most of the houses are built on the mountain side of the road because of the high seas and strong winds during the winter months of July and August. Australian pine trees and hedges of white lilies are planted on the beach side of the road to serve as wind breaks.

GETTING AROUND TUBUAI

    You will be met at the airport or boat dock by someone from the pension where you've reserved accommodations. Check with your host for car and bicycle rentals. There is no public transportation system.

    Juliette, *Tel. 95.04.12,* rents cars and 4WD vehicles for 7.000-8.000 CFP for a 24-hr. period. **Tupua Center** rents bicycles.

WHERE TO STAY

    CHEZ SAM ET YOLANDE, *B.P. 23, Mataura, Tubuai, 98754. Tel./Fax*

689/95.05.52. On the mountainside in Mataura, 2 km (1.2 mi.) from the airport and 3 km (1.9 mi.) from the boat dock. MAP 8.268 CFP per person; AP 9.646 CFP per person, including taxes. Round-trip transfers 1.100 CFP per person. No credit cards.

This modern, clean and attractive 2-story concrete house has 5 guest rooms with comfortable beds, A/C or ceiling fans, private bathrooms and hot water showers. A big open terrace and balcony overlook the beach and lagoon across the road. Yolande takes care of the students' meals in the school in Mataura village and she is also active in the Mormon Church. During her absence her pension guests are looked after by her employees. The maid will wash your clothes for 500 CFP per machine load and you can rent a bicycle for 1.500 CFP per day. Circle island tours, boat excursions and picnics on the motu can also be arranged. This pension has an excellent reputation for its cuisine.

PENSION VAITEA NUI, *B.P. 141, Mataura, Tubuai, 98754. Tel. 689/ 93.22.40; Fax 689/93.22.42; bodinm@mail.pf; www.vaiteanui.com. Beside the cross-island transversal road in Mataura, 5 km (3 mi.) from the airport and a 10-min. walk inland from the circle island road in the heart of Mataura village. EP 3.500 CFP sgl/57.50 CFP dbl; MAP add 3.400 CFP; AP add 5.300 CFP per person, transfers and taxes included. No credit cards.*

This is a 5-room motel-like concrete structure in a big yard behind the Bodin family house. The simply furnished rooms are built very close to the kitchen, which can be noisy, and the walls are thin, but the rooms are clean, with screened windows, a double bed with a foam rubber mattress, and a private bathroom with hot water shower. Meals are served in the family style dining room. Heinui Bodin runs the pension, which is conveniently located near the post office, food stores, banks, hospital, pharmacy, churches and town hall. Guests have free use of the bicycles and other activities can be arranged.

CHEZ KARINE & TALE, *B.P. 34, Mataura, Tubuai, 98754. Tel. 689/ 93.23.40; Fax 689/93.23.41; charles@mail.pf. On mountainside in Taahuaia, 6 km (3.7 mi.) from the airport and 2 km (1.2 mi.) from Mataura quay. EP 5.000 CFP sgl/ 8.000 CFP dbl, plus taxes. Breakfast included. No lunch or dinner served. No credit cards.*

This cute little bungalow is across the road from a white sand beach, furnished with a double bed and 2 single beds, living room, kitchen, private bathroom with hot water shower, and a terrace facing the lagoon. The windows are screened and there is a ceiling fan, plus a TV and washing machine. Bicycles rent for 1.000 CFP per day.

Karine Tahuhuterani is an American woman from California who grew up in Tahiti and married her childhood sweetheart from Tubuai. She and Charlie (Tale) live next door to the bungalow, and she is the Air Tahiti agent in Tubuai.

RAROATA DREAM, *B.P. 27, Mataura, Tubuai 98754. Tel. 689/95.07.12/ 73.10.02; maletdoom@mail.pf. On the mountainside in Mataura, 2 km (1.2 mi.) from the airport and 3 km (1.9 mi.) from the boat dock. 2008 Rates: Room and breakfast 4.400 CFP per person; Room and MAP 6.600 CFP, including taxes. No credit cards.*

This Bed and Breakfast is owned by Wilson Doom, who is president of the Tubuai Visitors Bureau. He lives next door to Chez Sam and Yolande and has his own white sand beach across the road. He rents 2 rooms to guests, 1 of which is on the mezzanine. There is a double bed in the room and 2-3 mattresses can be placed on the mezzanine. Wilson leads 1/2-day historical/archaeological excursions for 2.500 CFP, 4WD excursions for 2.500 CFP per person, and picnics on the motu for 8.000 CFP per person. In-house guests get a discount on the picnic outing. See details in the Wind's Islands Program Australs (W.I.P.A) listed under *Sports & Recreation* below.

WHERE TO EAT

Guests usually take their meals in the pension where they are staying unless they can prepare their own meals. Should you wish to dine at another pension, please reserve in advance. Snack stands open and close according to what is happening on the island. **Libre Service Tien Hing** in Mataura village is the biggest food store, and each morning they sell casse-croûte baguettes and prepared dishes such as chow mein and other Chinese dishes to take away.

SEEING THE SIGHTS

Mount Taitaa is an attraction for hikers, who will enjoy the view from the summit, which is 422 m. (1,384 ft.) high. Your pension host will drop you off beside the track and it's an easy round-trip hike of 3 hrs. to get to the top. Other hiking trails are also interesting and easily reached. Your pension can arrange car tours around the island and you can also bike around.

SPORTS & RECREATION
Lagoon Excursions & Picnics on the Motu

Wind's Islands Program Australs (W.I.P.A) is operated by Wilson Doom, *Tel./Fax 95.07.12, Cell 73.10.02; maletdoom@mail.pf.* He provides island tours inside the lagoon aboard his 24-ft. motorboat, transfers to Motu One for a 2-3-hr. swim, and a 9am-4pm excursion that takes you around the island, with a local style picnic lunch on the motu. Wilson serves poisson cru, *pahua* (reef clams) and freshly grilled fish. This all-day outing is 8.000 CFP per person. He also has a kite surfing group and welcomes international kite surfers from many countries.

Scuba Diving

La Bonne Bouteille, *Tel/Fax 95.08.41, cell 74.90.97; labonnebouteille@mail.pf; www.labonnebouteilleplongee.com.* "The Good Bottle" is operated by Laurent Juan de Mendoza, originally from Nice, who is a BEES 1 sports educator instructor and Sea Guide. His boat is specially equipped for scuba divers and he has all the necessary diving equipment available in his center located at Mataura Quay. He teaches scuba diving and also has free-dive outings, as well as diving with the humpback whales between July and late October.

SHOPPING

An artisan center is located beside the old town hall in the main village of Mataura, selling woven hats, mats, bags, clothing, *pareos* and *tifaifai* bed covers. Handcrafts are also on display at the airport prior to Air Tahiti arrivals and departures.

PRACTICAL INFORMATION

Banks

Banque Socredo, *Tel. 95.04.86,* has an agency in Mataura village behind the Protestant church. **Banque de Tahiti**, *Tel. 95.03.63,* is in Mataura village.

Doctors

There is a medical center in Mataura, which serves all the Austral Islanders, *Tel. 93.22.50.*

Police

French *gendarmerie, Tel. 93.22.05.*

Post Office

There is a Post Office and Telecommunications Center in Mataura, *Tel. 95.03.50.*

Tourist Bureau

The **Tubuai Visitors Bureau**, *Tel./Fax 95.07.12, Cell 73.10.02; maletdoom@mail.pf,* is in Mataura, presided by Wilson Doom, who speaks English.

RIMATARA

Located 538 km (334 mi.) southwest of Tahiti and 150 km (93 mi.) west-south-west of Rurutu, the circular island of Rimatara is the smallest and lowest of the inhabited Austral Islands. The land surface is only 8 sq. km. (3 sq. mi.) and Mount Vahu is the highest peak at 83 m. (274 ft.). A narrow fringing reef hugs the uneven shore of the island and there is no lagoon.

Far removed from the beaten path of tourists and even cruising yachts, Rimatara has no sheltered boat harbor or dock, and no hotel. For some of the island's 797 inhabitants (Sept. 2007 census), who live in blissful isolation from the world's problems and turmoil, Rimatara is a joyful and tranquil refuge. Several of the young people, however, are slowly leaving their island for Tahiti, where they can find jobs and a livelier lifestyle. Since the opening of an airport in 2006, the islanders now have more freedom of travel, and visitors can more easily get to Rimatara.

When the *Tuhaa Pae II* anchors offshore **Rimatara** every few weeks to bring supplies, the passengers come ashore by whaleboat, surfing over the reef in turbulent waves that beat against the island's limestone cliffs. Upon landing on the beautiful white sand beach of Amaru the visitors are required to follow an old custom of the island and walk through a cloud of smoke to purify them before being welcomed ashore.

ARRIVALS & DEPARTURES

Arriving By Air

The Mon. flight from Tahiti to Rimatara stops in Tubuai and Rurutu and the Wed. and Fri. flights are direct. Airfares from Tahiti are 21.900 CFP one-way and 39.700 CFP round-trip; and from Rurutu to Rimatara the one-way fare is 7.700 CFP, and from Tubuai to Rimatara the fare is 15.900 CFP. **Air Tahiti reservations** in Tahiti, *Tel. 86.42.42.*

Arriving By Boat

Tuhaa Pae II, *Tel. 41.36.06, Fax 42.06.09; snathp@mail.pf* makes 3 voyages a month from Tahiti to the Austral Islands, calling at Tubuai, Rimatara, Raivavae and Rurutu, then returning to Papeete. This itinerary changes according to the freight requirements of each voyage. The one-way fare to Rimatara is 3.817 CFP on the deck, and 7.348 CFP for a berth in a cabin. Meals are extra. See further information in Chapter 6, *Planning Your Trip.*

Departing By Air

There is a direct flight from Rimatara to Tahiti on Mon.; the Wed. flight stops in Rurutu, and the Fri. flight stops in Rurutu and Tubuai.

Departing By Boat

The **Tuhaa Pae II** calls at Rimatara enroute to the other Austral Islands or on its way back to Papeete. You can purchase your ticket on board the ship.

ORIENTATION/WHERE TO STAY

Amaru is the principal village, with the town hall, *gendarmerie*, post office and infirmary, plus a school and a couple of stores. **Anapoto** and **Mutuaura** villages are reached by dirt roads. There is a severe water shortage during dry seasons. At publication time there were no pensions, guesthouses, bed and breakfasts, restaurants and bars or rental bicycles and cars on Rimatara. However, if you really want to stay here and can communicate in French or Tahitian, the Polynesian people will always find a place for you to sleep.

RAIVAVAE

Raivavae is one of the most exquisite islands in the South Pacific, rivaling even Bora Bora with its natural beauty. Fern covered Mount Hiro reaches 437 m. (1,442 ft.) into the mist of clouds. Sea birds soar around some 2 dozen picturesque islets that seem to float on the emerald lagoon protected by a distant coral reef. Beaches of soft white powdery sand surround these motus, forming graceful swirling patterns of lagoons within lagoons.

Located 632 km (392 mi.) southeast of Tahiti, this island of 16 sq. km (6 sq. mi.) remained aloof from the world of tourism until 2002, when the small airport opened, providing Air Tahiti connections to Papeete 2-3 times a week, depending on the season. Although the airport represents a giant step forward into modern times, tranquility still reigns on Raivavae, even in the 4 pretty villages of **Rairua**, **Mahanatoa**, **Anatonu** and **Vaiuru**. These neat and clean villages, with their pastel colored limestone houses, are home to the island's 940 inhabitants. The women of Raivavae compete with one another to see who can make the most original hat to wear to the Evangelical church services. Some of the decorations consist of plastic fruit, golf balls and even blinking lights.

Raivavae has long held the attention of anthropologists, archaeologists and biologists, who come here to study the people and their customs, the remains of stone temples and tiki statures or to make an inventory of the birds, snails and aquatic insects. These included J. Frank Stimson in 1917, Thor Heyerdahl in 1956

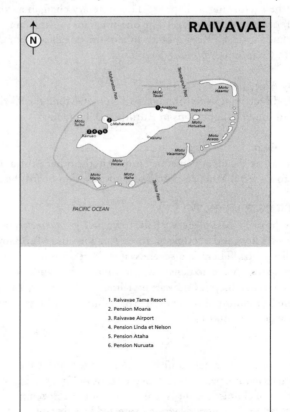

1. Raivavae Tama Resort
2. Pension Moana
3. Raivavae Airport
4. Pension Linda et Nelson
5. Pension Ataha
6. Pension Nuruata

and Donald Marshall in 1957. John Stokes of the Bishop Museum in Hawaii led an archaeological mission to Raivavae in 1921 to record the oral traditions and inventory the archaeological sites. The people agreed to loan 5 of their tikis to the Bishop Museum, which have never been returned. Thor Heyerdahl's expedition resulted in the loss of 7 more tikis that were carried away without permission of the local authorities and are now in the Museum of Oslo. 2 of the tikis from Raivavae were shipped to Tahiti in 1933 and are now standing on the grounds of the Paul Gauguin Museum in Tahiti. Chilean archaeologist Edmundo Edwards made an inventory of the sites in 1986 and 1991 on behalf of the Culture and Patrimony Service at the Museum of Tahiti and Her Islands and his findings are reported in his book published in September 2003: *Ra'ivavae: Archaeological Survey of Ra'ivavae, French Polynesia*. More than 600 archaeological structures have been found on Raivavae, including 80 marae still remaining. A short walk inland from the coastal road, just to the west of Mahanatoa village you can see Raivavae's only remaining tiki, which is 2 m. high. There are 20 tikis on Pomoavao marae, which is on the Matahariua land facing the airport, but these are incomplete fragments.

Raivavae's climate and fertile soil are ideal for growing crops of taro, potatoes, carrots, cabbages, coffee and citrus fruits. Sandalwood trees are also numerous on this island. There is a plentiful variety of seafood in the lagoon, including lobster, sea snails and tridacna clams. Due to a high level of ciguatera that affects the lagoon fish and clams, most of the family pensions serve only deep-sea fish at their tables.

ARRIVALS & DEPARTURES
Arriving By Air
Air Tahiti flies has a 1 hr. and 45-min. direct flight from Tahiti to Raivavae each Wed. and on Fri. There is also a flight each Mon. that stops in Rurutu and Tubuai. The one-way airfare from Tahiti to Raivavae is 23.900 CFP; the fare from Rurutu to Raivavae is 13.400 CFP, and from Tubuai to Raivavae it is 9.700 CFP. There is no flight between Raivavae and Rimatara. **Air Tahiti reservations:** *Tahiti Tel. 86.42.42/86.41.84; Raivavae Tel. 95.44.33.*

You can also get to Rurutu by chartering an airplane in Tahiti from **Air Archipels**, *Tel. 81.30.30*; or **Air Tahiti**, *Tel. 86.42.42.*

Arriving By Boat
Tuhaa Pae II, *Tel.41.36.06, Fax 42.06.09; snathp@mail.pf* makes 3 voyages a month from Tahiti to the Austral Islands, calling at Tubuai, Rimatara, Raivavae and Rurutu, then returning to Papeete. This itinerary changes according to the freight requirements of each voyage. The one-way fare to Raivavae is 5.502 CFP on the deck and 10.591 CFP for a berth in a cabin. Meals are extra. See further information in Chapter 6, *Planning Your Trip.*

Departing By Air
You can fly from Raivavae direct to Tahiti on Mon., and the Wed. flight stops

in Tubuai enroute to Tahiti. There is also a Fri. flight with stops in Tubuai and Rurutu. **Air Tahiti reservations** in Raivavae, *Tel. 95.44.33.*

Departing By Boat

The **Tuhaa Pae II** calls at Raivavae on its way back to Papeete or enroute to the other Austral Islands, according to the needs of the islanders. You can purchase your ticket on board the ship.

ORIENTATION

The island of Raivavae is 9 km. (5.6 mi.) long and 2 km. (1.2 mi.) wide. On the western shore of the island is Rairua village, where there is a port for cargo vessels, a *mairie* (town hall), small infirmary, post office, *gendarmerie*, primary school and a couple of old Chinese stores with a poor selection of supplies. A road, either concrete or dirt, connects the villages and a cross-island road provides a shortcut route over a mountain saddle from Rairua on the western side to Vaiuru on the southern coast. The airport is 6 km. (3.7 mi.) from the ship dock, built on a landfill between Rairua and Vaiuru.

Most of the houses are built on the mountain side of the coastal road and hedges of white spider lilies border the beach side to serve as a windbreak. Tall Australian pine trees also help to protect homes from the strong austral winds and big ocean swells that arrive during the winter months of July and August. Picturesque Protestant churches adorn each village, where the faithful parishioners gather several times a week to sing and pray.

GETTING AROUND RAIVAVAE

You will be met at the airport or boat dock by someone from the pension where you've reserved accommodations. There is no public transportation system on Raivavae and no taxi service outside the pensions. Check with your host for car and bicycle rentals or read information on *Where to Stay* in this chapter.

WHERE TO STAY & EAT

RAIVAVAE TAMA RESORT, *B.P. 17, Vaiuru, Raivavae 98750. Tel. 689/ 95.42.52/94.42.74 (evenings); Fax 689/95.42.52; raivavaetama@mail.pf; www. raivavaetama.com. Beside the sea in Anatonu village, 6 km (3.7 mi.) from the airport and 8 km (5 mi.) from the boat dock. 2008 Rates: MAP 8.500 CFP sgl, 15.000 CFP dbl; AP 10.000 CFP sgl, 18.000 CFP dbl, including taxes, transfers and bicycles. No credit cards.*

Emmy Teupoo White and her American husband, Dennis, have built 3 wooden bungalows overlooking the beach in Anatonu village, and plan to add 2 garden units. Each well-furnished bungalow has a double bed or two twin beds, mosquito nets, ceiling fan, TV, and a bathroom with hot water shower. There is also a sundeck where you can sit and watch the lagoon, or you can walk a few steps past a row of *aito* trees (Australian pines) and you are on a white sand beach. This is the only place on the island where you can stay beside the beach, and you are lulled to sleep at night by the gentle murmur of the waves.

Emmy's delicious and generous meals are served family style in their dining room or on the patio of the main house. She worked in the San Bernardino, California school system for 15 years, in nutrition, cafeteria and catering, before returning home to Raivavae in 2001. She was also president of the Friends of Tahiti association in California.

Fare Toa Angelique, a magasin store that is run by their daughter and son-in-law, is across the road from the bungalow, and besides being well stocked with supplies, provides fax service. A phone booth is on the corner and the Protestant church is just next door.

Emmy and Dennis will take you in one of their big 4WD's to visit the island and their 2 sons provide optional fishing trips and picnics on the motu. You will be able to visit the exquisitely lovely Motu Vaiamanu, which the residents of Raivavae call "la piscine", as it resembles a vast swimming pool. The Whites will also take you camping on Motu Ruahoa, where they will make a fire on the beach at night and you can sing under the stars. On request, Emmy will also drop you off at a motu all by yourself and bring you food every couple of days. Otherwise, you will have all the privacy you wish.

PENSION LINDA ET NELSON, *B.P. 45, Rairua, Raivavae 98750. Tel. 689/95.42.91; Fax 689/95.44.25; pensionlindanelson@yahoo.fr. Across the road from the lagoon in Rairua village, close to the airport. 2008 Rates: MAP 6.700 CFP sgl, 12.200 CFP dbl; AP 9.100 CFP sgl, 17.000 CFP dbl. Round-trip transfers and taxes included. No credit cards.*

Choices include a bungalow with private bathroom and ceiling fan in the garden and 4 rooms with a communal bathroom inside a big white concrete house. Double or twin beds can accommodate up to 3 people. Meals are served family style in the open sided dining room, which is covered by an immense roof and overlooks the beach across the road.

A circle island tour is offered guests free of charge. Paid activities include a visit to the archaeological sites, guided hiking excursions, and a picnic on the motu. The owners are now living in Maupiti, running Nelson's mother's pension, Fare Pa'eao, and Henriette Ruben is now in charge of the pension in Raivavae.

PENSION ATAHA, *B.P. 37, Rairua, Raivavae 98750. Tel./Fax 689/95.43.69. Across road from lagoon in Rairua village, 2.5 km (1.6 mi.) from the airport. 2008 Rates: Room and MAP 5.000 CFP per person; Room and AP 6.000 CFP per person. Cabin on Motu Rani 1.500 CFP per person. Round-trip airport or boat dock transfers included. Add taxes. No credit cards.*

Terani Tamaititahio and his wife Odile have 2 houses for guests. Ataha 1 is a one-story concrete house beside the road, with 2 bedrooms containing a double bed and fan, a shared bathroom with a very small bathtub and hot water, small living/dining area and an open terrace facing the lagoon. Ataha 2 is a new house containing 3 rooms, living room, dining room, shared bathroom and terrace. Local style meals are served, featuring tuna and mahi mahi. Guests can do their laundry in his washing machine for 1.000 CFP per load. He has 5 bicycles that he rents for 500 CFP for a half-day, and he charges 1.000 CFP per person for a cross-island tour by car. He has kayaks for guests located at Ataha 1 and also on Motu Rani, where Ataha 3 is located. This is a small cabin with no kitchen and no electricity. They will take you there by boat and you can buy a *casse croûte* sandwich and a bottle of water and spend the day by yourself on the motu. Or they will prepare a picnic for you.

Other Guest Lodgings

Pension Moana, Tel. 689/95.42.66, is a 3-bedroom concrete house with kitchen owned by Madame Haamoeura Teehu. Located on a private road near Mahanatoa village, between the airport and Rairua boat dock. Beach across road and food store nearby. 2008 Rates: EP Room 3.000 CFP sgl/5.000 dbl; Room and MAP 6.000 CFP per person; AP Room 8.500 CFP per person. Add taxes. No credit cards.

Pension Nuruata, Tel./Fax 689/95.42.83; cell 78.63.50. This is a new 2-story concrete house on the mountainside in Rairua near the airport, with 3 guest rooms, and 2 communal bathrooms with hot water. Free transfers and paid excursions to visit the island and lagoon. Rental car and bikes. 2008 Rates: Room and MAP 6.000 CFP sgl, 11.000 CFP dbl; Room and AP 8.500 CFP sgl, 15.000 CFP dbl. No credit cards.

SEEING THE SIGHTS

No matter where you stay in Raivavae your hosts can arrange for a circle island tour by 4WD and they can usually find someone with a boat who will take you to visit the fabulous motu islets on the southern and eastern parts of the reef. Do not miss going to Motu Vaiamanu, which the islanders call motu piscine. This is the most beautiful motu I have ever seen in all my island hopping days in the South Seas. You arrive by boat from the main island and step onto a perfect white sand beach of white powdery sand. Then you walk a few feet through the shady grove of ironwood trees (Australian pines) to the other side of the motu, and a breathtaking vision opens up before you that will make you very happy you brought your camera. This lagoon within a lagoon is even better than Blue Lagoon in Rangiroa. Miles of soft white sand beach mingle with the shallow water of the tides, which reflect the patterns of white clouds. You can walk across this swimming pool to another motu that is closer to the reef or you can follow the curve of the beach to the spot where the tridacna clams are still found in abundant plenty in knee-deep water. Unfortunately, 2007 studies have found that they have high levels of toxic ciguatera. You can picnic here or continue on to explore some of the other motus, and you can also camp out on many of these uninhabited islets.

Archaeological sites on the main island include the one remaining big stone tiki, in a clearing just west of Mahanatoa village, Marae Maunauto on the south coast, where there is the grave of a princess, and Marae Pomoavao, facing the airport. You'll need a guide to take you to Marae Poupou at Vai Otorani stream in the valley, a short walk inland from the transversal road. Many of the big slabs of volcanic stone are still standing around this immense structure. A private museum is operated by the Vavitu Association in the courtyard of the Vivi family home. This little bamboo structure has an exhibit of artifacts found around the island, including a rock that was supposedly used by a warrior from Mahanatoa to kill his enemy from Anatonu during a battle. There are also stones carved with petroglyphs and a stone tiki of a pregnant woman, as well as woven hats, purses, floor mats, hand embroidered fabrics, various seashell jewelry and a few sculptures. Entry is 300 CFP.

SHOPPING
Woven hats, bags and mats, as well as wood carvings are sold at the airport when Air Tahiti arrives. Handcrafts centers are located in Mahanatoa, Vaiuru, Rairua and Anatonu, but they are not open except for special occasions.

RAPA
Remote **Rapa** stands proudly alone 1,074 km. (666 mi.) southeast of Tahiti, below the tropical zone, where the temperature can drop to 5 degrees Celsius (41 degrees Fahrenheit) during the austral winter in July and August. Rapa-Iti, as the island is also called, has a strong cultural connection to Rapa-Nui, the Polynesian name for Easter Island. Archaeological ruins include strong *pa* fortresses built among volcanic pinnacles. **Mount Perehau**, the tallest of six peaks, reaches 650 m. (2,145 ft.) above the island, whose fjord-like coastline has 12 deeply indented bays. Several sugar loaf-shaped islets lie just offshore and there is no fringing reef in these cold waters. White puffs of sheep and wild goats perch on precipitous cliffs over the sea and bay, and herds of cattle roam the velvety green mountain ranges.

Rapa's 506 inhabitants live in **Haurei Village** and in the smaller village of Area, which is reached only by boat across Haurei Bay. There is a town hall, post office, infirmary, weather station and school. A cooperative store provides the villagers with basic supplies and many of the homes have television and telephone service. There is no airport in Rapa, and the *Tuhaa Pae II* supply ship docks in Haurei Bay every 6-8 weeks, the island's only regular connection to the outside world. This ship usually stays only a few hours at the dock before returning to Tahiti.

ARRIVALS & DEPARTURES
Tuhaa Pae II, *Tel. 41.36.06, Fax 42.06.09; snathp@mail.pf* calls at Rapa once every 2 months during its visits to the Austral Islands. The one-way fare from Tahiti to Rapa is 7.523 CFP on the deck, and 14.481 CFP for a berth in a cabin. Meals are extra. See further information in Chapter 6, *Planning Your Trip*.

WHERE TO STAY & EAT
   CHEZ JEAN TITAUA, Ahurei, Rapa 98751. Tel./Fax 689/95.72.59. Beside lagoon in Ahurei village. EP Rates 4.000 CFP sgl/dbl per day; 60.000 CFP per month. No credit cards.
   This is a 1-bedroom house with a living room, dining room, kitchen, terrace and private bathroom with hot water. House linens are furnished.

21. Glossary of Tahitian Terms

The **Tahitian alphabet** contains 13 letters. A is pronounced ah, as in father, E is pronounced e, as in fate, F is pronounced fa as in farm, H is pronounced he as in heaven, I is pronounced i as me, M is pronounced mo as in mote, N is pronounced nu as in noon, O is pronounced o as in go, P is pronounced p as in pat, R is pronounced ro as in rode, T is pronounced t as in time, U is pronounced u as in rule, V is pronounced v as in veer.

The Tahitian dialect abounds in vowels, such as Faaa, the name of Tahiti's largest commune, where the international airport is located. This is pronounced Fah-ah-ah, but most people lazily forget the last syllable. Tahitian words have no "s" for the plural. There are no hard consonants in the Tahitian alphabet, such as the letter "B;" however, the name Bora Bora is accepted as the legal name for the island that was formerly called Pora Pora.

a'ahi - tuna, *thon* on French menus

ahima'a - underground oven used for cooking traditional Polynesian food; also *hima'a*

ahu - the most sacred place on a marae, an altar that took many forms, including pyramid shaped

aita - Tahitian for "no"

aita e peapea - no problem; also used as "you're welcome"

aita maitai - no good

aito - ironwood tree, also a strong warrior

aparima - a Polynesian story-telling group dance

api - new, young

arii - Polynesian high chief, a sacred being or princely caste

arioi - a religious sect or fraternity in the Society Islands in pre-Christian days

atoll - a low coral island, usually no more than six feet above sea level

atua - Polynesian gods

baguette - long loaf of crusty French bread

barrier reef - coral reef between the shoreline and the ocean, separated from the land by a lagoon

belvédère - panoramic lookout

bonitier - bonito boat

BP - *bôite postale*, post office box

breadfruit - a football-size starchy green fruit that grows on a breadfruit tree, eaten as a staple with fish, pork or canned corned beef and coconut milk

bringue - a party or fête, usually with lots of music, singing, dancing and Hinano beer

cascade - French for waterfall

casse-croûte - sandwich made with *baguette* bread

CEP - *Centre d'expérimentation du Pacifique*; the French nuclear-testing program that was carried out in French Polynesia from 1966-1996

CFP - *cours de franc Pacifique*; the French Pacific franc is the local currency

chevrette - French for sea shrimp, as opposed to fresh water *crevettes*

CMAS - *Confédération Mondiale des Activités Subaquatiques*; the World Underwater Federation, France's scuba diving equivalent to PADI

copra - dried coconut meat used to make oil and monoi

coral - a white calcareous skeletal structure inhabited by Madreporaria, organisms that comprise the living polyps inside the skeletal pores, giving color to the coral

croque madame - also called *croque vahine*, is a toasted ham and cheese sandwich with a fried egg on top

croque monsieur - toasted ham and cheese sandwich

cyclone - tropical storm rotating around a low-pressure 'eye'; the equivalent to a typhoon in the western Pacific and a hurricane in the Caribbean

demi-pension - half board (bed, breakfast and dinner), see also *pension complète*

demis - half caste Tahitian-European

e - Tahitian for "yes"

espadon - French for sword fish

faa'amu -to feed; an informal child adoption system in Polynesia

faa'apu - farm

fafa - the green tops of the taro plant, similar to spinach

fafaru - stinky fish dish

fare - traditional Polynesian house, home, hut

fare iti - little house, outdoor toilet

fare manihini - visitor's bureau

fare moni - bank

fare ohipa - office

fare pape - bathroom

fare pote'e - chief's house or community meeting place, oval shaped

fare pure - church

fare purera'a rahi - cathedral

fare rata - post office

fare taoto -sleeping house

fare toa - store

fare tutu - kitchen

fei - plantain, Tahitian cooking banana

fête - festival, party, celebration

fiu - bored, fed up

fringing reef - a coral reef along the shoreline

FFESSM - *Fèderation Française des Activités Subaquatiques*, or French Underwater Federation of Scuba Divers

gendarmerie - French national police station

goëlette - French for schooner; inter-island cargo or freighter ships

haere mai - come here

haere maru - take it easy

haura - swordfish or marlin

heiva - festival, an assembly for dancing

heiva vaevae - big festival parade

here here - romance

high island - an island created by volcanic action or geological upheaval

himenes - Tahitian for songs or hymns

hinano - flower of the pandanus tree, girl's name, Tahiti's favorite beer

Hiro - Polynesian god of thieves; Raiatea's first king was named Hiro

hoa - shallow channel across the outer reef of an atoll that carries water into or out of the central lagoon at high tide or with big ocean swells

hoe - ceremonial canoe paddle

honu - turtle

ia ora na - hello, good morning, good afternoon, good evening, pronounced similar to "your honor" (yore-ronah)

ia'ota - marinated fish salad, *poisson cru*

ipo - a dumpling made with breadfruit and coconut water

iti - small, little

kaina - a slang term similar to hick or hillbilly, usually applied to out-islanders; country music

kava - mildly intoxicating drink made from the root of piper methysticum, the pepper plant; a fruit tree

kaveu - coconut crab

keshi - a pearl without a nucleus

lagoon - a body of normally calm water inside a coral reef

leeward - on the downwind side, sheltered from the prevailing winds

le truck - Tahiti's public transportation system

LMS - London Missionary Society, the first Protestants to bring the Gospel to Tahiti in 1797

ohipa - work

opani - out of order, broken, closed

maa - food, also spelled **ma'a**

maa tahiti - traditional Tahitian food

maa tinito - Chinese food

maa tinito haricots rouge - a popular dish with red beans, macaroni, pork or chicken

mabe - blister pearl that is grown inside the mother-of-pearl shell

maeva; manava - greetings, welcome

magasin - small food store

mahi mahi - dolphinfish, *dorade Coryphène*

mahu - Tahitian for transvestite or homosexual male

maitai - good; also a potent rum drink

maiore - another name for uru or breadfruit

mana - spiritual power

manahune - the common people or peasant class in pre-European Polynesia; servants, tillers of the soil, fishermen, prisoners of war and slaves

manuia - cheers, a toast to your health

mako, mao - shark

maniota - manioc root

manu - bird

maoa - sea snails

Maohi - Tahitian Polynesians; the ancestors of today's Tahitians, some of whom sailed to New Zealand and are called Maori

mape - Tahitian chestnut

maraamu - southeast trade winds that can often blow for days, bringing rain, rough seas and cooler weather

marae - traditional Polynesian temple of coral or basaltic stone, usually built with an ahu altar at one end

marara - flying fish

mauruuru - thank you

mauruuru roa - thank you very much

me'ae - Marquesan word for marae

mei'a - banana

meka - a melt-in-your-mouth swordfish from the ocean depths. French menus sometimes list it as *espadon de nuit*

miti ha'ari - fresh coconut milk poured over traditional Tahitian foods

miti hue - a fermented coconut milk used as a dipping sauce for breadfruit, taro, fei, bananas, fish, pork and canned corned beef

mona mona - sweet, candy

monoi - oil made from coconut oil, flavored with Tiare Tahiti, ylang ylang, pitate and other flowers, also with sandalwood powder or vanilla. It is used as an emollient, perfume, hair dressing, suntan oil and mosquito repellent

mo'o - lizard

mo'o rea - yellow lizard, name of the island of Moorea

more - Tahitian grass skirts made from the purau tree

mou'a - mountain

motu - a coral islet inside the lagoon, between the outer reef and a high island

mutoi - Tahitian municipal police

nacre - mother-of-pearl shell

naissain - larva of an oyster

nao nao -mosquito

navette - shuttle boat

nehenehe - pretty; handsome

neo neo - stinky smell

noa noa - fragrant, sweet smelling

nohu - stone fish

noni - Marquesan for *Morinda citrifolia*, a plant whose juice is used as a tonic

nono - sand flea; also Tahitian word for *Morinda citrifolia*

nucleus - a small sphere of calcium carbonate that is grafted into the gonads of the pearl oyster to produce a pearl. The fresh water mussel from the Mississippi River provides the best nucleus and helps to produce the finest black pearls

nui - big, new

oa oa - happy, joyful, merry

ono ono - barracuda

Oro - Polynesian god of war who demanded human sacrifices at the *marae* in pre-Christian days

otea - legendary group dance performed in grass skirts

PADI - Professional Association of Diving Instructors, the American system of scuba diving

pae pae - stone paved floor of pre-European houses or meeting platforms

pahua - clam; *bénitier* on French menus

painapo - pineapple, *anana*

pandanus - palm tree with aerial roots whose leaves are used for weaving roofs, hats, mats and bags

pape - water

pareo, pareu - a sarong-like garment that is hand-painted or tie-dyed

pass - channel through the outer reef of an atoll or the barrier reef around a high island that allows water to flow into and out of the lagoon

Paumotu - inhabitants of the Tuamotu atolls

peapea - problems, worries

pension - boarding house, hostel

pension complète - full-board (bed and all meals)

penu - pestle

pétanque - also known as *boules* or bocci-ball; a French game of bowls, where metal balls are thrown to land as near as possible to a target ball. A very competitive sport in Tahiti

peue - mats woven of coconut or pandanus fronds

pia - beer

pirogue - French word for outrigger canoe

PK - *poste kilometre*, the number of kilometers from the *mairie* or post office

plat du jour - daily special, plate of the day

po'e - a sticky pudding made with papaya, bananas or pumpkin, corn starch and coconut milk

poe rava - black pearl that comes from the *Pinctada Margaritifera,* the black-lip oyster

poisson cru - fish marinated in lime juice and served cold with tomatoes, onions, carrots, cucumbers and coconut milk. In Tahitian it's *i'a ota*

popaa - foreigner, Europeans, westerners, white people

popoi - fermented breadfruit eaten as a bread substitute or sweetened with sugar and coconut cream as a dessert

poulet - French for chicken

poulet fafa - chicken cooked with taro leaves and coconut milk

pu - conch shell blown to announce the arrival of a delegation, dancers, or the fish truck

puaa - pig, the basic food for all Tahitian *tamaara'a* feasts

pua'a'toro - beef; canned corned beef, the staple of the South Seas

purau - wild hibiscus tree, whose inner bark is used to make grass skirts

rae rae - a slang term for *mahu,* usually implying homosexuality

raatira - the intermediary caste of the ancient Polynesian society, between the *arii* and the *manahune*

rori - sea slug, sea cucumber

roulotte - mobile dining van

sennit - woven fiber from coconut husks

siki - dark skinned people

Taaroa - Polynesian creator god

tahua - priests of ancient Polynesian religion

taioro - fermented grated coconut sauce that may contain *pahua* clams or *maoa* sea snails

tamaara'a - Tahitian feast

tama'a maitai - enjoy your meal, *bon appetit*

tamure - Tahiti's national hip swiveling, rubber-legging dance

tane - man, husband, boyfriend, Mr.

tapa - bark-cloth, traditional clothing of the pre-European Polynesians; wall hangings

tapu - tabu, taboo, sacred, forbidden

taramea - crown-of-thorns starfish that eats the coral animals and destroys the reefs

taro - root vegetable that is one of the staple foods in Polynesia

tarua - a tuber usually cooked in the *ahima'a* oven

tatau - Tahitian word for tattoo

tiane'e - slipper lobster; *cigalle de mer* on French menus

tiare - flower

Tiare Tahiti - fragrant white petalled *gardenia taitensis,* Tahiti's national flower

tifaifai - colorful bed and cushion covers or wall hangings sewn in patchwork or appliquéd designs

tii - Tahitian name for human-like wooden or stone statues that had a religious significance in pre-European Polynesia

tiki - a Marquesan word for the Tahitian *tii*; some of these statues are still found on the *me'ae* in the Marquesas Islands

Tinito - Tahitian name for Chinese

tiurai - Tahitian for July, the major festival of July

TPE - *traitement paiement electronique*, an automatic teller machine equivalent to the ATM. Nobody calls this a TPE, however, but a *distributeur*

toe toe - cold

toere - wooden slit drum played for Tahitian dance shows

tohua - a place for meetings or festivals in pre-European Polynesia

tupa - land crab

tupapau - spirit ghosts of the Polynesian religion, still feared by some people

ufi - a huge root vegetable similar to yams, cooked in underground *ahima'a* oven

umara - sweet potato

umete - wooden dish or bowl used for serving foods or holding fruits and flowers

upa upa - music

uru - breadfruit

vaa - Tahitian word for outrigger canoe

vahine - Tahitian word for woman, wife, Ms.

vehine- Marquesan word for woman, wife, Ms.

vana- black sea urchin whose meat is good to eat

vanira - vanilla

varo - sea centipede, a gourmet's delicacy

V.A.T. - value added tax; called T.V.A. in French Polynesia

vea vea - hot

vivo - nose flute

VTT or vélo or tout terrain - mountain bike

windward - facing the wind; the opposite of leeward

4x4 or 4WD - a 4-wheel drive vehicle, such as a Land Rover, Jeep or pick-up truck

GENERAL INDEX

LODGING INDEX

Things Change!

Phone numbers, prices, addresses, quality of food, etc, all change. If you come across any new information, we'd appreciate hearing from you. No item is too small! Let Jan know at her webiste, **www.janprince.net**, where she'll be posting updates of this book. And you can always write us at:

Tahiti & French Polynesia Guide
Open Road Publishing, P.O. Box 284
Cold Spring Harbor, NY 11724

Travel Notes

Travel Notes

Travel Notes

Travel Notes

Travel Notes

About the Author

Jan Prince has lived in Tahiti and Moorea since 1971. She is a travel writer and journalist, and has also written about Tahiti for Fodor's travel guides, *The Los Angeles Times, Time Magazine, Tahiti Magazine, Pacific Islands Monthly*, and many other publications. She is currently the senior writer for the *Tahiti Beach Press,* a 20-page English-language magazine that is published once a month and distributed weekly in hotels and other tourist locations.

You may e-mail her at *janprincemoorea@mail.pf* only for questions and comments relating to this book – not to assist in travel or other arrangements. Please understand that she cannot help you with real estate, employment or immigration inquiries.

Jan's website is *www.janprince.net,* where she will post periodic updates for this book.

Open Road Publishing

Open Road has launched **a radical new concept in travel guides** that we call our *Best Of* guides: matching the time you *really* have for your vacation with the right amount of information you need for your perfect trip! No fluff, just the best things to do and see, the best places to stay and eat. Includes one-day, weekend, one-week and two-week trip ideas – in living color! Now what could be more perfect than that?

Best Of Guides

Open Road's Best of Arizona, $14.95
Open Road's Best of The Florida Keys, $14.95
Open Road's Best of Las Vegas, $14.95
Open Road's Best of New York City, $14.95
Open Road's Best of Southern California, $14.95
Open Road's Best of Belize, $14.95
Open Road's Best of Costa Rica, $14.95
Open Road's Best of Honduras, $14.95
Open Road's Best of Panama, $14.95
Open Road's Best of Ireland, $14.95
Open Road's Best of Italy, $16.95
Open Road's Best of Paris, $12.95
Open Road's Best of Provence & The French Riviera, $14.95
Open Road's Best of Spain, $14.95

Family Travel Guides

Open Road's Italy with Kids, $16.95
Open Road's Paris with Kids, $16.95
Open Road's Caribbean with Kids, $14.95
Open Road's London with Kids, $14.95
Open Road's New York City with Kids, $14.95
Open Road's Best National Parks With Kids, $14.95
Open Road's Washington, DC with Kids, $14.95
Open Road's Hawaii with Kids, $14.95

Order now at www.openroadguides.com